T0203693

Next Generation
of Data Mining

Chapman & Hall/CRC
Data Mining and Knowledge Discovery Series

SERIES EDITOR

Vipin Kumar

University of Minnesota
Department of Computer Science and Engineering
Minneapolis, Minnesota, U.S.A

AIMS AND SCOPE

This series aims to capture new developments and applications in data mining and knowledge discovery, while summarizing the computational tools and techniques useful in data analysis. This series encourages the integration of mathematical, statistical, and computational methods and techniques through the publication of a broad range of textbooks, reference works, and handbooks. The inclusion of concrete examples and applications is highly encouraged. The scope of the series includes, but is not limited to, titles in the areas of data mining and knowledge discovery methods and applications, modeling, algorithms, theory and foundations, data and knowledge visualization, data mining systems and tools, and privacy and security issues.

PUBLISHED TITLES

UNDERSTANDING COMPLEX DATASETS: Data Mining with Matrix Decompositions
David Skillicorn

COMPUTATIONAL METHODS OF FEATURE SELECTION
Huan Liu and Hiroshi Motoda

CONSTRAINED CLUSTERING: Advances in Algorithms, Theory, and Applications
Sugato Basu, Ian Davidson, and Kiri L. Wagstaff

KNOWLEDGE DISCOVERY FOR COUNTERTERRORISM AND LAW ENFORCEMENT
David Skillicorn

MULTIMEDIA DATA MINING: A Systematic Introduction to Concepts and Theory
Zhongfei Zhang and Ruofei Zhang

DATA MINING FOR DESIGN AND MARKETING
Yukio Ohsawa and Katsutoshi Yada

NEXT GENERATION OF DATA MINING
Hillol Kargupta, Jiawei Han, Philip S. Yu, Rajeev Motwani, and Vipin Kumar

Chapman & Hall/CRC
Data Mining and Knowledge Discovery Series

Next Generation of Data Mining

Edited by

Hillol Kargupta, Jiawei Han, Philip S. Yu,
Rajeev Motwani, and Vipin Kumar

 CRC Press
Taylor & Francis Group
Boca Raton London New York

CRC Press is an imprint of the
Taylor & Francis Group, an **informa** business
A CHAPMAN & HALL BOOK

Chapman & Hall/CRC
Taylor & Francis Group
6000 Broken Sound Parkway NW, Suite 300
Boca Raton, FL 33487-2742

First issued in paperback 2019

CRC Press is an imprint of Taylor & Francis Group, an Informa business

ISBN-13: 978-1-4200-8586-0 (hbk)
ISBN-13: 978-0-367-38605-4 (pbk)

Visit the Taylor & Francis Web site at
http://www.taylorandfrancis.com

and the CRC Press Web site at
http://www.crcpress.com

Dedication

To my daughter Priyanka

Hillol Kargupta

Contents

Preface

Data mining is changing the face of the world. This interdisciplinary field of extracting hidden patterns from data by paying attention to computing, communication, storage, and user interaction is playing an increasingly important role in solving many critical problems faced by the world today. For example, consider the grand challenges for engineering recently identified by the U.S. National Academy of Engineering to (1) make solar energy economical, (2) provide energy from fusion, (3) develop carbon sequestration methods, (4) manage the nitrogen cycle, (5) provide access to clean water, (6) restore and improve urban infrastructure, (7) advance health informatics, (8) engineer better medicines, (9) reverse-engineer the brain, (10) prevent nuclear terror, (11) secure cyberspace, (12) enhance virtual reality, (13) advance personalized learning, and (14) engineer the tools of scientific discovery. While some of these may have a more obvious need for data analysis than the rest, it is hard to imagine any of these problems solved without requiring any advanced analysis of data for modeling, classification, clustering, anomaly detection, and other applications. Mining large scientific simulation data for solving energy problems, modeling the geophysical processes, networking threat detection in a distributed environment while protecting privacy, adapting personalization for advanced human–computer interaction, sensor network–based monitoring of water supply systems, and mining of biomedical data—these are a few examples of how data mining may affect our lives today and in the future.

This book focuses on some of the emerging trends in the field of data mining. It deals with some of the directions along which the next generation of data mining technology is starting to shape up. The book emerged from the National Science Foundation supported Next Generation of Data Mining Symposium held in October, 2007 at Baltimore. The goal of this meeting was to identify the next generation of challenges faced by the field of data mining. Researchers and practitioners from different disciplines and different walks of life gathered at Baltimore over two and a half days to have a brainstorming session to discuss various possibilities. In many ways, the book documents this exploration. This is an edited volume that covers five emerging areas: (1) data mining in e-science and engineering; (2) ubiquitous, distributed, and high-performance data mining; (3) Web, semantics, and text data mining; (4) data mining in security, surveillance, and privacy protection; and (5) medicine, social science, finance, and spatial data mining. It shares the thoughts of some of the most interesting minds in this field and debates the upcoming challenges. This book should not be treated as a comprehensive treatise identifying all the emerging areas and applications of data mining. It offers one collection of thoughts, one set of perspectives, and hopefully one piece of the puzzle that may play a role in shaping the future of data mining.

This book is a result of the hard work of many individuals. All the contributors, who took the time to write the chapters deserve a lot of credit. Representatives of the publisher, Taylor & Francis, particularly Randi Cohen, must be congratulated for their hard work and patience.

We enjoyed putting this book together. We hope you will enjoy reading it.

Hillol Kargupta
University of Maryland, Baltimore County and Agnik

Jiawei Han
University of Illinois at Urbana-Champaign

Philip S. Yu
University of Illinois at Chicago

Rajeev Motwani
Stanford University

Vipin Kumar
University of Minnesota

Acknowledgments

The editors would like to thank the US National Science Foundation, SAIC, UMBC, and Agnik for supporting the NSF Next Generation Data Mining Symposium.

The authors would like to thank UbiqDesigns for designing the graphics on the cover.

Editors

Hillol Kargupta is an associate professor in the Department of Computer Science and Electrical Engineering, University of Maryland, Baltimore County. He received his PhD in computer science from the University of Illinois at Urbana-Champaign in 1996. He is also a co-founder of Agnik LLC, a data analytics company for distributed, mobile, and embedded environments. His research interests include mobile and distributed data mining. Dr. Kargupta won a U.S. National Science Foundation CAREER Award in 2001 for his research on ubiquitous and distributed data mining. He along with his co-authors received the best paper award at the 2003 IEEE International Conference on Data Mining for a paper on privacy-preserving data mining. His papers were also selected for Best of 2008 SIAM Data Mining Conference (SDM'08) and Most Interesting Paper of WebKDD'06. He won the 2000 TRW Foundation Award, 1997 Los Alamos Award for Outstanding Technical Achievement, and 1996 SIAM annual best student paper award. His research has been funded by the U.S. National Science Foundation, U.S. Air Force, Department of Homeland Security, NASA, Office of Naval Research, and various other organizations. He has published more than 90 peer-reviewed articles in journals, conferences, and books and has co-edited several books. He is an associate editor of *IEEE Transactions on Knowledge and Data Engineering*; *IEEE Transactions on Systems, Man, and Cybernetics, Part B*; and *Statistical Analysis and Data Mining Journal*. He is the program co-chair of the 2009 IEEE International Data Mining Conference, and was general chair of the 2007 NSF Next Generation Data Mining Symposium, program co-chair of the 2005 SIAM Data Mining Conference, program vice-chair of the 2005 PKDD Conference, program vice-chair of the 2008 and 2005 IEEE International Data Mining Conference, program vice-chair of the 2008 and 2005 Euro-PAR Conferences, and associate general chair of the 2003 ACM SIGKDD Conference, among others. More information about him can be found at http://www.cs.umbc.edu/~hillol.

Jiawei Han is a professor in the Department of Computer Science at the University of Illinois. He has been conducting research in data mining, data warehousing, stream data mining, spatiotemporal and multimedia data mining, biological data mining, social network analysis, text and Web mining, and software bug mining, with over 350 conference and journal publications. He has chaired or served on over 100 program committees of international conferences and workshops and also served or is serving on the editorial boards for *Data Mining and Knowledge Discovery*; *IEEE Transactions on Knowledge and Data Engineering*; *Journal of Computer Science and Technology*; and *Journal of Intelligent Information Systems*. He is the founding editor-in-chief of *ACM Transactions on Knowledge Discovery from Data* (TKDD).

Jiawei has received three IBM faculty awards, the Outstanding Contribution Award at the 2002 International Conference on Data Mining, the ACM Service Award (1999) and the ACM SIGKDD Innovation Award (2004), and the IEEE Computer Society Technical Achievement Award (2005). He is an ACM Fellow (2004). His book *Data Mining: Concepts and Techniques* (Morgan Kaufmann) has been used widely as a textbook.

Philip S. Yu received his MS and PhD in Electrical Engineering from Stanford University, and his MBA from New York University. He is a professor in the Department of Computer Science at the University of Illinois at Chicago and also holds the Wexler Chair in Information and Technology. He was manager of the software tools and techniques group at the IBM Thomas J. Watson Research Center. His research interests include data mining, Internet applications and technologies, database systems, multimedia systems, parallel and distributed processing, and performance modeling. Dr. Yu has published more than 500 papers in refereed journals and conferences. He holds or has applied for more than 300 U.S. patents. Dr. Yu is a fellow of the ACM and a fellow of the IEEE. He is an associate editor of *ACM Transactions on the Internet Technology* and *ACM Transactions on Knowledge Discovery from Data*. He is on the steering committee of IEEE Conference on Data Mining and was a member of the IEEE Data Engineering steering committee. He was the editor-in-chief of *IEEE Transactions on Knowledge and Data Engineering* from 2001 to 2004. He has received several IBM honors including two IBM Outstanding Innovation Awards, an Outstanding Technical Achievement Award, two Research Division Awards, and the 94th Plateau of Invention Achievement Award. He has been an IBM master inventor. Dr. Yu received a Research Contributions Award from IEEE International Conference on Data Mining in 2003 and also an IEEE Region 1 Award for "promoting and perpetuating numerous new electrical engineering concepts" in 1999.

Rajeev Motwani is a professor of computer science at Stanford University. He obtained his PhD in computer science from the University of California, Berkeley, in 1988. His research has spanned a diverse set of areas in computer science, including databases, data mining, and data privacy; Web search and information retrieval; and robotics, computational drug design, and theoretical computer science. He has written two books—*Randomized Algorithms* published by Cambridge University Press in 1995, and an undergraduate textbook published by Addison-Wesley in 2001. Motwani has received the Godel Prize, the Okawa Foundation Research Award, the Arthur Sloan Research Fellowship, the National Young Investigator Award from the National Science Foundation, the Distinguished Alumnus Award from IIT Kanpur, and the Bergmann Memorial Award. He is a fellow of the ACM and a fellow of the Institute of Combinatorics. He serves on the editorial boards of *SIAM Journal on Computing*; *Journal of Computer and System Sciences*; *ACM Transactions on Knowledge Discovery from Data*; and *IEEE Transactions on Knowledge and Data Engineering*.

Vipin Kumar is currently the William Norris professor and head of the Computer Science and Engineering Department at the University of Minnesota. Kumar's current research interests include data mining, bioinformatics, and high-performance computing. He has authored over 200 research articles, and has co-edited or co-authored nine books including the widely used textbooks *Introduction to Parallel Computing* and *Introduction to Data Mining*. Kumar is a founding co-editor-in-chief of *Journal of Statistical Analysis and Data Mining* and editor-in-chief of *IEEE Intelligent Informatics Bulletin*. He co-founded the SIAM International Conference on Data Mining, and serves on the steering committees of the IEEE International Conference on Bioinformatics and Biomedicine; the IEEE International Conference on Data Mining; and SIAM International Conference on Data Mining. Kumar is a fellow of the ACM, IEEE, and AAAS. He received the 2005 IEEE Computer Society's Technical Achievement Award for contributions to the design and analysis of parallel algorithms, graph partitioning, and data mining.

Contributors

Nitin Agarwal
Department of Computer Science
and Engineering
School of Computing and Informatics
Arizona State University
Tempe, Arizona

Anushka Anand
National Center for Data Mining
University of Illinois
Chicago, Illinois

Bettina Berendt
Department of Computer Science
Katholieke Universiteit Leuven
Heverlee, Belgium

Michael W. Berry
Department of Electrical Engineering
and Computer Science
University of Tennessee
Knoxville, Tennessee

Shyam Boriah
Department of Computer Science
and Engineering
University of Minnesota
Minneapolis, Minnesota

Kirk D. Borne
Department of Computational
and Data Sciences
George Mason University
Fairfax, Virginia

Gregory Buehrer
Microsoft Live Labs
Silicon Valley, California

Redmond P. Burke
Miami Children's Hospital
Miami, Florida

Doina Caragea
Department of Computing
and Information Sciences
Kansas State University
Manhattan, Kansas

Mete Celik
Department of Computer Science
and Engineering
University of Minnesota
Minneapolis, Minnesota

Alok Choudhary
Electrical Engineering and Computer
Science Department
Northwestern University
Evanston, Illinois

Chris Clifton
Department of Computer Science
Purdue University
West Lafayette, Indiana

Noshir Contractor
Northwestern University
Evanston, Illinois

Antoine Cornuéjols
Laboratoire de Recherche
en Informatique
LRI
Université de Paris-Sud
Orsay, France

Kamalika Das
Department of Computer Science
  and Electrical Engineering
University of Maryland
  Baltimore County
Baltimore, Maryland

Fernando Farfán
School of Computing and
  Information Sciences
Florida International University
Miami, Florida

Tim Finin
Computer Science and Electrical
  Engineering Department
University of Maryland
  Baltimore County
Baltimore, Maryland

João Gama
LIAAD - INESC PORTO LA
University of Porto
Porto, Portugal

Jing Gao
Department of Computer Science
University of Illinois
Urbana, Illinois

James E. Gentle
Computational and Data
  Sciences Department
George Mason University
Fairfax, Virginia

Amol Ghoting
IBM T. J. Watson Research Center
Hawthorne, New York

Fosca Giannotti
ISTI-CNR
Pisa, Italy

Tyrone Grandison
IBM Almaden Research Center
San Jose, California

Marc Greenblatt
Department of Medicine
University of Vermont
Burlington, Vermont

Robert L. Grossman
National Center for Data Mining
University of Illinois
Chicago, Illinois

Yunhong Gu
National Center for Data Mining
University of Illinois
Chicago, Illinois

Jiawei Han
Department of Computer Science
University of Illinois
Urbana, Illinois

Matt Handley
National Center for Data Mining
University of Illinois
Chicago, Illinois

Shoji Hirano
Department of Medical Informatics
Shimane University
Izumo, Japan

Vasant Honavar
Department of Computer Science
Iowa State University
Ames, Iowa

Daniel Honbo
Department of Electrical Engineering
  and Computer Science
Northwestern University
Evanston, Illinois

Andreas Hotho
Department of Electrical Engineering
  and Computer Science
University of Kassel
Kassel, Germany

Vagelis Hristidis
School of Computing and
  Information Sciences
Florida International University
Miami, Florida

Akshay Java
Department of Computer Science
  and Electrical Engineering
University of Maryland
  Baltimore County
Baltimore, Maryland

Wei Jiang
Department of Computer Science
Purdue University
West Lafayette, Indiana

Anupam Joshi
Department of Computer Science
  and Electrical Engineering
University of Maryland
  Baltimore County
Baltimore, Maryland

Anubhav Kale
Microsoft
Seattle, Washington

Hillol Kargupta
Department of Computer Science
  and Electrical Engineering
University of Maryland
Baltimore County
and
Agnik
Baltimore, Maryland

Steven Klooster
Science and Environmental Policy
California State University,
  Monterey Bay
Seaside, California

Pranam Kolari
Yahoo! Applied Research
Santa Clara, California

Vipin Kumar
Department of Computer Science
  and Engineering
University of Minnesota
Minneapolis, Minnesota

Amy N. Langville
Department of Mathematics
College of Charleston
Charleston, South Carolina

Huan Liu
Department of Computer Science
  and Engineering
School of Computing and Informatics
Arizona State University
Tempe, Arizona

Kun Liu
IBM Almaden Research Center
San Jose, California

Donato Malerba
Department of Computer Science
University of Bari
Bari, Italy

Sandeep Mane
Department of Computer Science
University of Minnesota
Twin Cities, Minnesota

Michael May
Fraunhofer Institute for Intelligent
  Analysis and Information Systems
Sankt Augustin, Germany

Leonard McMillan
Department of Computer Science
University of North Carolina
Chapel Hill, North Carolina

Ernestina Menesalvas
Facultad de Informática
Universidad Politécnica de Madrid
Madrid, Spain

Sanchit Misra
Electrical Engineering and
  Computer Science Department
Northwestern University
Evanston, Illinois

Katharina Morik
Artificial Intelligence Unit
Department of Computer Science
University of Dortmund
Dortmund, Germany

Rajeev Motwani
Department of Computer Science
Stanford University
Palo Alto, California

Mummoorthy Murugesan
Department of Computer Science
Purdue University
West Lafayette, Indiana

Ramanathan Narayanan
Electrical Engineering and
  Computer Science Department
Northwestern University
Evanston, Illinois

Olfa Nasraoui
Department of Computer Engineering
  and Computer Science
University of Louisville
Louisville, Kentucky

M. Ercan Nergiz
Department of Computer Science
Purdue University
West Lafayette, Indiana

Fernando Pardo-Manuel de Villena
Department of Genetics
University of North Carolina
Chapel Hill, North Carolina

Nishith Pathak
Department of Computer Science
  and Engineering
University of Minnesota
Twin Cities, Minnesota

Srinivasan Parthasarathy
Department of Computer Science
  and Engineering
The Ohio State University
Columbus, Ohio

Rasmus Pedersen
Department of Informatics
Copenhagen Business School
Copenhagen, Denmark

Scott Poole
Department of Communication
University of Illinois
Urbana-Champaign, Illinois

Christopher Potter
NASA Ames Research Center
Moffett Field, California

Anthony F. Rossi
Miami Children's Hospital
Miami, Florida

Michael Sabala
National Center for Data Mining
University of Illinois
Chicago, Illinois

Lorenza Saitta
Department of Computer Science
University of Piemonte Orientale
Alessandria, Italy

John Salerno
Air Force Research Laboratory/IFEA
Rome, New York

Yücel Saygin
Faculty of Engineering
 and Natural Sciences
Sabanci University
Istanbul, Turkey

Assaf Schuster
Computer Science Department
Technion, Israel Institute of Technology
Haifa, Israel

Shashi Shekhar
Department of Computer Science
 and Engineering
University of Minnesota
Minneapolis, Minnesota

Lisa Singh
Department of Computer Science
Georgetown University
Washington, DC

Maha Soliman
Department of Computer Engineering
 and Computer Science
University of Louisville
Louisville, Kentucky

Jaideep Srivastava
Department of Computer Science
 and Engineering
University of Minnesota
Twin Cities, Minnesota

Michael Steinbach
Department of Computer Science
 and Engineering
University of Minnesota
Minneapolis, Minnesota

Jeffrey E. Stone
Department of Computer Science
University of Vermont
Burlington, Vermont

Rajmonda Sulo
National Center for Data Mining
University of Illinois
Chicago, Illinois

Domenico Talia
Department of Electronics
 and Information Systems
University of Calabria
Cosenza, Italy

Pang-Ning Tan
Department of Computer Science
 and Engineering
Michigan State University
East Lansing, Michigan

Shirish Tatikonda
Department of Computer Science
 and Engineering
The Ohio State University
Columbus, Ohio

David Threadgill
Department of Genetics
University of North Carolina
Chapel Hill, North Carolina

Paolo Trunfio
Department of Electronics
 and Information Systems
University of Calabria
Cosenza, Italy

Shusaku Tsumoto
Department of Medical Informatics
Shimane University
Izumo, Japan

Koen Vanhoof
Department of Applied
 Economic Sciences
University of Hasselt
Diepenbeek, Belgium

Ranga Raju Vatsavai
Oak Ridge National Laboratory
Oak Ridge, Tennessee

Wei Wang
Department of Computer Science
University of North Carolina
Chapel Hill, North Carolina

Jeffrey A. White
Teges Corporation
Miami, Flordia

Lee Wilkinson
National Center for Data Mining
University of Illinois
Chicago, Illinois

Dmitri Williams
Annenberg School of Communication
University of Southern California
Los Angeles, California

Xindong Wu
Department of Computer Science
University of Vermont
Burlington, Vermont

Xifeng Yan
IBM T. J. Watson Research Center
Hawthorne, New York

Philip S. Yu
Department of Computer Science
University of Illinois
Chicago, Illinois

Feida Zhu
Department of Computer Science
University of Illinois
Urbana-Champaign, Illinois

Part I

Data Mining in e-Science and Engineering

Part I

Data Mining in e-Science and Engineering

Chapter 1

Research Challenges for Data Mining in Science and Engineering

Jiawei Han and Jing Gao

Contents

1.1   Introduction

It has been popularly recognized that the rapid development of computer and information technology in the last 20 years has fundamentally changed almost every field in science and engineering, transforming many disciplines from data-poor to increasingly data-rich, and calling for the development of new, data-intensive methods to conduct research in science and engineering. Thus, the new terms like, data science or data-intensive engineering, can be used to best characterize the data-intensive nature of today's science and engineering.

Disclaimer: Any opinions, findings, and conclusions or recommendations expressed in the chapter are those of the authors and do not necessarily reflect the views of the funding agencies.

Besides the further development of database methods to efficiently store and manage petabytes of data online, making these archives easily and safely accessible via the Internet or a computing grid, another essential task is to develop powerful data mining tools to analyze such data. Thus, there is no wonder that data mining has also stepped on to the center stage in science and engineering.

Data mining, as the confluence of multiple intertwined disciplines, including statistics, machine learning, pattern recognition, database systems, information retrieval, World Wide Web, visualization, and many application domains, has made great progress in the past decade [HK06]. To ensure that the advances of data-mining research and technology will effectively benefit the progress of science and engineering, it is important to examine the challenges on data mining posed in data-intensive science and engineering and explore how to further develop the technology to facilitate new discoveries and advances in science and engineering.

1.2   Major Research Challenges

In this section, we examine several major challenges raised in science and engineering from the data-mining perspective, and point out some promising research directions.

1.2.1   Information Network Analysis

With the development of Google and other effective Web search engines, information network analysis has become an important research frontier, with broad applications, such as social network analysis, Web community discovery, terrorist network mining, computer network analysis, and network intrusion detection. However, information network research should go beyond explicitly formed, homogeneous networks (e.g., Web page links, computer networks, and terrorist e-connection networks) and delve deeply into implicitly formed, heterogeneous, and multidimensional information networks. Science and engineering provide us with rich opportunities on exploration of networks in this direction.

There are a lot of massive natural, technical, social, and information networks in science and engineering applications, such as gene, protein, and microarray networks in biology; highway transportation networks in civil engineering; topic- or theme-author-publication-citation networks in library science; and wireless telecommunication networks among commanders, soldiers, and supply lines in a battle field. In such information networks, each node or link in a network contains valuable, multidimensional information, such as textual contents, geographic information, traffic flow, and other properties. Moreover, such networks could be highly dynamic, evolving, and interdependent.

Traditional data-mining algorithms such as classification, market basket analysis, and cluster analysis commonly attempt to find patterns in a data set containing independent, identically distributed samples. One can think of this process as learning a model for the node attributes of a homogeneous graph while ignoring the links between the nodes. A key emerging challenge for data mining is tackling the problem of mining richly structured, heterogeneous data sets [GD05]. The domains often consist of a variety of object types; the objects can be linked in a variety of ways. Naively applying traditional statistical inference procedures, which assume that instances are independent, can lead to inappropriate conclusions about the data. In fact, object linkage is knowledge that should be exploited.

Although a single link in a network could be noisy, unreliable, and sometimes misleading, valuable knowledge can be mined reliably among a large number of links in a massive information network. Our recent studies on information networks show that the power of such links in massive information networks should not be underestimated. They can be used for predictive modeling across multiple relations [YHYY06], for user-guided clustering across multiple relations [YHY05], for effective link-based clustering [JW02,YHY06], for distinguishing different objects with identical names [YHY07a], and for solving the veracity problem, that is, finding reliable facts among multiple conflicting Web information providers [YHY07b]. The power of such links should be thoroughly explored in many scientific domains, such as in protein network analysis in biology and in the analysis of networks of research publications in library science as well as in each science/engineering discipline.

The most well-known link mining task is that of link-based object ranking (LBR), which is a primary focus of the link analysis community. The objective of LBR is to exploit the link structure of a graph to order or prioritize the set of objects within the graph. Since the introduction of the most notable approaches, PageRank [PBMW98] and HITS [Kle99], many variations have been developed to rank one type [CDG+98,Hav02,RD02] or multiple types of objects in the graph [JW02, SQCF05]. Also, the link-based object classification (LBC) problem has been studied. The task is to predict the class label for each object. The discerning feature of LBC that makes it different from traditional classification is that in many cases, the labels of related objects tend to be correlated. The challenge is to design algorithms for collective classification that exploit such correlations and jointly infer the categorical values associated with the objects in the graph [CDI98]. Another link-related task is entity resolution, which involves identifying the set of objects in a domain. The goal of entity resolution is to determine which references in the data refer to the same real-world entity. Examples of this problem arise in databases (deduplication, data integration) [ACG02,DHM05], natural language processing (coreference resolution, object consolidation) [BG06,PMM+02], personal information management, and other fields. Recently, there has been significant interest in the use of links for improved entity resolution. The central idea is to consider, in addition to the attributes of the references to be resolved, the other references to which these are linked. These links may be, for example, coauthor links between author references in bibliographic data, hierarchical links between spatial references in geospatial data, or co-occurrence links between name references in natural language documents. Besides utilizing links in data mining, we may wish to predict the existence of links based on attributes of the objects and other observed links in some problems. Examples include predicting links among actors in social networks, such as predicting friendships; predicting the participation of actors in events [OHS05], such as e-mail, telephone calls, and coauthorship; and predicting semantic relationships such as advisor-of based on Web page links and content [CDF+00]. Most often, some links are observed, and one is attempting to predict unobserved links [GFKT01], or there is a temporal aspect.

Another important direction in information network analysis is to treat information networks as graphs and further develop graph mining methods [CH07]. Recent progress on graph mining and its associated structural pattern-based classification and clustering, graph and graph containment indexing, and similarity search will play an important role in information network analysis. An area of data mining that is related to link mining is the work on subgraph discovery. This work attempts to find interesting or commonly occurring subgraphs in a set of graphs. Discovery of these patterns may be the sole purpose of the systems, or the discovered patterns may be used for graph classification, whose goal is to categorize an entire graph as a positive or negative instance of a concept. One line of work attempts to find frequent subgraphs [KK01,YH07], and some other lines of work are on efficient subgraph generation and compression-based heuristic search [CH07,WM03]. Moreover, since information networks often form huge, multidimensional heterogeneous graphs, mining noisy, approximate, and heterogeneous subgraphs based on different applications for the construction of application-specific networks with sophisticated structures will help information network analysis substantially. Generative models for a range of graph and dependency types have been studied extensively in the social network analysis community [CSW05]. In recent years, significant attention has been focused on studying the structural properties of networks [AC05], such as the World Wide Web, online social networks, communication networks, citation networks, and biological networks. Across these various networks, general patterns such as power law degree distributions, small graph diameters, and community structure are observed. These observations have motivated the search for general principles governing such networks. The use of the power law distribution of many information networks and the rules on density evolution of information networks will help reduce computational complexity and enhance the power of network analysis. Finally, the studies of link analysis, heterogeneous data integration, user-guided clustering, and user-based network construction will provide essential methodology for the in-depth study in this direction.

Many domains of interest today are best described as a network of interrelated heterogeneous objects. As future work, link mining may focus on the integration of link-mining algorithms for a spectrum of knowledge discovery tasks. Furthermore, in many applications, the facts to be analyzed are dynamic and it is important to develop incremental link-mining algorithms. Besides mining knowledge from links, objects, and networks, we may wish to construct an information network based on both ontological and unstructured information.

1.2.2 Discovery, Understanding, and Usage of Patterns and Knowledge

Scientific and engineering applications often handle massive data of high dimensionality. The goal of pattern mining is to find itemsets, subsequences, or substructures that appear in a data set with frequency no less than a user-specified threshold. Pattern analysis can be a valuable tool for finding correlations, clusters, classification models, sequential and structural patterns, and outliers.

Frequent pattern mining has been a focused theme in data-mining research for over a decade [HCXY07]. Abundant literature has been dedicated to this research, and tremendous progress has been made, ranging from efficient and scalable algorithms for frequent itemset mining in transaction databases to numerous research frontiers, such as sequential pattern mining, structural pattern mining, correlation mining, associative classification, and frequent pattern-based clustering, as well as their broad applications.

The most focused and extensively studied topic in frequent pattern mining is perhaps scalable mining methods. There are also various proposals on reduction of such a huge set, including closed patterns, maximal patterns, approximate patterns, condensed pattern bases, representative patterns, clustered patterns, and discriminative frequent patterns. Recently, studies have proceeded to the development of scalable methods (1) for mining colossal patterns [ZYH$^+$07] where the size of the patterns could be rather large so that the step-by-step growth using an apriori-like approach does not work, and (2) for pattern compression and extraction of high-quality top-k patterns [XCYH06]. Much research is still needed to substantially reduce the size of derived pattern sets, mine such patterns directly and efficiently, and enhance the quality of retained patterns.

Moreover, frequent pattern mining could help in other data mining tasks and many such pattern-based mining methods have been developed. Frequent patterns have been used for effective classification by association rule mining (such as Ref. [LHM98]), top-k rule generation for long patterns (such as [CTTX05]), and discriminative frequent pattern-based classification [WK05]. Recent studies show that better classification models could be constructed using discriminative frequent patterns and such patterns could be mined efficiently and directly from data [CYHH07,CYHY08]. Frequent patterns have also been used for clustering of high-dimensional biological data [WWYY02]. Therefore, frequent patterns can play an essential role in these major data-mining tasks and the benefits should be exploited in depth.

We also need mechanisms for deep understanding and interpretation of patterns, for example, semantic annotation for frequent patterns, and contextual analysis of frequent patterns. The main research work on pattern analysis has been focused on pattern composition (e.g., the set of items in itemset patterns) and frequency. A contextual analysis of frequent patterns over the structural information can help respond to questions like "Why this pattern is frequent?" [MXC$^+$07]. The deep understanding of frequent patterns is essential to improve the interpretability and the usability of frequent patterns.

Besides studies on transaction data sets, much research has been done on effective sequential and structural pattern mining methods and the exploration of their applications [CH07,HCXY07]. Applications often raise new research issues and bring deep insight on the strength and weakness of an existing solution. Much work is needed to explore new applications of frequent pattern mining, for example, bioinformatics and software engineering.

The promotion of effective application of pattern analysis methods in scientific and engineering applications is an important task in data mining. Moreover, it is important to further develop efficient methods for mining long, approximate, compressed, and sophisticated patterns for advanced applications, such as mining biological sequences and networks and mining patterns related to scientific and engineering processes. Furthermore, the exploration of mined patterns for classification, clustering, correlation analysis, and pattern understanding will still be interesting topics of research.

1.2.3   Stream Data Mining

Stream data refers to the data that flows into and out of the system like streams. Stream data is usually in vast volume, changing dynamically, possibly infinite, and containing multidimensional features. Typical examples of such data include audio and video recording of scientific and engineering processes, computer network information flow, Web click streams, and satellite data flow. Such data cannot be handled by traditional database systems, and moreover, most systems may only be able to read a data stream once in sequential order. This poses great challenges on effective mining of stream data [Agg06,BBD$^+$02].

First, the techniques to summarize the whole or part of the data streams are studied, which is the basis for stream data mining. Such techniques include sampling [DH01], load shedding [TcZ$^+$03] and sketching techniques [Mut03], synopsis data structures [GKMS01], stream cubing [CDH$^+$02], and clustering [AHWY03]. Progress has been made on efficient methods for mining frequent patterns in data streams [MM02], multidimensional analysis of stream data (such as construction of stream cubes) [CDH$^+$02], stream data classification [DH00,KM05], stream clustering [AHWY03], stream outlier analysis, rare event detection [GFHY07], and so on. The general philosophy is to develop single-scan algorithms to collect information about stream data in tilted time windows, exploring microclustering, limited aggregation, and approximation.

The focus of stream pattern analysis is to approximate the frequency counts for infinite stream data. Algorithms have been developed to count frequency using tilted windows [GHP$^+$04] based on the fact that users are more interested in the most recent transactions, to approximate frequency counting based on previous historical data to calculate the frequent patterns incrementally [MM02], and to track the most frequent k items in the continuously arriving data [CM03].

Initial studies on stream clustering concentrated on extending K-means and K-median algorithms to stream environment [GMM$^+$03]. The main idea behind the developed algorithms is that the cluster centers and weights are updated after examining one transaction or a batch of transactions, whereas the constraints on memory and time complexity are satisfied by limiting the number of centers. Later, Aggarwal et al. (Ref. [AHWY03]) proposes to divide the clustering process into online microclustering process, which stores summarized statistics about the data streams, and the off-line microclustering process, which performs macroclustering on the summarized data according to a number of user preferences such as the time frame and the number of clusters. Projected clustering can also be performed for high-dimensional data streams [AHWY04].

The focus of stream classification of data streams is first on how to efficiently update the classification model when data continuously flow in. Very fast decision tree (VFDT) [DH00] is a representative method in this field where a incremental decision tree is built based on Hoeffding trees. Later, the concept drift problem in data-stream classification has been recognized, which refers to the unknown changes of the distribution underlying data streams. Many algorithms have been developed to prevent deterioration in predicting accuracy of the model [HSD01,KM05], by carefully selecting training examples that represent the true concept [Fan04] or combining multiple models to reduce variance in prediction [GFH07,WFYH03]. For skewed distribution of stream data, it is recommended to explore biased selective sampling and robust ensemble methods in model construction [GFHY07].

Stream data is often encountered in science and engineering applications. It is important to explore stream data mining in such applications and develop application-specific methods, for example, real-time anomaly detection in computer network analysis, in electric power grid supervision, in weather modeling, in engineering and security surveillance, and other stream data applications.

1.2.4 Mining Moving Object Data, RFID Data, and Data from Sensor Networks

With the popularity of sensor networks, global positioning system (GPS), cellular phones, other mobile devices, and RFID technology, tremendous amount of moving object data has been collected, calling for effective analysis. This is especially true in many scientific, engineering, business, and homeland security applications.

Sensor networks are finding increasing number of applications in many domains, including battle fields, smart buildings, and even the human body. Most sensor networks consist of a collection of light-weight (possibly mobile) sensors connected via wireless links to each other or to a more powerful gateway node that is in turn connected with an external network through either wired or wireless connections. Sensor nodes usually communicate in a peer-to-peer architecture over an asynchronous network. In many applications, sensors are deployed in hostile and difficult to access locations with constraints on weight, power supply, and cost. Moreover, sensors must process a continuous (possibly fast) stream of data. Data mining in wireless sensor networks (WSNs) is a challenging area, as algorithms need to work in extremely demanding and constrained environment of sensor networks (such as limited energy, storage, computational power, and bandwidth). WSNs also require highly decentralized algorithms.

Development of algorithms that take into consideration the characteristics of sensor networks, such as energy and computation constraints, network dynamics, and faults, constitute an area of current research. Some work has been done in developing localized, collaborative, distributed, and self-configuration mechanisms in sensor networks. In designing algorithms for sensor networks, it is imperative to keep in mind that power consumption has to be minimized. Even gathering the distributed sensor data in a single site could be expensive in terms of battery power consumed, therefore, some attempts have been made toward making the data collection task energy efficient and balancing the energy-quality trade-offs. Clustering the nodes of the sensor networks is an important optimization problem. Nodes that are clustered together can easily communicate with each other, which can be applied to energy optimization and developing optimal algorithms for clustering sensor nodes. Other works in this field include identification of rare events or anomalies, finding frequent itemsets, and data preprocessing in sensor networks.

Recent years have witnessed an enormous increase in moving object data from RFID records in supply chain operations, toll and road sensor readings from vehicles on road networks, or even cell phone usage from different geographic regions. These movement data, including RFID data, object trajectories, anonymous aggregate data such as the one generated by many road sensors, contain rich information. Effective management of such data is a major challenge facing society today, with important implications into business optimization, city planning, privacy, and national security. Interesting research has been conducted on warehousing RFID data sets [GHLK06], which could handle moving object data sets by significantly compressing such data, and proposing a new aggregation mechanism that preserves their path structures. Mining moving objects is a challenging problem due to the massive size of the data, and its spatiotemporal characteristics. The methods developed along this line include FlowGraph [GHL06b], which is a probabilistic model that captures the main trends and exceptions in moving object data, and FlowCube [GHL06a], which is a multidimensional extension of the FlowGraph and an adaptive fastest path algorithm [GHL+07] that computes routes based on driving patterns present in the data. RFID systems are known to generate noisy data so data cleaning is an essential task for the correct interpretation and analysis of moving object data, especially when it is collected from RFID applications and thus demands for cost-effective cleaning methods (such as Ref. [GHS07]). One important application with moving objects is automated identification of suspicious movements. A framework for detecting anomalies [LHKG07] is proposed to express object trajectories using discrete pattern fragments, to extract features to form a hierarchical feature space, and to learn effective classification rules at multiple levels of granularity. Another line of work on outlier detection in trajectories focuses on detecting outlying subtrajectories [LHL08] based on partition-and-detect framework, which partitions a trajectory into a set of line segments, and then detects outlying line segments for trajectory outliers. The problem of clustering trajectory data [LHW07] is also studied where common subtrajectories are discovered using the minimum description length principle.

Overall, this is still a young field with many research issues to be explored on mining moving object data, RFID data, and data from sensor networks. For example, how to explore correlation and regularity to clean noisy sensor network and RFID data, how to integrate and construct data warehouses for such data, how to perform scalable mining for petabyte RFID data, how to find strange moving objects, how to classify multidimensional trajectory data, and so on. With time, location, moving direction, speed, as well as multidimensional semantics of moving object data, multidimensional data mining is likely to play an essential role in this study.

1.2.5   Spatial, Temporal, Spatiotemporal, and Multimedia Data Mining

Scientific and engineering data is usually related to space, time, and in multimedia modes (e.g., containing color, image, audio, and video). With the popularity of digital photos, audio DVDs, videos, YouTube, Web-based map services, weather services, satellite images, digital earth, and many other forms of multimedia, spatial, and spatiotemporal data, mining spatial, temporal, spatiotemporal, and multimedia data will become increasingly popular, with far-reaching implications [MH01,SC03]. For example, mining satellite images may help detect forest fire, find unusual phenomena on Earth, predict hurricane landing site, discover weather patterns, and outline global warming trends.

Spatial data mining is the process of discovering interesting and previously unknown, but potentially useful, patterns from large spatial data sets [SZHV04]. Extracting interesting and useful patterns from spatial data sets is more difficult than extracting the corresponding patterns from traditional numeric and categorical data due to the complexity of spatial data types, spatial relationships, and spatial autocorrelation. Interesting research topics in this field include prediction of events at particular geographic locations, detecting spatial outliers whose values are extreme regarding to its neighbors, finding colocation patterns where instances containing the patterns often located in close geographic proximity, and grouping a set of spatial objects into clusters. Future research is needed to compare the difference and similarity between classical data mining and spatial data mining techniques, model semantically rich spatial properties other than neighborhood relationships, design effective statistical methods to interpret the mined spatial patterns, investigate proper measures for location prediction to improve spatial accuracy, and facilitate visualization of spatial relationships by representing both spatial and nonspatial features. The problem of incorporating domain knowledge into mining when data is scarce and integrating data collection with mining are worth studying in spatial data mining, and both theoretical analyses toward general studies of spatial phenomena and empirical model designs targeted for specific applications represent the trends for future research.

Time series data [SZ04], which represent sequences of recorded values, appear naturally in almost all fields of applications including physics, finance, medicine, and music. People have tried to obtain insights into the mechanism that generates time series and use the valuable information contained in time series to predict future values. In the last decade, there has been an explosion of interest in mining time series data. Literally, hundreds of papers have introduced new algorithms to preprocess, index, classify, cluster, and identify patterns or novelties from time series. As future work, the research on time series should consider mining multiple time series of the same type or of different types, incorporating domain knowledge into time series mining and facilitate real-time time series mining in some applications.

For applications involving multimedia data, we need tools for discovering relationships between objects or segments within multimedia document components, such as classifying images based on their contents, extracting patterns in sound, categorizing speech and music, and recognizing and tracking objects in video streams. In general, the multimedia files from a database must be first preprocessed to improve their quality. Subsequently, these multimedia files undergo various transformations and feature extractions to generate important features from the multimedia files. With the generated features, mining can be carried out using data-mining techniques to discover significant patterns. These resulting patterns are then evaluated and interpreted in order to obtain the final application knowledge. Numerous methodologies have been developed and many applications have been investigated, including organizing multimedia data indexing and retrieval, extracting representative features from raw multimedia data before the mining process and integrating features obtained from multiple modalities. For example, a moving picture experts group (MPEG-7) standard provides a good representative set of features. Automatic annotation, also referred to as concept mining, is one of the main tasks in multimedia mining. The methods developed for this task include supervised learning, unsupervised learning, and context-based approaches. In supervised learning, based on the annotated concepts for each multimedia document, the unclassified files are automatically categorized. In unsupervised learning, multimedia files are clustered and annotators assign keywords to each cluster, which could be used to extract rules for annotating future documents [SS03]. The third approach tries to mine concepts by looking at the contextual information [SW05], such as the text associated with images, to derive semantic concepts. Another important topic, detection of interesting or unusual events, has received considerable interest in multimedia research. In the future, multimedia mining will be continuously receiving attention, especially for its application in online video sharing, security surveillance monitoring, and effective image retrieval.

Spatiotemporal data mining [RHS01] is an emerging research area that is dedicated to the development of novel algorithms and computational techniques for the successful analysis of large spatiotemporal databases and the disclosure of interesting knowledge in spatiotemporal data. Much work has been done to modify the data-mining techniques so that they can, to the largest extent, exploit the rich spatiotemporal relationships/patterns embedded in the data sets. Spatiotemporal data-mining tasks and techniques can be roughly classified into indexing and searching, pattern analysis, clustering, compression, and outlier detection.

Both the temporal and spatial dimensions could add substantial complexity to data-mining tasks. First, the spatial and temporal relationships are information bearing and therefore need to be considered in data mining. Some spatial and temporal relationships are implicitly defined, and must be extracted from the data. Such extraction introduces some degree of fuzziness or uncertainty that may have an impact on the results of the data-mining process. Second, working at the level of stored data is often undesirable, and thus complex transformations are required to describe the units of analysis at higher conceptual levels. Third, interesting patterns are more likely to be discovered at the lowest resolution/granularity level, but large support is more likely to exist at higher levels. Finally, how to express domain independent knowledge and how to integrate spatiotemporal reasoning mechanisms in data-mining systems are still open problems.

Research in this domain needs the confluence of multiple disciplines including image processing, pattern recognition, geographic information systems, parallel processing, and statistical data analysis. Automatic categorization of images and videos, classification of spatiotemporal data, finding frequent/sequential patterns and outliers, spatial collocation analysis, and many other tasks have been studied popularly. With the mounting of such data, the development of scalable analysis methods and new data-mining functions will be an important research frontier for years to come.

1.2.6 Mining Text, Web, and Other Unstructured Data

Web is the common place for scientists and engineers to publish their data, share their observations and experiences, and exchange their ideas. There is a tremendous amount of scientific and engineering data on the Web. For example, in biology and bioinformatics research, there are GenBank, ProteinBank, GO, PubMed, and many other biological or biomedical information repositories available on the Web. Therefore, the Web has become the ultimate information access and processing platform, housing not only billions of link-accessed pages, containing textual data, multimedia data, and linkages, on the surface Web, but also query-accessible databases on the deep Web. With the advent of Web 2.0, there is an increasing amount of dynamic workflow emerging. With it penetrating deeply into our daily life and evolving into unlimited dynamic applications, the Web is central in our information infrastructure. Its virtually unlimited scope and scale render immense opportunities for data mining.

Text mining and information extraction [Ber03] have been applied not only to Web mining but also to the analysis of other kinds of semistructured and unstructured information, such as digital libraries, biological information systems, research literature analysis systems, computer-aided design and instruction, and office automation systems. Technologies in the text-mining process include information extraction, topic tracking, summarization, categorization, clustering, and concept linkage. Information extraction [Cha01] represents a starting point for computers analyzing unstructured text and identifying key phrases and relationships within text. It does it by looking for predefined sequences in the text, a process called pattern matching. A topic-tracking system [All02] keeps user profiles and based on the documents a user views, predicts other documents of interest to the user. Text summarization [ER04] helps users figure out whether a lengthy document meets their needs and is worth reading. With large-volume texts, text-summarization software processes and summarizes the document in almost no time. The key to summarization is reducing the length and detail of a document while retaining its main points and overall meaning. Categorization involves identifying the main themes of a document [WIZD04]. When categorizing particular documents, a computer program often treats them as a bag of words. The program does not attempt to process the actual information as information extraction does. Rather, categorization counts only words that appear and, from the counts, identifies the main topics covered in the document. Clustering is a technique used to group similar documents [DM01], but it differs from categorization in that documents are clustered on the fly instead of through predefined topics. Documents can also appear in multiple subtopics, ensuring that useful documents are not omitted from the search results. Some topic-modeling techniques [MZ05] connect related documents by identifying their shared concepts, helping users find information they perhaps would not have found through traditional search methods. It promotes browsing for information rather than searching for it.

Web mining [Cha03,KB00,Liu06] is the extraction of interesting and potentially useful patterns and implicit information from artifacts or activity related to the World Wide Web. There are roughly three knowledge discovery domains that pertain to Web mining: Web content mining, Web structure mining, and Web usage mining. Web content mining is an automatic process that goes beyond keyword extraction [QD07] to discover useful information from the content of a Web page. The type of the Web content may consist of text, image, audio, or video data in the web. The text content is the most widely researched area. Technologies that are normally used in Web content mining are natural language processing, information retrieval, and text mining. The strategies include directly mining the content of documents and improving on the content search of other tools like search engines. Web structure mining [FLGC02] can help reveal more information than just the information contained in documents. For example, links pointing to a document indicate the popularity of the document, while links coming out of a document indicate the richness or perhaps the variety of topics covered in the document. Counters of hyperlinks, in and out documents, retrace the structure of the Web artifacts summarized. Finally, Web usage mining [FL05] can help understand the user behavior and the Web structure by analyzing the Web access logs of different Web sites. There are two main tendencies in Web usage mining driven by the applications of the discoveries: general access pattern tracking, which analyzes the Web logs to understand access patterns and trends to construct better structure and grouping of resource providers, and customized usage tracking, which analyzes individual trends to customize Web sites to users.

There are lots of research issues in this domain [Cha03,Liu06], which takes collaborative efforts of multiple disciplines, including information retrieval, databases, data mining, natural language processing, and machine learning. For many scientific and engineering applications, the data is somewhat structured and semistructured, with designated fields for text and multimedia data. Thus, it is possible to mine and build relatively structured Web repositories. Some promising research topics include heterogeneous information integration, information extraction, personalized information agents, application-specific partial Web construction and mining, in-depth Web semantics analysis, development of scientific and engineering domain-specific semantic Webs, and turning Web into relatively structured information-base.

1.2.7   Data Cube-Oriented Multidimensional Online Analytical Mining

Scientific and engineering data sets are usually high dimensional in nature. Viewing and mining data in multidimensional space will substantially increase the power and flexibility of data analysis. Data-cube computation and OLAP (online analytical processing) technologies developed in data warehouse have substantially enhanced multidimensional analysis of large data sets.

Some researchers began to investigate how to conduct traditional data mining and statistical analysis in the multidimensional manner efficiently. For example, regression cube [CDH$^+$06] is designed to support efficient computation of the statistical models. In this framework, each cell can be compressed into an auxiliary matrix with a size independent of the number of tuples and then the statistical measures for any data cell can be computed from the compressed data of the lower level cells without accessing the raw data. In a prediction cube [CCLR05], each cell contains a value that summarizes a predictive model trained on the data corresponding to that cell and characterizes its decision behavior or predictiveness. The authors further show that such cubes can be efficiently computed by exploiting the idea of model decomposition. In Ref. [LH07], the issues of anomaly detection in multidimensional time-series data are examined. A time-series data cube is proposed to capture the multidimensional space formed by the attribute structure and facilitate the detection of anomalies based on expected values derived from higher level, more general time-series. Moreover, an efficient search algorithm is proposed to iteratively select subspaces in the original high-dimensional space and detect anomalies within each one. Recent study on sampling cubes [LHY$^+$08] discussed about the desirability of OLAP over sampling data, which may not represent the full data in the population. The proposed sampling cube framework could efficiently calculate confidence intervals for any multidimensional query and uses the OLAP structure to group similar segments to increase sampling size when needed. Further, to handle high-dimensional data, a sampling cube shell method is proposed to effectively reduce the storage requirement while still preserving query result quality. Such multidimensional, especially high-dimensional, analysis tools will ensure data can be analyzed in hierarchical, multidimensional structures efficiently and flexibly at user's finger tips. This leads to the integration of OLAP with data mining, that is, OLAP mining. Some efforts have been devoted along this direction, but grand challenges still exist when one needs to explore the large space of choices to find interesting patterns and trends [RC07].

We believe that OLAP mining will substantially enhance the power and flexibility of data analysis and lead to the construction of easy-to-use tools for the analysis of massive data with hierarchical structures in multidimensional space. It is a promising research field for developing effective tools and scalable methods for exploratory-based scientific and engineering data mining.

1.2.8   Visual Data Mining

A picture is worth a thousand words. There have been numerous data visualization tools for visualizing various kinds of data sets in massive amount and of multidimensional space [Tuf01]. Besides popular bar charts, pie charts, curves, histograms, quantile plots, quantile–quantile plots, boxplots, and scatter plots, there are also many visualization tools using geometric (e.g., dimension stacking and parallel coordinates), hierarchical (e.g., treemap), and icon-based (e.g., Chernoff faces and stick figures) techniques. Moreover, there are methods for visualizing sequences, time-series data, phylogenetic trees, graphs, networks, Web, as well as various kinds of patterns and knowledge (e.g., decision trees, association rules, clusters, and outliers) [FGW01]. There are also visual data-mining tools that may facilitate interactive mining based on user's judgment of intermediate data-mining results [AEEK99]. Recently, we have developed a DataScope system that maps relational data into two-dimensional maps so that multidimensional relational data can be browsed in Google map's way [WLX+07].

Most data analysts use visualization as part of a process sandwich strategy of interleaving mining and visualization to reach a goal, an approach commonly identified in many research works on applications and techniques for visual data mining [dOL03]. Usually, the analytical mining techniques themselves do not rely on visualization. Most of the papers describing visual data-mining approaches and applications found in the literature fall into two categories: either they use visual data-exploration systems or techniques to support a knowledge extraction goal or a specific mining task, or they use visualization to display the results of a mining algorithm, such as a clustering process or a classifier, and thus enhance user comprehension of the results. A classification of information visualization and visual data-mining techniques is proposed in Ref. [Kei02], which is based on the data type to be visualized, the visualization technique, and the interaction and distortion techniques. Mining tasks usually demand techniques capable of handling large amounts of multidimensional data, often in the format of data tables or relational databases. Parallel coordinates and scatter plots are much exploited in this context. Also, interaction mechanisms for filtering, querying, and selecting data are typically required for handling larger data sets [Ins97]. Another typical use of visualization in mining resides in visually conveying the results of a mining task, such as clustering or classification, to enhance user interpretation. One such example is given to the clustering algorithm [GSF97], BLOB, which uses implicit surfaces for visualizing data clusters. But rather than using visual data exploration and analytical mining algorithms as separate tools, a stronger data-mining strategy would be to tightly couple the visualizations and analytical processes into one data-mining tool. Many mining techniques involve different mathematical steps that require user intervention. Some of these can be quite complex and visualization can support the decision processes involved in making such interventions. From this viewpoint, a visual data-mining technique is not just a visualization technique being applied to exploit data in some phases of an analytical mining process, but is also a data-mining algorithm in which visualization plays a major role.

We believe that visual data mining is appealing to scientists and engineers because they often have good understanding of their data, can use their knowledge to interpret their data and patterns with the help of visualization tools, and interact with the system for deeper and more effective mining. Tools should be developed for mapping data and knowledge into appealing and easy-to-understand visual forms, and for interactive browsing, drilling, scrolling, and zooming data and patterns to facilitate user exploration. Finally, for visualization of large amount of data, parallel processing and high-performance visualization tools should be investigated to ensure high performance and fast response.

1.2.9 Domain-Specific Data Mining: Data Mining by Integration of Sophisticated Scientific and Engineering Domain Knowledge

Besides general data-mining methods and tools for science and engineering, each scientific or engineering discipline has its own data sets and special mining requirements, some could be rather different from the general ones. Therefore, in-depth investigation of each problem domain and development of dedicated analysis tools are essential to the success of data mining in this domain. Here, we examine two problem domains: biology and software engineering.

1.2.9.1 Biological Data Mining

The fast progress of biomedical and bioinformatics research has led to the accumulation and publication (on the Web) of vast amount of biological and bioinformatics data. However, the analysis of such data poses much greater challenges than traditional data analysis methods [BHLY04]. For example, genes and proteins are gigantic in size (e.g., a DNA sequence could be in billions of base pairs), very sophisticated in function, and the patterns of their interactions are largely unknown. Thus, it is a fertile field to develop sophisticated data-mining methods for in-depth bioinformatics research. We believe substantial research is badly needed to produce powerful mining tools in many biological and bioinformatics subfields, including comparative genomics, evolution and phylogeny, biological data cleaning and integration, biological sequence analysis, biological network analysis, biological image analysis, biological literature analysis (e.g., PubMed), and systems biology. From this point of view, data mining is still very young with respect to biology and bioinformatics applications. Substantial research should be conducted to cover the vast spectrum of data analysis tasks.

1.2.9.2 Data Mining for Software Engineering

Software program executions potentially (e.g., when program execution traces are turned on) generate huge amounts of data. However, such data sets are rather different from the data sets generated from the nature or collected from video cameras since they represent the executions of program logics coded by human programmers. It is important to mine such data to monitor program execution status, improve system performance, isolate software bugs, detect software plagiarism, analyze programming system faults, and recognize system malfunctions.

Data mining for software engineering can be partitioned into static analysis and dynamic/stream analysis, based on whether the system can collect traces beforehand for post-analysis or it must react at real time to handle online data. Different methods have been developed in this domain by integration and extension of the methods developed in machine learning, data mining, pattern recognition, and statistics. For example, statistical analysis (such as hypothesis testing) approach [LFY+06] can be performed on program execution traces to isolate the locations of bugs that distinguish program success runs from failing runs. Despite of its limited success, it is still a rich domain for data miners to research and further develop sophisticated, scalable, and real-time data-mining methods.

1.3 Conclusions

Science and engineering are fertile lands for data mining. In the last two decades, science and engineering have evolved to a stage that gigantic amounts of data are constantly being generated and collected, and data mining and knowledge discovery becomes the essential scientific discovery process. We have proceeded to the era of data science and data engineering.

In this chapter, we have examined a few important research challenges in science and engineering data mining. There are still several interesting research issues not covered in this short abstract. One such issue is the development of invisible data mining functionality for science and engineering that builds data-mining functions as an invisible process in the system (e.g., rank the results based on the relevance and some sophisticated, preprocessed evaluation functions) so that users may not even sense that data mining has been performed beforehand or is being performed and their browsing and mouse clicking are simply using the results of or further exploring of data mining. Another research issue is privacy-preserving data mining that aims to performing effective data mining without disclosure of private or sensitive information to outsiders. Finally, knowledge-guided intelligent human computer interaction based on the knowledge extracted from data could be another interesting issue for future research.

Acknowledgment

The work was supported in part by the U.S. National Science Foundation NSF IIS-05-13678 and BDI-05-15813.

References

[AC05]   E. M. Airoldi and K. M. Carley. Sampling algorithms for pure net-
            work topologies: A study on the stability and the separability of metric
            embeddings. *SIGKDD Explor. Newslett*, 7(2): 13–22, 2005.

[ACG02]   R. Ananthakrishna, S. Chaudhuri, and V. Ganti. Eliminating fuzzy
            duplicates in data warehouses. In *Proceedings of the 2002 Interna-
            tional Conference Very Large Data Bases (VLDB'02)*, pp. 586–597,
            Hong Kong, China, Aug. 2002.

[AEEK99]   M. Ankerst, C. Elsen, M. Ester, and H. P. Kriegel. Visual classification:
            An interactive approach to decision tree construction. In *Proceedings
            of the 1999 International Conference Knowledge Discovery and Data
            Mining (KDD'99)*, pp. 392–396, San Diego, CA, Aug. 1999.

[Agg06]   C. C. Aggarwal. *Data Streams: Models and Algorithms*. Springer, New York, 2006.

[AHWY03]   C. C. Aggarwal, J. Han, J. Wang, and P. S. Yu. A framework for clustering evolving data streams. In *Proceedings of the 2003 International Conference Very Large Data Bases (VLDB'03)*, pp. 81–92, Berlin, Germany, Sept. 2003.

[AHWY04]   C. C. Aggarwal, J. Han, J. Wang, and P. S. Yu. A framework for projected clustering of high dimensional data streams. In *Proceedings of the 2004 International Conference Very Large Data Bases (VLDB'04)*, pp. 852–863, Toronto, Canada, Aug. 2004.

[All02]   J. Allan. *Topic Detection and Tracking: Event-Based Information Organization*. Kluwer Academic, Norwell, MA, 2002.

[BBD$^+$02]   B. Babcock, S. Babu, M. Datar, R. Motwani, and J. Widom. Models and issues in data stream systems. In *Proceedings of the 2002 ACM Symposium on Principles of Database Systems (PODS'02)*, pp. 1–16, Madison, WI, June 2002.

[Ber03]   M. W. Berry. *Survey of Text Mining: Clustering, Classification, and Retrieval*. Springer, New York, 2003.

[BG06]   I. Bhattacharya and L. Getoor. A latent dirichlet model for unsupervised entity resolution. In *Proceedings of the 2006 SIAM International Conference Data Mining (SDM'06)*, pp. 47–58, Bethesda, MD, Apr. 2006.

[BHLY04]   P. Bajcsy, J. Han, L. Liu, and J. Yang. Survey of bio-data analysis from data mining perspective. In J. T. L. Wang, M. J. Zaki, H. T. T. Toivonen, and D. Shasha (Eds.), *Data Mining in Bioinformatics*, pp. 9–39. Springer, London, UK, 2004.

[CCLR05]   B. C. Chen, L. Chen, Y. Lin, and R. Ramakrishnan. Prediction cubes. In *Proceedings of the 2005 International Conference Very Large Data Bases (VLDB'05)*, pp. 982–993, Trondheim, Norway, Aug. 2005.

[CDF$^+$00]   M. Craven, D. DiPasquo, D. Freitag, A. McCallum, T. M. Mitchell, K. Nigam, and S. Slattery. Learning to construct knowledge bases from the World Wide Web. *Artif. Intell.*, 118: 69–113, 2000.

[CDG$^+$98]   S. Chakrabarti, B. E. Dom, D. Gibson, J. M. Kleinberg, P. Raghavan, and S. Rajagopalan. Automatic resource compilation by analyzing hyperlink structure and associated text. In *Proceedings of the 7th International World Wide Web Conference (WWW'98)*, pp. 65–74, Brisbane, Australia, 1998.

[CDH$^+$02]   Y. Chen, G. Dong, J. Han, B. W. Wah, and J. Wang. Multi-dimensional regression analysis of time-series data streams. In *Proceedings of the*

            2002 International Conference Very Large Data Bases (VLDB'02),
            pp. 323–334, Hong Kong, China, Aug. 2002.

[CDH⁺06]   Y. Chen, G. Dong, J. Han, J. Pei, B. W. Wah, and J. Wang. Regression
            cubes with lossless compression and aggregation. *IEEE Trans. Knowl-
            edge Data Eng.*, 18: 1585–1599, 2006.

[CDI98]   S. Chakrabarti, B. E. Dom, and P. Indyk. Enhanced hypertext
            classification using hyper-links. In *Proceedings of the 1998 ACM-
            SIGMOD International Conference Management of Data (SIG-
            MOD'98)*, pp. 307–318, Seattle, WA, June 1998.

[CH07]   D. J. Cook and L. B. Holder. *Mining Graph Data*. John Wiley & Sons,
            Hoboken, NJ, 2007.

[Cha01]   S. Chakrabarti. Integrating the document object model with hyper-
            links for enhanced topic distillation and information extraction. In
            *Proceedings of the 2001 International World Wide Web Conference
            (WWW'01)*, pp. 211–220, Hong Kong, China, May 2001.

[Cha03]   S. Chakrabarti. *Mining the Web: Discovering Knowledge from Hyper-
            tex Data*, Morgan Kaufmann, San Francisco, CA, 2003.

[CM03]   G. Cormode and S. Muthukrishnan. What's hot and what's not: Track-
            ing most frequent items dynamically. In *PODS '03: Proceedings of
            the 22nd ACM SIGMOD-SIGACT-SIGART Symposium on Principles
            of Database Systems*, pp. 296–306, ACM, New York, 2003.

[CSW05]   P. J. Carrington, J. Scott, and S. Wasserman. *Models and Methods
            in Social Network Analysis*. Cambridge University Press, New York,
            2005.

[CTTX05]   G. Cong, K. L. Tan, A. K. H. Tung, and X. Xu. Mining top-k cover-
            ing rule groups for gene expression data. In *Proceedings of the 2005
            ACM-SIGMOD International Conference Management of Data (SIG-
            MOD'05)*, pp. 670–681, Baltimore, MD, June 2005.

[CYHH07]   H. Cheng, X. Yan, J. Han, and C. W. Hsu. Discriminative frequent
            pattern analysis for effective classification. In *Proceedings of the
            2007 International Conference Data Engineering (ICDE'07)*, Istan-
            bul, Turkey, Apr. 2007.

[CYHY08]   H. Cheng, X. Yan, J. Han, and P. S. Yu. Direct discriminative pattern
            mining for effective classification. In *Proceedings of the 2008 Inter-
            national Conference Data Engineering (ICDE'08)*, Cancun, Mexico,
            Apr. 2008.

[DH00]   P. Domingos and G. Hulten. Mining high-speed data streams. In *Pro-
            ceedings of the 2000 ACM SIGKDD International Conference Knowl-
            edge Discovery in Databases (KDD'00)*, pp. 71–80, Boston, MA,
            Aug. 2000.

[DH01]   P. Domingos and G. Hulten. A general method for scaling up machine learning algorithms and its application to clustering. In *ICML '01: Proceedings of the 18th International Conference on Machine Learning*, pp. 106–113, Morgan Kaufmann Publishers, San Francisco, CA, 2001.

[DHM05]   X. Dong, A. Halevy, and J. Madhavan. Reference reconciliation in complex information spaces. In *SIGMOD '05: Proceedings of the 2005 ACM SIGMOD International Conference on Management of Data*, pp. 85–96, ACM, New York, 2005.

[DM01]   I. S. Dhillon and D. S. Modha. Concept decompositions for large sparse text data using clustering. *Mach. Learn.*, 42(1–2): 143–175, 2001.

[dOL03]   M. C. F. de Oliveira and H. Levkowitz. From visual data exploration to visual data mining: A survey. *IEEE Trans. Vis. Comput. Graph.*, 9(3): 378–394, 2003.

[ER04]   G. Erkan and D. R. Radev. Lexrank: Graph-based lexical centrality as salience in text summarization. *J. Artifi. Intell. Res.*, 22: 457–479, 2004.

[Fan04]   W. Fan. Systematic data selection to mine concept-drifting data streams. In *KDD '04: Proceedings of the 10th ACM SIGKDD International Conference on Knowledge Discovery and Data Mining*, pp. 128–137, ACM, New York, 2004.

[FGW01]   U. Fayyad, G. Grinstein, and A. Wierse. *Information Visualization in Data Mining and Knowledge Discovery*. Morgan Kaufmann, San Francisco, CA, 2001.

[FL05]   F. M. Facca and P. L. Lanzi. Mining interesting knowledge from weblogs: A survey. *Data Knowledge Eng.*, 53(3): 225–241, 2005.

[FLGC02]   G. Flake, S. Lawrence, C. L. Giles, and F. Coetzee. Self-organization and identification of web communities. *IEEE Comput.*, 35: 66–71, 2002.

[GD05]   L. Getoor and C. P. Diehl. Link mining: A survey. *SIGKDD Explor.*, 7: 3–12, 2005.

[GFH07]   J. Gao, W. Fan, and J. Han. On appropriate assumptions to mine data streams: Analysis and practice. In *Proceedings of the 2007 International Conference Data Mining (ICDM'07)*, pp. 143–152, Omaha, NE, Oct. 2007.

[GFHY07]   J. Gao, W. Fan, J. Han, and P. S. Yu. A general framework for mining concept-drifting data streams with skewed distributions. In *Proceedings of the 2007 SIAM International Conference Data Mining (SDM'07)*, pp. 3–14, Minneapolis, MN, Apr. 2007.

[GFKT01]   L. Getoor, N. Friedman, D. Koller, and B. Taskar. Learning prob-
            abilistic models of relational structure. In *Proceedings of the 2001
            International Conference Machine Learning (ICML'01)*, pp. 170–177,
            Williamstown, MA, 2001.

[GHL06a]   H. Gonzalez, J. Han, and X. Li. Flowcube: Constructuing RFID
            flowcubes for multi-dimensional analysis of commodity flows. In *Pro-
            ceedings of the 2006 International Conference Very Large Data Bases
            (VLDB'06)*, pp. 834–845, Seoul, Korea, Sept. 2006.

[GHL06b]   H. Gonzalez, J. Han, and X. Li. Mining compressed commodity
            workflows from massive RFID data sets. In *Proceedings of the 2006
            International Conference Information and Knowledge Management
            (CIKM'06)*, pp. 162–171, Arlington, VA, Nov. 2006.

[GHL⁺07]   H. Gonzalez, J. Han, X. Li, M. Myslinska, and J. P. Sondag. Adaptive
            fastest path computation on a road network: A traffic mining approach.
            In *Proceedings of the 2007 International Conference Very Large Data
            Bases (VLDB'07)*, pp. 794–805, Vienna, Austria, Sept. 2007.

[GHLK06]   H. Gonzalez, J. Han, X. Li, and D. Klabjan. Warehousing and anal-
            ysis of massive RFID data sets. In *Proceedings of the 2006 Interna-
            tional Conference Data Engineering (ICDE'06)*, p. 83, Atlanta, GA,
            Apr. 2006.

[GHP⁺04]   C. Giannella, J. Han, J. Pei, and P. S. Yu. Mining frequent patterns in
            data streams at multiple time granularities. In H. Kargupta, A. Joshi, K.
            Sivakumar, and Y. Yesha (Eds.), *Data Mining: Next Generation chal-
            lenges and Future Directions*, AAAI Press, Menlo Park, CA, 2004.

[GHS07]   H. Gonzalez, J. Han, and X. Shen. Cost-conscious cleaning of massive
            RFID data sets. In *Proceedings of the 2007 International Conference
            Data Engineering (ICDE'07)*, pp. 1268–1272, Istanbul, Turkey, Apr.
            2007.

[GKMS01]   A. C. Gilbert, Y. Kotidis, S. Muthukrishnan, and M. Strauss. Surfing
            wavelets on streams: One-pass summaries for approximate aggregate
            queries. In *Proceedings of the 2001 International Conference on Very
            Large Data Bases (VLDB'01)*, pp. 79–88, Rome, Italy, Sept. 2001.

[GMM⁺03]   S. Guha, A. Meyerson, N. Mishra, R. Motwani, and L. O'Callaghan.
            Clustering data streams: Theory and practice. *IEEE Trans. Knowledge
            Data Eng.*, 15: 515–528, 2003.

[GSF97]   M. H. Gross, T. C. Sprenger, and J. Finger. Visualizing information on
            a sphere. In *Proceedings of the 1997 IEEE Symposium on Information
            Visualization (InfoVis '97)*, pp. 11, Phoenix, AZ, 1997.

[Hav02]   T. H. Haveliwala. Topic-sensitive pagerank. In *WWW '02: Proceedings of the 11th International Conference on World Wide Web*, pp. 517–526, ACM, New York, 2002.

[HCXY07]   J. Han, H. Cheng, D. Xin, and X. Yan. Frequent pattern mining: Current status and future directions. *Data Min. Knowledge Discov.*, 15: 55–86, 2007.

[HK06]   J. Han and M. Kamber. *Data Mining: Concepts and Techniques* (2nd ed.). Morgan Kaufmann, San Francisco, CA, 2006.

[HSD01]   G. Hulten, L. Spencer, and P. Domingos. Mining time-changing data streams. In *Proceedings of the 2001 ACM SIGKDD International Conference Knowledge Discovery in Databases (KDD'01)*, San Francisco, CA, Aug. 2001.

[Ins97]   A. Inselberg. Multidimensional detective. In *Proceedings of the 1997 IEEE Symposium on Information Visualization (InfoVis '97)*, p. 100, Washington DC, 1997.

[JW02]   G. Jeh and J. Widom. SimRank: A measure of structural-context similarity. In *Proceedings of the 2002 ACM SIGKDD International Conference on Knowledge Discovery and Data Mining (KDD'02)*, pp. 538–543, Edmonton, Canada, July 2002.

[KB00]   R. Kosla and H. Blockeel. Web mining research: A survey. *SIGKDD Explor.*, 1: 1–15, 2000.

[Kei02]   D. A. Keim. Information visualization and visual data mining. *IEEE Trans. Vis. Comput. Graph.*, 8(1): 1–8, 2002.

[KK01]   M. Kuramochi and G. Karypis. Frequent subgraph discovery. In *Proceedings of the 2001 International Conference Data Mining (ICDM'01)*, pp. 313–320, San Jose, CA, Nov. 2001.

[Kle99]   J. M. Kleinberg. Authoritative sources in a hyperlinked environment. *J. ACM*, 46: 604–632, 1999.

[KM05]   J. Z. Kolter and M. A. Maloof. Using additive expert ensembles to cope with concept drift. In *Proceedings of the 2004 International Conference Machine Learning (ICML'05)*, pp. 449–456, Bonn, Germany, 2005.

[LFY+06]   C. Liu, L. Fei, X. Yan, J. Han, and S. P. Midkiff. Statistical debugging: A hypothesis testing-based approach. *IEEE Trans. Software Eng.*, 32: 831–848, 2006.

[LH07]   X. Li and J. Han. Mining approximate top-k subspace anomalies in multi-dimensional time-series data. In *Proceedings of the 2007 International Conference Very Large Data Bases (VLDB'07)*, Vienna, Austria, Sept. 2007.

[LHKG07]   X. Li, J. Han, S. Kim, and H. Gonzalez. Roam: Rule- and motif-based anomaly detection in massive moving object data sets. In *Proceedings of the 2007 SIAM International Conference Data Mining (SDM'07)*, Minneapolis, MN, Apr. 2007.

[LHL08]   J. G. Lee, J. Han, and X. Li. Trajectory outlier detection: A partition-and-detect framework. In *Proceedings of the 2008 International Conference Data Engineering (ICDE'08)*, Cancun, Mexico, Apr. 2008.

[LHM98]   B. Liu, W. Hsu, and Y. Ma. Integrating classification and association rule mining. In *Proceedings of the 1998 International Conference Knowledge Discovery and Data Mining (KDD'98)*, pp. 80–86, New York, Aug. 1998.

[LHW07]   J. G. Lee, J. Han, and K. Whang. Clustering trajectory data. In *Proceedings of the 2007 ACM-SIGMOD International Conference Management of Data (SIGMOD'07)*, Beijing, China, June 2007.

[LHY$^+$08]   X. Li, J. Han, Z. Yin, J. -G. Lee, and Y. Sun. Sampling cube: A framework for statistical olap over sampling data. In *Proceedings of the 2008 ACM-SIGMOD International Conference Management of Data (SIGMOD'08)*, pp. 779–790, Vancouver, Canada, June 2008.

[Liu06]   B. Liu. *Web Data Mining: Exploring Hyperlinks, Contents, and Usage Data*. Springer, Berlin, Germany, 2006.

[MH01]   H. Miller and J. Han. *Geographic Data Mining and Knowledge Discovery*. Taylor & Francis, New York, 2001.

[MM02]   G. Manku and R. Motwani. Approximate frequency counts over data streams. In *Proceedings of the 2002 International Conference Very Large Data Bases (VLDB'02)*, pp. 346–357, Hong Kong, China, Aug. 2002.

[Mut03]   S. Muthukrishnan. Data streams: Algorithms and applications. In *Proceedings of the 2003 Annual ACM-SIAM Symposium Discrete Algorithms (SODA'03)*, pp. 413–413, Baltimore, MD, Jan. 2003.

[MXC$^+$07]   Q. Mei, D. Xin, H. Cheng, J. Han, and C. Zhai. Semantic annotation of frequent patterns. *ACM Trans. Knowledge Discov. Data (TKDD)*, 15: 321–348, 2007.

[MZ05]   Q. Mei and C. X. Zhai. Discovering evolutionary theme patterns from text: An exploration of temporal text mining. In *KDD '05: Proceedings of the 11th ACM SIGKDD International Conference on Knowledge Discovery in Data Mining*, pp. 198–207, Chicago, IL, 2005.

[OHS05]   J. O'Madadhain, J. Hutchins, and P. Smyth. Prediction and ranking algorithms for event-based network data. *SIGKDD Explor. Newsl.*, 7(2): 23–30, 2005.

[PBMW98] L. Page, S. Brin, R. Motwani, and T. Winograd. The pagerank cita-
          tion ranking: Bringing order to the web. In Technical Report SIDL-
          WP-1999-0120, Computer Science Department, Stanford University,
          Palo Alto, CA, 1998.

[PMM$^+$02] H. Pasula, B. Marthi, B. Milch, S. J. Russell, and I. Shpitser. Identity
          uncertainty and citation matching. In *Advances in Neural Information
          Processing Systems 15 (NIPS'02)*, pp. 1401–1408, Vancouver, Canada,
          Dec. 2002.

[QD07]   X. Qi and B. D. Davison. Web page classification: Features and algo-
          rithms. In Technical Report LU-CSE-07-010, Computer Science and
          Engineering, Lehigh University, Bethlehem, PA, 2007.

[RC07]   R. Ramakrishnan and B. C. Chen. Exploratory mining in cube space.
          Data Min. Knowledge Discov., 15(1): 29–54, 2007.

[RD02]   M. Richardson and P. Domingos. The intelligent surfer: Probabilistic
          combination of link and content information in pagerank. In *Advances
          in Neural Information Processing Systems 14*, pp. 1441–1448,
          Vancouver, Canada, 2002.

[RHS01]   J. F. Roddick, K. Hornsby, and M. Spiliopoulou. An updated bibliog-
          raphy of temporal, spatial, and spatio-temporal data mining research.
          In *Lecture Notes in Computer Science 2007*, pp. 147–163, Springer,
          London, UK, 2001.

[SC03]   S. Shekhar and S. Chawla. *Spatial Databases: A Tour*. Prentice Hall,
          Upper Saddle River, NJ, 2003.

[SQCF05] J. Sun, H. Qu, D. Chakrabarti, and C. Faloutsos. Relevance search and
          anomaly detection in bipartite graphs. *SIGKDD Explor. Newslett*, 7(2):
          48–55, 2005.

[SS03]   D. Stan and I. K. Sethi. EID: A system for exploration of image
          databases. *Inf. Process. Manage.*, 39: 335–361, 2003.

[SW05]   C. Snoek and M. Worring. Multimodal video indexing: A review of
          the state-of-the-art. *Multimedia Tools Appl.*, 25(1): 5–35, 2005.

[SZ04]   D. Shasha and Y. Zhu. *High Performance Discovery in Time Series:
          Techniques and Case Studies*. Springer, New York, 2004.

[SZHV04] S. Shekhar, P. Zhang, Y. Huang, and R. R. Vatsavai. Trends in spatial
          data mining. In H. Kargupta, A. Joshi, K. Sivakumar, and Y. Yesha
          (Eds.), *Data Mining: Next Generation Challenges and Future Direc-
          tions*, pp. 357–380, AAAI/MIT Press, Menlo Park, CA, 2004.

[TcZ$^+$03] N. Tatbul, U. Çetintemel, S. Zdonik, M. Cherniack, and M. Stone-
          braker. Load shedding in a data stream manager. In *VLDB'2003: Pro-
          ceedings of the 29th International Conference on Very Large Data
          Bases*, pp. 309–320, Berlin, Germany, 2003.

[Tuf01]   E. R. Tufte. *The Visual Display of Quantitative Information* (2nd ed.). Graphics Press, Cheshire, CT, 2001.

[WFYH03]   H. Wang, W. Fan, P. S. Yu, and J. Han. Mining concept-drifting data streams using ensemble classifiers. In *Proceedings of the 2003 ACM SIGKDD International Conference Knowledge Discovery and Data Mining (KDD'03)*, pp. 226–235, Washington DC, Aug. 2003.

[WIZD04]   S. Weiss, N. Indurkhya, T. Zhang, and F. Damerau. *Text Mining: Predictive Methods for Analyzing Unstructured Information.* Springer, New York, 2004.

[WK05]   J. Wang and G. Karypis. HARMONY: Efficiently mining the best rules for classification. In *Proceedings of the 2005 SIAM Conference Data Mining (SDM'05)*, pp. 205–216, Newport Beach, CA, Apr. 2005.

[WLX⁺07]   T. Wu, X. Li, D. Xin, J. Han, J. Lee, and R. Redder. Datascope: Viewing database contents in google maps' way. In *Proceedings of the 2007 International Conference Very Large Data Bases (VLDB'07)*, pp. 1314–1317, Vienna, Austria, Sept. 2007.

[WM03]   T. Washio and H. Motoda. State of the art of graph-based data mining. *SIGKDD Explor.*, 5: 59–68, 2003.

[WWYY02]   H. Wang, W. Wang, J. Yang, and P. S. Yu. Clustering by pattern similarity in large data sets. In *Proceedings of the 2002 ACM-SIGMOD International Conference Management of Data (SIGMOD'02)*, pp. 418–427, Madison, WI, June 2002.

[XCYH06]   D. Xin, H. Cheng, X. Yan, and J. Han. Extracting redundancy-aware top-k patterns. In *Proceedings of the 2006 ACM SIGKDD International Conference Knowledge Discovery in Databases (KDD'06)*, pp. 444–453, Philadelphia, PA, Aug. 2006.

[YH07]   X. Yan and J. Han. Discovery of frequent substructures. In D. Cook and L. Holder (Eds.), *Mining Graph Data*, pp. 99–115, John Wiley & Sons, Hoboken, NJ, 2007.

[YHY05]   X. Yin, J. Han, and P. S. Yu. Cross-relational clustering with user's guidance. In *Proceedings of the 2005 ACM SIGKDD International Conference Knowledge Discovery in Databases (KDD'05)*, pp. 344–353, Chicago, IL, Aug. 2005.

[YHY06]   X. Yin, J. Han, and P. S. Yu. Linkclus: Efficient clustering via heterogeneous semantic links. In *Proceedings of the 2006 International Conference on Very Large Data Bases (VLDB'06)*, pp. 427–438, Seoul, Korea, Sept. 2006.

[YHY07a]   X. Yin, J. Han, and P. S. Yu. Object distinction: Distinguishing objects with identical names by link analysis. In *Proceedings* of the 2007 International Conference Data Engineering (ICDE'07), pp. 1242–1246, Istanbul, Turkey, Apr. 2007.

[YHY07b]   X. Yin, J. Han, and P. S. Yu. Truth discovery with multiple conflicting information providers on the web. In *Proceedings of the 2007 ACM SIGKDD International Conference Knowledge Discovery in Databases (KDD'07)*, pp. 1048–1052, San Jose, CA, Aug. 2007.

[YHYY06]   X. Yin, J. Han, J. Yang, and P. S. Yu. Efficient classification across multiple database relations: A crossmine approach. *IEEE Trans. Knowledge Data Eng.*, 18: 770–783, 2006.

[ZYH⁺07]   F. Zhu, X. Yan, J. Han, P. S. Yu, and H. Cheng. Mining colossal frequent patterns by core pattern fusion. In *Proceedings of the 2007 International Conference Data Engineering (ICDE'07)*, pp. 706–715, Istanbul, Turkey, Apr. 2007.

Chapter 2

Detecting Ecosystem Disturbances and Land Cover Change Using Data Mining

Shyam Boriah, Vipin Kumar, Michael Steinbach, Pang-Ning Tan,
Christopher Potter, and Steven Klooster

Contents

2.1 Introduction

Remote sensing data consisting of satellite observations of the land surface, biosphere, solid Earth, atmosphere, and oceans, combined with historical climate records and predictions from ecosystem models, offers new opportunities for understanding how the Earth is changing, for determining what factors cause these changes, and for predicting future changes. Data mining and knowledge discovery

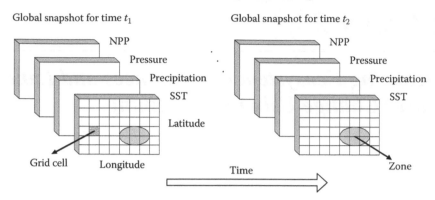

FIGURE 2.1: Simplified view of the problem domain.

techniques can aid this effort by discovering patterns that capture complex inter-actions among ocean temperature, air pressure, surface meteorology, and terrestrial carbon flux.

2.1.1 Earth Science Data

The Earth science data for our analysis consists of global snapshots of measure-ment values for a number of vegetation-related variables collected for all land sur-faces (see Figure 2.1). The data observations come from NASA's Earth Observation System (EOS) [1] satellites; data sets are distributed through the Land Processes Distributed Active Archive Center (LP DAAC) [2].

The historical data for our proposed work is measured at points on latitude–longitude grids of different resolutions. Historically, land measurements, such as temperature, were available at a spatial resolution of $0.5° \times 0.5°$, sea surface tem-perature was available for a $1° \times 1°$ grid, and sea level temperature was available for a $2.5° \times 2.5°$ grid. The temporal resolution was 1 month. Depending on the data set, this resulted in time series with lengths ranging from roughly 100 to 500 time steps (each time step corresponds to 1 month). More recently, however, NASA's EOS has been providing data with a higher spatial and temporal resolution, e.g., $250 \text{ m} \times 250 \text{ m}$ and every 16 days.

2.1.2 Challenges in Mining of Earth Science Data

There are a number of data mining challenges that are associated with Earth sci-ence data. The *spatiotemporal* nature of Earth science data is especially challeng-ing since traditional data mining techniques do not take advantage of the spatial and temporal autocorrelation present in such data. Furthermore—due to improvements in satellites, sensor instruments, and storage capabilities—the size of Earth science data sets has increased six orders of magnitude in 20 years and continues to grow with increasingly higher-resolution data being generated. For example, grid cells have gone from a resolution of $2.5° \times 2.5°$ (10K points for the globe) to $250 \text{ m} \times 250 \text{ m}$

(15M points for just California; 10B for the globe). Finally, there is the issue of high dimensionality since long time series are common in Earth science (and the temporal resolution is also increasing).

2.1.3   Contributions

In this chapter we discuss the analysis of satellite observations of the land surface with two important goals: to detect large-scale disturbances with natural and anthropogenic (due to human activity) causes using low-resolution data, and to detect changing land cover patterns using high-resolution data.

The first study discussed in this chapter was conducted to evaluate patterns in a 19 year record of global satellite observations of vegetation from the advanced very high resolution radiometer (AVHRR) as a means to characterize major ecosystem disturbance events and regimes. The goal of the study was to gain insight into a number of important Earth science issues in relation to ecosystem disturbances. Specifically, the goal was to detect and characterize sudden changes in greenness over extensive land areas due to ecosystem disturbances.

The second study discussed in this chapter deals with change detection for spatiotemporal data from the domain of Earth science, specifically land cover change. Determining where, when, and why natural ecosystem conversions occur is a crucial concern for Earth scientists because characteristics of the land cover can have important impacts on local climate, radiation balance, biogeochemistry, hydrology, and the diversity and abundance of terrestrial species. Consequently, understanding trends in land cover conversion at local scales is a requirement for making useful quantitative predictions about other regional and global changes. In this study we present preliminary results obtained by applying data mining techniques to the land cover change detection problem.

2.2   Detection of Ecosystem Disturbances

The goal of this study was to detect and characterize sudden changes in greenness over large land areas due to ecosystem disturbances. Ecosystem disturbances can have a variety of causes: physical (hurricanes, fires, floods, droughts, ice storms), biogenic (insects, mammals, pathogens), and anthropogenic (logging, drainage of wetlands, chemical pollution).

Understanding such changes can help provide deeper insight into the interplay among natural disasters, human activity, and the rise of CO_2. The use of satellite observations has the potential to reveal completely new pictures of ecological changes and disasters, particularly since many locations where such events occur may be sparsely populated or inaccessible and disturbances may have gone undetected. Furthermore, the CO_2 that may be released into the atmosphere as a result of an ecosystem disturbance can contribute to the current rise of CO_2 in the atmosphere, which has global implications.

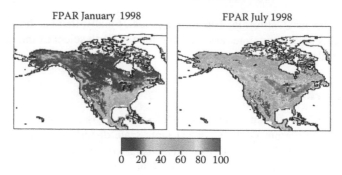

FIGURE 2.2: (See color insert following page 264.) FPAR data for North America.

2.2.1 Data

Earth-observing satellites have monitored daily leafy vegetation cover on land (also called "greenness" cover) for more than 20 years [3]. The fraction absorbed of photosynthetically active radiation (FPAR) by vegetation canopies worldwide has been computed at a monthly time interval from 1982 to 2000 and gridded at a spatial resolution of 8 km globally. FPAR is a common measure of greenness cover, ranging from zero (on barren land) to 100% (for dense cover). For this study we used the 8 km FPAR data set for North America. Figure 2.2 shows an image with 2 months of FPAR for North America; January has lower levels of FPAR and June has higher levels of FPAR in correspondence with the winter and summer seasons in the northern hemisphere. A typical time series is shown in Figure 2.3. The figure also shows a simplified view of what a hypothetical disturbance event might look like.

2.2.2 Algorithm

The observed FPAR time series at each pixel was first detrended using a linear adjustment, which is necessary to minimize the possibility that, in cases where there is a gradual but marked increase in monthly FPAR over the 18 years time series, any potential disturbance event occurring relatively near the end of the series is not overlooked. To remove the dominant seasonal oscillations in vegetation phenology observed throughout the globe, the detrended FPAR time series was subsequently "deseasonalized" by applying the 12 month moving average for every pixel location.

We hypothesized that significant declines in average annual FPAR levels can be defined to be greater than 1.7 standard deviations (SD) below (LO) the 18 years average FPAR computed for any specific pixel location. A "sustained" disturbance event would be defined as any decline in average annual FPAR levels (at an assigned significance level) that lasts for a temporal threshold value of at least 12 consecutive monthly observations at any specific pixel location. The reasoning used here was that an actual disturbance involves a sustained decline in FPAR because the structure of the vegetation cover has been severely altered or destroyed during the disturbance

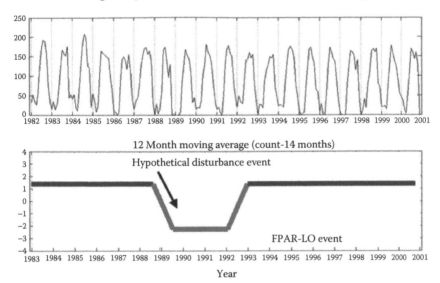

FIGURE 2.3:   Example of an FPAR-LO event.

event to a magnitude that lowers FPAR significantly for at least one seasonal growing cycle, after which time regrowth and recovery of the former vegetation structure may permit FPAR to increase again.

We then performed a one-sided statistical t-test, where rejection of the null hypothesis means that there is no difference between the 19 year average for the monthly FPAR level and the consistent FPAR-LO level identified in a string of 12 or more consecutive time steps. An absolute SD value of 1.7 or more represents the 95% confidence level, SD of 2.0 or more represents the 97% confidence level, and SD of 2.6 or more represents the 99% confidence level.

2.2.3   Results

We applied the algorithm described above to the 1982–2000 FPAR time series from AVHRR observations at 8 km resolution to identify potential disturbance events in terrestrial ecosystems of North America. At a level of SD of 1.7 or more (95% confidence) for definition of disturbance intensity, we detected 11,972 pixel locations at the threshold of 12 consecutive monthly time steps for FPAR-LO events. For all vegetated land areas of North America, the fraction of total land area that had at least one FRAR-LO event was 3.9%. Summed over 19 years, these pixels together cover a total area of just over 766,000 km^2, which is slightly larger than the state of Texas. In the sections that follow, we summarize regional disturbance types chronologically, with focus on well-documented tropical storms and wildfires during the 1980s and 1990s. For an extended discussion that includes coverage of droughts, heat waves, cold waves, and blizzards, see Ref. [4].

TABLE 2.1: Hurricanes (category 3 and higher) of the 1980s detected as FPAR-LO events.

Year	Hurricane	Category	Landfall Location	Landfall Latitude/Longitude
1983	Alicia	3	SE Texas, USA	28.9°N 95.0°W
1985	Elena	3	Mississippi, USA	30.2°N 88.8°W
1985	Gloria	3	East Coast, USA	35.5°N 75.5°W
1988	Gilbert	3	East Coast, Mexico	20.4°N 86.5°N
				23.9°N 97.0°W
1989	Hugo	4	North Carolina, USA	33.5°N 80.3°W

2.2.3.1 Tropical Storms

A series of major tropical storms in Category 3 or 4 (sustained winds in excess of 178 km/h) made landfall across the southeastern coast of the United States and along the Gulf Coasts of the United States and Mexico during the 1980s (Table 2.1). By locating 8 km pixels in the vicinity of documented landfall points of storms, five of the strongest hurricanes making North American landfall in the 1980s were readily detected as FPAR-LO events in the 19 years AVHRR time series. These five hurricanes (in order of occurrence) were called Alicia, Elena, Gloria, Gilbert, and Hugo.

The impacts of Hurricane Gilbert in 1988 on the Yucatán Peninsula of Mexico and Hurricane Hugo in 1989 on the North Carolina coast are representative of disturbance to forest ecosystems detected as FPAR-LO events throughout southeastern North America and Caribbean Islands during this period of severe tropical storm damage. The hurricane season in North America extends from June to November, with storms most common in September, when ocean temperatures are warmest. The FPAR time series in Figure 2.4 show this expected timing of FPAR-LO events detected in late summer or early autumn of 1988 and 1989.

Unlike the examples shown in Table 2.1, Hurricane Andrew, a Category 4 storm that struck southern Florida in 1992, could not be detected as a FPAR-LO event in the 19 years AVHRR time series. The probable explanation is that the landfall areas in southern Florida for Hurricane Andrew were not dominated by forest vegetation cover, but instead by grassland and wetland areas. Hence, the disturbance detection method with thresholds of SD of 1.7 or more, FPAR-LO lasting more than 12 consecutive months will not reveal areas of predominantly annual herbaceous cover that would only be disrupted for several weeks or a month due to a severe wind event.

2.2.3.2 Large-Scale Forest Fires

A critical set of historical disturbance events available for verification of FPAR-LO events as large-scale ecosystem disturbances are well-documented wildfires that burned areas reported to cover tens of thousands of hectares in a single year or growing season. A list of such events was compiled (Table 2.2) using publications and reports from the North American fire literature. The list in Table 2.2 is not intended to represent an exhaustive set of North American fire events over the 19 year period

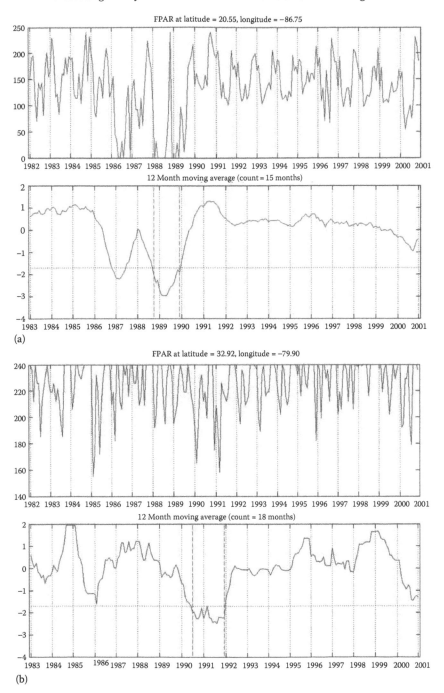

FIGURE 2.4: Disturbance detection algorithm applied to the FPAR time series for two locations. (a) Corresponds to a location in the Yucatán Peninsula of Mexico where a disturbance is sustained for 15 months; and (b) corresponds to a location on the coast of North Carolina where a disturbance lasted for 18 months.

TABLE 2.2: List of major forest wildfires for North America in the 1980s and 1990s.

Year	Location	Area Burned (ha)	Latitude/Longitude	Notes
1987	Stanislaus, California, USA	59,000	38°N 120°W	Stanislaus National Forest
1987	Siskiyou, Oregon, USA	51,000	42°N 124°W	Silver fire, Siskiyou National Forest
1988	Yellowstone, Wyoming, USA	>500,000	44.6°N 110.7°W	
1989	Manitoba, Canada	>400,000	51°N 97°W	Lake Manitoba (spread northward for 800 km)
1989 and 1991	Quebec, Canada	>200,000	52°N 75°W	
1997	Alaska, USA	>200,000	63°–64°N 159°W	Inowak fire (100 miles SW of McGrath); Simels and Magitchlie Creek fires, Galena District
1998	Mexico	>500,000	17°–22°N 94°–98°W	Chiapas, Oaxaca

of the FPAR record, but instead is a list of the largest fire events that could be confirmed for their timing of initiation (to about 3 months) and geographic location (to within approximately 1° latitude and longitude). Selected wildfire areas have been confirmed for timing and location using Landsat and other relatively high-resolution satellite images.

We find that within each geographic area of the confirmed wildfire events listed in Table 2.2, an FPAR-LO event was detected during the reported time period of actual wildfire activity. As an example, the FPAR time series for the Yellowstone National Park fire shows a significant FPAR-LO event (SD ± 2.0) beginning during the summer of 1988. This pixel location coincides with the North Fork fire that spread on the edge of the park toward West Yellowstone, Montana. The recovery back to long-term average FPAR required nearly 2 years.

2.2.4 Study Outcomes

There were several important outcomes from this study, some of which were highlighted in a press release by NASA [5]. One was the discovery that ecosystem disturbances can contribute to the current rise of CO_2 in the atmosphere, which has implications for atmospheric CO_2 studies. Specifically, it was estimated that 9 billion metric tons of carbon may have moved from the Earth's soil and surface life forms into the atmosphere in the 18 years beginning in 1982 due to wildfires and other disturbances. In comparison, fossil fuel emission of CO_2 to the atmosphere each year was about 7 billion metric tons in 1990.

Other unique aspects of the study were the long temporal range (covered more than a decade of analysis) and global coverage of the data, as well as the fact that the study encompassed all potential categories of major disturbances (physical, biogenic, and anthropogenic).

The limitations of the techniques used in the study were that some disturbances may have been missed and the algorithm may also produce false alarms. The estimation of the false negative and false positive rates are aspects of this work that need further study. Another limitation was that due to the coarse resolution of the data, smaller disturbances may not have been detected. For example, small-scale logging, flooding along rivers, ice and wind storms, and small wildfires probably cannot be detected at 8 km resolution. Such events are likely to be revealed by follow-up studies using higher-resolution data.

2.3 Land Cover Change Detection

The conversion of natural land cover into human-dominated cover types continues to be a change of global proportions with many unknown environmental consequences. For example, studies [6,7] have shown that deforestation has significant implications for local weather, and in places such as the Amazon rainforest, cloudiness and rainfall are greater over cleared land than over intact forest (see Figure 2.5).

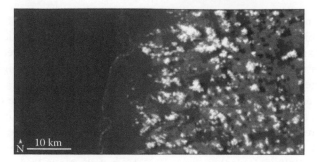

FIGURE 2.5: (See color insert following page 264.) Deforestation changes local weather. Cloudiness and rainfall can be greater over cleared land (image right) than over intact forest (left). (Courtesy of NASA Earth Observatory.)

Thus, there is a need in the Earth science domain to systematically study land cover change to understand its impacts on local climate, radiation balance, biogeochemistry, hydrology, and the diversity and abundance of terrestrial species. Land cover conversions include tree harvests in forested regions, urbanization (e.g., Figures 2.6 and 2.7), and agricultural intensification in former woodland and natural grassland areas. These types of conversions also have significant public policy implications due to issues such as water supply management and atmospheric CO_2 output. Consequently, understanding trends in land cover conversion at local scales is a requirement for making useful predictions about other regional and global changes.

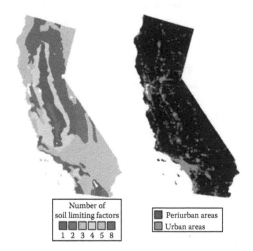

FIGURE 2.6: (See color insert following page 264.) This pair of images shows the suitability of California soils for farming on the left, and urban areas on the right. The Great Central Valley, where the state's best soils are and most of America's fresh vegetables are grown, is becoming increasingly urbanized. (1: best soil; 8: worst soil). (Courtesy of Marc Inoff, NASA GSFC, and Flashback Imaging Corporation, Ontario, Canada.)

FIGURE 2.7: (See color insert following page 264.) Urbanization. Between 1982 and 1992, 19,000 sq mi (equivalent to the area of half of Ohio) of rural cropland and wilderness were developed in the United states. This image shows the expansion of Plano (near Dallas) between 1974 and 1989. (Courtesy of NASA Earth Observatory.)

The land cover change detection problem is essentially one of detecting when the land cover at a given location has been converted from one type to another. Examples include the conversion of forested land to barren land (possibly due to deforestation or a fire), grasslands to golf courses, and farmlands to housing developments. There are a number of factors that make this a challenging problem including the nature of Earth science data. Change detection, in general, is an area that has been extensively studied in the fields of statistics [8], signal processing [9], and control theory [10]. However, most techniques from these fields are not well-suited for the massive high-dimensional spatiotemporal data sets from Earth science. This is due to limitations such as high computational complexity and the inability to take advantage of seasonality and spatiotemporal autocorrelation inherent in Earth science data. In our work, we seek to address these challenges with new change point detection techniques that are based on novel data mining approaches. Specifically, these techniques will take advantage of the inherent characteristics of spatiotemporal data and will be scalable so that they can be applied to increasingly high-resolution Earth science data sets. Preliminary results from this study have been presented in Ref. [11], where they are discussed from an Earth science point of view.

2.3.1 Data

The data set used for this analysis was the enhanced vegetation index (EVI) product measured by the moderate resolution imaging spectroradiometer (MODIS). EVI is a vegetation index that essentially serves as a measure of the amount and greenness of vegetation at a particular location. It represents the "greenness" signal (area-averaged canopy photosynthetic capacity), with improved sensitivity in high biomass cover areas. MODIS algorithms have been used to generate the EVI index at 250 m spatial resolution from February 2000 to the present. In this study, the data is from the time period February 2000 to May 2006. Figure 2.8 shows a global snapshot of EVI for 2 months in different seasons.

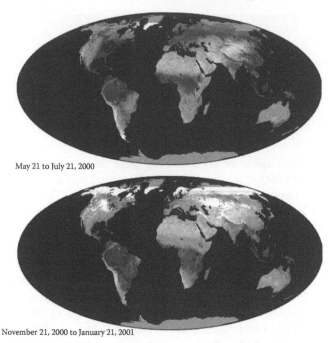

May 21 to July 21, 2000

November 21, 2000 to January 21, 2001

FIGURE 2.8: (See color insert following page 264.) The MODIS EVI provides a look at vegetation around the globe year round. As the seasons change, the mirror effect of seasonality is seen, and one hemisphere's vegetation is high while the other is low. The images show EVI during two different seasons. Vegetation ranges from 0, indicating no vegetation, to nearly 1, indicating densest vegetation. Gray areas indicate places where observations were not collected. (Courtesy of NASA Earth Observatory, GSFC, and University of Arizona.)

Figure 2.9 shows an example of land cover change of the type we are trying to detect in this study. The time series shows an abrupt jump in EVI in 2003; a land cover change pattern we are looking for. The location of the point corresponds to a new golf course, which was in fact opened in 2003. Changes of this nature can be detected only with high-resolution data.

In this preliminary study, we focussed our analysis on the state of California. We made this choice for two reasons: (1) the population of California has increased by 75% between 1970 and 2005, and (2) over half of all new irrigated farmland put into production was of lesser quality than prime farmland taken out of production by urbanization.

2.3.2   High-Level View of Land Cover in the San Francisco Bay Area via Clustering of EVI Data

We initially performed a clustering of the EVI data for the San Francisco Bay Area region in order to observe the high-level characteristics of the vegetation data.

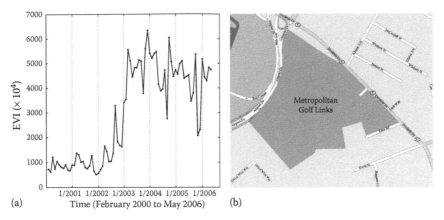

(a)   Time (February 2000 to May 2006)   (b)

FIGURE 2.9: This figure shows an example of a change point in the Bay Area that corresponds to a new golf course constructed in Oakland. This golf course was built in 2003, which corresponds to the time step at which the time series exhibits a change. (a) Time series of a point which shows a change; (b) Map of a region corresponding to the point above. (Courtesy of Google Maps.)

We used the k-means algorithm to cluster the 250 m EVI time series to produce a minimum number of distinct centroids (in this case, five centroids). A map of the Bay Area in Figure 2.10b shows the clusters represented by different colors (the colors match the centroids in Figure 2.10a). Large contiguous areas of the state were found to display temporally consistent timings of annual green-up and green-down cycles in the EVI profiles. This type of time series land cover map represents a new mapping approach to understanding how ecosystems within a region differ from one another in terms of green cover variations during a year.

2.3.3 Clustering-Based Land Cover Change Detection

In this section, we discuss two techniques based upon clustering of EVI data that we used for the land cover change detection problem.

2.3.3.1 Distance to Cluster Centroid

We used a clustering-based methodology to detect locations that exhibited land cover change. In Ref. [12], the authors proposed an outlier detection methodology based on clustering. Although outlier detection is a different problem from change detection, we nevertheless evaluated this scheme with EVI data since there is some overlap between outliers and change points. Specifically, if the majority of time series in a data set do not exhibit a change, then some outliers in such a data set will be change points.

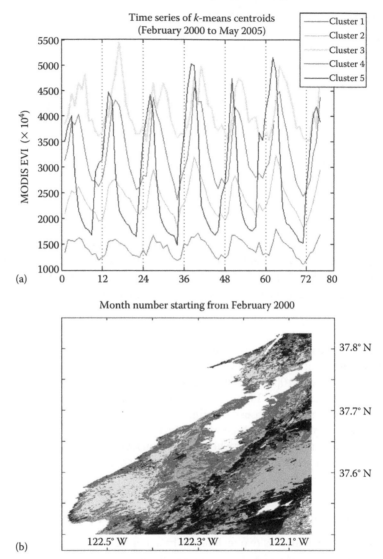

FIGURE 2.10: (See color insert following page 264.) (a) MODIS EVI time series separated as *k*-means cluster centroids. Attributes of biomass density and interannual variability are defined as follows, with a corresponding land cover type assigned: Cluster 1 is high seasonal biomass density, moderate interannual variability (shrub cover). Cluster 2 is moderate annual biomass density, moderate interannual variability (grass cover). Cluster 3 is high annual biomass density, low interannual variability (evergreen tree cover). Cluster 4 is low annual biomass density, low interannual variability (urbanized cover). Cluster 5 is high seasonal biomass density, high interannual variability (agricultural cover). (b) Map of MODIS EVI time series clusters for the San Francisco Bay Area, defined by the centroid lines and corresponding colors from Figure 2.10a.

The clustering-based methodology proceeds as follows. The points are first clustered into k major classes. Then the distance* is computed from each point to its nearest centroid. Finally, the outliers are extracted based on this distance.

Since clustering is the central component of this scheme, the quality of the results naturally depends on the quality of the clustering. We found that we were able to obtain a reasonable (from a domain perspective) clustering using the k-means clustering algorithm. This is the same clustering we previously discussed in Section 2.3.2 (shown in Figure 2.10b).

2.3.3.2   Confidence Intervals Around Cluster Centroids

We also devised another clustering-based methodology for change detection. This scheme is based on the assumption that most of the data can be grouped into well-defined clusters and that the majority of data does not exhibit a change.

The algorithm works as follows. The data is clustered into k major classes, as we had done previously in Section 2.3.3.1. For each cluster, an upper and lower interval is constructed based on the 5th and 95th percentile, i.e., for every month, the percentiles are computed from all the data points in the cluster. Data points are characterized as outliers based on their relationship to these intervals, using a numerical score that signifies the number of months a data point lies outside the interval.

Figure 2.11 shows an example of a change point that was discovered by this scheme. The figure shows how a point that is partially within the confidence interval

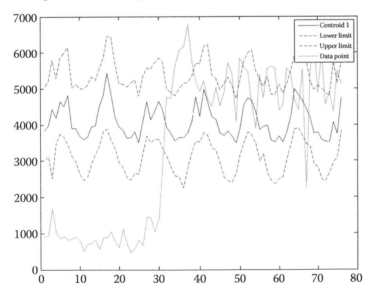

FIGURE 2.11: (See color insert following page 264.) This figure shows an example of a change point that was discovered by the confidence intervals around cluster centroids methodology.

---

* The distance measure used for all the land cover change analyses was the L_1 (Manhattan) distance.

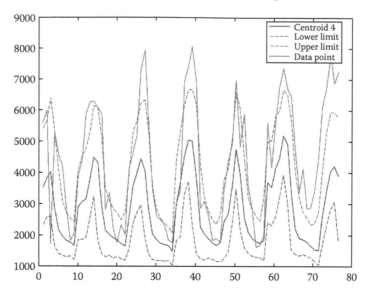

FIGURE 2.12: (See color insert following page 264.) This figure shows an example of a point that was discovered by the confidence intervals around cluster centroids methodology. It is evident from the time series that this point should not be considered a change point.

of a cluster and partially outside is likely to be a change point. The drawback of this scheme, as with the distance to centroid scheme, is that there is a heavy dependence on the quality of the clustering. If there is a group of points that have similar time series but are not in a cluster by themselves, then these points may be discovered as change points. For example, Figure 2.12 shows a time series that does not contain a change, but is likely to belong to a class of points that was not found as a cluster.

2.3.4   Preliminary Results

Early results from this land cover change detection study have been very encouraging. There were a number of interesting changes detected, many of which would not be detected without the use of high-resolution data (e.g., conversion to golf courses). Although some patterns detected by the techniques in our study can be found using simple techniques like comparing the beginning and end of the time series, there were several patterns that would not be detected by such techniques. For example, even though extensive agricultural land conversion has taken place in California in the last 5 years, it is not enough to look for locations whose EVI drops permanently from a high level. This is because even when such land is converted to housing or business developments, there may be an increase in vegetation.

We have also found our techniques to be scalable when applied to vegetation data sets with millions of locations (the California EVI data set contains over 5M locations). This aspect of the study is especially encouraging since the MODIS EVI data is available for the whole globe, and there are many more locations of interest across the world for studying land cover change.

2.4   Concluding Remarks

The two studies discussed in this chapter have shown the utility of data mining techniques in bringing new knowledge out of existing Earth observation data. In particular, these studies have demonstrated that the analysis of both high- and low-resolution data sets can provide Earth scientists with key insights into vegetation processes and phenomena, and that data mining plays a major role in these discoveries. These studies addressed a number of challenges that are posed by Earth science data. Specifically, the techniques we have used have been able to handle high-dimensionality, seasonality and have been scalable for the data sets under study.

There are a number of current challenges for both the problems discussed in this chapter that merit further study. Scalability is an important requirement when working with Earth science data due to the increasing dimensionality and data set sizes. A few interesting directions to pursue in relation to scalability are indexing (to perform efficient similarity queries by eliminating unnecessary comparisons), streaming algorithms, and parallel data mining techniques.

The evaluation methodology for both the studies also needs further study. In particular, while there are several approaches for estimating the accuracy of an algorithm, the problem of estimating the false negative rate also must be addressed. For the disturbance detection problem, since the same statistical test is applied many times, this may produce many false positives. Techniques such as Bonferroni correction could be used to address this issue, but the approach is too conservative, thus leading to large false negatives. A technique that handles this trade-off appropriately needs to be investigated.

An interesting extension of our work with ecosystem disturbances would be with regard to data fusion. The availability of a variety of climate variables in addition to vegetation data offers the potential for studying the relationship between disturbances and other variables such as precipitation. Additionally, the data sets corresponding to different variables are usually of different resolutions (climate data sets have a much coarser resolution than vegetation data sets). Data fusion is an emerging area of research, and its application to Earth science data can potentially lead to interesting discoveries.

For the change detection problem, an interesting extension would be context-based change detection. In the paradigm of context-based change detection, a change is defined in the context of other time series in the data set. The definition of what constitutes the context depends on the goals of the underlying analysis. For example, an Earth science researcher studying changes in the vegetation of a region may be interested in locations where the land cover changed but the neighboring locations did not. In other words, the researcher is interested in "small pockets" of changes.

Acknowledgments

We are grateful to the anonymous reviewers for their comments and suggestions, which improved this chapter. This work was supported by NOAA cooperative agreement NA06OAR4810187, NASA Grant NNA05CS45G, NSF Grant CNS- 0551551, NSF ITR Grant ACI-0325949, and NSF Grant IIS-0713227. This work was also supported by grants from NASA programs in Intelligent Systems and Intelligent Data Understanding, and the NASA Earth Observing System (EOS) Interdisciplinary Science Program. Access to computing facilities was provided by the University of Minnesota Digital Technology Center and Supercomputing Institute.

References

[1] NASA Earth Observing System. http://eospso.gsfc.nasa.gov.

[2] Land Processes Distributed Active Archive Center. http://edcdaac.usgs.gov.

[3] R. B. Myneni, C. J. Tucker, G. Asrar, and C. D. Keeling. Interannual variations in satellite-sensed vegetation index data from 1981 to 1991. *Journal of Geophysical Research*, 103(D6): 6145–6160, 1998.

[4] C. Potter, P.-N. Tan, V. Kumar, C. Kucharik, S. Klooster, V. Genovese, W. Cohen, and S. Healey. Recent history of large-scale ecosystem disturbances in North America derived from the AVHRR satellite record. *Ecosystems*, 8(7): 808–824, 2005.

[5] Press Release: NASA Data Mining Reveals a New History of Natural Disasters. http://www.nasa.gov/centers/ames/news/releases/2003/03_51AR.html.

[6] R. Dickinson and P. Kenneday. Impacts on regional climate of Amazon deforestation. *Geophysical Research Letters*, 19(19): 1947–1950, 1992.

[7] A. Henderson-Sellers, R. E. Dickinson, T. B. Durbidge, P. J. Kennedy, K. McGuffie, and A. J. Pitman. Tropical deforestation: Modeling local- to regional-scale climate change. *Journal of Geophysical Research*, 98: 7289–7315, 1993.

[8] C. Inclán and G. C. Tiao. Use of cumulative sums of squares for retrospective detection of changes of variance. *Journal of the American Statistical Association*, 89(427): 913–923, 1994.

[9] F. Gustafsson. *Adaptive Filtering and Change Detection*. John Wiley & Sons, New York, 2000.

[10] T. L. Lai. Sequential changepoint detection in quality control and dynamical systems. *Journal of the Royal Statistical Society. Series B (Methodological)*, 57(4): 613–658, 1995.

[11] C. Potter, V. Genovese, P. Gross, S. Boriah, M. Steinbach, and V. Kumar. Revealing land cover change in California with satellite data. *EOS, Transactions American Geophysical Union*, 88(26): 269, 2007.

[12] T. Yairi, Y. Kato, and K. Hori. Fault detection by mining association rules from house-keeping data. In *Proceedings of the 6th International Symposium on Artificial Intelligence, Robotics and Automation in Space*, pp. 18–21, European Space Agency Publications Division, Montreal, Canada, 2001.

Chapter 3

Efficient Data-Mining Methods Enabling Genome-Wide Computing

**Wei Wang, Leonard McMillan, David Threadgill,
and Fernando Pardo-Manuel de Villena**

Contents

3.1   Introduction

Understanding the complex interactions between genetic and environmental factors is the major challenge of the postgenome era. Doing so requires transformative approaches capable of integrating many high-throughput biological data sources. Major computational breakthroughs are required to shift from today's one gene-at-a-time studies to combinatorial analyses of all genes concurrently. Genome-wide approaches are our only hope for exposing the complexity of gene interactions that go undetected in single-gene knockout studies, yet they are essential for truly understanding how organisms operate.

In order to elucidate the complexity of gene and protein networks within multicellular organisms, a new animal model called the collaborative cross (CC) [14,39,40] has been proposed and is currently under development at the University of North

Carolina at Chapel Hill, North Carolina. This effort captures most of the known genetic variation in existing strains of laboratory mice and randomly redistributes it amongst 1000 new isogenic strains. The CC was designed specifically for whole-genome, combinatorial analysis. It will generate vast amounts of heterogeneous data including high-density genotypes and phenotypic measurements at the molecular, physiological, and environmental levels.

The CC provides a translational tool to integrate gene functional studies into genetic networks using realistic population structures, which will be essential to understand the intricacies of biological processes such as disease susceptibility. In turn, CC becomes the focal point for cumulative and integrated data collection, giving rise to the detection of networks of functionally important relationships among diverse sets of biological and physiological phenotypes and a new view of the mammalian organism as a whole and interconnected system. It has the potential to support studies by the larger scientific community incorporating multiple genetic, environmental, and developmental variables into comprehensive statistical-supported models describing differential disease susceptibility and progression. Equally important, the CC is an ideal test bed for predictive, or more accurately, probabilistic biology, which will be essential for the deployment of personalized medicine.

3.2   Research Issues in Data Mining

The volume, diversity, and complexity of the data collected in CC offers unique challenges, whose solutions will advance both our understanding of the underlying biology and the tools for computational analysis. For instance, it is commonplace to use clustering algorithms to search for patterns among homogeneous data sets, such as mRNA expression data. However, it is unclear how best to cluster, and thus find patterns within, multimodal data sets, such as those combining genomic, mRNA expression assays, and phenotypic measurements. Yet in their totality, these measurements surely tell hidden stories about cause and effect, identify biomarkers, or predict clinical course and outcome.

3.2.1   Analysis of High-Dimensional Data

It is widely recognized that noise and diversity are challenges when analyzing microarrays to discover those genes whose expression is modified by experimental conditions or when examining the genotypes of individuals raised in diverse environments to find the loci underlying complex traits. In both cases, exploratory, nonhypothesis driven, data analysis is a crucial first step.

Clustering has been the most popular approach of analyzing gene expression data and has proven successful in many applications, such as discovering gene pathway, gene classification, and function prediction. There is a very large body of literature on clustering in general and on applying clustering techniques to gene expression data in particular. Several representative algorithmic techniques have been developed and experimented in clustering gene expression data, which include but are not limited to hierarchical clustering, self-organizing maps [41], and graphic theoretic approaches (e.g., CLICK [35]). These clustering methods seek full space clusters across all genes and all experiments. When applied to microarrays, they often produce a partition of genes that both precludes the assignment of genes to different clusters and fails to exclude irrelevant experiments. They are incapable of discovering gene expression patterns visible in only a subset of experimental conditions. In fact, it is common that a subset of genes are coregulated and coexpressed under a subset of conditions, but tend to behave independently under other conditions.

Recently, biclustering has been developed to uncover the local structures inside the gene expression matrix. Cheng and Church [13] are among the pioneers in introducing this concept. Their biclusters are based on uniformity criteria, and they presented a greedy algorithm to discover them. Lazzeroni and Owen [22] presented another model to capture the approximate uniformity in a submatrix in gene expression data and look for patterns where genes differ in their expression levels by a constant factor. Ben-Dor et al. [7] discussed approaches to identify patterns in expression data that distinguish two subclasses of tissues on the basis of a supporting set of genes that results in high classification accuracy. Segal et al. [34] described rich probabilistic models for relations between expressions, regulatory motifs, and gene annotations. Its outcome can be interpreted as a collection of disjoint biclusters generated in a supervised manner. Tanay et al. [38] defined a bicluster as a subset of genes that jointly respond across a subset of conditions, where a gene is termed responding under some condition if its expression level changes significantly under that condition with respect to its normal level. Ben-Dor et al. [8] introduced the model of OPSM (order preserving submatrix) to discover a subset of genes identically ordered among a subset of conditions. It focuses on the coherence of the relative order of the conditions rather than the coherence of actual expression levels. For example, in the gene expression data of patients with the same disease, the genes interfering with the progression of this disease should behave similarly in terms of relative expression levels on this set of patients. These types of pattern can be observed in data from nominally identical exposure to environmental effects, data from drug treatment, and data representing some temporal progression, etc. One major drawback of this pioneering work is the strict order of the conditions enforced by the OPSM model.

Biclustering is also referred to as subspace clustering (SSC) or coclustering in the field of computer science, which has two main branches. One branch of SSC algorithms divides both the set of objects and the set of attributes into disjoint parti-tions, where the partitions maximize global objective functions [12,15]. Even though a globally optimal partition may be reached, the local properties of each cluster are hard to characterize. The other branch of SSC algorithms eliminates the restriction of disjoint partitions by looking for clusters satisfying desired properties. These clus-tering algorithms are also called pattern-based algorithms. Unlike partition-based algorithms that search for the best global partitions, pattern-based algorithms allow one object to be in multiple clusters in different subspaces. Several pattern-based algorithms have been developed for different cluster properties. A commonly adopted property is that the set of points in a cluster are spatially close to each other in some subspace of the original high-dimensional space [1–3]. Note that SSC based on spatial distance is limited in its ability to find clusters with high correlations. In biological applications, genes with different expression levels may still exhibit consistent up- and down-regulation patterns (called coregulation patterns) under a subset of conditions. Recently, algorithms such as residue-based biclustering [13], order preserving biclustering [8,24,26], and the search of shifting and scaling patterns [43–45] were developed to look for specific coregulation patterns. Our team at UNC is one of the leading groups conducting research in SSC and has made several key contributions [24,26,43–45] in pattern-based SSC algorithms.

3.2.2   Machine Learning Techniques in Prediction of Phenotypes

There has been extensive research in training classifiers for predicting phenotype values from gene expression data. Several classification techniques, including K-nearest neighbor classifier, decision tree, support vector machine (SVM), and logistic regression, have been widely used. Among them, the margin-based classifiers including the SVM and penalized logistic regression (PLR) have scored many successes. For example, SVM and PLR have been implemented with high accuracy using microarray gene expression data for cancer study [11,19,30,49]. In binary classification or supervised learning, margin-based techniques usually deliver high performance by implementing the idea of large margins. Specifically, given a training data set of n samples $\{(x_i, y_i), i = 1, \ldots, n\}$ obtained from unknown probability distribution $P(x,y)$, where $y_i \in \{+1, -1\}$ is the outcome (of a given phenotype) of individual i with input x_i, then the goal is to build a classifier to predict class y for a new subject with given x. For such a problem, machine learning is performed by constructing a function f, mapping from x to y, such that $\text{sign}[f(x)]$ is the classification rule. An important concept, the so-called margin $yf(x)$, is critical for the success of margin-based classifiers. For each sample pair (x_i, y_i), the margin $y_if(x_i)$ indicates the correctness and strength of classification of x_i by f.

A desirable classifier is one with good generalization ability, which is measured by the generalization error (GE). The GE, defined as the probability of misclassification, can be written as $\text{Err}(f) = P[yf(x) < 0] = 0.5E\{1 - \text{sign}[yf(x)]\}$. A margin-based classifier with a loss function $V(u)$ tries to minimize the GE by using the loss function V, which mimics the role of $1-\text{sign}$ or commonly called $0-1$ loss, that is, 0.5 $(1 - \text{sign})$. For example, SVM uses the hinge loss function with $V(u) = [1-u]_+$, see Ref. [23]; PLR adopts the logistic loss $V(u) = \log[1 + \exp(-u)]$, see Ref. [42]; AdaBoost employs the exponential loss function $V(u) = \exp(-u)$, see Ref. [18]; and the Ψ loss satisfies $U > \Psi(u) > 0$ if $u \in (0, \tau]$ and $V(u) = 1 - \text{sign}(u)$ otherwise [36].

Despite the success in predicting discrete phenotype classes, margin-based classifiers cannot be applied to estimate the probability distribution of a phenotype directly. In our study, we are interested in both. For instance, it is more important to estimate the susceptibility to cancer of a given mouse line than to only give a boolean classification. Therefore, significant additional development is required in order to use large margin classifiers.

3.2.3   Challenges

A number of computational challenges lie ahead. These include, but are not limited to, dealing with data heterogeneity, handling high complexity, and the presence of

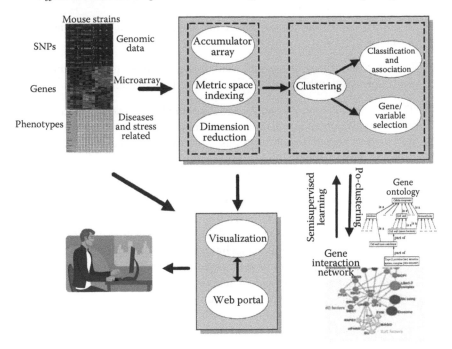

FIGURE 3.1:   Data-mining pipeline.

noise. This project aims to address these issues and provide data mining and statistical analysis tools to enable learning from multiple types of data. This will (1) provide a framework from which analytic models of the underlying biochemistry, genetics, and physiology can be developed; (2) lead to the identification of biomarkers for the disease; and (3) describe new methods for prediction of disease progression and classification of mouse lines. Conceptually, the data can be thought of as organized into a large matrix. Each mouse line corresponds to a column and the rows represent SNPs (single nucleotide polymorphisms), gene expressions, and phenotypic measurements captured, as illustrated in Figure 3.1.

Several key characteristics of this large data matrix complicate its analysis:

- The dimensionality is high since the data matrix contains massive amounts of information on (relatively) few subjects and there exist both complex correlations and causal relationships between variables.

- The data matrix is comprised of disparate measurements including both continuous and discrete variables, which may not be directly comparable to each other.

- The data matrix is not static, but growing, both in terms of adding new CC lines and measurements. The data will eventually contain high-density SNPs, or even whole genome sequences, for at least hundreds of CC lines and millions of phenotypic measurements (molecular and physiological) and other derived variables.

- Individual items may be contaminated, noisy, or simply missing, which makes detectable relationships hard to see, and thus hard to interpret.

- The number of unknowns far exceeds the number of knowns since relatively little is known about associations between polymorphisms to gene expression pathways to phenotypic observations. Moreover, it is likely that there is more than one pathway related to a given phenotypic observation, possibly characterized by different gene expression patterns.

Consequently, the number of potential hypotheses is extremely large, making it intractable to generate and test every possibility. New data structures and data-mining methods are needed to address these challenges. We need to develop novel and scalable data management and mining techniques to enable high-throughput genetic network analysis, real-time genome-wide exploratory analysis, and interactive visualization. This requires new methods to support instant access and computation for any user-specified regions and enable fast and accurate correlation calculation and retrieval of loci with high-linkage disequilibrium.

In the remainder of this chapter, we present some of our initial success within the research scope depicted in Figure 3.1.

3.3 Efficient Subspace Pattern Discovery for Genetic Network Analysis

Accurate modeling of gene regulation and association to phenotypes requires accurate representation of the sophisticate patterns exhibited in the data. We have exploited SSC techniques to model significant correlation patterns exhibited in any subspace of the high-dimensional feature space. SSC has the flexibility to elucidate the relationships among variables when only some genes and some experiments may exhibit the desired relationships. It does not rely on any additional categorization or labeling.

As a powerful method to identify distinguished regularities in the data matrix that may imply significant sample-variable associations, SSC provides far greater flexibility and far more complete information than the traditional methods for clustering and feature selection. The possibility of producing overlapping submatrices allows a single sample to be associated with many interactions (e.g., a phenotype could be associated with multiple genotypes).

Several key SSC features distinguish it from standard clustering methods, and enhance its utility in the analysis of high-dimensional data. First, the rows and columns of the resulting submatrices need not be contiguous; in principle, the number of possible submatrices grows exponentially with the number of rows and columns. Second, the submatrices need not be disjoint (they can overlap), and they need not cover the entire data matrix. This contrast with independent and two-way row–column clustering: after suitable reordering of rows and columns, these methods cover the data matrix with a rectangular grid of contiguous blocks. Third, SSC algorithms are exhaustive: when they exist, they find every (maximal) submatrix satisfying the given relation. This contrasts with clustering-and-search (e.g., variable selection) algorithms. These algorithms are commonly based on informed heuristics that operate in greedy fashion. They can be expected to work well in many cases, but do not come with quantifiable performance guarantees. Last, SSC is deterministic, adaptive, and data dependent. It identifies distinguished regularities in the data matrix that may point to significant sample–variable associations. As with traditional cluster analysis, clusters are a natural starting point for further exploratory analysis and for subsequent investigation. Although SSC is designed to handle unsupervised, exploratory analysis of large data sets, it can also be used in supervised analyses (e.g., classification).

We have explored the utilities of five SSC models including δ-cluster, pCluster, reg-cluster, order preserving cluster (OPCluster), and its extension tendency preserving cluster (TPCluster) to capture coherent patterns exhibited in submatrices. These models differ in the similarity and association criteria defined on the submatrices: The first three are aimed at modeling shifting-and-scaling patterns exhibited by a submatrix and the last two relax the model to tendency-based. Let $X = R \times C$ be the data matrix where R and C are the rows and columns. We use x_{ij} to refer to the entry of the ith row and jth column in X. Let $Y = I \times J$ denote a submatrix where $I \subset R$ and $J \subset C$. And let $\Phi(X)$ be the collection of submatrices that meet a given criterion; $|\Phi(X)|$ be the number of these submatrices.

1. δ-cluster [45]: Let the row base $\text{RB}_i = \frac{\Sigma_{j \in J} x_{ij}}{|J|}$ for each row $i \in I$, the column base $\text{CB}_j = \frac{\Sigma_{i \in I} x_{ij}}{|I|}$ for each column $j \in J$, and the cluster base $\text{YB} = \frac{\Sigma_{i \in I, j \in J} x_{ij}}{|I| \times |J|}$ for the submatrix Y. Y is a δ-cluster if for every entry x_{ij} in Y, $|x_{ij} - \text{RB}_i - \text{CB}_j + \text{YB}| < \delta$, given a user-specified threshold δ. Note that if the rows in Y exhibit perfect shifting patterns (i.e., $x_{i1,j} = x_{i2,j} + c$ for any pair of rows $i_1, i_2 \in I$), $x_{ij} - \text{CB}_j = \text{RB}_i - \text{YB}$ holds true. The parameter δ is introduced to tolerate noise. Scaling patterns (i.e., $x_{i1,j} = cx_{i2,j}$) can be handled since they can be transformed into shifting patterns by applying a logarithm function. The problem of mining all δ-clusters for a given threshold is NP hard. Existing algorithms for mining δ-clusters are greedy algorithms utilizing heuristics to look for a handful of large clusters. There is no guarantee neither to discover all δ-clusters, nor to discover the most significant δ-clusters.

2. pCluster [43]: Given a pair of rows $i_1, i_2 \in I$ and a pair of columns $j_1, j_2 \in J$, the pScore of the 2×2 submatrix is

$$\text{pScore}\left(\begin{bmatrix} x_{i_1 j_1} & x_{i_1 j_2} \\ x_{i_2 j_1} & x_{i_2 j_2} \end{bmatrix}\right) = |(x_{i_1 j_1} - x_{i_1 j_2}) - (x_{i_2 j_1} - x_{i_2 j_2})| \quad (3.1)$$

The submatrix Y is a pCluster if the pScore of every 2×2 submatrix of Y is less than a user-specified threshold δ. The algorithm bears complexity

$O[p^2 n \log n + n^2 p \log p + (n + p)|\Phi(X)|]$ to return all pClusters, given a user-specified threshold δ. Similar to δ-cluster model, pCluster model can capture shifting patterns or scaling patterns (after logarithm transformation) in any submatrices. They differ in their approaches to tolerate noise. One advantage of pCluster is that this model allows for polynomial algorithms.

3. reg-cluster [44]: The model of reg-cluster was proposed to represent scaling and shifting patterns in submatrices. That is, $x_{i1,j} = ax_{i2,j} + c$ for any pair of rows $i_1, i_2 \in I$ in submatrix Y. The reg-cluster model is more powerful than the previous two models. Both scaling and shifting patterns can be discovered simultaneously without logarithm transformation. However, finding all reg-clusters is an NP hard problem. Current algorithm can only handle data matrices of small to medium size.

4. OPCluster [24,26]: Different from the above three models focusing on scaling and shifting patterns, the model of OPCluster looks for submatrices in which the rows I (e.g., genes) show consistent trend on the columns J (e.g., experiments). A submatrix Y is an OPCluster if the relative orderings between columns are the same for the set of rows in Y. This model is very useful in studying up or down regulations of genes in response to environmental stimuli, where the trend is more important than the absolute expression level. Both heuristics and exhaustive algorithms have been developed to mine OPClusters, which took advantage of the property that an OPCluster can be efficiently represented by a single-ordered list of columns in the submatrix.

5. TPCluster [48]: We propose to develop a new cluster model, TPCluster. TPCluster relaxes the requirement of every row in Y complying to the same column order strictly. Instead, it allows noises that may disrupt the order to some extent. A submatrix Y is a TPCluster if, for every pair of rows $i_1, i_2 \in I$, the maximum common subsequence between the sorted column lists of i_1 and i_2 has length greater than $(1 - \varepsilon)|J|$. Note that there may not exist a common column ordering shared by every row in Y. OPCluster can be considered as a special case of TPCluster. We explored the properties held by TPClusters, which lead to an efficient algorithm that generate the complete set of TPClusters given a threshold ε.

3.4   Semisupervised Clustering with Gene Ontology

In unsupervised learning (such as clustering), unlabeled instances are grouped according to their similarity in symptoms and measurements in an automatic fashion; while in supervised learning (such as classification), a perfectly annotated training data set is required. In bioinformatics applications, a small subset but not all genes, metabolites, and proteins have already been well studied by biologists. This knowledge can be easily obtained from a number of databases, such as gene ontology and protein–protein interaction network databases. This knowledge is often ignored by unsupervised learning. On the other hand, it cannot constitute a perfect training set for supervised learning. In order to take advantage of existing knowledge, while still being faithful to empirical and clinical data sets, we have designed and implemented a semisupervised clustering method.

Semisupervised learning (SSL) is a recent branch of data mining that resides midway between supervised learning and unsupervised learning. Labeled instances, however, are often difficult, expensive, or time consuming to obtain, as they require the efforts of experienced human annotators. Meanwhile, unlabeled data may be relatively easy to collect, but they are inherently less useful. SSL addresses this problem by using large amounts of unlabeled data together with a small number of annotated instances, to build better predictive models. This approach is applicable to both the clustering and classification approaches described above. Because SSL enables a user-defined amount of supervision, it has great adaptability and online learning capabilities. SSL often gives better performance than both supervised and unsupervised learning. It can show our analyses are influenced by incorporating information about the likelihood that a gene or protein is a transcription factor at increasing levels of certainty to see how this information affects our ability to segregate data in meaningful ways. In addition, SSL is an important data-mining paradigm for analyzing dynamic data sets because it more readily integrates with visualization in a tightly coupled feedback loop. We use gene ontology as an example of existing knowledge during our initial algorithm development [25,27]. More specifically, we use the annotations available in gene ontology to guide/select the cluster structure construction so that only (subspace) clusters that are highly enriched by any gene annotations are retained to form the cluster hierarchy. Figure 3.2 shows an example of desired outcome.

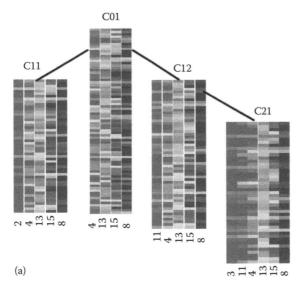

FIGURE 3.2: (See color insert following page 264.)   (a) List of four SSCs, each of which has consistent patterns of their gene expressions.

(continued)

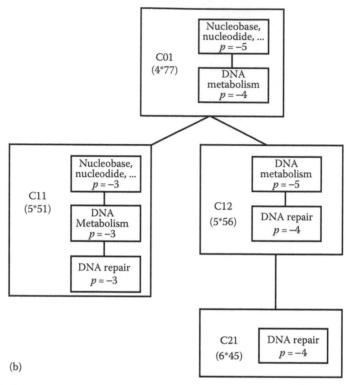

(b)

FIGURE 3.2: (continued)   (b) Annotation of each cluster using gene ontology. The significance of each annotation is 10^p.

3.5   Subspace Pattern-Based Classification

The success of any classification scheme depends on the existence of associations between the measurements and the response [4–6,9,10,32]. Regularities in the response should be associated with corresponding regularities in the measurements. The associations identified by SSC can provide a starting point for the classification of high-dimensional data: Among the distinguished submatrices, one can identify those strongly associated with a particular class, and use them to classify unlabeled samples. The data's high dimensionality poses a number of unique challenges including the following: (1) many of the measurements are uninformative, and most measurements are subject to noise; (2) there are typically large, highly correlated subgroups of measurements; and (3) the number of samples may be less than the number of measurements. Taken together, the cumulative effect of noninformative variables and noise is a problem for nearest neighbor classification methods, while the latter two issues rule out the use of traditional linear discriminant methods.

3.5.1 Phenotype Prediction and Ranking

Thus, we proposed a novel classification method based on SSCs [47]. Let X be a gene expression matrix where rows are strains and columns are genes, and $\Phi(X)$ be the set of SSCs discovered. Let T be a target phenotype. For simplicity, let us assume that T is binary $+1$, -1, indicating the presence or absence of, for example, certain diseases. The proposed method can be generalized to multi-category case. For a SSC $Y \in \Phi(X)$, let N_+ and N_- be the number of strains with positive response and negative response, respectively. The predictive power of the rule $Y \rightarrow (T = +1)$ can be measured by $2[N_+/(N_+ + N_-) - 0.5]$, which is a continuous variable between -1 and 1. Any value close to 0 suggests weak predictive power and any values close to -1 or 1 are considered strong predictive power. For a new strain s with unknown phenotype, let $\Phi_s(X) \subset \Phi(X)$ be the subset of SSCs that are compatible with s. We say a SSC $Y = I \times J$ is compatible with s if $(I \cup s) \times J$ is also a valid SSC. Classification of s can be accomplished by a voting scheme based on the predictive power of compatible SSCs. Note that this classification method can be easily generalized to give a quantitative estimation of the likelihood of phenotype values. In the context of our study, a large number of phenotypic measurements will be available. The SSC-based classification method can be extended to provide a ranking of all phenotypes or predict the top k phenotypes based on their likelihood of having positive response.

3.5.2 SSC-Based Gene Selection

An important goal of our research is to identify the genes that are most responsible for accurate prediction of a given phenotype. With this group of genes identified, one can further study the relationship of these genes with the phenotype that may provide means to develop more accurate predictions. There are methods proposed in the literature for gene selection in the context of microarray classification. Dudoit et al. [16] proposed a ranking method that ranks genes by the ratio of between to within sum-of-squares of each gene. Guyon et al. [20] proposed a recursive feature elimination method that starts with all genes and eliminates unimportant genes recursively.

Compared to prescreening methods for gene selection, it is desirable to have a classifier with built-in variable selection ability. One of the advantages of SSC is in its easy interpretability. Each SSC contains a subset of strains and genes. Intuitively, for a phenotype T, if a gene belongs to many SSCs that have strong (positive or negative) predictive power for T, it is likely that this gene plays a role in determining the phenotype response. Therefore, we can construct a simple yet power method for gene selection. The importance of a gene can be estimated by the number of SSCs it belongs to and the predictive power of these SSCs. We can then establish a ranking of all genes in descending order of their importance.

3.6   Fast Dimensionality Reduction Methods
for Interactive Visualization

High-throughput experimental methods have revolutionized the field of biology. Tools such as gene-expression microarrays and genotyping chips have enabled the systematic search for genetic links to disease and the analysis of drug effectiveness. These tools produce vast volumes of high-dimensional data that require computationally aided analysis to fathom their results. We have developed a series of visualization and data exploration tools focused on dynamic explorations of bioinformatics data. It is explicitly designed to aid investigators in tuning parameters and exploring their data for patterns and anomalies. Our tools provide interactive visualizations that allow users to gauge both local and global effects of the parameter selection, as well as the sensitivity of clustering and classification algorithms to parameter selection. As a result, we hope to implicitly reconnect the experimentalist with their data in an effort to provide intuition and to facilitate the modeling, understanding, and ultimate discovery of new biological relationships.

A wide range of visualization tools have been developed to aid biologists in exploring gene-expression microarrays. Saraiya et al. [33] give an overview of many public-domain and commercial visualization tools and evaluated the effectiveness in various real-world tasks. Clustering was one of the most commonly used techniques and it was integrated into nearly every tool, but they are processed off-line (over the period of a few seconds), require parameter tweaks, and the resulting visualizations are difficult to interpret. There are numerous other publicly available tools, as well as, those from the manufacturers of microarray chips. We have also developed tools that include clustering capabilities, but our goal is to allow the exploration of parameter spaces and assess their potential impact on clusters, or alternatively explore the evolution of existing clusters based on smooth parameter variations.

We employ dissimilarity matrices as an indirect means for visualizing the relationships between high-dimensional points, providing a dimension-independent display. Strehl and Ghosh [37] advocated using dissimilarity matrices for visualizing and reasoning about clusters. Our work extends this notion by providing the capability to combine multiple measures and interactively see their impact on the clustering. We also allow the user to directly specify clusters in an alternate view, where data points are depicted in a reduced-dimension presentation that respects the desired dissimilarity matrices.

A key component of our tool is its ability to interactively explore parameter spaces that combine various attributes of high-dimensional data points. We employ dimensionality reduction methods, specifically multidimensional scaling (MDS), to visualize the impact of these reweightings. MDS is a classical statistical analysis method that finds optimal (in the least-squares sense) lower dimensional embeddings compatible with a given dissimilarity matrix. The problem with MDS is that it does not easily scale well to large data sets. To address this problem, we have also developed a novel fast MDS approximation algorithm that is targeted at interactive display rates as well as handling large data sets.

One component of our approach is the ability to depict multiple views of relationships between point pairs. One of our primary views of the data is as a dissimilarity matrix. Dissimilarity matrices have the property that they reduce the relationships between each pair of points to a single scalar value regardless of the point's original dimension. This is valuable for many bioinformatics applications, such as multi-experiment gene-expression data, where expression levels of ten thousands of gene might be compared across tens or hundreds of mouse strains and tissues. A dissimilarity matrix represents the pairwise differences between either all possible gene pairs or all possible patent pairs.

Many common metrics, such as the Euclidean distance between points, or the Hamming distance between binary strings, can be represented in dissimilarity matrices. Any relationship that satisfies the following properties for the point-pair (x,y) is a valid dissimilarity matrix: $D[x,x] = 0$ and $D[x,y] = D[y,x]$. A dissimilarity matrix is metric if the triangle inequality holds: $D[x,y] + D[y,z] \geq D[x,z]$ for all y. Example dissimilarity matrices for 800 SNPs are shown in Figure 3.3.

Although visualization of high-dimensional data sets as dissimilarity matrices provides some useful insights, it is not sufficient for considering the evolution of clusters in response to parameter changes. We employ a dimensionality reduction

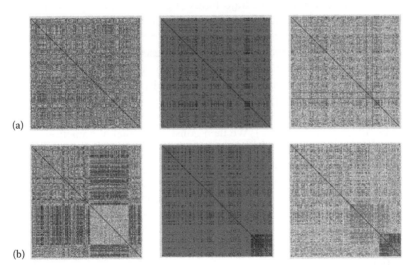

FIGURE 3.3: (See color insert following page 264.) Permutations of weighed dissimilarity matrices. Each row shows two separate dissimilarity matrices on the left and a combined dissimilarity matrix on right. The leftmost column represents the spatial relationships between SNPs according to their sequence position. The center column represents pairwise SNPs correlations weighted by a phenotype level. The top row is shown in the original sequence order, and the bottom row is permuted to expose the clusters resulting from a 50/50 weighting of spatial and phenotype matrices.

method to aid in this task. Our approach is to provide a lower dimensional point-cloud view of the high-dimensional data set that treats the dissimilarity matrices as the Euclidean distance between points. This visualization provides a spatial representation of the clusters in a low-dimensional setting suitable for direct viewing (either two or three dimensional). In this view, it is possible to see potential clusters as well as track the evolution of existing clusters due to parameter changes.

We use classical MDS to derive the point-cloud coordinates from dissimilarity matrices. MDS is a well-known statistical method for mapping pairwise relationships to meaningful coordinates. The coordinates that MDS generates are an optimal linear fit to the given dissimilarity matrix assuming it is treated as a Euclidean distance. The coordinates the MDS generates are only unique down to a rigid-body transformation, with a possible reflection.

The difficulty with MDS is that it does not scale well to large data sets, and it is generally too slow for interactive use. We have developed an approximation to MDS that can provide constant interactive feedback. Since we apply MDS dynamically, we also align successive runs to compensate for arbitrary rotations, translations, and reflections that vary from frame to frame. This is accomplished by finding a least-squares optimal, affine-alignment matrix between a random sample of the current point coordinates with those from the corresponding points in the previous frame. This provides smooth transitions as clustering parameters (feature weightings) are varied, making it easy to trace the trajectories of groups or individual points.

Our high-speed MDS approximation [46] is based on partitioning the dissimilarity matrix into submatrices along the diagonal. Note that each such submatrix is also a dissimilarity matrix. We then apply MDS to each submatrix. For each submatrix, we can estimate the sample dimensionality based on the goodness of fit measure (cumulative sum of the eigenvalues) returned by MDS. We next draw a sufficient number of samples from each submatrix to capture its inherent dimensionality (a minimum of $D+1$ samples from each submatrix is required, but we generally oversample by a factor of 2 or more). We then construct a final alignment-dissimilarity matrix from these samples by extracting their rows and columns from the original dissimilarity matrix. We perform MDS on this alignment matrix, and then compute an affine transform of each submatrix solution to best align its subsampled points to their corresponding coordinates in the alignment matrix solution.

The quality of the approximation depends on how representative each submatrix is of the entire data set. Ideally, all submatrices and the original dissimilarity matrix should appear as having been drawn from the same statistical distribution. Thus, clustered dissimilarity matrices, such as the one shown in Figure 3.3b, generally do not provide good approximations. We address this problem by randomizing the point order prior to partitioning the data set into submatrices.

For large data sets, generating the complete dissimilarity matrix can be extremely costly in terms of both time and space. Our fast MDS approximation allows for lazy evaluation of the dissimilarity matrix as needed. This permits the reuse of storage and avoids the computation of entries that are unused. However, we still have the problem of depicting the dissimilarity matrix in the weighted-dissimilarity-matrix view for large data sets. For this case, we use the alignment matrix in the dissimilarity-matrix visualization, and take care to reverse the permutations resulting from the randomized sampling. Our fast MDS approach typically achieves over a 100 speedup over traditional MDS, with suitable accuracy. This allows us to explore data sets with over 20,000 points at interactive rates. Our weighted-dissimilarity-matrix viewing and permutation tools as well as our MDS-based point-cloud viewer have been incorporated into several applications for visualizing and exploring bioinformatics data sets. It provides many approaches for navigating and visualizing data sets, and has been employed in a wide range of applications.

3.7   Conclusion and Discussion

In this chapter, we present our experience in developing data-mining methods for genome-wide analysis. We hope it serve as the starting point to inspire broad interests in developing and integrating novel techniques in bioinformatics, data management, data mining, statistics, and knowledge management, to discover, summarize, and use subspace patterns for efficient analysis and visualization. There are far more challenges and opportunities than solutions we have. The following are some critical issues we plan to invesitigate.

- *Robustness to noise.* Each model presented above has some built-in capability to handle small noise. We will simulate different types of noises at various severities to test their robustness to noise. The outcome is measured by the recoverability of embedded clusters and the generation of spurious clusters.

- *Scalability to large data.* Most of these models are inherently NP hard and existing algorithms can only apply to matrices of small to moderate size. They cannot be readily applied to the CC data. We plan to improve the scalability of these algorithms by identifying computational bottlenecks, introducing new optimization techniques, and employing parallel computing.

- *Statistical significance of result.* We plan to assess the statistical significance of the discovered SSCs. Resampling and simulation-based tests [17,21,31] will be used for validation: For each SSC model, we (1) simulate a large number of random data matrices (or permute the entries of a given matrix), (2) apply the SSC model to each simulated matrix, and (3) count the number of times we find a submatrix of the specified size and intensity.

- *Biological significance of result.* We plan to investigate the optimal model for discovering gene regulations and phenotype associations, which provides the best balance between the computational efficiency of SSC representation and mining and statistical significance of discovered correlations.

Acknowledgments

The authors would like to gratefully thank Jinze Liu, Kyle Moore, Feng Pan, Adam Roberts, Lynda Yang, Tynia Yang, Mengsheng Zhang, Qi Zhang, and Xiang Zhang for their contributions to this research. We also thank Yufeng Liu, Jan Prins, Ivan Rusyn, Fred Wright, and Fei Zou for their many thoughtful suggestions. The research was supported by NSF IIS 0448392, NSF IIS 0534580, EPA STAR RD832720, and NIH U01 CA105417.

References

[1] Aggarwal, C. C., Wolf, J. L., Yu, P. S., Procopiuc, C., and Park, J. S. (1999). Fast algorithms for projected clustering. In *SIGMOD '99: Proceedings of the 1999 ACM SIGMOD International Conference on Management of Data*, pp. 61–72, ACM Press, New York.

[2] Aggarwal, C. C. and Yu, P. S. (2000). Finding generalized projected clusters in high dimensional spaces. In *Proceedings of the 2000 ACM SIGMOD International Conference on Management of Data*, pp. 70–81, ACM Press, New York.

[3] Agrawal, R., Gehrke, J., Gunopulos, D., and Raghavan, P. (1998). Automatic subspace clustering of high dimensional data for data mining applications. In *SIGMOD Conference*, pp. 94–105, Seattle, Washington.

[4] Alter, O., Brown, P. O., and Botstein, D. (1997). Singular value decomposition for genome-wide expression data processing and modeling, *Proc. Natl. Acad. Sci. USA*, 97(18), 10101–10106.

[5] Ambroise, C. and McLachlan, G. (2002). Selection bias in gene extraction on the basis of microarray gene-expression data. *Proc. Natl. Acad. Sci. USA*, 99, 6562–6566.

[6] Bauer, E. and Kohavi, R. (1999). An empirical comparison of voting classification algorithms: Bagging, boosting, and variants. *Mach. Learn.*, 36, 105–139.

[7] Ben-Dor, A., Friedman, N., and Yakhini. Z. (2001). Class discovery in gene expression data. In *RECOMB 2001*, pp. 31–38, ACM, New York.

[8] Ben-Dor, A., Chor, B., Karp, R., and Yakhini, Z. (2002). Discovering local structure in gene expression data: The order-preserving submatrix problem. In *RECOMB 2002*, pp. 49–57, Washington, DC.

[9] Breiman, L. (2001). Random forests. *Mach. Learn.*, 45, 5–32.

[10] Brown, M. P. S., Grundy, W. N., Cristianini, N., Sugnet, C. W., Furey, T. S., Ares, M., and Haussler, D. (1997). Knowledge based analysis of microarray gene expression data by using support vector machine. *Proc. Natl. Acad. Sci. USA*, 97, 262–267.

[11] Brown, M., Grundy, W. N., Liu, D., Christianini, N., Sugnet, C., Ares, M., Jr., and Haussler, D. (1999). Support vector machine classification of microarray gene expression data. UCSC-CRL 99-09, Department of Computer Science, University of California, Santa Cruz, CA.

[12] Chakrabarti, D., Papadimitriou, S., Modha, D. S., and Faloutsos, C. (2004). Fully automatic cross-associations. In *KDD '04: Proceedings of the 10th ACM SIGKDD International Conference on Knowledge Discovery and Data Mining*, pp. 79–88, ACM Press, New York.

[13] Cheng, Y. and Church, G. (2000). Biclustering of expression data. In *ISMB 2000*, pp. 93–103, La Jolla, CA.

[14] Churchill, G. A. et al. (2004). The collaborative cross, a community resource for the genetic analysis of complex traits. *Nat. Genet.*, 36, 1133–1137.

[15] Dhillon, I. S. and Guan, Y. (2003). Information theoretic clustering of sparse co-occurrence data. In *Proceedings of the 3rd IEEE International Conference on Data Mining (ICDM-03)*, pp. 517–521.

[16] Dudoit, S., Fridlyand, J., and Speed, T. (2002). Comparison of discrimination methods for the classification of tumors using gene expression data. *J. Am. Stat. Assoc.*, 97, 77–87.

[17] Dudoit, S. and Fridlyand, J. (2003). Bagging to improve the accuracy of a clustering procedure, *Bioinformatics*, 19, 1090–1099.

[18] Friedman, J. H., Hastie, T., and Tibshirani, R. (2000). Additive logistic regression: A statistical view of boosting. *Ann. Stat.*, 28, 337–407.

[19] Furey, T., Cristianini, N., Duffy, N., Bednarski, D., Schummer, M. and Haussler, D. (2000). Support vector machine classification and validation of cancer tissue samples using microarray expression data. *Bioinformatics*, 16(10), 906–914.

[20] Guyon, I., Weston, J., Barnhill, S. and Vapnik. V. (2002). Gene selection for cancer classification using support vector machines. *Mach. Learn.*, 46, 389–422.

[21] Kerr, M. K. and Churchill, G. A. (2001). Bootstrapping cluster analysis: Assessing the reliability of conclusions from microarray experiments. *Proc. Natl. Acad. Sci. USA*, 98, 8961–8965.

[22] Lazzeroni, L. and Owen, A. (2000). Plaid models for gene expression data. Available at http://www.stanford.edu/owen/plaid/.

[23] Lin, Y. (2000). Some asymptotic properties of the support vector machine. Technical Report 1029, Department of Statistics, University of Wisconsin, Madison, WI.

[24] Liu, J. and Wang, W. (2003). Subspace clustering by tendency in high dimensional space. In *ICDM 2003*, pp. 187–194, Melbourne, FL.

[25] Liu, J., Yang, J., and Wang, W. (2004). Gene ontology friendly biclustering of expression profiles. In *Proceedings of the IEEE Computational Systems Bioinformatics Conference (CSB)*, pp. 436–447, IEEE Computer Society, Washington, DC.

[26] Liu, J., Yang, J., and Wang, W. (2004). Biclustering of gene expression data by tendency. In *Proceedings of the IEEE Computational Systems Bioinformatics Conference (CSB)*.

[27] Liu, J., Wang, W. and Yang, J. (2004). A framework for ontology-driven subspace clustering. In *Proceedings of the 10th ACM SIGKDD International Conference on Knowledge Discovery and Data Mining (SIGKDD)*, pp. 623–628, ACM, New York.

[28] Liu, J., Strohmaier, K., and Wang, W. (2004). Revealing true subspace clusters in high dimensions. In *Proceedings of the 4th IEEE International Conference on Data Mining (ICDM)*, pp. 463–466.

[29] Liu, J., Paulsen, S., Xu, X., Wang, W., Nobel, A., and Prins, J. (2006). Mining approximate frequent itemset in the presence of noise: Algorithm and analysis. In *Proceedings of the 6th SIAM Conference on Data Mining (SDM)*, pp. 405–416.

[30] Mukherjee, S., Tamayo, P., Slonim, D., Verri, A., Golub, T., Mesirov, J., and Poggio, T. (1999). Support vector machine classification of microarray data. Technical Report AI Memo1677, MIT, MA.

[31] Pollard, K.S. and van der Laan, M.J. (2002). Statistical inference for simultaneous clustering of gene expression data. *Math. Biosci.*, 176, 99–121.

[32] Qu, Y. et al. (2002). Boosted decision tree analysis of surface-enhanced laser desorption/ionization mass spectral serum profiles discriminates prostate cancer from noncancer patients. *Clin. Chem.*, 48, 1835–1843.

[33] Saraiya, P., North, C., and Duca, K. (2004). An evaluation of microarray visualization tools for biological in-sight. In *Proceedings of the IEEE Symposium on Information Visualization (Infovis'04)*, pp. 1–8.

[34] Segal, E., Taskar, B., Gasch, A., Friedman, N., and Koller, D. (2001). Rich probabilistic models for gene expression. *Bioinformatics*, 17, S243–S252.

[35] Sharan, R. and Shamir, R. (2000). Click: A clustering algorithm with applications to gene expression analysis. In *ISMB*, pp. 307–316.

[36] Shen, X., Tseng, G. C., Zhang, X., and Wong, W. H. (2003). On Ψ-learning. *J. Am. Stat. Assoc.*, 98, 724–734.

[37] Strehl, A. and Ghosh, J. (2003). Relationship-based clustering and visualization for high-dimensional data-mining, *INFORMS J. Comput.*, Spring, 208–230.

[38] Tanay, A., Sharan, R. and Shamir, R. (2002). Discovering statistically significant biclusters in gene expression data. *Bioinformatics*, 18, S136–S144.

[39] Threadgill, D. W. (2006). Meeting report for the 4th Annual Complex Trait Consortium Meeting: From QTLs to systems genetics. *Mamm. Genome*, 17, 2–4.

[40] Threadgill, D. W. et al. (2002). Genetic dissection of complex and quantitative traits: From fantasy to reality via a community effort. *Mamm. Genome*, 13, 175–178.

[41] Torkkola, K., Gardner, R. M., Kaysser-Kranich, T., and Ma, C. (2001). Self-organizing maps in mining gene expression data, *Inf. Sci.*, 139 (1–2), November, 79–96.

[42] Wahba, G. (1998). Support vector machines, reproducing kernel Hilbert spaces, and randomized GACV. In: B. Scholkopf, C. J. C. Burges, and A. J. Smola (Eds.), *Advances in Kernel Methods: Support Vector Learning*, MIT Press, pp. 125–143.

[43] Wang, H., Wang, W., Yang, J., and Yu, P. S. (2002). Clustering by pattern similarity in large data sets. In *SIGMOD '02: Proceedings of the 2002 ACM SIGMOD International Conference on Management of Data*, pp. 394–405, ACM Press, New York.

[44] Xu, X., Tung, A. K. H., Lu, Y., and Wang, W. (2006). Mining shifting-and-scaling co-regulation patterns on gene expression profiles. In *Proceedings of the 22nd IEEE International Conference on Data Engineering (ICDE)*.

[45] Yang, J., Wang, H. Wang, W., and Yu, P. (2005). An improved biclustering method for analyzing gene expression profiles. *Int. J. Artif. Intell. Tools (IJAIT)*, 14(5), 771–789.

[46] Yang, T., Liu, J., McMillan, L., and Wang, W. (2006). A fast approximation to multidimensional scaling. In *Proceedings of the ECCV Workshop on Computation Intensive Methods for Computer Vision (CIMCV)*.

[47] Zhang, X., Wang, W., and Huan, J. (2007). On demand phenotype ranking through subspace clustering. In *Proceedings of the 7th SIAM Conference on Data Mining (SDM)*.

[48] Zhang, M., Wang, W., and Liu, J. (2008). Mining approximate order preserving clusters in the presence of noise. In *Proceedings of the 24th IEEE International Conference on Data Engineering (ICDE)*.

[49] Zhu, J. and Hastie, T. (2004). Classification of gene microarrays by penalized logistic regression. *Biostatistics*, 5(3), 427–444.

Chapter 4

Mining Frequent Approximate Sequential Patterns

Feida Zhu, Xifeng Yan, Jiawei Han, and Philip S. Yu

Contents

4.1 Introduction

Frequent sequential pattern mining remains one of the most important data-mining tasks since its introduction in Ref. [1]. With the ubiquity of sequential data, it has found broad applications in customer analysis, query log analysis, financial stream data analysis, and pattern discovery in genomic DNA sequences in bioinformatics. Extensive research on the topic has brought about general sequential pattern mining algorithms like Refs. [2–7] and constraint-based ones like Refs. [8,9]. Periodic pattern mining in temporal data sequences has also been studied [10,11].

However, all these mining algorithms follow the exact matching sequential pattern definition. It has been shown that the capacity to accommodate approximation in the mining process has become critical due to inherent noise and imprecision in data, e.g., gene mutations in genomic DNA sequence mining. The notion of approximate sequential pattern has been proposed in Ref. [12], in which an algorithm called ApproxMap is designed to mine consensus patterns. While mining consensus patterns provide one way to produce compact mining result under general distance

69

measures, it remains a challenge how to efficiently mine the complete set of approximate sequential patterns under some distance measure that is stricter yet equally useful in many cases. The Hamming distance model, which counts only mismatches, is one of such.

We look at bioinformatics: for example (1) The identification of repeats serves as a critical step in many biological applications on a higher level such as a preprocessing step for genome alignment, whole genome assembly, and a postprocessing step for BLAST queries. For repeat families that are relatively new in the evolution, the set of repeats found under the Hamming distance model captures almost the complete set. (2) The limited knowledge that biologists currently have of these repeats makes it often hard for them to evaluate the relative significance among different repeats. It is therefore worth the effort to mine the complete set. Existing tools like RepeatMasker [13] only solve the problem of pattern matching, rather than pattern discovery without prior knowledge. (3) Many research works for the repeating patterns have been on an important subtype: the tandem repeats [14], where repeating copies occur together in the sequence. However, as shown by our experiments, these methods would miss those patterns whose supporting occurrences appear globally in the entire data sequence, which account for the majority of the complete set of frequent patterns.

REPuter [15] is the closest effort toward mining frequent approximate sequential patterns under the Hamming distance model. Unfortunately, REPuter achieves its efficiency by strictly relying on the suffix tree for constant-time longest common prefix computation in seed extension. Consequently, the type of approximate patterns that REPuter is able to mine is inevitably limited. In particular, it can only discover patterns with two occurrences and mismatches at identical positions across the support set. The mining problem targeted by REPuter is essentially a different one.

To uncover more interesting approximate patterns in DNA sequences, we establish a more general model for approximate sequential pattern mining problem. Our general philosophy is a "break-down-and-build-up" one based on the following observation. Although for an approximate pattern, the sequences in its support set may have different patterns of substitutions, they can in fact be classified into groups, which we call *strands*. Each strand is a set of sequences sharing a unified pattern representation together with its support. The idea is that by "breaking down" the support sets of the approximate patterns into strands, we are able to design efficient algorithms to compute them. Using a suffix-tree-based algorithm, we can in linear time mine out the initial strands, which are all the exact-matching repeats. These initial strands will then be iteratively assembled into longer strands in a local search fashion, until no longer strands can be found. In the second "build-up" stage, different strands are then grouped based on their constituting sequences to form a support set so that the frequent approximate patterns would be identified. By avoiding incremental growth and global search, we are able to achieve great efficiency without losing the completeness of the mining result. Instead of mining only the patterns repeating within a sliding window of some fixed size, our algorithm is able to mine all globally repeating approximate patterns.

4.2 Problem Formulation

In our problem setting, we focus on mining approximate sequential patterns under the Hamming distance model. Hamming distance, which is defined for two strings of equal length, is the number of substitutions required to change one into the other.

DEFINITION 4.1 **Hamming Distance**
For two strings $S = \langle s_1, s_2, \ldots, s_n \rangle$ *and* $P = \langle p_1, p_2, \ldots, p_n \rangle$ *of a same length n, the Hamming distance between them is defined as*

$$Dist(S,P) = |I|, \quad I = \{i | s_i \neq p_i, 1 \leq i \leq n\}$$

The Hamming distance between two strings S and P is denoted as $Dist(S,P)$. In our model, two sequential patterns are considered approximately the same if and only if they are of equal length and their distance is within a user-specified error tolerance. We therefore use string or substring to refer to all sequential patterns in the rest of the chapter. Given a string $S = \langle s_1, s_2, \ldots, s_n \rangle$ of length n, another string $Z = \langle z_1, \ldots, z_m \rangle$ is a substring of S if there exists an index i of S such that $z_j = s_{i+j}$ for all $1 \leq j \leq m$. In this case, S is a superstring of Z. We use $|S|$ to denote the length of a string S.

Given an input string S, we are interested in finding all frequent approximate substrings of S, i.e., for each such substring, the set of substrings that are considered approximately the same must be sufficiently large.

DEFINITION 4.2 **Frequent Approximate Substring**
Given a string S, a substring P of S is a frequent approximate substring if and only if there exists a set U of substrings of S and for each $W \in U$, $Dist(P,W) \leq |P| \delta$, and $|U| \geq \theta$, where θ is the minimum frequency threshold and δ is the error tolerance threshold. U is called the support set of P, denoted as P_{sup}.

Notice that U is represented as a set of indices of S as all substrings in U share the same length with P.

As in frequent itemset mining, the definition of frequent approximate substring also gives rise to redundancy in the mining result. Consider the three substrings in Figure 4.1.

Suppose S_1 is a frequent approximate substring, with its distances to S_2 and S_3 being both 2 in this case. If we delete the last character A from all three strings, the resulting substring S_1 is still a frequent approximate substring with its distances to S_2

$$S_1 = \boxed{A\,T\,C\,C\,G}\ T\,A\,C\,T\,A\,T\,G\ T\ T\,C\,A\,G\,T\,T\,G\,C\,A\,G\,C\,C\,A$$
$$S_2 = \boxed{A\,T\,C\,C\,G}\ G\ A\,C\,T\,A\,T\,G\ A\,T\,C\,A\,G\,T\,T\,G\,C\,A\,G\,C\,C\,A$$
$$S_3 = \boxed{A\,T\,C\,C\,G}\ A\ A\,C\,T\,A\,T\,G\,G\ T\,C\,A\,G\,T\,T\,G\,C\,A\,G\,C\,C\,A$$

FIGURE 4.1: Three substrings from input.

Gap = 0
P1 = $ATCCG$ P2 = $ACTATG$ P3 = $TCAGTTGCAGCCA$
Gap = 1
P4 = $ATCCGTACTATG$ P5 = $ACTATGTTCAGTTGCAGCCA$
Gap = 2
P6 = $ATCCGTACTATGT\ TCAGTTGCAGCCA$

FIGURE 4.2:   Ideal mining result.

and S_3 unchanged. This remains true as we delete more characters so long as the error
tolerance requirement is satisfied. It would be considered redundancy in many cases
if all such shorter substrings of S_1 are also reported. Ideally, we would like to report
a substring only when it can not be extended without changing its distance to some
substring in its support set. In the example of Figure 4.1, we would like to report
six frequent approximate substrings as shown in Figure 4.2. We therefore define the
closeness for a frequent approximate substring.

DEFINITION 4.3   Closed Frequent Approximate Substring
   *Given a string S, a frequent approximate substring P of S is closed if and only if
there exists no frequent approximate substring Z of S such that (1) Z is a superstring
of P, (2) there exists a bijection between Z_{sup} and P_{sup} such that for each $S_i \in P_{sup}$,
there exists a $S_i' \in Z_{sup}$ such that S_i' is a superstring of S_i, and (3) $Dist(Z,S_i') =
Dist(P,S_i)$ for some $S_i \in P_{sup}$.*

In this chapter, we study the problem of mining all closed frequent approximate
substrings from a given data string. For brevity, all frequent approximate substrings
mined by our algorithm are closed for the rest of the chapter. A frequent approximate
substring will be abbreviated as a FAS. Formally, the frequent approximate substring
mining problem (FASM) is defined as follows.

DEFINITION 4.4   FASM
   *Given a string S, a minimum frequency threshold θ and an error tolerance
threshold δ, the FASM problem is to find all closed frequent approximate substrings
P of S.*

4.3   Algorithm Design

In general, for a FAS P, consider any two substrings S_1 and S_2 in P_{sup}. Aligning
S_1 and S_2, we observe an alternating sequence of maximal-matching substrings and
gaps of mismatches: $Pattern(S_1,S_2) = \langle M_1,g_1,M_2,g_2,\ldots,M_k \rangle$, where $M_i,1 \le i \le k$
denote the maximal-matching substrings shared by S_1 and S_2. $g_i,1 \le i < k$ denote the

$$S_1 = \underline{ATCCG} \, T \, \underline{ACAG} \, T \, \underline{TCAGTAGCA}$$
$$S_2 = \underline{ATCC} \, G \, \underline{CAC} \, A \, \underline{GGTCAGTAGCA}$$
$$S_3 = \underline{ATC} \, T \, G \, \underline{CACAGGTCAGC} \, \underline{AGCA}$$
$$S_4 = \underline{ATC} \, A \, \underline{GCACAGGT} \, \underline{CAGG} \, \underline{AGCA}$$

FIGURE 4.3: Alignment of S_1, S_3, and S_4 against S_2.

number of mismatches in the ith gap. Consider four substrings S_1,S_2,S_3, and S_4 as shown in Figure 4.3.

In this case, $Pattern(S_1,S_2) = \langle ATCCG, 1, ACAG, 1, TCAGTTGCA \rangle$. All four substrings are of length 20. If the error tolerance threshold $\delta = 0.1$ and minimum frequency threshold $\theta = 4$, then S_2 is a FAS since the other three substrings are within Hamming distance 2 from S_2. For each substring, the bounding boxes indicate the parts that match exactly with S_2. We can therefore define the notion of a strand, which is a set of substrings that share one same matching pattern.

DEFINITION 4.5

A set U of substrings $U = \{S_1,\dots,S_k\}$ is a strand if and only if for any two pairs of substrings $\{S_{i_1},S_{j_1}\}$ and $\{S_{i_2},S_{j_2}\}$ of U, $Pattern(S_{i_1},S_{j_1}) = Pattern(S_{i_2},S_{j_2})$.

By definition, all the substrings in a strand U share the same alternating sequence of maximal-matching substrings and gaps of mismatches, which we call $Pat(U)$. We use $|Pat(U)|$ to denote the length of the substrings in U. We use $Gap(U)$ to denote the number of gaps in $Pat(U)$ and $Miss(U)$ to denote the number of total mismatches in $Pat(U)$. Given a strand U with its corresponding matching pattern $Pat(U) = \langle M_1,g_1,\dots,M_k \rangle$, $Dist(S_i,S_j) = Miss(U) = \sum_{i=1}^{k-1} g_i$, for all $S_i,S_j \in U$ and $i \neq j$. All substrings in a strand share a same distance from one another. Define $Plist(U)$ to be the support set of a strand U, i.e., $Plist(U)$ is the set of indices where each substring in U occurs. A strand U is represented by the pair $\langle Pat(U),Plist(U) \rangle$.

We call a strand U valid if the distance between any two substrings of U satisfy the user-specified error tolerance threshold, i.e., $Miss(U) \leq |Pat(U)|\delta$. Similar to the notion of the closeness of a FAS, we have the definition for the closeness of a strand. A strand U is closed if and only if there exists no strand U' such that (1) there exists a bijection between the set of substrings of U and U' such that for each $P \in U$, there is a $P' \in U'$ and P' is a superstring of P, and (2) $Miss(U) = Miss(U')$.

A FAS could belong to multiple strands. For any given FAS, the observation is that its support set is exactly the union of all its closed valid strands.

LEMMA 4.1

For a FAS P, its support set $P_{sup} = \cup_{U \in X} U$, where X is the set of all P's closed valid strands.

PROOF   We first prove $P_{sup} \subseteq \cup_{U \in X} U$. For any substring $W \in P_{sup}$, by the definition of P_{sup}, we have $Dist(P,W) \leq |P|\delta$. Let U be the strand uniquely defined by P and W. Then $Miss(U) = Dist(P,W) \leq |P|\delta$, which means U is valid. Since P is closed, extending P would change $Dist(P,W)$, and accordingly $Miss(U)$. As such U is also closed. Hence $W \in \cup_{U \in X} U$. We then show $\cup_{U \in X} U \subseteq P_{sup}$. For any substring $W \in \cup_{U \in X} U$, let U' be a valid and closed strand of P which contains W. Then $Dist(P,W) = Miss(U') \leq |P|\delta$ by the definition of a valid strand. Since P and W belong to a same strand, they are of equal length. The fact that U' is closed means that extending P would change $Dist(P,W)$. Hence $W \in P_{sup}$.   ☐

We therefore have the following approach to decide if a given substring P is a FAS: Find all the closed valid strands of P and let the union of them be X. P is a FAS if and only if the cardinality of X is at least θ. Consider the example in Figure 4.3 in which the error tolerance is 0.1 and minimum frequency threshold is 4. Both strands $\{S_1, S_2\}$ and $\{S_2, S_3, S_4\}$ are valid. Suppose these two strands are also closed, then combining them we get a support set of size 4, satisfying the frequency requirement. As such, S_2 is a FAS.

Our algorithm solves the FASM in two steps.

1. *Growing strand*: Compute a set of closed valid strands initially. The set of initial strands is the set of all maximal exact repeats. More precisely, for each initial strand U, $Pat(U) = \langle M_1 \rangle$, $Miss(U) = 0$, and U is closed. These initial strands are computed by *InitStrand* using the suffix tree of the input sequence S. Similar approach has been used in REPuter [15] to mine exact repeats. By a linear-time suffix tree implementation as in Ref. [16], we are able to identify all initial strands in time linear to the input size. To mine out all closed valid strands, we iteratively call the following procedure to grow the current set of strands until no new strands are found: We scan the entire tape and, for each strand encountered, checks on both ends to see if the current strand can be grown by assembling neighboring strands. Let the result set be X.

2. *Grouping strand*: Once we have mined out all the closed valid strands in the first step, we compute the support set for each frequent approximate substring. The idea of grouping the strands is the following. Given the set X of all closed valid strands, we construct a substring relation graph G from X. The vertex set is all the substrings in the strands of X, each vertex representing a distinct substring. There is an edge between two substrings if and only if the Hamming distance between two substrings is within the error tolerance. Since all the substrings in one valid strand share the same distance among each other and the distance is within the error tolerance, all corresponding vertices in G form a clique. After scanning all the strands in X, we would construct a graph G which is a union of cliques. Then by our observation, a substring is a frequent approximate substring if and only if the degree of the corresponding vertex is greater than or equal to the minimum frequency threshold. Figure 4.4 illustrates the idea.

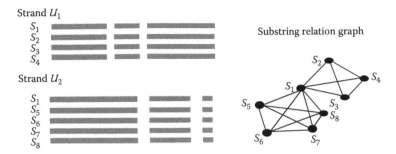

FIGURE 4.4:   Two strands U_1 and U_2 and their substring relation graph.

4.3.1   Growing Strand

The main algorithm for growing strands is shown in Algorithm 4.1. The procedure *GrowthOnce()* is shown in Algorithm 4.2.

ALGORITHM 4.1   StrandGrowth

Input: The original sequence S
        Error tolerance threshold δ
Output: $Tape[1 \ldots |S|]$

1: Tape $\leftarrow$ InitStrand(S);
2: **while** *new valid strands are found*
3:   *Tape $\leftarrow$ GrowthOnce(S,Tape,δ);*
4: **return** *Tape;*

ALGORITHM 4.2   GrowthOnce

Input: The original sequence S
        $Tape[1 \ldots |S|]$
        Error tolerance threshold δ
Output: Tape

1: **for** $i = 1$ **to** $|S|$
2:   **for each** *substring U_i*
3:   *Check for a distance d to the right of U_i*
4:   **for each** *U'_j found at distance d'*
5:   *$Pat(U'') \leftarrow \langle Pat(U),d',Pat(U') \rangle$*
6:   **if** *U'' is valid*
7:   *$Plist(U'') \leftarrow Plist(U) \otimes_{d'} Plist(U');$*

```
8:                  Insert Plist(U″) into Tape;
9:            Check for a distance d to the left of Uᵢ
10:      for each U′ⱼ found at distance d′
11:          Pat(U″) ← ⟨Pat(U′),d′,Pat(U)⟩
12:          if U″ is valid
13:              Plist(U″) ← Plist(U′) ⊗_{d′} Plist(U);
14:              Insert Plist(U″) into Tape;
15: return Tape;
```

Initial Strand Computation

The set of initial strands is the set of all maximal exact repeats. More precisely, for each initial strand U, $Pat(U) = \langle M_1 \rangle$, $Miss(U) = 0$, and U is closed. These initial strands are computed by *InitStrand* using the suffix tree of the input sequence S. Similar approach has been used in REPuter [15] to mine exact repeats. A suffix tree is a data structure that compactly encodes the internal structure of a string. As such, it can be used to solve some complicated string problems in linear time. In particular, it enables us to mine out all frequent maximal exact-matching substrings of S with a running time linear in the length of S. A suffix tree $\mathscr{T}$ for a string S of n characters is a rooted directed tree with exactly n leaves numbered 1 to n. Each internal node of $\mathscr{T}$, except for the root has at least two children. Each edge is labeled with a nonempty substring of S. No two edges going out of a node have the labels on the edge beginning with the same character. A suffix tree encodes all suffixes of S by the following: for any leaf node i, the concatenation of edge-labels on the path from the root to leaf i corresponds exactly to the suffix of S beginning from index i, which is $S[i,\dots,n]$. For instance, if $S = \langle ATTCGATTAC \rangle$, the suffix tree for S is as shown in Figure 4.5.

The first linear-time algorithm for constructing a suffix tree was given by Weiner [17] in 1973. We therefore have the following theorem:

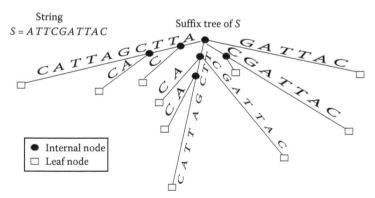

FIGURE 4.5:   Suffix tree for a string S.

THEOREM 4.1   (Weiner 1973 [17])

   Given a data sequence S, a suffix tree $\mathcal{T}$ can be constructed for S in $O(|S|)$ time. The size of $\mathcal{T}$ is $O(|S|)$.

   InitStrand mines out all maximal frequent exact-matching substrings of length at least l_{min} and occurs at least θ times. The algorithm first constructs in linear time a suffix tree for S and then use the same idea as in Ref. [16] to identify the left diverse nodes in linear time to find all maximal frequent exact-matching substrings, as shown in Algorithm 4.3. For each node v of a suffix tree, define the *label of the path* for v as the concatenation of edge labels from the root to v, and is denoted as $\Xi(v)$. Denote as $Child_{num}(v)$ the number of leaves in the subtree rooted at v. Notice that $Child_{num}(v)$ for each node v can be computed along the tree traversal. Once we find a set of substrings matching with each other exactly at a node v, we can create a valid strand U for the set by setting the strand's pattern $Pat(U)$ as $\Xi(v)$ and $Plist(U)$ as the list of the numbers of all the leaves in v's subtree sorted in increasing order.

ALGORITHM 4.3   InitStrand

Input: The original sequence S
            The minimum length threshold l_{min}
            The minimum frequency threshold θ
Output: $Tape[1 \ldots |S|]$

1: Build the suffix tree $\mathcal{T}$ for S
2: Traverse $\mathcal{T}$
3:    **for each** internal node v
4:       **if** $|\Xi(v)| \geq l_{min}$ **and** $Child_{num}(v) \geq \theta$
5:          Generate a strand U for $\Xi(v)$
6:          Insert U into Tape
7: **return** Tape;

   Notice that the suffix tree $\mathcal{T}$ can be built in linear time. Since Line 2 to Line 7 is a tree traversal and thus takes time proportional to the size of the tree, we conclude that *InitStrand* runs in time linear in the length of S. We have the following theorem from Ref. [16]. We conclude from Theorem 4.2 that *InitStrand* runs in time $O(|S|)$ for a given input string S.

THEOREM 4.2

   All maximal frequent repeats in S can be found in $O(|S|)$ time.

4.3.2   Grouping Strand

Once we have mined out all the closed valid strands in the first step, we use *StrandGroup* to compute the support set for each frequent approximate substring. The idea of grouping the strands is the following. Given the set X of all closed valid strands, we construct a substring relation graph G from X. The vertex set is all the substrings in the strands of X, each vertex representing a distinct substring. There is an edge between two substrings if and only if the Hamming distance between two substrings is within the error tolerance. Since all the substrings in one valid strand share the same distance among each other and the distance is within the error tolerance, all corresponding vertices in G form a clique. After scanning all the strands in X, we would construct a graph G which is a union of cliques. Then by Lemma 4.1, a substring is a frequent approximate substring if and only if the degree of the corresponding vertex is greater than or equal to the minimum frequency threshold, as illustrated in Figure 4.4. Algorithm 4.4 shows the following algorithm.

ALGORITHM 4.4   StrandGroup

Input: Tape[1 ... |S|]
              The minimum frequency threshold θ
Output: all frequent approximate substrings

1: **for each** *strand U found while scanning Tape*
2:      **for each** *substring* $P \in Plist(U)$
3:              *Add* $|Plist(U)| - 1$ *neighbors to P*
4: **for each** *substring P*
5:      **if** *P has at least* θ *neighbors*
6:              *Output P*

4.3.3   Completeness of Mining Result

We now prove that our algorithm would generate the complete set of FASs. The sketch of the proof is as follows. We first prove that *StrandGrowth* would generate all closed valid strands by induction on the number of gaps of the strands. Lemma 4.1 then tells us that we could compute the support sets of all FASs and identify them by grouping the strands by Algorithm 4.4.

LEMMA 4.2
   InitStrand would generate all closed valid strands U such that $Gap(U) = 0$.

PROOF   By Theorem 4.2, we know that *InitStrand* would generate all frequent maximal exact-matching substrings. By the definition of a strand, the strands formed by these exact-matching substrings would have their number of gaps to be zero since no mismatches exist in these substrings. Hence the validity of the strands. The fact that these frequent substrings are maximal means that the strands thus constructed are closed. $\square$

StrandGrowth discovers a new strand by always attempting to assemble two current closed valid strands. Before we prove the theorem, we need one more lemma to show that any closed valid strand can be generated from two shorter closed valid strands.

LEMMA 4.3
Given a closed valid strand U with $Pat(U) = \langle M_1, g_1, \ldots, M_m \rangle$. U can always be divided into two shorter closed valid strands U_1 and U_2 such that $Pat(U_1) = \langle M_1, g_1, \ldots, M_i \rangle$ and $Pat(U_2) = \langle M_{i+1}, g_{i+1}, \ldots, M_m \rangle$ for some $1 \leq i \leq m-1$.

PROOF Given a closed valid strand U with $Pat(U) = \langle M_1, g_1, \ldots, M_m \rangle$, let U_1 and U_2 be such that $Pat(U_1) = \langle M_1, g_1, \ldots, M_{m-1} \rangle$ and $Pat(U_2) = \langle M_m \rangle$. By definition, U_2 is a closed valid strand. If it is also true for U_1, we are done. Otherwise, the only possibility would be that U_1 is not valid. Since the entire strand U is valid, it follows that, if we move the last exact-matching substring M_{m-1} from $Pat(U_1)$ to $Pat(U_2)$ and obtain two new strands such that $Pat(U_1') = \langle M_1, g_1, \ldots, M_{m-2} \rangle$ and $Pat(U_2') = \langle M_{m-1}, g_{m-1}, M_m \rangle$, we must conclude that U_2' is again a closed valid strand. We then check if U_1' is valid. If not, we again move the last exact-matching substring M_{m-2} from $Pat(U_1')$ to $Pat(U_2')$, and so on so forth. Since at the end, if we have $Pat(U_1') = \langle M_1 \rangle$ and $Pat(U_2') = \langle M_2, g_2, \ldots, M_m \rangle$, both strands must be valid, we conclude that there exists some $i, 1 \leq i \leq m-1$, such that U can be divided into U_1 and U_2 where $Pat(U_1) = \langle M_1, g_1, \ldots, M_i \rangle$ and $Pat(U_2) = \langle M_{i+1}, g_{i+1}, \ldots, M_m \rangle$. $\square$

Now we are ready to show that we would be able to generate all the closed valid strands.

THEOREM 4.3
StrandGrowth would generate all closed valid strands.

PROOF We prove by induction on the number of gaps $Gap(U)$ for any closed valid strand U. When $Gap(U) = 0$, the claim is true by Lemma 4.2. Assume that the claim is true for $Gap(U) = k \geq 0$. When $Gap(U) = k+1$, by Lemma 4.3, U can be divided into two shorter closed valid strands U_1 and U_2 such that $Pat(U_1) = \langle M_1, g_1, \ldots, M_i \rangle$ and $Pat(U_2) = \langle M_{i+1}, g_{i+1}, \ldots, M_m \rangle$ for some $1 \leq i \leq m-1$. By induction, both U_1 and U_2 will be generated by *StrandGrowth*. As such, when d is large enough in *StrandGrowth*, U_1 and U_2 will be assembled into U. The claim is thus also true for $Gap(U) = k+1$. We therefore conclude that *StrandGrowth* would generate all valid canonical strands. $\square$

Since it is easy to verify the correctness of Algorithm 4.4 and we have proved Lemma 4.1, we would generate the support sets of all frequent approximate substrings and thus identify them. We therefore claim the following theorem for the completeness of our mining result.

THEOREM 4.4

Given an input data string S, StrandGrowth and StrandGroup would mine the complete set of frequent approximate substrings from S.

4.3.4   Local Search

One salient feature of *StrandGrowth* is that only local search is performed when checking on both ends of a strand for strand growth. We therefore need to determine the value of d in *GrowthOnce*. If d is set to be too big, then in the worst case, we would scan the entire data string each time we check for a strand. The running time of *GrowthOnce* would then be $\Omega(|X|^2)$, where X is the set of all valid canonical strands. On the other hand, if d is set to be too small, we could fail to guarantee the completeness of the mining result. Consider the following example in Figure 4.6. Suppose we have two valid strands U_1 and U_2 such that $|Pat(U_1)| = 20, Miss(U_1) = 0$ and $|Pat(U_2)| = 40, Miss(U_2) = 0$. There is a gap of 7 mismatches between them. Suppose the error tolerance is $\delta = 0.1$. Notice that a valid strand U can accommodate further mismatches on either ends up to a distance of $|Pat(U)|\delta - Miss(U)$. Then U_1 can accommodate $d_1 = 2$ extra mismatches and U_2 can accommodate $d_2 = 4$ extra mismatches.

However, as Figure 4.6 shows, the tricky part is that if we only search forward d_1 from U_1 and backward d_2 from U_2, we would fail to identify the chance to assemble them due to the fact that the gap is larger than the sum of d_1 and d_2. Even if we search forward from U_1 for a distance that doubles d_1, we could still miss U_2. Fortunately, searching backward from U_2 for a distance of $2d_2$ would let us reach U_1. Then how to decide on the value of d such that we would guarantee the completeness of the mining result, and at the same time, scan as small a portion of the data string as possible? It turns out we have the following theorem to help determine the value for d.

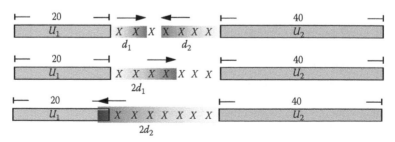

FIGURE 4.6:   Assembling two strands U_1, U_2.

THEOREM 4.5

Given the error tolerance δ and a strand U, searching for a distance $d = 2$ $(|Pat(U)|\delta - Miss(U))/(1 - \delta)$ would guarantee the completeness of the mining result.

PROOF Suppose a closed valid strand U can be assembled by two shorter strands U_1 and U_2. Assuming U_1 occurs before U_2 in the data sequence. We only need to show that one of the following must happen: (1) searching forward a distance d from the end of U_1 would reach U_2 (2) searching backward a distance d from the beginning of U_2 would U_1. Suppose when assembling U_1 and U_2 into U, the gap between them is g. Since U is valid, we have $Miss(U) \leq |Pat(U)|\delta$, i.e., $Miss(U_1) + Miss(U_2) + g \leq (|Pat(U_1)| + |Pat(U_2)| + g)\delta$. Therefore, $g \leq (|Pat(U_1)|\delta - Miss(U_1))/(1 - \delta) + (|Pat(U_2)|\delta - Miss(U_2))/(1 - \delta)$. Without loss of generality, assume $|Pat(U_1)| \geq |Pat(U_2)|$. As such, $g \leq 2(|Pat(U_1)|\delta - Miss(U_1))/(1 - \delta)$. This means U_2 would be encountered when searching forward a distance of $d = 2(|Pat(U_1)|\delta - Miss(U_1))/(1 - \delta)$ from U_1. $\Box$

Theorem 4.5 tells us that we do not have to search too far for us to guarantee the completeness. In fact, it is easy to observe that we at most search twice the distance of an optimal algorithm. Notice that any strand encountered within a distance of $\hat{d} = (|Pat(U)|\delta - Miss(U))/(1 - \delta)$ can be assembled with the current strand to form a new valid strand, since the current strand itself can accommodate all the mismatches in a gap of length $\hat{d}$. As such to guarantee a complete mining result, any algorithm would have to check at least a distance of $\hat{d}$. We therefore check at most twice the distance of an optimal algorithm.

4.4 Performance Study

We used a real soybean genomic DNA sequence, CloughBAC, for our experiment. CloughBAC is 103,334 bp in length. There are altogether 182,046 closed approximate sequences of length at least 5. The longest closed approximate sequence is of length 995. The error tolerance δ is set as 0.1. The minimum frequency threshold θ is set as 3.

Figure 4.7 shows those of size up to 40 while Figure 4.8 shows the rest of the mining result, which are of size from 40 to 995. It can be observed that, in this particular soybean genomic DNA sequence, the approximate sequences are dense around the size of 10 and become sparse from size 15 to form a long tail.

We define the *spread* for an approximate sequence to be the distance between the index of its first occurrence and that of its last occurrence. A globally repeating approximate sequence has a large spread since its occurrences are not confined to a particular portion of the data sequence. As such, the larger the spread, the harder it is to discover the sequence by a sliding-window-based method. The spreads of all the

Next Generation of Data Mining

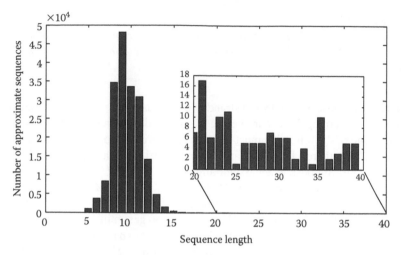

FIGURE 4.7:   Sequences of size up to 40 bps.

approximate sequences in the mining result are plotted in Figure 4.9. It is evident that the majority of them actually have spreads comparable to the length of the orginal data sequence. Indeed as shown in Figure 4.10, the advantage of our mining approach compared against a sliding-window-based approach manifests itself in the fact that even a sliding window half the size of the original data sequence would discover all the occurrences of only 30% of the complete mining result. Furthermore, Figure 4.11 shows the average gaps between two successive occurrences of the approximate sequences in the complete mining result. Most of the sequences have an average gap

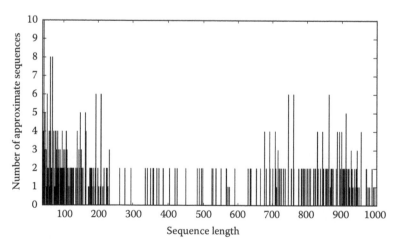

FIGURE 4.8:   Sequences of size from 40 to 1000 bps.

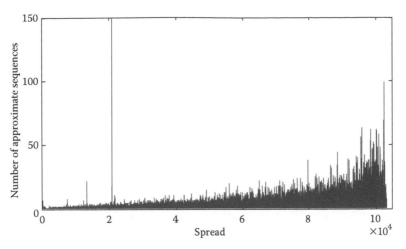

FIGURE 4.9: Spread of the mining result.

of size $1/10$ of the original data sequence, which makes it hard for any locally aware approaches with a fixed intelligence radius to identify any repeating occurrences.

Figure 4.12 shows the running time of our algorithm as the number of output approximate sequence increases. It is compared against the one without the local search technique to demonstrate its importance in boosting the mining efficiency. The running time of our algorithm is observed to be linear in the output size. Figure 4.13 illustrates the run time performance with varied error tolerance δ. The bar chart, with its y-axis on the right-hand side of the figure, shows the corresponding numbers of output sequences as δ increases. More lenient error tolerance results in more output sequences and consequently a longer running time. Figure 4.14 illustrates the run

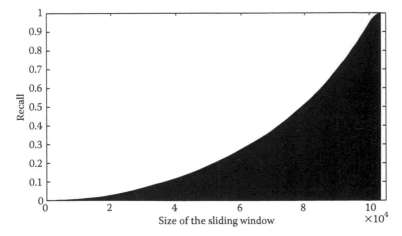

FIGURE 4.10: Recall of sliding window approach.

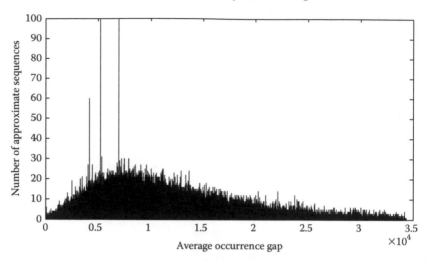

FIGURE 4.11: Average occurrence gap.

time performance with varied minimum frequency threshold θ. The bar chart, with its y-axis on the right-hand side of the figure, shows the corresponding numbers of output sequences as θ increases. Observe that as the minimum frequency threshold increases, the output size decreases sharply while the running time almost remains the same. This is because regardless of the minimum frequency threshold for the output, all sequences with at least two occurrences have to be computed during the strand growing stage, which is responsible for most of the mining cost. It is only in the strand grouping stage that a greater minimum frequency threshold helps to reduce the running time. The influence of θ on the mining cost is therefore less significant.

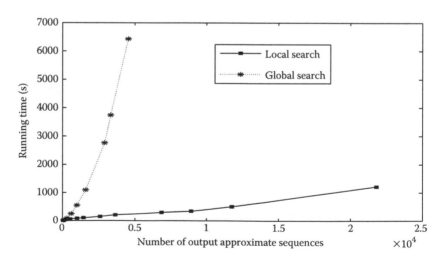

FIGURE 4.12: Run time.

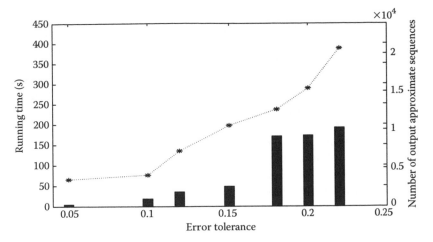

FIGURE 4.13: Run time with varied δ.

4.5 Related Work

Agrawal and Srikant first introduced the sequential pattern mining problem in Ref. [1], and later, based on the a priori property [18], continued to develop a generalized and improved algorithm [16]. A succession of sequential pattern mining algorithms have been proposed since then for performance improvements, including SPADE [5], PrefixSpan [6], and SPAM [7]. These algorithms either use a vertical id-list format (e.g., SPADE), a vertical bitmap data representation (e.g., SPAM), or a

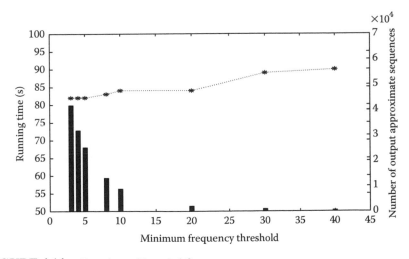

FIGURE 4.14: Run time with varied θ.

horizontal data set format (e.g., PrefixSpan) to enhance mining efficiency. There are also constraint-based ones like Refs. [8,9]. Periodic pattern mining in temporal data sequences have also been studied [10,11]. To make the mining result more friendly for user understanding, algorithms have been developed to mine frequent closed sequences. CloSpan [19] follows the candidate maintenance-and-test approach and uses techniques like CommonPrefix and Backward Sub-Pattern Pruning. BIDE [20] improves scalability by avoiding candidate maintenance and applying BI Directional Extension. When approximation is taken into consideration in the frequent sequential pattern definition, the size of the mining result could be prohibitively huge under a general distance measure. ApproxMap [12] approached this problem by mining instead the consensus patterns, which are a subset of long and representative patterns. Algorithms aimed at mining the complete answer set like Ref. [21], which have been studied in music information retrieval, suffer running time cost as high as $O(n^4)$ where n is the data sequence length. Algorithms in bioinformatics community have been focusing on approximate pattern matching and generate popular tools like RepeatMasker [13]. Most of these algorithms target at finding tandem repeats. REPuter [15] uses suffix tree to find maximal exact repeats and employs a suffix-tree-based constant time longest common prefix algorithm to extend them. However, REPuter cannot discover patterns with more than two occurrences and mismatches present at different positions across the support.

4.6   Future Work

The fast-growing data-intensive applications today present plenty of sequential pattern mining research problems for the new generation. Some future work directions include

1. *Multiple input sequences*: The current mining framework can be naturally extended to the multiple sequence scenario where the input is a set of long sequences. In many cases, the occurrences of a frequent substring in each input sequence are counted only once in the support computation. Suffix-tree with certain enhancement can handle repeats in multiple sequences. However, efficient discovery of frequent approximate substrings for multiple sequences requires further extension of the current algorithm.

2. *Other approximation definitions*: It is evident that there are many approximate sequential pattern definitions other than the Hamming distance model studied in this Chapter. In many bio-applications, the distance between two strings is defined in a much more complicated way than by gaps.

3. *Online sequential pattern mining*: The huge amount of data generated at a galloping speed in many real-life applications would eventually require efficient online mining algorithms for sequential patterns. It is interesting to study how to discover useful frequent patterns when only partial data can be stored and near-real-time response is desired.

4. *Anomaly mining*: In many trajectory data mining, e.g., commercial logistics applications, anomalous patterns (i.e., those outliers significantly deviate from the frequent patterns) are the mining targets. These patterns raise alert, drawing human attention for further examination.

4.7 Conclusions

Mining frequent approximate sequential pattern has been an important data-mining task. Its version in biological applications—finding repeats —has long been a topic of extensive research. Existing algorithms in bioinformatics communities solve pattern matching rather than mining. In particular, most algorithms are designed to find tandem repeats. In data-mining community, algorithms have been developed to mine a set representative patterns to avoid the combinatorial explosion due to the general distance definition. In this Chapter, we proposed the definition of *closed* frequent approximate sequential patterns. We aim to solve the problem of mining the complete set of frequent approximate sequential pattern mining under Hamming distance. Our algorithm is based on the notion of classifying a pattern's support set into *strands*, which makes possible both efficient computation and compact representation of it. By combining a suffix-tree-based initial strand mining and iterative strand growth, we adopt a local search optimization technique to reduce time complexity. We also proved that our local search strategy guarantees the completeness of the mining result. Our performance study shows that our algorithm is able to mine out globally repeating approximate patterns in biological genomic DNA data with great efficiency.

Acknowledgment

We are grateful to Professor Matt Hudson and Kranthi Varala for providing us with the genome sequence data and many helpful discussions and suggestions.

References

[1] R. Agrawal and R. Srikant. Mining sequential patterns. In *Proceedings of the 1995 International Conference on Data Engineering (ICDE'95)*, pp. 3–14, Taipei, Taiwan, March 1995.

[2] F. Masseglia, F. Cathala, and P. Poncelet. The PSP approach for mining sequential patterns. In *Proceedings of the 1998 European Symposium on Principle*

of Data Mining and Knowledge Discovery (PKDD'98), pp. 176–184, Nantes, France, September 1998.

[3] R. Srikant and R. Agrawal. Mining sequential patterns: Generalizations and performance improvements. In *Proceedings of the 5th International Conference on Extending Database Technology (EDBT'96)*, pp. 3–17, Avignon, France, March 1996.

[4] J. Han, J. Pei, B. Mortazavi-Asl, Q. Chen, U. Dayal, and M.-C. Hsu. FreeSpan: Frequent pattern-projected sequential pattern mining. In *Proceedings of the 2000 ACM SIGKDD International Conference on Knowledge Discovery in Databases (KDD'00)*, pp. 355–359, Boston, MA, August 2000.

[5] M. Zaki. SPADE: An efficient algorithm for mining frequent sequences. *Machine Learning*, 40: 31–60, 2001.

[6] J. Pei, J. Han, B. Mortazavi-Asl, H. Pinto, Q. Chen, U. Dayal, and M.-C. Hsu. PrefixSpan: Mining sequential patterns efficiently by prefix-projected pattern growth. In *Proceedings of the 2001 International Conference on Data Engineering (ICDE'01)*, pp. 215–224, Heidelberg, Germany, April 2001.

[7] J. Ayres, J. Flannick, J. E. Gehrke, and T. Yiu. Sequential pattern mining using bitmap representation. In *Proceedings of the 2002 ACM SIGKDD International Conference on Knowledge Discovery in Databases (KDD'02)*, pp. 429–435, Edmonton, Canada, July 2002.

[8] M. Garofalakis, R. Rastogi, and K. Shim. SPIRIT: Sequential pattern mining with regular expression constraints. In *Proceedings of 1999 International Conference on Very Large Data Bases (VLDB'99)*, pp. 223–234, Edinburgh, UK, September 1999.

[9] J. Pei, J. Han, and W. Wang. Constraint-based sequential pattern mining in large databases. In *Proceedings of the 2002 International Conference on Information and Knowledge Management (CIKM'02)*, pp. 18–25, McLean, VA, November 2002.

[10] J. Han, G. Dong, and Y. Yin. Efficient mining of partial periodic patterns in time series database. In *Proceedings of 1999 International Conference on Data Engineering (ICDE'99)*, pp. 106–115, Sydney, Australia, April 1999.

[11] C. Bettini, X. Sean Wang, and S. Jajodia. Mining temporal relationships with multiple granularities in time sequences. *Bulletin of the Technical Committee on Data Engineering*, 21:32–38, 1998.

[12] H.-C. Kum, J. Pei, W. Wang, and D. Duncan. ApproxMap: Approximate mining of consensus sequential patterns. In *Proceedings of the 2003 SIAM International Conference on Data Mining (SDM'03)*, pp. 311–315, San Francisco, CA, May 2003.

[13] Institute for Systems Biology. Repeatmasker. In http://www.repeatmasker. org/webrepeatmaskerhelp.html, 2003.

[14] G. M. Landau and J. P. Schmidt. An algorithm for approximate tandem repeats. In *Proceedings of the 4th Annual Symposium on Combinatorial Pattern Matching*, number 684, pp. 120–133, Padova, Italy, 1993. Springer-Verlag, Berlin.

[15] S. Kurtz, J. V. Choudhuri, E. Ohlebusch, C. Schleiermacher, J. Stoye, and R. Giegerich. Reputer: The manifold applications of repeat analysis on a genomic scale. *Nucleic Acids Research*, 22: 4633–4642, 2001.

[16] D. Gusfield. *Algorithms on Strings, Trees and Sequences, Computer Science and Computation Biology*. Cambridge University Press, 1997.

[17] P. Weiner. Linear pattern matching algorithms. In *Proceedings of the 14th IEEE Annual Symposium on Switching and Automata Theory*, pp. 1–11, 1973.

[18] R. Agrawal and R. Srikant. Fast algorithm for mining association rules in large databases. In Research Report RJ 9839, IBM Almaden Research Center, San Jose, CA, June 1994.

[19] X. Yan, J. Han, and R. Afshar. CloSpan: Mining closed sequential patterns in large datasets. In *Proceedings of the 2003 SIAM International Conference on Data Mining (SDM'03)*, pp. 166–177, San Fransisco, CA, May 2003.

[20] J. Wang and J. Han. BIDE: Efficient mining of frequent closed sequences. In *Proceedings of the 2004 International Conference on Data Engineering (ICDE'04)*, pp. 79–90, Boston, MA, March 2004.

[21] Jia-Lien Hsu, Arbee L. P. Chen, and Hung-Chen Chen. Finding approximate repeating patterns from sequence data. In *Proceedings of the 5th International Conference on Music Information Retrieval (ISMIR'04)*, pp. 246–250, Barcelona, Spain, October 2004.

Chapter 5

Scientific Data Mining in Astronomy

Kirk D. Borne

Contents

5.1 Introduction

It has been said that astronomers have been doing data mining for centuries: "the data are mine, and you cannot have them!" Seriously, astronomers are trained as data miners, because we are trained to (1) characterize the known (i.e., unsupervised learning, clustering), (2) assign the new (i.e., supervised learning, classification), and (3) discover the unknown (i.e., semisupervised learning, outlier detection) [1,2]. These skills are more critical than ever since astronomy is now a data-intensive science, and it will become even more data intensive in the coming decade [3–5].

We describe the new data-intensive research paradigm that astronomy and astrophysics are now entering [6]. This is described within the context of the largest data-producing astronomy project in the coming decade—the LSST (Large Synoptic Survey Telescope). The enormous data output, database contents, knowledge discovery, and community science expected from this project will impose massive data challenges on the astronomical research community. One of these challenge areas is the rapid machine learning (ML), data mining, and classification of all novel astronomical events from each 3 gigapixel (6 GB) image obtained every 20 s throughout every night for the project duration of 10 years. We describe these challenges and a particular implementation of a classification broker for this data fire hose. But, first, we review some of the prior results of applying data mining techniques in astronomical research.

5.2   Data Mining Applications in Astronomy

Astronomers classically have focused on clustering and classification problems as standard practice in our research discipline. This is especially true of observational (experimental) astronomers who collect data on objects in the sky, and then try to understand the objects' physical properties and hence understand the underlying physics that leads to those properties. This invariably leads to a partitioning of the objects into classes and subclasses, which reflect the manifestation of different physical processes that appear dominant in different classes of objects. Even theoretical astrophysicists, who apply pure physics and applied mathematics to astronomy problems, are usually (though not always) governed by the results of the experimentalists—to identify classes of behavior within their models, and to make predictions about further properties of those classes that will enhance our understanding of the underlying physics.

5.2.1   Clustering

Clustering usually has a very specific meaning to an astronomer—that is, spatial clustering (more specifically, angular clustering on the sky). In other words, we see groupings of stars close together in the sky, which we call star clusters. We also see groupings of galaxies in the sky, which we call galaxy clusters (or clusters of galaxies). On even larger spatial scales, we see clusters of clusters of galaxies (superclusters)—for example, our Milky Way galaxy belongs to the local group of galaxies, which belongs to the local supercluster. Most of these cluster classes can be further subdivided and specialized: for example, globular star clusters versus open star clusters, or loose groups of galaxies versus compact groups of galaxies, or rich clusters of galaxies versus poor clusters of galaxies. Two of the research problems that are addressed by astronomers who study these objects are discovery and membership—that is, discovering new clusters, and assigning objects as members of one or another cluster. These astronomical applications of clustering are similar to corresponding ML applications. Because clustering is standard research practice in astronomy, it is not possible to summarize the published work in this area, since it would comprise a significant fraction of all research papers published in all astronomy journals and conference proceedings over the last century. Specific data-mining applications of clustering in astronomy include the search for rare and new types of objects [7–9].

More generally, particularly for the ML community, clustering refers to class discovery and segregation within any parameter space (not just spatial clustering). Astronomers perform this general type of clustering also [6,10]. For example, there are many objects in the universe for which at least two classes have been discovered. Astronomers have not been too creative in labeling these classes, which include types I and II supernovae, types I and II Cepheid variable stars, populations I and II (and maybe III) stars, types I and II active galaxies, and so on, including further refinement into subclasses for some of these. These observationally different types of objects (segregated classes) were discovered when astronomers noticed clustering in various parameter spaces (i.e., in scatter plots of measured scientific parameters).

5.2.2 Classification

The other major dimension of astronomical research is the assignment of objects to classes. This was historically carried out one at a time, as the data were collected one object at a time. ML and data-mining classification algorithms were not explicitly necessary. However, in fact, the process is the same in astronomy as in data mining: (1) class discovery (clustering), (2) discover rules for the different classes (e.g., regions of parameter space), (3) build training samples to refine the rules, and (4) assign new objects to known classes using new measured science data for those objects. Hence, it is accurate to say that astronomers have been data mining for centuries. Classification is a primary feature of astronomical research. We are essentially zoologists—we classify objects in the astronomical zoo.

As the data sets have grown in size, it has become increasingly appropriate and even imperative to apply ML algorithms to the data in order to learn the rules and to apply the rules of classification. Algorithms that have been used include Bayesian analysis, decision trees, neural networks, and (more recently) support vector machines. The ClassX project has used a network of classifiers in order to estimate classes of x-ray sources using distributed astronomical data collections [11,12].

We now briefly summarize some specific examples of these. But first we present a more general survey of data-mining research in astronomy.

5.2.3 General Survey of Astronomical Data Mining

A search of the online astronomical literature database ADS (NASA's astrophysics data system) lists only 63 refereed astronomy research papers (765 abstracts of all types—refereed and unrefereed) that have the words "data mining" or "machine learning" in their abstracts. (Note that ADS searches a much broader set of disciplines than just astronomy when nonrefereed papers are included—most of these search results are harvested from the ArXiv.org manuscript repository.) Of course, there are many fine papers related to astronomical data mining in the *SIAM*, *ACM*, *IEEE*, and other journals and proceedings that are not harvested by ADS.

Within the ADS list of refereed papers, the earliest examples that explicitly refer to data mining in their abstract are two papers that appeared in 1997—these were general perspective papers. (Note that there are many papers, including Refs. [1,2] that were not in the refereed literature but that predate the 1997 papers.) The first of the refereed data-mining application papers that explicitly mentions data mining in the abstract and that focused on a specific astronomy research problem appeared in 2000 [13]. This paper described all-sky monitoring and techniques to detect millions of variable (transient) astronomical phenomena of all types. This was an excellent precursor study to the LSST (see Section 5.4.1).

Among the most recent examples of refereed papers in ADS that explicitly refer to data mining (not including this author's work [14]) is the paper [15] that addresses the same research problem as Ref. [13]: the automated classification of large numbers of transient and variable objects. Again, this research is a major contributor and precursor to the LSST research agenda (Section 5.4.3).

A very recent data-mining paper focuses on automatic prediction of solar coronal mass ejections, which lead to energetic particle events around the Earth–Moon–Mars environment, which are hazardous to astronauts outside the protective shield of the Earth's magnetosphere [16]. This is similar to the data-mining research project just beginning at George Mason University with this author [17].

Additional recent work includes investigations into robust ML for terascale astronomical data sets [18]. In addition to these papers, several astronomy-specific data-mining projects are underway. These include AstroWeka,* Grist† (Grid Data Mining for Astronomy), the Laboratory for Cosmological Data Mining,‡ the LSST Data Mining Research study group [19], the Transient Classification Project at Berkeley [20], and the soon-to-be commissioned Palomar Transient Factory.

We now look at more specific astronomical applications that employed ML and data-mining techniques. We have not covered everything (e.g., other methods that have been applied to astronomical data mining include principal component analysis, kernel regression, random forests, and various nearest-neighbor methods, such as Refs. [10,21–25]).

5.2.3.1 Bayesian Analysis

A search of ADS lists 575 refereed papers in which the words Bayes or Bayesian appear in the paper's abstract. For comparison, the same search criteria returned 2313 abstracts of all papers (refereed and nonrefereed). Seven of the refereed papers were published before 1980 (none published before 1970). One of these was by Sebok [26]. He applied Bayesian probability analysis to the most basic astronomical classification problem—distinguishing galaxies from stars among the many thousands of objects detected in large images. This is a critical problem in astronomy,

---

* http://astroweka.sourceforge.net/.

† http://grist.caltech.edu.

‡ http://lcdm.astro.uiuc.edu/.

since the study of stars is a vastly different astrophysics regime than the study of galaxies. To know which objects in the image are stars, and hence which objects are galaxies is critical to the science. It may seem that this is an obvious distinction, but that is only true for nearby galaxies, which appear large on the sky (with large angular extent). This is not true at all for very distant galaxies, which provide the most critical information about the origin and history of our universe. These distant galaxies appear as small blobs on images, almost indistinguishable from stars—nearly 100% of the stars are in our Milky Way galaxy, hence very very nearby (by astronomical standards), and consequently stars therefore carry much less cosmological significance.

A more recent example is the application of Bayesian analysis to the problem of star formation in young galaxies [27]: The authors applied a Bayesian Markov Chain Monte Carlo method to determine whether the stars in the galaxies form in one monolithic collapse of a giant gas cloud, or if they form in a hierarchical fashion (with stars forming in smaller galaxies forming first, then those galaxies merge to become larger galaxies, and so on). The latter seems to be the best model to fit the observational data.

The above examples illustrate a very important point. The large number of papers that refer to Bayes analysis does not indicate the number that are doing data mining. This is because Bayesian analysis is used primarily as a statistical analysis technique or as a probability density estimation technique. The latter is certainly applicable to classification problems, but not on a grand scale as we expect for data mining (i.e., discovering hidden knowledge contained in large databases).

One significant recent paper that applies Bayesian analysis in a data mining sense focuses on a very important problem in large-database astronomy: cross-identification of astronomical sources in multiple large data collections [28]. In order to match the same object across multiple catalogs, the authors have proposed the use of more than just spatial coincidence, which also include numerous physical properties, including colors, redshift (distance), and luminosity. The result is an efficient algorithm that is ready for petascale astronomical data mining.

5.2.3.2 Decision Trees

A search of ADS lists 21 refereed papers (166 abstracts of all types) in which decision tree appears in the abstract. One of the earliest (nonrefereed) conference papers was the 1994 paper by Djorgovski, Wier, and Fayyad [29], when Fayyad was working at NASA's Jet Propulsion Laboratory. This paper described the SKICAT classification system, which was the standard example of astronomical data mining quoted in many data-mining conference talks subsequently. The earliest paper we could find in astronomy was in 1975 [30], 16 years before the next paper appeared. The 1975 paper addressed a "new methodology to integrate planetary quarantine requirements into mission planning, with application to a Jupiter orbiter."

Decision trees have been applied to another critical research problem in astronomy by Ref. [31]—the identification of cosmic ray (particle radiation) contamination in astronomical images. Charge-coupled device (CCD) cameras not only make excellent light detectors, but they also detect high-energy particles that permeate space. Cosmic-ray particles deposit their energy and create spikes in CCD images (in the same way that a light photon does). The cosmic-ray hits are random (as the particles enter the detector randomly from ambient space)—they have nothing to do with the image. Understanding the characteristics of these bogus events (background noise) in astronomical images and being able to remove them are very important steps in astronomical image processing. The decision-tree classifiers employed by Ref. [31] produced 95% accuracy. Recently, researchers have started to investigate the application of neural networks to the same problem [32] (and others).

5.2.3.3 Neural Networks

A search of ADS lists 418 refereed papers in which the phrases "neural net" or "neural network" appear in the paper's abstract. For comparison, the same search criteria returned over 10,000 abstracts of all papers (refereed and nonrefereed, most of which are not in astronomy; see Section 5.2.3). The earliest of these refereed papers that appeared in an astronomical journal [33] (published in 1986) addressed neural networks and simulated annealing algorithms in general. One of the first real astronomical examples that was presented in a refereed paper [34] applied a neural network to the problem of rapid adaptive mirror adjustments in telescopes in order to dramatically improve image quality.

As mentioned above, artificial neural networks (ANNs) have been applied to the problem of cosmic-ray detection CCD images. ANNs have also been applied to another important problem mentioned earlier: star–galaxy discrimination (classification) in large images. Many authors have applied ANN to this problem, including Refs. [35–42]. Of course, this astronomy research problem has been tackled by many algorithms, including decision trees [43].

Two other problems that have received a lot of astronomical research attention using neural networks are as follows: (1) the classification of different galaxy types within large databases of galaxy data (e.g., Refs. [44–47]); and (2) the determination of the photometric redshift estimate, which is used as an approximator of distance for huge numbers of galaxies, for which accurate distances are not known (e.g., Refs. [48–51]). The latter problem has also been investigated recently using random forests [24] and support vector machines (SVMs).

5.2.3.4 Support Vector Machines

ADS lists 154 abstracts (refereed and nonrefereed) that include the phrase "support vector machine," of which 21 of these are refereed astronomy journal papers. Three of the latter focus on the problem mentioned earlier: determination of the photometric redshift estimate for distant galaxies [52–54]. Note that Ref. [54] also applies a kernel regression method to the problem—the authors find that kernel regression is slightly more accurate than SVM, but they discuss the positives and negatives of the two methods. SVM was used in conjunction with a variety of other methods to address the problem of cross-identification of astronomical sources in multiple data collections that was described earlier [55,56]. SVM has also been used by several authors for forecasting solar flares and solar wind-induced geostorms, including Refs. [16,57,58].

5.3 Data-Intensive Science

The development of models to describe and understand scientific phenomena has historically proceeded at a pace driven by new data. The more we know, the more we are driven to tweak or to revolutionize our models, thereby advancing our scientific understanding. This data-driven modeling and discovery linkage has entered a new paradigm [59]. The acquisition of scientific data in all disciplines is now accelerating and causing a nearly insurmountable data avalanche [60]. In astronomy in particular, rapid advances in three technology areas (telescopes, detectors, and computation) have continued unabated—all of these advances lead to more and more data [5]. With this accelerated advance in data-generation capabilities, humans will require novel, increasingly automated, and increasingly more effective scientific knowledge discovery systems [61].

To meet the data-intensive research challenge, the astronomical research community has embarked on a grand information technology (IT) program, to describe and unify all astronomical data resources worldwide. This global interoperable virtual data system is referred to as the National Virtual Observatory (NVO*) in the United States, or more simply the Virtual Observatory (VO). Within the international research community, the VO effort is steered by the International Virtual Observatory Alliance.† This grand vision encompasses more than a collection of data sets. The result is a significant evolution in the way that astrophysical research, both observational and theoretical, is conducted in the new millennium [62]. This revolution is leading to an entirely new branch of astrophysics research—Astroinformatics—still in its infancy, consequently requiring further research and development as a discipline in order to aid in the data-intensive astronomical science that is emerging [63].

The VO effort enables discovery, access, and integration of data, tools, and information resources across all observatories, archives, data centers, and individual projects worldwide [64]. However, it remains outside the scope of the VO projects to generate new knowledge, new models, and new scientific understanding from the huge data volumes flowing from the largest sky survey projects [5,60]. Even further beyond the scope of the VO is the ensuing feedback and impact of the potentially exponential growth in new scientific knowledge discoveries back onto those telescope instrument operations. In addition, while the VO projects are productive science-enabling IT research and development projects, they are not specifically scientific (astronomical) research projects. There is still enormous room for scientific data portals and

---

* www.us-vo.org.
† www.ivoa.net.

data-intensive science research tools that integrate, mine, and discover new knowledge from the vast distributed data repositories that are now VO-accessible [61].

The problem therefore is this: astronomy researchers will soon (if not already) lose the ability to keep up with any of these things—the data flood, the scientific discoveries buried within, the development of new models of those phenomena, and the resulting new data-driven follow-up observing strategies that are imposed on telescope facilities to collect new data needed to validate and augment new discoveries.

5.4   Astronomy Sky Surveys as Data Producers

A common feature of modern astronomical sky surveys is that they are producing massive (terabyte) databases. New surveys may produce hundreds of terabytes (TB) up to 100 (or more) petabytes (PB) both in the image data archive and in the object catalogs (databases). Interpreting these petabyte catalogs (i.e., mining the databases for new scientific knowledge) will require more sophisticated algorithms and networks that discover, integrate, and learn from distributed petascale databases more effectively [65,66].

5.4.1   LSST Sky Survey Database

One of the most impressive astronomical sky surveys being planned for the next decade is the LSST[*] project [67]. The three fundamental distinguishing astronomical attributes of the LSST project are as follows:

1. Repeated temporal measurements of all observable objects in the sky, corresponding to thousands of observations per each object over a 10-year period, expected to generate 10,000–100,000 alerts each night—an alert is a signal (e.g., XML-formatted news feed) to the astronomical research community that something has changed at that location on the sky, either the brightness or position of an object, or the serendipitous appearance of some totally new object.

2. Wide-angle imaging that will repeatedly cover most of the night sky within 3–4 nights (= tens of billions of objects).

3. Deep co-added images of each observable patch of sky (summed over 10 years: 2015–2025), reaching far fainter objects and to greater distance over more area of sky than other sky surveys [68].

Compared to other astronomical sky surveys, the LSST survey will deliver time-domain coverage for orders of magnitude more objects. It is envisioned that this project will produce ~30 TB of data per each night of observation for 10 years. The

---

[*] www.lsst.org.

final image archive will be ~70 PB (and possibly much more), and the final LSST astronomical object catalog (object-attribute database) is expected to be ~10–20 PB.

LSST's most remarkable data product will be a 10-year movie of the entire sky—cosmic cinematography. This time-lapse coverage of the night sky will open up time-domain astronomy like no other project has been able to do previously. In general, astronomers have a good idea of what things in the sky are varying and what things are not varying, as a result of many centuries of humans staring at the sky, with and without the aid of telescopes. But, there is so much more possibly happening that we are not aware of at the very faintest limits simply because we have not explored the sky systematically night after night on a large scale. When an unusual time-dependent event occurs in the sky (e.g., a γ-ray burst, supernova, or incoming asteroid), astronomers (and others) will not only want to examine spatial coincidences of this object within the various surveys, but they will also want to search for other data covering the same region of the sky that was obtained at the same time as this new temporal event. These contextual data will enable more robust classification and characterization of the temporal event. Because of the time criticality and potential for huge scientific payoff of such follow-up observations of transient phenomena, the classification system must also be able to perform time-based searches very efficiently and very effectively (i.e., to search all of the distributed VO databases as quickly as possible). One does not necessarily know in advance if such a new discovery will appear in any particular waveband, and so one will want to examine all possible astronomical sky surveys for coincidence events. Most of these targets of opportunity will consequently be added immediately to the observing programs of many ground-based and space-based astronomical telescopes, observatories, and ongoing research experiments worldwide.

5.4.2 LSST Data-Intensive Science Challenge

LSST is not alone. It is one (likely the biggest one) of several large astronomical sky survey projects beginning operations now or within the coming decade. LSST is by far the largest undertaking, in terms of duration, camera size, depth of sky coverage, volume of data to be produced, and real-time requirements on operations, data processing, event-modeling, and follow-up research response. One of the key features of these surveys is that the main telescope facility will be dedicated to the primary survey program, with no specific plans for follow-up observations. This is emphatically true for the LSST project [69]. Paradoxically, the follow-up observations are scientifically essential—they contribute significantly to new scientific discovery, to the classification and characterization of new astronomical objects and sky events, and to rapid response to short-lived transient sky phenomena.

Since it is anticipated that LSST will generate many thousands (probably tens of thousands) of new astronomical event alerts per night of observation, there is a critical need for innovative follow-up procedures. These procedures necessarily must include modeling of the events—to determine their classification, time criticality, astronomical relevance, rarity, and the scientifically most productive set of follow-up measurements. Rapid time-critical follow-up observations, with a wide range of timescales from seconds to days, are essential for proper identification, classification, characterization, analysis, interpretation, and understanding of nearly every astrophysical phenomenon (e.g., supernovae, novae, accreting black holes, microquasars, γ-ray bursts, gravitational microlensing events, extrasolar planetary transits across distant stars, new comets, incoming asteroids, trans-Neptunian objects, dwarf planets, optical transients, variable stars of all classes, and anything that goes bump in the night).

5.4.3   Petascale Data Mining with the LSST

LSST and similar large sky surveys have enormous potential to enable countless astronomical discoveries. Such discoveries will span the full spectrum of statistics: from rare one-in-a-billion (or one-in-a-trillion) type objects to a complete statistical and astrophysical specification of a class of objects (based upon millions of instances of the class). One of the key scientific requirements of these projects therefore is to learn rapidly from what they see. This means (1) to identify the serendipitous as well as the known, (2) to identify outliers (e.g., front-page news discoveries) that fall outside the bounds of model expectations, (3) to identify rare events that our models say should be there, (4) to find new attributes of known classes, (5) to provide statistically robust tests of existing models, and (6) to generate the vital inputs for new models. All of this requires integrating and mining of all known data: to train classification models and to apply classification models.

LSST alone is likely to throw such data mining and knowledge discovery efforts into the petascale realm. For example, astronomers currently discover $\sim$100 new supernovae (exploding stars) per year. Since the beginning of human history, perhaps $\sim$10,000 supernovae have been recorded. The identification, classification, and analysis of supernovae are among the key science requirements for the LSST project to explore dark energy—that is, supernovae contribute to the analysis and characterization of the ubiquitous cosmic dark energy. Since supernovae are the result of a rapid catastrophic explosion of a massive star, it is imperative for astronomers to respond quickly to each new event with rapid follow-up observations in many measurement modes (light curves, spectroscopy, images of the host galaxy's environment). Historically, with $<$10 new supernovae being discovered each week, such follow-up has been feasible. But now, LSST promises to produce a list of 1000 new supernovae each night for 10 years [68], which represent a small fraction of the total (10,000–100,000) alerts expected each night. Astronomers are faced with the enormous challenge of efficiently mining, correctly classifying, and intelligently prioritizing a staggering number of new events for follow-up observation each night for a decade.

The major features and contents of the LSST scientific database include the following:

- $>$100 database tables

- Image metadata = 675M rows

- Source catalog = 260B rows

- Object catalog = 22B rows, with 200+ attributes

- Moving object catalog

- Variable object catalog

- Alerts catalog

- Calibration metadata

- Configuration metadata

- Processing metadata

- Provenance metadata

Many possible scientific data mining use cases are anticipated with the LSST database, including the following:

- Provide rapid probabilistic classifications for all 10,000 LSST events each night

- Find new fundamental planes of parameters (e.g., the fundamental plane of elliptical galaxies)

- Find new correlations, associations, and relationships of all kinds from 100+ attributes in the science database

- Compute N-point correlation functions over a variety of spatial and astrophysical parameters

- Discover voids or zones of avoidance in multidimensional parameter spaces (e.g., period gaps)

- Discover new and exotic classes of astronomical objects, while discovering new properties of known classes

- Discover new and improved rules for classifying known classes of objects (e.g., photometric redshifts)

- Identify novel, unexpected behavior in the time domain from time-series data of all known variable objects

- Hypothesis testing—verify existing (or generate new) astronomical hypotheses with strong statistical confidence, using millions of training samples

- Serendipity—discover the rare one-in-a-billion type of objects through outlier detection

- Quality assurance—identify glitches, anomalies, and image-processing errors through deviation detection

Some of the data-mining research challenge areas posed by the petascale LSST scientific database include the following:

- Scalability (at petabytes scales) of existing ML and data-mining algorithms

- Development of grid-enabled parallel data-mining algorithms

- Designing a robust system for brokering classifications from the LSST event pipeline

- Multiresolution methods for exploration of petascale databases

- Visual data-mining algorithms for visual exploration of the massive databases

- Indexing of multiattribute multidimensional astronomical databases (beyond sky-coordinate spatial indexing)

- Rapid querying of petabyte databases

5.5   Classification Broker for Astronomy

We are beginning to assemble user requirements and design specifications for a ML engine (data-integration network plus data-mining algorithms) to address the petascale data-mining needs of the LSST and other large data-intensive astronomy sky survey projects. The data requirements surpass those of the current Sloan Digital Sky Survey (SDSS*) by 1,000–10,000 times, while the time-criticality requirement (for event/object classification and characterization) drastically drops from months (or weeks) down to minutes (or tens of seconds). In addition to the follow-up classification problem (described above), astronomers also want to find every possible new scientific discovery (pattern, correlation, relationship, outlier, new class, etc.) buried within these new enormous databases. This might lead to a petascale data-mining compute engine that runs in parallel alongside the data archive, testing every possible model, association, and rule. We focus here on the time-critical data-mining engine (i.e., classification broker) that enables rapid follow-up science for the most important and exciting astronomical discoveries of the coming decade, on a wide range of timescales from seconds to days, corresponding to a plethora of exotic astrophysical phenomena.

5.5.1   Broker Specifications: AstroDAS

The classification broker's primary specification is to produce and distribute scientifically robust near-real-time classification of astronomical sources, events, objects, or event host objects (i.e., the astronomical object that hosts the event; e.g., the host

---

galaxy for some distant supernova explosion—it is important to measure the redshift distance of the host galaxy in order to interpret and to classify properly the supernova). These classifications are derived from integrating and mining data, information, and knowledge from multiple distributed data repositories. The broker feeds off existing robotic telescope and astronomical alert networks worldwide, and then integrates existing astronomical knowledge (catalog data) from the VO. The broker may eventually provide the knowledge discovery and classification service for LSST, a torrential fire hose of data and astronomical events.

Incoming event alert data will be subjected to a suite of ML algorithms for event classification, outlier detection, object characterization, and novelty discovery. Probabilistic ML models will produce rank-ordered lists of the most significant or most unusual events. These ML models (e.g., Bayesian networks, decision trees, multiple weak classifiers, Markov models, or perhaps scientifically derived similarity metrics) will be integrated with astronomical taxonomies and ontologies that will enable rapid information extraction, knowledge discovery, and scientific decision support for real-time astronomical research facility operations—to follow up on the 10–100 K alertable astronomical events that will be identified each night for 10 years by the LSST sky survey.

The classification broker will include a knowledgebase to capture the new labels (tags) that are generated for the new astronomical events. These tags are annotations to the events. "Annotation" refers to tagging the data and metadata content with descriptive terms, which apply to individual data granules or to subsets of the data. For this knowledgebase, we envision a collaborative tagging system called AstroDAS (Astronomy Distributed Annotation System) [70]. AstroDAS is similar to existing science knowledgebases, such as BioDAS[*] (Biology Distributed Annotation System), WikiProteins,[†] the Heliophysics Knowledgebase (HPKB[‡]), and the Entity Describer [71]. AstroDAS is "distributed" in the sense that the source data and metadata are distributed, and the users are distributed. It is a system with a unified schema for the annotation database, where distributed data are perceived as a unified data system to the user. One possible implementation of AstroDAS could be as a Web 2.0 scientific data and information mashup (Science 2.0). AstroDAS users will include providers (authors) and annotation users (consumers). Consumers (humans or machines) will eventually interact with AstroDAS in four ways:

1. Integrate the annotation database content within their own data portals, providing scientific content to their own communities of users

2. Subscribe to receive notifications when new sources are annotated or classified

3. Use the classification broker as a data integration tool to broker classes and annotations between sky surveys, robotic telescopes, and data repositories

4. Query the annotation database (either manually or through Web services)

---

[*] http://biodas.org/.
[†] http://www.wikiprofessional.info/.
[‡] http://www.lmsal.com/helio-informatics/hpkb/.

In the last case, the users include the astronomical event message producers, who will want to issue their alerts with their best estimate for the astronomical classification of their event. The classification will be generated through the application of ML algorithms to the networked data accessible via the VO, in order to arrive at a prioritized list of classes, ordered by probability of certainty. In order to facilitate these science use cases (and others not listed here), AstroDAS must have the following features: (1) it must enable collaborative, dynamic, and distributed sharing of annotations; (2) it must access databases, data repositories, grids, and Web services; (3) it must apply ontologies, semantics, dictionaries, annotations, and tags; and (4) it must employ data/text mining, ML, and information extraction algorithms.

5.5.2 Collaborative Annotation of Classes

ML and data-mining algorithms, when applied to very large data streams, could possibly generate the classification labels (tags) autonomously. Generally, scientists do not want to leave this decision making to machine intelligence alone—they prefer to have human intelligence in the loop also. When humans and machines work together to produce the best possible classification labels, this is collaborative annotation. Collaborative annotation is a form of human computation [72]. Human computation refers to the application of human intelligence to solve complex difficult problems that cannot be solved by computers alone. Humans can see patterns and semantics (context, content, and relationships) more quickly, accurately, and meaningfully than machines. Human computation therefore applies to the problem of annotating, labeling, and classifying voluminous data streams. Of course, the application of autonomous machine intelligence (data mining and ML) to the annotation, labeling, and classification of data granules is also valid and efficacious. The combination of both human and machine intelligence is critical to the success of AstroDAS as a classification broker for enormous data-intensive astronomy sky survey projects, such as LSST.

5.5.3 Research Agenda

We identify some of the key research activities that must be addressed, in order to promote the development of a ML-based classification broker for petascale mining of large-scale astronomy sky survey databases. Many of these research activities are already being pursued by other data mining and computational science researchers—we hope to take advantage of all such developments, many of which are enabled through advanced next-generation data mining and cyberinfrastructure research:

1. Before the classification labels can be useful, we must reach community consensus on the correct set of semantic ontological, taxonomical, and classification terms. There are ontologies under development in astronomy already—their completeness, utility, and usability need to be researched.

2. Research into user requirements and scientific use cases will be required in order that we design, develop, and deploy the correct user-oriented petascale data-mining system.

3. A complete set of classification rules must be researched and derived for all possible astronomical events and objects. For objects and events that are currently unknown, we need to identify robust outlier and novelty detection rules and classifiers. These need to be researched and tested.

4. We need to research and collect comprehensive sets of training examples for the numerous classes that we hope to classify. With these samples, the classification broker will be trained and validated.

5. Algorithms for Web service-based (perhaps grid-based or peer-to-peer) classification and mining of distributed data must be researched, developed, and validated. These mining algorithms should include text mining as well as numeric data mining, perhaps an integrated text-numeric data-mining approach will be most effective and thus needs to be researched.

6. User interface and interaction models will need to be researched through prototypes and demonstrations of the classification broker.

7. Research into the robust integration of the many AstroDAS system components will be needed. This will require investigation of different modes of interaction and integration, such as grids, Web services, news feeds, ontologies, linked databases, etc.

8. Deploy a working classification broker on a live astronomical event message stream, to research its functionality, usefulness, bottlenecks, failure modes, security, robustness, and (most importantly) scalability (from the current few events per night, up to many tens of thousands of events per night in the coming decade). Fortunately, there are such event message feeds available today, though on a much smaller scale than that anticipated from LSST.

Clearly, this is an ambitious research agenda. It will not be fully accomplished in just a year or two. It will require several years of research and development. This is fortunate, since the most dramatic need for the classification broker system for astronomy will come with the start-up of LSST sky survey operations in 2015, lasting 10 years (until 2025). So, we have a few years to get it right, and we will need all of those years to complete the challenging research program described above.

5.6 Introducing the New Science of Astroinformatics

As described above, today's astronomical research environment is highly focused on the design, implementation, and archiving of very large sky surveys. Many projects today (e.g., Palomar-Quest Synoptic Sky Survey, SDSS, and 2-Micron All Sky Survey [2MASS]) plus many more projects in the near future (e.g., LSST, Palomar Transient Factory, Supernova Acceleration Probe, Panoramic Survey Telescope And Rapid Response System, and Dark Energy Survey) are destined to produce enormous catalogs of astronomical sources. The virtual collection of these gigabyte, terabyte, and (eventually) petabyte catalogs will significantly increase science return and enable remarkable new scientific discoveries through the integration and cross-correlation of data across these multiple survey dimensions. Astronomers will be unable to tap the riches of this data lode without a new paradigm for astroinformatics that involves distributed database queries and data mining across distributed virtual tables of decentralized, joined, and integrated sky survey catalogs. The challenges posed by this problem are daunting, as in most disciplines today that are producing data floods at prodigious rates.

The development and deployment of the astronomy VO is perceived by some as the solution to this problem. The VO provides one-stop shopping for all end-user data needs, including access to distributed heterogeneous data, services, and other resources (e.g., the GRID). Some grid-based data-mining services are already envisioned or in development (e.g., GRIST,[*] the Datamining Grid, and F-MASS[†]). However, processing and mining the associated distributed and vast data collections are fundamentally challenging since most off-the-shelf data-mining systems require the data to be downloaded to a single location before further analysis. This imposes serious scalability constraints on the data-mining system and fundamentally hinders the scientific discovery process. If distributed data repositories are to be really accessible to a larger community, then technology ought to be developed for supporting distributed data analysis that can reduce, as much as possible, communication requirements.

The new science of astroinformatics will emerge from this large and expanding distributed heterogeneous data environment. We define astroinformatics as the formalization of data-intensive astronomy for research and education. Astroinformatics will borrow heavily from concepts in the fields of bioinformatics and geoinformatics (i.e., GIS [geographic information systems]). The main features of this new science are as follows: it is data driven, data centric, and data inspired. As bioinformatics represents an entirely new paradigm for research in the biological sciences, beyond computational biology, so also does astroinformatics represent a new mode of data-intensive scientific research in astronomy that is cognizant of and dependent on the astronomical flood of astronomical data that is now upon us. Data mining and knowledge discovery will become the killer apps for this mode of scientific research and discovery. Scientific databases will be the virtual sky that astronomers will study and mine. New scientific understanding will flow from the discovered knowledge that is derived from the avalanche of information content, which is extracted from the massive data collections.

5.6.1   Distributed Scientific Data Mining

Distributed data mining (DDM) of large scientific data collections will become the norm in astronomy, as the data collections (from the numerous large sky surveys) become so large that they cannot all be downloaded to a central site for mining

---

[*] http://grist.caltech.edu/.

[†] http://www.itsc.uah.edu/f-mass/.

and analysis. DDM algorithms will be an essential tool to enable discovery of the hidden knowledge buried among geographically dispersed heterogeneous databases [9,73–76].

As an example of the potential astronomical research that DDM will enable, we consider the large survey databases being produced (now and in the near future) by various NASA missions. GALEX is producing all-sky surveys at a variety of depths in the near-UV and far-UV. The Spitzer Space Telescope is conducting numerous large-area surveys in the infrared, including regions of sky (e.g., the Hubble Deep Fields) that are well studied by the Hubble Space Telescope (optical), Chandra X-ray Observatory, and numerous other observatories. The WISE mission (to be launched circa 2009) will produce an all-sky infrared survey. The 2MASS has cataloged millions of stars and galaxies in the near-infrared. Each of these wavebands contributes valuable astrophysical knowledge to the study of countless classes of objects in the astrophysical zoo. In many cases, such as the young star-forming regions within starbursting galaxies, the relevant astrophysical objects and phenomena have unique characteristics within each wavelength domain. For example, starbursting galaxies are often dust-enshrouded, yielding enormous infrared fluxes. Such galaxies reveal peculiar optical morphologies, occasional x-ray sources (such as intermediate black holes), and possibly even some UV bright spots as the short-wavelength radiation leaks through holes in the obscuring clouds. All of these data, from multiple missions in multiple wavebands, are essential for a full characterization, classification, analysis, and interpretation of these cosmologically significant populations.

In order to reap the full potential of scientific data mining, analysis, and discovery that this distributed data environment enables, it is essential to bring together data from multiple heterogeneously distributed data sites. For the all-sky surveys in particular (such as 2MASS, WISE, GALEX, SDSS, and LSST), it is impossible to access, mine, navigate, browse, and analyze these data in their current distributed state. To illustrate this point, suppose that an all-sky catalog contains descriptive data for one billion objects, and suppose that these descriptive data consist of a few hundred parameters (which is typical for the 2MASS and SDSS). Then, assuming simply that each parameter requires just 2-byte representation, then each survey database will consume 1 TB of space. If the survey also has a temporal dimension (such as the LSST, which will reimage each object 1000–2000 times), then massively more data handling is required in order to mine the enormous potential of the database contents. If each of these catalog entries and attributes requires only one CPU cycle to process it (e.g., in a data mining operation), then many teraflops (up to petaflops) of computation will be required even for the simplest data-mining application on the full contents of the databases.

It is clearly infeasible, impractical, and impossible to drag these terabyte (and soon, petabyte) catalogs back and forth from user to user, from data center to data center, from analysis package to package, each time someone has a new query to pose against these various data collections. Therefore, there is an urgent need for novel DDM algorithms that are inherently designed to work on distributed data collections. We are consequently focusing our research efforts on these problems [9,76].

5.6.2 Beyond the Science

Before we conclude, it is important to mention how these scientific data mining concepts are also relevant to science, mathematics, and technical education in our society today. The concept of using data in the classroom is developing quite an appeal among inquiry-based learning proponents.[*] Astronomy data and images in particular have a special universal appeal to students, general public, and all technical experts. Student-led data-mining projects that access large astronomical databases may lead to discoveries of new comets, asteroids, exploding stars, and more. Members of both the LSST and the NVO project scientific teams are especially interested in this type of collaboration among scientists, data-mining experts, educators, and students. The classroom activities (involving cool astronomy data) are engaging and exciting to students and thus contribute to the overall scientific, technical, and mathematical literacy of the nation. Astroinformatics enables transparent data sharing, reuse, and analysis in inquiry-based science classrooms. This allows not only scientists, but also students, educators, and citizen scientists to tackle knowledge discovery problems in large astronomy databases for fun and for real. This integrated research and education activity matches well to the objectives of the new CODATA ADMIRE[†] (advanced data methods and information technologies for research and education) initiative. Students are trained (1) to access large distributed data repositories, (2) to conduct meaningful scientific inquiries into the data, (3) to mine and analyze the data, and (4) to make data-driven scientific discoveries.

5.6.3 Informatics for Scientific Knowledge Discovery

Finally, we close with discussions of BioDAS (the inspiration behind AstroDAS) and of the relevance of informatics (e.g., bioinformatics and astroinformatics) to the classification broker described earlier. Informatics is "the discipline of organizing, accessing, mining, analyzing, and visualizing data for scientific discovery." Another definition says informatics is "the set of methods and applications for integration of large datasets across spatial and temporal scales to support decision making, involving computer modeling of natural systems, heterogeneous data structures, and data-model integration as a framework for decision making" [77].

Massive scientific data collections impose enormous challenges to scientists: how to find the most relevant data, how to reuse those data, how to mine data and discover new knowledge in large databases, and how to represent the newly discovered knowledge. The bioinformatics research community is already solving these problems with BioDAS. The DAS provides a distributed system for researchers anywhere to annotate (markup) their own knowledge (tagged information) about specific gene sequences. Any other researcher anywhere can find this annotation information quickly for any gene sequence. Similarly, astronomers can annotate individual astronomical objects with their own discoveries. These annotations can be applied

---

[*] http://serc.carleton.edu/usingdata/.

[†] http://www.iucr.org/iucr-top/data/docs/codataga2006_beijing.html.

to observational data/metadata within distributed digital data collections. The annotations provide mined knowledge, class labels, provenance, and semantic (scientifically meaningful) information about the experiment, the experimenter, the object being studied (astronomical object in our case, or gene sequence in the case of the bioinformatics research community), the properties of that object, new features or functions discovered about that object, its classification, its connectiveness to other objects, and so on.

Bioinformatics (for biologists) and astroinformatics (for astronomers) provide frameworks for the curation, discovery, access, interoperability, integration, mining, classification, and understanding of digital repositories through (human plus machine) semantic annotation of data, information, and knowledge. We are focusing new research efforts on further development of astroinformatics as follows: (1) a new subdiscipline of astronomical research (similar to the role of bioinformatics and geoinformatics as stand-alone subdisciplines in biological and geoscience research and education, respectively), and (2) the new paradigm for data-intensive astronomy research and education, which focuses on existing cyberinfrastructure such as the astronomical VO.

References

[1] Borne, K. D. 2001, Science user scenarios for a VO design reference mission: Science requirements for data mining, in *Virtual Observatories of the Future*, San Francisco, CA, Astronomical Society of the Pacific, p. 333.

[2] Borne, K. D. 2001, Data mining in astronomical databases, in *Mining the Sky*, New York, Springer-Verlag, p. 671.

[3] Brunner, R. J., Djorgovski, S. G., Prince, T. A., and Szalay, A. S. 2001, Massive datasets in astronomy. Available at http://arxiv.org/abs/astro-ph/0106481.

[4] Szalay, A. S., Gray, J., and VandenBerg, J. 2002, Petabyte scale data mining: Dream or reality? in the *Proceedings of the SPIE*, Vol. 4836, Survey and Other Telescope Technologies and Discoveries, Bellingham, WA, SPIE, p. 333.

[5] Becla, J. et al. 2006, Designing a multi-petabyte database for LSST. Available at http://arxiv.org/abs/cs/0604112.

[6] Djorgovski, S. G. et al. 2001, Exploration of parameter spaces in a Virtual Observatory. Available at http://arxiv.org/abs/astro-ph/0108346.

[7] Djorgovski, S. G. et al. 2000, Searches for rare and new types of objects. Available at http://arxiv.org/abs/astro-ph/0012453.

[8] Djorgovski, S. G. et al. 2000, Exploration of large digital sky surveys. Available at http://arxiv.org/abs/astro-ph/0012489.

[9] Dutta, H., Gianella, C., Borne, K., and Kargupta, H. 2007, Distributed top-*k* outlier detection from astronomy catalogs using the DEMAC system, in *Proceedings of SIAM Scientific Data Mining*, Philadelphia, PA, SIAM, p. 473.

[10] Djorgovski, S. and Davis, M. 1987, Fundamental properties of elliptical galaxies, *Astrophysical Journal*, 313, 59.

[11] Suchkov, A. et al. 2002, Automated object classification with Class X. Available at http://arxiv.org/abs/astro-ph/0210407.

[12] Suchkov, A. A., Hanisch, R. J., and Margon, B. 2005, A census of object types and redshift estimates in the SDSS photometric catalog from a trained decision-tree classifier. Available at http://arxiv.org/abs/astro-ph/0508501.

[13] Paczynski, B. 2000, Monitoring all sky for variability, *Publications of the ASP*, 112, 1281.

[14] Borne, K. D. 2008, A machine learning classification broker for the LSST transient database, *Astronomische Nachrichten*, 329, 255.

[15] Mahabal, A. et al. 2008, Automated probabilistic classification of transients and variables, *Astronomische Nachrichten*, 329, 288.

[16] Qahwaji, R., Colak, T., Al-Omari, M., and Ipson, S. 2008, Automated prediction of CMEs using machine learning of CME flare associations, *Solar Physics*, 248, 471.

[17] Olmeda, O., Zhang, J., Wechsler, H., Poland, A., and Borne, K. 2008, Automatic detection and tracking of coronal mass ejections in coronagraph time series, *Solar Physics*, 248, 485.

[18] Ball, N. M., Brunner, R. J., and Myers, A. D. 2007, Robust machine learning applied to terascale astronomical datasets. Available at http://arxiv.org/abs/0710.4482.

[19] Borne, K. D., Strauss, M. A., and Tyson, J. A. 2007, Data mining research with the LSST. Available at http://adsabs.harvard.edu/abs/2007AAS...21113725B.

[20] Bloom, J. S. et al. 2008, Towards a real-time transient classification engine. Available at http://arxiv.org/abs/0802.2249.

[21] Whitmore, B. C. 1984, An objective classification system for spiral galaxies. I. The two dominant dimensions, *Astrophysical Journal*, 278, 61.

[22] Ferreras, I. et al. 2006, A principal component analysis approach to the star formation history of elliptical galaxies in compact groups. Available at http://arxiv.org/abs/astro-ph/0511753.

[23] Borne, K. D. and Chang, A. 2007, Data mining for extra-solar planets, *Astronomical Data Analysis Software and Systems XVI*, A.S.P. Conference Series, San Francisco, CA, Astronomical Society of the Pacific, Vol. 376, p. 453.

[24] Carliles, S., Budavari, T., Heinis, S., Priebe, C., and Szalay, A. 2007, Photometric redshift estimation on SDSS data using random forests. Available at http://arxiv.org/abs/0711.2477.

[25] Ball, N. M. et al. 2007, Robust machine learning applied to astronomical data sets—II. Quantifying photometric redshifts for quasars using instance-based learning, *Astrophysical Journal*, 663, 774.

[26] Sebok, W. 1979, Optimal classification of images into stars or galaxies—A Bayesian approach, *Astronomical Journal*, 84, 1526.

[27] Kampakoglou, M., Rotta, R., and Silk J. 2008, Monolithic or hierarchical star formation? A new statistical analysis, *Monthly Notices of the Royal Astronomical Society*, 384, 1414.

[28] Budavari, T. and Szalay, A. S. 2007, Probabilistic cross-identification of astronomical sources. Available at http://arxiv.org/abs/0707.1611.

[29] Djorgovski, S. G., Weir, N., and Fayyad, U. 1994, Cataloging of the northern sky from the POSS-II using a next-generation software technology, *Astronomical Data Analysis Software and Systems III*, A.S.P. Conference Series, San Francisco, CA, Astronomical Society of the Pacific, Vol. 61, p. 195.

[30] Howard, R. A., North, D. W., and Pezier, J. P. 1975, A new methodology to integrate planetary quarantine requirements into mission planning, with application to a Jupiter orbiter, Final Report Stanford Research Institute, Menlo Park, CA.

[31] Salzberg, S. et al. 1995, Decision trees for automated identification of cosmic-ray hits in the Hubble Space Telescope images, *Publications of the ASP*, 107, 279.

[32] Waniak, W. 2006, Removing cosmic-ray hits from CCD images in real-time mode by means of an artificial neural network, *Experimental Astronomy*, 21(3), 151.

[33] Jeffrey, W. and Rosner, R. 1986, Optimization algorithms—simulated annealing and neural network processing, *Astrophysical Journal*, 310, 473.

[34] Angel, J. R. P., Wizinowich, P., Lloyd-Hart, M., and Sandler, D. 1990, Adaptive optics for array telescopes using neural network techniques, *Nature*, 348, 221.

[35] Odewahn, S. C., Stockwell, E. B., Pennington, R. L., Humphreys, R. M., and Zumach, W. A. 1992, Automated star/galaxy discrimination with neural networks, *Astronomical Journal*, 103, 318.

[36] Odewahn, S. C., Humphreys, R. M., Aldering, G., and Thurmes, P. 1993, Star-galaxy separation with a neural network. 2: Multiple Schmidt plate fields, *Publications of the ASP*, 105, 1354.

[37] Bazell, D. and Peng, Y. 1998, A comparison of neural network algorithms and preprocesing methods for star-galaxy discrimination, *Astrophysical Journal Supplement*, 116, 47.

[38] Mahonen, P. and Frantti, T. 2000, Fuzzy classifier for star-galaxy separation, *Astrophysical Journal*, 541, 261.

[39] Andreon, S., Gargiulo, G., Longo, G., Tagliaferri, R., and Capuano, N. 2000, Wide field imaging—I. Applications of neural networks to object detection and star/galaxy classification, *Monthly Notices of the Royal Astronomical Society*, 319, 700.

[40] Cortiglioni, F., Mahonen, P., Hakala, P., and Frantti, T. 2001, Automated star-galaxy discrimination for large surveys, *Astrophysical Journal*, 556, 937.

[41] Philip, N. S., Wadadekar, Y., Kembhavi, A., and Joseph, K. B. 2002, A difference boosting neural network for automated star-galaxy classification, *Astronomy and Astrophysics*, 385, 1119.

[42] Qin, D.-M., Guo, P., Hu, Z.-Y., and Zhao, Y.-H. 2003, Automated separation of stars and normal galaxies based on statistical mixture modeling with RBF neural networks, *Chinese Journal of Astronomy and Astrophysics*, 3, 277.

[43] Ball, N. M., Brunner, R. J., Myers, A. D., and Tcheng, D. 2006, Robust machine learning applied to astronomical data sets—I. Star-galaxy classification of the Sloan Digital Sky Survey DR3 using decision trees, *Astrophysical Journal*, 650, 497.

[44] Storrie-Lombardi, M. C., Lahav, O., Sodre, L., and Storrie-Lombardi, L. J. 1992, Morphological classification of galaxies by artificial neural networks, *Monthly Notices of the Royal Astronomical Society*, 259, 8.

[45] Naim, A., Lahav, O., Sodre, L., and Storrie-Lombardi, M. C. 1995, Automated morphological classification of APM galaxies by supervised artificial neural networks, *Monthly Notices of the Royal Astronomical Society*, 275, 567.

[46] Goderya, S. N. and Lolling, S. M. 2002, Morphological classification of galaxies using computer vision and artificial neural networks: A computational scheme, *Astrophysics and Space Science*, 279, p. 377.

[47] Ball, N. M. et al. 2004, Galaxy types in the Sloan Digital Sky Survey using supervised artificial neural networks, *Monthly Notices of the Royal Astronomical Society*, 348, 1038.

[48] Firth, A. E., Lahav, O., and Somerville, R. S. 2003, Estimating photometric redshifts with artificial neural networks, *Monthly Notices of the Royal Astronomical Society*, 339, 1195.

[49] Collister, A. A. and Lahav, O. 2004, ANNz: Estimating photometric redshifts using artificial neural networks, *Publications of the ASP*, 116, 345.

[50] Vanzella, E. et al. 2004, Photometric redshifts with the multilayer perceptron neural network: Application to the HDF-S and SDSS, *Astronomy and Astrophysics*, 423, 761.

[51] Oyaizu, H. et al. 2008, A galaxy photometric redshift catalog for the Sloan Digital Sky Survey data release 6, *Astrophysical Journal*, 674, 768.

[52] Wadadekar, Y. 2005, Estimating photometric redshifts using support vector machines, *Publications of the ASP*, 117, 79.

[53] Way, M. J. and Srivastava, A. N. 2006, Novel methods for predicting photometric redshifts from broadband photometry using virtual sensors, *Astrophysical Journal*, 647, 102.

[54] Wang, D., Zhang, Y.-X., Liu, C., and Zhao, Y.-H. 2008, Two novel approaches for photometric redshift estimation based on SDSS and 2MASS, *Chinese Journal of Astronomy and Astrophysics*, 8, 119.

[55] Rohde, D. J. et al. 2005, Applying machine learning to catalogue matching in astrophysics, *Monthly Notices of the Royal Astronomical Society*, 360, 69.

[56] Rohde, D. J., Gallagher, M. R., Drinkwater, M. J., and Pimbblet, K. A. 2006, Matching of catalogues by probabilistic pattern classification, *Monthly Notices of the Royal Astronomical Society*, 369, 2.

[57] Gavrishchaka, V. V. and Ganguli, S. B. 2001, Support vector machine as an efficient tool for high-dimensional data processing: Application to substorm forecasting, *Journal of Geophysics Research*, 106, 29911.

[58] Qu, M., Shih, F. Y., Jing, J., and Wang, H. 2006, Automatic detection and classification of coronal mass ejections, *Solar Physics*, 237, 419.

[59] Mahootian, F. and Eastman, T. 2008, Complementary frameworks of scientific inquiry: Hypothetico-deductive, hypothetico-inductive, and observational-inductive, *World Futures Journal*, in press.

[60] Bell, G., Gray, J., and Szalay, A. 2005, Petascale computations systems: Balanced cyberinfrastructure in a data-centric world. Available at http://arxiv.org/abs/cs/0701165.

[61] Borne, K. D. 2006, Data-driven discovery through e-science technologies, in *Proceedings of the IEEE Conference on Space Mission Challenges for Information Technology*, Washington, DC, IEEE Computer Society.

[62] McDowell, J. C. 2004, Downloading the sky, *IEEE Spectrum*, 41, 35.

[63] Borne, K. D. and Eastman, T. 2006, Collaborative knowledge-sharing for e-science, in *Proceedings of the AAAI Conference on Semantic Web for Collaborative Knowledge Acquisition*, Menlo Park, CA, AAAI Press, p. 104.

[64] Plante, R. et al. 2004, VO resource registry, in *Proceedings of the ADASS XIII Conference*. Available at http://www.us-vo.org/pubs/index.cfm accessed on August 23, 2007.

[65] Gray, J. et al. 2002, Data mining the SDSS SkyServer database. Available at http://arxiv.org/abs/cs/0202014.

[66] Longo, G. et al. 2001, Advanced data mining tools for exploring large astronomical databases, in *Proceedings of the SPIE*, Vol. 4477, Astronomical Data Analysis, Bellingham, WA, SPIE, p. 61.

[67] Tyson, J. A. 2004, The Large Synoptic Survey Telescope: Science and design. Available at http://www.lsst.org/Meetings/CommAccess/abstracts. shtml accessed on August 23, 2007.

[68] Strauss, M. 2004, Towards a design reference mission for the LSST. Available at http://www.lsst.org/Meetings/CommAccess/abstracts.shtml accessed on August 23, 2007.

[69] Mould, J. 2004, LSST followup. Available at http://www.lsst.org/Meetings/ CommAccess/abstracts.shtml accessed on August 23, 2007.

[70] Bose, R., Mann, R., and Prina-Ricotti, D. 2006, AstroDAS: Sharing assertions across Astronomy Catalogues through Distributed Annotation, *Lecture Notes in Computer Science (LNCS)*, Berlin, Germany, Springer, Vol. 4145, p. 193.

[71] Good, B., Kawas, E., and Wilkinson, M. 2007, Bridging the gap between social tagging and semantic annotation: E.D. The Entity Describer. Available at http://precedings.nature.com/documents/945/version/2, accessed on September 26, 2007.

[72] von Ahn, L. and Dabbish, L. 2004, Labeling images with a computer game, in *Proceedings of the SIGCHI Conference on Human Factors in Computing Systems*, New York, ACM, p. 319.

[73] Borne, K. D. 2003, Distributed data mining in the National Virtual Observatory, in *Proceedings of the SPIE*, Vol. 5098, Data Mining and Knowledge Discovery: Theory, Tools, and Technology, Bellingham, WA, SPIE, p. 211.

[74] Borne, K. D. 2005, Data mining in distributed databases for interacting galaxies, *Astronomical Data Analysis Software and Systems XIV*, A.S.P. Conference Series, Vol. 347, San Francisco, CA, Astronomical Society of the Pacific, p. 350.

[75] McConnell, S. M. and Skillicorn, D. B. 2005, Distributed data mining for astrophysical datasets, *Astronomical Data Analysis Software and Systems XIV*, A.S.P. Conference Series, Vol. 347, San Francisco, CA, Astronomical Society of the Pacific, p. 360.

[76] Gianella, C., Dutta, H., Borne, K., Wolff, R., and Kargupta, H. 2006, Distributed data mining for astronomy catalogs, in *Proceedings of the 2006 SIAM International Conference on Data Mining*, Philadelphia, SIAM.

[77] Available at http://ag.arizona.edu/srnr/research/wr/breshears/informatics_UA accessed on August 23, 2007.

Part II

Ubiquitous, Distributed, and High Performance Data Mining

Chapter 6

Thoughts on Human Emotions, Breakthroughs in Communication, and the Next Generation of Data Mining

Hillol Kargupta

Contents

6.1 Introduction

Communication played a critical role in the development of human civilization. We cry, laugh, smile, talk, and write. Each of these dimensions makes what we are and also helps shaping what others are. We need others to shape our life and the vice versa. This fundamental need of our inner self has played a key role in priming the development of the communication technology since the days of cave dwelling homosapiens. Now that we have reached the era of almost instant communication through the Internet, cell phones, wireless networks, mobile ad hoc networks (MANET), and vehicular networks (VANET), what else we need to further explore what we are and how we interact.

This chapter argues that while we have become very good in almost instantly connecting an entity with another entity as long as the former knows the address of the latter, we have made little progress in taking the messages and services from one to some willing and interested parties hidden in a large population. This chapter also argues that the current client–server model of communication in the internet applications and social networking sites may not scale very well in connecting individuals over the next generation of the Internet using wired, wireless, and ad hoc networks.

Section 6.2 discusses some of the early breakthrough in communication technology and their local nature. Section 6.3 revisits some of the early efforts in expanding the range of local communication. Sections 6.4 and 6.5 identify some of the challenges for this age of internet-era communication. Section 6.6 makes a note of some lessons from the nature and discusses them on the ground of scalable local distributed algorithms. Section 6.7 identifies the role of data mining in the alternate communication architecture that attempts to bring people closer at a global range through local interaction in a scalable manner with less reliance on centralized controls. Section 6.8 discusses some of the algorithmic challenges and possible directions.

6.2   First Breakthrough: Speech and Local Communication

One of the biggest breakthroughs in the history of mankind was the evolution of language for communication. It is believed that the early forms of language evolved about 200,000 years ago in homosapiens. This gave us the capability to communicate among a relatively small group of individuals when they are in proximity. We could now smile, laugh, cry, and also talk for sharing different facets of our life with others. There is no doubt that speech revolutionized human civilization and played a key role in where we are today. Evolution of speech gave us a tool with a constraint—local proximity. We can talk to others; but in absence of any other technical aid we can communicate with only those who are physically nearby and can listen to what we are saying.

However, this was not sufficient. As relatively complex social structure developed, people felt the need for communicating with others who are at a remote place either spatially or temporally. Simple verbal communication was not sufficient. Then language started shaping up in the written form. Cave paintings started appearing around 30,000 BC (e.g., Chauvet Cave in Southern France). Petroglyphs, pictograms, and ideograms started emerging in different societies. This led to the invention of the first writing systems in the late fourth millennium BC. This allowed documentation of events and communications in a more permanent form. People learned how to communicate over time. For example, a cave dweller could then observe a hunting event and document that for the posterior generations. Although this allowed us to reach a bigger audience over time, the spatial locality constraint still remained. If a cave dweller had a message for you on the walls of a cave, you did have to go there in order to retrieve the message.

6.3 Distance Communication: One to Few More

Mankind tried to invent techniques for removing the restriction on spatial locality for communication. For example, smoke signals, fire beacons, and heliographs were used in early days for expanding the scope of the spatial locality. Courier-based postal systems emerged in Egypt during 2400 BC. Iran, India, and China are some of the places where matured postal systems were developed during 500–185 BC. The postal system gradually offered access to distance communication to common people. It made communication a lot more convenient. You can write a letter with an address, drop it at a fixed location, and it will most likely reach the destination if you are willing to pay for the stamps. The main constraint is that the postal system takes time, it is not very personalized, and you need the address before you can communicate with someone.

We wanted more convenience. We wanted instant distance communication from the convenience of our living room in our house or the workplace. Commercial telegraph system was invented in 1837. The telephone systems appeared in 1871. Around the same time radio was invented for wireless communication. All these technologies greatly enhanced the convenience of distance communication. It also gave the receiver some control. If you do not want to participate then you can opt out (e.g., hang up the phone, throw away the mail that you received from the post office). However, some of the fundamental constraints remained there:

1. You still needed to know the address of the destination in order to communicate with someone at a distance location.

2. It was still very hard to reach a very large number of people all over the world who are interested in listening to you message.

6.4 The Internet Era

The twentieth century offered us the computer-based communication technology. The Internet further enhanced the convenience factors of the distance communication. We can reach an even larger number of individuals all over the world; communication is cheaper; it is fast and multimedia friendly. However, the fundamental constraints are still prevalent. You need to know the address of the computer node where you are sending the message and it is still hard to get your message out there to an interested audience hidden in a large population. The current internet-era solutions for these problems are fundamentally similar to what we have in the postal system.

One of those is sending millions of junk mails to a large collection of addresses. Fundamentally this is very similar to the junk mails that we receive in our postal mailbox, only in a larger scale. This is a fairly primitive concept and unlikely to scale producing a large number of satisfactory clients. In fact, most individuals view spams as an unwelcome mode of communication.

Another emerging mechanism is based on the so-called social-networking Web sites. These Web sites allow you to sign-up, post-personal information, and other content. Others can search and browse your information. If there is a match of interest then the site typically offers a mechanism to connect them. This mechanism is gaining popularity among different sections of the society in absence of any better solutions for address-free communication with a large number of individuals all over the world and making your message heard by a lot of interested people. However, this approach has several problems. Section 6.5 discusses those.

6.5   Missing Piece of Puzzle: From One to Many among Too Many

Current client–server models for social networking type infrastructures have several problems:

1. Economics of mass communication: Often these sites have business interests that are driven by the economics. That means, if a matchmaking or a social communication creates value for the business then eventually those are the ones that will be promoted by the site. For example, these days many news-Web sites allow the readers to send images and make news. This is similar to the readers' columns in good old news papers. The important thing to note is that they moderate this news. The owner/editor of the Web site decides which one of your images, if any, gets posted. If you have a message for the world that does not help the economics of the news Web site then it is unlikely to be used.

2. Privacy and intellectual property issues: Many of these sites want you to publish your content on their Web site. There are contents from many aspects of life that you may want to control because of privacy or intellectual property issues. Existing business models basically expect you to trust the owner of the site with your content.

3. Not scalable: The biggest problem with the current centralized approach is that it is not very scalable. This is particularly troublesome for the next generation of internet based on wired, bandwidth-constrained wireless, and ad hoc networks. The approach is based on a centralized solution for a fundamentally large distributed environment. It is equivalent to saying that every node in the network must communicate with a single node and let that node handle all the data processing tasks. If I have a message that should reach a large audience of interested individuals and I do not have the addresses of these individuals then the site must be able to analyze content of the message and find the matches with the interest profiles of individuals. Doing this may require performing various data-mining tasks such as clustering, indexing, and classification among others. As the volume of data and the size of the Internet increases along with heterogeneity (e.g., wired and wireless), it will be harder to scale such a centralized approach. This will particularly be harder in the mobile wireless world.

6.6 Any Better Approach

Although we do not yet have an existing solution that can take someone's message to a large appropriate audience in a more efficient manner, we may have some clues toward alternate approaches. This section briefly outlines some of those.

Nature offers many scalable, large complex systems where a large number of entities interact with the others they need to in an efficient manner. Individuals become part of a network where messages from one entity get transformed and transmitted to other entities in the network through local interactions. For example, consider an ant colony. Large ant colonies are known to have hundreds of millions of ants. In a colony, ants locally interact with each other using a set of simple rules and the global behavior emerges out of this local behavior despite the lack of centralized control. In fact, human civilization is also an example of such behavior. Different parts of the world produced different societies and different cultures based on their local rules of interactions. The global pattern of behavior for the human race is indeed a result of such local interactions in an asynchronous manner. Such behavior of many natural complex systems such as schools of fishes, migratory birds, termite colonies, and many other species further strengthens the observation.

Global communication through local interactions also appears to have a strong theoretical basis. Early work of Holland [1] and his students on adaptation in natural and artificial systems explored this approach and offered several locally interacting adaptive learning systems such as cellular automata [2], genetic algorithms [1,3], and classifier systems [4]. Locally interacting distributed algorithms have also been developed for various computing and communication-related problems [5]. The limits of local interaction-based distributed computing has been explored elsewhere [6].

The literature on distributed algorithms and systems point out that synchronized communication through a single node does not usually produce reliable efficient algorithms for distributed applications. Local algorithms that work by binding the communication cost of each node to a reasonable amount often scale much better compared to a centralized solution in a large asynchronous distributed environment.

6.7 Global Communication through Local Interactions and Distributed Data Mining

In order to take someone's message, finding the appropriate audience, and delivering that worldwide in a scalable manner would require developing technology for the following key problems: (1) finding a balance between our reliance upon single-entity owned centralized client–server model of computation and decentralized emergence on global behavior through local interactions; (2) privacy-sensitive content analysis and matchmaking between the source and the interested parties in a distributed decentralized environment.

Although we have a long way to go in solving these problems, we are starting to see some possible directions. The methodology for achieving global communication through efficient but strictly local interactions is drawing attention in many domains. For example, peer-to-peer (P2P) networks have been gaining popularity in many domains. P2P systems work by using the computing power, storage, and bandwidth of the participants of a network. Unlike client–server systems, P2P systems do not rely upon the servers to carry out most of the computation and storage-intensive tasks. P2P systems such as Gnutella, Napster, e-Mule, Kazaa, and Freenet are increasingly becoming popular for many applications that go beyond downloading music without paying for it. Examples include P2P systems for network storage, Web caching, bioinformatics, astronomy, searching and indexing of relevant documents, and distributed network-threat analysis.

Matchmaking and personalized information retrieval in such P2P environments would require distributed data clustering, indexing, and classification of algorithm that work in a decentralized communication efficient manner. P2P distributed data-mining algorithms [7,8] offer many interesting applications such as client-side P2P Web mining. Many popular Web servers use web-mining applications to analyze and track users' click-stream behavior. Now imagine client-side Web mining that does the same for Web site visitors (rather than host servers) by analyzing the browsing histories of many users connected via a P2P network. Today, site visitors have no direct access to the results of Web mining algorithms running on the servers, but a client-side P2P Web mining system [9] could empower visitors with click-stream data mining for advanced applications such as P2P search, interest-community formation, and P2P electronic commerce.

For example, an application like this may be able to find the best deal in the cell phone market by analyzing the search history of multiple users in a privacy-preserving manner. Clearly, maintaining users' privacy will be an important issue, and the field of privacy-preserving distributed data mining may offer some solutions. Similar methodology can be used for matchmaking and finding consumers of other services or messages in a decentralized, distributed P2P-like environment. P2P News, P2P e-commerce, and P2P exploratory astronomy are some examples. We need more work along these directions for truly bringing the power to the people—linking producers of messages and services to interested consumers without relying too much upon a centralized entity while protecting the privacy of the involved parties. This should be a key focus for the next generation of data mining research.

6.8 Algorithmic Approaches

Although global communication in a distributed system through local asynchronous analysis of data is an attractive proposition, developing efficient algorithms for that is often nontrivial. One of the main problems of current local algorithms is that many of them are not communication efficient despite their operation based on local interaction with the neighboring entities. These algorithms may not perform the given task in bounded time, storage, and communication cost.

In order to achieve the goal of global address-free communication through local interaction, we must develop efficient algorithms that require time, storage, and communication cost bounded by some constant independent of the network size and other relevant parameters or some slow-growing polynomials of those. One possibility is to limit the cost per node.

Consider a distributed network comprised of N nodes $P_1, \ldots, P_N$ each initially holding data set S_i. Let S denote $\bigcup_{p=1}^{N} S_p$, i.e., the data set that would be obtained by centralizing the data sets. The P2P network can be represented by an abstract tuple $G = < V, E, C_{V,t}, S_V, P_E >$. V and E represent the vertex and edge sets of the undirected network graph; $C_{V,t}$ represents the set of all states $C_{v,t}$ of a vertex $v \in V$ at time t. $S_V = \{S_1, S_2, \ldots, S_N\}$ and P_E represents properties of every edge is E. The *distance* $(\text{dist}_G(u,v))$ between a pair of nodes u and v is the length of the shortest path between those vertices.

DEFINITION 6.1

α-neighborhood of a vertex Let $G = (V,E)$ be the graph representing the network where V denotes the set of nodes and E represents the edges between the nodes. The α-neighborhood of a vertex $v \in V$ is the collection of vertices at distance α or less from it in G: $\Gamma_\alpha(v, V) = \{u | \text{dist}(u, v) \leq \alpha\}$, where $\text{dist}(u, v)$ denotes the length of the shortest path in between u and v and the length of a path is defined as the number of edges in it.

DEFINITION 6.2

α-local query Let $G = (V,E)$ be a graph as defined in last definition. Let each node $v \in V$ store a data set X_{v,t_v} at local time t_v in node v. An α-local query by some vertex v is a query whose response can be computed using some function $f(X_\alpha(v,t_v))$ where $X_\alpha(v,t_v) = \{X_{v,t_u} | u \in \Gamma_\alpha(v,V)\}$ for some time t_v measured at node v.

DEFINITION 6.3

(α, β, γ)-local algorithm An algorithm is called (α,β,γ)-local if it never requires computation of a η-local query such that $\eta > \alpha$; the total size of the response to all such α-local queries sent out by a node is bounded by γ and the total time taken to compute the response for all these queries measured at the node is bounded by β. α can be a constant or a function parameterized by the size of the network while β and γ can be parameterized by both the size of the data of a peer and the size of the network.

We call such an (α, β, γ)-local algorithm *efficient* if α, β, and γ are either small constants or some slow-growing functions (sublinear) with respect to its parameters. In this definition, α bounds the size of the local neighborhood, β bounds the temporal locality, and γ bounds the communication cost within the local neighborhood.

Let $\Phi(X)$ be the function we need to compute for finding a match between the source of content and the desired destination. Since X is distributed over the network, in order to compute this function using efficient (α, β, γ)-local algorithms we need to construct a decomposition of the $\Phi(X)$ in terms of a collection of α-local queries with bounded response time and size:

$$\Phi(X) = \zeta \left(\bigcup_{u \in V' \subseteq V} f(X_\alpha(u, t_u)) \right)$$

where ζ is some function of the α-local queries that finally generates the overall output of the computation.

This can be viewed as a distributed representation construction problem where the goal is to decompose the overall task among a set of locally computable functions— the α-local queries. This is a classical problem that shows up in many domains. First of all, not all functions can be represented in this manner. For example, consider a network where each node has a data vector and the goal is to compute the pairwise inner product matrix. In other words, each node must communicate with every other node in the network and compute the inner product between the vectors stored in these two nodes. Clearly, $\alpha = N$ here. Therefore, it is not clear how we can design an efficient exact (α, β, γ)-local algorithm for this problem. One possibility is to explore probabilistic or deterministic approximation techniques. What if we are interested in just computing the top-k entries of the inner product matrix instead of computing the entire matrix? Will that make the algorithm (α, β, γ)-local?

Therefore, one may approach this problem using the following methodologies:

1. Exact algorithms

2. Approximation techniques

    a. Deterministic approximation algorithms

    b. Probabilistic approximation algorithms

The following discussion presents some examples of these methodologies and identifies some of the challenges.

6.8.1   Exact Algorithms

A large fraction of the distributed data mining algorithms that satisfy some form of locality are indeed exact in nature. Given sufficient time, they usually converge to the correct result. However, the problem is that most of them can be very inefficient depending upon the distribution of the data and the structure of the network topology. While these algorithms do work by directly communicating only with the immediate neighbors, that alone does not restrict a node from ending up communicating with every other node in the network.

Consider, the problem of computing the average of a collection of numbers where each number is stored at a node in the network. Let $x_1, \ldots, x_N$ be the numbers stored in nodes $P_1, \ldots, P_N$, respectively. Our goal is to compute the average of these numbers such that every node ends up getting a copy of this average value. There exist several algorithms for this problem and most of them share the the following idea. If $X_1[t],\ldots,X_N[t]$ be the state of the temporary variable at time t in nodes $P_1,\ldots,P_N$, respectively, then one can design an iterative algorithm as follows:

$$X_1[0] = x_1,\ldots,X_N[0] = x_N;$$

$$X_i[t] = \rho \sum_{j \in \Gamma_i} (X_i[t] - X_j[t]);$$

where ρ is a constant. $X_i[t]$ asymptotically converges to the average value.

In many cases, computing the exact value of the average is both costly and unnecessary. On the other hand, if we can cheaply find out if the average is within a certain threshold (sufficient in many applications), we can potentially solve many interesting problems as we later show. An algorithm (known as majority voting algorithm in the literature) for this decision version of the problem is proposed elsewhere [10,11]. This algorithm sends a message to its neighbor only if the change is going to change the majority decision. This is different from the previous approach where the difference is always sent to the neighbor.

The average computation and its decision version, the majority voting algorithm, serve as useful primitives for many advanced data mining operations in a distributed environment. For example, a distributed algorithm for a decision version of the L2 norm computing has been proposed elsewhere [12]. Similar algorithms for computing decision trees [13], eigen analysis [14], and multivariate regression [15] are also available.

We need to find more efficient algorithms for computing useful data-mining primitives in a distributed environment. Also, note that the algorithms discussed so far satisfy locality in a loose sense. Unlike (α, β, γ)-locality, many of these algorithms only offer bounded α. Neither overall communication cost nor the temporal locality is bounded. We need to design algorithms that offer locality in a more rigorous sense.

6.8.2 Approximate Local Algorithms for Peer-to-Peer Networks

As we noted earlier, exact local algorithms do not exist for many data-mining problems. For those, we may have to explore alternate choices that calls for approximation. Approximation can be introduced in distributed data mining through different means. We may design randomized algorithms that introduce approximations through probabilistic techniques such as sampling. We may also be able introduce deterministic approximations using techniques such as variational methods.

Probability theory and statistics offers a great deal of theoretical results for analyzing the randomized algorithms and quantifying performance bounds. Many of these results such as law of large numbers, central limit theorem, Chernoff bound, and Hoeffeding bound are based on independent sampling from a population. In order to make use of these tools we first need to develop local sampling techniques for distributed environments. Section 6.8.2.1 discusses some of the existing work and challenges in that area.

6.8.2.1   Local Algorithms for Sampling in a Distributed Environment

Sampling is one of the basic statistical tools used heavily in information integration and knowledge discovery for approximating results from large data set. A representative sample of data is often good enough for deriving basic trend and statistics about the data. However, collecting a uniform data sample form a network for approximation is a nontrivial problem due to nature of the network (varying degree of connectivity between peers, widely varying sizes of data shared, and changing network topology with time due to nodes dropping out of the network or new nodes joining the network). Designing various sampling algorithms that work through local interaction and offer bounded cost per node is of utmost importance.

Some progress have been made in the recent past in this area. Random walk-based techniques have been developed to collect uniform samples from the distributed data.

A random walk is a random process consisting of a sequence of discrete steps of fixed length, each in a random direction. In a graph G, a simple random walk is a sequence of nodes visited, where at each step, the next destination node is selected with a fixed probability. If the vertices of a graph can be thought of representing the state at time t, X_t in a finite state space, then a random walk on the graph represents a finite stochastic process, and can be modeled by a Markov chain. It has been shown by Motwani and Raghavan [16] that a long enough random walk on graph G will end up at node n_i randomly irrespective of its point of start, but the resulting sampling distribution is dependent on the degree of the node d_i.

Since degrees of nodes vary widely in a network, the sampling distribution is most likely to be nonuniform. Nodes with higher degree have more probability of being selected by a regular random walk, or in other words, the random sampling becomes biased. To make the resulting distribution uniform, the probability transition matrix P needs to be modified to remove the bias due to irregular degrees of nodes. The Matropolis–Hasting [17] algorithm offers one way to do that through a random walk with a duly modified transition probability matrix. This algorithm [18] can sample nodes from a graph uniformly randomly as long as the random walk length is of the order of $\log(n)$ for a network of size n as long as some assumptions about the network topology is satisfied. However, the same technique is applied to network with different amount of data at different peers, picking up a datapoint from each of the uniformly selected peers still gives a biased data sample.

In order to get rid of the bias in data sample due to different sizes of data stored in different nodes of a network, one may need to further change the state transition probability matrix and adapt the random walk accordingly. Recent work by Datta et al. [19] proposed a random walk based scheme similar to that of Matropolis–Hasting [17] which creates a transition probability matrix taking care of the bias introduced by the local data size as well. Conceptually, this is a random walk following Matropolis–Hasting algorithm on a virtual graph, where each datapoint represents one virtual node, and datapoints belonging to same peers forming a fully connected virtual subgraph upon which random walk-based virtual node sampling results in uniform selection of data. An approximate but efficient (α, β, γ)-local distributed association rule mining algorithm based on this sampling approach is also developed by Datta et al. [19].

While we now have a way to uniformly draw samples from a distributed environment, we need a lot of work in this area. We need major results of statistics and probability theory revisited in the light of distributed environments. We need to build this foundation in order to build the next generation of local approximation algorithms for distributed data mining.

We also need more approximate distributed data-mining algorithms that are local in a rigorous sense and guarantee performance bounds.

6.8.3 Deterministic Approximation

Approximation techniques can be either probabilistic or deterministic. Section 6.8.2 discussed the probabilistic approaches based on sampling techniques. This section explores some of the deterministic possibilities.

There are many ways in which one may introduce deterministic approximations in a data-mining algorithm. Replacing a complicated highly nonlinear function by a piecewise linear function is one example. If we need to optimize a complicated objective function, we may choose to replace the exact complicated expression by a relatively simpler approximation. This may introduce some error; but if this makes the distributed algorithm more communication efficient and local then this may a good trade-off.

Recently, Mukherjee and Kargupta [20] proposed a variational framework for local distributed multivariate regression algorithms. The variational method is a widely studied deterministic approximation technique, which is applied to many intractable optimization problems. The variational method involves defining an objective function that is optimized at the solution to the problem, and then searching for an optimum of that function. Often, this search is done in a restricted subset of the solution space, which makes the technique computationally tractable. Deterministic approximation techniques like this need to be developed for efficient local data analysis in a distributed environment.

6.9 Privacy Issues

Connecting a entity with another in this world of attention economy would certainly require distributed data analysis. However, data analysis alone may not work well unless the algorithms pay close attention to the social, cultural, and personal preferences. Privacy is one such important issue. The next generation of distributed data-mining algorithms for analyzing multiparty content must be privacy sensitive whenever appropriate.

The field of privacy-preserving data mining [21,22] has been growing fast. Most of the perturbation-based techniques [21,23] are primarily designed for one-time sanitization of privacy-sensitive data, not for distributed environments where communication cost must be minimized. Moreover, the model of privacy for such perturbation-based techniques in distributed environments is also not very clear.

For large-scale distributed systems, Gilburd et al. proposed a privacy model called k-TTP [24]. The intuition is that at any time each participant can only learn a combined statistics of a group of at least k participants, and therefore any specific participant's private input is hidden among at least $k-1$ other participants' input. The secure k-anonymity framework by Jiang and Clifton [25] proposes a two-party framework that generates k-anonymous data from two vertically partitioned sources without disclosing the data of one party to the other.

Secure multiparty computation (SMC) [22] offers a possibility for performing secure computation in a distributed environment. However, this suffers from several problems:

1. Most of the SMC techniques are synchronous in nature. In a large distributed asynchronous environment such techniques may not scale very well.

2. Most SMC techniques are not local and not very communication efficient.

We need local asynchronous algorithms for privacy-preserving distributed data-mining algorithms. In order to do that we need to explore several important issues. Some of these are listed below:

1. We need to acknowledge that in a multiparty diverse environment, different entities may have different notions of privacy. Privacy models are inherently going to be heterogeneous. We need to develop frameworks for handling such heterogeneous privacy models.

2. We need algorithmic primitives for local privacy-preserving data-mining operations.

Section 6.10 concludes this chapter.

6.10 Conclusions

This chapter pointed out the need for developing technology for taking the content of someone and delivering that to the interested parties in a large population with diverse interests in a distributed, decentralized environment. It argued that the existing client–server models may not work very well in solving this problem because of scalability and privacy issues.

This chapter noted that distributed data mining is likely to play a key role in indexing, searching, and linking the data located at different nodes of a network. The chapter underscored the need for designing local, asynchronous, and distributed data-mining algorithms. It discussed various avenues to cover both deterministic and probabilistic frameworks. Finally, the chapter the need for developing local, asynchronous, distributed privacy-preserving data-mining algorithms.

Acknowledgments

Partial support for this work was provided by MURI award FA9550-08-1-0265 from the Air Force office of Scientific Research and NASA Grant NNX07AV70G. The author also thanks Kamalika Das, Kun Liu, Kanishka Bhaduri, and Souptik Dutta.

References

[1] J. Holland. *Adaptation in Natural and Artificial Systems*. The MIT Press, 1975.

[2] T. Toffoli. Cellular automata mechanics, Ph.D. Thesis, University of Michigan, Technical report no. 208, Logic of computers group, 1977.

[3] D.E. Goldberg. *Genetic Algorithms in Search, Optimization, and Machine Learning*. Addison-Wesley, Reading, MA, 1989.

[4] L.B. Booker, D.E. Goldberg, and J.H. Holland. Classifier systems and genetic algorithms. *Artificial Intelligence*, 40(1–3):235–282, 1989.

[5] D. Peleg. *Distributed computing: A Locality-Sensitive Approach*. SIAM, Philadelphia, PA, 2000.

[6] M. Naor and L. Stockmeyer. What can be computed locally? *SIAM Journal on Computing*, 24:1259–1277, 1995.

[7] H. Kargupta and K. Sivakumar. Existential pleasures of distributed data mining. *Data Mining: Next Generation Challenges and Future Directions*, pp. 3–27, 2004.

[8] S. Datta, K. Bhaduri, C. Gianella, R. Wolff, and H. Kargupta. Distributed data mining in peer-to-peer networks. Invited submission to the *IEEE Internet Computing* special issue on distributed data mining, 10(4):18–26, 2006.

[9] K. Liu, K. Bhaduri, K. Das, P. Nguyen, and H. Kargupta. Client-Side web mining for Community formation in peer-to-peer environments. *SIGKDD Explorations*, 8(2):11–20, December 2006.

[10] Y. Birk, L. Liss, A. Schuster, and R. Wolff. A local algorithm for ad hoc majority voting via charge fusion. In *Proceedings of the 18th International Conference on Distributed Computing*, pp. 275–289, 2004.

[11] R. Wolff and A. Schuster. Association rule mining in peer-to-peer systems. In *Proceedings of the IEEE Conference on Data Mining ICDM*, pp. 2426–2438, 2003.

[12] R. Wolff, K. Bhaduri, and H. Kargupta. Local L2 thresholding based data mining in peer-to-peer systems. In *Proceedings of SIAM International Conference in Data Mining (SDM)*, pp. 430–440, Bethesda, MD, 2006.

[13] K. Bhaduri and H. Kargupta. Decision tree induction in peer-to-peer systems. *Statistical Analysis and Data Mining Journal*, 1(2):85–103, 2008.

[14] R. Wolff, K. Bhaduri, and H. Kargupta. A peer-to-peer distributed algorithm for eigenstate monitoring. *IEEE Transactions on Knowledge and Data Engineering*, pp. 363–370, 2008. In press.

[15] K. Bhaduri and H. Kargupta. A scalable local algorithm for distributed multivariate regression. *Statistical Analysis and Data Mining Journal*, In press, 2008.

[16] R. Motwani and P. Raghavan. Randomized algorithms. *ACM Computing Surveys*, 28(1):33–37, 1996.

[17] M.N. Rosenbluth, A.H. Teller, N. Metropolis, A.W. Rosenbluth, and E. Teller. Equations of state calculations by fast computing machines. *Journal of Chemical Physics*, 21(2):1087–1092, 1953.

[18] M. Zhong, K. Shen, and J. Seiferas. Non-uniform random membership management in peer-to-peer networks. In *Proceedings of the IEEE INFO-COM*, 2:1151–1161, Miami, FL, March 2005.

[19] S. Datta and H. Kargupta. Uniform data sampling from a peer-to-peer network. In *IEEE International Conference on Distributed Computing Systems (ICDCS 2007)*, p. 50, 2007.

[20] S. Mukherjee and H. Kargupta. Distributed probabilistic inferencing in sensor networks using variational approximation. *Journal of Parallel and Distributed Computing (JPDC)*, 68(1):78–92, 2008.

[21] R. Agrawal and R. Srikant. Privacy preserving data mining. In *Proceedings of the ACM SIGMOD Conference on Management of Data*, pp. 439–450, Dallas, TX, May 2000.

[22] C. Clifton, M. Kantarcioglu, J. Vaidya, X. Lin, and M. Zhu. Tools for privacy preserving distributed data mining. *ACM SIGKDD Explorations*, 4(2):28–34, 2003.

[23] H. Kargupta, S. Datta, Q. Wang, and K. Sivakumar. On the privacy preserving properties of random data perturbation techniques. In *Proceedings of the IEEE International Conference on Data Mining*, pp. 99–106, Melbourne, FL, November 2003.

[24] B. Gilburd, A. Schuster, and R. Wolff. k-TTP: A new privacy model for large-scale distributed environments. In *Proceedings of KDD'04*, pp. 563–568, Seattle, WA, 2004.

[25] W. Jiang and C. Clifton. A secure distributed framework for achieving k-anonymity. *The VLDB Journal*, 15(4):316–333, 2006.

Chapter 7

Research Challenges in Ubiquitous Knowledge Discovery

Michael May, Bettina Berendt, Antoine Cornuéjols, Jõao Gama,
Fosca Giannotti, Andreas Hotho, Donato Malerba, Ernestina Menesalvas,
Katharina Morik, Rasmus Pedersen, Lorenza Saitta, Yücel Saygin,
Assaf Schuster, and Koen Vanhoof

Contents

7.1 Ubiquitous Knowledge Discovery

7.1.1 Introduction

Knowledge discovery in ubiquitous (KDubiq) environments is an emerging area of research at the intersection of the two major challenges of highly distributed and mobile systems and advanced knowledge discovery systems.

Today, in many subfields of computer science and engineering, being intelligent and adaptive mark the difference between a system that works in a complex and changing environment and a system that does not work. Hence, projects across many areas, ranging from Web 2.0 to ubiquitous computing and robotics, aim to create systems that are smart, intelligent, adaptive, etc., allowing to solve problems that could not be solved before. A central assumption of ubiquitous knowledge discovery is that what seems to be a bewildering array of different methodologies and approaches for building smart, adaptive, and intelligent systems can be cast into a coherent, integrated set of key ideas centered on the notion of learning from experience.

Focusing on these key ideas, ubiquitous knowledge discovery aims to provide a unifying framework for systematically investigating the mutual dependencies of otherwise quite unrelated technologies employed in building next-generation intelligent systems: machine learning, data mining, sensor networks, grids, peer-to-peer (P2P), data stream mining, activity recognition, Web 2.0, privacy, user modeling, and others. Machine learning and data mining emerge as basic methodologies and indispensable building blocks for some of the most difficult computer science and engineering challenges of the next decade.

The first task is to characterize the objects of study for ubiquitous knowledge discovery more clearly. The objects of study

1. Exist in time and space in a dynamically changing environment

2. Can change location and might appear or disappear

3. Have information processing capabilities

4. Know only their local spatiotemporal environment

5. Act under real-time constraints

6. Are able to exchange information with other objects

Objects to which these characteristics apply are humans, animals, and, increasingly, various kinds of computing devices. It is the latter that form the objects of study for ubiquitous knowledge discovery.

7.1.2 Dimensions of Ubiquitous Knowledge Discovery Systems

Mainstream data mining and machine learning is focused centrally on the learning algorithm. Algorithms are typically treated as largely independent from the application domain and the system architecture in which the algorithm is later embedded. Thus, the same implementation of a support vector machine can be applied to texts, gene-expression data, or credit card transactions; the difference is in the feature extraction during preprocessing.

7.1.2.1 Design Space

Ubiquitous knowledge discovery challenges these independence assumptions in several ways. In the further sections, it will be argued that often the learning algorithms have to be tailored for a specific network topology characterized by communication constraints, reliability, or resource availability. Thus, when designing a ubiquitous knowledge discovery system, major design decisions in various dimensions have to be taken. These choices mutually constrain each other. Dependencies among them have to be carefully analyzed. For analyzing the different possible architectures of ubiquitous knowledge, the design space of ubiquitous knowledge discovery systems is factored into six dimensions:

1. Application area. What is the real-world problem being addressed?

2. Ubiquitous technologies. What types of sensors are used? What type of distributed technology is used?

3. Resource aware algorithms. Which machine learning or data mining algorithms are used? What are the resource constraints imposed by the ubiquitous technologies? How does the algorithm adapt to a dynamic environment?

4. Ubiquitous data collection. What issues arise from information integration of the sensors? Are the issues from collaborative data generation?

5. Privacy and security. Does the application create privacy risks?

6. Human–computer interaction (HCI) and user modeling. What is the role of the user in the system? How does he interact with the devices?

7.1.2.2 Ubiquity of Data and Computing

Two important aspects of ubiquity have to be distinguished, namely the ubiquity of data and the ubiquity of computing. In a prototypical application, the ubiquity of computing corresponds naturally to the ubiquity of the data: the data is analyzed when and where it is generated—the knowledge discovery takes place *in situ*, inside the interacting, often collaborating, distributed devices.

There exist however borderline cases that are ubiquitous in one way but not in the other, for example, clusters or grids for speeding up data analysis by distributing files and computations to various computers, or track mining from global positioning system (GPS) data where the data are analyzed on a central server in an off-line batch setting.

While research on this kind of systems is in several respects highly relevant for ubiquitous knowledge discovery, for the purpose of this chapter a more narrow point of view is adopted, and the following characterization is assumed: Ubiquitous knowledge discovery is part of machine learning and data mining that investigates learning *in situ*, inside a dynamic distributed infrastructure of interacting artificial devices.

7.2   Example 1: Autonomous Driving Vehicles

To provide a more specific description of the content of ubiquitous knowledge discovery, in the next sections, a number of examples are analyzed. The following selection criteria have been used: (1) each example focuses on a different domain, (2) it presents a challenging real-life problem, and (3) there is a body of prior technical work addressing at least some of the six dimensions of ubiquitous knowledge discovery, while other dimensions are not covered.

Contributions from various fields are analyzed: robotics, ubiquitous computing, machine learning, and data mining. Work is not necessarily done under the label of "ubiquitous knowledge discovery," since the subject is new and draws inspiration from work scattered around many communities. These examples provide material for discussing the general features of ubiquitous knowledge discovery in the next sections.

7.2.1   Application

Modern vehicles are a good starting point to discuss ubiquitous knowledge discovery systems, since they exist in a dynamic environment, move in time and space, and are equipped with a number of sensors. There are various directions to add to the intelligence of modern cars. An ambitious attempt is to construct autonomous driving vehicles. In the DARPA 2005 grand challenge, the goal was to develop an autonomous robot capable of traversing unrehearsed road-terrain: to navigate a 228 km long course through the Mojave desert in no more than 10 h. The challenge was won in 2005 by the robot, Stanley. What sets robots such as Stanley apart from traditional cars on the hardware side is the large number of additional sensors, computational power, and actuators.

7.2.2   Learning Component

Machine learning is a key component of Stanley, being used for a number of learning tasks, both off-line and online [28]. An off-line classification task solved with machine learning is obstacle detection, where a first-order Markov model is used. The use of machine learning is motivated by the fact that it would be impossible to train the system off-line for all possible situations the car might encounter.

More importantly for our discussion, a second online task is road finding: classifying images into drivable and nondrivable areas. Drivable terrain is globally represented by a mixture of n Gaussians defined in the RGB color space of pixels. A new image is mapped into a small number of k local Gaussians (where $k \ll n$); they are used to update the global model. This way, a distribution that changes over time can be modeled. During learning the mean and variance of the global Gaussian, a pixel count can be updated, and new Gaussians can be added and old Gaussians discarded. The decision whether to adapt or to add or forget is taken by calculating the Mahalanobis distance $d(i,j) = (\mu_i - \mu_j)^{\mathrm{T}}(\Sigma_i + \Sigma_j)^{-1}(\mu_i - \mu_j)$ between local and global Gaussians. Additionally, exponential decay is used for the counters in memory. An area is classified as drivable, if its pixel values are close to the learned Gaussians that characterize drivable terrain. Adapting the parameters helps to model slow changes in the terrain, while adding and forgetting can accommodate for abrupt changes.

The significance of Stanley for our present discussion is that it provides a very pictorial example of how acting in a dynamic environment combined with real-time constraints demands learning algorithms that have been a niche topic in machine learning so far: algorithms that can adapt to concept drift, that is, to distributions that can change slowly or abruptly over time. In the next examples, we see that this is an almost universal feature of ubiquitous knowledge discovery, and in Section 7.6.2 a general discussion can be found.

7.2.3 Communication

Autonomous robotics puts strong emphasis on planning and control to achieve the vision of autonomy, where for ubiquitous knowledge discovery full autonomy is normally not the goal. Instead, collaboration and interaction among humans and devices are stressed. The desert-driving scenarios are very limited in this respect if compared to a normal traffic scenario. The robot has no knowledge about the existence of other objects similar to itself (treating them as obstacle at best), not matching the HCI and user modeling characteristic mentioned above. The DARPA 2007 urban challenge was a step in that direction, since vehicles were required to navigate their way under normal traffic conditions, with other cars present, turns, etc. Thus, the vehicles needed modules for tracking other cars [27]. Yet cars were not able to communicate [7] or learn from each other. A distributed protocol of learning among cars was outside the scope of the challenge.

7.3 Example 2: Activity Recognition—Inferring Transportation Routines from GPS Data

7.3.1 Application

The widespread use of GPS devices has led to an explosive interest in spatial data. Classical applications are car navigation and location tracking. Intensive activity, notably in the ubiquitous computing community, is underway to explore additional application scenarios, for example, in assistive technologies or in building models of the mobile behavior of citizens, useful for various areas, including social research, planning purposes, and market research. We discuss an application from assistive technologies, analyze its strength and shortcomings, and identify research challenges from a ubiquitous knowledge discovery perspective.

The OpportunityKnocks prototype [21] consists of a mobile phone equipped with GPS and connected to a server in a mobile client/server setup. The mobile phone can connect to a server via genral packet radio service (GPRS) and transmit the GPS signals, thus tracking the person's behavior. The server analyzes the data, utilizing additional information about the street network or bus schedules from the Internet. Using this information, the person is located and the system makes inferences about his current behavior and gives suggestions what to do next. This information is sent back to the client and communicated to the user with the help of an audio/visual interface.

The system is able to give advice to persons, for example, which route to take or where to get off a bus, and it can warn the user in case he commits errors, for example, takes the wrong bus line. The purpose of the system is to assist cognitively impaired persons in finding their way through city traffic.

This application meets the main criteria for ubiquitous systems: the device is an object moving in space and time in a changing and unknown environment; it has computing power, and has a local view of its environment only; it reacts in real time and it is equipped with GPS sensors and exchanges information with other objects (e.g., satellites, the server, etc.). Compared to the last example, the current example does not aim for an autonomous device but is designed for interaction with a human.

7.3.2   Learning Components

Since both the environment and the behavioral patterns are not known in advance, it is impossible to solve this task without the system being able to learn from a user's past behavior. Thus, machine learning algorithms are used to infer likely routes, activities, transportation destinations, and deviations from a normal route. The basic knowledge representation mechanism is a hierarchical dynamic Bayesian network. The topology of the network is manually built and creates a hierarchy, with the upper level devoted to novelty detection, the middle layer responsible for estimating user's goals and trip segments, and the lowest level representing mode of transportation, speed, and location. Time is represented by arcs t and $t - 1$ connecting time slices. While the generic network design is specified in advance and is the same for every user, the specific parameters of the distribution are learned from the data in an unsupervised manner. Data comes in streams, but apparently the full information is stored in a database. For efficient online inference of the hidden variables given the GPS data, a combination of particle and Kalman filtering is employed [21].

Although innovative, the architecture of this prototype will face a number of practical problems. Thus, in absence of a phone signal, communication with the server is impossible, and the person may get lost. Similarly, when there is no reliable GPS signal, for example, in urban canyons or indoors, guidance is impossible. A further problem is that communicating via a radio network with a server consumes a lot of battery power, so that the system works only 4 h under continuous operation. Finally, continuous tracking of a person and centrally collecting the data creates strong privacy threats.

An implicit assumption of the prototype seems that sensing is always possible, that communication between client and server is generally reliable, and that power consumption does not play an important role. In other words, it assumes a setting as is appropriate in a local network. But these assumptions are invalid to a degree that would prevent a real-world deployment of the system. It should be noted that cognitive assistance is more demanding here than, for example, usual car navigation, because the people may be helpless without the device.

7.3.3   Moving the Learning to the Device

The significance of this example is that on the one hand it describes a highly interesting scenario for ubiquitous knowledge discovery and advanced machine learning methods, but on the other hand the design of the overall system does not match the constraints of a ubiquitous environment. Ubiquitous knowledge discovery starts with the observation that a learning algorithm cannot be designed in abstraction from the characteristics of the systems on which it is deployed (see Section 7.6.3).

The ubiquitous knowledge discovery paradigm asks for distributed, intelligent, and communicating devices integrating data from various sources. A KDubiq Upgrade would result in a much more satisfactory design for the prototype. It would be guided by the imperative to move the machine learning to the mobile device. If the major part of the learning is done on the mobile device—especially that part that refers to localization on the street map—there is no need for constant server communication, and assistance becomes more reliable.

Splitting the computation into an energy and computationally efficient onboard part yielding highly compressed models, transmitting only this compressed information and performing computationally intensive parts on the server would be a favorable solution. Section 7.5 discusses this in more detail.

7.3.4   Industrial Application

A GPS device that can do data mining *in situ* and on-the-fly has important industrial applications. Here, we describe one such scenario. The Arbeitsgemeinschaft Media-Analyse—a joint industry committee of around 250 principal companies of the advertising and media industry in Germany—commissioned in 2007 a nationwide survey about mobile behavior of the German population. This is the basis for determining performance characteristics in outdoor advertising (e.g., the percentage of the population that has had contact with a poster network within 1 week). The basic input are mobility data in form of GPS trajectories. Nationwide, the daily movements of about 30,000 people have been surveyed for up to 7 days.

In order to model the behavior of the overall German population from this sample, a number of data mining and modeling tasks had to be solved by Fraunhofer. Using techniques based on survival analysis and simulation techniques, the mobile behavior for all German cities is estimated [1]. A second data source is a sample of approximately 100,000 video measurements on traffic frequencies in German cities. A k-NN-based spatial data-mining algorithm has been developed that derives traffic frequency predictions for 4 Mio. street segments in German cities (see Ref. [23], Section 9.6). Track data and frequency estimates are combined in a data fusion step. Other tasks are related to spatial clustering. The application described so far is about analyzing data collected with ubiquitous mobile devices. Collectively, it took several month and several project partners to complete the data preparation. This project has a high impact because the pricing of posters is based on these models and a whole branch of German industry is based on the data-mining predictions.

A future scenario is to do all the track-related data preparation online. We are currently working on a scenario where data mining is done in the GPS device and annotated tracks are inferred on the fly. For applications where the user has agreed to make his or her data available, not the raw GPS data, but annotated diaries of activities, are sent to a server via a radio network and processed using a grid infrastructure [30]. This would not only shorten development time dramatically, but also allows the possibility to derive a snapshot of a population's mobility with very short delay.

7.4   Example 3: Ubiquitous Intelligent Media Organization

While the first example did not match the collaborative aspect of ubiquitous knowledge discovery and the second did not investigate learning *in situ*, the next two examples, while very different from each other, match all criteria of ubiquitous knowledge discovery.

7.4.1   Application

With the advent of Web 2.0, collaborative structuring of large collections of multimedia data based on metadata and media features has become a significant task. Nemoz (networked media organizer) [9] is a Web 2.0-inspired collaborative platform for playing music, browsing, searching, and sharing music collections. It works in a loosely coupled distributed scenario, using P2P technology. Nemoz combines Web 2.0-style tagging, with automatic audio classification using machine learning techniques. This application is a representative of a innovative subclass of applications in a Web 2.0 environment. Whereas most Web 2.0 tagging applications use a central server where all media data and tags are consolidated, the current application is fully distributed.

The application differs from the preceding ones in that the (geo)spatiotemporal position of the computing devices does not play an important role; the devices and the media file collections they contain are stored somewhere on some node in the network. Yet, it is a defining characteristic of the application that two collections $\mathscr{C}_i$ and $\mathscr{C}_j$ are stored at different places, and it is important whether or not two collections are connected via a neighborhood graph.

Also in contrast to the other examples, the fully distributed nature of the problem is a defining characteristic of the application. In a P2P environment, computing devices might be connected to a network only temporarily, communication is unreliable, and the collections are evolving dynamically; items are added and deleted, and also classifications can change. In many distributed data-mining applications, originally centralized data are distributed for improving the efficiency of the analysis. The current application is different because first, the data are inherently distributed, and second, there is no intention to come up with a global model. Thus, it is, as discussed in the introduction, a system where the ubiquity of computing naturally corresponds to the ubiquity of data.

7.4.2   Learning Components

Nemoz is motivated by the observation that a globally correct classification for audio files does not exist, since each user has its own way of structuring the files, reflecting his own preferences and needs. Still, a user can exploit labels provided by other peers as features for his own classification: the fact that Mary, who structures her collection along mood, classifies a song as melancholic might indicate to Bob, who classifies along genre, that it is not a Techno song. To support this, Nemoz nodes are able to exchange information about their individual classifications. These added labels are used in a predictive machine-learning task. Thus, the application is characterized by evolving collections of large amounts of data, scattered across different computing devices that maintain a local view of a collection, exchanging information with other nodes. It is a crucial aspect of this application that the nodes maintain a local view, incorporating information from other nodes. We are not aware of other solutions that are able to automatically learn from other user's classifications while maintaining a local or subjective point of view.

The significance of this example is that Nemoz introduces a new class of learning problems: the collaborative representation problem and localized alternative cluster ensembles for collaborative structuring [33]. From the perspective of ubiquitous knowledge discovery, this is important, since in a nondistributed environment, these new learning scenarios would be very hard to motivate. This new class is relevant for both examples discussed above. If a mobile device is used in city traffic, it could be very helpful if the device would be able to exchange information with other devices. In this case, each device would maintain a local model of the surrounding traffic partially by exchanging information with other devices. It can also be imagined that a future competition on autonomous vehicle driving that includes communication among cars would include learning of local, subjective views in a collaborative setting.

This potential transfer of learning scenarios from seemingly very unrelated areas, mobile assistive technology, autonomous robots, and music mining is made possible by analyzing the applications in a common framework.

7.5   Example 4: Real-Time Vehicle Monitoring

7.5.1   Application

The vehicle data stream mining system VEDAS [18] is a mobile and distributed data stream mining application. It analyzes and monitors the continuous data stream generated by a vehicle. It is able to identify emerging patterns and reports them back to a remote control center over a low-bandwidth wireless network connection. Applications are real-time onboard health monitoring, drunk-driving detection, driver characterizations, and security-related applications for commercial fleet management.

VEDAS uses a PDA or other lightweight mobile device installed in a vehicle. It is connected to the on board diagnostic system (OBD-II); other sensory input comes from a GPS device. Significant mining tasks are carried out onboard, monitoring the state of transmission, engine, and fuel systems. Only aggregated information is transmitted to a central server via a wireless connection. The data mining has to be performed onboard using a streaming approach, since the amount of data that would have to be transmitted to the central server is too huge.

7.5.2 Learning Components

The basic idea of the VEDAS data-mining module is to provide distributed mining of multiple mobile data sources with little centralization. The data-mining algorithms are designed around the following ideas: minimize data communication, minimize power consumption, minimize onboard storage, minimize computing usage, and respect privacy constraints.

VEDAS implements incremental principal component analysis, incremental Fourier transform, online linear segmentation, incremental k-means clustering, and several lightweight statistical techniques. The basic versions of these algorithms are of course well known and precede the data-mining age. The innovation lies here in adapting to a resource-constrained environment, resulting in new approximate solutions.

A comparison of this example with the activity recognition scenario reveals resources to improve the latter scenario. It offers a solution that locally computes and preaggregates results and communicates only few data via the radio network, splitting the computation into an energy and computationally efficient onboard part yielding highly compressed models, transmitting only this compressed information, and performing computationally intensive parts on the server.

However, an additional price is paid: for the onboard part, new algorithms are necessary that trade accuracy against efficiency. The specific trade-off is dictated by the application context, and the choice made in the vehicle monitoring application would be hard to motivate in an off-line context (or even for the current application).

The significance of this example is as a template how to design resource-aware mobile data-mining solutions and it avoids some of the pitfalls of the activity recognition scenario.

7.6 Research Challenges

The ubiquitous knowledge discovery paradigm asks for distributed, intelligent, and communicating devices integrating data from various sensor sources. The learning takes place *in situ*. Privacy has to be addressed.

The examples discussed match that paradigm to various degrees. Example 1 showed the importance of algorithms that can inference in real time, inside the device, paying attention to concept drift. To turn this into a realistic scenario, communication among cars would be needed. Example 2 used a mobile client–server scenario. However, for a realistic deployment, it would be necessary to move the algorithms to the device. Additionally, privacy constraints have to be addressed. Example 3 was an example for a fully distributed scenario in which nodes learn from each other and build a local subjective model. Example 4 finally provided a template for building resource-aware approximate algorithms for monitoring the state of a system.

In Section 7.6.1 the general characteristics and challenges that emerge for research in ubiquitous knowledge discovery are discussed.

7.6.1   Resource Constraints

In applications comprising mobile or small devices, limitations in storage, processing and communication capabilities, energy supply and bandwidth, combined with a dynamic and unreliable network connectivity are a major constraining factor. Optimizing a learning algorithm for such systems often leads to a coupling of application semantics and the system layers.

In many cases, the best available algorithm might be too demanding in terms of computational or memory resources to be run on the designated device. Thus, an approximation has to be designed. The approximation might depend on the exact configuration of the system and on specifics about the application. For example, in Example 4, the state of the vehicle is monitored in real time. To monitor a set of variables, a principal component analysis is performed. Changes in driving characteristics result in changes in the eigenvectors of the covariance matrix. Because constant recomputation would be too costly, the system determines only the upper bounds on changes in eigenvalues and eigenvectors over time, and initiates a recomputation only if necessary [18]. Other examples for the use of approximation in order to save resources are in Ref. [26], where a trade-off between accuracy and communication load for monitoring threshold functions in various kinds of distributed environments is discussed. For a general overview on resource-aware computing in sensor networks, see Ref. [34].

7.6.2   Beyond Identically Distributed Data

An important challenge is that ubiquitous knowledge discovery focuses on learning beyond independent and identically distributed (iid) data. Although work in this area exists, this implies a significant shift in focus from the current mainstream in data mining and machine learning. At the core of the problem is the following observation: In a ubiquitous setting, we cannot assume anymore to have an iid sample of the underlying distribution. The reason is that inference takes place under real-time constraints in a dynamically changing environment, as has been describe in Example 1.

A collection of random variables $X_1,...,X_n$ is said to be iid if each X_i has the same distribution function f and the X_i are mutually independent. Each of the two

TABLE 7.1: Violating the iid assumption gives rise to different areas of machine learning and statistics.

	Independent	Not Independent
Identical	Statistical learning theory, PAC, and mainstream data mining	Simple kriging, stationary time series, statistical relational learning, and Markov chains
Not identical, slowly changing	PAC online learning	ARIMA, state space models, and Kalman filter
Not identical, abrupt changes	Concept drift and CUSUM	Piecewise ARIMA

conditions—independence and identical distribution—may be violated separately, or both may be violated at the same time. This gives rise to distinct areas of machine learning and statistics (Table 7.1).

Most practical and theoretical results in machine learning depend on the iid assumption (top left corner of the table). The main body of probably approximately correct (PAC) learning [15] and statistical learning theory [29] are crucially based on it. The reason is that if we sample independently from a distribution that is supposed to be fixed and invariant with respect to time (i.e., if the process is iid), all necessary information about the future behavior of a signal can in principle be obtained from a (sufficiently large) sample of past or present values. This justifies to attempt forecasting. Moreover, techniques such as cross-validation can be used to assess the prediction error on future instances.

7.6.2.1 Dependent Data

If the independence assumption is invalid but the distribution is fixed, sampling instances become autocorrelated (top right corner of Table 7.1). Traditionally, the theory of stationary time series [5] and spatial statistics (e.g., simple kriging) [6] deal with temporally and spatially autocorrelated variables, respectively. Markov chains are widely employed to model sequential data, and some extensions of PAC learning for this setting exist [11]. More recently, statistical relational learning starts investigating scenarios that violate the independence assumption [13,22].

7.6.2.2 Slowly Changing Distributions

Some extensions of learning theory cover slowly changing sequences of concepts [16], where the instances of a concept are drawn at random (middle left cell of Table 7.1). It derives bounds on how fast a concept can change so that learning is still possible.

Very common in econometrics and engineering are approaches that combine both autocorrelation and slowly changing distributions, especially ARIMA (autoregressive integrated moving average) and state space models [5] (middle right cell). In an ARIMA model, although the input signal can have a trend or cycles, it is assumed that after taking differences finitely many times (usually just one or two), the signal becomes stationary. So there is at least some component of the original signal that gives information useful for forecasting. The trick here is that we can recover stationarity in some way, so that stationary time-series analysis becomes applicable again.

7.6.2.3 Abrupt Changes

The least explored but for ubiquitous knowledge discovery most relevant and interesting part of Table 7.1 is where we face abrupt changes in the distribution (bottom row of Table 7.1).

An important distinction concerns the available information: are only the past values available (forecasting), a measurement of the current value (filtering) or past, future, and present values (smoothing)? As we move down the table, prediction becomes increasingly difficult, and for the case of abrupt changes, the typical setting is that of monitoring or filtering, instead of prediction. Thus, Examples 1, 2, and 4 are all cases for monitoring or filtering. Breaks are detected but not predicted. All examples use online algorithms.

A body of work in machine learning on concept drift addresses this scenario. It assumes nonstationarities, breaks, but assumes the data in between to be independent [19,31]. The predictive accuracy is monitored and once it drops a new model is learned. The main objective is to automatically keep an up-to-date model over time, for example, in a spam filtering scenario. A streaming scenario is explicitly addressed in Refs. [12,17]. Although designed for scalability in terms of data size, the various approaches assume sufficient compute power and are not designed, for example, for a mobile solution.

Control charts and the CUSUM method (that calculates the cumulative sum of differences between the current and average value) are more traditional approaches to this problem for univariate data [2], often used to monitor industrial processes. Example 4 [18] discusses vehicle monitoring and break detection in a multivariate setting.

Severo and Gama [25] combine machine learning and traditional approaches in a generic scenario where a regression algorithm, for example, a regression tree, is used as a basic learner, its residuals are monitored, and thresholds adapted using a Kalman filter; CUSUM is used for deciding whether a break occurred. If the performance degrades, a new tree is learned.

The most general setting allows data to be dependent and distributions to be nonstationary, with both slow and abrupt changes. There is a recent work that combines elements from statistics and machine learning on piecewise ARIMA models that can model both slow and abrupt changes [8]. The breaks are identified using genetic algorithms and the minimum description length principle. However, it presupposes that the full series is available, so breaks can be modeled only *a posteriori*; thus it is not applicable in a typical ubiquitous knowledge discovery scenario.

In contrast, the drivable terrain detection algorithm that has been described in Section 7.2 allows for an evolving stream of data, since it detects both slow and abrupt changes in an online setting. Also the activity recognition would fall under this scenario, since a person might abruptly change his or her behavior (e.g., his or her daily routine after changing job), but also more gradually (e.g., undertaking longer walks when it becomes summer).

This shows how common and important this last scenario is. A more systematic and unified approach is needed in the machine learning and data mining community to develop methods for detecting slow and abrupt changes in possibly dependent data. It would be important to address this in a typical data-mining scenario where a large number of variables can be included, and no *a priori* knowledge about their relevance is available.

7.6.3 Locality

A third central feature is various forms of locality. Locality and the stationarity assumption are in fact closely linked. The assumption that a process is spatiotemporally stationary implies that we can make a translation on the time scale or in the spatial coordinates and the autocorrelation structure remains invariant. Thus, we can take a sample at some place on Earth at the beginning of the twenty-first century and can draw valid inferences about the process in some distant galaxy, from the stone age to the end of days. While this proved to be a powerful assumption for fundamental physical processes, it leads into trouble for areas related to human activities. Assuming iid data is a way of removing spatiotemporal boundaries from our inference capabilities. Embracing dependent data and nonstationary distributions with breaks leads us to inference in temporally or spatially local environments. The associated challenges are discussed in the following subsections.

7.6.3.1 Temporal Locality

The first aspect is temporal locality. In a typical scenario for ubiquitous knowledge discovery, the learner has access to past and maybe present data from a time-varying distribution (see Section 7.7), and has to make inferences about the present (filtering) or future (forecasting). In a memory-constrained environment, typically, a data-stream setting is assumed. This setting leads to incremental and online learners, time-window approaches, weighting, etc. (for an overview on data streams see Ref. [10]), as already discussed in various examples.

7.6.3.2 Spatial Locality

There is a second aspect of locality that derives from spatial locality and distributedness. For example, in a sensor network, the reach of a sensor is restricted so that it can sense only the local environment. In the case of terrain finding Example 1, the vehicle is moving, having just a local snapshot of the terrain. The nodes in Nemoz have full access only to their own collection.

If the task is to have a global model about the whole terrain, locality is related to the iid assumption. None of the nodes has access to the full distribution. Instead, each node has (often highly autocorrelated) measurements coming from a small range of the full distribution. In P2P networks, neighboring nodes will in some case share other relevant features as well (e.g., the kind of music they like in the Nemoz application) so that sampling values from neighbor nodes gives a biased sample.

To share this local view with others and to come up finally with a global model, a node has to communicate. But for small devices dependent on battery power, communication is costly. It has been shown that in many scenarios a fully centralized solution involves too much communication overhead to be feasible. Along the same lines fully reliable, globally synchronized networking is not attainable in many P2P scenarios [32].

7.6.3.3 Distributed Learning Algorithms

Under this condition, the task is to find a near optimal solution to the inference problem that takes account of specific constraints in communication and reliability. Solutions may be either exact or approximate. Local communication leads, in some cases, to totally different algorithms than their counterparts in centralized scenarios. As a result, algorithms appear that would make no sense in a globally centralized, static environment.

An example is the large-scale distributed association-rule mining algorithm by Wolff and Schuster [32]. It relies on a distributed local majority voting protocol to decide whether some item is frequent. It is applicable to networks of unlimited size. Distributed monitoring of arbitrary threshold functions based on geometric considerations is described in Sharfman et al. [26]. The case is considered where $X_1, X_2, ..., X_d$ are frequency counts for d items and where we are interested to detect whether a nonlinear function $f(X_1, X_2, ..., X_d)$ rises or falls below a threshold. It is pointed out that for a nonlinear function in general it is not possible to deduce, for example, the average of two counts at X_1 and X_2, if they are passed through the function f, by just looking at the local values. This observation is, for example, relevant for a distributed spam-filter, where a system of agents is installed on a number of distributed mail servers. The task is to set up the learning systems in such a way that by monitoring the threshold at local nodes, we can be sure that if the constraints are met at all local nodes, no global violation has occurred, and thus no communication across nodes is necessary. The solution is based on a geometric approach to monitor threshold violations. Further examples for local inference algorithms that depend on network characteristics and involve either geometric or graph theoretic considerations are described in Ref. [34].

It is claimed that in sensor networks, the topology of the network cannot be decoupled from application semantics [34]. This statement takes over to ubiquitous knowledge discovery: the network topology, the information processing, and the core learning algorithms become mutually dependent. This fact is a deeper reason why we cannot design ubiquitous learning algorithms independently from considerations about the underlying distributed technology, the specific data types, privacy constraints, and user modeling issues.

7.6.4 Further Challenges

In this section, further challenges are shortly summarized. From the discussion it emerges that ubiquitous knowledge discovery requires new approaches in spatiotemporal data mining, privacy-preserving data mining, sensor data integration, collaborative data generation, distributed data mining, and user modeling. The most successful approaches will be those that combine several aspects. Thus, ubiquitous knowledge discovery holds the potential as an integrated scenario for various or otherwise fragmented directions of current research.

Spatiotemporal Mining. Examples 1 and 2 highlighted the central role of spatiotemporal data mining, especially GPS track data. For an overview on recent developments in this area, see Refs. [14,20,23].

Data Collection. On the data collection side two major issues arise. The first issue is collection and integration of data collected from heterogeneous sensors as in Examples 1, 2, and 4. Example 3 highlights data collection issues in a collaborative Web 2.0 environment.

Privacy. All examples proved to be privacy sensitive, since ubiquitous devices reveal highly sensitive information about the persons that carry them. Privacy-preserving data mining in a distributed, spatiotemporal environment poses many challenges [4,24]. Privacy issues will become even more pressing once the application migrates from a research prototype status to real products.

User Modeling. Finally, user modeling and HCI are particularly challenging, for example, since not only experts but also technically nonskilled end users will be confronted with those systems [3]. For example, once autonomous cars would go into production, HCI and user modeling (as well as privacy) will play a central role: There are many questions starting from user acceptance (the autonomy of the car diminishes the autonomy of the user) to liability and legal issues.

7.7 Summary

In this section, common lessons from the examples are drawn and research challenges identified.

We reviewed examples from data mining, machine learning, probabilistic robotics, ubiquitous computing, and Web 2.0. Collectively, these applications span a broad range of ubiquitous knowledge discovery applications from vehicle driving, assistive technologies, transportation, and leisure. This showed that across a large sector of challenging application domains, further progress depends on advances in the fields of machine learning and data mining; increasing the ubiquity sets the directions for further research and improved applications.

Ubiquitous knowledge discovery investigates learning *in situ*, inside distributed interacting devices and under real-time constraints. From this characterization, the major challenges follow:

- *Devices are resource constrained.* This leads to a streaming setting and to algorithms that may have to trade off accuracy and efficiency by using sampling, windowing, approximate inference, etc.

- *Data is nonstationary and nonindependent.* The distribution may be both temporally and spatially varying, and it may change both slowly or abruptly.

- *Locality.* Temporal locality combined with real-time properties leads to online algorithms and to a shift from prediction to monitoring, change detection, filtering, or short-term forecasts. Spatial locality (combined with resource constraints) leads to distributed algorithms that are tailored for specific network topologies and that make use of graph theoretic or geometric properties.

At the heart of the algorithmic challenges for KDubiq is thus local inference beyond iid data in resource-constrained environments. While inference on iid data occupies only one-sixth of the cells in Table 7.1, by far the most amount of work in data mining and machine learning is devoted to this topic so far. There are large areas of unexplored terrain that wait for research from the data mining and machine learning community.

From a systems perspective, the challenge consists in building learning algorithms for distributed, multidevice, multisensor environments. While partial suggestions exist on how to implement privacy-preserving, distributed, collaborative algorithms, respectively, there is hardly any existing work that properly addresses all the dimensions at the same time in an integrated manner. Yet as long as one of these dimensions is left unaddressed, the ubiquitous knowledge discovery prototype will not be fully operational in a real-world environment. We need both new algorithms—including analysis and proof about their complexity and accuracy—and an engineering approach for integrating the various partial solutions—algorithms, software, and hardware—in working prototypes.

Acknowledgments

This chapter has been funded by the European Commission under IST-FP6-021321 KDubiq Coordination Action. The KDubiq research network (www.kdubiq.org) was launched in 2006 to stimulate research in this area. Currently, it has more than 50 members. This chapter is based on the discussions in the network, and contributions from project partners are gratefully acknowledged.

References

[1] Arbeitsgemeinschaft Media-Analyse (ag.ma). Kontakt und Reichweitenmodell Plakat. Available at http://www.agma-mmc.de/03_forschung/plakat/erhebung_methode/abfragemode ll.asp?topnav=10&subnav=199, 2008.

[2] M. Basseville and I. Nikiforov. *Detection of Abrupt Changes: Theory and Application*. Prentice Hall, Upper Saddle River, NJ, 1993.

[3] B. Berendt, A. Kröner, E. Menasalvas, and S. Weibelzahl (Eds.). *Proceedings of the Knowledge Discovery for Ubiquitous User Modeling '07*. Available at http://vasarely.wiwi.hu-berlin.de/K-DUUM07/, 2007.

[4] F. Bonchi, Y. Saygin, V.S. Verykios, M. Atzori, A. Gkoulalas-Divanis, S. Volkan Kaya, and E. Savas. Privacy in spatio-temporal data mining. In F. Giannotti and D. Pedreschi (Eds.), Geography, Mobility, and Privacy: A Knowledge Discovery Vision. Springer, New York, pp. 253–276, 2008.

[5] P.J. Brockwell and R.A. Davis. *Introduction to Time Series and Forecasting*. Springer, 2nd edition, New York, 2002.

[6] N. Cressie. *Statistics for Spatial Data*. Wiley, New York, 1993.

[7] DARPA. Darpa urban challenge rules. Available at http://www.darpa.mil/grandchallenge/rules.asp, 2007.

[8] R.A. Davis, T. Lee, and G. Rodriguez-Yam. Structural break estimation for nonstationary time series models. *J. Am. Statist. Assoc.*, 11: 229–239, 2006.

[9] O. Flasch, A. Kaspari, K. Morik, and M. Wurst. Aspect-based tagging for collaborative media organization. In B. Berendt, A. Kröner, E. Menasalvas, and S. Weibelzahl (Eds.), *Proceedings of the Knowledge Discovery for Ubiquitous User Modeling '07*. Available at http://vasarely.wiwi.hu-berlin.de/K-DUUM07/, 2007.

[10] J. Gama and M. Garber (Eds.). *Learning from Data Streams: Processing Techniques in Sensor Networks*. Springer, New York, 2007.

[11] D. Gamarnik. Extension of the PAC framework to finite and countable Markov chains. In *COLT: Proceedings of the Workshop on Computational Learning Theory*, pp. 308–317, Morgan Kaufmann, San Francisco, CA, 1999.

[12] J. Gao, W. Fan, J. Han, and P.S. Yu. A general framework for mining concept-drifting data streams with skewed distributions. In *SIAM International Conference on Data Mining (SDM)*, Minneapolis, MN, 2007.

[13] L. Getoor and B. Taskar (Eds.). *Introduction to Statistical Relational Learning*. MIT Press, Cambridge, MA, 2007.

[14] F. Giannotti and D. Pedreschi (Eds.). *Geography, Mobility, and Privacy: A Knowledge Discovery Vision.* Springer, New York, 2008.

[15] D. Haussler. Probably approximately correct learning. In *National Conference on Artificial Intelligence*, pp. 1101–1108, AAAI Press, Menlo Park, CA, 1990.

[16] D.P. Helmbold and P.M. Long. Tracking drifting concepts by minimizing disagreements. Technical Report UCSC-CRL-91-26, University of California, 1991.

[17] G. Hulten, L. Spencer, and P. Domingos. Mining time-changing data streams. In *Proceedings of the 7th ACM SIGKDD International Conference on Knowledge Discovery and Data Mining*, pp. 97–106. ACM Press, San Francisco, CA, 2001.

[18] H. Kargupta, R. Bhargava, K. Liu, M. Powers, P. Blair, S.Bushra, J. Dull, K. Sarkar, M. Klein, M. Vasa, and D. Handy. Vedas: A mobile and distributed data stream mining system for real-time vehicle monitoring. In *Proceedings of the SIAM International Data Mining Conference*, Orlando, FL, 2004.

[19] R. Klinkenberg and T. Joachims. Detecting concept drift with support vector machines. In Pat Langley (Ed.), *Proceedings of ICML-00, 17th International Conference on Machine Learning*, pp. 487–494, Morgan Kaufmann Publishers, San Francisco, CA, 2000.

[20] B. Kuijpers, M. Nanni, C. Körner, M. May, and D. Pedreschi. Spatio-temporal data mining. In *Geography, Mobility, and Privacy: A Knowledge Discovery Vision*, Springer, New York, pp. 277–306, 2008.

[21] L. Liao, D.J. Patterson, D. Fox, and H. Kautz. Learning and inferring transportation routines. *Artificial Intelligence*, 171(5–6):311-331, 2007.

[22] J. Neville and D. Jensen. Relational dependency networks. In L. Getoor and B. Taskar (Eds.), Introduction to Statistical Relational Learning, MIT Press, Cambridge, MA, pp. 239–268, 2007.

[23] S. Rinzivillo, S. Turini, V. Bogorny, C. Körner, B. Kuijpers, and M. May. Knowledge discovery from geographical data. In F. Giannotti and D. Pedreschi (Eds.) *Geography, Mobility, and Privacy: A Knowledge Discovery Vision*, Springer, New York, pp. 253–276, 2008.

[24] A. Schuster, R. Wolff, and B. Gilburd. Privacy-preserving association rule mining in large-scale distributed systems. In *Proceedings of CCGRID'04*, Chicago, IL, 2004.

[25] M. Severo and J. Gama. Change detection with Kalman filter and CUSUM. In *Discovery Science'06*, Springer, New York, pp. 243–254, 2006.

[26] I. Sharfman, A. Schuster, and D. Keren. A geometric approach to monitoring threshold functions over distributed data streams. *ACM Transactions on Database System*, 32(4), 2007.

[27] Stanford Racing Team. Stanford's robotic vehicle "Junior": Interim report. Available at www.darpa.mil/GRANDCHALLENGE/TechPapers/Stanford.pdf, 2007.

[28] S. Thrun, et al. Stanley: The robot that won the DARPA grand challenge. *Journal of Field Robotics*, 23(9): 661–622, 2006.

[29] V.N. Vapnik. *Statistical Learning Theory*. Springer, New York, 1998.

[30] D. Wegner, D. Hecker, C. Koerner, M. May, and M. Mock. Parallel grid-applications with R: An industrial case study. Proceedings of the 1st Ubiquitous Knowledge Discovery Workshop (UKD'08) at ECML/PKDD'08, Antwerp, Belgium, 2008.

[31] G. Widmer and M. Kubat. Learning in the presence of concept drift and hidden contexts. *Machine Learning*, 23(1): 69–101, 1996.

[32] R. Wolff and A. Schuster. Association rule mining in peer-to-peer systems. In *Proceedings of the IEEE Conference on Data Mining ICDM*, Melbourne, FL, 2003.

[33] M. Wurst, K. Morik, and I. Mierswa. Localized alternative cluster ensembles for collaborative structuring. *ECML/PKDD 2006*, Springer, New York, 2006.

[34] F. Zhao and L. Guibas. *Wireless Sensor Networks. An Information Processing Approach*. Morgan Kaufman, San Francisco, CA, 2004.

Chapter 8

High-Performance Distributed Data Mining

Sanchit Misra, Ramanathan Narayanan, Daniel Honbo, and Alok Choudhary

Contents

8.1   Introduction

Data mining, a technique to understand and convert raw data into useful information, is increasingly being used in a variety of fields like marketing, business intelligence, scientific discoveries, biotechnology, Internet searches, and multimedia. Data mining is an interdisciplinary field combining ideas from statistics, machine learning, and natural language processing. Advances in computing and networking technologies have resulted in many pervasive distributed computing environments. The Internet, intranets, LANs, WANs, and peer-to-peer (P2P) networks are all rich sources of vast distributed databases. These distributed data sets provide ample opportunities for large-scale data-driven knowledge discovery, as well as the potential for fundamental advances in science, business, and medicine. Data mining in such environments requires a judicious use of the available resources. Typical sequential data mining algorithms are conceived with the assumption that data is memory resident, making them unable to cope with the exponentially increasing size of data sets. Therefore, the use of parallel and distributed systems has gained significance.

There is a subtle yet significant difference between algorithms designed for parallel and distributed systems. Generally, parallel data mining algorithms deal with tightly coupled custom-made shared memory systems or distributed-memory systems with fast interconnects. Distributed data mining generally deals with cluster-like loosely coupled systems connected over a slow Ethernet LAN or WAN. The main differences between parallel and distributed systems are scale, communication costs, interconnect speed, and data distribution. For example, the amount of communication feasible in a shared-memory parallel system can be large, whereas it might not be practical to do the same in a distributed cluster over the Internet. Large-scale real-world data mining systems typically use a combination of both parallel and distributed data mining systems. The parallel techniques are used for optimizing mining at a local hub, whereas distributed techniques are useful for aggregating information across geographically distributed locations. In this chapter, we focus on distributed implementations of data mining techniques.

The shift toward intrinsically distributed, complex, heterogeneous computing environments has thrown up a range of new data mining research challenges. This chapter explores the different paradigms and trade-offs when designing distributed data mining algorithms. Particularly, we discuss data generation/replication, static and dynamic workload distribution, database formats, exact versus heuristic techniques, and different parallelization paradigms.

The remainder of this chapter is organized as follows: Section 8.2 describes the challenges in designing distributed data mining algorithms. Section 8.3 discusses distributed classification. We then give an overview of high-performance distributed association rule mining algorithms in Section 8.4 and clustering algorithms in Section 8.5, followed by conclusions and future challenges in Section 8.6.

8.2　Challenges in Distributed Data Mining

8.2.1　Peer-to-Peer Data Mining

Conventional data mining is often associated with analyzing large amounts of data, usually in the form of centralized database tables, for useful and interesting information. On the other hand, P2P networks consist mostly of file sharing networks consisting of point-to-point connections without any central server. Together, they store vast amounts of data collected from different sources, which if integrated and mined, will provide useful information about various aspects of these networks. However, it is impossible to move all this data to one centralized server where data mining algorithms can be run to extract information. Still, if the same result or a close approximation of the algorithms can be obtained without moving too much data from P2P, we can use it for very exciting applications (e.g., searching documents on P2P networks using distributed clustering). Abundance of such interesting research problems has encouraged researchers to develop data mining algorithms for data distributed in P2P networks (also known as P2P data mining).

A primary goal of P2P data mining is to achieve similar results as the centralized approach without moving any actual data from its original location. Peers should work by exchanging some information about their corresponding data items but should not move the actual data items. Moreover, P2P networks are very unstable and volatile in nature. Peers may leave or join the network during the execution of the algorithms. This necessitates the design of robust algorithms that are able to recover from failures of peers, and subsequent loss of data.

8.2.2　Data Mining in Sensor Networks

Sensor networks are also an example of P2P networks. Sensor networks are becoming increasingly popular with applications in many domains, including habitat monitoring, traffic control, and even for monitoring the human body. Most sensor networks contain a collection of lightweight sensors connected through wireless links to each other or to a more powerful gateway node. Sensors are often constrained by weight, power supply, and cost and must process a continuous and fast stream of data. This makes P2P data mining in sensor networks even more challenging. A sensor network is most commonly used in some high-level information processing tasks like environmental monitoring, tracking, and classification. Hence, a prominent research area in distributed data mining is the development of algorithms that take into account the characteristics of sensor networks, like energy and computation constraints, network dynamics, and faults. As we know that, in terms of energy used, communicating messages over sensor networks is much more expensive than computation. Hence algorithms, which perform localized collaborative processing, tend to be much better in terms of robustness and scalability. In such algorithms, each node interacts only with its small neighborhood, while working on the global problem.

8.2.3 Grid Data Mining

Current scientific research is generating data at an exponential rate and hence needs more and more computational power and storage facilities. Data in the range of terabytes to petabytes is being generated by many scientific projects including astronomy and physical science projects, bioinformatics projects, gene and protein archives, meteorological and environmental surveys, etc. Grid computing provides a shared distributed computing infrastructure to scientists from different geographical areas to do collaborative research. Several research projects like Knowledge Grid, Grid Miner, DataCutter, etc. have focused on providing systems that facilitate data mining and knowledge discovery on top of a grid-based system. Hence, there is a need for efficient distributed data mining algorithms that work well on a grid.

8.2.4 Privacy Preserving Data Mining

Recent application of data mining technology for the collection and analysis of data in security-, medicine-, and business-related applications has raised serious concerns over privacy issues. This has made transferring or sharing raw data undesirable. Moving the input data set to a central location for unification prior to processing, for example, may expose the data to eavesdropping. This could amount to a loss of some competitive advantage in a business setting, for instance, or a breach of privacy if the data in question were individual patient medical records. A local site involved in a distributed data mining effort often cannot guarantee the privacy of the link over which it communicates with the central processing site, or cannot trust the central site itself. The former issue can be mitigated to an extent by encrypting or otherwise obscuring the data sent over the link, but the latter effectively dictates that information shared with a the central site cannot be used to reconstruct individual objects. In practice, this means that abstract representations of local data are preferred when trust between sites is in question.

8.2.5 Data Stream Mining

A data stream is an ordered sequence of items appearing in a timely manner. Data streams are continuous, unbounded, and have distributions that often change with time. An example of such a data set is the generation of data streams by traffic sensors on a highway. Mining data streams pose several challenges: there is insufficient time for multiple passes over a data stream. Moreover, there is not enough space to store the entire stream for online processing. The limited amount of processing power and high-communication costs complicate the problem further. Algorithms also need to adapt to changing distributions of the data stream. The emergence of several stream data sets (emanating from multiple geographically distributed sources) motivates the need for efficient algorithms for distributed stream mining.

A more detailed overview of various challenges in distributed data mining, with corresponding bibliography, is given in [34].

8.3 Distributed Classification

Classification is a widely studied problem in data mining. A classification problem consists of a set of classes and a set of records (training set), labeled with these classes. The task is to build a model using the training set to be able to predict labels for new records whose class is unknown. Each record consists of a number of attributes that can be classified as ordered and unordered; or continuous and discrete attributes. Various techniques have been proposed to solve the classification problem including decision trees, Bayesian networks, neural networks, rule induction, support vector machines, regression models, and genetic algorithms. All of these initial algorithms rely on integrating the data at a central location, which is infeasible in a distributed environment. This brings us to the distributed classification algorithms.

8.3.1 Distributed Classification Overview

Considerable research has been done to design new classification algorithms for distributed data sets. The main goal of these algorithms have been to come up with same (or nearly same) results as the algorithms that work on a centralized database. When the number of nodes in the distributed systems is limited, many algorithms work by sharing information and data across a number of nodes and synchronizing the results with all nodes. But these techniques cease to work for larger networks like P2P or sensor networks. For such networks, the algorithms should work without moving too much data and should avoid using global synchronization. The following subsection gives some examples of the state-of-the-art distributed classification algorithms.

8.3.2 Examples of Distributed Classification Algorithms

8.3.2.1 Decision-Tree-Based Algorithms

Decision trees are very popular for data mining applications since they obtain reasonable accuracy and are relatively less computationally expensive to construct and use. A decision tree consists of internal nodes and leaves. Each of the internal nodes has a splitting decision and splitting attribute associated with it. The leaves have a class label assigned to them. Once a decision tree is built, the prediction process is relatively straightforward: the classification process begins at the root, and a path to a leaf is traced by using the splitting decision at each internal node. The class label attached to the leaf is then assigned to the incoming record.

There is inherent parallelism in decision tree construction algorithms, since all the children of a node can be processed concurrently. This technique is known as

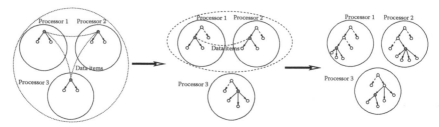

FIGURE 8.1:   Parallel tree construction approach.

partitioned tree construction approach [31]. This approach starts with all the processors cooperating to expand the root node. The processors are then divided among the child nodes and each division works on its part of the subtree. This process is recursively repeated until each processor has its own subtree. Figure 8.1 shows an example. Initially all three processors work together to expand the root node to get two child nodes. Processors 1 and 2 are assigned the left child, while processor 3 gets the right child. The left child is further expanded to get two children that are distributed to processors 1 and 2. Each processor now goes on to build its subtree using the sequential algorithm.

Another approach, called synchronous tree construction [31], concurrently constructs the tree on all processors. For each node of the tree, all the processors exchange local class distribution information in order to select the appropriate attribute. Figure 8.2 displays an example where the current node is the leftmost child of the root. All the processors collaborate to expand this node to get three children. Again the leftmost node of these child nodes is the current node and the processors work together to expand it.

Hybrid parallel formulation [31] combines both the approaches to get a more efficient technique. The communication cost of synchronous tree construction approach becomes very high with the increase in the frontier of the tree. On the other hand, the partitioned tree construction method incurs heavy costs in moving the corresponding data to different processor groups when a partition is done. Hybrid formulation

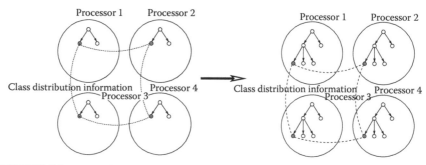

FIGURE 8.2:   Synchronous tree construction approach.

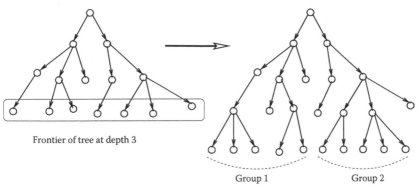

Frontier of tree at depth 3

Group 1   Group 2

Synchronous tree construction method   Partition tree construction method

FIGURE 8.3: Hybrid tree construction approach.

continues to apply the synchronous tree construction approach as long as the communication cost is within limits. When the communication cost becomes prohibitive, the current frontier of the tree is partitioned into two parts; one part is assigned to one half of the processors and other part to the other half (Figure 8.3).

Clearly, deciding on an appropriate time to partition is very crucial for the hybrid approach. In the hybrid algorithm, the tree is split once the accumulated cost of communication equals that of moving records and load balancing in the partition phase. Decision trees can have highly irregular shapes that depend on the input data. The hybrid approach works very well in most conditions. It uses synchronous tree construction approach for skinny trees and partitioned tree construction approach if the tree turns bushy. In case the tree has irregular depth leading to some of the processor groups finishing their job a lot earlier than others, it performs dynamic load balancing by moving idle processors to groups with more work.

The above algorithms were initially designed for parallel implementations, but have been very well adapted in distributed systems. Caragea et al. [5] noted in their paper that the evaluation of an effective splitting criteria is the most computationally intensive part of a decision tree algorithm. The authors proposed to move the summary statistics, in terms of local class distribution information, to a centralized site. This technique saves a lot of communication cost as compared to centralizing all the data. Moreover, the decision tree induced using the summary statistics is same compared to the one with centralized data. Giannella et al. [9] used Gini information gain as the splitting criteria and showed that Gini score between two attributes can be calculated as the dot product between two binary vectors. The communication cost was reduced by calculating the dot product after projecting the vectors in a random low-dimensional subspace. Hence the authors send these low-dimensional projected vectors instead of raw data or the high-dimensional original vectors. Thus, with only 20% of the communication cost, they build trees that are at least 80% accurate compared to those built on centralized data. More recently, a distributed decision tree algorithm for large P2P networks has been proposed in Ref. [3].

8.3.2.2   Multivariate-Regression-Based Algorithms

Multivariate regression (MR) is an effective statistical and machine learning tool, which is widely used in classification. It involves modeling a function on the various attributes by using the training data and classifying the data based on the value of the function obtained. MR has been sufficiently studied for centralized data. A technique to calculate global MR in a distributed scenario, considering a vertically partitioned data, is presented in Ref. [13]. The authors proposed a wavelet transform of the data to create local MR models, which are then moved to the central site to combine into a global MR model. A local distributed algorithm for large-scale distributed systems is proposed in Ref. [2]. This algorithm works in two steps: First, a local distributed algorithm is used to monitor the quality of current regression model. If the model is found to be outdated, then the monitoring algorithm is used as a feedback loop to come up with a new regression model. A number of other techniques using distributed kernel regression have been proposed in Refs. [10] and [12].

8.3.2.3   Ensemble Classifier-Based Algorithms

Ensemble classifiers or meta classifiers are another emerging group of classification algorithms. A meta classification algorithm learns a weak classifier on every partition of data and then combines each of these weak classifiers into a global classifier [4,8]. Various criteria can be applied to combine the weak classifiers. One such criteria is distributed plurality voting [23], which combines the weak classifiers by taking the majority of their outcomes on any new data.

8.3.2.4   Classification in Large-Scale Distributed Systems

Many modern distributed systems have a large number of nodes. For example, P2P networks of computers connected through Kaaza, sensor networks, and mobile embedded devices. Classification in such networks requires algorithms that are asynchronous, fully decentralized, and can handle rapidly changing data. Most of the distributed algorithms for such networks work on three main concepts—local algorithms, gossip- and flood-based computations and best effort heuristics. In local algorithms, as we already discussed before [23], every node collects statistics of just a few of its neighboring nodes. Hence, the overhead of each node is independent of the size of the network. These statistics need to be updated after every change in data. But if the change does not affect the statistics, then no communication is needed. In a typical best effort heuristic, each node samples data of its own partition and that of many of its neighbors and assumes that this data represents that on the entire set of nodes. Flooding algorithms flood the entire network with data so that every node has a copy of the entire data of the network. Clearly, flooding is not feasible for large distributed systems. Hence randomized flooding (called gossip) is used, in which every node sends its statistics to a random node. This technique can be used to calculate a number of aggregated statistics [17], but can require hundreds of messages per node to compute just one statistic and hence can turn out to be expensive.

8.4 Distributed Association Rule Mining

8.4.1 Problem Definition

Association rule mining (ARM) is the automatic discovery of groups of elements that tend to appear together in a common context. The ARM problem is formally defined as follows: Let $I = i_1, i_2, ..., i_n$ be a set of distinct items in a certain domain. An itemset is a subset of items in I. A transaction T consists of a subset of I along with a unique transaction identifier TID, that is, each transaction is of the form $< \text{TID}, i_1, i_2, ..., i_k >$. An itemset with k-items is called a k-itemset. A database is a list of transactions, and the size of a database $|\text{DB}|$ is the number of transactions it contains. An itemset i is said to have a support s in database DB, if $s\%$ transactions in DB contain all items in i. The frequency of an itemset i in DB is denoted by $\text{Freq}(i,\text{DB}) = (\text{Support}(i,\text{DB})/100) * |\text{DB}|$. We say that an itemset i is frequent in database DB if the frequency of i exceeds a minimum threshold f_{min}, that is, $\text{Freq}(i,\text{DB}) > f_{min}$ or $\text{Support}(i,\text{DB}) > f_{min} * |\text{DB}|$. An association rule is an expression $A \Rightarrow B$, where $A, B \subseteq I$ and $A \cap B = \Phi$. The confidence of an association rule is defined as the conditional probability that a transaction contains B, given that it contains A, that is, the confidence of a rule $A \Rightarrow B$ is defined as $\text{Support}(A \cup B, \text{DB})/\text{Support}(A, \text{DB})$. The association rule discovery is composed of two stages: the first stage involves computing all frequent itemsets (which have support greater than a specified threshold). The second stage involves generating association rules from the frequent itemsets. The computation intensive step is the generation of frequent itemsets, while the association rule discovery is relatively inexpensive.

8.4.2 Distributed ARM: Definition and Challenges

There are a large number of serial algorithms for discovering frequent itemsets. Since the problem was introduced, a number of approaches like Apriori, Partition, dynamic itemset count (DIC), dynamic hashing and pruning (DHP), and FP-growth [1,11,20,27,29] have been proposed. Sequential ARM algorithms do not scale well with increasing data size and dimensionality. Parallel algorithms for ARM make use of shared interconnect and shared memory of parallel machines. However, parallel machines are costly; and as distributed databases gain significance, it becomes imperative to develop distributed ARM algorithms that can handle the unique problems posed by such repositories. Most parallel/distributed ARM algorithms are variants of their sequential equivalents. In this section, we focus on distributed ARM algorithms designed for machines with no shared memory, and limited communication bandwidth. The main challenges in designing distributed ARM algorithms include communication cost, workload distribution, minimizing disk I/O, and efficient data layout.

8.4.3   Examples of Distributed ARM Algorithms

8.4.3.1   Apriori-Based Algorithms

The first class of distributed ARM algorithms we will study are those based on apriori and its variants. The classic apriori algorithm uses breadth first search and a hash tree structure to count candidate itemsets. The Apriori algorithm works as follows:

Compute F_1, the set of all frequent-1 itemsets

for (k = 2; $F_{k-1} \neq \phi$; k++) {
Generate C_k, the set of candidate itemsets of length k from F_{k-1}
Scan the database to compute counts of candidate itemsets in C_k
$F_k = \{c \in C_k | count(c) > s\}$
}
Frequent_Itemsets = $\bigcup F_k$

The algorithm makes an initial pass over the transaction database and computes the frequent 1-itemsets. In the kth iteration of the *for* loop, the algorithm initially generates *candidate* itemsets of size-k by extending $k - 1$-frequent itemsets. This step makes use of the anti-monotone property to ensure that all $k - 1$ subsets of a candidate k-itemset are themselves frequent. The supports of each of the candidate itemsets are estimated, and those with frequencies less than the minimum support criterion are discarded. This step is repeated till there are no more itemsets satisfying the minimum support threshold. Computing the support of the candidate itemsets is accomplished by maintaining a candidate hash tree.

In general, there are two main paradigms for distributed ARM algorithms based on Apriori: data distribution and task distribution.

Data distribution: In this parallel/distributed formulation, the database is equally partitioned among the processors. Each processor works on its local partition of the database but performs the same task of counting support for the global candidate itemsets.

The count distribution [26] algorithm is a distributed formulation of the Apriori algorithm, in which each processor generates its own version of the candidate hash tree. The counts of the candidates are estimated by performing a single pass over the local database, and a global reduction operation is then performed to estimate the global support of the candidate itemsets. When the globally frequent itemsets at level-k have been discovered, each processor generates the $k + 1$-candidate itemsets in parallel, and repeats the process till all frequent itemsets have been found. Figure 8.4 illustrates the working of this algorithm. A detailed scalability analysis of the count distribution algorithm shows that the parallel run time of the algorithm is $\frac{T_{serial}}{P} + O(C)$, where T_{serial} is the serial run time, P the number of processors, and C is the number of candidates generated. While this algorithm is scalable in the number of transactions, it does not parallelize the candidate hash tree generation process.

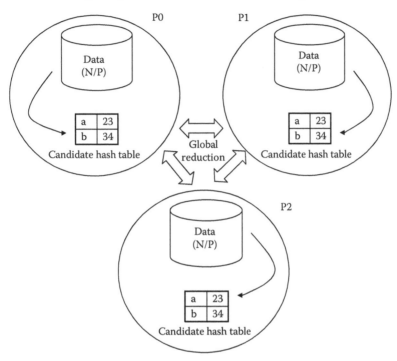

FIGURE 8.4: Count distribution.

This step becomes a bottleneck as the number of processors increase, and when the candidate hash tree is too large to fit in memory.

The PDM algorithm [21] is a parallel implementation of the serial DHP algorithm. While it is similar in nature to count distribution, the major difference is the use of a parallel hash table. The database is distributed among the processors, and each processor generates disjoint candidate itemsets. As in DHP, the hash table built during the candidate counting phase is used to prune candidates in the subsequent generation phase. For this to happen, each processor needs to have a copy of the global hash table. Since PDM maintains parallel hash tables, this requires communicating the counts of each location in the hash table by a global exchange. Communicating the entire hash table is inefficient, but there are several optimizations that can reduce communication. For instance, an entry in the local hash table will be globally frequent only if its support exceeds s/p on at least one processor. This fact is used to prune the entries that require a global broadcast. Effective parallelization of the hash table construction process makes PDM more efficient than other algorithms which use the data distribution paradigm.

Task distribution: Another parallelization paradigm is to replicate the candidate generation process on each processor, and parallelize the support counting process. The processors will then perform different computations independently, but will need access to the entire database.

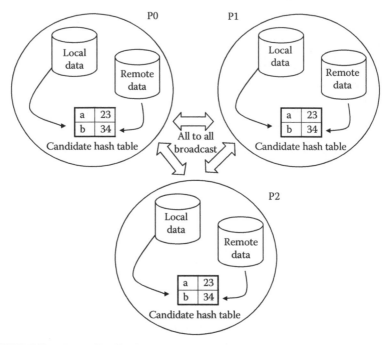

FIGURE 8.5:   Data distribution.

The Data Dist [26] algorithm addresses the memory problem of the count distribution algorithm by splitting the candidate generation process among the processors. The candidate itemsets are distributed among the processors in a round-robin manner (shown in Figure 8.5), and each processor computes the global counts of the candidates assigned to it. In order to do this, each processor needs to scan the transactions belonging to all the other processors. This is done by an asynchronous send–receive policy, wherein each processor allocates *P* buffers to read and write transactions from other processors. While this scheme allows each processor to handle a greater number of candidates, the communication overheads make it an order of magnitude slower than the count distribution algorithm.

There are a number of other algorithms (IDD, HD, ParEclat) based on the task distribution paradigm. These algorithms allow each processor to handle a subset of the candidate itemset and attempt to minimize communication and achieve load balance. The manner in which the database is replicated also impacts performance. A detailed summary of these techniques is available in Ref. [32].

8.4.3.2   Sampling-Based Algorithms

The sequential sampling [14] algorithm uses a random sample of the database to predict all candidate frequent itemsets, which are then validated in a single database scan. This single-scan property reduces I/O costs tremendously and makes it an attractive alternative to apriori-based algorithms. Using a random sample to generate itemsets is probabilistic and fallible, therefore not only are candidate itemsets counted but also their negative borders. If an itemset belonging to the negative border is classified as frequent, a second scan of the database is required to confirm all frequent itemsets. To further reduce the chance of failure, the authors describe a heuristic to determine the value of the minimum support, and guarantee theoretical bounds on the error limit. The D-sampling [30] algorithm effectively parallelizes the sampling algorithm by achieving a coherent view of the distributed random sample at reasonable communication costs. Not only does this algorithm divide the disk-I/O costs of the single scan by partitioning the database among several machines but also uses the combined memory to linearly increase the size of the sample. As a result, the D-sampling algorithm is able to generate high-quality results, because the error margin of the sampling algorithm decreases on increasing the sample size.

8.4.3.3 FP-Tree-Based Algorithms

The FP-tree algorithm [11] is a radically different way of mining frequent itemsets without candidate generation. The database is condensed into a compact FP-tree data structure, which avoids costly repeated database scans. A pattern-fragment growth technique is applied to avoid the costly generation of a large number of candidate itemsets. The weakness of apriori-based algorithms lies primarily in the exponential number of candidate itemsets, which severely increase I/O and impacts performance. Frequent itemsets are then mined from the FP-tree using a partitioning-based, divide-and-conquer method which decomposes the mining task into a set of smaller tasks for mining confined patterns in conditional databases, dramatically reducing the search space. The main challenge in parallelizing FP-growth lies in distributing the load equally among the processors, and allowing the local FP-tree segments to fit in memory. The FMGFI algorithm [12] is a recent distributed version of the FP-tree algorithm, in which each node identifies the locally frequent itemsets. Then, top-down and bottom-up approaches are used to efficiently prune the set of possible globally frequent itemsets. Globally frequent itemsets are then identified, while keeping communication costs at a minimum. There are several other distributed variants of the FP-tree algorithm, which focus on techniques to efficiently partition the FP-tree among sites, and minimizing communication while generating globally frequent itemsets.

8.4.3.4 Other Techniques

In Ref. [33], a family of hierarchical algorithms (ParEclat, ParMaxEclat, ParClique, ParMaxClique) is described. These algorithms use novel itemset clustering techniques based on equivalence classes and maximal hypergraph cliques to approximate the set of potentially maximal frequent itemsets. In addition, they adopt intelligent lattice traversal techniques so that each processor needs to scan its local database only twice. The fast distributed mining (FDM) algorithm is designed for highly distributed networks, where communication costs are high. FDM is based on count distribution and use local pruning and count polling strategies to minimize communication costs. Distributed ARM is a well-studied problem, and there is a vast amount of literature this chapter does not discuss.

8.5 Distributed Clustering

Clustering—the process of partitioning data into subsets based on similarity—is a well-studied topic in data mining. Conventional clustering techniques typically assume that the input data set resides, in its entirety, on the site where it is processed. This data locality provides the processing task with quick, private access to every record in the data set. But in many real-world applications, the data to be analyzed is stored on multiple independent computing systems that communicate over LAN or WAN connections.

Due to the loosely coupled nature of such computing environments, the cost of communication among processing elements is expected to be particularly high. An algorithm that relies on frequent synchronization, or one that requires the movement of large amounts of data among sites, will thus be unsuitable from the performance standpoint. Such constraints on data exchange in distributed computing environments have lead to the development of distributed clustering techniques. These techniques seek to achieve high-quality clusterings while minimizing the amount and frequency of data transmission between processing elements.

Distributed clustering techniques bear many resemblances to parallel clustering techniques, which have been well studied. Both distribute data and computational tasks across multiple processing elements, and many distributed clustering algorithms are based on parallel clustering algorithms. The most important distinction between distributed and parallel clustering is that the input data set is effectively pre-partitioned in the case of distributed clustering. As communication costs and data security demands preclude the movement of large amounts of raw data between sites, each local site is responsible for processing the portion of the data set present in its own local store. This is in contrast to a strictly parallel clustering situation, in which data is often assumed to exist initially in a central location and communication among processing elements takes place over a comparatively fast interconnect.

8.5.1 Distributed Clustering Overview

To explore the details of distributed clustering techniques, we begin by formulating the challenge of distributed clustering. Given a data set initially partitioned across multiple loosely coupled sites, how can you calculate an efficient and effective clustering of the data set as a whole? The naive option of unifying the data at a central site and processing it with a conventional clustering technique is immediately ruled out due to the complications associated with moving large amounts of data. Instead, distributed clustering algorithms apply the following computational model. First, each local site creates a representation of its data. Often, this representation is based on the result of a local clustering operation performed at each site. Next, the local representations of all sites participating in the clustering operation are gathered at a central location. The local representations are then aggregated to generate a global clustering of the data set.

Specific distributed clustering algorithms differ primarily in the method of local model representation and global aggregation that follows it. The selection of these methods is motivated by differing assumptions regarding data security requirements and the way in which the input data set is partitioned across sites.

The partitioning scheme of the data set across the local sites is an important consideration for distributed clustering. In practice, the partitioning scheme drives the choice of clustering algorithm, in that many distributed clustering algorithms designed with a horizontal partitioning scheme in mind will not produce meaningful clusters on a vertically partitioned data set.

Most existing distributed clustering algorithms focus on horizontally partitioned data. When horizontal partitioning is implemented, each site uses the same schema for the input data set. In other words, each site has local access to all relevant features of its stored objects. In this case, the primary difficulty of clustering relates to data dependencies that exist between data points stored on different sites. A global cluster whose member elements are dispersed across many sites may be interpreted as local noise at each site, instead of a cluster candidate. Identifying noise as potential local clusters requires more data to represent the local distributions, and more processing time to generate the global cluster labels. So there is a trade-off between clustering quality and performance. At the far end of the spectrum, a high-quality clustering can be achieved by identifying all noise as cluster candidates; but doing so increases the amount of data transmitted to the aggregation site and may inadvertently expose individual records to scrutiny.

In the case of vertical data partitioning, each site has access to some subset of the features of the data set. In order to generate a meaningful clustering of the entire data set, it is assumed that each site stores a unique ID feature, which consistently identifies objects across sites.

8.5.2 Examples of Distributed Clustering Algorithms

The various methods of local representation and global aggregation used by distributed clustering algorithms draw heavily upon existing conventional clustering techniques. In fact, most examples of distributed clustering algorithms employ some well-known form of conventional clustering at the local or global level.

8.5.2.1 *k*-Means

k-means [24] is one of the simplest and most widely deployed algorithms for partitional clustering. The algorithm arbitrarily chooses k initial cluster centroids and iteratively refines their locations based on how well they fit the natural distribution of the input data set. The distributed fast and exact *k*-means (DFEKM) algorithm [18] is a modification of *k*-means for a data set partitioned horizontally across multiple sites. It is based on the premise that a decent approximation of cluster locations can be calculated from a small sample of the entire data set, and that the locations can then be iteratively distributed to and refined by the local sites to produce the same results as k-means.

In order to generate the approximate centroid locations, each site sends a sample of its data to a central location, and the samples are then clustered with k-means. The refinement process requires each local site to make at least one pass through its data and track all points that fall near cluster boundaries. This information is used by the global site to update the global cluster centroids and test for convergence. Since both the sampling and fitting operations involve the transmission of individual records, this algorithm is suitable only for applications that do not require data privacy.

In terms of performance and cluster quality, DFEKM is still at its core, k-means, so many of the same benefits and drawbacks associated with k-means also apply to DFEKM. For instance, DFEKM is fast, but the number of clusters must be known beforehand and the results are often sensitive to the initial selection of cluster centroids.

8.5.2.2   Model-Based Clustering

The expectation-maximization (EM) algorithm [6] is commonly applied to data clustering. The goal is to model the data set as a mixture of k Gaussian distributions. Each distribution represents a cluster, and the assignment of objects to clusters is determined by the probability of membership. The distributed model-based clustering (DMBC) algorithm [22] for horizontally partitioned data executes the EM algorithm locally at each site, then aggregates the local models at a central site. The aggregation process is driven by the likelihood of two local clusters representing the same global cluster.

One benefit of DMBC is that is actively addresses the trade-off between performance and data privacy. At each site, the EM algorithm is executed potentially multiple times to find the most compact representation (i.e., the lowest input value of k) that adequately models the local data. At this point, the model used to represent the site's local data typically provides a good enough level of abstraction of the original data to prevent the reconstruction of individual objects.

The one exception occurs when the variance between objects of a cluster is very small. A small variance in all dimensions implies that at least one object is very similar to the cluster representation. Often this results from a cluster fitting a very tight grouping of data points, or from a very aggressive quality demand from the previous step that causes an artificially high number of clusters to be identified. In such cases, the cluster in question is not transmitted to the global site. By changing the thresholds that determine whether the overall model is suitable and whether individual clusters can be transmitted, the user is allowed to control the trade-off between privacy and performance.

8.5.2.3   Density-Based Clustering

Density-based clustering algorithms locate clusters by grouping representative points within densely populated regions. Density-based distributed clustering (DBDC) [15] applies the popular density-based spatial clustering of applications with noise (DBSCAN) algorithm [7] to a horizontally partitioned data set. At each site, DBSCAN is executed and its results are used to build a model of the local data set. This model consists of a set of representatives, each with an associated range. Each representative and range pair represents an area of high object density in the local data set. Since the representatives are actual local objects, absolute data privacy cannot be guaranteed. The local models from all sites are gathered at a central site, where they are subjected to a global clustering with DBSCAN. The scalable density-based distributed clustering (SDBDC) algorithm [16] is a refinement of DBDC, using an alternative method for local model generation and a modified version of DBSCAN for global aggregation.

8.5.2.4 Hierarchical Clustering

Hierarchical clustering techniques generate a representative dendogram by creating successive mergings (agglomerative) or divisions (divisive) of subclusters based on a similarity metric. Recursive agglomeration of clustering hierarchies by encircling tactic (RACHET) [28] and collective hierarchical clustering (CHC) [19] are two examples of distributed hierarchical clustering algorithms. RACHET assumes a horizontal partitioning of the data set, while CHC operates on a vertically partitioned data set. In the case of CHC, it is assumed that each site shares a common unique ID field that can be used to merge records at the global level.

Both RACHET and CHC apply agglomerative hierarchical clustering at each site to generate local dendograms. These dendograms store descriptive information about the cluster represented at each node, instead of the actual objects represented. In the case of RACHET, descriptive statistics of the representative cluster are stored at each node, which is typically a sufficient abstraction for data privacy toward the root of the dendogram. At the global level, the local dendograms are merged to create a global dendogram representing the entire data set.

8.6   Conclusion and Future Challenges

As the amount of data available in distributed databases increases exponentially, effective knowledge discovery is becoming a critical task. In this chapter, we have motivated the need for efficient algorithms capable of mining knowledge from vast distributed databases. The data to be mined is stored on distributed computing environments on diverse platforms. It cannot be moved to one central location due to technical and organizational reasons. We highlight the challenges faced in designing algorithms for various hctcrogeneous distributed data sets (P2P systems, sensor networks), with different communication/latency costs and other considerations (privacy, security). In addition, we provide examples of distributed algorithms for classification, clustering, and ARM. Design paradigms, performance trade-offs, and scalability issues of state-of-the-art techniques are also analyzed.

Distributed data mining techniques will continue to evolve to combat existing and future challenges. There are a number of problem domains that will require the use of powerful, scalable distributed data mining algorithms. Distributed streams, P2P networks, sensor networks are all examples of distributed architectures that require considerable research attention. Data privacy is an important issue that also needs to be addressed, in order to address privacy laws, protect business secrets and other social issues. The widespread proliferation of intelligent embedded devices provides yet another rich source of information that needs to be exploited. Designing distributed data mining algorithms suitable for embedded devices is another challenging problem that researchers face. Overall, the field of distributed data mining is evolving rapidly and presents numerous challenges for researchers to solve.

References

[1] A. Savasere, E. Omiecinski, and S.B. Navathe. An efficient algorithm for mining association rules in large databases. In *proceedings of the 21st International Conference on Very Large Databases*, pp. 432–444, Zurich, Switzerland, 1995.

[2] K. Bhaduri and H. Kargupta. An efficient local algorithm for distributed multivariate regression in peer-to-peer networks. *SIAM Data Mining Conference 2008*, Atlanta, GA, 2008.

[3] K. Bhaduri, R. Wolff, C. Giannella, and H. Kargupta. Distributed decision tree induction in peer-to-peer systems. *Statistical Analysis and Data Mining Journal*, 1(2):85–103, 2008.

[4] L. Breiman. Bagging predictors. *Machine Learning*, 24(2):123–140, 1996.

[5] D. Caragea, A. Silvescu, and V. Honavar. A framework for learning from distributed data using sufficient statistics and its application to learning decision trees. *International Journal of Hybrid Intelligent Systems*, 1(1–2):80–89, 2004.

[6] A.P. Dempster, N.M. Laird, and D.B. Rubin. Maximum likelihood from incomplete data via the EM algorithm. *Journal of the Royal Statistical Society, Series B*, 39(1):1–38, 1977.

[7] M. Ester, H. Kriegel, J. Sander, and X. Xu. A density-based algorithm for discovering clusters in large spatial databases with noise. In *Proceedings of the 2nd International Conference on Knowledge Discovery and Data Mining*, pp. 226–231, Portland, OR, 1996.

[8] J. Friedman, T. Hastie, and R. Tibshirani. Additive logistic regression: A statistical view of boosting, *Annals of Statistics*, 28, 2000.

[9] C. Giannella, K. Liu, T. Olsen, and H. Kargupta. Communication efficient construction of decision trees over heterogeneously distributed data. In *ICDM '04: Proceedings of the 4th IEEE International Conference on Data Mining*, pp. 67–74, Washington, DC, 2004. IEEE Computer Society.

[10] C. Guestrin, P. Bodi, R. Thibau, M. Paski, and S. Madde. Distributed regression: an efficient framework for modeling sensor network data. In *IPSN '04: Proceedings of the 3rd International Symposium on Information Processing in Sensor Networks*, pp. 1–10, New York, NY, 2004. ACM.

[11] J. Han, J. Pei, and Y. Yin. Mining frequent patterns without candidate generation. In *2000 ACM SIGMOD International Conference on Management of Data*, pp. 1–12, Dallas, TX, May 2000. ACM Press.

[12] B. He, Y. Wang, W. Yang, and Y. Chen. Fast algorithm for mining global frequent itemsets based on distributed database. *Rough Sets and Knowledge Technology*, 4062:415–420, 2006.

[13] D.E. Hershberger and H. Kargupta. Distributed multivariate regression using wavelet-based collective data mining. *Journal of Parallel and Distributed Computing*, 61(3):372–400, 2001.

[14] H. Toivonen. Sampling large databases for association rules. In *Proceedings of the 22nd International Conference on Very Large Databases*, 134–145, Bombay, India, 1996.

[15] E. Januzaj, H. Kriegel, and M. Pfeifle. Scalable density based distributed clustering. In *Proceedings of EDBT*, volume 2992 of *Lecture Notes in Computer Science*, pp. 88–105, Crete, Greece, March 2004.

[16] E. Januzaj, H. Kriegel, and M. Pfeifle. Scalable density-based distributed clustering. In *The 15th European Conference on Machine Learning*, Pisa, Italy, 2004.

[17] M. Jelasity, A. Montresor, and O. Babaoglu. Gossip-based aggregation in large dynamic networks. *ACM Transactions on Computer Systems*, 23(3):219–252, 2005.

[18] R. Jin, A. Goswami, and G. Agrawal. Fast and exact out-of-core and distributed k-means clustering. *Knowledge and Information Systems*, 10(1):17–40, 2006.

[19] E. Johnson and H. Kargupta. Collective, hierarchical clustering from distributed, heterogeneous data. In *Large-Scale Parallel Data Mining*, pp. 221–244, 1999. Springer.

[20] J.S. Park, M.S. Chen, and P.S. Yu. An effective hash-based algorithm for mining association rules. In *Proceedings of the ACM SIGMOD International Conference on Management of Data*, pp. 175–186, San Jose, California, May 1995.

[21] J.S. Park, M.S. Chen, and P.S. Yu. Efficient parallel data mining for association rules. In *Proceedings of the ACM International Conference on Information and Knowledge Management*, pp. 31–36, New York, 1995.

[22] H. Kriegel, P. Kroger, A. Pryakhin, and M. Schubert. Effective and efficient distributed model-based clustering. In *Proceedings of the 5th IEEE*

International Conference on Data Mining, pp. 258–265, Houston, TX, 2005. IEEE Computer Society.

[23] P. Luo, H. Xiong, K. Liu, and Z. Shi. Distributed classification in peer-to-peer networks. In *KDD '07: Proceedings of the 13th ACM SIGKDD International Conference on Knowledge Discovery and Data Mining*, pp. 968–976, New York, 2007. ACM.

[24] J.B. MacQueen. Some methods for classification and analysis of multivariate observations. In *Proceedings of the 5th Berkeley Symposium on Mathematical Statistics and Probability*, volume 1, pp. 281–297, Berkeley, CA, 1967. University of California Press.

[25] J.B. Predd, S.R. Kulkarni, and H.V. Poor. Distributed kernel regression: An algorithm for training collaboratively. CoRR, abs/cs/0601089, 2006.

[26] R. Agrawal and J. Shafer. Parallel mining of association rules. *IEEE Transactions on Knowledge and Data Engineering*, 8(6):962–969, 1996.

[27] R. Agrawal and R. Srikant. Fast algorithms for mining association rules. In *Proceedings of the 20th International Conference on Very Large Databases*, pp. 487–499, Santiago, Chile, 1994.

[28] N. Samatova, G. Ostrouchov, A. Geist, and A. Melechko. Rachet: An efficient cover-based merging of clustering hierarchies from distributed datasets. *Distributed and Parallel Databases*, 11(2):157–180, 2002.

[29] S. Brin, R. Motwani, J. Ullman, and S. Tsur. Dynamic itemset counting and implication rules for market basket data. *SIGMOD Record*, 6(2):962–969, June 1987.

[30] A. Schuster and R. Wolff. Communication-efficient distributed mining of association rules. *Data Mining and Knowledge Discovery*, 8(2):171–196, March 2004.

[31] A. Srivastava, E.-H. Han, V. Kumar, and V. Singh. Parallel formulations of decision-tree classification algorithms. *Data Mining and Knowledge Discovery: An International Journal*, 3(3):237–261, September 1999.

[32] Mohammed J. Zaki. Parallel and distributed association mining: A survey. *IEEE Concurrency*, 7(4):14–25, 1999.

[33] M.J. Zaki, S. Parthasarathy, M. Ogihara, and W. Li. Parallel algorithms for discovery of association rules. *Data Mining and Knowledge Discovery*, 1(4): 343–373, 1997.

[34] Distributed and Ubiquitous Data Mining. http://www.umbc.edu/ddm/wiki/Distributed-and-Ubiquitous-Data-Mining.

Chapter 9

User-Centered Biological Information Location by Combining User Profiles and Domain Knowledge

Jeffrey E. Stone, Xindong Wu, and Marc Greenblatt

Contents

9.1   Introduction

The burgeoning amount of biological information (e.g., the published literature, genome and proteome projects) is confronting researchers with challenges in dealing with this large volume of complicated data. With the advance of technologies in both the biological and computer sciences, universities and research centers are producing a huge amount of experimental data, diverse new discoveries, and related publications. For instance, the BioNetbook (BioNetbook) has recognized and collected biological information databases around the world, now totaling 1750 and growing. In addition, they have recognized 8048 relevant Web pages including bibliographical materials, analysis tools, software, and courses in biological research. In their 2004 annual database issue, *Nucleic Acids Research* has recognized biological information storage sites around the world, classified them into 11 categories of biological information, and listed 548 Web sites under operation (Galperin, 2004). These databases, dispersed in different locations, serve important roles in modern research including the storage of experimental data, the maintenance of information, and the integration of diverse data sources. Researchers often review multiple publications and other databases to arrive at a comprehensive understanding and generate or validate their hypotheses. In this model, biological phenomena may be viewed as being composed of a number of subdisciplines (e.g., structural biology, genomics, proteomics, and biochemistry). However, to obtain a coherent picture of biological phenomena at the molecular, cellular, and organism levels, one must look at both the attributes and the relationships among them. To do that currently requires finding which databases contain the relevant information and then searching through the databases one by one.

Biological information is a knowledge-intensive subject. Some Web sites provide biological information by listing a number of databases, arranged by category, and entrust the user with all the search responsibilities. Although public data repositories such as the National Center for Biotechnology Information (NCBI) and the Protein Data Bank (PDB) integrate several databases on one site and contain much of the publicly held biological data, these sites still face difficult problems caused by a flood of new and diverse data and variation in format. In addition, they suffer from a lack of robustness in search techniques for highly interconnected databases, such as being stranded during a series of search processes. Some requests inherently require going through a complicated serial search on highly interrelated databases. Under these circumstances, researchers have a hard time locating useful information in an efficient way and keeping themselves informed of updates. As data acquisition from new experimental techniques (such as microarrays) flourishes, the problem of finding the right information gets worse.

Our digital library approach in this chapter begins with a centralized, structured view of a conventional library, and provides access to the digital library via the Internet, thus maintaining the advantages of decentralization, rapid evolution, and flexibility of the Web. The application is a J2EE Web application built using the model view controller (MVC) architecture on a Tomcat server with JDBC connections to a MySQL database. The core of our project is a knowledge object modeling of data repositories, and an agent architecture that provides advanced services by combining data mining capabilities. The knowledge objects are defined to be an integration of the object-oriented paradigm with rules, the proper integration of which provides a flexible and powerful environment for deductive retrieval and pattern matching.

To make personalized service possible, a user profile representing the preferences of an individual user is constructed based upon past activities, goals indicated by the user, and options. Utilizing these user profiles, our system will make relevant information available to the user in an appropriate form, amount, and level of detail, and especially with minimal user effort.

The rest of this chapter is organized as follows. Section 9.2 describes the concept of object modeling and how it relates to our system. Section 9.3 demonstrates how a semantic network can be used to provide a knowledge base for our system and to control the vocabulary of our system. Section 9.4 begins with a discussion of common user profiling techniques and then describes the decision tree algorithm for generating user rules. We then describe the system architecture for our digital library in Section 9.5. Section 9.6 provides a comparison of related systems and we conclude in Section 9.7 with a description of how our digital library works and some areas where it can be improved upon.

9.2   Knowledge Object Modeling

Biological information can be broken down and represented in forms of objects with the integration of logic rules. Each object can have a set of rules that govern its behavior and appearance, as well as communication to other objects. Association links between objects can be represented in the form of rules in knowledge objects and used to conduct heuristic search over the databases.

The first task in developing a knowledge object model for Web-based biological information is to include a means for working with different forms of media. This model will be the first step toward building a manageable system for our digital library system in which biological data can be easily stored, extended, reordered, assembled, and disassembled on a component basis. The model will also make accessible properties that might be important to the user, especially in searching or classifying biological information.

The design criteria of the model will be completeness, compactness, and simplicity. In this project, the model is restricted to cover a few different media types

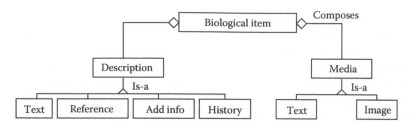

FIGURE 9.1:   Schema of a knowledge object model for biological information.

including images and text. The number of classes, their attributes, and methods will be kept to the minimum. Generic classes will be used wherever possible, inheritance will be used, composition of different building blocks may be merged into one class, and convenience functions and attributes will ideally be kept to none.

Based on previous work on object-oriented modeling of paper-based documents (Nguyen et al., 1998), Figure 9.1 shows a preliminary design of the object diagram of our biological object model, using the object modeling technique notation (Rumbaugh et al., 1991).

According to this model, a biological item will be decomposed into knowledge objects (classes or objects for short), each holding an internal state and a well-defined behavior. The object's internal state will be defined by attributes and constraints, and its behavior by rules and methods. The biological item object will represent a variety of biological data including annotation and publications, and will be constructed by the basic building block of description. Instances of the biological item class at the top level of the hierarchy will correspond to the most general form of biological data. It will be designed to completely cover all types of biological data in digital libraries, including images and text, and ranging from page images to interactive and compound documents. The biological item object can be composed of some description objects and some media objects, or just one or the other.

A description object, inheriting the aggregation relationship to itself from the biological item, can in turn contain itself recursively. A biological item will thus be composed of a recursive chain of description objects, which can be assembled, disassembled, and reordered, allowing for the whole document to be modified, extended, or truncated on a component basis, without losing the coherence of its overall structure. Description will be the generic class for all structural components of a biological item, such as text, reference, additional information, and so on. Our model will therefore allow for organizational components such as a description containing several parts, a part containing several subparts, etc., commonly found in biological databases. Since all these structural components share the same properties and behavior, it is most appropriate to have one single representative class. This design will make the model simpler and more compact. It will give authors more flexibility when defining their own biological item since the model will not differentiate between various structural components. It will also support the interconnected nature of biological information that refers and reuses passages and components in an integrated Web structure.

The above model will also make available presentation components, by defining them as child classes of description. A description object can thus be presented in a number of different ways: text chunks, references, additional information, and so on.

Media objects will hold the real contents that make up the digital library. Their content can be unstructured, raw materials that will be used to fill in the biological item objects or their description components. The actual data type of the content will be defined in the offspring classes of media. It can be any multimedia type such as text or images. This content can be semantically incomplete, that is, not meaningful to human readers. For example, it can be a fragment of text, which is a part of a paper. This semantic incompleteness will be reflected in the object design by the fact that no title or heading is required for an object of the media branch. Offspring objects of the media class, representing different media types, can therefore be inserted at arbitrary places in a biological item object. This concept will be applicable to all kinds of media types. Consider a paper with an image inserted halfway. If the paper is defined as one biological item object, then it must consist of three media objects of two broken text pieces and one image. We assume in our project that database personnel can index every document object and its parts in some way and save them in the database.

The design of our knowledge object model will allow the mapping of all types of biological data. The classes will account for any type of biological items and their relationships. Each offspring class will actually be a merge of many detailed parts that are to be composed in the form of a URL list to describe the biological information under consideration. New classes will be created if there are important properties or methods that need to be distinguished between them. The model will thus be both complete and compact, since it covers all biological items within the scope while the number of classes is kept minimal. Simplicity will be achieved by compactness, and also by the fact that the model design is based on the familiar and well-developed object-oriented paradigm and technologies of database systems, with many *de facto* standards for structural and presentational components. With this solid base, the model will be robust to changes and simple to use.

A significant problem for most biological databases and libraries is that of annotation. The detailed information needed to describe biochemical processes and genetics is much more complex than the information of the taxonomy of living species that Linnaeus developed in the eighteenth century. We need ways to transfer this information efficiently and without propagating error. Figure 9.2 shows a preliminary design of the knowledge structure of our targeted biological information. This design is based on the biological structures embodied in the target databases and is represented as a class hierarchy. At the top is the most general knowledge concept that could be decomposed into detailed and related knowledge modules. Each node in this structure is represented as a biological item introduced above.

Biologists are interested in specific genes and their products. Therefore, a biological object is divided into genetic information, gene ontology, and structure information. Each of these classes is further divided into more detailed classes that give the finer details of biological information. The genetic information will contain the DNA sequence, the gene's location in the genome, and its homologues. The gene ontology

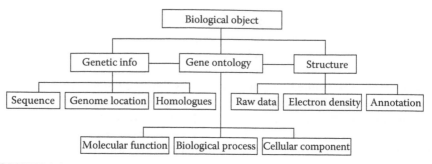

FIGURE 9.2:   Biological knowledge structures.

information comes from the Gene Ontology Consortium and contains information about molecular functions, biological processes, and cellular components. The structure information will include raw data, electron density, and structure annotation. Other information provided will be text, references, history, and information about possible relations to diseases. With this approach we will attempt to outline a biologist's view of the gene.

The design of the knowledge structure will allow both the depiction of the overall knowledge underlying the biological process and allow the system to efficiently search the right information in the databases. This structure will help achieve a more focused, context-based retrieval over the dispersed databases.

9.2.1   Dealing with Documents Prepared in Different Formats

Biological items linked to our digital library system are simple Web links, but our object model approach could be further developed to allow their content to be assembled into a composite Web page. The objects would be allowed to take a selection of different popular formats (such as HTML, SGML, and XML), and conversion from one format to another will not be necessary. This would provide authors with flexibility in preparing their data. Allowing items in different formats requires the agents in the digital library system to be familiar with these formats. For example, the indexing agent will traverse and index all relevant items linked to the digital library system. Future projects will design an interface for each allowed format to facilitate the agents to visit and process items in these formats. Since systems that can convert their files to HTML exist, it seems possible to study our research issues using only HTML in this project. However, making everyone use HTML (or any other format) would limit the presentation medium substantially and increase the overhead for authors. The premise of the World Wide Web and Internet was to allow heterogeneous formats. The idea of allowing different formats in this project is to free the authors of any indexing burden and make formats, like images, all indexable.

Unfortunately, not all resources are indexable. For sites that are not indexable, our library will use the entry page as the resource. While this may not seem like the ideal solution, there is in fact a considerable need for a way to search for appropriate databases. Most people know about the NCBI site, but there are literally thousands of relevant biological portals available now. Many of these go unnoticed by the vast majority of researchers.

9.2.2 Deriving the Knowledge Structure from Biologists

The knowledge structure will need to be designed through consultation between biologists and computer scientists. The need for this representation quickly increases with data complexity. This is due to many factors including the absence of permanent and unique identification of the objects, the existence of many-to-many relationships between different biological concepts such as genes and proteins and their relations to diseases and drugs, the quickly evolving knowledge of biological phenomena and data, the complex relationships between biological elements and phenomena, and the large variety of biological data types. The knowledge structure would have categories such as resource type, organism, biological domain, relationships, and associations. Some nodes might contain many or even all of these categories while others may have only one or two (Figure 9.3).

A hierarchy structure will further define each of these subcategories. For example, when a document about a specific gene is included in our system the biological domain would be genomic. However, we can further classify a gene by molecular functions, biological processes, and cellular components. Each of these in turn can be subdivided further. Molecular functions could be any number of functions such as transcription factors, cell adhesion molecule, etc.

We will be using the Unified Medical Language System (UMLS) semantic network as a base for our knowledge structure. To this base, we will be adding additional nodes where appropriate to better describe the disparate databases used in our system. Where applicable we will use established open-source schemas such as the Gene Ontology Consortium and the Object Protocol Model.

The knowledge object modeling in Wu and Cai (2000) is an integration of the object-oriented paradigm with logic rules, in which the class and inheritance features

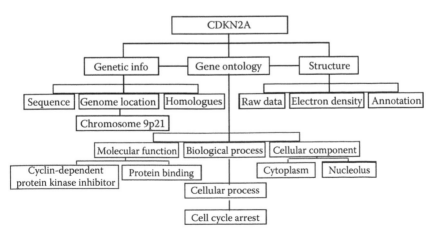

FIGURE 9.3: Knowledge structure for the CDKN24 gene.

of the object-oriented paradigm can assist users to describe and define biological information more naturally and to emphasize the semantic rather than the syntactic content of applications. The encapsulation and dynamic binding of the object-oriented paradigm will make the resultant software more maintainable, adaptable, and recyclable. Rule-based programming, meanwhile, can express constraints within and between biological information components very efficiently in its rules and provides inference power to the system. The proper integration of the object-oriented paradigm and rule-based programming will provide a flexible and powerful environment, as rule-based components provide facilities for deductive retrieval and pattern matching, and object-oriented components provide a clear intuitive structure for documents in the form of class hierarchies.

9.2.3   Alternatives to Knowledge Objects

There have been many research efforts reported in the literature (Bouziane and Hsu, 1997; May and Lausen, 2000) on the integration of the rule-based paradigm with object-oriented programming and on coupling rule bases and databases using either the entity-relationship or object-oriented data models, as thoroughly reviewed in Wu and Cai (2000). There have also been quite a number of commercial software packages (such as KEE, Prolog++ (Moss, 1994), ILOG Rules (ILOG, 1998), and CLIPS (Giarratano, 1993)) that support both rules and objects. Among others, agent-oriented programming (Shoham, 1993) and frame-based systems (Fikes and Kehler, 1985) are along the line of incorporating rules into objects. However, in our knowledge object modeling, we do not specialize the object-oriented features in any way, in contrast to agent-oriented programming and frame-based systems.

In knowledge objects, rules access objects' internal states and their global contexts. The rules in knowledge objects derive new data from existing data as well as expressing constraints of the object model. Objects' constraints are relationships between entities of an object model—entities here are objects, classes, attributes, links, and associations. Constraints exist both inside and outside objects. An important characteristic of knowledge object modeling is that users can be given explicit control of the object hierarchy to customize the system to their particular needs, which includes letting users select among different methods for a particular task such as displaying the results.

9.3   Semantic Network

In the construction of a dictionary, we encountered several difficulties due to the complex nature of biological data. These problems include multiple names for the same entity, the dependency of the biological state in which the function is taking place, and multiple functions for the same protein. To overcome these difficulties and to add additional functionality to our digital library, we have developed our dictionary as a semantic network.

Although there have been several ontologies developed for describing biological data, there is still no published knowledge base that can be used to cover the number of disparate databases that are used by biomedical professionals. Yu et al. (1999) adapted the UMLS semantic network to cover genomic knowledge and Hafner et al. (1994) also used the UMLS as a basic building block for their system of representing biomedical literature. Most other biomedical resource systems such as Genbank and the PDB contain crucial facts, but do not contain information about the concepts and relationships of the many interrelated terms (PDB).

The Gene Ontology Consortium has developed a large controlled vocabulary for the unification of genetic concepts and terminology. This controlled vocabulary along with several others is now part of the massive UMLS metathesaurus. These ontologies provide the vocabulary for the description of many biological concepts such as the annotation of the molecular function, biological process, and cellular component of gene products. This metathesaurus is a big step toward the unification of biological knowledge; however, it is simply far too complex to provide a federated solution to unify biological databases.

The structure of the gene ontology vocabulary provides a good example of the vocabularies that make up the UMLS metathesaurus. The gene ontology controlled vocabulary is based on the annotation of gene products. A gene product is a physical entity. Gene products may be RNA or proteins. These gene products may have many molecular functions. A molecular function is a description of what a gene product does. One drawback of the gene ontology system is that the molecular function only describes what a gene product has the potential to do without regard to where or when this function may take place. Such semantics as to where and when a function takes place could be contained within a semantic network.

The National Library of Medicine (NLM) has a long-term project to build a UMLS that is comprised of three major parts: the UMLS metathesaurus, the SPECIALIST Lexicon, and the UMLS semantic network. The metathesaurus provides a large integrated distribution of over 100 biomedical vocabularies and classifications. The lexicon contains syntactic information for many terms, component words, and English words, including verbs not contained in the metathesaurus. The semantic network contains information about the types or categories to which all metathesaurus concepts have been assigned and the permissible relationships among these types (UMLS). The UMLS has been used successfully in many applications mostly involving scientific literature.

The UMLS semantic network provides an ideal framework for federating disparate databases. However, the current structure of the UMLS semantic network is most useful for scientific literature and clinical trial information. If one is trying to use the UMLS semantic network for federation of several disparate databases, they will find the network is not sufficiently broad to cover the multiple items in all of these databases.

We have therefore decided that to best suit the needs of our digital library system, we must develop our own controlled language system. To do this, we have started with the basic framework of the UMLS semantic network and then pruned some of the less important details and added new concepts and relationships where needed to cover the databases in our digital library.

9.3.1 UMLS Semantic Network

Our semantic network is comprised of nodes representing semantic types and relationships between these nodes. Each node represents a category of either a biological entity or an event. The entities and events used in our semantic network result from a merging of some of the concept names in the NLM's UMLS and the Gene Ontology Consortium's controlled vocabulary.

Most relationships in our system will be of the is-a variety, such as a human is-a organism. However, many biological entities do not fit into a simple hierarchical structure. Therefore, we need additional relationships between multiple hierarchies to accurately represent the complexity of biological data. These interconnecting relationships and hierarchies make up our semantic network.

The first major entity category is that of an organism. This represents a simple taxonomic hierarchy of organisms. Another category is that of anatomical structure. This hierarchy represents embryonic structures, anatomical abnormalities, body parts, organs, organ components, tissues, cells, and cellular components including genes. The cellular component hierarchy will be mostly taken from the Gene Ontology Consortium's hierarchy. A third major category is that of a conceptual entity. This category will include items such as temporal, qualitative, quantitative, functional, and spatial concepts. We will also have a category for medical findings including symptoms and laboratory results.

We also have categories of events including activities, phenomena, and processes. Activities include health care activities such as laboratory, diagnostic, therapeutic, and preventative procedures; and research activities, such as research techniques and methods. The phenomenon or process category includes biological functions and pathologic functions. Biological functions include physiologic functions such as organ or tissue functions, cellular functions or subcellular component function, and molecular functions such as genetic function.

The events category is a crucial component of our semantic network since the information in many of the most important databases of interests to biologists relate to the information in this category. This is also the most difficult category to design due to the lack of a clear hierarchical structure of events. Again, we have borrowed from the Gene Ontology Consortium to develop the molecular and biological functions; however, we have chosen to truncate the tree structure of their system to prevent the relationships between these functions from getting too complex.

The relationships that tie all of these hierarchies together complete our semantic network. The relationship links between these hierarchies allow us to represent knowledge about an entity or an event. For example, we may represent a gene as a cellular component that is in the hierarchy of anatomical structures. This gene will produce a gene product. That gene product is also a cellular component that may have a biological function and possibly a molecular function. The gene may be part of many different organisms and it may be associated with a pathological function.

Initially we will start with very basic relationships among these hierarchies. We will rely on only top-level relationships such as the is-a relationships that make up the various hierarchies and the associated-with relationships that tie these hierarchies together. We will also build the next layer of relationships below the associated-with layer. This will comprise of physically related-to, spatially related-to, functionally related-to, temporally related-to, and conceptually related-to relationships. These relationship links have been built through a restructuring of the UMLS concepts and the Gene Ontology Consortium's hierarchy.

Our semantic network is similar in structure to the UMLS, but is able to classify the biological information in far greater detail. This is especially true with genomic data. The UMLS was designed by the NLM and has naturally taken the view of that institution on how to classify data. We have focused more on the end users and how they would view the data. Therefore, we have removed many of the nodes that have to deal with government regulation, legal information, and health care institution information and have focused more on pure biomedical research information. Other controlled vocabularies are specific for one branch of biomedical research such as the genomic research modeled by the Gene Ontology Consortium. Our system is based not on the research areas themselves, but rather on the data that will be included in our digital library system. Therefore, our system will evolve over time as more items are added to our digital library.

9.3.2 Dictionary Terms Reside at Each Node

Every node in our system will have a list of distinct concept classes. Each distinct concept class will have a list of synonymous words and phrases. These terms are primarily obtained from the medical subject headings compiled by the NLM. Every separate meaning will appear as its own concept class, but a node may have multiple concept classes. All the concept classes taken together will contain the entire set of terms in our dictionary. It is at this level that each item in our digital library will be classified into our semantic network.

Every entry in our digital library will have a list of these terms associated with it. Most items in biological databases are designed for keyword-based queries and therefore already have this information associated with them.

9.3.3 Decisions on What Concepts and Relationships to Include

As stated earlier, we have started with the basic structure of the UMLS. Starting with this system we remove those items that are too detailed to be included in such a system by manually pruning the "entity" and "associated-with" hierarchies. This careful pruning is done with a base set of databases in mind. These include the popular PDB, the Online Mendelian Inheritance in Man (OMIM), and mutation databases for the p53 and CDKN2a (p16) tumor suppressor genes (OMIM)(p53DB)(CDKN2a) to demonstrate our network's usefulness with private data.

Using these databases, we identify the corresponding types in our truncated UMLS semantic network along with any concepts not included by manual inspection. Where no concepts are included, we add new types and determine where they should be placed in the semantic network (Figures 9.4 and 9.5).

We have found that many of the entity semantic types of the UMLS semantic network are beyond the scope of our project. We have therefore performed a careful manual pruning of the network to remove those nodes that are not of interest. Most of the items removed pertained to specific medical equipment and physical health care facilities. We removed the node for the manufactured object and all the children of this node. However, since the node for clinical drug fell under this node, we would have to reinsert this node elsewhere in the network. The most logical place for this is a new node under chemical substance. We also removed the nodes of Finding, and several of the subnodes under the Event category such as a machine activity and an educational activity.

We inspected likewise the semantic relationships of the UMLS for areas to prune. We found less to prune here, but there were a few items, such as evaluation-of, analyzes, assesses-effect-of, and measures (Figure 9.6 and 9.7).

The information contained in the PDB is primarily structural data of proteins. However, the current UMLS semantic network does not contain structural information. We therefore have added a node for protein structure under the anatomical structure node. This new node will have four child nodes for primary, secondary, tertiary, and quaternary structure protein structures. The typical item in the PDB will be a "three-dimensional (3D) structure" and it will have an associated "1D structure" and a "2D structure". Items within the PDB might also have the relationship of being similar to another protein's structure or function. We therefore added semantic relationships for similarly-related-to, with its child nodes of physically-similar-to and functionally-similar-to.

We used a similar approach with information contained in the OMIM database (OMIM). This database of genetic disorders in man is rich in information; however, most of this information is structured in the form of text documents. This creates some difficulty in mapping the information to the semantic network since these pages are dynamic and the underlying database is not accessible to the public. Nonetheless, there is some basic information available on each document that can be searched efficiently. This information includes allelic variants, gene map disorders, clinical synopsis, and references. The allelic variants are a "physical" relationship whereas the clinical synopsis fits into the "causes" relationship and also under the disease or syndrome event. Much of the information within the OMIM database would fit nicely under the Gene Ontology Consortium's controlled vocabulary, which has been incorporated into our system.

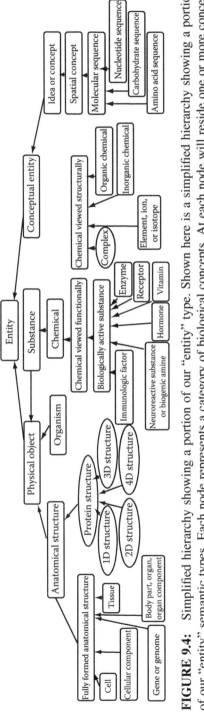

FIGURE 9.4: Simplified hierarchy showing a portion of our "entity" type. Shown here is a simplified hierarchy showing a portion of our "entity" semantic type. Each node represents a category of biological concepts. At each node will reside one or more concept classes, which will contain different terminology with the same or similar meaning. The hierarchical structure is represented by means of "is-a" linkages. The rectangular boxes come from the NLM's UMLS project. Oval nodes are new types that come from different ontologies outside of the UMLS project as well as types that we have designed ourselves.

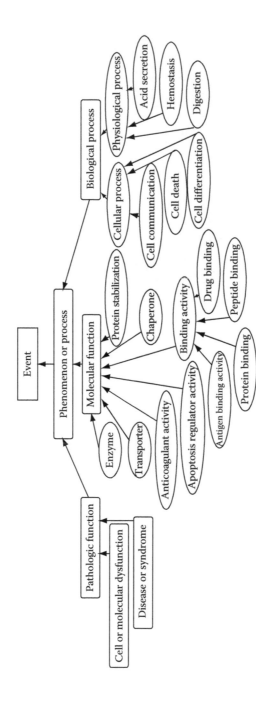

FIGURE 9.5: Semantic types to represent events. Another important semantic type is that of an "event." Many of the added nodes for the event type originate from the Gene Ontology Consortium's controlled vocabulary. The hierarchy shown is only a small portion of the entire event hierarchy. Each child of the event type has several children, many of whom have several children of their own.

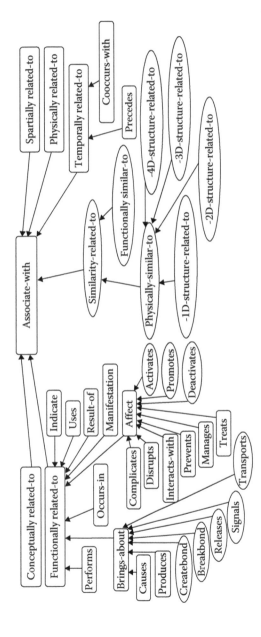

FIGURE 9.6: Semantic relationships to tie the semantic net together. In addition to the "is-a" relationships that represent a hierarchical structure, we also have "associate-with" relationships to represent the many nonhierarchical relationships biological items may have to one another. The importance of these relationships is one of the reasons why we chose a semantic network to represent the terms in our dictionary.

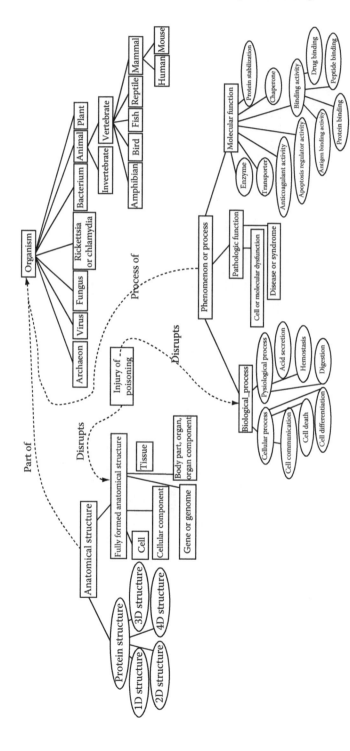

FIGURE 9.7: Partial schema of the overall semantic network. Shown here is a partial schema of the overall semantic network. Solid lines are is-a links whereas the dashed lines indicate a category of associate-with relationships. A user friendly interface is being developed through which the user may browse the semantic network or enter terms to find relationships to these terms.

9.4 User Profiling and Recommendation Agents

9.4.1 Collecting User Information

Capturing user preferences and providing adaptive information access to digital libraries (Brusilovsky et al., 2007) can be difficult tasks. Simply asking the users what they want can be obtrusive and error prone. In fact, the user might not even know what they really want. On the other hand, monitoring user behavior may be unobtrusive but can also be computationally time consuming and discovering meaningful patterns is difficult. Yet capturing user information is critical for the recommender system of our digital library.

User profiling methods can be classified as either knowledge based or behavior based. Knowledge-based methods employ questionnaires or interviews to dynamically match users to one of a number of different static models of users. Behavior-based approaches seek to capture the user's behavior and apply machine learning techniques to discover useful patterns in the behavior. This approach will need to log the user's behavior in some manner.

The user profiling employed by recommendation agents is primarily behavior based. With most recommendation agents, a binary, two-class model that represents what a user likes or dislikes is used. Machine learning techniques are then used to discover meaningful information about the user. In our system this meaningful information is in the form of rules. The recommendation agent will then use these rules to recommend items that he or she may be interested in.

The user knowledge can be collected either implicitly or explicitly. Implicit knowledge acquisition would be the preferred mechanism since it has little or no impact on the user's normal work. Analyzing the click stream as a user navigates through our system might provide one method to collect this information in an unobtrusive manner. This type of knowledge acquisition requires some degree of interpretation to understand the user's real interests. This is an inherently error-prone process. How do we, for instance, determine if a user is lingering on one item because they are truly interested or if they were interrupted while navigating the site?

Explicit knowledge acquisition, on the other hand, requires the user to interrupt their normal work to provide feedback. This may be undesirable, but will generally provide the system with high confidence information since the users themselves provide the information. This feedback is most often in the form of a questionnaire on the relevance, interest, and quality of an item. It may also come in the form of programming where the user is asked to create filter rules either visually or via a programming language.

Our system utilizes a combination of these different systems. When the user performs a search on our system, they may mark items as interesting. These items are then saved in the user profile. At any time the user may choose to use this profile to generate new rules. Due to the imprecision of this method, there is a third step where the user provides additional feedback on which rules to add to the profile.

9.4.2 Weka Data Mining Package

The Weka machine learning libraries (Witten and Frank, 2000) are an open source collection of data mining programs implemented in Java and issued under the GNU General Public License. Since they are open source, the algorithms can either be applied directly to a dataset or called from your own Java code. Weka contains tools for data preprocessing, classification, regression, clustering, association rules, and visualization. It is also well suited for developing new machine learning schemes. This system is available free of charge and provides tools for a good number of the machine learning algorithms that have been developed to date.

Data that are used by the system are described by a specific ASCII text file called an attribute-relation file format (ARFF) file. This format requires each attribute to be declared with an "@attribute" tag. The format also expects a name for each attribute and a set of allowable values. This could be real numbers, but it is most often a set of classifications. The data section of the file is denoted with an "@data" tag and the data is entered in a comma-delimitated fashion matching the order of the @attribute tags.

Our system creates this ARFF file dynamically based on the user profile and knowledge information contained in each object in the library. The attributes are all of the keywords used to describe the items in our digital library. Each of these attributes is a Boolean, true or false attribute. The final attribute is the class for the item. For the recommendation agent, this class is either a yes or a no indicating the interest the user has for this item. For the data section of the ARFF file, each item in our library is listed with the set of attributes pertaining to which keywords are associated with the item and a yes or no depending on the user's prior interest to this item.

9.4.3 J48 Decision Tree Algorithm

Our system builds user rules with the C4.5 tree algorithm developed by Quinlan (1993). The Weka implementation of the C4.5 algorithm is contained in the J48 package. The basic algorithm for decision tree induction is a greedy algorithm that constructs decision trees in a top-down recursive divide-and-conquer manner. The C4.5 algorithm is summarized in Figure 9.8.

9.4.3.1 Basic Strategy for Decision Trees

The basic strategy for building decisions trees can be described as follows:

- The tree starts as a single node representing the training samples (Step 1 in Figure 9.8).

- If the samples are all of the same class, then the node becomes a leaf and is labeled with that class (Steps 2 and 3).

- Otherwise, the algorithm uses an entropy-based measure known as gain ratio (Quinlan 1993) as a heuristic for selecting the attribute that will best separate the samples into individual classes (Step 6). This attribute becomes the "test"

Algorithm: Generate_decision_tree. Generate a decision tree from the given training data.

Input: The training samples, *samples*, represented by discrete-valued attributes; the set of candidate attributes, *attribute-list*.

Output: A decision tree.

Method:

(1)   create a node N;
(2)   if *samples* are all of the same class, C, then
(3)   return N as a leaf node labeled with the class C;
(4)   if *attribute-list* is empty then
(5)   return N as a leaf-node labeled with the most common class
                in *samples*;
//majority voting
(6)   select *test-attribute*, the attribute among *attribute-list* with the highest
                information gain;
(7)   label node N with *test-attribute*;
(8)   for each known value a_i of *test-attribute* //partition the samples
(9)   grow a branch from node N for the condition *test-attribute* = a_i;
(10)   let s_i be the set of samples in *samples* for which *test-attribute* =
                a_i; //a partion
(11)   if s_i is empty then
(12)   attach a leaf labeled with the most common class in
                        samples;
(13)   else attach the node returned by Generate_decision_tree(s_i,
                attribute-list-test-attribute);

FIGURE 9.8:   C4.5 decision tree algorithm.

or "decision" attribute at the node (Step 7). In this version of the algorithm, all attributes are categorical, that is, discrete valued. Continuous-valued attributes must be discretized.

- A branch is created for each known value of the test attribute, and the samples are partitioned accordingly (Steps 8 through 10).

- The algorithm uses the above process recursively to form a decision tree for the samples at each partition. Once an attribute has occurred at a node, it need not be considered in any of the node's descendents (Step 13).

- The recursive partitioning stops only when any one of the following conditions is true:

  - All samples for a given node belong to the same class (Steps 2 and 3).

  - There are no remaining attributes on which the samples may be further partitioned (Step 4). In this case, majority voting is employed (Step 5). This involves converting the given node into a leaf and labeling it with the class in majority among the samples. Alternatively, the class distribution of the node samples may be stored.

- There are no samples for the branch *test-attribute* = a_i (Step 11). In this case, a leaf is created with the majority class in samples (Step 12).

9.4.3.2 Extracting Classification Rules from Decision Trees

The knowledge represented in decision trees can be extracted and represented in the form of classification IF–THEN rules. One rule is created for each path from the root to a leaf node. Each attribute-value pair along a given path forms a conjunction in the rule antecedent ("IF" part). The leaf node holds the class prediction, forming the rule consequent ("THEN" part). The IF–THEN rules may be easier for humans to understand, particularly if the given tree is very large.

9.5 System Architecture

There are many factors involved in determining the architecture of a digital library. In making this decision, one must determine how the system will be used and who the users will be. We want the system to be robust and scalable, but we also have to face the reality of a limited budget. We also want the system to be available to users throughout the University of Vermont (UVM) campus and also users from other institutions. The system must also combine several different agents together in a seamless manner, some of which may be difficult to modify.

Based on an analysis of the use of a system such as ours, we decided that a Web application would be the ideal architecture for our digital library. Since the Weka data mining package was written in Java, we decided on a J2EE application server. We used the Tomcat server to host our Web application. This server is a free, open-source system available under the GNU Public License and is the reference implementation of the servlet 2.3 and JSP 1.2 specifications. Tomcat is quite powerful as either a stand-alone Web server or embedded within an Apache server.

Tomcat can recognize standard HTML files, Java server pages (JSP) or Java servlets. Servlets are Java technology's answer to common gateway interface (CGI) programming. They are programs that run on a Web server, acting as a middle layer between a request coming from a Web browser or other HTTP client and databases or applications on the HTTP server. It can be argued that Java servlets are more efficient, easier to use, more powerful, more portable, safer, and cheaper than traditional CGI and other technologies. JSP allow one to include Java code inside an HTML page. This provides the author with close control over the Web design.

9.5.1 MVC Architecture Design

Several problems can arise when applications contain a mixture of data access code, business logic code, and presentation code. Such applications are difficult to maintain, because interdependencies between all of the components cause strong ripple effects whenever a change is made anywhere. High coupling makes classes difficult or impossible to reuse because they depend on so many other classes. Adding new data views often requires reimplementing or cutting and pasting business logic code, which then requires maintenance in multiple places. Data access code suffers from the same problem, being cut and pasted among business logic methods.

The MVC design pattern solves these problems by decoupling data access, business logic, and data presentation and user interaction. As the name suggests, there are three main components of the MVC design. The model, view, and controller are described as follows:

- Model: The model represents enterprise data and the business rules that govern access to and updates of this data. Often the model serves as a software approximation to a real-world process, so simple real-world modeling techniques apply when defining the model.

- View: The view renders the contents of a model. It accesses enterprise data through the model and specifies how that data should be presented. It is the view's responsibility to maintain consistency in its presentation when the model changes. This can be achieved by using a push model, where the view registers itself with the model for change notifications, or a pull model, where the view is responsible for calling the model when it needs to retrieve the most current data.

- Controller: The controller translates interactions with the view into actions to be performed by the model. In a stand-alone GUI client, user interactions could be button clicks or menu selections, whereas in a Web application, they appear as GET and POST HTTP requests. The actions performed by the model include activating business processes or changing the state of the model. Based on the user interactions and the outcome of the model actions, the controller responds by selecting an appropriate view.

The separation of model and view allows multiple views to use the same enterprise model. Consequently, an enterprise application's model components are easier to implement, test, and maintain, since all access to the model goes through these components. In addition, the MVC architecture promotes reuse of model components. To support a new type of client, you simply write a view and some controller logic and wire them into the existing enterprise application. This type of design pattern will introduce some extra classes due to the separation of model, view, and controller. However, the benefits of code of reuse and ease of maintenance more than make up for this increase in complexity.

9.5.2 Components of Our Digital Library

The primary feature that sets our system apart from other systems is the recommendation agent. This agent will generate rules about the users and learn about the users' interests and preferences. The rules will be refined and improved through two learning processes: interactive incremental learning and silent incremental learning. Our system will first learn about a user's areas of interest by analyzing the user's declared interest topics and the user's visit records, and then assist the user in retrieving the right information. The user profile is composed of a set of biological terminologies coming from the knowledge structure and the dictionary. Interactive incremental learning will function in cycles that interact with the user. The system will prompt the user with a set of related documents that are likely of the user's interest, and ask for feedback on the level of interest in each of these documents. Considering the feedback, the system will make changes to its search and selection heuristics and improve its performance.

Our system will work differently from search engines and other kinds of agents like WebWatcher (Joachims et al., 1995) and World Wide Web Worm (World Wide Web Worm) that help the user on the global Web. First, through incremental learning of the user's characteristics or interest areas, the system will become an assistant to the user in retrieving relevant information. Second, our library will have the potential to reduce user accessing and retrieval time, by displaying a list of changes that have been made since the user's last visit. Finally, the system can be easily adopted for other digital libraries. This can be accomplished by adding a different knowledge source for the dictionary.

Figure 9.9 shows the design of our digital library system structure, which is a modification of an existing prototype (Ngu and Wu, 1997).

9.5.2.1   Access Log

Most Web sites allow global user access and have logging facilities in place (Pitkow and Bharat, 1994) to record users' access details. The access log of a Web site records all Web transaction/request services by the Web server. The three main elements for each record are: the machine name with its Internet address from which the access is performed, the date/time of access, and the Web page being accessed.

9.5.2.2   Dictionary

The dictionary has been a key focus of our research. The dictionary is implemented as a semantic network of biological terminology and represents the knowledge source for our library. It will be used by various agents including the recommendation agent. All keywords that describe items in our digital library must come from this dictionary; however, the use of concept classes allows for broad leeway in these keywords. Section 9.3 discusses the design and implementation of the dictionary in detail.

As described in Section 9.3, the semantic network not only contains the terminology used in the keywords, but also their relationships. This will allow for the implementation of several intelligent agents to provide additional functionality in future versions of the library. In this version of the library, the primary relationship is at the concept class level. For each keyword, we search the metathesaurus for the preferred term and substitute this term for the keyword. This will allow the system

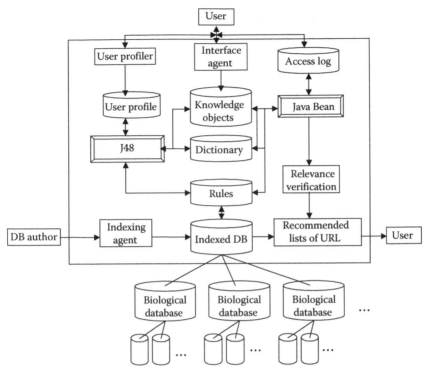

FIGURE 9.9: System architecture design. An overall schema of our digital library system. The J48 induction engine will be the "brain" of the digital library. It will generate rules in the form of conjunctions of keywords in the dictionary to identify the user's areas of interest, and forward the rules to the user profiles. The dictionary component of our digital library will be provided by the terminology contained at the nodes of our semantic network.

to find not only those items that have the same keywords, but also those that share the same meaning. This is a large improvement over the standard keyword searching employed by most library systems. We have chosen to do this keyword substitution at runtime and not by altering the keywords associated with an item. Although this will make the system a little slower, it will allow for changes in the semantic network to propagate throughout the application and will preserve the original information provided with each item in the library.

In our system we have implemented the semantic network in a relational database. This database includes tables for both the semantic network and for the metathesaurus of terms at the concept class level. Each term has a unique identifier and a concept identifier. All terms that have the same concept identifier have similar meanings and make up the concept class for those terms. Each concept class has one and only one term that is the preferred term for that concept class and is stored in a table of preferred terms indexed by the unique concept identifiers. A separate table links the concept identifiers to a list of different relationship identifiers. These relationship identifiers are stored in a table structure similar to that of the concepts.

9.5.2.3 Weka Data Mining Package

The Weka data mining package will serve as the "brain" of the discovery agent. It will take two input sets of documents; one set the user has seen and selected as interesting, and the other the user has not visited or has not found to be of interest. It will generate rules in the form of conjunctions of keywords in the dictionary to identify the user's areas of interest, and forward the rules to the user profiles.

9.5.2.4 Indexed Database

The indexed database will have an entry/index for each biological item in the digital library. We are using the MySQL database for the semantic network described, the user profile, and items in our library. Each entry in the database will have a pointer to the corresponding item, with a set of keywords from the dictionary to index the biological item, a date and time to show when the item was last modified, and a format indicator. The entries can be nested to allow for compound documents to be searched. In the future, we plan to employ the resource description framework (RDF) (W3C) to describe keyword properties of documents and compound documents, and integrate a commercial object-oriented database system for the indexed database, in order to manipulate large collections of documents effectively (Schatz et al., 1996).

9.5.2.5 Indexing Agent

Future versions of the library will employ this agent to traverse the digital library and index all relevant biological information according to the dictionary and store the results in the indexed database. It will incrementally refresh the indexes and automatically update indexing when document updates are forwarded by the database authors or administrators. How to generate and maintain the list of keywords for each document will be a crucial issue in future versions of this project.

9.5.2.6 Interface Agent

The interface, that is, what the user sees, will be developed using the "view" component of the MVC design and is implemented with JSP. The goal is to allow the user to interact easily with the system. The agent will provide the user with functions for navigation of the library, evaluation of retrieved documents, setting up user preferences, and a help system with hyperlinks using the semantic links between the keywords in the dictionary. We will also have a facility on the digital library interface for biological authors to submit relevant materials directly in electronic format.

9.5.2.7 User Profiles

Gathering the information that is thought to be of interest to the user is one of the most difficult tasks in digital library system development. A user profile will consist of the user's account details, areas of interest, access history, and the rules generated by Weka. Information about a user's interests describes the user's information needs in terms of information types and types of contents, and short-term and long-term interests. Since the domain is restricted to a very specific area of research, it would be useful in constructing user profiles to have information about each user. This personal data is a collection of user's personal identification data, such as user's name, status (student, researcher, etc.), user's current field of research, etc. More sophisticated information about user's interests are established by referring both to the knowledge structure and the dictionary. Each user can maintain more than one user profile, which enables the user to work on multiple subjects. One of them is assigned as a default profile that is running without specific selection of choice. To make this possible, we will provide an interface in which the user can switch the preference. Whenever the user switches the profile, the session is closed and a new session begins with the new profile.

9.5.2.8   User Machine with Web Browser

A Web user can access our digital library through a Java-enabled Web browser. Most modern Web browsers such as Microsoft Internet Explorer, Mozilla, and Netscape support Java.

9.5.3   Indexing Biological Information and Reporting Updates

How to generate and maintain the list of keywords for individual biological information is a crucial issue to the project, because the keywords are the indicators of information content to which the digital library is to have access, and if relevant keywords are missing, the system will not be able to assist the user. We assume that all the information in the databases is completely indexed by the database authors and database administrators. Any updates made by them are notified and sent to the indexed databases to appropriately update the indexing. At the same time, the updates are consulted with the user profiles and corresponding users for update notification are determined. During this decision making process, keywords in the user profiles are compared with those in the keyword dictionary and semantic links between these keywords. The relevance verification agent in Figure 9.9 will make use of the indexing facility. If a new document cannot be indexed properly by the keywords in the dictionary, the document will be considered irrelevant to the digital library.

9.6   Comparison with Related Work

A crucial factor in sharing of biological information among users in a consistent manner is whether a standardized framework exists and unambiguous information can be expressed and communicated. One existing method to capture the concepts

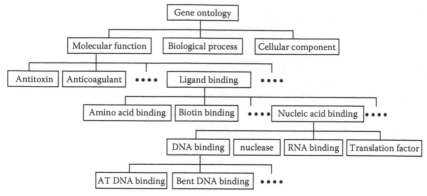

FIGURE 9.10: Gene ontology hierarchy.

and relationships between them is ontology. Ontologies have been used in artificial intelligence to describe a variety of domains. Initial endeavors to include ontology for biology can be found in Schulze-Kremer (1998) and Altman et al. (1998).

A dictionary for biology is one possibility for biological knowledge representation that reflects a specific view of the data. This ontology has been adopted in the TAMBIS project and the Gene Ontology Consortium's controlled vocabulary system. Stevens et al. (2000) designed a three-model hierarchy (Figure 9.10). Among the three models, the biological concept model, a knowledge base of biological terminology, is central to its architecture. This is basically used to drive query formulation and facilitate source integration in their system. However, in our project we will have an additional use for this, which is building and maintaining user profiles. Since the dictionary provides a scheme that can reason about the relationships between terms and their components, the terminologies in the dictionary can indicate the possible interests of the user at multiple levels of the subject category.

Assisting Web users by identifying their areas of interest has attracted the attention of quite a few recent research efforts. Several recent research projects (Balabanovic and Shoham, 1995) and Yan et al. (1996); WebMate (Chen and Sycara, 1998); Three-Descriptor Representation (Widyantoro et al., 2001); and Web Learner (Pazzani et al. 1995) also share similar ideas.

Balabanovic and Shoham (1995) developed a system that helps a Web user discover new sites that are of the user's interest. The system presents the user every day with a selection of Web pages that it thinks the user would find interesting. The user evaluates these Web pages and provides feedback for the system. The user's areas of interest are represented in the form of (keyword, weight) pairs, and each Web page is represented as a vector of weights for the keywords in a vector space.[*] From the user's feedback, the system knows more about his or her areas of interest and better serves the users in the future. If the user's feedback on a particular Web page is

---

[*] The vector space approach is one of the most promising paradigms and the best-known technique in information retrieval.

positive, the weights for relevant keywords of the Web page are increased, otherwise they are decreased. This system adds learning facilities to existing search engines, and as a global Web search agent does not avoid the general problems associated with search engines and Web robots. In addition, compared to our system, the (keyword, weight) pairs used in this system cannot represent logical relations between different keywords, such as ("data mining" AND "Internet") OR "rule induction." This type of logical expressions will be the starting point for knowledge representation and data mining in our system.

Yan et al. (1996) investigated a way to record and learn user access patterns in the area of designing online catalogues for electronic commerce. This approach identifies and categorizes user access patterns using unsupervised clustering techniques. User access logs are used to discover clusters of users that access similar pages. When a user comes, the system first identifies the user's pattern, and then dynamically reorganizes itself to suit the user by putting similar pages together. An (item, weight) vector, similar to the (keyword, weight) vector used to represent each Web page in Balabanovic and Shoham (1995), is used in Yan et al. (1996), to represent a user's access pattern. The system views each Web page as an item, and the weight of a user on the item is the number of times the user has accessed the Web page. This system does not use semantic information (such as areas of interest) to model user interests, but just actual visits. Also, it does not aim to provide users with newly created or updated Web pages when they visit the same Web site again. This is a significant difference in design between this system and ours.

WebWatcher (Armstrong et al., 1995) is an agent that helps the user in an interactive mode by suggesting pages relevant to the current page the user is browsing. It learns by observing the user's feedback to the suggested pages, and it can guide the user to find a particular target page. Users can specify their areas by providing a set of keywords when they enter WebWatcher, mark a page as interesting after reading it, and leave the system at any time by telling whether the search process was successful or not. WebWatcher creates and keeps a log file for each user and from the users' areas of interest and the "interesting" pages they have visited, it highlights hyperlinks on the current page and adds new hyperlinks to the current page. WebWatcher is basically a search engine, and therefore has the general problems associated with search engines and Web robots. Although it has been extended to act as a tour guide (Joachims et al., 1997), it does not support incremental exploration of all relevant, newly created, and updated pages at a local site.

Three-Descriptor Representation (Widyantoro et al., 2001) learns the areas that are of interest to a user, by recording the user's browsing behavior. It performs some tasks at idle times (when the user is reading a document and is not browsing). These tasks include looking for more documents that are related to the user's interest or might be relevant to future requests. Different from WebWatcher, Three-Descriptor Representation is a user interface that has no predefined search goals, but it assumes persistence of interest, that is, when the user indicates interests by following a hyperlink or performing a search with a keyword, their interests in the keyword topic rarely end with the returning of the search results. There are no specific learning facilities in Three-Descriptor Representation (but just a set of heuristics like the persistence of interest plus a best-first search), and therefore it does not perform incremental learning as our system will.

Web Learner (Pazzani et al., 1995) is similar to our system in that it learns about what a user is interested in and decides what new Web pages might interest the user. However, Web Learner generates keywords (called a feature vector) automatically from pages on the global Web, and does not provide facilities for incremental learning. Furthermore, none of the extensions mentioned in Issue II(c) of Section D.2.2 have been addressed in Web Learner.

Our localized digital library agent will start with the same idea of assisting Web users by learning and identifying their areas of interest. However, the agent will work with a centralized digital library server which contains indexes to Web pages on the Web by using a keyword dictionary local to the digital library. Further, based on the indexing of the Web pages on and linked to the digital library server, our system will support interactive and incremental learning. The rules with logical conditions in our system will be more powerful than the (keyword, weight) pairs used in some existing systems in representing users' areas of interest.

Our system will be different from existing search engines and robots on the World Wide Web. It does not traverse the global Web, but acts as a housekeeper for a centralized digital library server and as a helper for the user who visits the digital library to find relevant information, with particular attention to the newly developed and modified documents in the digital library.

9.7   Results and Future Work

9.7.1   Content of Our Library

To illustrate the digital library system developed in this project, we have built a specialized digital library for gene analysis. Databases of literature, sequence, structure, and others will be used, including GenBank, dbSNP, the Molecular Modeling Database, PubMed, OMIM, the p53 mutation database (http://www.iarc.fr/p53/), and a p16 mutation database compiled by Dr. Greenblatt (Murphy et al., 2004). We will demonstrate the flexibility of our system by including multiple types of information including text, sequence information, 3D protein structure information and even entire databases. All items were entered into the system using the add items interface in the administrative window.

9.7.2   Digital Library Interface

Our system (http://www.cs.uvm.edu:9180/library) has two entry points: one for general users and one for administrators. Figure 9.11 shows the entry to the site for general users. From entry point, new users can create an account by clicking on the "New Users: Please Register" or they can enter the system anonymously. Anonymous users will not be able to use the recommendation agents until they open an

FIGURE 9.11: The entry page for general users.

account on the system. They will however have the ability to use the search capabilities of the site and can browse the site as they wish.

Users who register with the system will fill out a short questionnaire that collects demographic information as well as a username and password for the system (Figure 9.12). Once the user is registered with the system, they will have full access to all nonadministrative functions of the library. The system will create a user profile in XML format and will add the user to the database of library users.

After a user account has been created, the user can enter the digital library by providing their username and password. They will then find themselves on the main search page for the digital library. From this page they can access all other functions of the digital library including searching the library, browsing the semantic network, generating new rules based on their profiles, and viewing items recommended by the system.

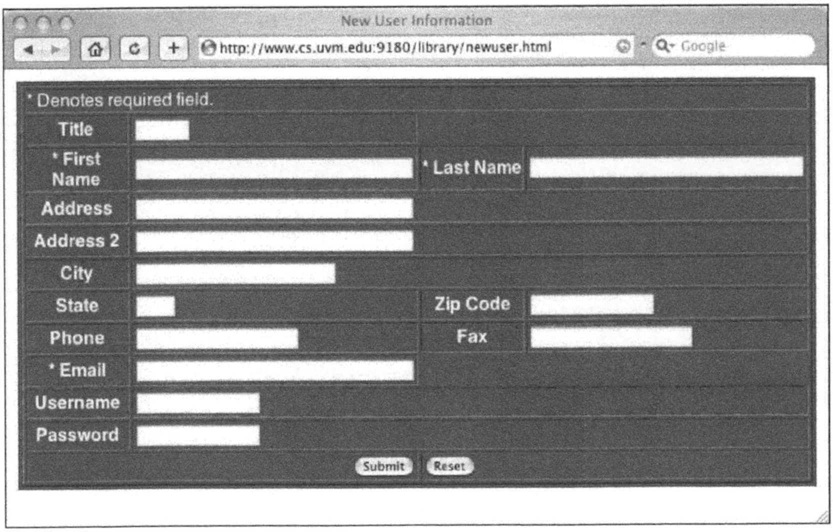

FIGURE 9.12: New user questionnaire.

The left-hand portion of the main page includes a number of links to information about the digital library and different functions for the library in general. These functions include browsing the library by data type, subject, or database. These functions print out to the screen all data in the site organized by the parameter selected. This functionality will become nearly useless in a large library system, but could be subdivided in future versions of the system to provide a clickable map of the data by utilizing the relationships in the semantic network.

This section also includes the function to view your user profile. This will open a window displaying your user profile in XML format. This is the file used by the intelligence agents of the system. It is also used to display your user profile at the bottom of the right-hand side of the page (Figure 9.13).

The upper right-hand side of this page provides the search interface to the library. You can search the library by title, semantic type, subject keyword, or author. At the top of this section there is a selector for the database that you want to search. In addition to searching our library, you can use this interface to search several other databases including the very popular NCBI Entrez site. When searching

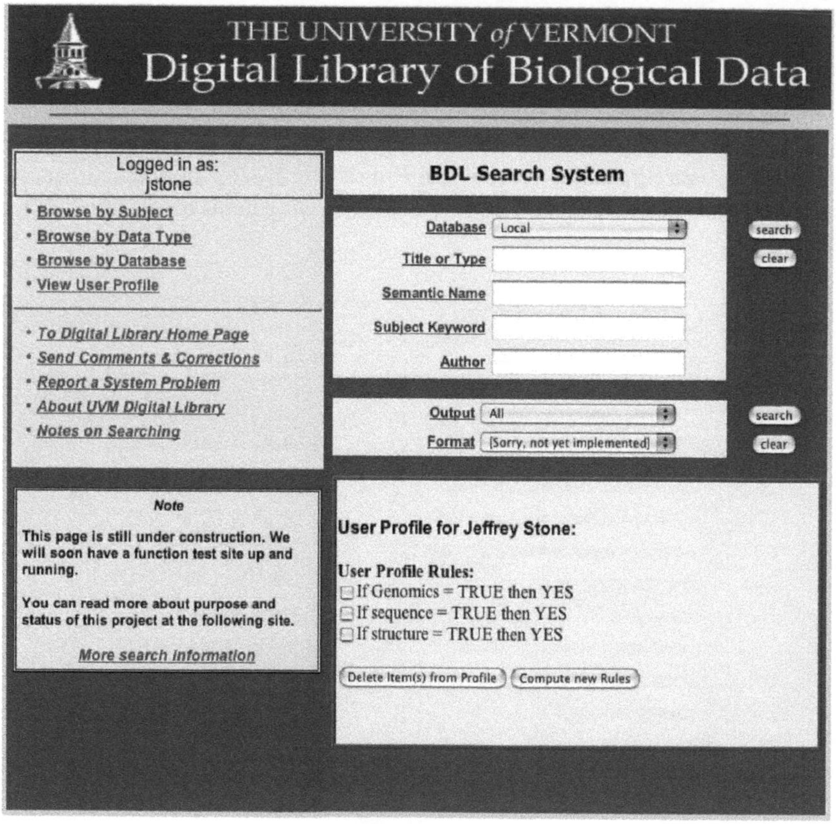

FIGURE 9.13:   The main page for the library.

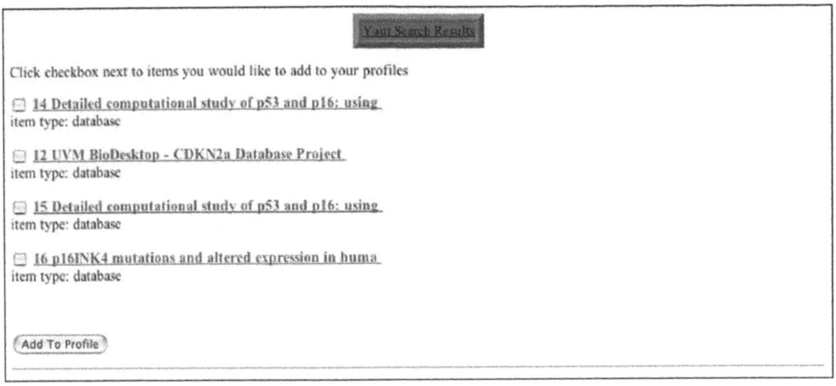

FIGURE 9.14:   Search results for p16.

off-site databases, control will be transferred to the off-site system in a new window. In addition to searching the off-site database with the search criteria specified, your user profiles will also be used to recommend other items on those sites. This provides a valuable additional functionality over using those Web sites directly.

The results of a search are presented in a new separate window (Figure 9.14). The results will be shown as a list of Web links to the items located on the Internet. Each item will also have a short description and a check box beside it to indicate if the item was helpful or not. Selecting an item will open up the Web page for that item in a separate window. This allows you to open several items at a time and still have your result list available to refer back to. In addition to this format, you may also select an alternate output format such as XML or the ANS 1.1 format used by NCBI.

In addition to displaying the items found in your search, two other sections are displayed. The first of these is the listing of items previously selected as interesting (Figure 9.15). You may choose to delete any of these from you profile. Future versions of this system will also include an update agent that will notify the users of new information on a selected item. At the bottom of the page are the items that the system has recommended to you. This recommendation is based on the user rules in your profile.

In addition to searching by author, keyword or title, you may also search by semantic type. This is a distinct search type that is unlike the others. Figure 9.16 shows an example of searching the semantic type for p16. This search will return all terms that are related to p16. This list can be quite exhaustive, but is helpful for finding items that are at the "tip of your tongue."

At the bottom of the main page is a window that provides the user interface for controlling their profile. This section uses an XSLT transformation to generate this section based on your XML formatted user profile. You can see your raw XML file by clicking on "View User Profile" on the upper left-hand panel (Figure 9.17). XSLT transformations use this XML file to build an HTML formatted section with a list of your user rules and buttons for removing rules from your profile or computing new rules. When you compute new rules, the Weka J48 algorithm is used to generate a

Results Page
http://www.cs.uvm.edu:9180/library/servlet/dlibrary.getUMLSInfo

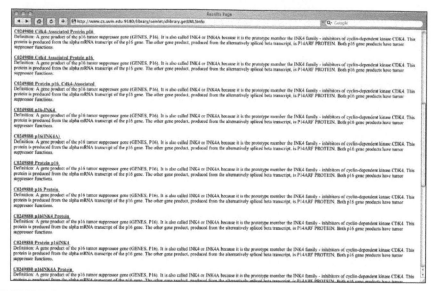

FIGURE 9.15: Items previously selected are also displayed.

decision tree based on your profile and then uses this decision tree to generate the new rules.

Since many researchers would be concerned by ad hoc generation of new rules, and because of the imprecision in the generation of these rules, user feedback is again requested. The list of rules found is displayed for the user to view. The user is then asked to select those rules that are meaningful for their research (Figure 9.18).

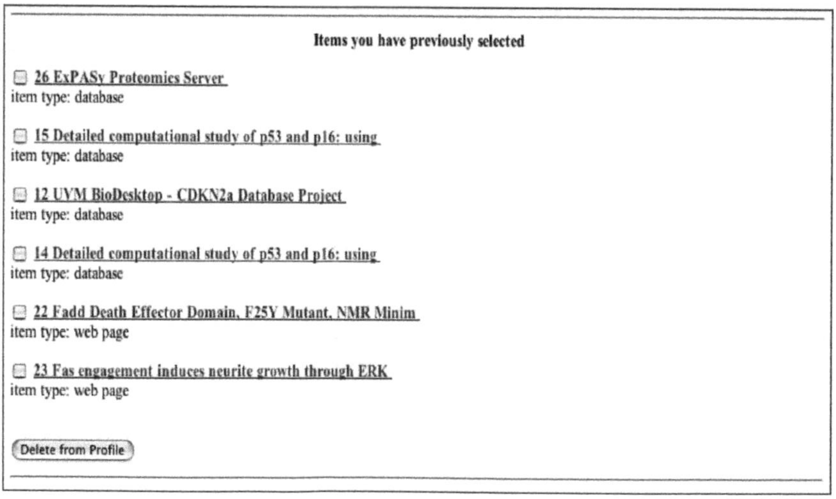

Items you have previously selected
26 ExPASy Proteomics Server
item type: database
15 Detailed computational study of p53 and p16: using
item type: database
12 UVM BioDesktop - CDKN2a Database Project
item type: database
14 Detailed computational study of p53 and p16: using
item type: database
22 Fadd Death Effector Domain, F25Y Mutant, NMR Minim
item type: web page
23 Fas engagement induces neurite growth through ERK
item type: web page
Delete from Profile

FIGURE 9.16: Partial display of the semantic search for "p16."

```
- <user-profile xsi:noNamespaceSchemaLocation="user_profile.xsd">
  - <name>
      <firstName>Jeffrey</firstName>
      <lastName>Stone</lastName>
  </name>
  - <address>
      <street>10 Railroad Street</street>
      <city>South Hero</city>
      <state>VT</state>
      <postal-code>054886</postal-code>
  </address>
  <phone/>
  <email>jestone@zoo.uvm.edu</email>
  - <history>
      <rule>If sequence = TRUE then YES</rule>
      <rule>If structure = TRUE then YES</rule>
  </history>
</user-profile>
```

FIGURE 9.17: A sample user profile in raw XML format.

9.7.3 Future Research Directions

The portion of the existing library that needs the most immediate attention is the database of items. This database is small at this time. We hope that this system will grow in the very near future to provide a valuable asset not only to the UVM research community, but indeed to all others. Some of the specific areas where future versions of this system may evolve are described below.

9.7.3.1 Sophisticated Data Entry for Populating the Library

At this time, the administrative page for logging items into the library is an HTML-form page. This process is very tedious and error prone. We would like to

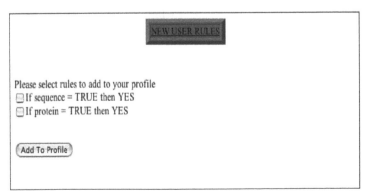

FIGURE 9.18: Generation of new user rules. Users can select which rules they would like to add to their profile. In addition to simple rules as shown above, J48 can discover complex rules such as the conjunction of rules.

create an agent for the automatic entry of these items. Potentially, some of the emerging Web services will provide some tools or methods for entering this information directly from trusted sites.

9.7.3.2 Improvement in Semantic Searching

The current method for searching the semantic network for relationships is quite slow. This is due in part to the large size of the semantic network database (roughly 3 million entries). Some effort needs to be put in to improve the performance of this semantic search. Perhaps there may be better ways of implementing the semantic network via Java object creation in memory.

9.7.3.3 Emerging Semantic Web Technologies

One of the more exciting areas of research is in the semantic Web technologies. New means of annotating Web resources are promising to revolutionize the way we use the Internet. The current Internet is designed mostly in markup languages to format this information for human consumption. With a new focus on Web services and XML technologies, researchers are looking into ways to create a Web designed by machines for machines.

Semantic Web technologies such as DAML and OIL could potentially be used for the generation of our semantic net (Berners-Lee et al., 2001). This would allow this net to extend beyond our own system to include other semantic networks and Web services by searching the descriptors such as RDFs for these systems for common nodes in the networks.

9.7.3.4 Expanding the Ontology

The current ontology contains information primarily designed for describing molecular biologists. Expanding this ontology can be achieved by either adding new nodes to the semantic network, or by adding whole new semantic networks to the system. The modular design of our system allows one to plug in any semantic network that fits the general schema outlined in Section 9.3. This would allow our library to be used outside of its intended biological domain to any domain that one would want.

9.7.3.5 Additional User Agents

There are several additional user agents that could be developed for our system. The most important among these would be an update agent. This agent would notify the user of updates to items that fit their profile. The semantic network contains a valuable knowledge base that could be further exploited. An agent for navigating the semantic neighborhood of an item in a graphical map might also prove interesting.

References

Altman, R. B., Benton, D., Karp, P. D., and Schulze-Kreoner, S., Eds. (1998). Workshop on Semantic foundations for Molecular Biology: Schemata, Controlled Vocabularies and Ontologies. Montreal, Canada, ISMB'98 Workshop.

R. Armstrong, D. Freitag, T. Joachims, and T. Mitchell, WebWatcher: A learning apprentice for the World Wide Web, *AAAI Spring Symposium on Information Gathering from Heterogeneous, Distributed Environments*, March 1995.

M. Balabanovic and Y. Shoham, Learning information retrieval agents: Experiments with automated Web browsing, In *On-line Working Notes of the AAAI Spring Symposium Series on Information Gathering from Distributed, Heterogeneous Environments*, Stanford, CA, March 1995.

T. Berners-Lee, J. Hendler, and O. Lassila, The semantic Web, *Scientific American*, May 2001.

BioNetbook, http://www.pasteur.fr/recherche/BNB/bnb-en.html.

M. Bouziane and C. Hsu, A rulebase management system using conceptual rule modeling, *International Journal on Artificial Intelligence Tools*, 6(1): 37–61, 1997.

P. Brusilovsky, J. Ahn, and R. Farzan, Accessing educational digital libraries through adaptive information visualization, *Proceedings of the 10th DELOS Thematic Workshop on Personalized Access, Profile Management, and Context Awareness in Digital Libraries (PersDL 2007)*, 2007.

L. Chen and K. Sycara, WebMate: A personal agent for browsing and searching, *Proceedings of the 2nd International Conference on Autonomous Agents*, Minneapolis, MN, pp. 132–139, 1998.

R. Fikes and T. Kehler, The role of frame-based representation in reasoning, *Communications of the ACM*, 28(9): 904–920, 1985.

M. Y. Galperin, The molecular biology database collection: 2004 update, *Nucleic Acids Research*, January 1, 32 Database issue: D3–22 2004.

J. Giarratano, *CLIPS User's Guide (CLIPS Ver 6.0)*, Lyndon B. Johnson Space Center, Information Systems Directorate, *Software Technology*, NASA, USA, 1993.

ILOG Rules, 1998. Available at http://www.ilog.com/html/products/infrastructure/rules.htm.

T. Joachims, T. Mitchell, D. Freitag, and R. Armstrong, WebWatcher: Machine learning and hypertext, *GI Fachgruppentreffen Maschinelles Lernen*, K. Morik and J. Herrmann (Eds.), University of Dortmund, Dortmund, Germany, August 1995.

T. Joachims, D. Freitag, and T. Mitchell, WebWatcher: A tour guide for the World Wide Web, *Proceedings of the 15th International Conference on Artificial Intelligence*, Nagoya, Japan, August 23–29, pp. 770–775, 1997.

W. May and G. Lausen, Information extraction from the Web, Technical Report No. 136, Institut fur Informatik, Saarbrücken Germany, March, 2000.

C. Moss, *Prolog++: The Power of Object-Oriented and Logic Programming*, Addison-Wesley, 1994.

J. A. Murphy, R. Barrantes-Reynolds, R. Kocherlakota, J. P. Bond, M. S. Greenblatt, The CDKN2A database: Integrating allelic variants with evolution, structure, function, and disease association, *Human Mutation*, 24: 296–304, 2004.

D. S. W. Ngu and X. Wu, SiteHelper: A localized agent that helps incremental exploration of the World Wide Web, *Proceedings of the 6th International World Wide Web Conference (www6)*, Santa Clara, CA, April 7–11, pp. 691–700, 1997.

T.-L. Nguyen, X. Wu, and S. Sajeev, Object-oriented modeling of multimedia documents, *Proceedings of the 7th International World Wide Web Conference (WWW7)* (Brisbane, Queensland, Australia, 14–18), published in *Computer Networks and ISDN Systems: The International Journal of Computer and Telecommunications Networking*, 30: 578–582, April 1998.

Online Mendelian Inheritance in Man (OMIM), *NCBI*. Available at http://www.ncbi.nlm.nih.gov/omim.

M. Pazzani, L. Nguyen, and S. Mantik, Learning from hot lists and cold lists: Towards a WWW information filtering and seeking agent, *Proceedings of IEEE 1995 International Conference on Tools with AI*, November 14–16, 1995.

J. E. Pitkow and K. A. Bharat, WebViz: A tool for WWW access log analysis, *Proceedings of the 1st International World Wide Web Conference*, Geneva, Switzerland, May 1994.

J. R. Quinlan, *C4.5: Programs for Machine Learning*, Morgan Kaufmann, San Mateo, CA, 1993.

J. Rumbaugh, M. Blaha, W. Premerlani, F. Eddy, and W. Lorensen, *Object-Oriented Modeling and Design*, Prentice-Hall, Englewood Cliffs, NJ, 1991.

B. Schatz, W. H. Mischo, T. W. Cole, J. B. Hardin, A. P. Bishop, and H. Chen, Federating diverse collections of scientific literature, *Computer*, 29(5): 28–36, 1996.

S. Schulze-Kremer, Ontologies for molecular biology, *Proceedings Of the 3rd Pacific Symposium on Biocomputing*, AAAI Press, Maui, Hawaii, pp. 693–704, 1998.

Y. Shoham, Agent-oriented programming, *Artificial Intelligence*, 60: 51–92, 1993.

R. Stevens, P. Baker, S. Bechhofer, G. Ng, A. Jacoby, N. W. Paton, C. A. Goble, and A. Brass, TAMBIS: Transparent Access to Multiple Bioinformatics Information Sources, *Bioinformatics*, 16(2): 118–186, 2000.

J. Stone, X. Wu, and M. Greenblatt, An Intelligent Digital Library System for Biologists, *Proceedings of the 2004 IEEE Computational Systems Bioinformatics Conference (CSB 2004)*, 491–492.

W3C, http://www.w3.org/RDF/Overview.html.

D. H. Widyantoro, T. R. Ioerger, J. Yen, Learning user interest dynamics with a three-descriptor representation, *Journal of American Society of Information Science and Technology*, 52(3): 212–225, 2001.

I. H. Witten and E. Frank, *Data Mining: Practical Machine Learning Tools with Java Implementations*, Morgan Kaufmann, San Francisco, CA, 2000.

World Wide Web Worm http://www.cs.colorado.edu/home/mcbryan/WWWW.html.

X. Wu and K. Cai, Knowledge object modeling, *IEEE Transactions on Systems, Man, and Cybernetics Part A: Systems and Humans*, 30(2): 96–107, 2000.

T. W. Yan, M. Jacobsen, H. Garcia-Molina, and U. Dayal, From user access patterns to dynamic hypertext linking, *Proceeding of the 5th International World Wide Web Conference*, Paris, France, May 1996.

Chapter 10

Issues and Challenges in Learning from Data Streams

João Gama

Contents

10.1 Introduction

Machine learning studies automatic methods for acquisition of domain knowledge with the goal improving systems performance as the result of experience. In the last two decades, machine learning research and practice have focused on batch learning usually with small datasets. In batch learning, the whole training data is available to the algorithm, that outputs a decision model after processing the data eventually (or most of the times) multiple times. The rationale behind this practice is that examples are generated at random according to some stationary probability distribution. Most learners use a greedy, hill-climbing search in the space of models. They are prone to overfitting, local maximas, etc.

The development of information and communication technologies dramatically change the data collection and processing methods. Advances in miniaturization and sensor technology lead to sensor networks, collecting detailed spatiotemporal data about the environment.

An illustrative application is the problem of mining data produced by sensors distributed all around electrical-power distribution networks. These sensors produce streams of data at high speed. From a data-mining perspective, this problem is characterized by a large number of variables (sensors), producing a continuous flow of data, in a dynamic nonstationary environment. Companies analyze these data streams and make decisions for several problems. They are interested in identifying critical points in load evolution, for example, picks on the demand. These aspects are related to anomaly detection, extreme values, failures prediction, outliers, and abnormal activities detection. Other problems are related to change detection in the behavior (correlation) of sensors. Cluster analysis can be used for the identification of groups of high-correlated sensors, corresponding to common behaviors or profiles (e.g., urban, rural, industrial, etc.). Decisions to buy or sell energy are based on the predictions on the value measured by each sensor for different time horizons. Data mining in this context requires continuous processing of the incoming data monitoring trends, and detecting changes. Traditional one-shot systems that are memory based, trained from fixed training set, and generating static models are not prepared to process the high-detailed data available, are not able to continuously maintain a predictive model consistent with the actual state of the nature, and are not quick to react to changes. Moreover, with the evolution of hardware components, these sensors are acquiring computational power. The challenge will be to run the predictive model in the sensors itself.

In this chapter we discuss the issues and challenges on learning from data streams, discussing limitations of current learning systems, and pointing out possible research lines for next generation data-mining systems. How to learn from these distributed continuous streaming data? Which are the main characteristics of a learning algorithm acting in sensor networks? What are the relevant issues, challenges, and research opportunities?

10.2 Machine Learning and Data Streams

The goal of machine learning is to build a computational model from what has been observed, for example, data. Nowadays the processes to collect data are radically changing. We have all kind of sensors sensing the environment and collecting data; and we are witness to an explosion of all types of networks (Web, peer-to-peer, wireless) that dramatically changed the data transmission processes. What distinguishes current data sets from earlier ones are the continuous flow of data and the automatic data feeds. We do not just have people who are entering information into a computer, instead, we have computers entering data into each other [1]. Nowadays there are applications in which the data is modeled best not as persistent tables but rather as transient data streams. In some applications it is not feasible to load the arriving data into a traditional database management systems (DBMS) [2], and traditional DBMS are not designed to directly support the continuous queries required in these applications [3].

10.2.1   Streaming Algorithms

In the streaming model, the input elements $a_1, a_2, \ldots, a_j$ arrive sequentially, item by item and describe an underlying function A [1]. We can distinguish between

1. Insert only model: once an element a_i is seen, it cannot be changed

2. Insert–delete model: elements a_i can be deleted or updated

From the view point of a data streams management system (DSMS) several research issues emerge, for example, approximate query processing techniques to evaluate continuous queries that require unbounded amount of memory. Sampling has been used to handle situations where the flow rate of the input stream is faster than the query processor. Another relevant issue is the definition of the semantics (and implementation) of blocking operators (operators that only return an output tuple after processing all input tuples, like aggregation and sorting) in the presence of unending streams [3].

Algorithms that process data streams deliver approximate solutions, providing a fast answer using few memory resources; they relax the requirement of an exact answer to an approximate answer within a small error range with high probability. In general, as the range of the error decreases the space of computational resources goes up.

Illustrative example.   Suppose the problem of counting the number of distinct pairs of IP addresses from the network traffic that crosses a server. This is a trivial problem, if we do not consider restrictions in space. The number of distinct pairs of IPs can be very large, and an exact answer is not mandatory.

Hash functions are a powerful tool in stream processing. They are used to project huge domains into lower space dimensions. One of the earlier results is the Hash (aka FM) sketches for distinct-value counting in one pass while using only a small amount of space [4]. Suppose the existence of a hash function $h(x)$ that maps incoming values $x \in [0, \ldots, N-1]$ uniformly across $[0, \ldots, L-1]$, where $L = O(logN)$. Let lsb(y) denote the position of the least-significant 1 bit in the binary representation of y. A value x is mapped to lsb$(h(x))$. The algorithm maintains a bitmap vector of L bits, initialized to zero. For each incoming value x, set the lsb$(h(x))$ bit of L to 1. At each time-stamp t, let R denote the position of rightmost zero in the bitmap. R is an indicator of log(d), where d denotes the number of distinct values in the stream.

In some applications, mostly database oriented, an approximate answer should be within an admissible error margin. DSMS developed a set of techniques that store compact stream summaries enough to approximately solve queries. All these approaches require a trade-off between accuracy and the amount of memory used to store the summaries, with an additional constrain of small time to process data items [1]. The most common problems end up to compute quantiles [5], frequent item sets [6–8], and to store frequent counts along with error bounds on their true frequency [9]. The techniques developed in DSMS can provide tools for designing machine learning algorithms in very high dimensions, both in the number of examples and in the cardinality of the variables. On the other hand, machine learning provides compact descriptions of the data than can be useful for answering queries in DSMS.

The following table summarizes the main differences between traditional and stream data processing:

	Traditional	**Stream**
Number of passes	Multiple	Single
Processing time	Unlimited	Restricted
Available memory	Unlimited	Fixed
Result	Accurate	Approximate
Distributed	No	Yes

Streaming data and domains offer a nice opportunity for a symbiosis between SDMS and machine learning. The techniques developed in DSMS to estimate synopsis and sketches requiring counts over very high dimensions, both in the number of examples and in the domain of the variables, can provide tools for designing machine learning algorithms in these domains. On the other hand, machine learning provides compact descriptions of the data than can be useful for answering queries in DSMS.

10.2.2   Algorithms for Learning in from Data Streams

The ultimate goal of data mining is to develop systems and algorithms with high level of autonomy. These systems address the problems of data processing, modeling, prediction, clustering, and control in changing and evolving environments. They self-evolve their structure and knowledge on the environment.

Recent developments in machine learning point out directions for learning in streaming environments. In the following subsections we present two general approaches.

10.2.2.1   Mining Infinite Data in Finite Time

In Ref. [10] the authors present a general method to learn from arbitrarily large databases. The method consists of deriving an upper bound for the learner's loss as a function of the number of examples used in each step of the algorithm. Then use this to minimize the number of examples required at each step, while guaranteeing that the model produced does not differ significantly from the one that would be obtained with infinite data. This general methodology has been successfully applied in k-means clustering [10], hierarchical clustering of variables [11], decision trees [12–14], etc.

Illustrative example. VFDT [12] is a decision-tree learning algorithm that dynamically adjusts its bias whenever new examples are available. In decision tree induction, the main issue is the decision of when to expand the tree, installing a splitting-test and generating new leaves. The basic idea of VFDT consists of using a small set of examples to select the splitting-test to incorporate in a decision tree node. If after seeing a set of examples, the difference of the merit between the two best splitting-tests does not satisfy a statistical test (the Hoeffding bound), VFDT proceeds by examining more examples. VFDT only makes a decision (i.e., adds a splitting-test in that node), when there is enough statistical evidence in favor of a particular test. This strategy guarantees model stability (low variance), controls over-fitting, while it may achieve an increased number of degrees of freedom (low bias) with increasing number of examples.

VFTD has been extended to deal with continuous attributes [13,15], functional leaves [13], and nonstationary data streams in Refs. [14,15]. An interesting characteristic of VFDT is the ability to freeze less promising leaves, when working in memory-restricted environments.

10.2.2.2 Approximation and Randomization

Approximation and randomization techniques have been used to solve distributed streaming learning problems [16]. While approximation allows answers that are correct within some fraction ε of error, randomization allows a probability δ of failure. The base idea consists of mapping a very large input space to a small synopsis of size $O(\frac{1}{\varepsilon^2}\log(\frac{1}{\delta}))$. Approximation and randomization techniques have been used to solve problems like measuring the entropy of a stream [17], association rule mining frequent items [18], k-means clustering for distributed data streams using only local information [19], etc.

Illustrative example. Cormode and Muthukrishnan [20] present a data stream summary, the so-called Count-Min sketch. It can be used to approximately count the number of packets from the set of IPs that cross a server in a network. More general, the Count-Min sketch can be used to approximately solve point queries, range queries, and inner product queries.[*] The Count-Min sketch data structure is an array of $w \times d$ in size, where $d = \log(1/\delta)$, and $w = 2/\varepsilon$. For each incoming value of the stream, the algorithm use d hash functions to map vector entries to $[1,\ldots,w]$. The counters in each row are incremented to reflect the updated. From this data structure, we can estimate the number of occurrences of any item $\hat{j}$ by taking $\min_d CM[d,h_d(j)]$. The error of the estimate is at most $n\varepsilon$ with probability at least $1-\delta$ in space $O(\frac{1}{\varepsilon}\log(\frac{1}{\delta}))$.

10.3 Algorithm Issues in Learning from Data Streams

The challenge problem for data mining is the ability to permanently maintain an accurate decision model. This issue requires learning algorithms that can modify

---

[*] Consider a random variable **a**, whose domain is $\{a_1,\ldots,a_n\}$. A point query returns an approximation of a_i, a range query returns an approximation of $\sum_{i=l}^{r} a_i$, and an inner product query returns an approximation of $\sum_1^n a_i.b_i$.

the current model whenever new data is available at the rate of data arrival. Moreover, they should forget older information when data is outdated. In this context, the assumption that examples are generated at random according to a stationary probability distribution does not hold, at least in complex systems and for large periods of time. In the presence of a nonstationary distribution, the learning system must incorporate some form of forgetting past and outdated information. Learning from data streams requires incremental learning algorithms that take into account concept drift. Solutions to these problems require new sampling and randomization techniques, and new approximate, incremental and decremental algorithms. The authors of Ref. [10] identify desirable properties of learning systems that are able to mine continuous, high-volume, open-ended data streams as they arrive. Learning systems should be able to process examples and answering queries at the rate they arrive. Some desirable properties for learning in data streams include incrementality, online learning, constant time to process each example, single scan over the training set, and taking drift into account.

10.3.1 Cost–Performance Management

Incremental learning is one fundamental aspect for the process of continuous adaptation of the decision model. The ability to update the decision model whenever new information is available is an important property, but it is not enough, it also requires operators with the ability to *forget* past information [21]. Some data stream models allow delete and update operators. Sliding windows models require forgetting old information. In all these situations the incremental property is not enough. Learning algorithms need forgetting operators that reverse learning: decremental unlearning [22].

The incremental and decremental issues require a permanent maintenance and update of the decision model as new data is available. Of course, there is a trade-off between the cost of update and the gain in performance we may obtain. Learning algorithms exhibit different profiles. Algorithms with strong variance management are quite efficient for small training sets. Very simple models, using few free-parameters, can be quite efficient in variance management, and effective in incremental and decremental operations being a natural choice in the sliding windows framework. The main problem with simple representation languages is the boundary in generalization performance they can achieve, since they are limited by high bias while large volumes of data require efficient bias management. Complex tasks requiring more complex models increase the search space and the cost for structural updating. These models, require efficient control strategies for the trade-off between the gain in performance and the cost of updating.

In most applications, we are interested in maintaining a decision model consistent with the current status of the nature. This leads us to the sliding window models where data is continuously inserted and deleted from a time window. Learning algorithms must have operators for incremental learning and forgetting. Incremental learning and forgetting are well defined in the context of predictive learning. The meaning or the semantics in other learning paradigms (like clustering) are not so well understood, very few works address this issue.

10.3.2 Monitoring Learning

When data flows over time, and at least for large periods of time, the assumption that the examples are generated at random according to a stationary probability distribution is highly unprovable. At least in complex systems and for large time periods, we should expect changes in the distribution of the examples. A natural approach for these incremental tasks are adaptive learning algorithms, incremental learning algorithms that take into account concept drift.

Concept drift means that the concept related to the data being collected may shift from time to time, each time after some minimum permanence. Changes occur over time. The evidence for changes in a concept are reflected in some way in the training examples. Old observations, that reflect the past behavior of the nature, become irrelevant to the current state of the phenomena under observation and the learning agent must forget that information.

The nature of change is diverse, they may occur in the context of learning, due to changes in hidden variables, or in the characteristic properties of the observed variables.

10.3.2.1 Methods and Algorithms for Change Detection

Most learning algorithms use blind methods that adapt the decision model at regular intervals without considering whether changes have really occurred, much more interesting is explicit change detection mechanisms. The advantage is that they can provide meaningful description (indicating change-points or small time-windows where the change occurs) and quantification of the changes. They may follow two different approaches:

1. Monitoring the evolution of performance indicators adapting techniques used in statistical process control

2. Monitoring distributions on two different time windows

The main research issue is how to incorporate change detection mechanisms in the learning algorithm, embedding change detection methods in the learning algorithm is a requirement in the context of continuous flow of data. The level of granularity of decision models is a relevant property, because it can allow partial, fast, and efficient updates in the decision model instead of rebuilding a complete new model whenever a change is detected. The ability to recognize seasonal and reoccurring patterns is an open issue.

Concept drift in the predictive classification setting is a well-studied topic. In other learning scenarios, like clustering, very few works address the problem. The main research issue is how to incorporate change detection mechanisms in the learning algorithm for different paradigms.

10.3.3 Novelty Detection

Novelty detection [23–25] refers to learning algorithms being able to identify and learn new concepts. Intelligent agents that act in dynamic environments must be able to learn conceptual representations of such environments. Those conceptual descriptions of the world are always incomplete, they correspond to what it is *known* about the world. This is the *open* world assumption as opposed to the traditional *closed* world assumption,* where what is to be learnt is defined in advance. In open worlds, learning systems should be able to extend their representation by learning new concepts from the observations that do not match the current representation of the world. For example, suppose a classification task where the training examples are samples from a subset of the set of classes. The learning algorithm must be able to infer new classes from unlabeled examples. This is a difficult task. It requires to identify the *unknown*, that is, the limits of the current model. In that sense, the unknown corresponds to an *emerging pattern* that is different from noise, or drift in previously known concepts.

10.3.4 Distributed Streams

Data streams are distributed in nature. When learning from distributed data streams, we need efficient methods to minimize the communication overheads between nodes [26].

The strong limitations of centralized solutions is discussed in depth in Refs. [27,28]. The authors point out a mismatch between the architecture of most off-the-shelf data-mining algorithms and the needs of mining systems for distributed applications. Such mismatch may cause a bottleneck in many emerging applications, namely hardware limitations related to the limited bandwidth channels. Most important, in applications like monitoring, centralized solutions introduce delays in event detection and reaction, that can make mining systems useless.

Another direction, for distributed processing, explore multiple models. In Ref. [29], the authors proposed a method that offer an effective way to construct a redundancy-free, accurate, and meaningful representation of large decision-tree ensembles often created by popular techniques such as bagging, boosting, random forests, and many distributed and data stream mining algorithms.

10.4 Online, Anytime, and Real-Time Data Mining

Data mining in a batch scenario is an iterative process, evolving sequences of data processing steps to achieve the goal of extracting useful information. In which way a streaming environment changes these processes? This section discusses some of the new challenges in the data mining-process.

---

* The *closed world* assumption assumes that the data-warehouse is the universe, while in the *open world* view the data-warehouse is a sample from the universe.

10.4.1 Feature Selection and Preprocessing

Selection of relevant and informative features, discretization, noise, and rare events detection are common tasks in machine learning and data mining. They are used in a one-shot process. In the streaming context, the semantics of these tasks changes drastically. Consider the feature selection problem. In streaming data the concept of irrelevant or redundant features are now restricted to a certain period of time. Features previously considered irrelevant may become relevant, and vice-versa to reflect the dynamics of the process generating data. Furthermore, in sensor networks, the number of sensors is variable (usually increasing) over time. While in standard data mining, an irrelevant feature could be ignored forever, in the streaming setting we need to still monitor the evolution of those features. Recent work based on the fractal dimension [30] could point out interesting directions for research.

10.4.2 Evolving Feature Spaces

In the static case, similar data can be described with different schemata. In the case of dynamic streams, the schema of the stream can also change. The distributed nature of development of Web-based information lead to the development of large databases about similar domains using different terminologies and described by different ontologies. With the advent of the semantic Web and Web services, a relevant research area is the semantic identification of correspondences between attributes across multiple database schemas. This task is designated as semantic matching [31]. We need algorithms that can deal with evolving feature spaces over streams. There is very little work in this area, mainly pertaining to document streams [32].

10.4.3 Evaluation Methods and Metrics

An important aspect of any learning algorithm is the hypothesis evaluation criteria. Most evaluation methods and metrics were designed for the static case and provide a single measurement about the quality of the hypothesis. In the streaming context, we are much more interested in how the evaluation metric evolves over time. Results from the sequential statistics [33] may be much more appropriate.

There is a fundamental difference between learning from small datasets and large datasets. As pointed out by some researchers [34], current learning algorithms emphasize variance reduction. However, learning from large datasets may be more effective when using algorithms that place greater emphasis on bias management.

10.5 Emerging Challenges and Future Issues

Simple objects that surround us are changing from static, inanimate objects into adaptive, reactive systems with the potential to become more and more useful and efficient. Smart things associated with all sort of networks offers new unknown possibilities for the development and self-organization of communities of intelligent communicating appliances. The dynamic characteristics of data flowing over time require adaptive algorithms. While the languages used to represent generalizations from examples are well understood, next generation data-mining algorithms should care, at least, about the cost–performance management; the limitations in working in an open world that implies limitations in the knowledge about the learning goals and the limitations in all aspects of computational resources.

It is therefore clear that a wide spectrum of learning abilities is in demand for these new developments to take place. Learning algorithms must be able to adapt continuously to changing environmental conditions (including their own condition) and evolving user habits and needs. Learning must consider the real-time constraints of limited computer, battery power, and communication resources. Intelligent agents that adapt over time in a dynamic and sometimes in adversary conditions, should be capable of self-diagnosis. A significant and useful intelligence characteristic is diagnostics—not only after failure has occurred, but also predictive (before failure) and advisory (providing maintenance instructions). The development of such self-configuring, self-optimizing, and self-repairing systems is a major scientific and engineering challenge. All these aspects require monitoring the evolution of learning process itself, and the ability of reasoning and learning about it.

References

[1] S. Muthukrishnan, 2005. *Data Streams: Algorithms and Applications.* Now Publishers, New York.

[2] N. Chaudhry, K. Shaw, and M. Abdelguerf, 2005. *Stream Data Management.* Springer Verlag, New York.

[3] B. Babcock, S. Babu, M. Datar, R. Motwani, and J. Widom, 2002. Models and issues in data stream systems. In Kolaitis, P. G., editor, *Proceedings of the 21st Symposium on Principles of Database Systems*, pp. 1–16. ACM Press, Madison, WI.

[4] P. Flajolet and G. N. Martin, 1985. Probabilistic counting algorithms for database applications, *Journal of Computer and System Sciences*, 31(2): 182–209.

[5] A. Arasu and G. Manku, 2004. Approximate counts and quantiles over sliding windows. *ACM Symposium on Principles of Database Systems*, pp. 286–296. ACM Press, Paris , France.

[6] N. Alon, Y. Matias, and M. Szegedy, 1999. The space complexity of approximating the frequency moments. *Journal of Computer and System Sciences*, 58: 137–147.

[7] B. Babcock and C. Olston, 2003. Distributed top K monitoring. *ACM International Conference on Management of Data*, pp. 28–39. ACM Press, San Diego, CA.

[8] G. Cormode and S. Muthukrishnan, 2003. What's hot and what's not: Tracking most frequent items dynamically. *ACM Symposium on Principles of Database Systems*, pp. 296–306. ACM Press, San Diego, CA.

[9] A. Metwally, D. Agrawal, and A. El Abbadi, 2005. Efficient computation of frequent and top-k elements in data streams. *International Conference on Database Theory*, pp. 398–412. Springer, Edinburgh, UK.

[10] G. Hulten and P. Domingos, 2002. Mining complex models from arbitrarily large databases in constant time. In *proceedings of the Eighth ACM SIGKDD International Conference on Knowledge Discovery and Data Mining*, pp. 525–531. ACM Press.

[11] P. Rodrigues, J. Gama, and J. P. Pedroso, 2008. Hierarchical clustering of time series data streams. *IEEE Transactions on Knowledge and Data Engineering*, 20(5):615–627.

[12] P. Domingos and G. Hulten, 2000. Mining high-speed data streams. In I. Parsa, R. Ramakrishnan, and S. Stolfo, editors, *Proceedings of the ACM 6th International Conference on Knowledge Discovery and Data Mining*, pp. 71–80. ACM Press, Boston, MA.

[13] J. Gama, R. Rocha, and P. Medas, 2003. Accurate decision trees for mining high-speed data streams. In *Proceedings of the 9th ACM SIGKDD International Conference on Knowledge Discovery and Data Mining*, pp. 523–528. ACM Press, Washington, DC.

[14] G. Hulten, L. Spencer, and P. Domingos, 2001. Mining time-changing data streams. In *Proceedings of the 7th ACM SIGKDD International Conference on Knowledge Discovery and Data Mining*, pp. 97–106. ACM Press, San Francisco, CA.

[15] J. Gama, P. Medas, and R. Rocha, 2004. Forest trees for on-line data. In *Proceedings of the 2004 ACM Symposium on Applied Computing*, pp. 632–636. ACM Press, Nicosia, Cyprus.

[16] R. Motwani and P. Raghavan, 1997. *Randomized Algorithms*. Cambridge University Press, New York.

[17] A. Chakrabarti, G. Cormode, and A. McGregor, 2007. A near-optimal algorithm for computing the entropy of a stream. In *Proceedings of SIAM Symposium on Discrete Algorithms*, pp. 328–335. ACM Press, New Orleans, LA.

[18] G. S. Manku and R. Motwani, 2002. Approximate frequency counts over data streams. In *Proceedings of the 28th International Conference on Very Large Data Bases*, pp. 346–357. Morgan Kaufmann, Vienna, Austria.

[19] G. Cormode, S. Muthukrishnan, and W. Zhuang, 2007. Conquering the divide: Continuous clustering of distributed data streams. In *Proceedings of the International Conference on Data Engineering (ICDE)*, pp. 1036–1045, IEEE, Istanbul, Turkey.

[20] G. Cormode and S. Muthukrishnan, 2005. An improved data stream summary: The count-min sketch and its applications. *Journal of Algorithms* 55(1):58–75, Elsevier Science.

[21] D. Kifer, S. Ben-David, and J. Gehrke, 2004. Detecting change in data streams. In *Proceedings of the 30th International Conference on Very Large Data Bases*, pp. 180–191. Morgan Kaufmann, Toronto, Canada.

[22] G. Cauwenberghs and T. Poggio, 2000. Incremental and decremental support vector machine learning. In *Proceedings of the 13th Neural Information Processing Systems*, pp. 409–415. MIT Press, Oregon.

[23] J. Ma and S. Perkins, 2003. Online novelty detection on temporal sequences. *International Conference on Knowledge Discovery and Data Mining*, pp. 613–618. ACM Press, Washington, DC.

[24] B. Schölkopf, R. Williamson, A. Smola, J. Shawe-Taylor, and J. Platt, 2000. Support vector method for novelty detection. Advances in *Neural Information Processing Systems*, 582–588, Oregon.

[25] E. Spinosa, A. Carvalho, and J. Gama, 2008. Cluster-based novel concept detection in data streams applied to intrusion detection in computer networks. *ACM Symposium on Applied Computing*, pp. 976–980. ACM Press, Fortaleza, Brazil.

[26] A. Bar-Or, D. Keren, A. Schuster, and R. Wolff, 2005. Hierarchical decision tree induction in distributed genomic databases. *IEEE Transactions on Knowledge and Data Engineering*, 17(8):1138–1151, IEEE Press.

[27] H. Kargupta, A. Joshi, K. Sivakumar, and Y. Yesha, 2004. *Data Mining: Next Generation Challenges and Future Directions*. AAAI Press and MIT Press.

[28] B. Park and H. Kargupta, 2002. Distributed data mining: Algorithms, systems, and applications. In N. Ye (Ed) *Data Mining Handbook*, pp. 341–358. Lawrence Erlbaum Associates.

[29] H. Kargupta and H. Dutta, 2004. Orthogonal decision trees. In *Proceedings of the 4th IEEE International Conference on Data Mining*, pp. 427–430. IEEE Press, Brighton, UK.

[30] D. Barbara and P. Chen, 2000. Using the fractal dimension to cluster datasets. In *Proceedings of the 6th International Conference on Knowledge Discovery and Data Mining*, pp. 260–264. ACM Press, Boston, MA.

[31] A. Doan, J. Madhavan, P. Domingos, and A. Halevy, 2004. Ontology matching: A machine learning approach. In *Handbook on Ontologies*, pp. 385–404. Springer.

[32] S. Jaroszewicz, L. Ivantysynova, and T. Scheffer, 2008. Schema matching on streams with accuracy guarantees. *Intelligent Data Analysis Journal*, 12(3):253–270.

[33] A. Wald, 1947. *Sequential Analysis*. John Wiley & Sons, New York.

[34] D. Brain and G. Webb, 2002. The need for low bias algorithms in classification learning from large data sets. In T. Elomaa, H. Mannila, and H. Toivonen, editors, *Principles of Data Mining and Knowledge Discovery PKDD-02*, pp. 62–73. LNAI 2431, Springer Verlag, Helsinki, Finland.

Chapter 11

Service-Oriented Architectures for Distributed and Mobile Knowledge Discovery

Domenico Talia and Paolo Trunfio

Contents

11.1 Introduction

Computer science applications are becoming more and more network centric, ubiquitous, knowledge intensive, and computing demanding. Hardware evolution toward small devices and multicore processors combined with network-oriented middleware, services, and applications embodying intelligent and semantic-based processing are changing the way of developing novel applications. This trend will result soon in an ecosystem of pervasive applications and services that professionals and end users can exploit everywhere. A long-term perspective can be envisioned where a collection of services and applications will be accessed and used as public utilities, like water, gas, and electricity are used today.

This research work is partially carried out under the FP6 Network of Excellence CoreGRID funded by the European Commission (Contract IST-2002-004265) and the TOCAI.IT project funded by MIUR.

Key technologies for implementing that scenario are service-oriented architectures (SOAs) and Web services (WSs), semantic Web and ontologies, pervasive computing, peer-to-peer systems, grid computing, ambient intelligence architectures, data mining and knowledge discovery tools, Web 2.0 facilities, mashup tools, and decentralized programming models. In fact, it is mandatory to develop solutions that integrate some or many of those technologies to provide future knowledge-intensive software utilities. In such scenario, grid technologies can contribute by providing a cyber infrastructure for efficiently supporting execution of distributed services and applications.

In the area of grid computing, a proposed approach in accordance with the trend outlined above is the service-oriented knowledge utilities (SOKU) model [1] that envisions the integrated use of a set of technologies that are considered as a solution to information, knowledge, and communication needs of many knowledge-based industrial and business applications. The SOKU approach stems from the necessity of providing knowledge and processing capabilities to everybody, thus supporting the advent of a competitive knowledge-based economy. Although the SOKU model is not yet implemented, grids are increasingly equipped with data management tools, semantic technologies, complex workflows, data-mining systems, and other Web intelligence solutions. These technologies can facilitate the process of having grids as a strategic component for pervasive knowledge-intensive applications and utilities.

Grids were originally designed for dealing with problems involving large amounts of data or compute-intensive applications. Today, however, grids enlarged their horizon as they are going to run business applications supporting consumers and end users [2]. To face those new challenges, grid environments must support adaptive data management and data analysis applications by offering resources, services, and decentralized data access mechanisms. In particular, according to the SOA model, data-mining tasks and knowledge-discovery processes can be delivered as services in grid-based infrastructures.

Through a service-oriented approach we can define integrated services for supporting distributed business intelligence tasks in grids. Those services can address all the aspects that must be considered in data mining and in knowledge-discovery processes such as data selection and transport, data analysis, knowledge model representation, and visualization. Our work in these areas has been focused in providing grid-based architectures and services for distributed knowledge discovery such as the Knowledge Grid [3,4], Weka4WS [5,6], and mobile grid services for data mining [7].

This chapter discusses how grid frameworks such as those mentioned above can be developed as a collection of grid services and how they can be used to develop distributed data analysis tasks and knowledge-discovery processes exploiting the SOA model.

The rest of the chapter is organized as follows: Section 11.2 introduces grids as new infrastructures for running data-mining applications. Section 11.3 discusses a strategy based on the use of grid services for the design of distributed knowledge-discovery services. Sections 11.4, 11.5, and 11.6 describe the grid services implemented, respectively, in Weka4WS, the Knowledge Grid, and the mobile data-mining framework. Finally, Section 11.7 concludes the chapter.

11.2   Grids and Data Mining

Grid computing represents the natural evolution of distributed computing and parallel processing technologies. The grid is a distributed computing infrastructure that enables coordinated resource sharing within dynamic organizations consisting of individuals, institutions, and resources. The main aim of grid computing is to give organizations and application developers the ability to create distributed computing environments that can utilize available computing resources on demand. Grid computing can leverage the computing power of a large numbers of server computers, desktop PCs, clusters, and other kind of hardware. Therefore, it can increase the efficiency and reduce the cost of computing networks by decreasing data-processing time and optimizing resources and distributing workloads, thereby allowing users to achieve much faster results on large operations and at lower costs.

Data-mining algorithms and knowledge-discovery applications demand for both computing and data-management facilities. Therefore, the grid is a good candidate offering a computing and data-management infrastructure for supporting decentralized and parallel data analysis. The opportunity of utilizing grid-based data-mining systems, algorithms, and applications is valuable to users wanting to analyze data distributed across geographically dispersed heterogeneous hosts. For example, grid-based data mining would allow corporate companies to distribute compute-intensive data analysis among a large number of remote resources. At the same time, it can lead to new algorithms and techniques that would allow organizations to mine data where it is stored. This is in contrast to the practice of selecting data and transferring it into a centralized site for mining. As we know, centralized analysis is difficult to perform because data is becoming increasingly larger and geographically dispersed, and because of security and privacy considerations.

Several research frameworks have been proposed for deploying distributed data-mining applications in grids (see Ref. [8] for a quick survey). Some of them are general environments supporting execution of data-mining tasks on machines that belong to a grid, others are single-mining tasks for specific applications that have been gridfied, and some others are implementations of single data-mining algorithms. As the grid is becoming a well-accepted computing infrastructure in science and industry, it is necessary to provide general data-mining services, algorithms, and applications that help analysts, scientists, organizations, and professionals to leverage grid capacity in supporting high-performance distributed computing for solving their data-mining problem in a distributed way and according to a service-oriented approach.

The grid community has adopted the Open Grid Services Architecture (OGSA) [9] as an implementation of the SOA model within the grid context. In OGSA, every resource is represented as a WS that conforms to a set of conventions and supports standard interfaces. OGSA provides a well-defined set of WS interfaces for the development of interoperable grid systems and applications. Recently, the Web Services Resource Framework (WSRF) [10] has been adopted as an evolution of early OGSA implementations. WSRF defines a family of technical specifications for accessing and managing stateful resources using WSs. The composition of a WS and a stateful resource is termed as WS-Resource.

The possibility to define a state associated to a service is the most important difference between WSRF compliant WSs and pre-WSRF services. This is a key feature in designing grid applications, since WS-Resources provide a way to represent, advertise, and access properties related to both computational resources and applications.

Besides our systems described in Sections 11.4, 11.5, and 11.6, two related systems exploiting the SOA model for supporting grid-based data-mining services that should be mentioned are Discovery Net [11] and GridMiner [12].

Discovery Net allows users to integrate data analysis software and data sources made available by third parties. The building blocks are the so-called knowledge discovery services, distinguished in computation services and data services. Discovery Net provides services, mechanisms, and tools for specifying knowledge-discovery processes. The functionalities of Discovery Net can be accessed through an interface exposed as an OGSA-compliant grid service. However, Discovery Net currently uses an early implementation of OGSA—namely, the Open Grid Services Infrastructure (OGSI)—which has been replaced by WSRF for lack of compatibility with standard WS technologies.

GridMiner aims at covering the main aspects of knowledge discovery on grids. Key components in GridMiner are mediation service, information service, resource broker, and on-line analytical processing (OLAP) cube management. These are the so-called GridMiner base services, because they provide basic services to GridMiner core services. GridMiner core services include services for data integration, process management, data mining, and OLAP. The services themselves do not communicate with each other. No service is aware of any other existing service. Hence, each of them is able to run completely independently. To support the individual steps of knowledge discovery in database (KDD) processes, the output of each service can be used as input for the subsequent service. Like Discovery Net, also GridMiner has been implemented on OGSI.

Another service-oriented toolkit for data mining in distributed systems and grid environments is FAEHIM (Federated Analysis Environment for Heterogeneous Intelligent Mining) [13]. This toolkit consists of a set of data-mining services and a set of tools to interact with these services. FAEHIM does not include a user interface for composing services and tools. To provide this facility, it uses the Triana problem-solving environment [14]. FAEHIM exposes data-mining services as WSs (mostly derived from Weka [15]) to enable easy integration with other third-party services, allowing data-mining algorithms to be embedded within existing applications.

11.3   Data Mining Grid Services

The WSRF can be used to define basic services for supporting distributed data-mining tasks in grids. Those services can address all the aspects that must be considered in knowledge-discovery processes from data selection and transport, to data analysis, knowledge model representation, and visualization. This can be done by designing services corresponding to

- Single steps that compose a KDD process such as preprocessing, filtering, and visualization

- Single data-mining tasks such as classification, clustering, regression, outlier detection, and rule discovery

- Distributed data-mining patterns such as collective learning, parallel classification, and meta-learning models

- Data-mining applications including all or some of the previous tasks expressed through multistep scientific workflows

This collection of data-mining services can constitute an open service framework for grid-based data mining. Such a framework can allow developers to design distributed KDD processes as a composition of single services that are available over a grid. At the same time, those services should exploit other basic grid services for data transfer and management such as Reliable File Transfer, Replica Location Service, Data Access and Integration, and Distributed Query Processing. Moreover, distributed data-mining algorithms can optimize the exchange of data needed to develop global knowledge models based on concurrent mining of remote data sets.

This approach also preserves privacy and prevents disclosure of data beyond the original sources. Finally, basic grid mechanisms for handling security, trustiness, monitoring, and scheduling distributed tasks can be used to provide efficient implementation of high-performance distributed data analysis.

In the next three sections, we describe the service-oriented systems Weka4WS, the Knowledge Grid, and the mobile data-mining framework that we developed according to the service-based model.

11.4   Weka4WS

Weka [15] provides a large collection of machine-learning algorithms written in Java for data preprocessing, classification, clustering, association rules, and visualization, which can be invoked through a common graphical user interface (GUI). In Weka, the overall data-mining process takes place on a single machine, since the algorithms can be executed only locally. The goal of Weka4WS [5] is to extend Weka to support remote execution of the data-mining algorithms in service-oriented grid environments.

To enable remote invocation, all the data-mining algorithms provided by the Weka library (WL) are exposed as a WSRF-compliant WS, which can be easily deployed on the available grid nodes. Thus, Weka4WS also extends the Weka GUI to enable

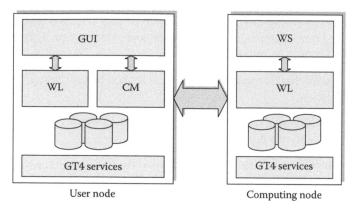

FIGURE 11.1: Software components of user nodes and computing nodes in the Weka4WS framework.

the invocation of the data-mining algorithms that are exposed as WSs on remote machines.

Weka4WS has been developed by using the Java WSRF library provided by Globus Toolkit (GT4) [16]. Moreover, all nodes involved in Weka4WS applications use the GT4 services for standard grid functionality, such as security, data management, and so on. These nodes are distinguished in two categories on the basis of the available Weka4WS components: user nodes that are the local machines providing the Weka4WS client software and computing nodes that provide the Weka4WS WS allowing for the execution of remote data-mining tasks. Data can be located on computing nodes, user nodes, or third-party nodes (e.g., shared data repositories). If a data set to be mined is not available on a computing node, it can be uploaded on it by means of the GT4 data-management services.

Figure 11.1 shows the software components of user nodes and computing nodes. Computing nodes include two components: WS and WL. The WS exposes all the data-mining algorithms provided by the underlying WL. Therefore, requests to the WS are executed by invoking the corresponding WL algorithms.

User nodes include three components: GUI, client module (CM), and WL. The GUI is an extended version of the Weka GUI to support the execution of both local and remote data-mining tasks. Local tasks are executed by directly invoking the local WL, while remote tasks are executed through the CM, which operates as an intermediary between the GUI and the WSs on remote computing nodes.

11.4.1 Implementation

Weka includes two main user interfaces: the Explorer and the KnowledgeFlow. The Explorer provides several panels, each one devoted to one of the steps that constitute the KDD process: preprocessing, data mining (classification, clustering, and association rules discovery), and visualization. The KnowledgeFlow allows users to select the Weka algorithms from a tool bar, place them onto a panel, and connect

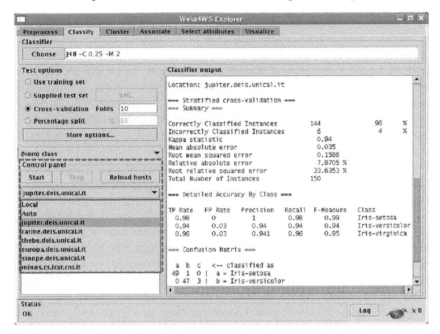

FIGURE 11.2: Weka4WS Explorer user interface. The broken box shows the panel that allows users to select a grid node where to run the data-mining task.

them together in order to form a workflow for processing and analyzing data. Weka4WS provides an extended version of both the Explorer and KnowledgeFlow interfaces to support the execution of remote and distributed data-mining tasks.

Figure 11.2 shows a snapshot of the Weka4WS Explorer interface. As highlighted by the broken box, a control panel has been added to the original Weka Explorer environment. This panel includes (1) a drop-down list to choose the grid node to which the data-mining task has to be submitted, (2) a Reload hosts button to update the list of available computing nodes, and (3) the Start and Stop buttons to start and stop the data-mining task.

Through the drop-down list the user can select one of the following items:

- *Local*: The task will be executed on the local machine, as in the standard Weka environment.

- *Auto*: The task will be submitted to one of the listed hosts; the host is selected automatically using a round-robin strategy (i.e., at each invocation, the next host in the list is chosen).

- *One of the listed hosts*: The task will be submitted to the grid node selected by the user.

Each data-mining task is managed by an independent thread. Therefore, a user can start multiple tasks in parallel on different nodes, this way taking full advantage of the distributed grid environment. Whenever the output of a data-mining task has been received from a remote computing node, it is visualized in the standard Output panel (on the right of Figure 11.2).

Like the Explorer, the original Weka KnowledgeFlow run locally. The Weka4WS KnowledgeFlow extends the original KnowledgeFlow to enable the execution of data-mining algorithms defined in a knowledge flow on multiple WSs. In this way, the overall execution time can be significantly reduced because different parts of the computation are executed in parallel on different grid nodes. This approach exploits also data locality.

Figure 11.3 shows a snapshot of the Weka4WS KnowledgeFlow interface. As in the original KnowledgeFlow environment, a user can compose a knowledge flow as a workflow linking together data loaders, filters, data-mining algorithms, and results visualizers. The new feature in the Weka4WS KnowledgeFlow is that for each algorithm in the application flow, the user can specify where such algorithm must be executed. A user can do that by right-clicking on the node that represents the algorithm, and then selecting the location of its execution through a control panel similar to that provided by the Weka4WS Explorer environment. As in the Explorer, the location can be set either to Local, Auto, or to a node specified by the user.

As an example, the distributed knowledge flow in Figure 11.3 represents a data-mining application in which a data set (covertype) is analyzed by using four different classification algorithms (J48, Random Forest, Decision Stump, and Naive

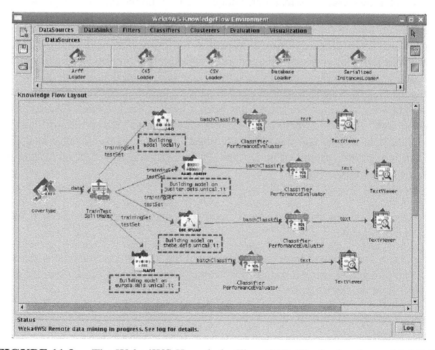

FIGURE 11.3:   The Weka4WS KnowledgeFlow GUI. The broken boxes highlight the hosts where the single data-mining tasks are running.

Bayes). The flow starts (on the left) with an ArffLoader node, used to load the data set, which is connected to a TrainTest SplitMaker node that splits the data set into training set and test set. The TrainTest SplitMaker node is connected to four nodes, each one performing a given classification algorithm. These are in turn connected to a ClassifierPerformanceEvaluator node for the model validation, and then to a TextViewer node for results visualization. The user can see the results of the data-mining tasks by clicking on the TextViewer nodes. When the application is started, the four branches of the knowledge flow are executed in parallel on four grid nodes, selected as specified by the user. As highlighted Figure 11.3, during the application execution, the environment shows the names of the hosts on which the single data mining algorithms are running.

A recent paper [6] discusses some data-mining applications developed using Weka4WS, as well as a performance analysis of the WSRF-distributed execution mechanisms implemented by Weka4WS. The experimental results demonstrate the low overhead of the WSRF WS invocation mechanisms with respect to the execution time of data-mining algorithms on large data sets, and confirms the efficiency of WSRF as a means for executing data-mining tasks on remote resources. By exploiting such mechanisms, Weka4WS provides an effective way to perform compute-intensive distributed data analysis on large-scale grid environments. The Weka4WS code is open source and it can be downloaded from http://grid.deis.unical.it/weka4ws.

11.5 Knowledge Grid

The Knowledge Grid [3] is a grid service-based environment providing knowledge-discovery services that can be used in high-performance-distributed applications. It includes high-level abstractions and a set of services by which users can integrate grid resources to be used in each phase of a knowledge-discovery process. The Knowledge Grid supports such activities by providing mechanisms and higher level services for searching resources (data, algorithms, etc.), representing, creating, and managing knowledge-discovery processes; for composing existing data services and data-mining services in a structured manner; and for allowing designers to plan, store, document, verify, share, and re-execute their workflows as well as manage their output results.

The Knowledge Grid architecture is composed of two groups of services, classified on the basis of their roles and functionalities. Indeed, two main aspects characterize a knowledge-discovery process performed in accordance with the Knowledge Grid philosophy. The first is the management of data sources, data sets, and tools to be employed in the whole process. The second is concerned with the design and management of a knowledge flow that is the sequence of steps to be executed in order to perform a complete knowledge-discovery process by exploiting the advantages coming from a grid environment. Notice that such a division has also a functional meaning, because a Knowledge Grid user first looks for data sets and tools to be used in the knowledge-discovery process, then defines the knowledge flow to be executed (by using the resources found in the first step). On the basis of such rationale, there are two distinct groups of services composing the Knowledge Grid architecture: the Resource Management Services (RMSs) and the Execution Management Services (EMSs).

The RMS group is composed of services that are devoted to the management of resources, like data sets, tools, and algorithms involved in a KDD process performed by the Knowledge Grid, as well as models inferred by previous analysis. Due to the heterogeneity of such resources, metadata represents a suitable descriptive model for them, in order to provide information about their features and their effective use. In this way, all the relevant objects for knowledge-discovery applications, such as data sources, data-mining software, tools for data preprocessing, and results of computation, are described by their metadata. RMSs comprise services that make a user able to store resource metadata and perform different kinds of resource discovery tasks. Such tasks may typically include queries on resources availability, resource location, as well as their access properties.

The EMS group is concerned with the design and management of the knowledge-discovery flow. A knowledge flow in the Knowledge Grid is modeled by the so-called execution plan that can be represented by a direct graph describing interactions and data flows between data sources, extraction tools, data-mining tools, and visualization tools. The execution graph describes the whole flow of the knowledge-discovery process, the resources involved, the data-mining steps, etc. The EMS module contains services that are devoted to create an execution plan, and to transform and execute it, on the basis of the available resources and the basic Grid services running on the host. It is worth noticing that when a user submits a knowledge-discovery application to the Knowledge Grid, he or she has no knowledge about all the low-level details needed by the execution plan. More precisely, the client submits to the Knowledge Grid a high-level description of the KDD application, named conceptual model, more targeted to distributed knowledge-discovery aspects than to grid-related issues. A specific function of the EMSs is to create an execution plan on the basis of the conceptual model received from the user, and execute it by using the resources effectively available. To realize this logic, the EMS module follows a two-step approach: it initially models an abstract execution plan that in a second step is resolved into a concrete execution plan.

Figure 11.4 shows the architecture of the Knowledge Grid. A client application that wants to submit a knowledge-discovery computation to the Knowledge Grid does not need to interact with all of these services, but just with a few of them. Inside each group, in fact, there are two layers of services: high-level services and core-level services. The design idea is that user-level applications directly interact with high-level services that, in order to perform client requests, invoke suitable operations exported by the core-level services. In turn, core-level services perform their operations by invoking basic services provided by available grid environments running on the specific host, as well as by interacting with other core-level services. In other words, operations exported by high-level services are designed to be invoked by user-level applications, whereas operations provided by core-level services are thought to be invoked both by high-level and core-level services.

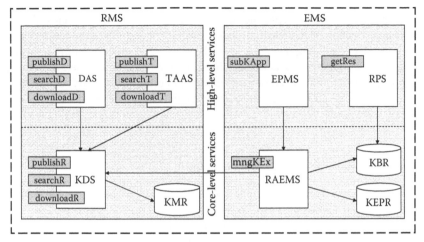

FIGURE 11.4:   Knowledge Grid architecture.

Before giving further details about the Knowledge Grid services, we would like to point out that the Knowledge Grid prototype has been used to implement distributed data-mining applications in different fields.

A first example is a classification task performed on a large set of data generated by monitoring a network environment subject to simulated intrusion [8]. Through the Knowledge Grid, the original data set has been first partitioned and distributed on a set of nodes. Then, a number of independent classifiers have been computed by applying in parallel the same learning algorithm over the set of distributed training sets. Afterward, the best classifier has been chosen by means of a voting operation. This application has been tested on Grid deployments ranging from three to eight nodes. The measured speedup ranged from about two to five compared to the sequential execution on a single node.

Another applications developed on the Knowledge Grid has been focused on bioinformatics, in particular a proteomics application [17]. This application carries out the clustering of human-protein sequences using TribeMCL, a clustering method through which it is possible to cluster correlated proteins into groups termed "protein family." Similar to the previous application, the overall data set is partitioned and distributed on different nodes, where the clustering task is performed in parallel. The application has been tested on a small Knowledge Grid deployment including three nodes, obtaining an execution time reduced by a factor of about 2.3 with respect to the sequential execution.

The last application we mention here is the integration of a query-based data-mining system into the Knowledge Grid [18]. KDDML-MQL is a system for the execution of complex mining tasks expressed as high-level queries. A KDDML query has the structure of a tree in which each node is a KDDML operator specifying the execution of a KDD task or the logical combination of results coming from lower levels of the tree. To achieve its integration into the Knowledge Grid, KDDML has been modified into a distributed application composed of three independent phases: query entering and splitting, query executor, and results visualization. The distributed execution of KDDML has been modeled according to the master–worker paradigm, a worker being an instance of the query executor. In addition, a proper allocation policy for the subqueries has been implemented. It is based both on optimization criteria and on the structure of the tree, in order to correctly reconstruct the final response combining the partial results. Details about experimental results can be found in Ref. [18].

11.5.1   Resource Management Services

This group of services includes basic and high-level functionalities for managing different kinds of Knowledge Grid resources. Among such resources, data sources and algorithms are of main importance, for this reason the Knowledge Grid architecture provides ad-hoc components, namely Data Access Service (DAS) and Tools and Algorithms Access Service (TAAS), for dealing with data, tools, and algorithms.

DAS. It is concerned with the publishing, searching, and transferring of data sets to be used in a KDD application, as well as the search for inferred models (resulting from the mining process). The DAS exports the publishData, searchData, and downloadData operations. The publishData is invoked by a user-level application to publish metadata about a data set; as soon as a publish operation is requested, it passes the corresponding metadata to the local Knowledge Directory Service (KDS) by invoking the publishResource operation. The searchData operation is invoked by a client interface that needs to locate a data set on the basis of a specified set of criteria. The DAS submits its request to the local KDS, by invoking the corresponding searchResource and, as soon as the search is completed, it receives the result from the KDS. Such a result consists in a set of references to the data sets matching the specified search criteria. It is worth noticing that the search operation is not just handled on the local host, but it is also remotely forwarded to other hosts. Finally, the downloadData operation works similarly to the previous operations: it receives the reference of the data set to be download and forwards the request to the downloadResource of the local KDS component. The DAS is, together with the TAAS, a high-level service of the RMS group.

TAAS. It is concerned with the publishing, searching, and transferring of tools to be used in a knowledge-discovery application. Such tools can be extraction tools, data-mining tools, and visualization tools. It has the same basic structure as the DAS and performs the main tasks by interacting with a local instance of the KDS, which in turn may invoke one or more other remote KDS instances. The operations that are exported by the TAAS are publishTool, searchTool, and downloadTool. They have similar functionalities and similar behavior as DAS operations, with the difference that TAAS operations are concerned with tools and not with data.

KDS. It is the only core-level service of the RMS group. It manages metadata describing Knowledge Grid resources. Such resources comprise hosts, repositories of data to be mined, tools and algorithms used to extract, analyze, and manipulate data, and knowledge models obtained as results of mining processes. Such information is stored in a local repository, the Knowledge Metadata Repository (KMR). The KDS exports the publishResource, searchResource, and downloadResource operations. As previously noticed, they are invoked by the high-level services, DAS or TAAS (to perform operations on data sets or tools, respectively). The publish Resource operation is invoked to publish information (metadata) about a resource; the publish operation is made effective by storing their metadata in the local KMR. The searchResource operation is invoked to retrieve a resource on the basis of a given set of criteria represented by a query. An important aspect to be pointed out is that the KDS performs such a searching task both locally, by accessing the local KMR, and remotely, by querying other remote KDSs (that in turn will access their local KMR). The downloadResource operation asks that a given resource is downloaded to the local site; also in this case, if the requested resource is not stored on the local site, the KDS will forward such a request to other remote KDS instances.

11.5.2 Execution Management Services

Services belonging to this group allow a user to design and execute KDD applications, as well as delivering and visualizing the computation result.

EPMS. The Execution Plan Management Service (EPMS) allows for defining the structure of an application by building the corresponding execution graph and adding a set of constraints about resources. This service, on the basis of a conceptual model received from the client, generates its corresponding abstract execution plan that is a more formal representation of the structure of the application. Generally, it does not contain information on the physical grid resources to be used, but rather constraints and other criteria about them. Nevertheless, it can include both well-identified resources and abstract resources, that is, resources that are defined through logical names and quality-of-service requirements. The EPMS exports the submit KApplication operation, through which it receives a conceptual model of the application to be executed and transforms it into an abstract execution plan for subsequent processing by the Resource Allocation and Execution Management Service (RAEMS). The mapping between the abstract execution plan and a more concrete representation of it, as well as its execution, is delegated to the RAEMS.

RPS. The Results Presentation Service (RPS) offers facilities for presenting and visualizing the extracted knowledge models (e.g., association rules, clustering models, and decision trees), as well as to store them in a suitable format for future reference. It is pointed out that the results stage-out, often needed for delivering results to the client, is an important task of this service. Indeed, a user can remotely interact with the Knowledge Grid and, as soon as the final result is computed, it is delivered to the client host and made available for visualization.

RAEMS. It is used to find a suitable mapping between an abstract execution plan (received from the EPMS) and available resources, with the goal of satisfying the constraints (CPU, storage, memory, database, and network bandwidth requirements) imposed by the execution plan. The output of this process is a concrete execution plan, which explicitly defines the resource requests for each data-mining process. In particular, it matches requirements specified in the abstract execution plan with real names, location of services, data files, etc. From the interface viewpoint, the RAEMS exports the manageKExecution operation, which is invoked by the EPMS and receives the abstract execution plan. Starting from it, the RAEMS queries the local KDS (through the searchResource operation) to obtain information about the resources needed to create a concrete execution plan from the abstract execution plan. As soon as the concrete execution plan is obtained, the RAEMS coordinates the actual execution of the overall computation. For this purpose, the RAEMS invokes the appropriate services (data-mining services and basic grid services) as specified by the concrete execution plan. As soon as the computation terminates, the RAEMS stores its results into the Knowledge Base Repository (KBR), while the execution plans are stored into the Knowledge Execution Plan Repository (KEPR). As a final operation, in order to publish results obtained by the computation, the RAEMS publishes their metadata (result metadata) into the KMR (by invoking the publishResource operation of the local KDS).

11.6 Mobile Data-Mining Services

After the description of two frameworks for designing data-mining applications on wired grids, in this section, we present a mobile data-mining system based on a wireless SOA. Here, we refer to mobile data mining as the process of using mobile devices for running data-mining applications involving remote computers and remote data. The availability of client programs on mobile devices that can invoke the remote execution of data-mining tasks and show the mining results is a significant added value for nomadic people and organizations. Those users need to perform analysis of data stored in repositories far away from the site where they work, thus mobile-mining services allow them to generate knowledge regardless of their physical location.

This section shortly discusses pervasive data mining of databases from mobile devices through the use of WSRF-compliant WSs. By implementing mobile WSs, the system allows remote users to execute data-mining tasks on a grid from a mobile phone or a personal digital assistant (PDA) and receive on those devices the results of a data analysis task.

The system is based on the client–server architecture shown in Figure 11.5 [7]. The architecture includes three types of components:

- *Data providers*: Applications that generate the data to be mined

- *Mobile clients*: Applications that require the execution of data mining computations on remote data

- *Mining servers*: Server nodes used for storing the data generated by data providers and for executing the data-mining tasks submitted by mobile clients

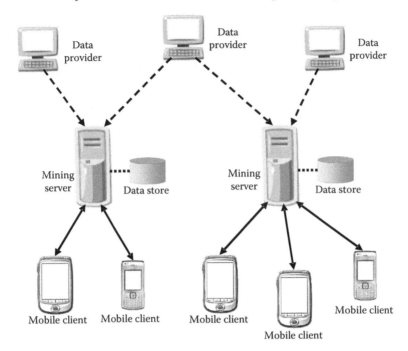

FIGURE 11.5: Mobile data-mining services framework.

As shown in Figure 11.5, data generated by data providers is collected by a set of mining servers that store it in a local data store. Depending on the application requirements, data coming from a given provider could be stored in more than one mining server.

The main role of mining servers is allowing mobile clients to perform data mining on remote data by using a set of data-mining algorithms. Once connected to a given server, the mobile client allows a user to select the remote data to be analyzed and the algorithm to be run. When the data-mining task has been completed on the mining server, the results of the computation are visualized on the user device either in textual or visual form.

11.6.1 Mining Server

Each mining server exposes its functionalities through two WSs: the Data Collection Service (DCS) and the Data Mining Service (DMS). Figure 11.6 shows the DCS and DMS and the other software components of a mining server.

The DCS is invoked by data providers to store data on the server. The DCS interface defines a set of basic operations for uploading a new data set, updating an existing data set with incremental data, or deleting an existing data set. These operations are overally indicated as DCS ops in Figure 11.6. Data uploaded through the DCS is stored as plain data sets in the local file system. As shown in Figure 11.6, the

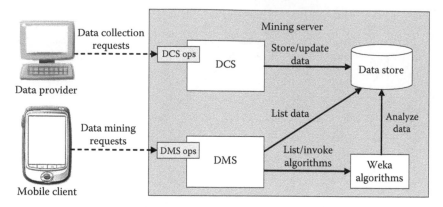

FIGURE 11.6:   Software components of a mining server.

DCS performs either store or update operations on the local data sets in response to data providers requests.

The DMS is invoked by mobile clients to perform data-mining tasks. Its interface defines a set of operations (DMS ops) that allow to obtain the list of the available data sets and algorithms, submit a data-mining task, get the current status of a computation, and get the result of a given task.

The data analysis is performed by the DMS using a subset of the algorithms provided by the WL. When a data-mining task is submitted to the DMS, the appropriate algorithm of the WL is invoked to analyze the local data set specified by the mobile client.

11.6.2   Mobile Client

The mobile client is composed by three components: the MIDlet, the DMS stub, and the RMS (Figure 11.7)

The MIDlet is a J2ME application allowing the user to perform data-mining operations and visualize their results. The DMS stub is a WS stub allowing the MIDlet to invoke the operations of a remote DMS. Even if the DMS stub and

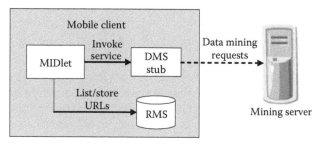

FIGURE 11.7:   Software components of a mobile client.

the MIDlet are two logically separated components, they are distributed and installed as a single J2ME application.

The RMS is a simple record-oriented database that allows J2ME applications to persistently store data across multiple invocations. In our system, the MIDlet uses the RMS to store the URLs of the remote DMSs that can be invoked by the user. The list of URLs stored in the RMS can be updated by the user using a MIDlet functionality.

11.6.3 Implementation

The WSs discussed above have been implemented using the WSRF Java library provided by GT4 and a subset of the WL as data-mining algorithms. The mobile client has been implemented by the Sun Java Wireless Toolkit, a widely adopted suite for the development of J2ME applications.

The small size of the screen is one of the main limitations of mobile device applications. In data-mining tasks, in particular, a limited screen size can affect the appropriate visualization of complex results representing the discovered model. In our system, we overcome this limitation by splitting the result in different parts and allowing a user to select which part to visualize at one time. Moreover, users can choose to visualize the mining model (e.g., a cluster assignment or a decision tree) either in textual form or as an image. In both cases, if the information does not fit the screen size, the user can scroll it by using the normal navigation facilities of the mobile device.

As an example, Figure 11.8 shows two screenshots of the mobile client taken from a test application. The screenshot on the left shows the menu for selecting which part

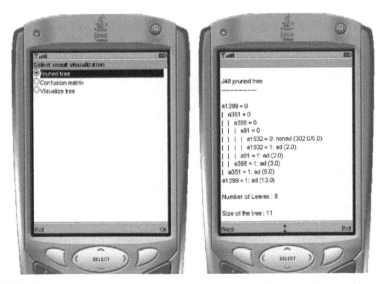

FIGURE 11.8: Two screenshots of the client applications running on the emulator of the Sun Java Wireless Toolkit.

of the result of a classification task must be visualized, while the screenshot on the right shows the result, in that case the pruned tree resulting from classification.

Our early experiments show that the system performance depends almost entirely on the computing power of the server on which the data-mining task is executed. On the contrary, the overhead due to the communication between MIDlet and DMS does not affect the execution time in a significantly way, since the amount of data exchanged between client and server is very small. In general, when the data-mining task is relatively time consuming, the communication overhead is a negligible percentage of the overall execution time.

11.7   Conclusions

Grid-computing systems and data analysis techniques are two primary technologies for implementing innovative data- and knowledge-intensive applications. The main thesis of this chapter is that the grid can be used as an effective cyber infrastructure for implementing and deploying geographically distributed data-mining and knowledge-discovery services and applications. Future uses of the grid are mainly related to the ability to utilize it as a knowledge-oriented platform that is able to run world-wide complex distributed applications. Among those, knowledge-discovery applications are a major goal. To reach this goal, the grid needs to evolve toward an open decentralized platform based on interoperable high-level services that make use of knowledge both in providing resources and in giving results to end users [19].

Software frameworks and technologies for the implementation and deployment of knowledge services, as those we discussed in this chapter, provide key elements to build up data analysis applications on enterprise or campus grids or on a world-wide grid. Those models, techniques, and tools can be instrumented in grids as decentralized and interoperable services that enable the development of complex systems such as distributed knowledge-discovery suites and knowledge-management systems offering pervasive access, adaptivity, and high performance to single users, professional teams, and virtual organizations in science, engineering, and industry that need to create and use knowledge-based applications.

References

[1] Next Generation Grids Expert Group Report 3. Future for European Grids: Grids and Service-Oriented Knowledge Utilities, January 2006.

[2] M. Cannataro and D. Talia. Semantics and knowledge grids: Building the next-generation grid. *IEEE Intelligent Systems and Their Applications*, 19(1): 56–63, 2004.

[3] M. Cannataro and D. Talia. The knowledge grid. *Communications of the ACM*, 46(1): 89–93, 2003.

[4] A. Congiusta, D. Talia, and P. Trunfio. Distributed data mining services leveraging WSRF. *Future Generation Computer Systems*, 23(1): 34–41, 2007.

[5] D. Talia, P. Trunfio, and O. Verta. Weka4WS: A WSRF-enabled Weka toolkit for distributed data mining on grids. In *Proceedings of the 9th European Conference on Principles and Practice of Knowledge Discovery in Databases (PKDD 2005)*, Vol. 3721 of *LNCS*, pp. 309–320, Springer, Porto, Portugal, 2005.

[6] D. Talia, P. Trunfio, and O. Verta. The Weka4WS framework for distributed data mining in service-oriented grids. *Concurrency and Computation: Practice and Experience*. To appear.

[7] D. Talia and P. Trunfio. Mobile data mining on small devices through Web services. In L. T. Yang, A. Borgy Waluyo, J. Ma, L. Tan, and B. Srinivasan (Eds.), *Mobile Intelligence: Mobile Computing and Computational Intelligence*. Wiley, New York. To appear.

[8] M. Cannataro, A. Congiusta, A. Pugliese, D. Talia, and P. Trunfio. Distributed data mining on grids: Services, tools, and applications. *IEEE Transactions on Systems, Man, and Cybernetics: Part B*, 34(6): 2451–2465, 2004.

[9] I. Foster, C. Kesselman, J. Nick, and S. Tuecke. The physiology of the grid. In F. Berman, G. Fox, and A. Hey (Eds.), *Grid Computing: Making the Global Infrastructure a Reality*, pp. 217–249. Wiley, New York, 2003.

[10] K. Czajkowski, D. Ferguson, I. Foster, J. Frey, S. Graham, I. Sedukhin, D. Snelling, S. Tuecke, and W. Vambenepe. The WS-Resource Framework— Version 1.0, 2004. Available at http://www.ibm.com/developerworks/library/ws-resource/ws-wsrf.pdf.

[11] S. Al Sairafi, F.-S. Emmanouil, M. Ghanem, N. Giannadakis, Y. Guo, D. Kalaitzopoulos, M. Osmond, A. Rowe, J. Syed, and P. Wendel. The design of discovery net: Towards open grid services for knowledge discovery. *International Journal of High Performance Computing Applications*, 17(3): 297–315, 2003.

[12] P. Brezany, J. Hofer, A. M. Tjoa, and A. Woehrer. GridMiner: An infrastructure for data mining on computational grids. In *APAC Conference and Exhibition on Advanced Computing, Grid Applications and eResearch*, Queensland, Australia, 2003.

[13] A. S. Ali, O. F. Rana, and I. J. Taylor. Web services composition for distributed data mining. In *Workshop on Web and Grid Services for Scientific Data Analysis*, pp. 11–18, Oslo, Norway, 2005.

[14] I. Taylor, M. Shields, I. Wang, and A. Harrison. The Triana workflow environment: Architecture and applications. In I. Taylor, E. Deelman, D. Gannon,

and M. Shields (Eds.), *Workflows for E-Science*, pp. 320–339. Springer, New York, 2007.

[15] I. H. Witten and E. Frank. *Data Mining: Practical Machine Learning Tools and Techniques*, 2nd edn. Morgan Kaufmann, San Francisco, CA, 2005.

[16] I. Foster. Globus Toolkit Version 4: Software for service-oriented systems. In *International Conference on Network and Parallel Computing (NPC'05)*, Vol. 3779 of *LNCS*, pp. 2–13, Springer, Beijing, China, 2005.

[17] M. Cannataro, C. Comito, A. Congiusta, and P. Veltri. PROTEUS: A bioinformatics problem solving environment on grids. *Parallel Processing Letters*, 14(2): 217–237, 2004.

[18] G. Bueti, A. Congiusta, and D. Talia. Developing distributed data mining applications in the KNOWLEDGE GRID framework. In *High Performance Computing for Computational Science—VECPAR'04*, Vol. 3402 of *LNCS*, pp. 156–169, Springer, Valencia, Spain, 2004.

[19] F. Berman. From TeraGrid to knowledge grid. *Communications of the ACM*, 44(11): 27–28, 2001.

Chapter 12

Discovering Emergent Behavior from Network Packet Data: Lessons from the Angle Project

Robert L. Grossman, Michael Sabala, Yunhong Gu, Anushka Anand, Matt Handley, Rajmonda Sulo, and Lee Wilkinson

Contents

12.1   Introduction

There are millions of computers connected to the Internet and billions of network flows that access them. Unfortunately, not all these flows are benign, and an increasing number of them are associated with some type of anomalous behavior, such as sending spam, probing for system vulnerabilities, attempting to install malware, and related behavior. Detecting suspicious flows across the Internet is a challenging problem in high-performance analytics.

One of the reasons the problem is challenging is because the types of suspicious flows change all the time. One of the goals in this project was to detect behavior that is suspicious and different than the type of behavior that has been seen before. We call this type of suspicious behavior *emergent* and give a precise definition of it in Section 12.4.

There were three technical challenges in this project:

1. The first challenge was to develop an architecture for the system that supports discovery from very large, geographically distributed data sets.

2. The second challenge was how to define emergent behavior in a meaningful way and to develop algorithms to detect it.

3. The third challenge was to develop a visual analytics interface that could be used effectively by analysts.

There was also one practical challenge in the project:

4. The organizations we worked with were very reluctant to share data, due to the privacy required when working with IP traffic. A practical challenge was to develop an anonymization procedure and policies for handling data that are protective enough of privacy that institutions would share IP data but that left enough information so that sharing data was still useful.

In this chapter, we introduce a system called Angle for making discoveries about emergent behavior from distributed IP data. Angle is based upon a framework so that information from geographically distributed locations can be combined together easily in order to detect emergent behavior that may not be readily apparent simply by analyzing data from one location.

The majority of prior work in this area is what is usually called signature based. Signatures of specific attacks are created and IP data is screened using these signatures. Snort is one of the most widely deployed systems for analyzing IP packet data using signatures [1]. There are also a variety of statistical-based techniques (see, for example, Ref. [2] and the references cited therein). Angle is a statistical-based system.

This chapter is organized as follows: Section 12.2 includes some background materials and describes related work. Section 12.3 describes the Angle architecture. Section 12.4 describes the data analysis methodology used by Angle. Section 12.5 describes the visual analytics interface. Section 12.6 describes several experimental studies and the status of the project. Section 12.7 includes some lessons learned and contains a summary and conclusion.

12.2   Background and Related Work

12.2.1   Emergent Behavior

There are many ways that emergent behavior can be defined. Our approach is to define emergence based upon two abstractions: windows and models (or summarizations).

We give several examples below. Given these abstractions, assume that we have a sequence of windows w_1, w_2, w_3, ... and a sequence of corresponding models M_1, M_2, M_3, ... Loosely speaking, we say that there is emergent behavior at $\gamma > 1$ in case (1) the models M_i for $i \leq \gamma$ are similar; and (2) the models M_γ and $M_{\gamma+1}$ are dissimilar. More precisely, assume also that there is a distance function defined on the models:

$$d(M_i,M_j) \geq 0, \quad d(M_i,M_j) = d(M_j,M_i), \quad i \neq j, \quad d(M_i,M_i) = 0.$$

More precisely, we say there is emergent behavior at $\gamma > 1$ in case there are constants $B_0 > 0$, $B_1 > 0$, and $D > 1$ such that

$$d(M_{i-1},M_i) \leq B_0, \quad i = \gamma - D, \gamma - D + 1, \ldots, \gamma - 1.$$

$$d(M_{\gamma-1},M_\gamma) \geq B_1.$$

Of course, as a variant, we could require that the models M_i are uniformly similar within the windows $w_{\gamma-D}$, ..., $w_{\gamma-1}$.

Example. The setup for this example is that we have time-stamped events and given a collection of events one can compute feature vectors. In the first example, we assume that the windows w_j are temporal and that each event can be assigned to one window. For each time window w_j, collect all the events that fall within the window and compute feature vectors. Let the model associated with window w_j be defined by a cluster model M_j containing k clusters, with centers $a_{j,1}, a_{j,2}, \ldots, a_{j,k}$, that is computed from the feature vectors associated with the window. Define a distance function

$$d(M_i,M_j) = \sum_{\alpha=1}^{k} \left(\min_\beta ||a_{i,\alpha} - a_{j,\beta}||^2 \right). \tag{12.1}$$

There are many variants of this example, depending upon how we define the clusters and how we measure the similarity (and dissimilarity) of two or more cluster models.

There is a large literature on outliers. A good overview of the subject is Ref. [3]. A standard definition is to define an outlier as an observation (or set of observations) that appears to be inconsistent with the remainder of that set of data [3] (page 7). Although one could argue that any method used to identify outliers could be used to identify emergent behavior, we are only interested in this chapter in the much more narrow definition of emergent behavior defined above.

12.2.2   Algorithms for Detecting Emergent Behavior

The point γ at which emergent behavior occurs is an example of a change point [4]. Given any distance function $d(\cdot,\cdot)$, a variety of algorithms for the quickest detection of a change point could be applied to the time series $x_i = d(M_{i-1},M_i)$. In general, these require some assumptions about the statistical properties of the time series x_i (see, for example, Ref. [4]).

Detecting emergent behavior is related to novelty detection. Reference [5] also uses models to detect new or novel behavior. The idea is to sound an alarm when a model no longer matches the observed data well, whereas the idea here is to look at the distance between models that describe the data in a sequence of windows.

Reference [6] also focuses on aggregate behavior in windows but, in contrast to the work described in this chapter, is interested in the efficient detection of bursts in data streams.

Our preliminary studies involving Angle have primarily used cluster models. Using a large number of clusters to identify new types of behavior has been used previously in Refs. [7,8]. The approach described here is similar to these approaches in two ways: First, data points that are not closely associated with clusters are considered as candidates for emergent behavior. Second, data points belonging to clusters with small cardinality are also considered candidates for emergent behavior. The approach described above is different than Refs. [7,8] in that we analyze large numbers of different clusters (indeed on cluster model for each window) and analyze the behavior of these different cluster models to identify periods of stability followed by behavior that may be identified as emergent (see Figure 12.2).

Another approach that is sometimes used is to use a one-class learning method, such as one-class support vector machine (SVM) [9–11]. With this approach, *all* data in a training period is considered to be positive and a one-class SVM is used to find the boundary of the positively labeled data. This one-class SVM is then used to score data, and anything not assigned by the SVM to the positive class is considered emergent.

12.2.3   Cloud-Based Computing Platforms for Data Mining

The most common platform for data mining is a single workstation. There are also several data-mining systems that have been developed for local clusters of workstations, distributed clusters of workstations, and grids [12]. More recently, data-mining systems have been developed that use Web services and, more generally, a service-oriented architecture.

By and large, data-mining systems that have been developed to date for clusters, distributed clusters, and grids have assumed that the processors are the scarce resource, and hence shared. When processors become available, the data is moved to the processors, the computation is started, and results are computed and returned [13]. To simplify, this is the supercomputing (and distributed supercomputing) model. With this approach, in practice for many computations, a good portion of the time is spent transporting the data.

An alternative approach has become more common during the last few years. In this approach, the data is persistently stored and computations take place over the data when required. In this model, the data waits for the task or query. To simplify, this is the data center (and distributed data center) model. This is an example of what is sometimes called a cloud-computing model. A storage or data cloud is used to manage the persistent data. A compute cloud is layered over the storage cloud and provides computing services. Examples of data or storage clouds include Amazon's S3 [14], the Google file system [15], and the open source Hadoop system [16].

To date, work on data clouds [14–16] has assumed relatively small bandwidth between the distributed clusters containing the data. In contrast, the Sector storage cloud used for the Angle application is designed for wide-area, high-performance 10 Gbps networks and employs specialized protocols such as UDP-based data transport (UDT) [17] to utilize the available bandwidth on these networks.

The most common way to compute these days over storage clouds is to use MapReduce [18]. In Angle, the Sphere compute cloud is designed to use a style of high-performance distributed computing which is a generalization of MapReduce in which both the Map and Reduce functions are replaced by user-defined functions that can be executed simply over the Sector storage cloud using the Sphere libraries.

12.3 Angle Architecture

In this section, we describe the architecture of the Angle system. Angle consists of three types of nodes:

1. *Sensor nodes.* The first type of nodes are sensor nodes that are attached to the commodity Internet and collect IP data.

2. *Cloud nodes.* The second type of nodes are connected via a wide-area, high-performance network and run cloud-based storage and computing services. Each sensor node is associated to a cloud node and data is passed from the sensor node to this node for processing. The nodes in the cloud can be used both for processing data locally as well as for the distributed processing of data. It is important feature of this architecture that nodes in the cloud also provide persistent storage for data collected by the associated sensor node.

3. *Grid nodes.* The third type of nodes are pools of nodes that run grid services. Grid nodes are used for specialized compute intensive tasks, such as the reanalysis of previously collected data. Data is moved to grid nodes as required.

Figure 12.1 contains a diagram of this architecture. If a computer has two network cards, one for the commodity Internet and one for a high-performance network connecting the Angle cloud nodes, then an Angle sensor node and an Angle cloud node may both share the same physical computer.

Angle cloud nodes run a peer-to-peer storage system called Sector that is designed to manage large remote and distributed data over wide-area, high-performance networks [19]. Sector is based on the Chord peer-to-peer routing API [20]. All participating cloud nodes belong to the storage system, which uses the Chord-routing API to locate files by their names. A data channel is then set up between the Sector node that a storage client connects to and the Sector storage server node that holds the desired file. To transport data efficiently over high-performance networks with high bandwidth delay products, Angle uses a network transport protocol called UDT [21], for the data channel.

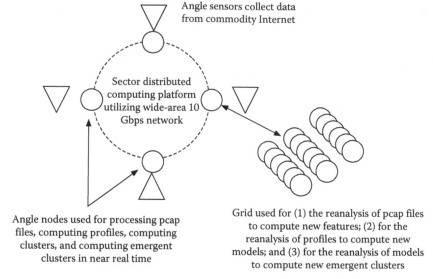

Angle sensors collect data
from commodity Internet

Sector distributed
computing platform
utilizing wide-area 10
Gbps network

Angle nodes used for processing pcap
files, computing profiles, computing
clusters, and computing emergent
clusters in near real time

Grid used for (1) the reanalysis of pcap files
to compute new features; (2) for the
reanalysis of profiles to compute new
models; and (3) for the reanalysis of models
to compute new emergent clusters

FIGURE 12.1: This is an overview of the Angle architecture. Data is collected in near real time from sensors located on the commodity Internet. Each Angle sensor node is paired to an Angle cloud node on a distributed computing platform running Sector and UDT middleware. Data analysis is done using the Angle cloud nodes.

Angle Sensors, running on sensor nodes, collect IP packet data and buffer it. In addition, Angle Sensors run code that extract features from IP packet data belonging to a rolling window and transport it to an Angle cloud node running Sector.

We close this section with three remarks.

First, a simple generalization of this architecture is to replace sensor nodes with data ingestion nodes whose purpose is to ingest data into the Sector cloud. Once ingested, the data is managed persistently by the Sector cloud and compute services are provided as required by the Sphere cloud. We have used this architecture to manage, analyze, and mine a variety of different e-science data sets, including data sets from biology, astronomy, and Earth science.

Second, in contrast to a grid computing architecture where data is generally moved to a shared pool of compute nodes as required by computing tasks [8], the Angle cloud-based infrastructure provides long-term persistence for data and exploits locality whenever possible. Sphere compute services are designed so that as much as the computation as possible is done without moving the data. This is an important benefit of this type of architecture, as compared, for example, with grid services as commonly deployed.

Third, it is important to note that some of the Angle cloud nodes are connected by a 10 Gbps network, which is faster than the backplane of some computers. This type of wide-area distributed computer was first popularized by the OptIPuter [22], and

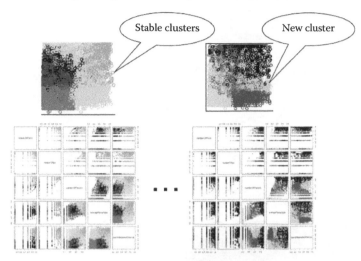

FIGURE 12.2: (See color insert following page 264.) At the bottom of the figure are two scatter matrix plots (sploms). On the lower left is a splom from a period in which the clusters are stable. On the lower right is a splom as a new cluster emerges after the period of stability illustrated in the left splom. Above the sploms is a blow up in which the new cluster can be seen (the gray cluster).

with the proper middleware, such as Sector and UDT, enables certain data-intensive computing tasks to be completed almost as efficiently as if the data were colocated in one place.

12.4 Angle Data Analysis Methodology

12.4.1 Overview

In this section, we describe the approach used by Angle to analyze distributed IP data.

Collecting and processing packets. Network data is captured by independently managed network monitoring servers running IP packet capture software that we have developed. Typically we use fast servers that monitor a port-mirror of an output port of a switch or router on the edge of a network.

Angle capture software was designed to preserve privacy while capturing sufficient packet information to allow behavioral data mining. Source and destination IP addresses are hashed using a randomly generated salt, which is changed automatically by the software every time it is restarted or when the previous salt is 1 week old. Payload checksum is computed and stored, and the payload itself is nulled. MAC address fields along with checksum are nulled. Geolocation information is looked up

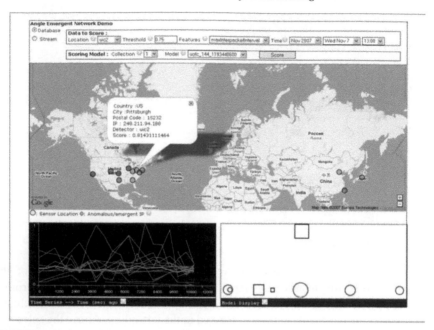

FIGURE 12.3:   This is a screen shot from Angle that shows the visual analytics interface.

based on IP addresses prior to their hashing and includes country, state, city, and zip code (as available). The captured data is stored in a standard pcap format [23] to allow processing with standard tools and at no time are nonanonymized packets stored on disk. Furthermore, salts are nonrecoverable. Uploads of pcap files are

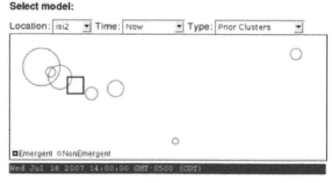

FIGURE 12.4:   This is a view of one of the Angle models. Squares represent emergent clusters, while circles represent regular clusters. The Angle system currently has access to over 100,000 separate models that can be selected and used to look for anomalies and emergent behavior in near real time or from historical data.

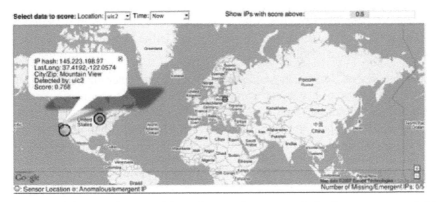

FIGURE 12.5: In the Map View above of emergent behavior, once a model is selected, emergent or anomalous IPs are identified in pink.

handled automatically by a data collection tool that manages a queue of files on the local disk of the sensor, spools the files, and uploads them to a near-by Angle cloud node. Care was required to build a tool that captures all the required data despite the variety of failures that happen from time to time at each site. Examples of failures machines going down, networks going down, disks getting full, etc. Currently a compressed pcap file is sent every 10 min by each monitoring location.

Temporal aggregation. We then choose a window length d and aggregate the data in pcap files into temporal windows of length d. Call these: w_1, w_2, w_3, etc.

Computing profiles. The next step is that the pcap data for each temporal window w_i is processed to produce profiles maintained by Angle, by which we mean summary data associated with a specific entity of interest as defined by one or more features associated with the entity of interest.[*] In the experimental studies described below, we compute profiles associated with Source IP addresses, but other types of profiles can be easily generated using the Angle.

As an example of the features that we have used to compute profiles, some of our experimental studies have used the following eight features: number of ports touched by the IP, number of destination IPs touched by the IP, number of packets sent, average packet size, average data size, maximum packets per destination, maximum packets per port, and maximum interpacket interval. The features are normalized using data collected over a period of time and over several locations. The Angle system is designed so that features can be easily added or removed.

The pcap queuing process running on the Angle Sensor receives pcap files and queues them for processing by the Angle Cloud nodes that compute profiles. The results are stored in files and are also tracked in a SQL database. The database stores

---

[*] Currently, since we are still performing experiment studies to determine the optimal window size d, we compute feature vectors for each pcap file and then aggregate these feature vectors as required.

information about each pcap file—site, time interval, number of packets, number of dropped packets, and number of hosts—and stores URLs to the pcap file along with URL to the computed profile file.

Computing models. Next each profile file is processed to determine clusters, which we view as a convenient way of summarizing the behavior at a particular sensor location over a particular time period. Currently, clusters are computed using the k-means algorithm, but other algorithms can also be easily used. More generally, from the viewpoint of Angle as a system, the k-means algorithm can be replaced by any algorithm that processes a dataset of profiles and produces a model that can be used for scoring, say as specified by PMML standard [24,25].

More specifically, for the feature vectors associated with each window w_i, clusters are computed with centers $a_{i,1}$, $a_{i,2}$, ..., $a_{i,k}$ and the temporal evolution of these clusters is used to identify certain clusters called emergent clusters.

Meta-analysis of models. Next collections of models are analyzed to determine emergent behavior. Emergent clusters can be defined in various ways. As described above, our approach is to look for a period in which collections of clusters are relatively stable, and, then, after a period of such stability, to define as emergent any new cluster that arises. The details are in Section 12.4.2.

Real-time scoring of profiles. The Angle system allows models to be browsed, visualized, and selected. Once a model is selected, emergent clusters in the model are scored using the Angle scoring functions. This process is described below.

12.4.2   Computing Stable and Emergent Clusters

As mentioned above, a set of clusters for a selected combination of sensor locations and time window w_i are an example of a "model" M_i in the Angle application. As above, let $a_{i,\alpha}$ denote the centers (for $\alpha = 1,2, ..., k$) of the cluster model M_i associated with window w_i.

For example, if the clusters are relatively stable for windows w_1, w_2, ..., $w_{\gamma-1}$, but there is a statistically significant change at w_γ, then one or more clusters from model $M_{\gamma+1}$ associated with window $w_{\gamma+1}$ can be identified. These are the simply clusters that are responsible for the jump in the function $d(M_{\gamma-1},M_\gamma)$ (see Equation 12.1). These clusters are called emergent clusters (see Figure 12.2).

In the experimental studies reported here, we identify emergent behavior using the statistic (compare Equation 12.1)

$$\delta_i = \sum_{\alpha=1}^{k} \left(\min_\beta ||a_{i,\alpha} - a_{i-1,\beta}||^2 \right) \qquad (12.2)$$

Figure 12.6 shows this statistic δ_i for windows of length d equals 10 min. Notice that it is quite choppy. On the other hand, Figure 12.7 shows the same statistic for windows of length d equals 1 day, where it is easy to identify three period of emergent behavior.

receiving these requests performs an analysis using the user's parameters. Once the analysis is complete, the results are returned to client's Web browser and appropriate views are updated.

To use the interface, the first task for the user is to select a model to determine emergent behavior. This is accomplished using the lower-right Model View panel of the interface. Next, the user selects the type of comparison to occur (Prior Clusters, Common Clusters or Daily Average) and the data capture location for Angle to use for signaling emergent behavior. Data sets captured at any interval may be specified to search for emergent clusters.

Once emergent behavior is located, a user can determine which IP address hashes (IPhash) are involved in the anomalous activity. The upper Map View panel, showing a map of the world, is utilized to place anomalous IPhashes onto the world map. The angle score slider at the upper-right corner of the panel controls the threshold of Angle scores to be visualized. The user can experiment with this slider, starting it near 0, and moving it up to filter visualization of low-scoring IPhashes. Clicking on red circular icons reveals information about the selected IPhash.

12.6 Experimental Studies

12.6.1 Angle Data Collection

Angle Sensors are currently installed at four locations: the University of Illinois at Chicago, the University of Chicago, Argonne National Laboratory, and the ISI/University of Southern California.

Each day, Angle processes approximately 575 pcap files totaling approximately 7.6 GB and 97 million packets. To date, we have collected approximately 140,000 pcap files which we compress to about 1 TB. For each pcap file, we aggregate all the packet data by source IP (or other specified entity), compute features, and then cluster the resulting points in feature space. This produces approximately 140,000 cluster models which we store in a database for subsequent analysis.

12.6.2 Experimental Studies: Detecting Emergent Behavior

We did a series of experiments to determine an appropriate window size for computing summary models. If the window is too short, there is not enough structure to the data to be useful. On the other hand, if the window is too long, interesting emergent behavior is lost.

We determined an appropriate window size empirically by varying the window size d from 10 min to 24 h. For each fixed window size d, we divided the data into windows w_1, w_2, w_3, ... each of size d and computed clusters as described above for the data in each window w_i. Let $a_{i,\alpha}$ be the centers of the k clusters (as $\alpha = 1, \ldots, k$) computed for the data in window w_i. We then computed the following statistic (compare Equation 12.2):

TABLE 12.1:   The time spent clustering
using sphere scales as the number of records
increases is illustrated from 500 records
to 100,000,000 records.

Number Records	Time	Average Error
500	1.9 s	0.021
1,000	4.2 s	0.021
1,000,000	85 min	0.028
100,000,000	178 h	0.036

$$\delta_i = \sum_{\alpha=1}^{k} \left(\min_{\beta} ||a_{i,\alpha} - a_{i-1,\beta}||^2 \right).$$

Figure 12.6 shows this graph for windows of length $d = 10$ min. Notice that the statistic δ_i is not well-enough behaved to draw any conclusions. On the other hand, Figure 12.7 shows the same statistic for windows of length $d = 1$ day. We manually investigated the packet behavior when the statistic δ_i crossed a threshold, as illustrated in Figure 12.7.

As a result of these manual investigations, we identified a variety of suspicious behavior, including port scans, e-mail spam, and the probing of our network for vulnerabilities associated with a known Trojan attack.

12.6.3   Scalability of the Cloud Infrastructure

One of the ways this project is different than previous work in high-performance, distributed data mining is the use of a cloud computing platform instead of Web-service-based or grid-based computing platform. We also performed several experimental studies to understand the scalability of the Sector/Sphere cloud. As illustrated in Table 12.1 we computed cluster models from the distributed pcap files ranging in size from 500 points to 100,000,000 points using Sector/Sphere. As the table indicates, the time required for this computation scales in an acceptable manner.

We are continuing to explore the use of Sector/Sphere for computing cluster and related statistical models.

12.7   Conclusions

12.7.1   Lessons Learned

During the past year or so of the project as we developed a preliminary prototype of the system, we have learned several lessons.

Lesson 1. The current grid-based distributed computing infrastructure is well suited for sharing cycles, but less suited for making discoveries using distributed data. With the Angle architecture, a persistent distributed infrastructure is used to store and manage the distributed data over a wide-area, high-performance network (Sector). With Sector, computations can be performed locally using Cloud Nodes or data may be moved using specialized protocols (UDT) when data is required to be colocated for computation.

Lesson 2. Much of the power of Angle derives from the ability to work with many different analytic models (there are currently over 100,000 different models available for identifying emergent behavior). It has been recognized for some time the necessity of developing algorithms that scale as the number of records increases and as the number of dimensions increases. Applications such as Angle also show the desirability of developing algorithms and infrastructure that scale as the number of analytic models increase.

Lesson 3. The Angle system is designed in a flexible way so that properly anonymized data can be shared, as well as models that contain no identifying information. Note that models built locally can be built on a richer set of features than models built on shared data. Even with this design, a great deal of effort was spent on developing policies and procedures so that anonymized data could be shared between organizations. This process substantially slowed the pace at which the project could proceed, which is an important lesson to be kept in mind when designing projects that require sharing data.

12.7.2 Summary

In this chapter, we have described the Angle project that identifies emergent behavior in distributed IP data. Angle is noteworthy for several reasons.

First, Angle employs a distributed, cloud-based computing architecture called Sector that is designed to provide persistent storage for large distributed data sets. Layered over Sector is a compute cloud called Sphere that moves the analytic computation to the data whenever possible. In contrast, many grid-based distributed computing systems are designed to move data to pools of compute servers when they become available.

Second, the Angle middleware supports computing with a large number of different analytic models, an approach, which for some applications, can lead to discoveries that are quite difficult when just one or a few analytic models are used, as is usually done. Angle also persists these models into a model repository, which simplifies their analysis, management, and deployment.

Third, Angle introduces statistical algorithm for identifying new types of behavior that have not been previously seen. This is an example of what is sometimes called emergent behavior. Angle also employs visual analytic techniques for identifying emergent behavior.

A fruitful area for research is to develop new algorithms for identifying emergent behavior. It is important to note that by emergent we do not simply mean anomalous behavior, but more specifically emergent behavior as defined in Section 12.2.1. The reasons for the importance of this area is very simple. First, there is very little work in the area. Second, the impact of many data-mining problems is often gated by the number of analysts who can look at alerts generated by data-mining systems in detail. Typically these analysts have to balance two types of investigations: investigations that look at instances related to *known* behavior of interest and those that look at instances of interesting behavior that is *unknown* in that it has not been seen previously. Algorithms to detect emergent behavior is targeted at the later type of behavior.

Another fruitful area of research is to develop high-performance data-mining systems that use cloud-based architectures. Again the reason is simple. Work to date in high-performance data mining has focused primarily on data mining using high-performance clusters and grids. With both of these systems, the "cycles usually wait for the data." In contrast, with a cloud-based system, a storage cloud can provide long-term persistent storage for data, and a compute cloud can be layered over the storage cloud and designed to exploit data locality whenever possible. This leads in practice to good end-to-end performance, that includes not just the time required to compute a model once the data has reached the cluster, but the entire time required, including the time to transport the data, compute the model, and return the results.

Acknowledgments

This work was supported in part by the National Science Foundation through grants SCI-0430781, CNS-0420847, and ACI-0325013.

References

[1] Snort. www.snort.com, retrieved on September 1, 2007.

[2] A. Lazarevic, L. Ertoz, A. Ozgur, J. Srivastava, and V. Kumar. Evaluation of outlier detection schemes for detecting network intrusions. In *Proceedings of the Third SIAM International Conference on Data Mining*, San Francisco, CA, 2003.

[3] V. Barnett and T. Lewis. *Outliers in Statistical Data*, third edition. John Wiley & Sons, New York, 1994.

[4] H. V. Poor and O. Hadjiliadis. *Quickest Detection*. Cambridge University Press, New York, 2008.

[5] J. Ma and S. Perkins. Online novelty detection on temporal sequences. In *KDD '03: Proceedings of the Ninth ACM SIGKDD International Conference on Knowledge Discovery and Data Mining*, pp. 613–618, New York, 2003. ACM.

[6] Y. Zhu and D. Shasha. Efficient elastic burst detection in data streams. In *KDD '03: Proceedings of the Ninth ACM SIGKDD International Conference on Knowledge Discovery and Data Mining*, pp. 336–345, New York, 2003. ACM.

[7] C. C. Aggarwal, J. Han, J. Wang, and P. S. Yu. A framework for clustering evolving data streams. In *VLDB*, pp. 81–92, 2003.

[8] M. M. Gaber and P. S. Yu. Detection and classification of changes in evolving data streams. *International Journal of Information Technology and Decision Making*, 5(4):659–670, 2006.

[9] B. Scholkopf, J. Platt, J. Shawe, A. Smola, and R. Williamson. Estimating the support of a high-dimensional distribution. Technical Report MSR-TR-99-87, Microsoft Research, 1999.

[10] L. Manevitz and M. Yousef. One class SVMS for document classification. *Journal of Machine Learning Research*, 2:139–154, 2001.

[11] K. Crammer and G. Chechik. A needle in a haystack: Local one-class optimization. In *ICML*, 2004.

[12] R. L. Grossman. Standards, services and platforms for data mining: A quick overview. In *Proceedings of the 2003 KDD Worskhop on Data Mining Standards, Services and Platforms (DM-SSP 03)*, Washington, D.C., 2003.

[13] I. Foster and C. Kesselman. *The Grid 2: Blueprint for a New Computing Infrastructure*. Morgan Kaufmann, San Francisco, CA, 2004.

[14] Amazon. Amazon simple storage service (amazon s3). www.amazon.com/s3 retrived on May 15, 2008.

[15] S. Ghemawat, H. Gobioff, and S.-T. Leung. The Google file system. In *SOSP*, 2003.

[16] D. Borthaku. The hadoop distributed file system: Architecture and design. Retrieved from lucene.apache.org/hadoop, May 15, 2008.

[17] R. L. Grossman, Y. Gu, X. Hong, A. Antony, J. Blom, F. Dijkstra, and C. de Laat. Teraflows over gigabit wans with UDT. *Journal of Future Computer Systems*, 21(4):501–513, 2005.

[18] J. Dean and S. Ghemawat. Mapreduce: Simplified data processing on large clusters. In *OSDI'04: Sixth Symposium on Operating System Design and Implementation*, San Francisco, CA, 2004.

[19] R. L. Grossman, Y. Gu, D. Handley, M. Sabala, J. Mambretti, A. Szalay, A. Thakar, K. Kumazoe, O. Yuji, M. Lee, Y. Kwon, and W. Seok. Data mining middleware for wide area high performance networks. *Journal of Future Generation Computer Systems (FGCS)*, 22(8):940–948, 2006.

[20] I. Stoica, R. Morris, D. Karger, M. F. Kaashoek, and H. Balakrishnan. Chord: A scalable peer-to-peer lookup service for internet applications. In *Proceedings of ACM SIGCOMM'01*, pp. 149–160, San Diego, CA, 2001.

[21] Y. Gu and R. L. Grossman. UDT: UDP-based data transfer for high-speed wide area networks. *Computer Networks*, 51(7):1777–1799, 2007.

[22] L. L. Smarr, A. A. Chien, T. DeFanti, J. Leigh, and P. M. Papadopoulos. The optiputer. *Communications of the ACM*, 46(11):58–67, New York, 2003.

[23] Programming with pcap. www.tcpdump.org/pcap.htm, retrieved on September 1, 2007.

[24] R. L. Grossman, S. Bailey, A. Ramu, B. Malhi, P. Hallstrom, I. Pulleyn, and X. Qin. The management and mining of multiple predictive models using the predictive model markup language (pmml). *Information and Software Technology*, 41:589–595, 1999.

[25] Data Mining Group. Predictive Model Markup Language (PMML), version 3.2. www.dmg.org, retrieved on May 15, 2008.

Chapter 13

Architecture Conscious Data Mining: Current Progress and Future Outlook

Srinivasan Parthasarathy, Shirish Tatikonda, Gregory Buehrer, and Amol Ghoting

Contents

13.1 Introduction

Advances in technology have enabled us to collect vast amounts of data across a myriad of domains for various purposes, ranging from astronomical observations to health screening tests, from computational fluid simulations to network flow data, from genomic data to large-scale interaction networks, at an ever-increasing pace. To benefit from these large data stores often housing tera- and even petascale data sets, organizations and individuals have increasingly turned to knowledge discovery and data-mining (KDD) methods, to extract vital information and knowledge from such data stores.

At an abstract level, the KDD process is concerned with extracting actionable knowledge from data stores efficiently. Over the last 15 years or more much progress has been made. New and efficient KDD algorithms have been developed and deployed. Key scientific, engineering, financial, and economic breakthroughs have been enabled by various data mining and data preprocessing techniques. That said we are still a very young field and there is indeed a long laundry list of objectives to be met, ranging from improved theoretical foundations in key KDD subfields to a better understanding of how to define and determine pattern interestingness, from

---

This chapter is based upon the work supported by NSF grants CCF-0702587, CNS-0406386, IIS-0347662, RI-CNS-0403342, IBM Faculty Partnership award, IBM PhD fellowship award (granted to Amol Ghoting), and Microsoft research fellowship award (granted to Gregory Buehrer).

261

new application domains such as interaction graphs and proteomics to biomedical knowledge discovery, and from better visualization methods that can aid in data and model understanding to developing even more efficient and scalable algorithms capable of handling petabytes of scientific and Web data. The last of these, efficiency, is the primary focus of this chapter.

Efficiency is critical to the KDD process since the process is iterative (repetitive) and involves a human-in-the-loop (interactive). In fact, interactivity is often the key to facilitating effective data understanding and knowledge discovery since lengthy time delay between responses of two consecutive user requests can disturb the flow of human perception and formation of insight. KDD researchers have tackled the problem of scalability and efficiency in numerous ways: through the development of innovative algorithms that reduce the theoretical or empirical complexity, through the use of compression and sampling techniques to reduce memory and I/O costs, and through the use of parallel and distributed algorithm designs. In this chapter, we submit that an orthogonal design strategy—architecture conscious algorithm designs—in addition to the aforementioned ones needs to be investigated and integrated with mainstream KDD algorithms. There are two reasons for this argument: (1) it is a very fruitful endeavor often yielding performance improvements of up to three orders of magnitude and (2) with impending commodity multicore technology, it more or less becomes a necessity.

Over the past several years, architectural innovation in processor design has led to new capabilities in single-chip commodity processing and high-end compute clusters. Examples include hardware prefetching, simultaneous multithreading (SMT), and more recently true chip multiprocessing (CMP). At the very high end, systems area networking technologies like InfiniBand have spurred the development of affordable cluster-based supercomputers capable of storing and managing petabytes of data. We contend that data-mining algorithms often require significant computational, I/O, and communication resources, and thus stand to benefit from such innovations if appropriately leveraged. The challenges to do so are daunting.

First, a large number of state-of-the-art data-mining algorithms grossly underutilize modern processors, the building blocks of current generation commodity clusters. This is due to the widening gap between processor and memory performance and the memory and I/O intensive nature of these applications. Second, the emergence of multicore architectures to the commodity market bring with them further complications. Key challenges brought to the fore include the need to enhance available fine-grained parallelism and to alleviate memory bandwidth pressure. Third, parallelizing data-mining algorithms on a multilevel cluster environment is a challenge given the need to share and communicate large sets of data and to balance the workload in the presence of data skew.

In this chapter, we discuss progress made in the context of these challenges and attempt to demonstrate that architecture-conscious solutions are both viable and necessary. We attempt to separate general methodologies and techniques from specific instantiations whenever it makes sense. We conclude with a discussion on future outlook, both in the context of system's support for cyber discovery—enabling the development of new algorithms on emerging architectures—as well as in terms of educational objectives brought to the fore in this context.

13.2 Mining on Modern Uniprocessors

Over the past decade, processor speeds have increased 40-fold according to Moore's law. However, DRAM speeds have not kept up. Consequently, programs that exhibit poor cache locality tend to keep the processor stalled, waiting on the completion of a main memory access, for a large fraction of the time. This is often referred to as the memory wall problem and results in poor CPU utilization. Modern processors typically have deep pipelines and thus need a large pool of schedulable instructions at any given instant of time. A program's inability to provide such a pool often results in an excessive number of pipeline stalls from a low degree of instruction level parallelism.

There has been a number of recent efforts in database systems to deal with the memory wall problem. Ailamiki et al. [1,2] showed that poor cache utilization is the primary cause of extended query execution time on modern architectures. They also presented cache-conscious layouts for database tables. Shatdal et al. [3] showed that the use of well-known optimization techniques such as blocking, partitioning, extracting relevant data, loop fusion, and data clustering can significantly improve cache performance of join and aggregation operations. Bender et al. [4] presented cache-oblivious B-trees so that the number of memory transfers between any two levels in the memory hierarchy is within a constant factor of the optimal. These bounds on the number of memory transfers hold across all block sizes. Consequently, cache-oblivious algorithms do not need to be aware of any memory hierarchy parameters such as cache size, line size, and associativity. Lattner and Adve present automatic pool allocation [5], a method that automatically partitions heap-based data structures into separate pools in a locality-enhancing fashion.

Rao and Ross [6,7] proposed new data structures: cache-sensitive search trees and cache-sensitive B+ trees. This work builds on the premise that the optimal tree node size is equal to the natural data transfer size. Cache-sensitive search trees provide a cache-conscious data layout for a binary search. Chen et al. [8] further improved upon the performance of index and range searches by leveraging prefetching. For index search, they propose to increase tree node size to be more than the cache line size. Prefetching helps in hiding latency on a cache miss when fetching these large B+ tree nodes. They have also used prefetching to improve the performance of hash-join operations [9]. Chilimbi et al. [10] improve the benefits from prefetching by remapping dynamic data structures. They describe ccmalloc, a malloc-based library that allows the user to provide hints to the memory allocator regarding candidates for colocation. The approach is localized in that it does not allow for the global restructuring of a large dynamic data structure.

Lo et al. [11] analyzed the performance of database workloads on SMT processors. They concluded that the improved cache performance is necessary to leverage the abilities of multiple threads in a SMT environment. Zhou et al. [12] evaluate several techniques for effectively using SMT processors for database operations. For example, they propose to use helper threads that aggressively prefetch the data for database operations.

We showed that the gap between processor performance and memory subsystem performance on modern systems is a critical bottleneck limiting the performance of data-intensive applications [13]. Further hampering performance is the parameter and data-dependent aspects of data-mining algorithms that makes predicting access patterns very difficult, thus leading to poor data locality. The reliance on dynamic data structures to house important metainformation to prune the search space often limits available instruction level parallelism while also hampering data locality leading to poor processor utilization. The challenges to overcome are daunting and below we identify several simple strategies that seem to be quite useful for a range of data analysis and management applications.

The first strategy is to improve the spatial locality within such algorithms. The basic idea is to ensure that once a data object is read or written to, objects located in spatial proximity to said object will also be touched soon. Exploiting this strategy requires an understanding of the access patterns in the algorithm, identifying the dominant access patterns (to make the common case fast), and then realizing a memory placement that matches the dominant access patterns [14]. We found this strategy to be useful for a host of algorithms including frequent pattern mining, clustering, and outlier detection. For instance, it improved the performance of FPGrowth [15], a state-of-the-art frequent itemset mining algorithm, by up to 50% [13]. FPGrowth summarizes the data set into a succinct prefix tree or FP-tree. While generating new candidate itemsets, FP-tree is traversed in a bottom-up fashion from leaf nodes to the root node. However, the pointer-based nature of FP-tree makes these traversals very expensive. We address this problem by proposing a cache-conscious prefix tree or CP-tree [13]. It stores the tree nodes on each branch (i.e., root-to-leaf path) in consecutive blocks of memory so that the memory placement matches the dominant access pattern. Such a data layout not only improves instruction level parallelism and spatial locality, but also benefits from hardware prefetching.

The second strategy is to improve the temporal locality within data-mining algorithms. The objective here is to schedule all the operations on a data object as close as possible (in time). Exploiting this strategy requires the ability to partition the data (or the data structure) and operate on a partition-by-partition basis, that is, process a partition completely before moving on to the next partition. Such a strategy minimizes the number of times one has to cross different levels of the memory hierarchy. Note that partitions may be overlapping but the key is to minimize the degree of overlap. Furthermore, partitions may be a natural cut of the data (or the data structure) or alternatively may be constructed on the fly through suitable hash or approximate ordering functions. We applied this strategy, under the name "path tiling," to CP-tree-based itemset mining algorithm. We break down the tree into relatively fixed sized blocks of memory (tiles) along paths of the tree from leaf nodes to the root. The mining algorithm is then restructured to access these tiles iteratively so that the reuse of CP-tree is maximized once it is loaded into cache. Path tiling improved the temporal locality, giving up to twofold runtime improvement for in-core data sets [13] (see Figure 13.2) and up to a 400-fold improvement for out-of-core data sets [16]. Figure 13.1 demonstrates the effect of this strategy on runtime and memory performance by comparing the same against state-of-the-art algorithms like

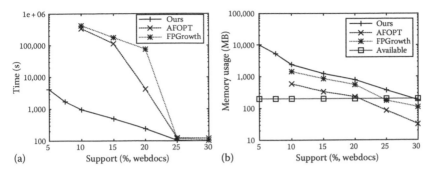

FIGURE 13.1: Effect of locality in frequent itemset mining (out of core).

AFOPT [17] and FPGrowth [15]. Note that the Y-axis is in log scale. At 20% support, all three algorithms must use disk resident memory. The slowdowns in AFOPT and FPGrowth are attributed to the fact that they do not exhibit high spatial and temporal locality, and thus do not utilize the memory hierarchy efficiently. In fact, we have tested all the implementations from the FIMI repository, including algorithms such as Apriori [18] and Eclat [19], and all exhibited the behavior seen from AFOPT and FPGrowth when they go out of core. However, our optimized algorithm maintains its efficiency even as it spills into disk resident memory, resulting in over a 400-fold performance improvement.

The third strategy is to leverage key features of such architectures effectively. For example, improving spatial locality can have the added benefit of effectively leveraging hardware prefetching, a latency tolerating mechanism available in modern architectures. Another recent innovation is SMT—a mechanism that enables one to place multiple thread contexts in hardware with a goal of increasing available instruction level parallelism. A naive realization for data mining, essentially deploying parallel independent threads (tasks), often fails to achieve the desired effect due to cache conflicts and data stalls. However, we find that coscheduling tasks that operate on identical or related pieces of data limits the number of data stalls and conflict misses, yielding close to ideal performance for some applications [20]—up to 30%–60% improvement (Figure 13.2). When hardware prefetching is enabled, there is an additional 10%–25% speedup. Temporal locality and SMT-related strategies gave cumulative speedups of up to 3.2- and 4.8-fold, respectively.

The fourth strategy, one that requires an in-depth knowledge of the algorithm, is to examine alternative design strategies that limit the use of pointer-based data structures with the potential to yield algorithms with smaller memory footprints and better ILP. As an example, we recently considered the problem of mining frequent trees within a forest of trees (e.g., XML repository). Our approach relies on a concise bijection between trees and sequences with appropriate structural information embedded in the representation. The key to our approach is the ability to traverse the search space of trees by exploring in the space of sequences. Subsequently, we designed a dynamic programming-based algorithm that finds frequent patterns by

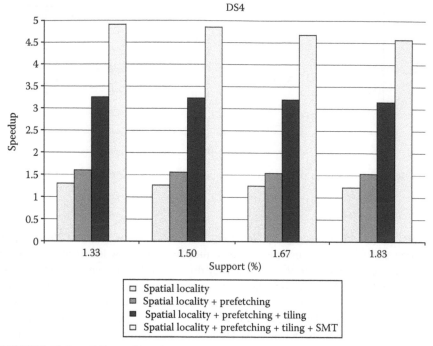

FIGURE 13.2:   Effect of locality in frequent itemset mining (in core).

recasting a specialized case of subtree isomorphism problem to a much simpler problem of subsequence matching. We also designed several memory-conscious optimizations that, irrespective of mining parameters like support threshold, result in
constant-sized memory footprints [21,22]. Our algorithms showed more than three
orders of magnitude improvement in runtime and memory usage, when compared
to state-of-the-art algorithms such as TreeMiner [23] and iMB3Miner [24]
(Figure 13.3). As it turns out, this approach has an even more general appeal in

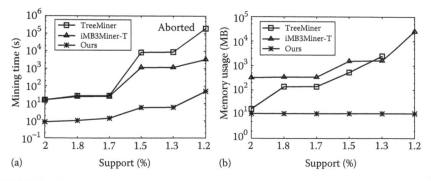

FIGURE 13.3:   Effectiveness of algorithmic improvements (tree-mining workload).

that a similar strategy proved to be extremely effective for indexing XML data [25]. Once again we found that the approach outperforms the state-of-the-art XML indexing strategies by up to three orders of magnitude while utilizing significantly less memory and disk resources.

13.3   Mining on Emerging CMP Architectures

Further complicating the already difficult task of utilizing modern architectural platforms efficiently is the recent emergence of true CMP, often referred to as multicore chips. Designs range from the general purpose (AMD, Intel) to the specialized (Sony-Toshiba-IBM Cell, Sun) to the niche markets (GPUs). AMD released dual-core workstation and desktop processors in 2005. Intel's first desktop dual-dye quad core CPU, Kentsfield, was released in November 2006. Sun Microsystems recently developed a eight-core system called Niagara. Although current designs have four to eight cores, Intel's 2015 processor road map proposes CMPs with hundreds of cores.*

Parallelizing existing algorithms is an obvious objective in this context. While much work has been done on this, there are some important challenges. Paramount to leveraging the additional compute capability is an effective task partitioning mechanism to distribute the work among individual processing elements so that they all are kept busy for as long as possible. This can be particularly challenging in the presence of data and control dependencies. Moreover, the data- and parameter-dependent aspects of data-mining workloads make estimating the lifetime of a task difficult. As several recent researchers have pointed out, there is a need to expose and subsequently exploit fine-grained parallelism on CMP architectures [26]. Further, the ability to pack multiple cores on a single silicon dye introduces new set of challenges. Since all the cores now share a common front-side bus, bandwidth to main memory is likely to be a precious shared commodity [27,28]. As a result, cache locality and working set size may become key factors in achieving efficient performance.

To address the challenge of load balancing, we believe adaptable algorithm designs must take center stage. For example, to handle the issue of task granularity, we have proposed schemes that allow the size of a task to morph depending on the state of the system. We term this scheme moldable task partitioning, where each task makes a decision at preset points during its runtime whether it needs to further break up into subtasks, which can subsequently be enqueued on a distributed shared task queue or to continue processing. This decision would be based on the current load balance in the system. Adaptive partitioning not only affords a dynamic granularity to accommodate variability in the associativity of the data set, but it also can improve cache performance [29]. The cost of context switch between different task

---

* http://www.intel.com/technology/magazine/computing/platform-2015-0305.htm.

granularities directly affects the effective performance. Care must be taken to ensure that the cost is significantly lower than the amount of time required to execute the task to its completion.

Processors, in this scheme, can operate in two different modes, namely task parallel and data parallel. In task parallel mode, different processors work on different tasks. Each task is executed till its completion or to a point where it forks off new subtasks. In contrast, processors operating in data parallel mode execute the same task, that is, same set of instructions but each processor acts on a distinct portion of the data set. We find that such an adaptive moldable task partitioning is both necessary and extremely effective when processing highly skewed data sets in the context of graph and tree mining [21,29]. As shown in Figure 13.4a, static or levelwise partitioning on a graph-mining workload provided at most a four-fold speedup over sequential execution, whereas adaptive partitioning showed a 22.5-fold speedup. As the number of partition levels increases from one to five, scalability generally increases, but it does not approach adaptive partitioning. Adaptive partitioning not only improves load balance in the system, but also affords the benefit of improved temporal locality. Figure 13.4b emphasizes the viability of this strategy for current day multicore architectures. We observed near-linear speedups while mining frequent trees from two highly skewed data sets, Cslogs and Treebank [21].

It is common that algorithms can trade increased memory usage for improved execution times. We seek to leverage this principle to improve run times for datamining applications by maintaining additional state when it is inexpensive to do so. Architectures today provide us with performance counters to estimate bandwidth utilization at runtime. We propose to develop solutions that can trade-off algorithmic state for reduced bandwidth consumption thereby facilitating execution on CMPs. If there is sufficient memory bandwidth available in the system, then we can choose to increase state for future use. Furthermore, in the presence of contention, we can limit or reduce state as needed. We term this adaptive state management.

We evaluated the benefits of using adaptive state management by mining real-world data sets for substructure (graphs and trees) mining. The task-level

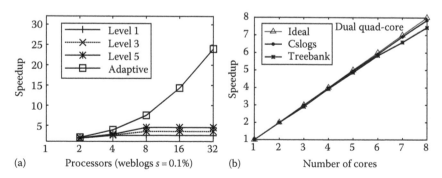

FIGURE 13.4: Adaptive task partitioning: (a) graph mining (on a SMP) and (b) tree mining (on a CMP).

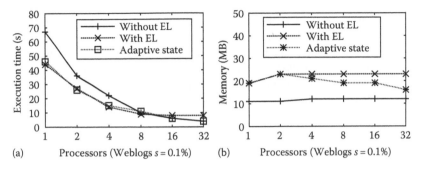

FIGURE 13.5: Adaptive state management (graph-mining workload).

metadata structure is called an embedding list (EL), which maps discovered graphs to their mappings in the data set. The EL reduces the search space of a task at the expense of maintaining increased state. We compared the performance of three algorithms, one that always maintains the state (gaston [30]—with EL in Figure 13.5), one that never maintains the state (gSpan [31]—labeled without EL), and one that adaptively maintains state (ours). Notably, our adaptive algorithm is always the most efficient, and when operating on smaller number of cores the algorithm adaptively maintains more state and when operating on large number of cores the algorithm adaptively maintains less state trading memory off for computation. Overall, the adaptive approach makes near-optimal use of the available hardware resources [29]. This result, particularly the implicit cross-over in performance between gaston (better on lower number of cores) and gSpan (better on higher number of cores), underscores an important point in that simpler algorithm designs with smaller memory footprints are likely to be the norm for deployment on emerging architectures.

Thus far, we have discussed the performance of data-mining algorithms on general purpose emerging architectures. A joint venture by Sony, Toshiba, and IBM (STI) has produced a nine-core architecture called the Cell BDEA. This architecture represents an interesting design point along the spectrum of chipsets with multiple processing elements. The STI Cell has one main processor and eight support processing elements (SPEs)—over 200 gigaflops of compute power—and with explicit memory management—25 GB/s off-chip bandwidth. The layout of Cell lies somewhere between other modern CMP chips and a high-end GPU. Unlike GPUs, however, the Cell can chain its processors in any order, or have them operate independently. While most CMPs are MIMD with POSIX-style threading models, the Cell's eight cores are SIMD (single instruction multiple data) vector processors, and must get specialized task modules passed to them by the PPE. Several workloads seem quite amenable to its architecture. For example, high floating-point workloads with streaming access patterns are of particular interest [32]. These workloads could leverage the large floating-point throughput, and because their access pattern is known *a priori*, they can use software-managed caches for good bandwidth utilization. Kunzman et al. [33] adapted their parallel runtime framework CHARM++, a parallel object-oriented C++ library, to provide portability between the Cell and other platforms. In particular, they proposed the Offload API, a general-purpose API to prefetch data, encapsulate data, and peek into the work queue.

In recent work, we have sought to map and evaluate several important data-mining application workloads on the Cell, namely clustering (kMeans), classification (kNN), and anomaly detection (ORCA), and PageRank computation. Developing algorithms on the Cell requires three components: (1) parallelizing the workload, (2) designing an efficient data transfer mechanism to move data from main memory to local store of each SPE, and (3) restructuring the algorithm to leverage the SIMD intrinsics of Cell. We investigated the above-mentioned data-mining workloads along the axes of performance, programming complexity, and algorithm design [34]. Specifically, we develop data transfer and SIMD optimizations for these applications and evaluate them in detail to determine the benefits as well as the inherent bottlenecks of the Cell processor for data-intensive applications. As part of our comparative analysis, we juxtapose these algorithms with similar ones implemented on modern architectures including the Itanium, AMD Opteron, and Pentium architectures.

For the first three workloads, we consider the Cell processor is up to 50 times faster than competing technologies, when the underlying algorithm uses the hardware efficiently (Figure 13.6). Restructuring computation to incorporate SIMD instructions improved execution times by 2.3-fold over single-data instructions. Loop unrolling sped up the runtimes by more than two times. Further, parallelizing on the Cell results in a nearly sixfold performance improvement when using the six available SPUs. However, in case of PageRank computation, its performance is quite low because of frequent nonstreaming writes, that is, random writes to main memory. In particular for this workload, execution stalls on writes, since it may be necessary to rewrite to the same 16-byte block in the next instruction.

An important outcome of the study, beyond the results on these particular algorithms, is that we answer several higher level questions, which are designed

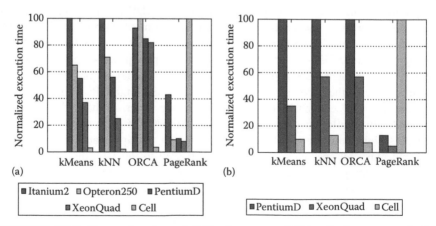

FIGURE 13.6: (See color insert following page 264.) Performance of Cell against (a) single-core processors and (b) multicore processors.

to provide a fast and reliable estimate to application designers for how well other workloads will scale on the Cell. For instance, we found that any metadata that grows with the size of the data set cannot be stored locally. Also, the metadata associated with a data item should be inlined with that item, and must be moved to main memory whenever the item is ejected from local store of a SPE. This restricts the usability of Cell for a number of pattern-mining algorithms (e.g., graphs and trees), which make use of potentially large metastructures, such as ELs. Cell may not be the right platform for applications whose access pattern is not predictable. We also believe that in cases where it is predictable, one can chunk the data elements and the algorithm can be restructured to operate chunks.

13.4   Mining on Emerging Clusters

Mining truly large data sets is extremely challenging. The computational complexity of many data-mining algorithms makes them scale nonlinearly with the data set size. A cost-effective and viable solution to this problem is to use a tightly interconnected distributed cluster of shared memory processors. In this regard, a number of researchers over the last decade have developed innovative parallel or distributed algorithms for various data-mining algorithms including association mining [14,35–42], sequence mining [43–45], classification [46–50], clustering [51–53], multivariate discretization [54,55], similarity discovery [56], and Bayesian network learning [57]. Zaki presents a detailed survey on parallel and distributed association mining [58]. However, we argue that here too, in most of the algorithms reviewed to date, architectural resources are not being fully utilized. A multilevel—within a multicore chip, across multiple chips on a shared memory workstation, and across a cluster of workstations—design strategy is needed to fully utilize such a supercomputing resource. Hybrid systems further add to the complexity. An example of such a hybrid supercomputer is the proposed IBM Roadrunner system, comprising AMD CMPs along with Cell accelerator blades to be delivered to Los Alamos National Laboratory [59]. It is designed to achieve a sustained performance of 1 petaflops/s. For such systems, load balancing in the presence of data skew, accommodating data and task parallelism across multiple levels, minimizing the communication overhead, and effectively leveraging strategies like remote memory paging are key to efficient utilization. For instance, one needs to identify coarse-grained tasks so that each task has a sufficient amount of work to fully utilize a multicore node in the cluster. However, given the scale of data sets involved, acquiring data resources for tasks can be very expensive. In such a situation, we believe that a global form of affinity scheduling can improve the performance. This is because one has more time to determine a better scheduling policy at the cluster level, as opposed to the multicore or node level where time to schedule is very limited.

We have recently presented a parallelization of a fast frequent itemset mining algorithm FPGrowth to enable efficient mining of very large, out-of-core data sets [36]. In a distributed setting where the data is distributed across multiple cluster nodes, the key challenge is to be able to obtain global knowledge required to discredit an itemset as infrequent. A naive solution may potentially incur a significant communication overhead, thereby affecting the scalability. We designed a strategy strip marshaling that significantly reduces the number of messages transferred among compute nodes. It concisely encodes the metadata structures of FPGrowth before they are shared among different processors. More interestingly, the resulting encoding can be processed in an online fashion so that one can effectively overlap communication with computation. We also designed a set of pruning techniques that not only reduce the amount of redundant computations but also enables memory hierarchy-conscious mining. In other words, our strategies simultaneously exploit and utilize memory, processing, storage, and networking resources while minimizing I/O and communication overheads. The experimental evaluation of such multilevel architecture-conscious algorithms using state-of-the-art commodity cluster and large data sets illustrates linear scale up and very good system utilization (up to an order of magnitude improvement over competing strategies) (Figure 13.7). Yet, another result from this study is that our strategies could easily mine a terabyte data set on a 48-node cluster. The amount of reduction in communication due to strip marshaling at different support levels is demonstrated in Figure 13.7a. Weak scalability, that is, execution time performance as the data set is progressively increased proportional to the number of machines is shown in Figure 13.7b. Our distributed itemset mining algorithm (DFP) leverages the available memory space by building a data structure that eliminates the need to repeatedly scan the disk. Also, it effectively circulates sufficient global information through strip marshaling to allow machines to mine tasks independently, unlike other extant algorithms such as DD [35] and IDD [60].

A lot of research is also performed in developing scalable data-mining algorithms for grid environments [61–64]. Applications in such environments must develop efficient and scalable mechanisms to access remote data repositories and to manage large pool of shared resources. However, these issues are outside the scope of this review, which is primarily focusing on leveraging advancements in computer (both serial and parallel) architectures.

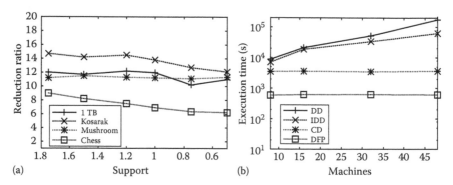

FIGURE 13.7: Distributed itemset mining: (a) effect of strip marshaling and (b) runtime improvement.

13.5 Future Outlook

On the research front, the future outlook for architecture-conscious data mining is clearly very encouraging. Quite simply, it offers a new and orthogonal approach to enhance the efficiency with which algorithms can compute and tackle large data sets. Moreover, with the advent of multicore processors to the commodity computing market, it more or less becomes a necessity since algorithm developers will need to attune themselves to the novel features and limitations of these architectures. There are clearly several directions of work to look at in the future.

While the early signs are encouraging, deployment on other data-mining techniques in novel application settings is still needed and very challenging. In many cases, there are strong dependency structures at a conceptual or algorithmic level limiting available parallelism that need to be overcomed (e.g., exact inference in graphical models). Innovative algorithmic restructuring, resorting to approximate solutions to enhance parallelism, proactive or speculative methods all have a role to play in this context.

A fundamental question to ask here is moving forward what have we learnt from these successful architecture-conscious implementations? What can we take away for future algorithms and realizing architecture-conscious implementations on emerging and next generation platforms? The general principles, outlined earlier, such as improving spatial locality, improving temporal locality, minimizing the use of pointer-based dynamic data structures, lowering memory footprints and trading off memory for computation, reducing off-chip bandwidth, and minimizing communication offer a good starting point, but more needs to be done.

This question and the basic solutions outlined lead us to the related question of whether cyberinfrastructure support for realizing architecture conscious KDD implementations is feasible? It is our opinion that a service-oriented architecture holds significant promise in this context. Such an architecture could include services for data access and partitioning (e.g., hash-sorting, sampling, memory placement, and distributed shared data structures), services for data and knowledge reuse and caching, services for scheduling and load balancing, etc. We recently proposed such an architecture and started building some of the services [65,66] (Figure 13.8). The data storage service implements strategies for managing and accessing data in distributed disk space. It includes basic data preprocessing, data replication, declustering, data-distribution services along with update-propagation trigger services for dynamic data sets [37]. The objective of data distribution is to balance the storage and I/O load across the nodes so that the maximum aggregate disk bandwidth can be used, while minimizing communication overhead [67]. Caching services provide support to maintain duplicate data and result summaries for reuse. Data-mining algorithms can benefit from two types of caching services: data caching and knowledge caching. Data caching,which caches subsets and summaries of data sets used across multiple data-mining operations, is a general-purpose caching strategy. Knowledge caching services, which caches recently constructed or used knowledge objects, are particularly important due to iterative nature of data mining [68]. The scheduling

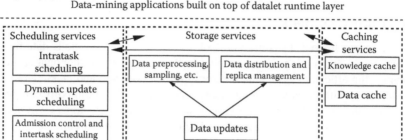

FIGURE 13.8: Service-oriented system architecture.

services address admission control of data-mining jobs, and intratask scheduling for both static and dynamic data-mining tasks. It also provides support for automated execution of system level datalets (lightweight objects customized for user-defined processing) for data distribution, summary computation, data replication, and data caching.

Various data mining and visualization modules can be implemented on top of these basic services and can in turn serve as front ends for more complex knowledge-discovery tasks. The plug-and-play nature of the services is ideally suited to the interactive and iterative nature of KDD algorithms. Further, each individual service can be attuned to the architecture upon which it is built with the potential to yield architecture-conscious solutions for a wide range of data-mining techniques and end applications. Such a services-oriented approach also ensures useful utilization of computational resources.

On the educational front, the multicore architectures are essentially bringing the parallel computing into main-stream commodity market. Designers must be aware of the basic principles underlying parallel algorithm design, and be familiar with important architectural advances and features, in addition to having an innate understanding of data-mining principles. Colearning group projects where groups are formed by matching students with strong systems and architecture background along with students more familiar with data mining and statistical learning algorithms are a useful mechanism in this context. Such efforts are essential and must go hand-in-hand with research advances.

References

[1] A. Ailamaki, D.J. DeWitt, M.D. Hill, and D.A. Wood. DBMSs on a modern processor: Where does time go. *Proceedings of the 25th International Conference on Very Large Data Bases*, pp. 266–277, Edinburg, Scotland, 1999.

[2] A. Ailamaki, D.J. DeWitt, M.D. Hill, and M. Skounakis. Weaving relations for cache performance. *Proceedings of the 27th International Conference on Very Large Data Bases (VLDB)*, pp. 169–180, San Francisco, CA, 2001.

[3] A. Shatdal, C. Kant, and J.F. Naughton. Cache conscious algorithms for relational query processing. *Proceedings of the 20th International Conference on Very Large Data Bases (VLDB)*, pp. 510–521, Santiago de Chile, Chile, 1994.

[4] M.A. Bender, E.D. Demaine, and M. Farach-Colton. Cache-oblivious B-trees. *Proceedings of the 41st Annual Symposium on Foundations of Computer Science*, p. 399, Redondo Beach, CA, 2000.

[5] C. Lattner and V. Adve. Automatic pool allocation: Improving performance by controlling data structure layout in the heap. *ACM SIGPLAN Notices*, 40(6): 129–142, 2005.

[6] J. Rao and K.A. Ross. Cache conscious indexing for decision-support in main memory. *Proceedings of the 25th International Conference on Very Large Data Bases (VLDB)*, pp. 78–89, Edinburg, Scotland, 1999.

[7] J. Rao and K.A. Ross. Making B+trees cache conscious in main memory. *ACM SIGMOD Record*, 29(2): 475–486, 2000.

[8] S. Chen, P.B. Gibbons, and T.C. Mowry. Improving index performance through prefetching. *ACM SIGMOD Record*, 30(2): 235–246, 2001.

[9] S. Chen, A. Ailamaki, P.B. Gibbons, and T.C. Mowry. Improving hash join performance through prefetching. *ACM Transactions on Database Systems (TODS)*, 32(3):17, 2007.

[10] T.M. Chilimbi, M.D. Hill, and J.R. Larus. Cache-conscious structure layout. *Proceedings of the ACM SIGPLAN 1999 Conference on Programming Language Design and Implementation*, pp. 1–12, 1999.

[11] J.L. Lo, L.A. Barroso, S.J. Eggers, K. Gharachorloo, H.M. Levy, and S.S. Parekh. An analysis of database workload performance on simultaneous multithreaded processors. *ACM SIGARCH Computer Architecture News*, 26(3): 39–50, 1998.

[12] J. Zhou, J. Cieslewicz, K.A. Ross, and M. Shah. Improving database performance on simultaneous multithreading processors. *Proceedings of the 31st International Conference on Very Large Data Bases*, pp. 49–60, Trondheim, Norway, 2005.

[13] A. Ghoting, G. Buehrer, S. Parthasarathy, D. Kim, A. Nguyen, Y.K. Chen, and P. Dubey. Cache-conscious frequent pattern mining on a modern processor. *Proceedings of the 31st International Conference on Very Large Data Bases*, pp. 577–588, Trondheim, Norway, 2005.

[14] S. Parthasarathy, M.J. Zaki, M. Ogihara, and W. Li. Parallel data mining for association rules on shared-memory systems. *Knowledge and Information Systems*, 3(1): 1–29, 2001.

[15] J. Han, J. Pei, Y. Yin, and R. Mao. Mining frequent patterns without candidate generation: A frequent-pattern tree approach. *Data Mining and Knowledge Discovery*, 8(1): 53–87, 2004.

[16] G. Buehrer, S. Parthasarathy, and A. Ghoting. Out of core frequent pattern mining on a commodity PC. *Proceedings of the 12th ACM SIGKDD International Conference on Knowledge Discovery and Data Mining*, pp. 86–95, New York. ACM, 2006.

[17] G. Liu, H. Lu, J.X. Yu, W. Wei, and X. Xiao. AFOPT: An efficient implementation of pattern growth approach. In *ICDM Workshop on Frequent Itemset Mining Implementations*, Melbourne, FL, 2003.

[18] R. Agrawal and R. Srikant. Fast algorithms for mining association rules. *Proceedings of 20th International Conference on Very Large Data Bases (VLDB)*, pp. 487–499, Santiago de Chile, Chile, 1994.

[19] M.J. Zaki, S. Parthasarathy, M. Ogihara, and W. Li. New algorithms for fast discovery of association rules. *Proceedings of 3rd International Conference on Knowledge Discovery and Data Mining*, pp. 283–286, Newport beach, CA, 1997.

[20] A. Ghoting, G. Buehrer, S. Parthasarathy, D. Kim, A. Nguyen, Y.K. Chen, and P. Dubey. Cache-conscious frequent pattern mining on Modern and emerging processors. *VLDB Journal*, 16(1):77–96, 2007.

[21] S. Tatikonda and S. Parthasarathy. An efficient parallel tree mining algorithm for emerging commodity processors. *Proceedings of the 13th ACM SIGPLAN Symposium on Principles and Practice of Parallel Programming*, pp. 263–264, Salt Lake City, UT, 2008.

[22] S. Tatikonda, S. Parthasarathy, and T. Kurc. TRIPS and TIDES: New algorithms for tree mining. *Proceedings of the 15th ACM International Conference on Information and Knowledge Management*, pp. 455–464, Arlington, VA, 2006.

[23] M.J. Zaki. Efficiently mining frequent trees in a forest: Algorithms and applications. *IEEE Transactions on Knowledge and Data Engineering (TKDE)*, 17(8): 1021–1035, 2005.

[24] H. Tan, T.S. Dillon, F. Hadzic, E. Chang, and L. Feng. IMB3-Miner: Mining induced/embedded subtrees by constraining the level of embedding.

Proceedings of Pacific-Asia Conference on Knowledge Discovery and Data Mining, pp. 450–461, Singapore, 2006.

[25] S. Tatikonda, S. Parthasarathy, and M. Goyder. LCS-Trim: Dynamic programming meets XML indexing and querying. *Proceedings of 33rd Conference on Very Large Data Bases (VLDB)*, pp. 63–74, Vienna, Austria, 2007.

[26] B. Saha, A.R. Adl-Tabatabai, A. Ghuloum, M. Rajagopalan, R.L. Hudson, L. Petersen, V. Menon, B. Murphy, T. Shpeisman, E. Sprangle, A. Rohillah, D. Carmean, and J. Fang, Enabling scalability and performance in a large scale CMP environment. *Proceedings of the 2007 Conference on EuroSys*, pp. 73–86, Lisbon, Portugal, 2007.

[27] R. Kumar, K.I. Farkas, N.P. Jouppi, P. Ranganathan, and D.M. Tullsen. Single-ISA heterogeneous multi-core architectures: The potential for processor power reduction. *Proceedings of 36th Annual IEEE/ACM International Symposium on Microarchitecture*, pp. 81–92, San Diego, CA, 2003.

[28] C. McNairy and R. Bhatia. Montecito: A dual-core, dual-thread Itanium processor. *Micro, IEEE*, 25(2): 10–20, 2005.

[29] G. Buehrer, S. Parthasarathy, and Y.K. Chen. Adaptive parallel graph mining for CMP architectures. *Proceedings of the 6th International Conference on Data Mining (ICDM)*, pp. 97–106, Hong Kong, 2006.

[30] S. Nijssen and J.N. Kok. A quickstart in frequent structure mining can make a difference. *Proceedings of the 2004 ACM SIGKDD International Conference on Knowledge Discovery and Data Mining*, pp. 647–652, Seattle, WA, 2004.

[31] X. Yan and J. Han. gSpan: Graph-based substructure pattern mining. *Proceedings of International Conference on Data Mining (ICDM)*, pp. 721–724, Maebashi City, Japan, 2002.

[32] S. Williams, J. Shalf, L. Oliker, S. Kamil, P. Husbands, and K. Yelick. The potential of the cell processor for scientific computing. *Proceedings of the 3rd Conference on Computing Frontiers*, pp. 9–20, Ischia, Italy, 2006.

[33] D. Kunzman, G. Zheng, E. Bohm, and L. Kale. Charm++, offload API, and the cell processor. In *Proceedings of Super Computing (SC)*, pp. 135, Tampa Bay, 2006.

[34] G. Buehrer, S. Parthasarathy, and M. Goyder. Data mining on the cell broadband engine. *Proceedings of the 19th Annual International Conference on Supercomputing (ICS)*, Island of Kos, Greece, June 2008.

[35] R. Agrawal and J.C. Shafer. Parallel mining of association rules. *IEEE Transactions on Knowledge and Data Engineering (TKDE)*, 8(6): 962–969, 1996.

[36] G. Buehrer, S. Parthasarathy, S. Tatikonda, T. Kurc, and J. Saltz. Toward terabyte pattern mining: An architecture-conscious solution. *Proceedings of*

the *12th ACM SIGPLAN Symposium on Principles and Practice of Parallel Programming*, pp. 2–12, San Jose, CA, 2007.

[37] H. Wang, S. Parthasarathy, A. Ghoting, S. Tatikonda, G. Buehrer, T. Kurc, and J. Saltz. Design of a next generation sampling service for large scale data analysis applications. *Proceedings of the 19th Annual International Conference on Supercomputing (ICS)*, pp. 91–100, Cambridge, MA. ACM Press, 2005.

[38] M.J. Zaki, W. Li, and S. Parthasarathy. Customized dynamic load balancing for a network of workstations. *Journal of Parallel and Distributed Computing (JPDD)*, 43(2): 156–162, 1997.

[39] M.J. Zaki, S. Parthasarathy, M. Ogihara, and W. Li. Parallel algorithms for discovery of association rules. *Data Mining and Knowledge Discovery*, 1(4): 343–373, 1997.

[40] D.W. Cheung, J. Han, V.T. Ng, A.W. Fu, and Y. Fu. A fast distributed algorithm for mining association rules. *Proceedings of the 4th International Conference on Parallel and Distributed Information Systems*, pp. 31–43, Tokyo, Japan, 1996.

[41] E.H. Han, G. Karypis, V. Kumar, et al. Scalable parallel data mining for association rules. *IEEE Transactions on Knowledge and Data Engineering (TKDE)*, 12(3): 337–352, 2000.

[42] T. Shintani and M. Kitsuregawa. Hash based parallel algorithms for mining association rules. *Proceedings of the 4th International Conference on Parallel and Distributed Information Systems*, pp. 19–30, Tokyo, Japan, 1996.

[43] A. Sohn and Y. Kodama. Load balanced parallel radix sort. *Proceedings of the 12th International Conference Supercomputing (ICS)*, pp. 305–312. ACM, Melbourne, Australia, July 1998.

[44] M.J. Zaki. Parallel sequence mining on shared-memory machines. In *Jouranl of Parallel and Distributed Computing (JPDC)*, 61(3): 401–426, 2001.

[45] V. Guralnik, N. Garg, G. Karypis, Army High Performance Computing Research Center, and University of Minnesota. *Parallel Tree Projection Algorithm for Sequence Mining*. Springer, 2001.

[46] J. Shafer, R. Agrawal, and M. Mehta. SPRINT: A scalable parallel classifier for data mining. *Proceedings of the 22th International Conference on Very Large Data Bases*, pp. 544–555, Seoul, Korea, 1996.

[47] R. Kufrin. Decision trees on parallel processors. *Parallel Processing for Artificial Intelligence*, 3: 279–306, 1997.

[48] S. Goil and A. Choudhary. Efficient parallel classification using dimensional aggregates. *Large-Scale Parallel Data Mining*, 10: 50, 2000.

[49] M. Mehta, R. Agrawal, and J. Rissanen. SLIQ: A fast scalable classifier for data mining. *Proceedings of 5th International Conference on Extending Database Technology*, pp. 18–34, Avignon, France, 1996.

[50] M.J. Zaki and C.T.H.R. Agrawal. Parallel classification for data mining on shared-memory multiprocessors. *Proceedings of 15th International Conference on Data Engineering (ICDE)*, pp. 198–205, 1999.

[51] X. Li and Z. Fang. Parallel clustering algorithms. *Parallel Computing*, 11(3): 275–290, 1989.

[52] C.F. Olson. Parallel algorithms for hierarchical clustering. *Parallel Computing*, 21(8): 1313–1325, 1995.

[53] I.S. Dhillon and D.S. Modha. A data-clustering algorithm on distributed memory multiprocessors. In *Lecture Notes on Computer Science*, pp. 245–260, 2000.

[54] S. Parthasarathy. Active mining in a distributed setting. PhD dissertation, University of Rochester, Rochester, 2000.

[55] S. Parthasarathy and A. Ramakrishnan. Parallel incremental 2D-discretization on dynamic datasets. *International Conference on Parallel and Distributed Processing Systems*, pp. 247–254, Florida, 2002.

[56] S. Parthasarathy and M. Ogihara. Clustering distributed homogeneous datasets. *Proceedings of the 4th European Conference on Principles of Data Mining and Knowledge Discovery*, pp. 566–574, Lyon, France, 2000.

[57] D. Foti, D. Lipari, C. Pizzuti, and D. Talia. Scalable parallel clustering for data mining on multicomputers. *Proceedings of the Workshop on High Performance Data Mining, IPDPS 2000*, LNCS Vol. 1800, pp. 390–398, Cancun, Mexico, 2000.

[58] M.J. Zaki. Parallel and distributed association mining: A survey. *Concurrency, IEEE*, 7(4): 14–25, 1999 (see also *IEEE Parallel and Distributed Technology*).

[59] K. Koch. The new roadrunner supercomputer: What, when, and how. *Presented at Super Computing (SC)*, 2006.

[60] E.H. Han, G. Karypis, and V. Kumar. Scalable parallel data mining for association rules. *Proceedings of ACM SIGMOD International Conference on Management of Data (SIGMOD)*, pp. 277–288, Tucson, AZ. ACM Press, 1997.

[61] P. Brezany, J. Hofer, A.M. Tjoa, and A. Woehrer. GridMiner: An infrastructure for data mining on computational grids. *Australian Partnership for Advanced Computing (APAC)*, 6: 10, 2003.

[62] M. Cannataro, A. Congiusta, A. Pugliese, D. Talia, and P. Trunfio. Distributed data mining on grids: Services, tools, and applications. *IEEE Transactions on Systems, Man, and Cybernetics, Part B: Cybernetics*, 34(6): 2451–2465, 2004.

[63] A. Chervenak, I. Foster, C. Kesselman, C. Salisbury, and S. Tuecke. The data grid: Towards an architecture for the distributed management and analysis of large scientific datasets. *Journal of Network and Computer Applications*, 23(3): 187–200, 2000.

[64] L. Glimcher, R. Jin, and G. Agrawal. Middleware for data mining applications on clusters and grids. *Journal of Parallel and Distributed Computing*, 68(1): 37–53, 2008.

[65] H. Wang, A. Ghoting, G. Buehrer, S. Tatikonda, S. Parthasarathy, T. Kurc, and J. Saltz. A services oriented architecture for next generation data analysis centers. *Next Generation Software Workshop Held with IPDPS*, pp. 212.2, Colorado, 2005.

[66] A. Ghoting, G. Buehrer, M. Goyder, S. Tatikonda, X. Zhang, S. Parthasarathy, T. Kurc, and J. Saltz. Knowledge and cache conscious algorithm design and systems support for data mining algorithms. *Proceedings of the IPDPS Workshop on Next Generation Software*, pp. 1–6, Rome, Italy, March 2007.

[67] G. Buehrer and S. Parthasarathy. A placement service for data mining centers. Technical Report OSU-CISRC-11/07-TR75, Ohio State University, 2007.

[68] A. Ghoting and S. Parthasarathy. Knowledge-conscious data clustering. *Proceedings of 10th European Conference on Principles of Data Mining and Knowledge Discovery (PKDD)*, pp. 511–519, Berlin, Germany, 2006.

Part III

The Web, Semantics, and Text Data Mining

Chapter 14

Web 2.0 Mining: Analyzing Social Media

Anupam Joshi, Tim Finin, Akshay Java, Anubhav Kale, and Pranam Kolari

Contents

14.1 Introduction

The past few years have seen the advent of Web-based social-media systems such as blogs, wikis, media-sharing sites, and message forums. Such Web 2.0 systems have a significant amount of user-generated content, and have become an important new way to publish information, engage in discussions, and form communities on the Internet. Their reach and impact is significant with tens of millions of people providing content on a regular basis around the world. Governments, corporations, traditional-media companies, and NGOs are working to understand how to adapt them and use them effectively. Citizens, both young and old, are also discovering how social-media technology can improve their lives and give them more voice in the world.

We must better understand the information ecology of these new publication methods in order to make them and the information they provide more useful, trustworthy, and reliable. Doing this requires mining such systems to find various kinds of information, including finding communities based on a combination of topic, bias, and underlying beliefs; identifying influential authors and blogs within a community; discovering the source of beliefs and monitoring their diffusion; determining trustworthy sources of information about a particular topic; and learning what opinions and beliefs characterize a community and how do these opinions change.

We use the term "social media" for this new class of Web sites, although the term is not universally adopted nor does it have a consensus definition. While social-media sites are still evolving, it is possible to identify a number of different types of genres and subgenres. Perhaps the most popular, if not the most representative, social-media genre is the weblog or blog. Following the current fashion, we will refer to the set of weblogs as blogosphere. This is more than just a name coined to reference a set of Web pages—the rich interlinking of blogs does make it seem like a distinct network of resources embedded into the larger Web. While every social-media genre has its unique and interesting features, the blogosphere does embody many of the key features that typify social media in general. In this chapter, we focus our discussions on blogs and the blogosphere, but the issues and techniques we describe are applicable, with some modification, to a wider range of social-media systems.

In the rest of this chapter, we present a brief overview of the blogosphere and discuss our ongoing research in analyzing its properties and extracting useful information from it. We begin by describing an overarching task of discovering which blogs and bloggers are most influential within a community or about a topic. Pursuing this task uncovers a number of problems that must be addressed, several of which we describe here. These include recognizing spam in the form of blogs and comments, and developing more effective techniques to recognize the social structure of blog communities.

14.2   Brief Overview of the Blogosphere

As a social-media genre, blogs have many ancestors, most of which still exist today. These include message forums, topical mailing lists, newsgroups, and bulletin board systems. As the Internet and Web became widely available and used in the mid-1990s, a number of people began to maintain sites as personal diaries in which they made chronologically organized records of interesting Web resources discovered, thoughts on current events, and activities. In 1997, one of them, Jorn Barger, coined the term "weblog" to describe his diary site, which was subsequently shortened to blog. During the late 1990s, the appearance of hosted and open-source blogging platforms like Open Diary, LiveJournal, and Blogger made it easy for people to adopt the form. At the same time, the now common blog structure, protocols, and supporting infrastructure—comments, feeds, permalinks, blogrolls, trackbacks, pings, ping servers, etc.—became standardized.

Since 2000, the blogosphere has seen a continuous, exponential grown, doubling every 6 months for most of this period and only within the last year beginning to tapper off. Technorati[*] claimed [1] in the Spring of 2007 to be following over 70 M blogs that are generating about 1.5 M posts per day. This report also shows evidence that blogging has become a global activity by analyzing the most common languages used

---

[*] Technorati was one of the early search engines and is located at http://technorati.com/.

in blogs: Japanese 37%; English 36%; Chinese 8%; Spanish 3%; Russian, French, and Portuguese 2%; German and Farsi 1%; and all others 5%.

One reason that the blogosphere continues to grow is that popular blogging platforms like Blogspot, WordPress, and TypePad can serve as simple content management systems and for many provide a very easy way to add content to the Web. Moreover, the ping-based infrastructure exploited by blog search engines means that it provides the fastest way to get that content indexed by major search engines.*

The blogosphere is part of the Web and therefore shares most of its general characteristics. It differs, however, in ways that impact how we can model it and use the model to help extract information. The common model for the Web in general is as a graph of Web pages with undifferentiated links between pages. The blogosphere has a much richer network structure in that there are more types of nodes that have more types of relations between them. For example, the people who contribute to blogs and author blog posts form a social network with their peers, which can be induced by the links between blogs. The blogs themselves form a graph, with direct links to other blogs through blogrolls and indirect links through their posts. Blog posts are linked to their host blogs and typically to other blog posts and Web resources as part of their content.

A typical blog post has a set of comments that link back to people and blogs associated with them. The blogosphere trackback protocol alerts a blog site that it is being linked to from another blog and enables it to create a back link. Still more detail can be added by taking into account post tags and categories, syndication feeds, and semistructured metadata in the form of XML and RDF content. Finally, a link's anchor text as well as the text around the link provide significant information. We believe that adapting and extending the work done by many subcommunities in the data-mining arena can help develop new techniques to analyze social media.

The blogosphere, and social media in general, continue to evolve. For example, many major newspapers and magazines have blogs authored by their staff writers and are incorporating blog-like features such as user comments into their articles published online. New platforms like Facebook offer a blend of traditional blogs and social-networking sites. There is also a growing interest in enabling the integration of information in different social-media systems to produce what many refer to as a social graph. Finally, users are increasingly interested in being able to extract and use the data that social-media sites have about them.

14.3 Modeling Influence in the Blogosphere

The blogosphere provides an interesting opportunity to study social interactions including spread of information, opinion formation, and influence. Through original

---

* Experiments done by the authors in the mid-2007 showed that posts added to our research blog were indexed by major blog search engines in less than 10 min and typically showed up in Google's main search index within 2 h.

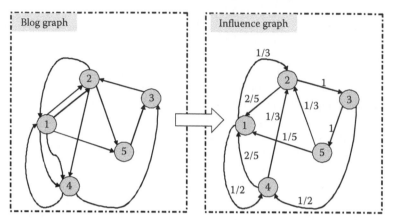

FIGURE 14.1: This diagram shows the conversion of a blog graph into an influence graph. A link from u to v indicates that u is influenced by v. The edges in the influence graph are reverse of the blog graph to indicate this influence. Multiple edges indicate stronger influence and are weighed higher.

content and commentary on topics of current interest, bloggers influence each other and their audience. We aim to study and characterize this social interaction by modeling the blogosphere and providing novel algorithms for analyzing social-media content. Figure 14.1 shows a hypothetical blog graph and its corresponding flow of information in the influence graph.

Studies on influence in social networks and collaboration graphs have typically focused on the task of identifying key individuals (influentials) who play an important role in propagating information. This is similar to finding authoritative pages on the Web. Epidemic-based models like linear threshold and cascade models [2–4] have been used to find a small set of individuals who are most influential in social network. However, influence on the Web is often a function of topic. For example, a post contrasting the positions of republicans and democrats on Engadget[*] is not likely to be influential even though it is one of the most popular blogs on the Web. A post comparing the Apple iPhone with the Nokia N95 will likely be influential. With Daily Kos,[†] the situation will be reversed.

This issue also arises with blogs in niche areas with small readership. A blog that is relatively low ranked on conventional measures can be highly influential in this small community of interest. In addition, influence can be subjective and based on the interest of the users. Thus, by analyzing the readership of a blog, we can gain some insights into the community likely to be influenced by it. We have implemented a system called Feeds That Matter[‡] [5] that aggregates subscription information across thousands of users to automatically categorize blogs into different topics.

---

[*] http://www.engadget.com/.

[†] http://dailykos.com/.

[‡] Feeds That Matter site is available at http://ftm.umbc.edu/.

TABLE 14.1: These were the top 10 political blogs in 2006 based on readership metrics from the feeds that matter [5] system.

1	http://www.talkingpointsmemo.com/
2	http://www.dailykos.com/
3	http://atrios.blogspot.com/
4	http://www.washingtonmonthly.com/
5	http://www.wonkette.com/
6	http://instapundit.com/
7	http://www.juancole.com/
8	http://powerlineblog.com/
9	http://americablog.blogspot.com/
10	http://www.crooksandliars.com/

Table 14.1 shows the top political blogs ranked using readership-based influence metrics derived by this system.

An important component in understanding influence is to detect sentiment and opinions. An aggregated opinion over many users is a predictor for an interesting trend in a community, and may indicate the emergence of a new meme. Sufficient adoption of this meme could lead to a tipping point and consequently influence the rest of the community.

The BlogVox system [6] retrieves opinionated blog posts specified by ad hoc queries. After retrieving posts relevant to a topic query, the system processes them to produce a set of independent features estimating the likelihood that a post expresses an opinion about the topic. These are combined using an support vector machine (SVM)-based system and integrated with the relevancy score to rank the results.

Since blog posts are often informally written, poorly structured, rife with spelling and grammatical errors, and feature nontraditional content, they are difficult to process with standard language analysis tools. Performing linguistic analysis on blogs is plagued by two additional problems: (1) the presence of spam blogs and spam comments, and (2) extraneous noncontent including blogrolls, linkrolls, advertisements, and sidebars. In the next section, we describe techniques designed to eliminate spam content from a blog index. This is a vital task before any useful analytics can be supported on social-media content.

In the following sections, we also discuss link polarity in blog graphs. We represent each edge in the influence graph with a vector of topic and corresponding weights indicating either positive or negative sentiment associated with the link for a topic. Thus, if a blog A links to a blog B with a negative sentiment for a topic T, influencing B would have little effect on A. Opinions are also manifested as biases. A community of ipod fanatics, for example, needs little or no convincing about the product. Thus, influencing an opinion leader in such already positively biased communities is going to have less significant impact for the product. Using link polarity and trust propagation, we demonstrate how like-minded blogs can be discovered and the potential of using this technique for more generic problems such as detecting trustworthy nodes in Web graphs [7].

Existing models of influence have considered a static view of the network. The blogosphere, on the other hand, is extremely buzzy and dynamic. New topics emerge and blogs constantly rise and fall in popularity. By considering influence as a temporal phenomenon, we can find key individuals that are early adopters or buzz generators for a topic. We propose an abstract model of the blogosphere that provides a systematic approach to modeling the evolution of the link structure and communities. Thus, in order to model influence on the blogosphere, we need to consider topic, readership, community structure, sentiment, and time.

In the following sections, we provide a brief description of various issues that need to be handled in order to model influence.

14.4   Detecting Blog Spam

As with other forms of communication, spam has become a serious problem in blogs and social media, effecting both users and systems that harvest, index, and analyze blog content. Two forms of spam are common in blogs: spam blogs, or splogs, where the entire blog and hosted posts consist of machine-generated spam, and spam comments attached by programs to authentic posts on normal blogs (Figure 14.2). Though splogs continue to be a problem for Web search engines and are considered a special case of Web spam, they present a new set of challenges for blog analytics. Given the context of this chapter and the intricacies of indexing blogs [8], we limit our discussion to that of splogs.

Blog search engines index new blog posts by processing pings from update ping servers, intermediary systems that aggregate notifications from updated blogs. Pings from spam pages increase computational requirements, corrupt results, and eventually reduce user satisfaction. We estimate that more than 50% of all pings are from spam sources [9].

14.4.1   Detecting Splogs

Over the past two years, we have developed techniques to detect spam blogs. We discuss highlights of our effort based on splog detection using blog home pages with local and relational features. Interested readers are referred to Refs. [10,11] for further details.

Results reported in the rest of this section are based on a seed dataset of 700 positive (splogs) and 700 negative (authentic blog) labeled examples containing the entire HTML content of each blog home page. All of the models are based on SVMs [12]. We used a linear kernel with top features chosen using mutual information and models evaluated using onefold cross-validation. We view detection techniques as local and relational, based on feature types used.

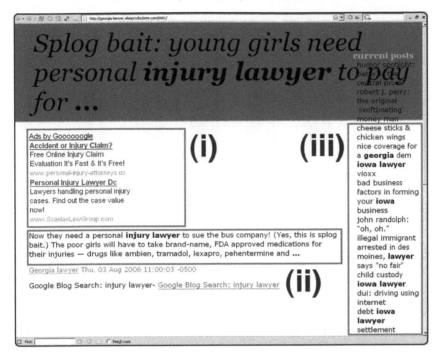

FIGURE 14.2:   This example of a splog, plagiarizes content (ii), promotes other spam pages (iii) and (i) hosts high-paying contextual advertisements.

14.4.2   Local Features

A blog's local features can be quite effective for splog detection. A local feature is one that is completely determined by the contents of a single Web page. A local model built using only these features can provide a quick assessment of the degree to which a blog appears to be spam. These features include bag-of-words, word *n*-grams, anchor text, and URLs. We have experimented with many such models, and our results are summarized in Figure 14.3.

1. *Words*. To verify their utility, we created bag-of-words for the samples based on their textual content. We also analyzed discriminating features by ordering features based on weights assigned to them by the linear kernel. It turns out that the model was built around features that the human eye would have typically overlooked. Blogs often contain content that expresses personal opinions, so words like I, we, my, and what appear commonly on authentic blog posts. To this effect, the bag-of-words model is built on an interesting blog-content genre. In general, such a content genre is not seen on the Web, which partly explains why spam detection using local textual content is less effective there.

2. *Word* n-*grams*. An alternative methodology to using textual content for classification is the bag-of-word-*n*-grams, where *n* adjacent words are used as a feature.

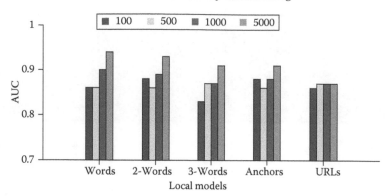

FIGURE 14.3: The performance of local models, as measured by the standard AUC metric, varies for different feature types and sizes.

We evaluated both bag-of-word-2-grams and bag-of-word-3-grams, which turned out to be almost as effective as bag-of-words. Interesting discriminative features were observed in this experiment. For instance, text like comments-off (comments are usually turned-off in splogs), new-york (a high paying advertising term), and in-uncategorized (spammers do not bother to specify categories for blog posts) are features common to splogs, whereas text like 2-comments, 1-comment, i-have, and to-my were some features common to authentic blogs. Similar features ranked highly in the 3-word gram model.

3. *Tokenized anchors.* Anchor text is the text that appears in an HTML link (i.e., between the <a...> and </a> tags) and is a common link-spamming technique around profitable contexts. We used a bag-of-anchors feature, where anchor text on a page, with multiple word anchors split into individual words, is used. Note that anchor text is frequently used for Web page classification, but typically to classifying the target page rather than the one hosting the link. We observed that comment and flickr were among the highly ranked features for authentic blogs.

4. *Tokenized URLs.* Intuitively, both local and outgoing URLs can be used as effective attributes for splog detection. This is motivated by the fact that many URL tokens in splogs are in profitable contexts. We term these features as bag-of-urls, arrived at by tokenizing URLs using "/" and ".". Results indicate this can be a useful approach complementing other techniques.

14.4.3 Relational Features

A global model is one that uses some nonlocal-features, that is, features requiring data beyond the content of Web page under test. We have investigated the use of link distributions to see if splogs can be identified once they place themselves on the blog (Web) hyperlink graph. The intuition is that authentic blogs are very unlikely to link to splogs and that splogs frequently do link to other splogs. We have evaluated this approach by extending our seed dataset with labeled in-links and out-links, to achieve AUC^* values of close to 0.85. Interested readers are referred to Ref. [11] for further details.

Though current techniques work well, the problem of spam detection is an adversarial challenge. In our continuing efforts, we are working toward better addressing concept drift and leveraging community and relational features. The problem of spam in social media is now extending well beyond the blogs and is quite common in popular social tools like MySpace and Facebook. The nature of these social tools demand additional emphasis on relational techniques, a direction we are exploring as well.

14.5 Communities and Polarization of Opinion

Communities [13], especially on deeply held issues, tend to be like-minded, and often critical of those outside. Our approach uses this idea by associating sentiment (positive or negative) with the links connecting two blogs. By "link" we mean the URL that blogger *A* uses in his or her blog post to refer to a post by blogger *B*. We call this sentiment as link polarity and the sign and magnitude of this value is based on the sentiment of text surrounding the link. This can be obtained using shallow natural-language processing techniques. These polar edges indicate the bias/trust/distrust between respective blogs. We then use trust propagation models (in particular, one described by Guha et al. [14]) to spread the polarity values from a subset of nodes that refer to one another to all possible pairs of nodes. We evaluate the idea of using trust propagation on polar links in the domain of political blogosphere by predicting the like-mindedness of democratic and republican blogs. In order to determine if a given blog is left or right leaning, we compute the trust/distrust score for it from a seed set of influential blogs and use a hand-labeled dataset from Ref. [15] to validate our results. More generally, we address the problem of detecting all such nodes that a given node would trust even if it is not directly connected to them.

We choose political blogs as our test domain; one of the major goals of the experiments was to validate that our proposed approach can correctly classify the blogs into two sets: republican and democratic.

Adamic and Glance [15] provided us with a reference dataset of 1490 blogs with a label of democratic or republican for each blog. Their data on political learning is based on analysis of blog directories and manual labeling and has a time frame of 2004 presidential elections.

Our test dataset from BuzzMetrics [16] did not provide a classified set of political blogs. Hence, for our experiments, we used a snapshot of BuzzMetrics that had a complete overlap with our reference dataset to validate the classification results. The

---

* Area under the receiver-operating characteristic (ROC) curve.

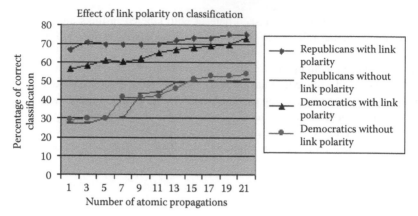

FIGURE 14.4: Our experiments show that using polar links for classification yields better results than plain link structure.

snapshot contained 297 blogs, 1309 blog–blog links, and 7052 post–post links. The reference dataset labeled 132 blogs as republicans and 165 blogs as democratics (there did not exist any neutral labels).

The results in Figure 14.4 show one of our experiments. They indicate a clear improvement on classifying republican and democratic blogs by applying polar weights to links followed by trust propagation compared to using the link structure alone. Further results and details are described in Ref. [7].

14.6 Conclusions

Social-media systems are increasingly important on the Web today and account for the majority of new content. The various kinds of social media are alike in that they all have rich underlying network structures that provide metadata and context that can help when extracting information from their content. We have described some initial results from ongoing work that is focused on extracting and exploiting this structural information. We note that there is a lack of adequate datasets to fully test the new approaches. To some extent, synthetic blog graphs can be useful to this end. In recent work [17], we have shown that existing graph-generation techniques do not work well for this, and proposed a new model.

As the Web continues to evolve, we expect that the ways people interact with it, as content consumers as well as content providers, will also change. The result, however, will continue to represent an interesting and extravagant mixture of underlying networks—networks of individuals, groups, documents, opinions, beliefs, advertisements, and scams. These interwoven networks present new opportunities and challenges for extracting information and knowledge from them.

Acknowledgments

We thank Dr. James Mayfield, Justin Martineau, and Sandeep Balijepalli for their contributions to the work on sentiment detection, and Amit Karandikar for his work on the generative model. Partial support for this research was provided by the National Science Foundation (awards ITR-IIS-0325172 and NSF-ITR-IDM-0219649) and IBM.

References

[1] D. Sifry. Available at http://www.sifry.com/alerts/archives/000493.html, April 2007.

[2] D. Kempe, J. M. Kleinberg, and É. Tardos. Maximizing the spread of influence through a social network. In *Proceeding of the 9th ACM SIGKDD International Conference on Knowledge Discovery and Data Mining*, pp. 137–146, New York, 2003. ACM Press.

[3] D. Kempe, J. M. Kleinberg, and É. Tardos. Influential nodes in a diffusion model for social networks. In *Proceedings of the Internatonal Colloquium on Automata, Languages and Programming*, pp. 1127–1138, Berlin/Heidelberg, Germany, 2005. Springer.

[4] J. Leskovec, M. McGlohon, C. Faloutsos, N. Glance, and M. Hurst. Cascading behavior in large blog graphs. In *SIAM International Conference on Data Mining (SDM 2007)*, Philadelphia, PA, 2007. SIAM.

[5] A. Java, P. Kolari, T. Finin, A. Joshi, and T. Oates. Feeds That Matter: A study of bloglines subscriptions. In *Proceedings of the International Conference on Weblogs and Social Media (ICWSM 2007)*, Menlo Park, CA, March 2007. AAAI Press.

[6] A. Java, P. Kolari, T. Finin, A. Joshi, J. Martineau, and J. Mayfield. The BlogVox opinion retrieval system. In *Proceedings of the 15th Text Retrieval Conference (TREC 2006)*, Gaithersburg, MD, February 2007.

[7] A. Kale, A. Karandikar, P. Kolari, A. Java, A. Joshi, and T. Finin. Modeling trust and influence in the blogosphere using link polarity. In *Proceedings of the International Conference on Weblogs and Social Media (ICWSM 2007)*, Menlo Park, CA, March 2007. AAAI Press.

[8] G. Mishne. Applied text analytics for blogs. PhD thesis, University of Amsterdam, January 2007.

[9] P. Kolari, A. Java, and T. Finin. Characterizing the splogosphere. In *WWW 2006, 3rd Annual Workshop on the Weblogggging Ecosystem: Aggregation, Analysis and Dynamics*, Edinburgh, UK, 2006. W3C.

[10] P. Kolari, T. Finin, and A. Joshi. SVMs for the blogosphere: Blog identification and splog detection. In *AAAI Spring Symposium on Computational Approaches to Analyzing Weblogs*, Menlo Park, CA, 2006. AAAI Press.

[11] P. Kolari, A. Java, T. Finin, T. Oates, and A. Joshi. Detecting spam blogs: A machine learning approach. In *Proceedings of the 21st National Conference on Artificial Intelligence (AAAI 2006)*, Menlo Park, CA, 2006. AAAI Press.

[12] B. E. Boser, I. M. Guyon, and V. N. Vapnik. A training algorithm for optimal margin classifiers. In *COLT '92: Proceedings of the 5th Annual Workshop on Computational Learning Theory*, pp. 144–152, New York, 1992. ACM Press.

[13] A. Java, A. Joshi, and T. Finin. Approximating the community structure of the long tail. In *Proceedings of the 2nd International Conference on Weblogs and Social Media (ICWSM 2008)*, Menlo Park, CA, March 2008. AAAI Press (poster paper).

[14] R. Guha, R. Kumar, P. Raghavan, and A. Tomkins. Propagation of trust and distrust. In *WWW '04: Proceedings of the 13th International Conference on World Wide Web*, pp. 403–412, New York, 2004. ACM Press.

[15] L. A. Adamic and N. Glance. The political blogosphere and the 2004 U.S. election: Divided they blog. In *LinkKDD '05: Proceedings of the 3rd International Workshop on Link Discovery*, pp. 36–43, New York, 2005. ACM Press.

[16] Nielsen BuzzMetrics. Available at http://www.nielsenbuzzmetrics.com.

[17] A. Karandikar, A. Java, A. Joshi, T. Finin, Y. Yesha, and Y. Yesha. Second space: A generative model for the blogosphere. In *Proceedings of the International Conference on Weblogs and Social Media (ICWSM 2008)*, Menlo Park, CA, March 2008. AAAI Press (poster paper).

Chapter 15

Searching for "Familiar Strangers" on Blogosphere

Nitin Agarwal, Huan Liu, John Salerno, and Philip S. Yu

Contents

15.1 Familiar Strangers on Blogosphere

The advent of Web 2.0 [1] has started a surge of open-source intelligence via online media such as blogs. Since more and more people are participating in Web 2.0 activities, it has generated enormous amounts of collective wisdom or open-source intelligence. Web 2.0 has allowed the mass not only to contribute and edit posts/articles through blogs and wikis, but also enrich the existing content by providing tags or labels, hence turning the former information consumers to the new producers. Allowing the mass to contribute or edit has also increased collaboration among the people unlike Web 1.0 where the access to the content was limited to a chosen few. Blogs are invigorating this process by encouraging the mass to document their ideas, thoughts, opinions, views reverse chronologically, called blog posts, and share them with other bloggers. These blog posts are published on blog sites and the universe of these blog sites is called blogosphere. Familiar strangers on blogosphere are not directly connected, but share some patterns in their blogging activities.

Blogosphere contains both single-authored blog sites known as individual blog sites and multiauthored blog sites or community blog sites. In individual blog sites, only one author creates blog posts and readers are allowed to comment on these posts, but the readers cannot create new entries. In community blog sites, several authors can create blog posts and comments. Readers are allowed to comment but only registered members of the community can author blog posts. Based on these different entities on the blogosphere we have two types of familiar strangers on blogosphere: groups and individuals. It is highly likely that both these types of familiar strangers occur in the Long Tail [2] as depicted in Figure 15.1, because the bloggers in the Short Head are highly authoritative, which means they are highly connected, hence less chances of being strangers. Moreover, existing search engines return relevant results only from the Short Head, so it is interesting and challenging to study the ones that appear in the Long Tail. In this Chapter we focus on individual familiar strangers.

Given a blogger b, we aim to find b's familiar strangers, and together, they form critical mass such that (1) the understanding of one blogger gives us a sensible and representative glimpse to all, (2) more data about familiar strangers can be collected for better customization and services (e.g., personalization and recommendation), (3) the nuances among them present new business opportunities, and (4) knowledge about them can facilitate predictive modeling and trend analysis.

Familiar strangers on blogosphere are the niches of business opportunities. They are distributed over the blogosphere and each is in a small group. Each group is isolated and its size is also small such that the need for a zoom-in study is often ignorable. For example, it is not cost effective to hire an expert to personally study a single blogger. However, aggregating familiar strangers can open up new opportunities. For the same example, the knowledge of one blogger's personalization can now be transferred to these familiar strangers so that the previous worthless zoom-in study becomes meaningful. In addition, their aggregation can provide a rich body of data that can be used for accurate personalization and mining for patterns. Next, we study the purposes of finding familiar strangers on the blogosphere.

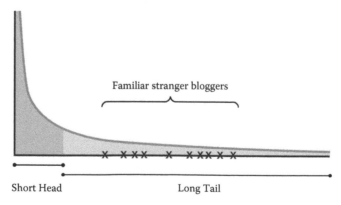

FIGURE 15.1:   Familiar stranger bloggers and Long Tail distribution.

15.2   Need for Aggregating Familiar Strangers

As we know, the Web follows the distribution of a power law. Since the blogosphere is a part of the Web, the power law naturally applies to the blogosphere in the sense that except for a small percentage of blog sites, the majority of blog sites belong to the Long Tail. In particular, many bloggers are active locally with limited connections to other bloggers. Here is the dilemma: Before a blogger becomes prominent or in the Short Head, it is not worth paying particularly customized attention to the blogger; and the blogger cannot be well targeted for otherwise potential business opportunities (i.e., niches). As depicted in Figure 15.2, advertisements generated by Google AdSense are not relevant. A not-well-connected post (in the Long Tail) does not have sufficient information for link-based approaches to find relevant advertisements. To do better requires a good number of bloggers who can provide more data for accurate automatic personalization for targeted marketing. Now we elaborate the impact of finding familiar strangers on the blogosphere from the perspective of marketing with Web 2.0.

Uncle Walt says the new iMac rocks Vista

Posted Aug 25th 2007 7:00PM by Mat Lu
Filed under: OS, Switchers, iMac

Ever since Boot Camp was released it has been no surprise to find out that the Intel Macs also make for some of the best Windows machines too (well, if you can bring yourself to install it, that is). Anyway, Walt Mossberg, dean of tech writers, has gotten one of the new iMacs and for kicks installed Vista via Boot Camp. And sure enough, Uncle Walt says he tested it "using Vista's built-in Windows Experience Index, a rating system that goes from 1 to 5.9, with scores above 3.0 generally required for full, quick performance. My iMac scored a 5.0, the best score of any consumer Vista machine I have tested." This was apparently the 2.8GHz machine as he says it was the top-of-the-line model. I know some folks were disappointed with the new iMacs slightly anemic graphics cards, but it's good to know they can still rock Vista if called upon to do so.

[via MacVolPlace]

Read　　　　　　Permalink | Email this | Linking Blogs | Comments [11]

FIGURE 15.2:   Blog post with irrelevant advertisements.

The underlying concept of familiar strangers is that they share some patterns and routines (or commonalities), although they are not directly connected. Connecting them to form critical mass will not only expand a blogger's social network but also increase participation to move from the Long Tail toward the Short Head. With Web 2.0, the new marketing 4Ps [3] are personalization, participation, peer-to-peer, and predictive modeling. Personalization is to customize products and services through the use of the Internet with emerging social media and advanced algorithms. The pervasive use of the Web technologies extends the Long Tail even longer, which makes personalization more important as well as more difficult in a cost-effective sense. It is important because impersonalized advertisements will likely be ignored and hence it defeats the purposes of attaching advertisements in the first place. It is difficult because the data is too sparse to be useful for accurate personalization. Participation allows a customer to participate in what the brand should stand for; what should be the product directions, or which advertisements to run. Finding familiar strangers on the blogosphere can increase the customer base of similar interests, which can encourage participation due to the crowd effect as reputation can significantly increase as the customer base expands. Reputation and expression are among major motivations for bloggers to engage in activities; and shared interests will encourage them to participate more actively. Finding familiar strangers makes peer-to-peer feasible, which refers to customer networks and communities where advocacy happens. Peers usually trust peers. Knowledge transfer or information flow among peers becomes smoother and more likely to be useful. Familiar strangers share some commonalities but can have varied deviations. The differences among them can be considered relevant niches for new business. Predictive modeling refers to employing inductive algorithms to learn predictive models from data in order to predict trends. Typical examples of predictive modeling include regression, classification, clustering, association rule mining, and other induction-based learning algorithms. Predictive modeling helps figure out what is going on or likely to happen and get ready to be among the first who act on the new business opportunities when it does happen. Alternatively, one can proactively prepare effective measures to respond and react in shortest time possible. Without being discovered from the Long Tail, it is hard to be differentiated from other fellow members in the Long Tail, one is less likely to receive necessary attention that warrants better services.

Aggregating familiar strangers can have significant impact on moving from the Long Tail to the Short Head. However, the mere fact that they are strangers presents challenges to reach many disconnected bloggers over the blogosphere effectively and efficiently. We next examine some challenges.

15.3 Problem and Challenges

Having discussed the need for identifying familiar strangers on the blogosphere, we try to formally define them here. Bloggers, with their blogging behavior, tend to create social relationships with peer bloggers. However, most of them ($\sim$97%)

are locally connected with limited links to other bloggers, thus in the Long Tail. The goal of this work is to aggregate familiar strangers. Given a blogger b, familiar strangers to b are a set of bloggers $B = b_1, b_2, ..., b_n$, who share common patterns as b, like blogging on similar topics, but have never come across each other or have never related to each other. Basically, every pair b, b_j of bloggers, where $1 \leq j \leq n$, blog on similar topics making them familiar or sharing the latent process that inspires them to do so. Similarity will be discussed in Section 15.4. Nevertheless, b, b_j still remain strangers because of no direct interaction between them either in terms of links in their blog posts or each one's presence in the other's social network. For the pair of b, b_j to be total strangers, two conditions should hold true:

1. b should not appear in b_j's social network

2. b_j should not appear in b's social network

Failing one of the two conditions would make them partial strangers. For example, many adults in the United States know of President Bush, but not vice versa. Henceforth, strangers are total strangers.

Since these familiar strangers are identified on the blogosphere, organizational differences in the blogosphere eventuate disparate types of familiar stranger bloggers. There are several social networking sites like MySpace,* Orkut,† Facebook,‡ etc. Each of these sites and others allow users to form communities of like-minded people to share ideas, thoughts, and views. These communities host their discussions and interactions on community blog sites or multiauthor blog sites. Multiauthor blog sites, a venue for community members to discuss and interact is unlike individual blog sites with greater interaction between community members. This community-wide interaction helps in understanding the individuals better. We divide familiar strangers into three broad categories:

1. Community-level familiar strangers—two bloggers b_{ix} and b_{iy} of the same community C_i (as shown in Figure 15.3)

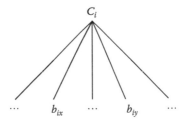

FIGURE 15.3:   Community-level familiar stranger bloggers.

---

* http://www.myspace.com.
† http://www.orkut.com.
‡ http://www.facebook.com.

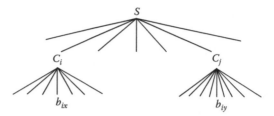

FIGURE 15.4:   Network-site level familiar strangers.

2. Networking-site-level familiar strangers—two bloggers b_{ix} and b_{jy} of different communities C_i and C_j, respectively, on the same site (shown in Figure 15.4)

3. Blogosphere-level familiar strangers—two bloggers b_{ix}^m and b_{jy}^n in two different communities C_i and C_j which are under different social networking sites, S_m and S_n, respectively (as shown in Figure 15.5)

Clearly, community-level familiar strangers are the easiest to find by studying one community at a social networking site. Identifying networking-site-level familiar strangers is still relatively easy. Identifying blogosphere-level familiar strangers is the most challenging. When we span across different social networking sites, we run into various problems like blogger identity mapping, related community identification, etc. The same blogger could use different identities on different social networking sites. It is challenging to make sure we are dealing with the same blogger, or two seemingly different bloggers on two different networking sites may be the same person. On the other hand, it would be exemplar to be able to find those bloggers using different identities at disparate networking sites as familiar strangers to themselves.

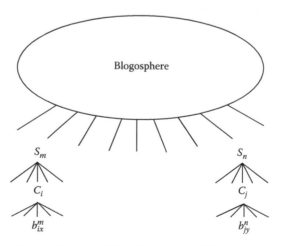

FIGURE 15.5:   Blogosphere-level familiar stranger blogger.

Examples of these different types of familiar strangers are

1. Community-level familiar stranger bloggers—on MySpace a community called "A group for those who love history" has 38 members; 2 members, Maria and John blog profusely on the similar topic, but they are not in each other's social network.

2. Networking-site level familiar strangers—we considered two groups on MySpace, The Samurai and The Japanese Sword consisting of 32 and 84 members, respectively. These communities are located at the same networking site, and the two bloggers discuss about Japanese martial arts. We looked at the social network of the top bloggers in these groups, Marc from The Samurai and Jeff from The Japanese Sword. Neither of them is in the other's social network. This implies, though being active locally and discussing on the same theme, the two bloggers are still strangers.

3. Blogosphere-level familiar strangers—We consider two different social networking sites, MySpace and Orkut. We manually search for similar communities on both networking sites. We picked The Samurai from MySpace and Samurai Sword from Orkut. The Samurai contains 32 members and Samurai Sword contains 29 members, which means both would lie in the Long Tail. Both groups are located in completely different networking sites. Top bloggers from the respective communities in MySpace and Orkut, Marc (the United States) and Anant (India), respectively, share the blogging theme but they are not in each others' social network. The above example illustrates the existence of blogosphere-level familiar strangers.

The problem of finding familiar strangers can be formulated as: Given a blogger b, identifying a set of bloggers B, such that every pair of bloggers b, b_j, where $1 \leq j \leq n$, satisfies the definition of familiar stranger bloggers mentioned above. Similarity can be defined by topics, bag of words, tag clouds, etc., and is discussed in Section 15.4.

One challenge is that a fragmented Web entails the fragmented blogosphere. Finding familiar strangers is essentially a problem of searching the Long Tail: Starting from a given blogger, we want to find familiar strangers. Given that a blogger has a social network, it seems sensible to start the search with the social network. The hope is that a familiar stranger is the blogger's friend's friend (or nth friend's social network), i.e., a familiar stranger of blogger b's can be found in the social network of blogger c who is in b's social network. However, this seemingly simple idea is practically infeasible. It is a type of naive link analysis that entails exhaustive search. Assuming each blogger has a social network of 10 friends, the search cost is $O(10^{10})$ after exhausting bloggers who are 10 links away from the first blogger. It might very likely find familiar strangers, but incur the unbearable search cost.

Another reason that naive link analysis cannot help much is that the Web is not a random network. Its power law distribution suggests that more often than not, a blogger or group is in the Long Tail and not in the Short Head. In other words, they are largely disconnected as only those in the Short Head are well connected.

Finding familiar strangers on the blogosphere differs from classic data mining tasks. There are no typical training and test data. Hence, it requires innovative ways of evaluating and validating the end results. We will have to address this challenge in order to demonstrate the efficacy of various approaches and comparative findings.

15.4   Finding Familiar Strangers

The Long Tail phenomenon demands novel ways to find and connect little ones so that together they can emerge to become true niches as business opportunities. Given the definitions of familiar strangers, we generally have access to three types of information and data:

1. Blogger b's social network or b's immediate links to other bloggers or posts

2. b's Blog posts

3. Blogger b's context

For each type, we investigate how to leverage the existing search engines and APIs to develop algorithms such that the feasibility and potentials of the corresponding approaches can be evaluated.

The first approach is link based. It searches for familiar strangers via a blogger's social network, or naive link analysis. Conceptually, it can be formulated as a matrix analysis problem as follows: Given a blogger-to-blogger $d \times d$ matrix A of d bloggers representing pair-wise direct links, A_h will reveal who can be reached via h hops. Challenges are

1. Finding the link information at each step from step 1 to step n

2. Making the huge, sparse matrix multiplication practical and efficient

This is basically an exhaustive search process. The complexity of this approach is $O(d^h)$ for h hops and d bloggers. This approach does not scale well with increasing number of bloggers because the matrix A gets more sparse.

The second approach is similarity based. It searches via a blogger b's posts, as illustrated in Figure 15.6. Intuitively, b's posts, $p_1, p_2, ..., p_n$ contain a rich amount of information such as text, links, and tags. In absence of tags, existing approaches like Ref. [4] can be used to discover topic structures of the blog posts. One way of finding familiar strangers is to use the tag cloud [5] or topics of b's post as query terms (or query expansion) to find those highly similar posts $q_1, q_2, ..., q_n$ by employing search engines or metasearch engines. Since we basically use the ranking functions of the search engines, the top-ranked ones might miss those in the Long Tail. Top results would always have high authority or linked by several authoritative blog posts. Hence existing search engines tend to produce results from the Short Head. If we remove the top results from the search, we may end up with irrelevant results. This results in a dilemma. A first step is to evaluate the posts returned by representative search

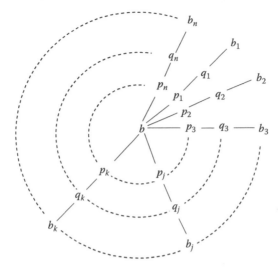

FIGURE 15.6: Searching via blogger's blog post.

engines and metasearch engines in a controlled domain to observe how disparate types of results are distributed in terms of relevance. Once related and relevant blog posts are obtained we can study the authors of these blog posts, $b_1,b_2,...,b_n$ and look for familiar strangers, as defined in Section 15.3. The complexity of this approach is not exponential with respect to h where $h = 1$ since the links are not traversed beyond the first hop of similar bloggers. However, it depends on the complexity of similar blog post search algorithms used. In terms of scalability, this approach does not scale well with number of blog posts submitted. Both large and small numbers of blog posts hurt the search performance. With large numbers of blog posts we have a problem of too many results. On the other hand, too few blog posts do not give robust and reliable estimation.

The third approach is context based, which makes use of a blogger's context as displayed in Figure 15.7. The context of a blogger could be gleamed from the community he is a part of. Using the community tag information, the search for familiar strangers and bloggers could be restricted to other communities of a similar category. The key is to use local information that can be identified through each individual to guide a directed search. Directly searching the Long Tail for familiar strangers turns this approach to the first approach—exhaustive search. The alternative is to use the tag information to determine those relevant categories that can be found in the Short Head, then lead the blogger to those reachable via some sites in the Short Head. This way, it avoids exhaustive search. First, we use the context information to find relevant sites in the Short Head. Second, we further filter those groups/bloggers at each relevant site in the Short Head that act as connectors (e.g., b_s in Figure 15.7) between familiar strangers in the Long Tail (e.g., b and b'). If the familiarity between blogger b, and his/her familiar stranger from the Long Tail, b' is depicted by $b \sim b'$ then the lower bound to this similarity can be $b \sim b_s$, where b_s is the connector from

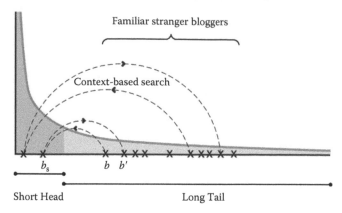

FIGURE 15.7:   Searching via blogger's context.

the Short Head. This approach is the least complex and scales well. Identifying context and building a profile for a blogger requires a linear number of operations. The search space for finding bloggers in the Long Tail is also pruned by constraining the search in related categories. Then using the Short Head bloggers help in further reducing the search space when searching the Long Tail.

Some intuitive baseline methods for finding familiar strangers for comparative study are related to recommending and searching/ranking. The first is Amazon's recommendation-based approach. Each blogger could be represented with a unique profile, and bloggers can be compared based on the similarity between their profiles. But the obvious problems are (1) whether there exist databases of blogger profiles, and (2) how to construct profiles for each blogger in advance. This approach may be feasible for a limited-size domain, but will encounter a scaling-up problem when searching the blogosphere. A changing profile could cause a severe problem. Another baseline approach could be to use searching/ranking engines and obtain the blogs/bloggers similar to the one at hand. But as mentioned before, the results obtained will, more often than not, belong to the Short Head. The key issue is whether it can find those relevant ones in the Long Tail. These research issues await interesting solutions.

15.5   An Empirical Study

We now describe an approach to finding Type 3 familiar strangers, i.e., blogosphere-level familiar strangers (Figure 15.5). We use data from a blog site directory available at BlogCatalog.* BlogCatalog organizes the blog sites under prespecified categories as shown in Figure 15.8. Bloggers can specify the categories where a blog site should be categorized. The number of categories keeps increasing as more blog sites are

---

* http://www.blogcatalog.com/.

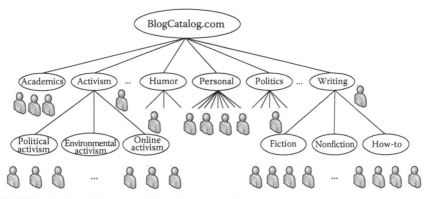

FIGURE 15.8:   Glimpse of BlogCatalog with its categories.

submitted to BlogCatalog, although in a controlled fashion. At the time of writing, BlogCatalog had in total 56 categories. These categories could be denoted as $c_1, c_2, ..., c_n$ and $n = 56$. The directory structure of BlogCatalog is relatively shallow, with 33 categories having no subcategories. The maximum depth of the category structure is 3 and only two categories have that depth. Bloggers submit the blog sites to BlogCatalog. Blog sites could be denoted as $S_1, S_2, ..., S_m$. Each site is authored by a blogger denoted by $b_1, b_2, ..., b_m$. Each blog site contains some blog posts of which last five are displayed on BlogCatalog. Other blog posts could also be crawled from respective blog sites which could be further pursued in future work. These blog posts could be denoted as $p_{11}, p_{12}, ..., p_{15}, p_{21}, p_{22}, ..., p_{25}, ..., p_{m1}, p_{m2}, ..., p_{m5}$, i.e., sets of blog posts for blog site $S_1, S_2, ..., S_m$, respectively.

Additional information collectable from BlogCatalog includes blogger name, rank of blog sites, number of views/hits of blog sites, time stamp of each blog posts, social network of each blogger, categories under which the blogger lists his/her blog site, blog post level tags, blog site level tags, and snippets of last five blog posts for each blog site. Both blog site level tags and blog post level tags are not necessarily available.

Searching for familiar–stranger bloggers for a given blogger requires searching exhaustively in the blogosphere. However, due to the excessively large search space, it should be pruned so that the search can be focused on those potentially similar blog sites. Here we assume that the familiar–stranger bloggers blog on similar contents. Finding similar blog sites to the given blogger's requires the clustering of blog sites into groups so that the search can be conducted in individual groups to avoid exhaustive search.

15.5.1   Blog Category Clustering

Clustering the similar categories can be formulated as an optimization problem. Assume 56 categories are clustered into k clusters, $C_1, C_2, ..., C_k$, optimal clustering is obtained if, for any two categories c_i and c_j,

$$\min \sum d(c_i, c_j), \forall (c_i, c_j) \in C_m, \quad i \neq j \tag{15.1}$$

$$\max \sum d(c_i, c_j), \forall c_i \in C_m, \forall c_j \in C_n, \forall (m,n), \quad m \neq n \tag{15.2}$$

Here $d(a,b)$ refers to a distance metric between a and b. The first condition minimizes the within-cluster distance between the cluster members and the second condition maximizes the between-cluster distance. Finding an efficient optimal solution for the above min–max conditions is infeasible.

Another approach to cluster the blog categories is based on the tags assigned to the blog posts and the blog site that belong to these categories. Each category can be profiled based on these accumulated tags. A simple cosine similarity distance metric could be used to find similarity between different categories. However, the document term representation of the categories based on the tags is high dimensional and sparse.

In light of the above challenges, we propose an approach to achieve category clustering based on the collective wisdom of the bloggers available on the Blog-Catalog. Often bloggers specify the categories that a particular blog site belongs to, which helps establish links between different categories. If there are many blog sites that construct links between more than one category then, these categories could be treated as a part of one cluster. For example, categories like Computers and Technology, Computers and Internet, and Blogging and Computers were linked by many bloggers via tagging their blog sites. Using the collective wisdom of the bloggers, these pairs of categories can be clustered. The number of blog sites that create the links between various categories is termed as Link strength. We call this link-based clustering WisClus. An instance of link-based clustering is shown in Figure 15.9 with edges between categories showing the links between the categories and edge weights represent the link strength. Using bloggers' collective wisdom for link-based clustering would help us in identifying the blogging patterns and the categories that are generally related by bloggers' activities.

Once we have formed the clusters of similar categories, we restrict the search space for familiar strangers of a blogger to his/her related categories. One way to evaluate the similarity of bloggers is via the comparison of their profiles.

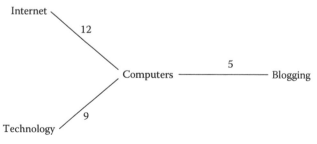

FIGURE 15.9:   WisClus: link-based clustering using collective wisdom.

15.5.2 Blogger Profile

We can construct a blogger's profile based on three types of information: blog post level tags, blogger level tags, and blog post snippets. Blog post level tags are highly dynamic in nature. A blogger could blog on completely different topics at different times. But he may follow a common theme throughout. For example, a blogger who is a baseball fan may blog on various things, though his focus is around baseball. All the blog posts for each blogger are available at BlogCatalog and construct a matrix, T_p, each row of which represents a term vector for a particular blogger. Every blog site is also associated with certain tags. These tags are assigned by the bloggers. These tags are not as time sensitive as blog post level tags but they give precise information about the blog site as a whole. Dominant themes of the blog site can be gauged with these tags. A blogger's main theme can be profiled based on these tags. We construct a matrix, T_s, each row of which represents a term vector for a particular blogger. The third type of information, blog post snippets, could also be used for profiling a blogger. These snippets are extracted from the blogger's five most recent blog posts and they contain first few words of the blog post. These snippets are pieces of texts that require some preprocessing before they can be used. We remove the stopwords from these pieces of texts, perform stemming and compute *tf–idf* to reduce the dimensionality. Once preprocessing is done we combine all the words from all the snippets for each blogger and construct a matrix, S_p, each row of which represents a term vector for a particular blogger.

Since the three types of information may not be present, we consider a linear combination of these three information sources. If all the three information sources are represented as document term matrices, i.e., blog site level tags ($T_{s,i}$), blog post level tags ($T_{p,i}$) and blog post snippets ($S_{p,i}$), then mathematically, the profile for the blogger-*i* (P_i) can be represented as

$$P_i = \alpha T_{s,i} + \beta T_{p,i} + \gamma S_{p,i} \qquad (15.3)$$

where α, β, and γ represent the weights for corresponding information sources, respectively.

Based on these different types of information sources, the blogger profile can be constructed. Depending upon the kind of profile needed and the type of information available, weights α, β, and γ and could be adjusted to emphasize more on dynamic and "fresh" tags or more stable tags.

15.5.3 Profile Similarity

Once the bloggers are profiled, we can match the profiles of other bloggers with that of blogger A. We can rank the results based on the similarity between profiles. A similarity function between bloggers could be simply the typical cosine similarity. However, the profiles that we have are very sparse and high dimensional. Moreover, naive term matching does not include the context information and does not perform well for problems like polysemy. To resolve sparsity, high dimensionality, and contextual ambiguity we use latent semantic indexing (LSI)-based approach for evaluating similarity between bloggers. Let X denote the term document matrix, where cell (i,j) denotes the frequency of term i in document j. Each column in X represents a blogger and the terms in rows represent his/her profile. We transform the matrix X to a concept space which is less sparse and low dimensional. This concept space also handles the context ambiguity. The matrix X is decomposed,

$$X = U \sum V^{\mathrm{T}} \tag{15.4}$$

where

U denotes the concept space transformation for the profile terms of the blogger

Σ is a diagonal matrix of the singular vectors

V^{T} denotes the concept space transformation of the bloggers' profiles

A cosine similarity in V^{T} matrix would give us the most similar bloggers but in the concept space. If X is $d \times m$ matrix, where m denotes the total number of bloggers and d denotes the total number of terms in the profiles, then matrix U is $d \times l$, Σ is $l \times l$, and V^{T} is $l \times m$. Here l is the total number of concepts in the reduced space. We can select the k largest singular values which would further reduce the concept space from l to k. This would give us the rank k approximation with smallest error.

Now we look at an example discovered in BlogCatalog by WisClus. Here the seed blogger "akridiy" blogs about "unusual business ideas that work" which is about making money by selling unusual stuff or providing curious services online. This blog site is listed under Innovation and Small Business categories. WisClus returns results as shown in Figure 15.10. Both first and third results talk about how to make money online through blogging and share at least one category with the seed blogger, i.e., Small Business and Innovation, respectively. However, second result is the most interesting one, which does not share any categories with the seed blogger but was returned as the search result. His blog site was listed under Blogging and Internet

Seed Blogger (Query)	Results (Broadcast Search)
Blogger: akridiy Categories: Innovation, Small Business Title: Unusual Business Ideas That Work URL: http://greatmoneynow.blogspot.com	*First result:* **Blogger: Emmanuelcee** Categories: Blogging, Small Business Title: Unique Opportunity URL: http://uniqueopportunity.blogspot.com
	Second Result: **Blogger: MMO** Categories: Blogging, Internet Title: Best ways to make money online URL: http://makemoneythebestway.blogspot.com
	Third Result: **Blogger: David Van Hulst** Categories: Marketing, Innovation Title: The Simple Truth About Making Real M*oney Online URL: http://netprofit-secrets.blogspot.com

FIGURE 15.10:   Example of familiar stranger in BlogCatalog.

categories and talks about best ways to make money online, which aligns with the context of the seed blogger. Although the second result and seed blogger do not share categories but their categories are linked by our link clustering method. Both Innovation and Small Business are linked to Blogging and Internet. This example validates the existence of familiar strangers on BlogCatalog and also shows that WisClus can find them whether or not they share any categories.

15.6 Research Issues

We introduce the problem, challenges, and an empirical study of searching for familiar strangers on the blogosphere. It is only the tip of an iceberg as there are many pertinent research issues that remain to be answered. We present some of them next.

15.6.1 Trust and Reputation

According to an article published in azcentral,* "A survey by Scottsdale-based iCrossing indicated that 59% of adults look for health and wellness information on the Internet through search engines, social-networking sites, bulletin boards and other online forums." The easier it gets to publish the information the more difficult to discern each piece's credibility. The open standards and low barrier to publishing in the blogosphere makes the content susceptible to false information and spam. This makes it harder for an ordinary user to decide which information to trust or not. We discuss the issue of spamming in the blogosphere in Section 15.6.2.

Trust on blogosphere is an important issue. It tries to answer the question whether we could trust the familiar strangers returned by WisClus or by any algorithm. When there are several appropriate familiar strangers for a particular blogger, which one should we trust the most? Since these bloggers are strangers and not even acquaintances, the blogger needs to feel safe when facing serious matters.

Trust can be defined as the relationship of reliance between two parties or individuals. Alice trusts Bob implies Alice's reliance on the actions of Bob, based on what they know about each other. Trust is basically prediction of an otherwise unknown decision made by a party or an individual based on the actions of another party or individual.

Trust is a promising area of research in social networks especially the blogosphere where many assumptions from friendship networks are absent.

1. Social friendship networks assume initial trust values are assigned to the nodes of the network. Unless some social networking Web sites allow their members to explicitly provide trust ratings for other members, it is a topic of research and exploration to compute initial trust scores for the members. Moreover, in blogosphere it is even harder to implicitly compute initial trust scores.

---

* http://www.azcentral.com/business/articles/0114biz-talker0115-ON.html.

2. Social friendship networks assume an explicit relationship between members of the network. However, in blogosphere there is no concept of explicit relationship between bloggers. Many times these relationships have to be estimated using link structures in the blogs or blogging characteristics of the bloggers.

3. Existing trust propagation algorithms assume an initial starting point. In blogosphere, where both network structures and initial ratings are not explicitly defined, it is challenging to tackle the trust aspect. A potential approach could be to use influential members [6] of a blog community as the seeds for trustworthy nodes.

4. Quantifying and computing trust in social networks is hard because concepts like trust are fuzzy, and are being expressed in a social way. The definitions and properties are not mathematical formalisms but social ones.

Trust can be considered as binary-valued with 1 indicating trust and 0 indicating "not-trusted." Trust can also be evaluated as continuous valued. Moreover, binary-valued trust is little more complicated than meets the eye. A value of 0 could be a little vague as it could represent both "no-opinion" or "distrust." To qualify this notion, often researchers use -1 to represent distrust and 0 as missing value or no-opinion. Researchers model the propagation of distrust the same way as the propagation of trust.

Existing works like Ref. [7] proposed a NodeMatching algorithm to compute the authority or reputation of a node based on its location in the social friendship network. A node's authority depends upon the authority of the nodes that relate to this node and also on other nodes that this node relates to. The basic idea is to propagate the reputation of nodes in the social friendship network. Others [8] developed a model for reputation management based on the Dempster–Shafer theory of evidence in the wake of spurious testimonies provided by malicious members of the social friendship network. In Ref. [9], authors consider those social friendship networking sites where users explicitly provide trust ratings to other members. However, for large social friendship networks it is infeasible to assign trust ratings to each and every member so they propose an inferring mechanism which would assign binary trust ratings (trustworthy/nontrustworthy) to those who have not been assigned one. Guha et al. [10] proposed another trust propagation scheme in social friendship networks based on a series of matrix operations but they included the element of distrust along with the trust scores. The next two issues can be considered the two extremes in trust research in the blogosphere.

15.6.2   Adversarial Blogging Patterns

Spam blogs should not be trusted. These blog posts usually do not have any meaningful content. Not only spam content but there could be some link spamming that could mislead the search through link analysis.

Spam blogs, often called splogs, is one of the major concerns in the blogosphere. Besides degrading search quality results it also wastes the network resources.

So a lot of researchers are looking into this aspect of the blogosphere. Although it is a relatively new phenomena, researchers have compared it with the existing work on Web (link) spam detection. For Web spam detection authors in Ref. [11] distinguish between normal Web pages and spam Web pages based on the statistical properties like, number of words, average length of words, anchor text, title keyword frequency, and tokenized URL. Some works [12,13] also use PageRank to compute the spam score of a Web page. Some researchers consider splogs as a special case Web spam. Authors in Refs. [14,15] consider each blog post as a static Web page and use both content and hyperlinks to classify a blog post as spam using a support vector machine (SVM-based classifier). However, there are some critical differences between web spam detection and splog detection. The content on blog posts is very dynamic as compared to Web pages, so content-based spam filters are ineffective. Moreover, spammers can copy the content from some regular blog post to evade content-based spam filters. Link-based spam filters can easily be beaten by creating links pointing to the splogs. Authors in Ref. [16] consider the temporal dynamics of blog posts and propose a self-similarity-based splog detection algorithm based on characteristic patterns found in splogs like, regularities/patterns in posting times of splogs, content similarity in splogs, and similar links in splogs.

15.6.3 Influential Bloggers

As communities evolve over time, so do the bellwethers or leaders of the communities who possess the power to influence the mainstream. According to the studies in Ref. [17], 83% people prefer consulting family, friends, or an expert over traditional advertising before trying a new restaurant, 71% people prefer to do so before buying a prescription drug or visiting a place, 61% of people prefer to do so before watching a movie. This style of marketing is known as word-of-mouth. Word-of-mouth has been found to be more effective than the traditional advertising in physical communities. Studies from Ref. [17] show that before people buy, they talk and they listen. These experts can influence decisions of people. For this reason these experts are aptly termed, *The Influentials*. Influential bloggers tend to submit influential blog posts that affect other members' decisions and opinions. Influential bloggers are often trustworthy. However, trustworthy bloggers may not be influential.

We can use the influential bloggers from community blog sites as the representatives or more appropriately the Short Heads. These few Short Heads could be used to find the Long Tail bloggers who are familiar strangers to the original blogger. These influential bloggers could be used to extend the idea of familiar stranger bloggers to familiar stranger communities. Each community could be represented by its influential bloggers and then we could search for other bloggers who are familiar stranger for this influential blogger. The structure of blogosphere can be considered recursive with even Long Tail communities having Short Head or influential bloggers that can be used to connect to the Long Tail bloggers of those communities.

Agarwal et al. [6] have proposed a framework of identifying influential bloggers in a community (multiauthored) blog site.

A straightforward way of defining an influential blogger is to check if the blogger has any influential blog post: A blogger can be influential if he or she submits even a single influential blog post. Formally, the problem of identifying an influential blogger can be stated as follows: Given a set of bloggers (u) at a blog site, we search for a subset of bloggers (k) such that $k \subset u$, which exhibit influential properties discussed below.

The influence of a blog post is best seen from the reactions of other fellow bloggers. Clearly, it is a subjective matter. Now we examine what are some sensible factors related to blog-post influence.

- An influential blog post can be referenced in many other blog posts, which means its number of inlinks (ι) is large. The more influential the blog posts that refer to this blog post, the more influential this blog post becomes.

- An influential blog post can receive many comments (γ) by fellow bloggers. That is, the influence of a blog post could depend on the amount of discussion it initiated.

- An influential blog post usually does not have many outlinks (θ). If a blog post refers to many articles or other blog posts, it is less likely to be an innovative piece.

- An influential blog post is often well written. Given the nature of the blogosphere, there is no incentive for a blogger to write a lengthy one that bores the readers. If one writes a long post, it often suggests some necessity of doing so. Hence, the length of a blog post (λ) is a heuristic measure checking if a post is influential or not.

Identifying influential blog posts could be visualized in terms of an influence graph or *i*-graph. Each node of an *i*-graph represents a single blog post characterized by ι, θ, γ, and λ. *i*-Graph is a directed graph with ι and θ representing the incoming and outgoing traffic flows of a node, respectively.

This work differs from several existing works. Authors in Refs. [18,19] maximize the total influence among the nodes (blog sites) by selecting a fixed number of nodes in the network using a greedy approach to select the most influential node in each iteration after removing the selected nodes. Some works like Ref. [20] try to find influential blog sites (both individual and community blog sites), in the entire blogosphere and study how they influence the external world and within the blogosphere. Some recent works [21,22] suggests to add implicit links to increase the density of link information based on topic propagation [23,24].

15.7 Conclusion

Based on the power law distribution of the blogosphere and motivated by discovering and connecting niches in the Long Tail, we identify a new problem—searching for familiar strangers on the blogosphere—which presents technical challenges and beckons innovative solutions and effective approaches. We describe the need for searching the Long Tail, offer working definitions, delineate three types of familiar strangers on the blogosphere, illustrate the challenges, and provide some potential solutions with baseline approaches. The three approaches employ different types of information such as links, similarity, and context. We then suggest some pertinent research issues including trust, adversarial blogging, and influential bloggers for further research in search of familiar strangers on the blogosphere.

15.8 Acknowledgments

We would like to thank Shankar Bhargav and Sanjay Sundararajan for facilitating the study of familiar strangers and implementing the system to acquire data from BlogCatalog. The second author would acknowledge his ASEE summer faculty fellowship at ARFL, Rome, NY in 2007 and the extension grant by AFRL that inspired in part this work. This work is in part supported by AFOSR and ONR.

References

[1] Tim O'Reilly. What is Web 2.0-design patterns and business models for the next generation of software. Available at http://www.oreillynet.com/pub/a/oreilly/tim/news/2005/09/30/what-is-web-20.html, September 2005.

[2] C. Anderson. *The Long Tail: Why the Future of Business is Selling Less of More*, New York, Hyperion, 2006.

[3] Idris Mootee. *High Intensity Marketing*, Canada, SA Press, 2001.

[4] J. Allan. *Topic Detection and Tracking: Event-Based Information Organization*, Massachusetts, Kluwer, 2002.

[5] B.Y.-L. Kuo, T. Hentrich, B. Good, and M. Wilkinson. Tag clouds for summarizing web search results. In *Proceedings of the World Wide Web*, pp. 1203–1204, Banff, Canada, 2007.

[6] N. Agarwal, H. Liu, L. Tang, and P. S. Yu. Identifying the influential bloggers. In *Proceedings of Web Search and Data Mining*, pp. 207–218, Stanford, CA, 2008.

[7] J.M. Pujol, R. Sangesa, and J. Delgado. Extracting reputation in multi agent systems by means of social network topology. In *AAMAS '02: Proceedings of*

the 1st International Joint Conference on Autonomous Agents and Multiagent Systems, pp. 467–474, New York, 2002. ACM Press.

[8] B. Yu and M.P. Singh. Detecting deception in reputation management. In *AAMAS '03: Proceedings of the 2nd International Joint Conference on Autonomous Agents and Multiagent Systems*, pp. 73–80, New York, 2003. ACM Press.

[9] J. Golbeck and J. Hendler. Inferring binary trust relationships in web-based social networks. *ACM Trans. Internet Technol.*, 6(4):497–529, 2006.

[10] R. Guha, Ravi Kumar, P. Raghavan, and A. Tomkins. Propagation of trust and distrust. In *WWW '04: Proceedings of the 13th International Conference on World Wide Web*, pp. 403–412, New York, 2004. ACM Press.

[11] A. Ntoulas, M. Najork, M. Manasse, and D. Fetterly. Detecting spam web pages through content analysis. In *Proceedings of the 15th International Conference on World Wide Web (WWW)*, pp. 83–92, Edinburgh, Scotland, 2006.

[12] Z. Gyongyi, P. Berkhin, H. Garcia-Molina, and J. Pedersen. Link spam detection based on mass estimation. In *Proceedings of the 32nd International Conference on Very Large Data Bases (VLDB)*, pp. 439–450, Seoul, Korea, 2006.

[13] Z. Gyongyi, H. Garcia-Molina, and J. Pedersen. Combating web spam with trustrank. In *Proceedings of the 30th International Conference on Very Large Data Bases (VLDB)*, pp. 576–587, Toronto, Canada, 2004.

[14] P. Kolari, T. Finin, and A. Joshi. SVMs for the blogosphere: Blog identification and splog detection. In *AAAI Spring Symposium on Computational Approaches to Analyzing Weblogs*, Stanford, CA, 2006.

[15] P. Kolari, A. Java, T. Finin, T. Oates, and A. Joshi. Detecting spam blogs: A machine learning approach. In *Proceedings of the 21st National Conference on Artificial Intelligence (AAAI)*, Boston, MA, 2006.

[16] Y.-R. Lin, H. Sundaram, Y. Chi, J. Tatemura, and B.L. Tseng. Splog detection using self-similarity analysis on blog temporal dynamics. In *AIRWeb '07: Proceedings of the 3rd International Workshop on Adversarial Information Retrieval on the Web*, pp. 1–8, New York, 2007. ACM Press.

[17] E. Keller and J. Berry. *One American in Ten Tells the Other Nine How to Vote, Where to Eat and, What to Buy. They are the Influentials*, New Yrok, Free Press, 2003.

[18] M. Richardson and P. Domingos. Mining knowledge-sharing sites for viral marketing. In *KDD '02: Proceedings of the 8th ACM SIGKDD International Conference on Knowledge Discovery and Data Mining*, pp. 61–70, New York, 2002. ACM Press.

[19] D. Kempe, J. Kleinberg, and E. Tardos. Maximizing the spread of influence through a social network. In *Proceedings of the KDD*, pp. 137–146, New York, 2003. ACM Press.

[20] K. E. Gill. How can we measure the influence of the blogosphere? In *WWW'04: Workshop on the Weblogging Ecosystem: Aggregation, Analysis and Dynamics*, New York, 2004.

[21] A. Kritikopoulos, M. Sideri, and I. Varlamis. Blogrank: Ranking weblogs based on connectivity and similarity features. In *AAA-IDEA '06: Proceedings of the 2nd International Workshop on Advanced Architectures and Algorithms for Internet Delivery and Applications*, p. 8, New York, 2006. ACM Press.

[22] E. Adar, L. Zhang, L. Adamic, and R. Lukose. Implicit structure and the dynamics of blogspace. In *Proceedings of the 13th International World Wide Web Conference*, New York, 2004.

[23] D. Gruhl, D. Liben-Nowell, R. Guha, and A. Tomkins. Information diffusion through blogspace. *SIGKDD Explorations Newslett.*, 6(2):43–52, 2004.

[24] J. Goldenberg, B. Libai, and E. Muller. Talk of the network: A complex systems look at the underlying process of word-of-mouth. *Mark. Lett.*, 12:211–223, 2001.

... ...
... ...

Chapter 16

Toward Semantics-Enabled Infrastructure for Knowledge Acquisition from Distributed Data

Vasant Honavar and Doina Caragea

Contents

16.1   Introduction

Recent development of high-throughput data-acquisition technologies in a number of domains (e.g., biological sciences, atmospheric sciences, space sciences, and commerce) together with advances in digital storage, computing, and communication technologies have resulted in the proliferation of a multitude of physically distributed data repositories created and maintained by autonomous entities (e.g., scientists and organizations). The resulting increasingly data-rich domains offer unprecedented opportunities in computer assisted data-driven knowledge acquisition in a number of applications including, in particular, data-driven scientific discovery in bioinformatics (e.g., characterization of protein sequence–structure–function relationships in computational molecular biology), environmental informatics, and health informatics. Machine-learning algorithms [1–4] offer some of the most cost-effective approaches to knowledge acquisition (discovery of features, correlations, and other complex relationships and hypotheses that describe potentially interesting regularities) from large data sets. However, the applicability of current approaches to machine learning in emerging data-rich applications in practice is severely limited by a number of factors:

- Data repositories are large in size, dynamic, and physically distributed. Consequently, it is neither desirable nor feasible to gather all of the data in a centralized location for analysis. In some domains, the ability of autonomous organizations to share raw data may be limited due to a variety of reasons (e.g., privacy considerations) [5]. In both cases, there is a need for efficient algorithms for learning from multiple distributed data sources without the need to transmit large amounts of data.

- Autonomously developed and operated data sources often differ in their structure and organization (relational databases, flat files, etc.). Furthermore, the data sources often limit the operations that can be performed (e.g., types of queries—relational queries, restricted subsets of relational queries, and statistical queries; and execution of user-supplied code to compute answers to queries that are not directly supported by the data source). Hence, there is a need for effective strategies for efficiently obtaining the information needed for learning under the operational constraints imposed by the data sources, and theoretical guarantees about the performance of the resulting classifiers relative to the setting in which the learning algorithm has unconstrained access to a centralized data set.

- Autonomously developed data sources differ with respect to data semantics. The semantic Web enterprise [6] is aimed at making the contents of the Web machine interpretable. Data and resources on the Web are annotated and linked by associating metadata that make explicit the ontological commitments of the data source providers or in some cases, the shared ontological commitments of a small community of users. The increasing need for information sharing between organizations, individuals, and scientific communities has led to several community-wide efforts aimed at the construction of ontologies in several domains. Explicit specification of the ontology associated with a data repository helps standardize the semantics to an extent. Collaborative scientific discovery applications often require users to be able to analyze data from multiple, semantically disparate data sources from different perspectives in different contexts. In particular, there is no single privileged perspective that can serve all users, or for that matter, even a single user, in every context. Hence, there is a need for methods that can efficiently obtain from a federation of autonomous, distributed, and semantically heterogeneous data sources, the information needed for learning (e.g., statistics) based on user-specified semantic constraints between user ontology and data-source ontologies.

Against this background, we consider the problem of data-driven knowledge acquisition from autonomous, distributed, and semantically heterogeneous data sources.

16.2   Learning from Distributed Data

Given a data set D, a hypothesis class H, and a performance criterion P, an algorithm L for learning (from centralized data D) outputs a hypothesis $h \in H$ that optimizes P. In pattern classification applications, h is a classifier (e.g., a decision tree.) The data D consists of a multiset of training examples. Each training example is an ordered tuple of attribute values, where one of the attributes corresponds to a class label and the remaining attributes represent inputs to the classifier. The goal of learning is to produce a hypothesis that optimizes the performance criterion (e.g., minimizing classification error on the training data) and the complexity of the hypothesis. In a distributed setting, a data set D is distributed among the sites $1, \ldots, n$ containing data set fragments $D_1, \ldots, D_n$. Two simple (and common) types of data fragmentation are horizontal fragmentation and vertical fragmentation. More generally, the data may be fragmented into a set of relations (as in the case of tables of a relational database, but distributed across multiple sites). We assume that the individual data sets $D_1, \ldots, D_n$ collectively contain (in principle) all the information needed to construct the data set D.

The distributed setting typically imposes a set of constraints Z on the learner that are absent in the centralized setting. For example, the constraints Z may prohibit the transfer of raw data from each of the sites to a central location while allowing the learner to obtain certain types of statistics from the individual sites (e.g., counts of instances that have specified values for some subset of attributes), or in the case of knowledge discovery from clinical records, Z might include constraints designed to protect the privacy of patients.

The problem of learning from distributed data can be stated as follows: Given the fragments $D_1, \ldots, D_n$ of a data set D distributed across the sites $1, \ldots, n$, a set of constraints Z, a hypothesis class H, and a performance criterion P, the task of the learner L_d is to output a hypothesis that optimizes P using only operations allowed by Z. Clearly, the problem of learning from a centralized data set D is a special case of learning from distributed data where $n = 1$ and $Z = \phi$. Having defined the problem of learning from distributed data, we proceed to define some criteria that can be used to evaluate the quality of the hypothesis produced by an algorithm L_d for learning from distributed data relative to its centralized counterpart. We say that an algorithm L_d for learning from distributed data sets $D_1, \ldots, D_n$ is exact relative to its centralized counterpart L if the hypothesis produced by L_d is identical to that obtained by L from the data set D obtained by appropriately combining the data sets $D_1, \ldots, D_n$.

Example [7]: Let L be a centralized algorithm for learning a decision tree classifier (Quinlan, 1993) $h : \mathbf{X} \to C$ (where $\mathbf{X}$ is an instance space and C is a finite set of class labels) from data set $D \subset \mathbf{X} \times C$. Let L_d be an algorithm for learning a decision tree classifier $h_d : \mathbf{X} \to C$ under a set of specified constraints Z from horizontally fragmented distributed data $D_1, \ldots, D_n$, where each $D_i \subset D \subset \mathbf{X} \times C$. Suppose further that $D = \cup_{i=1}^{n} D_i$. Then we say that L_d is exact with respect to L if and only if $\forall X \in \mathbf{X}, h(X) = h_d(X)$.

Proof of exactness of an algorithm for learning from distributed data relative to its centralized counterpart ensures that a large collection of existing theoretical (e.g., sample complexity, error bounds) as well as empirical results obtained in the centralized setting carry over to the distributed setting.

16.2.1 General Strategy for Transforming Centralized Learners into Distributed Learners

Our general strategy for designing an algorithm for learning from distributed data that is provably exact with respect to its centralized counterpart (in the sense defined above) follows from the observation that most of the learning algorithms use only some statistics computed from the data D in the process of generating the hypotheses that they output. (Recall that a statistic is simply a function of the data.) This yields a natural decomposition of a learning algorithm into two components (Figure 16.1):

1. Information extraction component that formulates and sends a statistical query to a data source

2. Hypothesis generation component that uses the resulting statistic to modify a partially constructed hypothesis (and further invokes the information extraction component as needed)

A statistic $s(D)$ is called a sufficient statistic for a parameter θ if $s(D)$, loosely speaking, provides all the information needed for estimating the parameter from data D [9]. Thus, sample mean is a sufficient statistic for the mean of a Gaussian distribution.

Inspired by theoretical work on probably approximately correct (PAC) learning from statistical queries [10], we have generalized this notion of a sufficient statistic for a parameter θ into a sufficient statistic $s_{L,h}(D)$ for learning a hypothesis h using a learning algorithm L applied to a data set D [7,11]. Trivially, the data D and the hypothesis h are both sufficient statistics for learning h using L. We are typically interested in statistics that are minimal or, at the very least, substantially smaller in size (in terms of the number of bits needed for encoding) than the data set D. In some simple cases, it is possible to extract a sufficient statistic $s_{L,h}(D)$ for constructing a

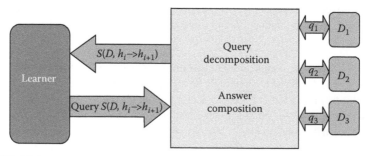

FIGURE 16.1:   Learning $=$ statistical query answering $+$ hypothesis construction.

hypothesis h in one step (e.g., by querying the data source for a set of conditional probability estimates when L is the standard algorithm for learning a naive Bayes classifier). In a more general setting, h is constructed by L by interleaving information extraction (statistical query) and hypothesis construction operations. Thus, a decision-tree learning algorithm would start with an empty initial hypothesis h_0, obtain the sufficient statistics (expected information concerning the class membership of an instance associated with each of the attributes) for the root of the decision tree (a partial hypothesis h_1), and recursively generate queries for additional statistics needed to iteratively refine h_1 to obtain a succession of partial hypotheses $h_1, h_2, \ldots$ culminating in h (Figure 16.2).

In this model, the only interaction of the learner with the repository of data D is through queries for the relevant statistics. Information extraction from distributed data entails decomposing each statistical query q posed by the information extraction component of the learner into subqueries $q_1, \ldots, q_n$ that can be answered by the individual data sources $D_1, \ldots, D_n$, respectively, and a procedure for combining the answers to the subqueries into an answer for the original query q (see Figure 16.2).

We have shown that this general strategy for learning classifiers from distributed data is applicable to a broad class of algorithms for learning classifiers from data [7]. Consequently, for these algorithms, we can devise a strategy (plan) for computing h from the data D using sufficient statistics. When the learner's access to data sources is subject to constraints Z, the resulting plan for information extraction has to be executable without violating the constraints Z. Given provably correct query decomposition and answer composition procedures, it is easy to establish the exactness of the algorithm L_d for learning from distributed data relative to its centralized counterpart.

We have applied the general framework described above for construction of algorithms for learning classifiers from distributed data to design provably exact algorithms for learning naive Bayes, nearest neighbor, Bayes network, neural network, and decision tree classifiers from distributed data under horizontal and vertical data fragmentation [7], and support vector machine (SVM) classifiers under horizontal data fragmentation (at the expense of multiple passes through the distributed data). We have also established the precise conditions under which the proposed

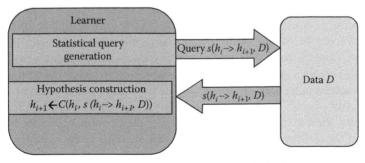

FIGURE 16.2: Learning from distributed data = statistical query answering from distributed data + hypothesis construction.

algorithms offer significant savings in bandwidth, memory, and computation time (relative to their centralized counterparts) [7].

16.2.2   Related Work on Learning Classifiers from Distributed Data

Srivastava et al. [12] propose methods for distributing a large centralized data set to multiple processors to exploit parallel processing to speed up learning. Grossman and Guo [13] and Provost and Kolluri [14] survey several methods that exploit parallel processing for scaling up data-mining algorithms to work with large data sets. In contrast, the focus of our work is on learning classifiers from a set of autonomous distributed data sources. The autonomous nature of the data sources implies that the learner has little control over the manner in which the data are distributed among the different sources. Distributed data mining has received considerable attention in the literature [15]. Domingos [16] and Prodromidis et al. [17] propose an ensemble of classifiers approach to learning from horizontally fragmented distributed data, which essentially involves learning separate classifiers from each data set and combining them typically using a weighted voting scheme. This requires gathering a subset of data from each of the data sources at a central site to determine the weights to be assigned to the individual hypotheses (or shipping the ensemble of classifiers and associated weights to the individual data sources where they can be executed on local data to set the weights). In contrast, our approach is applicable even in scenarios that preclude transmission of data or execution of user-supplied code at the individual data sources but allow transmission of minimal sufficient statistics needed by the learning algorithm. A second potential drawback of the ensemble of classifiers approach to learning from distributed data is that the resulting ensemble of classifiers is typically much harder to comprehend than a single classifier. A third important limitation of the ensemble classifier approach to learning from distributed data is the lack of strong guarantees concerning accuracy of the resulting hypothesis relative to the hypothesis obtained in the centralized setting. Bhatnagar and Srinivasan [18] propose an algorithm for learning decision-tree classifiers from vertically fragmented distributed data. Kargupta et al. [19] describe an algorithm for learning decision trees from vertically fragmented distributed data using a technique proposed by Mansour [20] for approximating a decision tree using Fourier coefficients corresponding to attribute combinations whose size is at most logarithmic in the number of nodes in the tree. At each data source, the learner estimates the Fourier coefficients from the local data, and transmits them to a central site where they are combined to obtain a set of Fourier coefficients for the decision tree (a process that requires a subset of the data from each source to be transmitted to the central site). However, a given set of Fourier coefficients can correspond to multiple decision trees. Furthermore, there are no guarantees concerning the performance of the hypothesis obtained in the distributed setting relative to that obtained in the centralized setting.

Relative to the large body of work on learning classifiers from distributed data, the distinguishing feature of our approach is a clear separation of concerns between hypothesis construction and extraction of sufficient statistics from data. This makes it possible to explore the use of sophisticated techniques for query optimization that yield optimal plans for gathering sufficient statistics from distributed data sources under a specified set of constraints describing the query capabilities of the data sources, operations permitted by the data sources, and available computation, bandwidth, and memory resources. It also opens up the possibility of exploring algorithms that learn from distributed data a hypothesis h_ε whose error is small relative to the error of a hypothesis h (obtained in the setting when the learner has unrestricted access to D), in scenarios where the constraints Z make it impossible to guarantee exactness in the sense defined above. Our approach also lends itself to adaptation to learning from semantically heterogeneous data sources.

16.3   Learning from Semantically Heterogeneous Data

In order to extend our approach to learning from distributed data (which assumes a common ontology that is shared by all of the data sources) into effective algorithms for learning classifiers from semantically heterogeneous distributed data, techniques need to be developed for answering the statistical queries posed by the learner in terms of the learner's ontology O from the heterogeneous data sources (where each data source D_i has an associated ontology O_i). Thus, we have to solve a variant of the problem of integrated access to distributed data repositories—the data integration problem [21,22] in order to be able to use machine-learning approaches to acquire knowledge from semantically heterogeneous data.

This problem is best illustrated by an example (Figure 16.3). Consider two academic departments that independently collect information about their students. Suppose a data set D_1 collected by the first department is organized in two tables: Student, and Outcome, linked by a Placed-In relation using ID as the common key.

	ID	Major	GPA	Ethnicity	Inten	Placed-in	ID	Outcome
D1							384	Grad Stud
	325	ComS	3.80	White	Yes		725	Employed
	673	Biol	3.50	Hispanic	No			
D2	Soc Sed	Field	Gender	Work Experience	Grade	Has-Status	Soc Sec	Status
							564	PhD
	564	Math	F	No	3.30		832	Industry
	832	ComS	M	Yes	3.78			
User	Stud ID	Major	Gender	Ethnicity	Grade	Intership	Employment Status	
	106	ComS	F	Afr Amer	3.60	Yes	PhD	
	278	Math	M	Asian	3.73	No	Industry	

FIGURE 16.3:   Student data collected by two departments from a statistician's perspective.

Students are described by ID, Major, GPA, Ethnicity, and Intern. Suppose a data set D_2 collected by the second department has a Student table and a Status table, linked by Has-Status relation using Soc Sec as the common key. Suppose Student in D_2 is described by the attributes Soc Sec, Field, Gender, Work Experience, and Grade.

Consider a user, for example, a university statistician, interested in constructing a predictive model based on data from two departments of interest from his or her own perspective, where the representative attributes are Student ID, Major, Gender, Ethnicity, Grade, Internship, and Employment Status. For example, the statistician may want to construct a model that can be used to infer whether a typical student (represented as in the entry corresponding to D_U in Figure 16.3) is likely to go on to get a PhD. This requires the ability to perform queries over the two data sources associated with the departments of interest from the user's perspective (e.g., fraction of students with internship experience that go onto PhD). However, because the structure (schema) and data semantics of the data sources differ from the statistician's perspective, he or she must establish the correspondences between the attributes of the data and the values that make up their domains.

We adopt a federated, query-centric approach to answering statistical queries from semantically heterogeneous data sources, based on ontology-extended relational algebra [23]. Specifically, we associate explicit ontologies with data sources to obtain ontology-extended relational data sources (OERDS). An OERDS is a tuple $\mathcal{D} = \{D,S,O\}$, where D is the actual data set in the data source, S the data source schema, and O the data source ontology [7,24].

A relational data set D is an instantiation $I(S)$ of a schema S. The ontology O of an OERDS $\mathcal{D}$ consists of two parts: structure ontology, O_S, that defines the semantics of the data-source schema (entities and attributes of entities that appear in data-source schema S), and content ontology, O_I, that defines the semantics of the data instances (values and relationships between values that the attributes can take in instantiations of schema S). Of particular interest are ontologies that take the form of is-a hierarchies and has-part hierarchies. For example, the values of the Status attribute in data source D_2 are organized in an is-a hierarchy. A user's view of data sources $D_1, D_2, \ldots, D_n$ is specified by user schema S_U, user ontology O_U, together with a set of semantic constraints IC, and the associated set of mappings from the user schema S_U to the data-source schemas $S_1, \ldots, S_n$ and from user ontology O_U to the data-source ontologies $O_1, \ldots, O_n$ [24]. Figure 16.4 shows examples of ontologies that take the form of is-a hierarchies over attribute values. Figure 16.5 shows some simple examples of user-specified semantic constraints between the user perspective and the data sources D_1 and D_2, respectively.

How can we answer a statistical query in a setting in which autonomous data sources differ in terms of the levels of abstraction at which data are described? For example, consider the data source ontologies O_1 and O_2 and the user ontology O_U shown in Figure 16.4. The attribute Status in data source D_2 is specified in greater detail (lower level of abstraction) than the corresponding attribute Outcome is in D_1. That is, data source D_2 carries information about the precise status of students after they graduate (specific advanced degree program, e.g., PhD, MS, that the student has been accepted into, or the type of employment that the student has accepted),

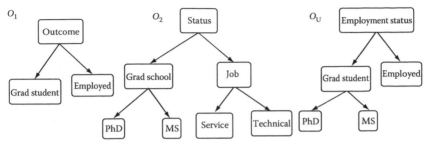

FIGURE 16.4: Attribute value taxonomies (ontologies) O_1 and O_2 associated with the attributes Outcome and Status in two data sources of interest. O_U is the ontology for Employment Status from the user's perspective.

whereas data source D_1 makes no distinctions between the types of graduate degrees or types of employment. Suppose we want to answer the query: What fraction of the students in the two data sources got into a PhD program? Answering this query is complicated by the fact that the Outcome of students in data source D_1 are only partially specified [25–27] with respect to the ontology O_U. Consequently, we can never know the precise fraction of students that got into a PhD program based on the information available in the two data sources. In such cases, answering statistical queries from semantically heterogeneous data sources requires the user to supply not only the mapping between the ontology and the ontologies associated with the data sources but also additional assumptions of a statistical nature (e.g., that grad program admits in D_1 and D_2 can be modeled by the same underlying distribution). The validity of the answer returned depends on the validity of the assumptions and the soundness of the procedure that computes the answer based on the supplied assumptions.

Given a means of answering statistical queries from semantically heterogeneous data, we can devise a general framework for learning predictive models from such data (Figure 16.6). Based on this framework, we have implemented a prototype of

$O_1 \rightarrow O_U$	$O_2 \rightarrow O_U$
ID:O_1 = Student ID:O_U	Soc Sec:O_2 = Student ID:O_U
Major:O_1 = Major:O_U	Field:O_2 = Major:O_U
GPA:O_1 = Grade:O_U	Grade:O_2 = Grade:O_U
Ethnicity:O_1 = Ethnicity:O_U	
	Gender:O_2 = Gender:O_U
Intern:O_1 = Internship:O_U	Work Experience:O_2 = internship:O_U
Outcome:O_1 = Employment Status:O_U	Status:O_2 = Employment Status:O_U

FIGURE 16.5: Example of user-specified semantic correspondences between the user ontology O_U and data-source ontologies.

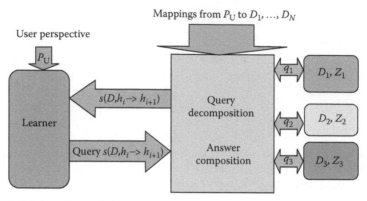

FIGURE 16.6: General framework for learning classifiers from semantically heterogeneous distributed data.

an intelligent data understanding system (INDUS) that supports execution of statistical queries against semantically heterogeneous ontology extended data sources and the construction of predictive models (e.g., classifiers) from such data sources (Figure 16.7). More precisely, INDUS system enables a user with some familiarity with the relevant data to query multiple data sources from his or her own point of view by selecting data sources of interest, specifying the user perspective, and the necessary mappings all without having to write any code. Queries posed by the user are sent to a query-answering engine (QAE) that automatically decomposes the user query q_U expressed in terms of the user ontology O_U into queries $q_1, \ldots, q_n$ that can be answered by the individual data sources. QAE combines the answers to individual queries (after applying the necessary mappings) to generate the answer for the

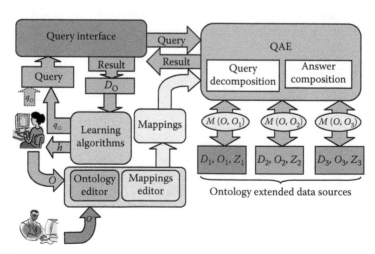

FIGURE 16.7:   INDUS system.

user query q_U. The soundness of the data-integration process (relative to a set of user-specified mappings between ontologies) follows from the soundness of the query-decomposition procedure, the correctness of the behavior of the QAEs associated with the individual data sources, and the answer composition procedure [24,28]. The current implementation of INDUS (http://www.cild.iastate.edu/ software/indus.html) that has been released under GNU public license includes support for the following:

- Import and reuse of selected fragments of existing ontologies and editing of ontologies. We have more recently developed semantic importing mechanism (based on a formalization of localized semantics) [29–31].

- Specification of semantic correspondences between a user ontology O_U and data-source ontologies [7]. Semantic correspondences between ontologies can be defined at two levels: schema level (between attributes that define data-source schemas) and attribute level (between values of attributes). Implementation of an efficient reasoning algorithm for verifying the consistency of subsumption and equivalence relationships [32].

- Registration of a new ontology-extended data source using a data-source editor for defining the schema of the data source, location, data-source ontology, and data-source constraints (Z).

- Specification and execution of queries across multiple semantically heterogeneous, distributed data sources. Each user can choose relevant data sources from a list of data sources that have been previously registered with INDUS and specify a user perspective (by selecting a user schema and user ontology from a list of available options or defining new ones if needed). The user can map between user perspective and data sources by choosing from existing mappings (or defining new mappings).

- Storage and further manipulation of results of queries. The results returned by a user query can be temporarily stored in a local relational database. This, in effect, represents a materialized relational view (modulo the mappings between user- and data-source-specific ontologies) across distributed, heterogeneous (and not necessarily relational) data repositories.

In summary, INDUS offers the basic functionality necessary to flexibly integrate information from multiple heterogeneous data sources and structure the results according to a user-supplied ontology.

16.3.1   Related Work on Data Integration

Hull [33], Davidson et al. [34], Eckman [35], Calvanese and De Giacomo [21], Doan and Halevy [36], and Halevy et al. [37] survey alternative approaches to data integration. These include multidatabase systems [38–40] and mediator-based approaches [41–48]. Tomasic et al. [49] proposed an approach to scaling up access to heterogeneous data sources. Haas et al. [50,51] investigated optimization of queries across heterogeneous data sources. Rodriguez-Martinez and Roussoloulos [52] proposed a code shipping approach to design an extensible middleware system for distributed data sources. Lambrecht et al. [53] proposed a planning framework for gathering information from distributed sources. Lenzerini [54], Dou et al. [55], Cali et al. [56], and Calvanese et al. [21,57] have developed logic-based approaches to data integration. Bonatti et al. [23] proposed ontology-extended relational algebra for integrating relational data sources. These efforts addressed, and, to varying degrees, solved the following problems in data integration: design of query languages and rules for decomposing queries into subqueries and composing the answers to subqueries into answers to the initial query through schema integration. Maluf and Wiederhold [58] proposed an ontology algebra for merging of ontologies. Others have explored approaches to mapping between schema [59–61] and discovering or learning mappings [62,63]. The design of INDUS [24,28,64,65] was necessitated by the lack of publicly available open-source data-integration platforms that could be used as a basis for learning classifiers from semantically heterogeneous distributed data. The INDUS approach to data integration draws on logic-based approaches to ontology-based schema integration and ontology-based relational algebra for bridging gaps in data semantics. To the best of our knowledge, INDUS is one of the few systems that support bridging of semantic gaps in both schema and data semantics.

16.4   Summary

The research summarized in this chapter has led to the following:

1. The development of a general theoretical framework for learning predictive models (e.g., classifiers) from large, physically distributed data sources where it is neither desirable nor feasible to gather all of the data in a centralized location for analysis [11]. This framework offers a general recipe for the design of algorithms for learning from distributed data that are provably exact with respect to their centralized counterparts (in the sense that the model constructed from a collection of physically distributed data sets is provably identical to that obtained in the setting where the learning algorithm has access to the entire data set). A key feature of this framework is the clear separation of concerns between hypothesis construction and extraction and refinement of sufficient statistics needed by the learning algorithm from data that reduces the problem of learning from data to a problem of decomposing a query for sufficient statistics across multiple data sources and combining the answers returned by the data sources to obtain the answer for the original query. This work has resulted in the identification of sufficient statistics for a large family of learning algorithms including, in particular, algorithms for learning decision trees [11], neural networks, SVMs, and Bayesian networks, and, consequently,

provably exact algorithms for learning the corresponding classifiers from distributed data [28].

2. The development of theoretically sound yet practical variants of a large class of algorithms [11,28] for learning predictive models (classifiers) from distributed data sources under a variety of assumptions (motivated by practical applications) concerning the nature of data fragmentation, and the query capabilities and operations permitted by the data sources (e.g., execution of user supplied procedures), and precise characterization of the complexity (computation, memory, and communication requirements) of the resulting algorithms relative to their centralized counterparts.

3. The development of a theoretically sound approach to formulation and execution of statistical queries across semantically heterogeneous data sources [24]. This work has demonstrated how to use semantic correspondences and mappings specified by users from a set of terms and relationships among terms (user ontology) to terms and relations in data-source-specific ontologies to construct a sound procedure for answering queries for sufficient statistics needed for learning classifiers from semantically heterogeneous data. An important component of this work has to do with the development of statistically sound approaches to learning classifiers from partially specified data resulting from data described at different levels of abstraction across different data sources [25–27].

4. The development of INDUS, a modular, extensible, open-source software toolkit,[*] for data-driven knowledge acquisition from large, distributed, autonomous, semantically heterogeneous data sources [24,64].

5. Applications of the resulting approaches to computational biology applications involving exploration of protein sequence–structure–function relationships [64]. Examples include construction of classifiers for assigning proteins to functional families [66,67] and for sequence-based prediction of protein–protein [68,69], protein–DNA [70], and protein–RNA [71,72] interfaces.

Work in progress is aimed at the following:

1. Design, implementation, and evaluation of scalable algorithms with provable performance guarantees (in terms of accuracy of results, bandwidth, and computational efforts), relative to their centralized counterparts, for learning predictive models from distributed, semantically heterogeneous, alternately structured data, including, in particular, multirelational data, sequence data, network data (e.g., three-dimensional molecular structures, social networks, and macromolecular interaction networks), multimodal data (e.g., text and images) sources under a variety of constraints on the operations supported by

---

[*] http://www.cild.iastate.edu/software/indus.html.

the data sources (queries for data, constraints on the types of queries allowed, queries for statistics, and execution of user-supplied code at the data source).

2. Systematic experimental analysis of the resulting algorithms on both real-world and synthetic data sets as a function of the characteristics of data sources (complexity of data-source schema, ontologies, and mappings; data-source query and processing capabilities; size of the data sets; and prevalence of partially missing attribute values as a consequence of integration of data described at multiple levels of granularity); errors or inconsistencies in semantic interoperation constraints and mappings; characteristics of the algorithms (e.g., types of statistics needed for learning) and performance criteria (quality of results produced relative to the centralized counterparts, computational resource, bandwidth, and storage usage); and different sets of data-source access, processing, and bandwidth constraints captured by alternative cost models.

3. Investigation of ontology and interontology mapping languages, including, in particular, distributed and modular ontology languages, distributed description logics [73], e-connections [74], and package-based description logics [29] to support selective integration of ontologies in open environments (e.g., the World Wide Web).

The resulting algorithms and software for information integration and distributed data mining will not only advance the state of the art in machine learning but also extend the range of applications of machine learning in emerging data-rich domains (e.g., bioinformatics, security informatics, materials informatics, and social informatics). These technical advances, together with a distributed testbed for experimenting with the resulting algorithms, will contribute to the development of critical elements of the cyberinfrastructure for e-science [75–77].

Acknowledgments

This research has been supported in part by grants from the National Science Foundation (NSF IIS 0219699, NSF IIS 0639230, and NSF IIS 0711356). Several current and former members of the Iowa State University Artificial Intelligence Research Laboratory have contributed to the work summarized in this chapter. We would like to acknowledge, in particular, the contributions of Jie Bao (modular ontologies, INDUS implementation), Cornelia Caragea (bioinformatics applications and relational learning), Drena Dobbs (bioinformatics applications), Neeraj Koul (INDUS implementation), Jyotishman Pathak (INDUS implementation), Jaime Reinoso-Castillo (an early prototype of the data-integration component of INDUS), Adrian Silvescu (learning from distributed and partially specified data), Gioea Slutzki (modular ontologies), George Voutsadakis (modular ontologies), and Jun Zhang (learning from partially specified data).

References

[1] C. M. Bishop. *Pattern Recognition and Machine Learning.* Springer-Verlag, Berlin, 2006.

[2] T. Hastie, R. Tibshirani, and J. Friedman. *The Elements of Statistical Learning: Data Mining, Inference, and Prediction.* Springer-Verlag, Berlin, 2001.

[3] T. M. Mitchell. *Machine Learning.* McGraw Hill, New York, 1997.

[4] S. Thrun, C. Faloutsos, M. Mitchell, and L. Wasserman. Automated learning and discovery: State-of-the-art and research topics in a rapidly growing field. *AI Magazine,* 20: 78–82, 1999.

[5] J. Vaidya and C. Clifton. Privacy-preserving data mining: Why, how, and when. *IEEE Security and Privacy,* 2(6): 19–27, 2004.

[6] T. Berners-Lee, J. Hendler, and O. Lassila. The semantic Web. *Scientific American,* 284(5):34–43, May 2001.

[7] D. Caragea. Learning classifiers from distributed, semantically heterogeneous, autonomous data sources. PhD thesis, Department of Computer Science, Iowa State University, Ames, IA, 2004.

[8] J. R. Quinlan, *C4.5 Programs for Empirical Learning.* Morgan Kaufman, 1993.

[9] R. A. Fisher. On the mathematical foundations of theoretical statistics. *Philosophical Transactions of the Royal Society,* 222: 309–368, 1922.

[10] M. Kearns. Efficient noise-tolerant learning from statistical queries. *Journal of the ACM,* 45(6): 983–1006, 1998.

[11] D. Caragea, A. Silvescu, and V. Honavar. A framework for learning from distributed data using sufficient statistics and its application to learning decision trees. *International Journal of Hybrid Intelligent Systems,* 1(2): 80–89, 2004.

[12] A. Srivastava, E. Han, V. Kumar, and V. Singh. Parallel formulations of decision-tree classification algorithms. *Data Mining and Knowledge Discovery,* 3(3): 237–261, 1999.

[13] L. R. Grossman and Y. Guo. Parallel methods for scaling data mining algorithms to large data sets. In *Handbook on Data Mining and Knowledge Discovery.* J. M. Zytkow (Ed.), pp. 433–442. Oxford University Press, London, U.K., 2001.

[14] F. J. Provost and V. Kolluri. A survey of methods for scaling up inductive algorithms. *Data Mining and Knowledge Discovery,* 3(2): 131–169, 1999.

[15] B. Park and H. Kargupta. Constructing simpler decision trees from ensemble models using Fourier analysis. In *Proceedings of the 7th Workshop on Research Issues in Data Mining and Knowledge Discovery (DMKD'2002)*, pages 1823, Madison, WI, 2002.

[16] P. Domingos. Knowledge acquisition from examples via multiple models. In *Proceedings of the 14th International Conference on Machine Learning*, pp. 98–106, Nashville, TN, 1997. Morgan Kaufmann.

[17] A. L. Prodromidis, P. Chan, and S. J. Stolfo. Meta-learning in distributed data mining systems: Issues and approaches. In H. Kargupta and P. Chan (Eds.), *Advances in Distributed and Parallel Knowledge Discovery*, pp. 81–114. AAAI Press, 2000.

[18] R. Bhatnagar and S. Srinivasan. Pattern discovery in distributed databases. In *Proceedings of the 14th National Conference on Artificial Intelligence*, pp. 503–508, Providence, RI, 1997. AAAI Press.

[19] H. Kargupta, B. H. Park, D. Hershberger, and E. Johnson. Collective data mining: A new perspective toward distributed data mining. In H. Kargupta and P. Chan (Eds.), *Advances in Distributed and Parallel Knowledge Discovery*. pp. 133-184, MIT Press, 2000.

[20] J. Mansour. Learning Boolean functions via the Fourier transform. In V. P. Roychodhury, K-Y. Siu, and A. Orlitsky (Eds.), *Theoretical Advances in Neural Computation and Learning*, pp. 391–424. Kluwer, New York, 1994.

[21] D. Calvanese and D. De Giacomo. Data integration: A logic-based perspective. *AI Magazine*, 26: 59–70, 2005.

[22] A. Levy. Logic-based techniques in data integration. In *Logic-Based Artificial Intelligence*, pp. 575–595. Kluwer Academic, New York, 2000.

[23] P. Bonatti, Y. Deng, and V. Subrahmanian. An ontology-extended relational algebra. In *Proceedings of the IEEE Conference on Information Integration and Reuse*, pp. 192–199, Las Vegas, NV, 2003. IEEE Press.

[24] D. Caragea, J. Pathak, and V. Honavar. Learning classifiers from semantically heterogeneous data. In *Proceedings on the Move to Meaningful Internet Systems: CoopIS, DOA, and ODBase*, Vol. 3291, pp. 963–980, Agia Napa, Cyprus, 2004. Springer-Verlag, Lecture Notes in Computer Science.

[25] J. Zhang and V. Honavar. Learning decision tree classifiers from attribute-value taxonomies and partially specified data. In T. Fawcett and N. Mishra (Eds.), *Proceedings of the International Conference on Machine Learning*, pp. 880–887, Washington DC, 2003. AAAI Press.

[26] J. Zhang and V. Honavar. AVT-NBL: An algorithm for learning compact and accurate naive Bayes classifiers from attribute value taxonomies and data. In *Proceedings of the 4th IEEE International Conference on Data Mining*, pp. 289–298, Brighton, United Kingdom, 2004. IEEE Press.

[27] J. Zhang, A. Silvescu, D.-K. Kang, and V. Honavar. Learning compact and accurate naive Bayes classifiers from attribute value taxonomies and partially specified data. *Knowledge and Information Systems*, 9: 157–179, 2006.

[28] D. Caragea, J. Zhang, J. Bao, J. Pathak, , and V. Honavar. Algorithms and software for collaborative discovery from autonomous, semantically heterogeneous, distributed information sources. In *Proceedings of the Conference on Algorithmic Learning Theory*, Vol. 3734, pp. 13–44, Singapore, 2005. Springer-Verlag, Lecture Notes in Computer Science.

[29] G. Bao, J. Slutzki, and V. Honavar. A semantic importing approach to knowledge reuse from multiple ontologies. In *Proceedings of the 22nd Conference on Artificial Intelligence*, pp. 1304–1309, Vancouver, Canada, 2007. AAAI Press.

[30] J. Bao, D. Caragea, and V. Honavar. Modular ontologies—A formal investigation of semantics and expressivity. In *Proceedings of the 1st Asian Semantic Web Conference*, Vol. 4185, pp. 616–631, Beijing, China, 2006. Springer-Verlag, Lecture Notes in Computer Science.

[31] J. Bao, D. Caragea, and V. Honavar. On the semantics of linking and importing in modular ontologies. In *Proceedings of the International Semantic Web Conference*, Vol. 4273, pp. 72–86, Athens, GA, 2006. Springer-Verlag, Lecture Notes in Computer Science.

[32] J. Bao, D. Caragea, and V. Honavar. A tableau-based federated reasoning algorithm for modular ontologies. In *Proceedings of the ACM/IEEE/WIC Conference on Web Intelligence*, pp. 404–410, Hong Kong, China, 2006.

[33] R. Hull. Managing semantic heterogeneity in databases: A theoretical perspective. In *Proceedings of the 16th ACM SIGACT-SIGMOD-SIGART Symposium on Principles of Database Systems*, pp. 51–61, Tucson, AZ, 1997. ACM Press.

[34] S. Davidson, J. Crabtree, B. Brunk, J. Schug, V. Tannen, G. Overton, and C. Stoeckert. K2/Kleisli and GUS: Experiments in integrated access to genomic data sources. *IBM Journal*, 40(2):512–531, 2001.

[35] B. Eckman. A practitioner's guide to data management and data integration in bioinformatics. In Z. Lacroix and T. Critchlow (Eds.), *Bioinformatics: Managing Scientific*, pp. 3–74. Morgan Kaufmann, San Francisco, CA, 2003.

[36] A. Doan and A. Halevy. Semantic integration research in the database community: Abrief survey. *AI Magazine*, 26(1): 83–94, 2005.

[37] A. Halevy, A. Rajaraman, and J. Ordille. Data integration: The teenage years. In *Proceedings of 24th International Conference on Very Large Data Bases*, p. 916, Seoul, Korea, 2006. ACM Press.

[38] T. Barsalou and D. Gangopadhyay. M(dm): An open framework for interoperation of multimodel multidatabase systems. In *IEEE Conference on Data Engineering*, pp. 218–227, Tempe, AZ, 1992.

[39] M. W. Bright, A. R. Hurson, and S. H. Pakzad. A taxonomy and current issues in multidatabase systems. *Computer Journal*, 25(3): 5–60, 1992.

[40] A. Sheth and J. Larson. Federated databases: Architectures and issues. *ACM Computing Surveys*, 22(3): 183–236, 1990.

[41] Y. Arens, C. Chin, C. Hsu, and C. Knoblock. Retrieving and integrating data from multiple information sources. *International Journal on Intelligent and Cooperative Information Systems*, 2(2): 127–158, 1993.

[42] C. K. Chang and H. Garcia-Molina. Mind your vocabulary: Query mapping across heterogeneous information sources. In *Proceedings of the ACM SIGMOD International Conference On Management of Data*, pp. 335–346, Philadelphia, PA, June 1999, ACM Press.

[43] D. Draper, A. Y. Halevy, and D. S. Weld. The nimble XML data integration system. In *Proceedings of the 17th International Conference on Data Engineering*, pp. 155–160, Heidelberg, Germany, 2001. IEEE Computer Society.

[44] H. Garcia-Molina, Y. Papakonstantinou, D. Quass, A. Rajaraman, Y. Sagiv, J. Ullman, V. Vassalos, and J. Widom. The TSIMMIS approach to mediation: Data models and languages. *Journal of Intelligent Information Systems, Special Issue on Next Generation Information Technologies and Systems*, 8(2): 117–132, 1997.

[45] C. A. Knoblock, S. Minton, J. L. Ambite, N. Ashish, I. Muslea, A. Philpot, and S. Tejada. The Ariadne approach to Web-based information integration. *International Journal of Cooperative Information Systems*, 10(1–2): 145–169, 2001.

[46] A. Levy. The information manifold approach to data integration. *IEEE Intelligent Systems*, 13:12–16, 1998.

[47] J. Lu, G. Moerkotte, J. Schue, and V. S. Subrahmanian. Efficient maintenance of materialized mediated views. In *Proceedings of 1995 ACM SIGMOD Conference on Management of Data*, pp. 340–351, San Jose, CA, 1995. ACM Press.

[48] G. Wiederhold and M. Genesereth. The conceptual basis for mediation services. *IEEE Expert*, 12: 38–47, 1997.

[49] A. Tomasic, L. Rashid, and P. Valduriez. Scaling heterogeneous databases and design of DISCO. *IEEE Transactions on Knowledge and Data Engineering*, 10(5): 808–823, 1998.

[50] L. Haas, M. Hernndez, H. Ho, L. Popa, and M. Roth. Clio grows up: From research prototype to industrial tool. In *Proceedings of the ACM SIGMOD International Conference on Management of Data*, pp. 805–810, Baltimore, ML, 2005. ACM Press.

[51] L. M. Haas, D. Kossmann, E. Wimmers, and J. Yan. Optimizing queries across diverse sources. In *Proceedings of 23rd International Conference on Very Large Data Bases*, pp. 267–285, Athens, Greece, 1997. Morgan Kaufmann.

[52] M. Rodriguez-Martinez and R. Roussopoulos. MOCHA: A self-extensible database middleware system for distributed data sources. In *Proceedings of the 2000 ACM SIGMOD International Conference on Management of Data*, pp. 213–224, Dallas, TX, 2000. ACM Press.

[53] E. Lambrecht, S. Kambhampati, and S. Gnanaprakasam. Optimizing recursive information-gathering plans. In *Proceedings of the 16th International Joint Conference on Artificial Intelligence*, pp. 1204–1211, Stokholm, Sweden. 1999. AAAI Press.

[54] M. Lenzerini. Data integration: A theoretical perspective. In *Proceedings of the 21st ACM SIGACT-SIGMOD-SIGART Symposium on Principles of Database Systems*, pp. 233–246, Madison, WI, 2002. ACM Press.

[55] D. Dou, D. McDermott, and P. Qi. Ontology translation on the semantic Web. *Journal of Data Semantics*, 2: 35–57, 2005.

[56] A. Cali, D. Calvanese, G. De Giacomo, and M Lenzerini. Data integration under integrity constraints. *Information Systems*, 29(2): 147–163, 2004.

[57] D. Calvanese, G. De Giacomo, M. Lenzerini, and R. Rosati. Logical foundations of peer-to-peer data integration. In *Proceedings of the 23rd ACM SIGACT-SIGMOD-SIGART Symposium on Principles of Database Systems*, pp. 241–251, Paris, France, 2004. ACM Press.

[58] D. Maluf and G. Wiederhold. Abstraction of representation in interoperation. In *Proceedings of the 10th International Symposium on Foundations of Intelligent Systems*, Vol. 1315, pp. 441–455, 1997. Springer-Verlag, Lecture Notes in Computer Science.

[59] A. Cali, D. Calvanese, G. De Giacomo, and M. Lenzerini. Accessing data integration systems through conceptual schemas. In *Decimo Convegno Nazionale su Sistemi Evoluti per Basi di Dati*, pp. 161–168, Isola d'Elba, Italy, 2002.

[60] J. Madhavan, P. Bernstein, P. Domingos, and A. Halevy. Representing and reasoning about mappings between domain models. In *Proceedings of the 18th National Conference on Artificial Intelligence and 14th Conference on Innovative Applications of Artificial Intelligence*, pp. 80–86, Edmonton, Alberta, 2002. AAAI Press.

[61] E. Rahm and P. Bernstein. A survey of approaches to automatic schema matching. *VLDB Journal*, 10(4): 334–350, 2001.

[62] R. Dhamankar, Y. Lee, A. Doan, A. Halevy, and P. Domingos. imap: Discovering complex mappings between database schemas. In *Proceedings of the ACM SIGMOD International Conference on Management of Data*, pp. 383–394, Paris, France, 2004. ACM Press.

[63] A. Doan, J. Madhavan, P. Domingos, and A. Halevy. Ontology matching: A machine learning approach. In *Handbook on Ontologies in Information Systems*, S. Staab and R. Studer (Eds.), pp. 397–416. Springer-Velag, Berlin, 2004.

[64] D. Caragea, A. Silvescu, J. Pathak, J. Bao, C. Andorf, D. Dobbs, and V. Honavar. Information integration and knowledge acquisition from semantically heterogeneous biological data sources. In *Proceedings of the Second International Workshop on Data Integration in Life Sciences, (DILS 2005)*, vol. 3615, pp. 175–190, San Diego, CA, 2005. Springer-Verlag, Lecture Notes in Computer Science.

[65] J. Reinoso-Castillo, A. Silvescu, D. Caragea, J. Pathak, and V. Honavar. Information extraction and integration from heterogeneous, distributed, autonomous information sources: A federated, query-centric approach. In *IEEE International Conference on Information Integration and Reuse*, pp. 183–191, Las Vegas, NV, November 2003. IEEE Press.

[66] C. Andorf, D. Dobbs, and V. Honavar. Exploring inconsistencies in genome-wide function annotations. *BMC Bioinformatics*, 8: 284, 2006. doi: 10.1186/1471-2105-8-284.

[67] X. Wang, D. Schroeder, D. Dobbs, and V. Honavar. Automated data-driven discovery of motif-based protein function classifiers. *Information Sciences*, 155: 1–18, 2003.

[68] C. Yan, D. Dobbs, and V. Honavar. A two-stage classifier for identification of protein-protein interface residues. *Bioinformatics*, 20: 371–378, 2004.

[69] C. Yan, V. Honavar, and D. Dobbs. Identifying protein-protein interaction sites from surface residues—A support vector machine approach. *Neural Computing Applications*, 13: 123–129, 2004.

[70] C. Yan, M. Terribilini, F. Wu, R. L. Jernigan, D. Dobbs, and V. Honavar. Identifying amino acid residues involved in protein-DNA interactions from sequence. *BMC Bioinformatics*, 2006. 7: 262. doi: 10.1186/1471-2105-7-262.

[71] M. Terribilini, J.-H. Lee, C. Yan, S. Carpenter, R. Jernigan, V. Honavar, and D. Dobbs. Identifying interaction sites in recalcitrant proteins: Predicted protein and RNA binding sites in HIV-1 and EIAV agree with experimental data. In *Pacific Symposium on Biocomputing*, Vol. 11, pp. 415–426, Hawaii, 2006. World Scientific.

[72] M. Terribilini, J. H. Lee, C. Yan, R. Jernigan, V. Honavar, and D. Dobbs. Computational prediction of protein-RNA interfaces. *RNA Journal*, 12: 1450–1462, 2006.

[73] A. Borgida and L. Serafini. Distributed description logics: Directed domain correspondences in federated information sources. In *Proceedings on the Move to Meaningful Internet Systems: CoopIS, DOA, and ODBase*, Vol. 2519,

pp. 3653, Irvine, CA, 2002. Springer-Verlag, Lecture Notes in Computer Science.

[74] B. Parsia and B. C. Grau. Generalized link properties for expressive e-connections of description logics. In *Proceedings of the 20th National Conference on Artificial Intelligence and the 17th Innovative Applications of Artificial Intelligence Conference*, pp. 657–662, Pittsburgh, PA, 2005. AAAI Press.

[75] D. E. Atkins, K. K. Droegemeier, S. I. Feldman, H. Garcia-Molina, P. Klein, and M. L. Messina. Revolutionizing science and engineering through cyberinfrastructure. In *Report of the National Science Foundation Blue-Ribbon Advisory Panel on Cyberinfrastructure*. National Science Foundation, Washington DC, 2003.

[76] J. Hendler and D. De Roure. E-science: The grid and the semantic Web. *IEEE Intelligent Systems*, 19(1): 65–71, 2004.

[77] T. Hey and A. E. Trefethen. Cyberinfrastructure for e-Science. *Science*, 308 (5723): 817–821, 2005.

Chapter 17

Nonnegative Matrix Factorization for Document Classification

Amy N. Langville and Michael W. Berry

Contents

17.1   Introduction

Future approaches to text mining and document classification will better address the interpretability of document clusters and perhaps solicit the growing number of domain-specific ontologies (e.g., genomics, proteomics, and medical education) for the automated labeling of documents. Computational models such as the nonnegative matrix factorization (NMF) offer a promising technological advancement in producing document clusters with immediate metadata that can be easily interpreted for concept/topic extraction purposes. As the volume of digital (text-based) information continues to grow exponentially, so too does the need for more automated document labeling or *tagging* systems.

In this chapter, we discuss different mathematical formulations of the NMF model that vary according to the objective function minimized in the underlying constrained optimization problem. The effects of these formulations on the computability and quality of the resulting matrix factors needed for document interpretation (i.e., the metadata) and clustering are discussed. The success of future document classification systems based on such factor analytic approaches will greatly depend on how well the corresponding mathematical formulations capture both obvious and latent semantic information subject to time and space constraints of the available computing environment.

The goal of NMF is to produce a factorization $\mathbf{WH}$ of a nonnegative matrix $\mathbf{A}_{m \times n}$ such that the factors $\mathbf{W}_{m \times k}$ and $\mathbf{H}_{k \times n}$ are both nonnegative matrices and the error between the original matrix $\mathbf{A}$ and the low rank approximation $\mathbf{WH}$ is minimized. The scalar k is a parameter that the user sets to determine the rank of the low rank approximation.

The matrix $\mathbf{A}$ is an $m \times n$ data matrix. In this chapter, specifically in Section 17.4, we examine a term-by-document matrix $\mathbf{A}$, but $\mathbf{A}$ could be any data matrix, such as a user-by-item matrix of ratings or purchase history. The columns of $\mathbf{W}$ contain latent basis vectors that every column of $\mathbf{A}$ can be built from, and $\mathbf{H}$ is the mixing matrix. A column of $\mathbf{H}$ contains the contribution of each basis vector in $\mathbf{W}$ to the corresponding column of $\mathbf{A}$. For example, as Section 17.4 describes in further detail, when $\mathbf{A}$ is the Aviation Safety Reporting System (ASRS) matrix of 773 terms and 100 recall documents, $\mathbf{W}$ is a term-by-topic matrix and $\mathbf{H}$ is a topic-by-document matrix.

The NMF can be used as a clustering or classification tool. To do the so-called hard clustering, where each document is assigned to one and only one cluster, one can simply assign document i to cluster j if H_{ij} is the maximum element in column i of $\mathbf{H}$. On the other hand, for soft clustering (as in the case of ASRS document classification), each document may belong to one or more clusters (or document anomaly categories).

Since the NMF is created so that the difference between the original data matrix $\mathbf{A}$ and its low rank approximation $\mathbf{W}$ and $\mathbf{H}$ is minimized, there are many ways to measure the error between $\mathbf{A}$ and $\mathbf{WH}$. The matrix L_2 norm or the Frobenius norm has received the most attention [2,13–15,17,18,23,24,26]. The L_2 formulation of the problem is

$$\min \|\mathbf{A} - \mathbf{WH}\|_F^2$$
$$s.t. \quad \mathbf{W} \geq \mathbf{0},$$
$$\mathbf{H} \geq \mathbf{0}.$$

We refer to this as the L_2 formulation rather than the Frobenius formulation because in this chapter it will be helpful to write this objective function as the sum of individual components in the matrix.

L_2 formulation:

$$\min \|\mathbf{A} - \mathbf{WH}\|_F^2 = \min \sum_{i=1}^{m} \sum_{j=1}^{n} ([\mathbf{A}]_{ij} - [\mathbf{WH}]_{ij})^2. \tag{17.1}$$

The individual component representation (above) is equally illuminating for the two other formulations. So while technically in matrix notation these are entrywise

1-norm and the delta (Δ) norm [10] formulations, we refer to them as L_1 and L_∞ formulations due to their componentwise representation. This chapter focuses on the two most common other p-norms, the L_1 and L_∞ norms. These two formulations simply change the error measurement in the objective function. That is, the objective function for the L_1 formulation is

L_1 formulation:

$$\min \|\mathbf{A} - \mathbf{WH}\|_1 = \min \sum_{i=1}^{m} \sum_{j=1}^{n} |[\mathbf{A}]_{ij} - [\mathbf{WH}]_{ij}|,$$

while the objective function for the L_∞ formulation is

L_∞ formulation:

$$\min \|\mathbf{A} - \mathbf{WH}\|_\Delta = \min \left(\max_{i,j} |[\mathbf{A}]_{ij} - [\mathbf{WH}]_{ij}| \right).$$

The goal of this chapter is to demonstrate, using the ASRS dataset described in Section 17.4, the differences between and relative merits of these three p-norm formulations. We note that p-norms are not the only possibilities for objective functions of the NMF problem. While the L_p norm for $p = 2$ has received the most attention, there are many alternative non-p-norm objective functions. For instance, recently, there has been a focus on the class of divergence or Bregman objectives [5,7].

17.2   Related Work

While this chapter focuses on applying the NMF to textual data, researchers studying factorizations for image processing have noted the differences in low rank image reconstruction that are apparent when using different objective function formulations. For instance, Harb uses wavelets to approximate images and in this setting compares the results of wavelets designed for the three different p-norms [12]. One set of images from his experiments (see Figure 17.1) visually demonstrates our point that different formulations give different results.

This image is particularly challenging for low rank approximations due to the background, which transitions from gray to white, and the white and black text on an opposite background. In this case, the L_∞ approximation produces the most useful low rank representation of the original image because it has the most readable text in both English and Chinese. The L_∞ approximation wins in this case because it does not bother to capture the background's gradual transition from gray to white. Instead the L_∞ optimization is best satisfied by choosing only two background colors, a medium gray and a soft white. In this way, the error between a dark gray pixel of the original image and a medium gray pixel of the approximated image is mitigated, so that no one pixel has a huge error. Notice that both the L_1 and L_2 approximations try to capture the gray–white transition of the background, but at the expense of the text.

Original Image

L_1 L_2 L_∞

FIGURE 17.1:   Effect of various objective function formulations on reconstructed text image using a wavelet basis. (From Guha, S. and Harb, B., Nonlinear approximation and image representation using wavelets. In *Dagstuhl Seminar Proceedings, Web Information Retrieval and Linear Algebra Algorithms*, Dagstuhl, Germany, February 2007.)

This example also demonstrates the possible applicability of L_∞ NMF compression techniques for images such as Web pages that involve both text and figures.

Harb's experiments make our case well, namely that it is worth pursuing other p-norm formulations for the NMF problem because, depending on the application and the modeler's goal, one error measure may be more appropriate than the others. As a result, the L_1 and L_∞ formulations of the NMF deserve more attention and research, which brings us to Section 17.3 and the question of the solvability of these new NMF formulations.

17.3   Solving the NMF Problem: The Method of Alternating Variables

As far as optimization problems go, optimization of a convex function over a convex set is the best scenario, because in this case, every local extremum is a global extremum. While the feasible region of the NMF optimization problem forms a convex set, unfortunately, regardless of the p-norm used, the objective function is not convex.[*] The NMF problem is not convex in both **W** and **H**, but it is, however,

---

[*] When one matrix variable is fixed, then the optimization problem has no interaction terms (**W** times **H**).

convex in $\mathbf{W}$ or $\mathbf{H}$. This fact forms the basis of many algorithms designed to solve the NMF problem. These algorithms use a method called the method of alternating variables [3]. To exploit the convexity in one variable, the method fixes one variable at a time, say $\mathbf{W}$, and solves for the other variable, $\mathbf{H}$, then fixes $\mathbf{H}$ and solves for $\mathbf{W}$. This alternating continues until convergence. Because each subproblem (i.e., solve for $\mathbf{H}$ when $\mathbf{W}$ is fixed) is convex, it can be solved optimally. Grippo and Sciandrone [11] have proven that this method is guaranteed to converge to a stationary point of the overall original problem when (1) only two variables are involved and (2) each subproblem is solved optimally (see also Refs. [18,20]). Kim and Park [18] provide suggestions for convergence criteria that are tailored to the NMF problem and this method of alternating variables.

17.3.1 Subproblems for the L_2 Formulation of the NMF Problem

The next three subsections present the method of alternating variables for each p-norm formulation of the NMF. The L_2 norm formulation is considered first, since it has received the most attention. L_2 NMF algorithms alternate between the following two subproblems, Subproblem $\mathbf{H}$ and Subproblem $\mathbf{W}$.

L_2 formulation:

Subproblem $\mathbf{H}$ | Subproblem $\mathbf{W}$

$$\min_{\mathbf{H}} \|\mathbf{A} - \mathbf{W}\mathbf{H}\|_F \qquad\qquad \min_{\mathbf{W}} \|\mathbf{A}^{\mathrm{T}} - \mathbf{H}^{\mathrm{T}}\mathbf{W}^{\mathrm{T}}\|_F$$
$$\mathbf{H} \geq \mathbf{0} \qquad\qquad\qquad\qquad \mathbf{W} \geq \mathbf{0}$$

The literature shows that there have been two approaches to solving these L_2 subproblems: the exact approach and the inexact approach. The exact approach aims to solve each subproblem exactly using a nonnegative least squares method. For example, in this case, the columns of $\mathbf{H}$, denoted $\mathbf{h}_j$, in Subproblem $\mathbf{H}$ can be found one column at a time by solving the following problem (recall that $\mathbf{W}$ is fixed):

$$\min_{\mathbf{h}_j} \|\mathbf{a}_j - \mathbf{W}\mathbf{h}_j\|_2$$

$$\mathbf{h}_j \geq \mathbf{0}.$$

The above problem is a nonnegatively constrained least squares (NNLS) problem and has been well studied. Algorithms exist for solving such a problem exactly. Unfortunately, these methods are known to be very slow [2,18,21]. The two fastest existing NNLS algorithms are the method of Bro and de Jong [4] and the method of van Benthem and Keenan [28]. Very recently, Kim and Park [17,18] have applied the method of van Benthem and Keenan to the NMF L_2 subproblems, with a smart implementation that exploits structure in the problem, and report nice results and improved convergence speed.

The second approach to solving the NNLS subproblems in the L_2 formulation involves inexact methods. These methods sacrifice accuracy and convergence theory for speed and approximate results. Rather than running a time-consuming NNLS algorithm to solve the subproblems exactly, instead, the NNLS problem is treated as a standard least squares problem. That is, the nonnegativity constraint is ignored. At any subproblem iteration, the output of a standard least squares algorithm may contain some negative elements, and these are handled by a simple speedy projection step, which sets each negative element to 0, and thus, projects the least squares solution into the nonnegative orthant. While this is inexact, and Dhillon et al. [16] show the error that can occur with each subproblem, inexact methods are extremely fast, and for some applications, have been shown to give reliable approximate results [19,20,26,27]. Methods falling under the classification of inexact L_2 methods are Refs. [2,20,22,26].

17.3.2   Subproblems for the L_1 Formulation of the NMF Problem

When the objective function changes from the L_2 to the L_1 formulation, rather than solving alternating (nonnegative) least squares problems, alternating linear programs are solved instead. The two subproblems for the L_1 formulation are below.

L_1 formulation:

Subproblem **H**

$$\min_{\mathbf{H}} \|\mathbf{A} - \mathbf{WH}\|_1$$
$$\mathbf{H} \geq 0$$

Subproblem **W**

$$\min_{\mathbf{W}} \|\mathbf{A}^{\mathsf{T}} - \mathbf{H}^{\mathsf{T}}\mathbf{W}^{\mathsf{T}}\|_1$$
$$\mathbf{W} \geq 0$$

Consider Subproblem **H**. To formulate a L_1 objective function as a linear program, another variable **R** is introduced to deal with the absolute values in the formulation. Matrix **R** can be thought of as a residual or error matrix because each element contains the error between the approximation $\mathbf{A}_{ij}$ and the actual value $[\mathbf{WH}]_{ij}$. Thus, the linear program that finds **H** is

$$\min_{\mathbf{H},\mathbf{R}} \mathbf{e}^{\mathsf{T}}\mathbf{Re}$$
$$-\mathbf{R} \leq \mathbf{A} - \mathbf{WH} \leq \mathbf{R}$$
$$\mathbf{H} \geq \mathbf{0},$$
$$\mathbf{R} \geq \mathbf{0},$$

where **e** is a column vector of all ones. Most linear programming software packages require that the program be written in standard form. Thus, for the NMF problem involving $\mathbf{A}_{m \times n}$, $\mathbf{W}_{m \times k}$, and $\mathbf{H}_{k \times n}$, the standard form for the L_1 subproblem is

$$\min_{\mathbf{H},\mathbf{R}} \mathbf{e}^{\mathsf{T}}\mathbf{Re}$$
$$\begin{pmatrix} -\mathbf{I}_{m \times m} & -\mathbf{W}_{m \times k} \\ -\mathbf{I}_{m \times m} & \mathbf{W}_{m \times k} \end{pmatrix} \begin{pmatrix} \mathbf{R}_{m \times n} \\ \mathbf{H}_{k \times n} \end{pmatrix} \leq \begin{pmatrix} -\mathbf{A}_{m \times n} \\ \mathbf{A}_{m \times n} \end{pmatrix}$$
$$\begin{pmatrix} \mathbf{R}_{m \times n} \\ \mathbf{H}_{k \times n} \end{pmatrix} \geq \mathbf{0},$$

where **I** is the identity matrix. Similar to the L_2 subproblem, the unknown matrix $(\mathbf{R}\ \mathbf{H})^{\mathsf{T}}$ in the above linear program can be found one column at a time, sequentially or in parallel. Of course, if parallel processing is available, this drastically improves the runtime.

17.3.3   Subproblems for the L_∞ Formulation of the NMF Problem

The L_∞ formulation is very similar to the L_1 formulation because alternating linear programs are also used. The two subproblems for the L_∞ formulation are below.

L_∞ formulation:

Subproblem **H**   Subproblem **W**

$$\min_{\mathbf{H}} \|\mathbf{A} - \mathbf{WH}\|_\Delta \qquad\qquad \min_{\mathbf{W}} \|\mathbf{A}^{\mathrm{T}} - \mathbf{H}^{\mathrm{T}}\mathbf{W}^{\mathrm{T}}\|_\Delta$$
$$\mathbf{H} \geq \mathbf{0} \qquad\qquad\qquad\qquad \mathbf{W} \geq \mathbf{0}$$

Again, let us consider only Subproblem **H**, which can be written as

$$\min_{\mathbf{H},r} \; r$$
$$-r\mathbf{E} \leq \mathbf{A} - \mathbf{WH} \leq r\mathbf{E}$$
$$\mathbf{H} \geq \mathbf{0},$$
$$r \geq 0,$$

where **E** is the matrix of all ones. One immediate observation is that the linear program for the L_∞ formulation requires only one additional scalar decision variable r, whereas the linear program for the L_1 formulation needs an $m \times n$ matrix decision variable **R**. Because all the subproblems in both the L_1 and L_∞ formulations are linear programs, the nonnegativity constraints are handled exactly, which means that no approximate (e.g., projection) steps are used, and therefore all alternating linear programming methods are guaranteed to converge to a stationary point.

17.4   Experiments with L_1, L_2, and L_∞ Objectives for the NMF Problem

Following the performance methodology presented in Ref. [1], we applied all three NMF formulations (L_1, L_2, and L_∞) in the classification of documents by anomaly from the ASRS corpus (see also Ref. [25]). Three parameters used to achieve such a classification are α, a threshold on the relevance score or (target value) t_{ij} for document i and anomaly/label j; δ, a threshold on the column elements of **H**, which will filter out the association of features with both the training (**R**) and test (**T**) documents; and σ, the percentage of documents used to define the training set (or number of columns of **R**).

17.4.1   Anomaly Classification Problem

Although a rank-40 model (i.e., $k = 40$ features) was exclusively used in Ref. [1] to classify anomalies spanning as many as 21,519 ASRS documents, we consider only the first 100 documents (and corresponding 733 terms) of that collection with 70 (i.e., $\sigma = .70$) randomly selected documents used for training and the remainder (30) used for testing. The **W** and **H** matrix factors generated by all three formulations were $773 \times k$ and $k \times 100$, respectively, for ranks[*] $k = 10, 20, 40$. Each element a_{ij} of the sparse term-by-document matrix $\mathbf{A} = [\mathbf{a_{ij}}]$, whose NMF factorization is computed, defines a weighted frequency of the occurrence of term i in document j. Following the experiments in Ref. [1], we define $a_{ij} = l_{ij}g_i$, where

$$l_{ij} = \log(1 + f_{ij}) \quad \text{and} \quad g_i = 1 + \left[\sum_j \hat{p}_{ij} \log(\hat{p}_{ij}) / \log n \right].$$

Namely, l_{ij} is the local (logarithmic) weight for term i occurring in document j and g_i is the global entropy weight for term i in small ASRS document subset. We note that the component $\hat{p}_{ij} = f_{ij} / \sum_j f_{ij}$ is essentially the probability of term i appearing in document j, provided the frequency of occurrence of term i in document j is given by f_{ij}.

The GTP software environment [9], along with a 493-word stoplist[†] for filtering out unimportant terms, was used to parse the small 100-document ASRS subset and obtain the 773×100 term-by-document matrix **A**. For all three NMF formulations, columnwise pruning of the elements in the resulting coefficient matrix **H** was also tested with the setting $\delta = .30$. This parameter effectively determines the number of features (among the $k = 10, 20, 40$ possible) that any document (training or test) can be associated with. As δ increases, so does the sparsity of **H** (see Ref. [1]). The α parameter, defined to be .40 in Ref. [1], is the prediction control parameter that ultimately determines whether or not document i will be given label (anomaly) j, i.e., whether $p_{ij} = +1$ or $p_{ij} = -1$ for the cost function

$$Q = \frac{1}{C} \sum_{j=1}^{C} Q_j,$$

$$Q_j = (2A_j - 1) + \frac{1}{D} \sum_{i=1}^{D} q_{ij} t_{ij} p_{ij},$$

(17.2)

where
  C is the number of labels (anomalies),
  D is the number of test documents,

---

[*] Determining the optimal rank (or number of features) to achieve the highest-possible accuracy in NMF-based document classification remains an open problem.
[†] See SMART's English stoplist at ftp://ftp.cs.cornell.edu/pub/smart/english.stop.

$q_{ij} \in [0,1]$ is the classifier's confidence of the value p_{ij}, and

A_j is the area under each receiver operating characteristic (ROC) curve* for the classifier's predictions for anomaly/label j.

For the small ASRS subset considered in this study, $D = 30$ and $C = 14$ (out of a possible 22). The overall cost function Q in Equation (17.2), which is the average of all intermediate cost functions Q_j, is used to account for both the accuracy and confidence of the NMF classifier (see Ref. [25] for more details).

17.4.2 NMF Classifier Performance

For each NMF classifier (L_1, L_2, and L_∞), the 30 documents not selected for training defined the test subset **T** and the same random training subset **R** (of 70 documents) was used by each classifier. Exactly five (outer) iterations were used for each formulation to produce $k = 10, 20, 40$ feature vectors (columns of **W**) which are used to cluster test documents among the training documents (whose corresponding anomalies are known). For reliable assessments of overall computing time, 10 repetitions of each NMF computation using MATLAB (version 7.5) were performed on on a Dell OptiPlex 745 (2.4 GHz dual processor, 4 MB cache, 2 GB RAM) workstation. The accuracy of each NMF classifier is compared (per anomaly) using the area under each ROC curve. All alternating linear programming problems associated with the L_1 and L_∞ formulations of NMF were solved using the CVX MATLAB-based modeling software for convex optimization† developed by Grant, Boyd, and Ye at Stanford University.

Fourteen (of the twenty-two) event types (or anomaly descriptions) listed in Table 17.1 were obtained from the Distributed National ASAP Archive (DNAA) maintained by the University of Texas Human Factors Research Project.‡ The performance of each NMF classifier (by p-norm formulation) is presented in Tables 17.2 and 17.3 for $k = 10, 20, 40$ features (or rank). Table 17.2 also lists the distributions of anomalies across the same training (**R**) and test (**T**) document subsets used for each classifier. Tables 17.4 and 17.5 demonstrate the wide variation in runtimes that can be expected for the different norms and the slight improvement in sparsity of **W** and **H** obtained for the L_1 formulation. Notice that for the smaller ranks of $k = 10, 20$, there are several instances (anomalies) in which the formulations based on L_1 and L_∞ objective functions actually achieve higher accuracies than the L_2 formulation (which was the only formulation deployed in Ref. [1] for the complete ASRS document collection). The most notable improvements (in accuracy) by the L_1- and L_∞-based NMF classifiers were for the most populated anomalies (e.g., 2,6,8) in the 70-document training subset. The high computational price paid for

---

* Recall that an ROC curve illustrates how the true positive rate (TPR) of the classifier on the y-axis varies with its corresponding false positive rate (FPR) on the x-axis so that a perfect classifer achieves an area score of 1. Both the TPR and FPR are defined on the interval [0,1].

† See http://www.stanford.edu/~boyd/cvx.

‡ See http://homepage.psy.utexas.edu/HomePage/Group/HelmreichLAB.

TABLE 17.1: DNAA event types
for selected anomalies.

Anomaly	DNAA Event Type
1	Airworthiness event
2	Noncompliance (policy)
4	Excursion (loss of control)
5	Incursion (collision hazard)
7	Altitude deviation
9	Speed deviation
10	Uncommanded (no control)
11	Terrain proximity event
12	Traffic proximity event
13	Weather issue
15	Approach/arrival problems
18	Aircraft damage/encounter
21	Illness/injury event
22	Security concern/threat

those improvements, however, is clearly illustrated in Table 17.4. Clearly, the need for high-performance computing or parallelization with these alternative formulations is justified.

17.5 Improving the L_1 and L_∞ Methods

The experiments of the previous section made it clear that while the new L_1 and L_∞ formulations can give better performance on document classification tasks at lower ranks than the L_2 formulation, they are orders of magnitude more costly. However, because our implementations of the L_1 and L_∞ formulations are unsophisticated, there is room for optimism about their potential. To demonstrate this point, we briefly summarize the dramatic progress that has been made with the L_2 methods since their inception.

An enormous amount of research has been done on the L_2 formulation of the NMF problem. In fact, now scores of algorithms exist to solve the L_2 NMF problem [2,5,7,16–20,22,24,26,27]. Dhillon makes a helpful distinction between these algorithms by dividing them into two classes, exact and inexact methods [16]. Exact methods solve each subproblem exactly, which usually requires more work per iteration (often times orders of magnitude more), but results in better more accurate factorizations and sound convergence theory (recall Section 17.3).

Inexact methods sacrifice accuracy and convergence theory for speed and solve the subproblems inexactly, i.e., approximately. Most early NMF algorithms were slow inexact methods. Then researchers created several much faster inexact methods. As convergence theory became an issue, the focus shifted from speedy inexact methods to exact methods. The first exact methods were slow. But very recently, several

TABLE 17.2: Performance of rank-10 NMF classifier with L_1, L_2, and L_∞ objective functions.

Anomaly	Area (ROC)			Anomaly Count in	
	L_1	L_2	L_∞	Training Set	Test Set
1	0.5862	0.8621	**0.8966**	5	1
2	<u>0.6124</u>	0.3971	**0.6986**	46	11
3					
4					
5	**0.6914**	0.6173	0.2099	5	3
6	**0.6425**	0.5566	0.4796	28	13
7	0.4560	0.5600	0.5360	11	5
8	**0.7037**	0.3580	**0.5062**	9	3
9					
10	0.6071	0.6071	0.3929	1	2
11					
12	**0.5900**	0.5650	0.3900	10	10
13	**0.7500**	0.6964	0.6607	7	2
14	0.4938	<u>0.7778</u>	0.5309	7	3
15					
16					
17					
18	**0.8750**	0.4286	**0.6429**	2	2
19	0.7037	0.5556	0.3951	16	3
20					
21	<u>0.8571</u>	<u>0.8571</u>	<u>0.8571</u>	0	2
22	0.2759	0.2759	0.2759	0	1

Notes: Boldfaced entries indicate cases in which the accuracy of the L_1- or L_∞-based NMF classifiers exceeded that of the L_2-based NMF classifier. Maximum classification accuracies for a given anomaly (regardless of rank) are underlined.

fast exact methods have been discovered. Using the gradient descent-constrained least squares (GD-CLS) formulation [27] of the NMF based on Equation (17.1), it is possible to recast the subproblems in Section 17.3.1 so that parallel/distributed computing can be used to generate the n columns of $\mathbf{H}$ and m rows of $\mathbf{W}$ for the $m \times n$ nonnegative matrix $\mathbf{A}$ in parallel. Of course, the parallel formulation is faster than a serial formulation. However, rather than computing $\mathbf{H}$ and $\mathbf{W}$ vector by vector (either in series or in parallel), a matrix view is particularly efficient. Matrix formulations of GD-CLS only require the solutions of $k \times k$ linear systems which typically pose no computational constraint when k is order of magnitude smaller than m and n.

In summary, in the past decade the improvements in both speed and quality of the resulting factorization have been impressive, which makes us optimistic that with similar attention, using for instance, the suggestions of Sections 17.5.1 and 17.5.2, the new L_1 and L_∞ formulations can exhibit equally dramatic improvements.

TABLE 17.3: Performance of rank-20 and rank-40 NMF classifiers with L_1, L_2, and L_∞ objective functions.

	Area (ROC) for Rank-20			Area (ROC) for Rank-40		
Anomaly	L_1	L_2	L_∞	L_1	L_2	L_∞
1	**0.8966**	0.1724	**0.9310**	0.2414	<u>1.0000</u>	0.3103
2	0.4067	0.5981	0.3062	**0.5215**	0.4593	**0.5550**
3						
4						
5	0.3951	0.6543	0.5679	0.3704	<u>0.7037</u>	0.6296
6	0.4661	0.5294	0.3846	0.3077	<u>0.6878</u>	0.3846
7	0.5200	0.5680	0.4160	0.3040	<u>0.6320</u>	0.4080
8	0.6296	<u>0.7160</u>	0.5556	0.4815	0.5062	0.3951
9						
10	<u>0.6786</u>	0.5357	**0.6429**	0.6429	0.5714	<u>0.6786</u>
11						
12	0.5200	0.6950	0.5000	0.6800	<u>0.7600</u>	0.6400
13	**0.4464**	0.4286	**0.6429**	0.6071	<u>1.0000</u>	0.5179
14	0.3086	0.3580	**0.7531**	**0.4691**	0.4198	0.1975
15						
16						
17						
18	**0.6786**	0.2679	**0.6607**	0.8036	<u>0.9107</u>	0.6964
19	**0.4444**	0.3827	0.2222	0.4198	0.3210	0.1481
20						
21	0.8750	0.8750	<u>0.8571</u>	<u>0.8571</u>	0.8750	<u>0.4286</u>
22	0.3103	0.3103	**0.3448**	0.2759	0.3448	0.3793

Note: Boldfaced entries indicate cases in which the accuracy of the L_1- or L_∞-based NMF classifiers exceeded that of the L_2-based NMF classifier. Maximum classification accuracies for a given anomaly (regardless of rank) are underlined.

17.5.1 Speed Improvements for the L_1 Formulation That Exploit Structure

The experiments of Section 17.4 showed the major drawback of the L_1 and L_∞ formulations, lengthy execution time. With careful thought, it is likely that this can be improved because there is significant structure in the linear programming formulation of these subproblems that can be exploited.

The subproblems in the L_1 formulation contain linear programs with matrix decision variables, yet the simplex method and interior point methods are designed to handle vector decision variables. One simple solution is to view the matrix of decision variables as a set of vector decision variables by considering one column of the matrix at a time. In fact, the matrix linear program is totally separable, meaning that the vector of decision variables for one column is completely decoupled from the other columns. Perhaps the best way to see this total separability is with the *vec*

TABLE 17.4: Computational cost of computing a rank-40 NMF on a dell OptiPlex 745 (2.4 GHz dual processor, 4 MB cache, 2 GB RAM) using L_1, L_2, and L_∞ objective functions.

	Computation of $X = WH$		
	L_1	L_2	L_∞
Mean (s)	1416.255	0.047	2236.850
Mean (min)	23.604	0.001	37.281
Variance	81.124	0	163.147
StdDev	9.007	0.002	12.773
	Computation of W		
	L_1	L_2	L_∞
Mean (s)	782.658		1499.436
Mean (min)	13.044		24.991
Variance	29.792		186.865
StdDev	5.4458		13.670
	Computation of H		
	L_1	L_2	L_∞
Mean (s)	633.597		737.413
Mean (min)	10.560		12.290
Variance	24.701		12.615
StdDev	4.970		3.552

Notes: The standard deviation (stdDev) and variance (Variance) of the runtimes (s) among 10 repetitions are reported.

TABLE 17.5: Sparsity of NMF factors of different ranks generated from the 773×100 ASRS subset with L_1, L_2, and L_∞ objective functions.

		Number of Nonzeros		
Rank	Factor	L_1	L_2	L_∞
10	W	7730	7730	7730
10	H	728	1000	1000
20	W	15140	15460	15460
20	H	1182	2000	2000
40	W	27831	30920	30920
40	H	70	4000	4000

operation. $vec(\mathbf{X})$ creates a vector from the matrix $\mathbf{X}$ by stacking its columns one on top of the other. Thus, if $\mathbf{X}$ is $m \times n$, then $vec(\mathbf{X})$ is $mn \times 1$. Recall the standard form of the linear program for the L_1 subproblem $\mathbf{H}$ in Section 17.3.2. For notational convenience, let

$$C = \begin{pmatrix} -I & -W \\ -I & W \end{pmatrix}$$

be the coefficient matrix, $X = \begin{pmatrix} R \\ H \end{pmatrix}$ be the matrix of decision variables, and $B = \begin{pmatrix} -A \\ A \end{pmatrix}$ be the matrix of righthand sides. Applying the *vec* operation creates the following vectorized linear program for the L_1 subproblem H. Here x_i is the ith column of X, b_i is the ith column of B, and $f^T = (e\ 0 \mid e\ 0 \mid \cdots \mid e\ 0)$.

$$\min f^T e$$

$$\begin{pmatrix} C & & & \\ & C & & \\ & & \ddots & \\ & & & C \end{pmatrix} \begin{pmatrix} x_1 \\ x_2 \\ \vdots \\ x_n \end{pmatrix} \leq \begin{pmatrix} b_1 \\ b_2 \\ \vdots \\ b_n \end{pmatrix}$$

$$vec(X) \geq 0.$$

The perfect block diagonal structure reveals the complete separability of the problem. As a result, each L_1 subproblem H contains n vector linear programs that can be solved in parallel. (Exploiting this parallelism would drastically improve the runtimes listed in Table 17.4. Instead the runtimes reported came from sequential solves of vector linear programs due to the absence of a machine with parallel processing capabilities.)

Even if the columns of the decision matrix are found sequentially, there is another potential for speedup. Notice that the coefficient matrix in the linear programming inequalities is constant, only the right-hand side changes from one sequential solve to the next. Such a situation is excellent news when one is solving a series of systems of linear equations. Thus, it is tempting to hope that this situation will be equally beneficial when solving a series of linear programs. Unfortunately, it is not as clear how this fact (constant C, changing b) can be used to improve linear programming computations involving a series of linear programs because the optimal basis may change when b changes. There are a few existing techniques that may be helpful. For instance, two papers [8,29] discuss *bunching*, a technique that bunches righthand side vectors that have the same optimal basis, and hence, same solution. It is also possible that ideas from parametric programming or the Dantzig–Wolfe decomposition may be helpful as well [6].

17.5.2 Speed Improvements for the L_∞ Formulation That Exploit Structure

Similarly, applying this *vec* operation to the L_∞ subproblem H also helps reveal some hidden structure. In the following linear program for the L_∞ subproblem H,

$\mathbf{f}^T = \begin{pmatrix} \mathbf{0}^T & \mathbf{0}^T \cdots & \mathbf{0}^T & 1 \end{pmatrix}.$

$$\min \mathbf{f}^T \mathbf{e}$$

$$\begin{pmatrix} -\mathbf{W} & & & & -\mathbf{e} \\ & -\mathbf{W} & & & -\mathbf{e} \\ & & \ddots & & \vdots \\ & & & -\mathbf{W} & -\mathbf{e} \\ \mathbf{W} & & & & -\mathbf{e} \\ & \mathbf{W} & & & -\mathbf{e} \\ & & \ddots & & \vdots \\ & & & \mathbf{W} & -\mathbf{e} \end{pmatrix} \begin{pmatrix} vec(\mathbf{H}) \\ r \end{pmatrix} \leq \begin{pmatrix} -vec(\mathbf{A}) \\ vec(\mathbf{A}) \end{pmatrix}$$

$$\begin{pmatrix} vec(\mathbf{H}) \\ r \end{pmatrix} \geq \mathbf{0}.$$

Notice that the L_∞ subproblem has many fewer decision variables than the L_1 subproblem. Yet unfortunately, the problem is not totally separable, the way the L_1 subproblem for $\mathbf{H}$ is, because the last column of the coefficient matrix $\mathbf{C}$ links the columns of the decision matrix $\mathbf{H}$.

Another potential for speedup appears in the structure of the coefficient matrix. The upper and lower halves of this coefficient matrix contain the so-called block angular structure, first defined by Dantzig. When just one angle appears in the coefficient matrix (rather than two in this case), the Dantzig–Wolfe or Bender decomposition can be used to exploit this structure [6]. In fact, such decompositions use the common sense approach that since the subproblems are lightly coupled, each can be solved separately to create a good approximation to the overall optimal solution.

17.6 Conclusions

Two new *p*-norm formulations of the NMF problem were presented. These formulations, the L_1 and L_∞ formulations, give results that differ from the popular L_2 formulation and may be useful in certain applications or when the modeler has explicit knowledge about the errors of the given data. For example, if the goal is minimizing the maximum error, then the L_∞ norm is the perfect choice. When compared to the standard L_2 formulation, the new L_1 and L_∞ formulations also seem to give superior results at lower ranks, an observation that is useful for storage-intensive applications. Unfortunately, the first implementations of the L_1 and L_∞ formulations presented in this chapter are not yet comparable in terms of runtimes to the current fast L_2 implementations. However, since L_1 and L_∞ formulations use alternating linear programs that have striking structural properties, it is possible that such structure can be exploited to dramatically reduce runtimes, perhaps making the two new methods practical competitors with the standard L_2 methods. Exploiting the structure of the linear programs is the subject of future work.

Acknowledgments

Amy Langville thanks Jim Cox and Russ Albright of SAS Institute for passing along their colleague Warren Searle's comment about using linear programs in place of least squares problems. Her research is supported in part by the National Science Foundation under grant No. CAREER-CCF-0546622. Michael Berry's research in text mining was sponsored in part by the National Aeronautics and Space Administration (NASA) Ames Research Center under contract No. 07024004.

References

[1] E.G. Allan, M.R. Horvath, C.V. Kopek, B.T. Lamb, T.S. Whaples, and M.W. Berry. Anomaly detection using non-negative matrix factorization. In M.W. Berry and M. Castellanos, editors, *Survey of Text Mining: Clustering, Classification, and Retrieval*, Second Edition pp. 203–217. Springer, New York, 2008.

[2] M.W. Berry, M. Browne, A.N. Langville, V.P. Pauca, and R.J. Plemmons. Algorithms and applications for approximate nonnegative matrix factorization. *Computational Statistics and Data Analysis*, 52(1):155–173, 2007.

[3] D. Bertsekas. *Nonlinear Programming*. Athena Scientific, Belmont, MA, 1999.

[4] R. Bro and S. de Jong. A fast non-negativity constrained linear least squares algorithm. *Journal of Chemometrics*, 11:393–401, 1997.

[5] A. Cichocki, R. Zdunek, and S.I. Amari. Csiszar's divergences for non-negative matrix factorization: Family of new algorithms. In *Proceedings of the sixth International Conference on Independent Component Analysis and Blind Signal Separation*, pp. 32–39, Charleston, SC, 2006. Springer LNCS 3889.

[6] G.B. Dantzig. *Linear Programming and Extensions*. Princeton University Press, Princeton, NJ, 1963.

[7] I.S. Dhillon and S. Sra. Generalized nonnegative matrix approximations with Bregman divergences. In *Proceedings of the Neural Information Processing Systems (NIPS) Conference*, Vancouver, BC., 2005.

[8] H.I. Gassmann and S.W. Wallace. Solving linear programs with multiple right-hand sides: Pricing and ordering schemes. *Annals of Operations Research*, 64(1):237–259, 2005.

[9] J.T. Giles, L. Wo, and M.W. Berry. GTP (General Text Parser) software for text mining. In H. Bozdogan, editor, *Software for Text Mining, in Statistical Data Mining and Knowledge Discovery*, pp. 455–471. CRC Press, Boca Raton, FL, 2003.

[10] G.H. Golub and C.F. Van Loan. *Matrix Computations*. Johns Hopkins University Press, Baltimore, MD, 1996.

[11] L. Grippo and M. Sciandrone. On the convergence of the block nonlinear Gauss-Seidel method under convex constraints. *Operations Research Letters*, 26(3):127–136, 2000.

[12] S. Guha and B. Harb. Nonlinear approximation and image representation using wavelets. In *Dagstuhl Seminar Proceedings, Web Information Retrieval and Linear Algebra Algorithms*, Dagstuhl, Germany, Available at http://drops.dagstuhl.de/opus/volltexte/2007/1063, February 2007.

[13] P. Hoyer. Non-negative matrix factorization with sparseness constraints. *Journal of Machine Learning Research*, 5:1457–1469, 2004.

[14] P.O. Hoyer. Non-negative sparse coding. In *Neural Networks for Signal Processing XII (Proceedings of the IEEE Workshop on Neural Networks for Signal Processing)*, pp. 557–565, Martigny, Switzerland, 2002.

[15] J. Karvanen and A. Cichocki. Measuring sparseness of noisy signals. In *Proceedings of the Fourth International Symposium on Independent Component Analysis and Blind Signal Separation (ICA2003)*, pp.125–130, Nara, Japan, 2003.

[16] D. Kim, S. Sra, and I.S. Dhillon. Fast Newton-type methods for the least squares nonnegative matrix approximation problem. In *Proceedings of the 2007 SIAM Data Mining Conference*, Minneapolis, MN, 2007.

[17] H. Kim and H. Park. Cancer class discovery using non-negative matrix factorization based on alternating non-negativity-constrained least squares. In *Proceedings of the International Symposium on Bioinformatics Research and Applications*, Atlanta, GA, Lecture Notes in Computer Science, Springer, Berlin, 4463, pp. 477-487, 2007.

[18] H. Kim and H. Park. Sparse non-negative matrix factorizations via alternating non-negativity-constrained least squares for microarray data analysis. *Bioinformatics*, 23(12):1495–1502, 2007.

[19] A.N. Langville. Experiments with the nonnegative matrix factorization and the reuters10 dataset, February 2005. Slides from SAS Meeting.

[20] A.N. Langville, C.D. Meyer, R. Albright, J. Cox, and D. Duling. Alternating least squares algorithms for the nonnegative matrix factorization. Unpublished, 2006.

[21] C.L. Lawson and R.J. Hanson. *Solving Least Squares Problems*. SIAM, Philadelphia, 1995.

[22] D. Lee and H. Seung. Algorithms for non-negative matrix factorization. *Advances in Neural Information Processing Systems*, 13:556–562, 2001.

[23] D.D. Lee and H.S. Seung. Learning the parts of objects by non-negative matrix factorization. *Nature*, 401:788–791, 1999.

[24] C.-J. Lin. Projected gradient methods for non-negative matrix factorization. Technical Report Information and Support Services Tech. Report ISSTECH-95-013, Department of Computer Science, National Taiwan University, Taipei, Taiwan, (R.O.C.), 2005.

[25] M.E. Otey, A.N. Srivastava, S. Das, and P. Castle. Appendix: SIAM Text Mining Competition 2007. In M.W. Berry and M. Castellanos, editors, *Survey of Text Mining: Clustering, Classification, and Retrieval*, Second Edition, pp. 233–235. Springer, New York, 2008.

[26] V.P. Pauca, J. Piper, and R.J. Plemmons. Nonnegative matrix factorization for spectral data analysis. *Linear Algebra and Its Applications*, 416(1):29–47, 2006.

[27] F. Shahnaz, M.W. Berry, V.P. Pauca, and R.J. Plemmons. Document clustering using nonnegative matrix factorization. *Information Processing and Management*, 42(2):373–386, 2006.

[28] M.H. van Benthem and M.R. Keenan. Fast algorithm for the solution of large-scale non-negativity-constrained least squares problems. *Journal of Chemometrics*, 18:441–450, 2004.

[29] R. Wets. Solving stochastic programs with simple recourse. *Stochastics*, 10:219–242, 1983.

Part IV

Data mining in Security, Surveillance, and Privacy Protection

Chapter 18

Is Privacy Still an Issue for Data Mining?

Chris Clifton, Wei Jiang, Mummoorthy Murugesan, and M. Ercan Nergiz

Contents

18.1 Introduction

Five years ago, the National Science Foundation held a workshop on "Next generation data mining." At that time, privacy was a relatively new issue to the data mining community; there had been half a dozen research papers on privacy-preserving data mining techniques [1–7] and even a couple of articles in the popular press [8,9]. The ensuing years have seen substantial research in privacy-preserving data mining techniques, several workshops on the subject. At the same time, data mining has been vilified as a threat to privacy and civil liberties—witness the 2003 letter from the USACM suggesting that data mining technology could contribute to the growth of privacy-compromising databases [10] (and the ensuing response from SIGKDD [11]), and perhaps more critically, the continuing efforts to restrict data mining in the U.S. Senate. The proposed Data Mining Moratorium Act of 2003 [12] would have banned data mining by the Department of Defense. The (more reasonable) Data Mining Reporting Act of 2007, now law in the United States, requires a report to Congress when "a department or agency of the Federal Government, or a non-Federal entity acting on behalf of the Federal Government, is conducting the queries, searches, or other analyses to discover or locate a predictive pattern or anomaly indicative of terrorist or criminal activity on the part of any individual or individuals"; that (among other things) gives

> An assessment of the impact or likely impact of the implementation of the data mining activity on the privacy and civil liberties of individuals, including a thorough description of the actions that are being taken or will be taken with regard to the property, privacy, or other rights or privileges of any individual or individuals as a result of the implementation of the data mining activity [13].

While the domain of this act is limited, it is clear that we need the ability to understand and mitigate the privacy impact of data mining.

What has been the impact of privacy-preserving data mining research over the last 5 years? In commercial terms, the answer is little or none—privacy-preserving data mining technology is still in the research paper, or at best research prototype, stage. However, the research may have had an impact on the privacy versus data mining debate; researchers have pointed out the privacy implications of data mining technology, and the debate had become more reasoned. For example, the Moratorium Act of 2003 banned data mining, with exceptions for computer searches of public information or computer searches that are based on a particularized suspicion of an individual. By the 2007 Act, the term "data mining" had been limited to pattern-based "queries, searches, or other analyses to discover or locate a predictive pattern or anomaly indicative of terrorist or criminal activity on the part of any individual or individuals." This is much more specific than the research community's view of data mining, and shows recognition that data mining technology is not inherently bad, but is (perhaps unusually) subject to misuse.

Where does this leave privacy-preserving data mining research? While it could be argued that the direction of the debate makes such research irrelevant, an alternative view is that the debate has led to a better framework for research in the next 5 years. In particular, the following have emerged from the debate, and can serve as guidance for privacy research in the data mining community:

- Misuse of data does not require data mining.

- Misunderstanding data mining technology can lead to misuse.

- Privacy is about individually identifiable data.

The following sections elaborate on these points, with suggestions on how research can address them as well as points to successes. The goal is to identify key issues that must be considered in pursuing the next generation of privacy-preserving data mining research.

18.2 Misuse of Data Does Not Require Data Mining

Most high-profile cases of misuse of private data appear to have nothing to do with data mining. Instead, it is problems with security of the database that lead to security breach and misuse. The USACM letter questioning the Total Information Awareness program recognized this [10]; it is unfortunate that the term "data mining" was featured so prominently, as the security risks described by the letter were based on potential for misuse of the immense databases proposed by the program, rather than the technology to analyze them. Identity theft is an aggravating and expensive problem, but results from direct disclosure of information about individuals (the underlying database) rather than analysis of that data. Most high-profile privacy breaches are similar; it is poor security of the database (contained on laptops, backup tapes, or through electronic break-in) that leads to the breach.

Does this mean data mining can be exonerated? Unfortunately, the answer is no. One of the highest profile cases was the 2005 theft of credit card information from CardSystems, a credit card transaction processing company [14]. A breach of such magnitude should not have been able to happen; CardSystems was only supposed to use the data to process the transaction, not store it. However, CardSystems stored data on some transactions "for research purposes in order to determine why these transactions did not successfully complete" [14]. Without data mining technology, meaningful analysis of such a large amount of data (at least 263,000 records were stolen) would have been difficult or impossible. Without data mining, there would have been no reason to keep the data, and thus nothing to steal.

18.2.1 How to Prevent Data Misuse

Most privacy-preserving data mining research to date can be used to address this problem. Much of the work falls in two basic categories. The first approach was exemplified by two papers titled "Privacy preserving data mining" that appeared in 2000 [2,4]. In Ref. [2], data was distorted before placing it in the database, obscuring actual values. Privacy-preserving data mining techniques on such data recover the correct data mining results, based on the data and knowledge of the process by which it was distorted, but recovery of actual data values (even knowing the distortion process) is (presumably) impossible. If CardSystems had used such a technique to save distorted transactions, theft of the data would have had no (privacy) impact.

The second approach, exemplified by Ref. [4], is to mine data from distributed sources without requiring the sources to disclose the data (even to each other). Such approaches could alleviate the need for the immense databases that raised concerns with the Total Information Awareness program. Techniques have been developed that replicate the results of several data mining algorithms, while allowing data about an individual to be split among several sites (starting with Ref. [6]); gathering enough information about an individual to result in a serious invasion of privacy would require compromising several databases.

18.2.2   Challenges to the Current Techniques

There have been techniques developed to support many types of data mining in these two approaches. For a more detailed discussion and citations to much of the research see Ref. [15]. However, work is not done: Additive random noise must be used carefully, as in some cases (e.g., attempting to mask correlated data items) signal processing techniques can be used to recover original values with relatively high accuracy [16]. Multiplicative randomization techniques can help this problem [17], but further investigation is needed.

The secure multiparty computation approach also has weaknesses. Much of what has been published has only been proven secure in the semihonest model; the assumption that parties will not cheat to try to obtain private information is not sufficient for many practical applications. Methods proven secure under the malicious model have not yet shown the efficiency needed for practical applications. Intermediate approaches such as accountable computing (AC) [18] has been proposed to circumvent these shortcomings. In addition, SMC techniques do not prevent any participating parties from modifying his or her input data before executing the SMC protocol. However, utilizing the concept of noncooperative computation (NCC) [19] could prevent this input modification problem.

The idea behind the AC framework is that a party who correctly followed the protocol can be proven to have done so and consequently prove that it did not know (and thus could not have disclosed) private data. This provides substantial practical utility over a semihonest protocol. Although a malicious adversary participating in an AC protocol may learn things they should not know and damage the result, such a behavior could be detected under the AC framework. Since the AC framework does not need to prevent disclosure to a malicious adversary, protocols can be less complex, with much of the added cost over a semihonest protocol pushed to a verification phase, which only needs to be run for auditing or to expose the culprit when disclosure is detected; development of protocols under these models is needed.

The NCC model can be seen as an example of applying game theoretical ideas in the distributed computation setting where each party participates in a protocol to learn the output of some given function f over the joint inputs of the parties. The NCC model assumes that every party wants to learn the result correctly, but at the same time, prefers to learn it exclusively. Informally speaking, if f is in the NCC model, it is impossible for parties who lie about their inputs to compute the correct output based on their original inputs and the incorrect final results. While the SMC-based PPDM protocols cannot prevent input modification, in the NCC model, parties are expected to provide their true inputs to correctly evaluate a function. Therefore, by combining the concept of SMC and NCC, we could implement PPDM tasks that guarantee that participating parties provide truthful inputs to construct legitimate data mining models.

18.2.3   Challenges in Acceptance of Current Techniques

Although the existing PPDM techniques are not perfect, they do prevent data misuse to certain degree. Nontheless, the deployment of such techniques is very difficult because of their associated costs in the real world. The key to the acceptance of this technology as a viable alternative to the monolithic (and vulnerable) data warehouse is to develop tools that make business sense. Two key possibilities are (1) enhancing user trust to get better data and (2) corporate collaboration using sensitive business data.

Studies suggest that reputation and ability to protect privacy result in a greater willingness to provide accurate personal data [20]. Businesses that use privacy-preserving data mining technologies should convince users' efficacy of that technology. This can be achieved by clearly documenting the steps of analysis and their results, and making them public to show how the users' privacy will not be affected. A well-informed user places more trust on the data collector; hence, the willingness to provide better data compared to that of a suspicious user.

Companies may need to keep data secret from collaborators, but still wish to use shared data for common analysis purposes. This is commonly done using a trusted broker to manage information, but is such trust necessary (or cost effective)? One area where this has been investigated (and found corporate interest) is in supply chain management [21]. Another area is related to independent trucking companies who have separate pickup and delivery tasks, and wish to identify potential efficiency enhancing task swaps, while limiting the information that the companies must reveal to identify these swaps [22]. It has shown that the use of cryptographic techniques can attain the same result without the use of a broker. Other areas surely exist where a business case can be made for development and use of privacy-preserving data analysis.

The goal of research on privacy-preserving data mining techniques needs to go beyond developing the basic techniques. The future lies with developing technology that ties to a business model where privacy is a demonstrable asset.

18.3 Misunderstanding Data Mining Technology Can Lead to Misuse

A key component of the Data Mining Reporting Act of 2007 [13] is a requirement that agencies give

> An assessment of the efficacy or likely efficacy of the data mining activity in providing accurate information consistent with and valuable to the stated goals and plans for the use or development of the data mining activity.

Predictive data mining techniques typically give at best a probability that the given prediction is correct. While this is of some value, it is not sufficient. For example, "X is a member of a terrorist organization with 50% probability" is much less actionable than saying "X is a member of a terrorist organization with 50% probability, and a dangerous crackpot with 50% probability" versus "X is a member of a terrorist organization with 50% probability, and a Senator with 50% probability."

The first step is understanding what can be expected of data mining technology. Classical work on limits of learning and sample complexity generally talks of the expected accuracy of a prediction and the confidence that the expected accuracy will be met. Work such as that of Ref. [23] can form a much better basis for justifying both the value and privacy implications of data mining in privacy-sensitive situations. Methodologies to apply such theory in the early stages of a data mining project are needed; only when we can justify the value and quantify the privacy risk should we begin the process of collecting data.

While most concerns focus on the potential inaccuracy of data mining, the converse is also important to privacy. Highly accurate predictive modeling can be a threat to privacy, if the prediction is with respect to sensitive information. We cannot just assume that data mining results are not sensitive; based on results from Ref. [24], it is clear that data mining results may violate privacy. A pattern of the form $a_1 \wedge a_2 \wedge a_3 \Rightarrow a_4$ with high support (sup) and confidence (conf) can be used to inter the support of the pattern $a_1 \wedge a_2 \wedge a_3 \wedge \neg a_4$. It is important to be aware of the implications of inference from data mining results. In Ref. [25], a suppression-based scheme is presented to remove the itemsets that cause this inference problem.

In this case, we need to be concerned not about average accuracy (which may be sufficient to report on the efficacy of a method), but the expected accuracy of a particular prediction. It is of little comfort to say that on average sensitive data will have low accuracy if you are one of the individuals for whom sensitive data can be predicted. While some work has been done that can be applied to this problem [26], more is needed.

There may be other times when accuracy alone cannot justify use of data mining outcomes. Private information may well be legally protected; for example, use of race or gender in decision making is often illegal. Note that it can be illegal to use apparently innocuous information that has the effect of introducing a bias on such a protected attribute, witness the ban on redlining in mortgage lending. The idea behind redlining was to reject loans from neighborhoods with a high rate of default (i.e., draw a red line around such areas in precomputer days). The problem was that the neighborhoods redlined tended to have high minority populations, leading to de facto discrimination based on race. This could easily arise in data mining; nonprivate information that correlates highly with private/protected data could lead to outcomes equivalent to misusing the protected data. Metrics that judge the difference between a model and one built using protected data could well be an outcome of a better understanding of both the efficacy and privacy impact of data mining methods.

18.4   Privacy Is about Individually Identifiable Data

Having explored some of the issues involved in data mining and privacy, we now return to the key question: What exactly is privacy? For many data mining tasks, the key question to ask is if any kind of information about a population[*] is subject

---

[*] Population here shall mean sufficiently large group of people.

to privacy concerns. Fortunately, the answer to this question seems to be no. The European Community Directive 95/46/EC [27] protects only personal data that can be tied to (individual) persons. Similarly, the U.S. Healthcare Insurance Portability and Accountability Act (HIPAA) privacy rules [28] state that the privacy standards apply to individually identifiable health information; other information, including de-identified personal data, is not subject to privacy regulations. For example, it is prohibited to disclose information that some U.S. citizen is diabetics, but it may be safe to release information saying 7% of U.S. citizens are diabetics. De-identification can protect privacy while allowing use of (personal) data.

However, recent research showed that de-identification is not an easy task. Trivial approach of simply removing unique identifiers (SSN, name, etc.) from data is not sufficient; external information can still be used to reidentify data by linking information to individuals. In the United States, the combination of zip code, and birth date is unique for 87% of the citizens [29]. Sweeney et al. showed that they could reidentify supposedly anonymous health records via linking them to a publicly available voter registration list.

As an example, in Figure 18.1, suppose dataset PT is publicly available, and a diabetes hospital has a private subset dataset T of diabetic patients. Note that in T, unique identifiers are removed and sensitive information (type of diabetes) is present. Suppose hospital wants to release T. However, even though T does not contain any unique identifiers, given PT, it is not safe to release T as it is. The reason is that quasi-identifiers (zip, age, and nation) in T and PT can be used by an adversary to identify, for example, tuple c of T as Carl and thus learn that Carl is Type 2 diabetic.

Anonymization techniques such as k-anonymity [30] have been proposed to address this issue by restricting linkage to groups of people. A dataset is said to be k-anonymous if every record projected over quasi-identifiers appears at least k times. Surely in a k-anonymous dataset, any information can at best be linked to k people. One way of k-anonymizing a given dataset is through generalization of values. Table $T^*_{(k)}$ shows a two-anonymization of T. Note that Carl can be mapped to one of the tuples b and c in $T^*_{(k)}$ as opposed to c only.

k-anonymity is a first response to the problem of identification. However, this problem needs much more attention in order to come up with a reasonable solution that will address public concerns. In the following sections, we present a couple of challenges researchers face: definition of identification and risk of identification.

18.4.1 Defining Identification

Even though laws and rules demand protection against identification, there may be many ways to interpret the notion of identification depending on the context. As it can be argued that Carl being identified as a Type 1 diabetic is a problem, Carl being identified as diabetic (regardless of the type) can also be considered to be a problem. Later research built upon k-anonymity focused on different interpretation of identification.

PT

	Publicly known data		
Name	Zip	Age	Nation
Bob	47903	48	Canada
Carl	47906	56	USA
Dirk	47630	42	Brazil
Frank	47633	53	Peru
Harry	48972	47	Bulgaria
Iris	48970	49	France
Gail	48973	33	Spain
Alice	47906	35	USA
Eunice	47630	22	Brazil

T

	Private data			
	Zip	Age	Nation	Diabetes
b	47903	48	Canada	T1
c	47906	56	USA	T2
d	47630	42	Brazil	G
f	47633	53	Peru	G
h	48972	47	Bulgaria	T2
i	48970	49	France	G

$T^*_{(k)}$

	Released data			
	Zip	Age	Nation	Diabetes
b	4790*	40–60	North America	T1
c	4790*	40–60	North America	T2
d	4763*	40–60	South America	G
f	4763*	40–60	South America	G
h	4897*	40–50	Europe	T2
i	4897*	40–50	Europe	G

$T^*_{(\ell)}$

	Released data			
	Zip	Age	Nation	Diabetes
b	47*	40–50	USA	T1
c	47*	40–60	USA	T2
d	47*	40–50	USA	G
f	47*	40–60	USA	G
h	4897*	40–50	Europe	T2
i	4897*	40–50	Europe	G

$T^*_{(a)}$

	Released data			
	Zip	Age	Nation	Diabetes
b	47903	48	Canada	T1, G
d	47630	42	Brazil	
c	47906	56	USA	T2, G
f	47633	53	Peru	
h	48972	47	Bulgaria	T2, G
i	48970	49	France	

$T^*_{(d)}$

	Released data		
	Zip	Age	Nation
b	47*	20–60	USA
c	47*	20–60	USA
d	47*	20–60	USA
f	47*	20–60	USA
h	4897*	30–50	Europe
i	4897*	30–50	Europe

FIGURE 18.1: Public table PT: the whole population. Private table T: diabetes patients in the population. Diabetes attribute specifies the type of the diabetes: T1, T2, or G. Released tables $T^*_{(k)}$, $T^*_{(\ell)}$, $T^*_{(a)}$, and $T^*_{(\delta)}$: different anonymizations of T.

18.4.1.1   Identification against Sensitive Attributes

Even though k-anonymity ensures that any public information joins with groups of at least k tuples, it does not enforce any constraint on the values of sensitive attributes in the group. As an example, in T and $T^*_{(k)}$, even though Dirk can be mapped to one of the tuples d and f, both tuples are Type G diabetics. This implies that Dirk is definitely Type G diabetic. Privacy models such as ℓ diversity [31] and t closeness [32] further enforce diversity in sensitive values within an anonymization group. Dataset $T^*_{(\ell)}$ is an example anonymization of T where tuples in each group have different sensitive values. Further research on these models (anatomization [33]) improves utilization by not generalizing on QI attributes. For example in $T^*_{(a)}$, QI attributes for Carl is released as they are and it is still not clear whether Carl is Type 1 or G diabetic. By assuming the insensitivity of QI attributes, anatomization totally separates identification against sensitive attributes from identification against membership, which we cover next.

18.4.1.2 Identification against Membership

For certain applications to be identified as in or not in the dataset is a risk. Privacy models above do not necessarily protect against such attacks toward membership disclosure. For example, given the public table PT and the released data $T^*_{(k)}$ (or $T^*_{(\ell)}$ or T^*_b), it is certain that Carl is in the diabetics dataset ($\mathscr{P}(\text{Carl} \in T \mid \text{PT}, T^*_{(k)}) = 1$). This is because all people with age > 40 are in $T^*_{(k)}$. δ-presence [34] addresses this issue by bounding the probability of a given person being in a private dataset with δ parameters (e.g., $\delta_{\min} \le \mathscr{P}(t \in T \mid \text{PT}, T^*) \le \delta_{\max}$ for any tuple $t \in \text{PT}$). For instance, all existence probabilities given PT and $T^*_{(\delta)}$ are $\frac{2}{3}$.

Problem of identification takes different forms under different adversary models. There has been work [35,36] on privacy protection against adversaries with additional background knowledge. (An adversary may have the knowledge that Carl is Type 2 diabetic, or he is so if Dirk is not.) Nonetheless, modeling arbitrary adversary background knowledge is still an open problem.

18.4.2 Building the Bridge between the Privacy Model and the Real World: Risk of Identification

On the one hand, the intent of HIPAA safe harbor rules is stated as "providing a means to produce some de-identified information that could be used for many purposes with a very small risk of privacy violation." On the other hand, how much small is very small? Implying that 99.9% of the patients in a given hospital are diabetics certainly exposes private information even if the group is very large. Most techniques above do not provide a statistical way of reasoning about the amount of disclosure inherent in the size of the groups.

A better approach is to work with the risk of reidentification. In Ref. [34], this issue is addressed by bounding the probability of a given person being in a private dataset so that risk of identification can be controlled. Diabetes dataset example is used to demonstrate how to bound probability of disclosure in ways that correspond to real risk of misuse.

Let I_p be the event that person p has diabetes. Since the rate of diabetes in all U.S. population is public information [37], any adversary will have a prior belief b_r on I_p given the public dataset P:

$$b_r = \mathscr{P}(I_p) = 0.07$$

The private dataset T is a subset of the set of all diabetes patients in P. Seeing some anonymization T^* of T, attacker will have a posterior belief b_o on I_p:

$$b_o = \mathscr{P}(I_p \mid T^*)$$
$$= \mathscr{P}(I_p \mid p \in T) \cdot \mathscr{P}(p \in T \mid T^*) + \mathscr{P}(I_p \mid p \notin T) \cdot \mathscr{P}(p \notin T \mid T^*)$$
$$= 1 \cdot \mathscr{P}(p \in T \mid T^*) + \frac{\mathscr{P}(I_p) \cdot |P| - |T|}{|P| - |T|} \cdot [1 - \mathscr{P}(p \in T \mid T^*)]$$
$$= \mathscr{P}(p \in T \mid T^*) \cdot \frac{|P| \cdot (1 - b_r)}{|P| - |T|} + \frac{b_r \cdot |P| - |T|}{|P| - |T|}$$

We start with an acceptable cost due to misuse. Assume a hiring decision, and that a \$100 annual difference in total cost of employee is noise (difference in productivity, taking an extra sick day, salary negotiation, etc.) Thus, if expected annual cost of medical treatment of diabetes based on misuse of the database is $c < \$100$, the risk of misuse is acceptably small. The total cost of diabetes per person is around $d = \$10,000$ [38]. The probabilistic acceptable misuse, m, is then $\frac{c}{d} = \frac{1}{100}$; we must ensure

$$b_o \cdot d - b_r \cdot d \leq c$$
$$b_o - b_r \leq m$$
$$\mathscr{P}(p \in T \mid T^*) \cdot \frac{(1 - b_r)|P|}{|P| - |T|} + \frac{b_r |P| - |T|}{|P| - |T|} - b_r \leq m$$
$$\mathscr{P}(p \in T \mid T^*) \leq \frac{m|P| + (1 - m - b_r)|T|}{(1 - b_r)|P|}$$

Letting $|T| \simeq 0.04|P|$ as in our experiments and applying the above numbers, we get

$$\mathscr{P}(p \in T \mid T^*) \lesssim 0.05$$

This gives us the minimum δ_{max} parameter to protect against substantial misuse when hiring a single job applicant. However, the upper bound does not protect against misuse when comparing two job applicant, p_1 and p_2. The reason is that in this setting, an anonymization that gives $b_o = 0.032$ for p_1 (this happens when $\mathscr{P}(p_1 \in T \mid T^*) \simeq 0$) and $b_o = b_r = 0.07$ for p_2 is perfectly okay, which implies p_2 is much more likely to have diabetes than p_1. We need to ensure that the company cannot cherry-pick employees known not to be in the database. As a result, the posterior belief should not be arbitrarily low. If we let probabilistic acceptable misuse $m = \frac{200}{10,000} = 0.02$, then

$$b_r - b_o \leq m$$
$$\mathscr{P}(p \in T \mid T^*) \geq \frac{-m|P| + (1 + m - b_r)|T|}{(1 - b_r)|P|}$$
$$\gtrsim 0.02$$

This gives us a maximum δ_{min} parameter.

Still the risk of identification is not well studied in the literature. It is certain that the risk is very dependent on the prior knowledge of adversaries and may be different for each individual in the data. For example, risk of identification is different for a young and old person when we identify the person as being a diabetic with 21% probability. The reason is that the probability of being a diabetic is publicly known to be 9.6% for a young person. This probability increases to 20.9% for an old person [37]. A second issue is to evaluate the cost of disclosure on an individual basis. The real cost (in terms of factors like economics, sociology, etc.) of being identified or in other words, the risk from identification should be studied. Finally, the trade-off between the risk and benefit (e.g., from any data mining operation on de-identified data) should be taken into consideration.

18.5   Quantification of PPDM Techniques

To better understand privacy-preserving data mining technology, we need a comprehensive view on how to evaluate effectiveness of the methodology. Unfortunately, there does not exist a single metric that can be used universally. Nevertheless, a few common metrics and criteria have been identified to evaluate the effectiveness of PPDM techniques [39]. In general, the main goals a PPDM algorithm should enforce are the following:

- Preventing the discovery of sensitive information

- Being resistant to the various data mining techniques

- Not compromising the access and the use of nonsensitive data

- Not having an exponential computational complexity

From these goals, the following set of criteria has been identified, and a PPDM algorithm can be evaluated based on these criteria: (1) Privacy level, (2) Hiding failure, (3) Data quality, and (4) Complexity.

18.5.1   Privacy Level

It indicates how closely the sensitive information, that has been hidden, can still be estimated. It takes into account two aspects: sensitive or private information that can be contained in the original dataset and private information that can be discovered from the data mining results. The first one is referred as data privacy and the latter is referred as result privacy. The quantification used to measure data privacy is generally the degree of uncertainty, according to which original private data can be inferred. The higher the degree of uncertainty is, the better the data privacy is protected by the PPDM algorithm. For various types of PPDM algorithms, the degree of uncertainty is estimated in different ways.

18.5.2 Hiding Failure

The percentage of sensitive information still discoverable after the data has been sanitized gives an estimate of the hiding failure parameter. Most of the developed privacy-preserving algorithms are designed with the goal of obtaining zero hiding failure. Thus, they hide all the sensitive patterns. However, it is well known that the more sensitive information we hide, the more nonsensitive information we miss. Thus, some PPDM algorithms have been recently developed that allow one to choose the amount of sensitive data that should be hidden in order to find a balance between privacy and knowledge discovery.

18.5.3 Data Quality

Many PPDM algorithms modify the database through insertion of false information or through the blocking of data values in order to hide sensitive information. Such perturbation techniques cause a decrease in data quality. It is obvious that the more the changes are made to the database, the less the database reflects the domain of interest. Therefore, data-quality metrics are very important in the evaluation of PPDM techniques. Since the data is often sold for making profit, or shared with others in the hope of leading to innovation, data quality should have an acceptable level according to the intended data usage. Data quality can be classified into the quality of the data resulted from PPDM process and the quality of the data mining results. In existing works, several data-quality metrics have been proposed that are either generic or data-use-specific. However, currently, there is no metric that is widely accepted by the research community.

18.5.4 Complexity

It measures the efficiency and scalability of a PPDM algorithm. Efficiency indicates whether the algorithm can be executed with good performance, generally assessed in terms of space and time. Space requirements are assessed according to the amount of memory that must be allocated in order to implement the given algorithm. Scalability describes the efficiency trends when data sizes increase. Such parameter concerns the increase of both performance and storage requirements as well as the costs of the communications required by a distributed technique with the increase of data sizes.

Although these measures provide insights into the effectiveness of PPDM technology, they are still difficult to interpret for common users. What we need is a graphic tool visualizing these measures, their differences, and trade-offs.

18.6 Complex Data

In recent times, more complex types of data are getting attention due to privacy concerns. Increased online activities give rise to more private data snippets being made available online. These small set of data are not harmful, but a collection of such data over time invariably build up into sensitive private information. A classic example is the query-oriented Web search, where users issue text queries to a search engine. It has been recently proven that from a log of Web queries, an adversary could identify the individual who issued the queries. The AOL query log release incident [40] is an example of how a set of collected queries could affect individual privacy. By performing simple analysis on the (supposedly) anonymized AOL data, a *New York Times* reporter was able to identify the owner of a set of queries [41]. This incident has also contributed to increased attention to the subject of privacy in complex data. Though it is rather hard to define what is private and what is public in such data, it is important to be aware of the privacy issues of complex data.

In Ref. [42], it is shown that token-based hashing technique to anonymize a query log is ineffective against statistical matching attacks. Recently, two solutions [43] have been proposed for anonymizing query log. In the first solution based on secret sharing, the query is replaced with the one of t secret shares. To reconstruct the query at least t shares are required, and thus a constraint is enforced that at least t users should have issued the query in order for it to be known. The second solution involves constructing query groups based on the topics of queries. The actual user id is replaced with a different random id for each of these sets of queries. The idea is not to reveal a whole variety of interests of a particular user, thus making the reidentification difficult.

There are more types of complex data coming out of social networks, personalization of services, and location-based services. Graph mining can be used to find the patterns, and also could reveal private and sensitive relationships from a social networks data. Recent works [44–46] have proposed techniques for anonymizing social networks data in order to hide sensitive relationships. In personalization of services, users often use various services such as e-mail, Web search, maps, weather forecast, etc. of a particular provider. Therefore, the data collected is often in the form of a multirelational table. A technique presented in Ref. [47] could be used in such cases where private data are stored in many related tables. Users of location-based services leave traces of information that could be combined over time to create user profiles, and thus poses serious privacy concerns. One type of solutions make an assumption that there is a trusted server that modifies the user requests to provide anonymity [48,49]. The second type of solutions [50–52] anonymize the data after the collection. More research is needed in this direction to find efficient techniques for de-identification of complex data.

In addition to the open issue of understanding when data is individually identifiable (and thus subject to privacy laws), recognizing that the goal of privacy is to protect individually identifiable data (and not necessarily anything more) could open the door for more efficient privacy-preserving data mining techniques. For instance, combining k-anonymity and homomorphic encryption could lead to more efficient solutions than currently envisioned by secure multiparty computation-based techniques.

18.7 Conclusions

Privacy-preserving data mining still has room to grow, but needs to become focused to have impact. As the privacy debate is growing more reasoned, the need for privacy is becoming more clear and succinct. Researchers must look to the privacy debate to ensure that privacy-preserving data mining research meets real privacy needs. This is both a challenge and an opportunity; while much has been done, the new problems that are arising are even greater.

Though designing efficient PPDM schemes is the main goal, clear understanding of the results from the mining process is required. Researchers must be familiar with the individually identifying information and be aware of the risk of identification. Overall, the key factors that need to be considered in privacy-preserving data mining research are listed below:

1. *Privacy level*: How well can an adversary estimate private information about an individual? Definitions are needed; cryptographic-style definitions give an all-or-nothing result that would prevent any use of data (due to the inherent knowledge contained in results.) Unfortunately, the many definitions in place do not adequately capture the risk from disclosing private information; this is an open research topic.

2. *Hiding failure*: Is disclosure possible in some situations? For example, given an adversary with sufficient background knowledge, can we accept disclosure (e.g., knowing your own information, you can discern yourself)? Is it okay to say "95% of individuals do not have their information disclosed?" (Many attempts at quantitative privacy definitions implicitly allow such disclosure.)

3. *Quality*: How are results impacted by privacy-preserving data mining? Are the results comparable to what we would expect without working about privacy?

4. *Complexity*: Is the use of privacy-preserving techniques feasible, or is the cost prohibitive? One must keep an entire system in mind—if the time/cost for running a data mining algorithm goes up by several orders of magnitude, but the time to acquire data is cut in half because of the privacy-sensitive approach, the overall time to obtain results may still be reduced.

The first generation of privacy-preserving data mining has generated techniques and solutions, but in the process has opened up more research challenges than were foreseen when the field began. The next generation of privacy-preserving data mining research will need to keep all of these challenges in mind to ensure that research leads to real-world impact.

References

[1] D. Agrawal and C. C. Aggarwal. On the design and quantification of privacy preserving data mining algorithms. In *Proceedings of the 20th ACM SIGACT-SIGMOD-SIGART Symposium on Principles of Database Systems*, pp. 247–255, Santa Barbara, CA, May 21–23, 2001. ACM.

[2] R. Agrawal and R. Srikant. Privacy-preserving data mining. In *Proceedings of the 2000 ACM SIGMOD Conference on Management of Data*, pp. 439–450, Dallas, TX, May 14–19, 2000. ACM.

[3] M. Kantarcioğlu and C. Clifton. Privacy-preserving distributed mining of association rules on horizontally partitioned data. In *The ACM SIGMOD Workshop on Research Issues on Data Mining and Knowledge Discovery (DMKD'02)*, pp. 24–31, Madison, WI, June 2, 2002.

[4] Y. Lindell and B. Pinkas. Privacy preserving data mining. In *Advances in Cryptology—CRYPTO 2000*, pp. 36–54, August 20–24, 2000. Springer-Verlag, Santa Barbara, CA.

[5] S. J. Rizvi and J. R. Haritsa. Maintaining data privacy in association rule mining. In *Proceedings of 28th International Conference on Very Large Data Bases*, pp. 682–693, Hong Kong, China, August 20–23, 2002. VLDB.

[6] J. Vaidya and C. Clifton. Privacy preserving association rule mining in vertically partitioned data. In *8th ACM SIGKDD International Conference on Knowledge Discovery and Data Mining*, pp. 639–644, Edmonton, AB, Canada, July 23–26, 2002.

[7] K. Muralidhar, R. Sarathy, and R. A. Parsa. An improved security requirement for data perturbation with implications for e-commerce. *Decision Science*, 32(4): 683–698, Fall 2001.

[8] A. Eisenberg. With false numbers, data crunchers try to mine the truth. *New York Times*, July 18, 2002.

[9] S. Lohr. Online industry seizes the initiative on privacy. *The New York Times on the Web*, October 11, 1999.

[10] B. Simons and E. H. Spafford. Letter from the USACM to the Senate Committee on Armed Services, January 23, 2003.

[11] W. Kim, R. Agrawal, C. Faloutsos, U. Fayyad, J. Han, G. Piatetsky-Shaprio, D. Pregibon, and R. Uthurasamy. "Data mining" is not against civil liberties. Open Letter from the Directors of the Executive Committee of ACM SIGKDD, July 28, 2003.

[12] R. Feingold, J. Corzine, R. Wyden, and B. Nelson. Data Mining Moratorium Act of 2003. U.S. Senate Bill (proposed), January 16, 2003.

[13] R. Feingold, J. Sununu, P. Leahy, D. Akaka, E. Kennedy, B. Cardin, D. Feinstein, and S. Whitehouse. Federal Agency Data Mining Reporting Act of 2007. U.S. Senate Bill (introduced), January 10, 2007. Incorporated as Sec. 804 of H.R. 1, signed into public law 110–153 August 3.

[14] J. M. Perry. Statement of John M. Perry, President and CEO, CardSystems Solutions, Inc. before the United States house of representatives subcommittee on oversight and investigations of the committee on financial services. Available at http://financialservices.house.gov/media/pdf/072105jmp.pdf, July 21, 2005.

[15] J. Vaidya, C. Clifton, and M. Zhu. *Privacy Preserving Data Mining*, Volume 19 of *Advances in Information Security*. Springer, New York, 2006.

[16] H. Kargupta, S. Datta, Q. Wang, and K. Sivakumar. Random data perturbation techniques and privacy preserving data mining. *Knowledge and Information Systems*, 7(4): 387–414, May 2004.

[17] K. Liu, H. Kargupta, and J. Ryan. Random projection-based multiplicative data perturbation for privacy preserving distributed data mining. *IEEE Transactions on Knowledge and Data Engineering*, 18(1): 92–106, January 2006.

[18] W. Jiang, C. Clifton, and M. Kantarcioglu. Transforming semi-honest protocols to ensure accountability. *Data and Knowledge Engineering*, 65(1): 57–74, Elsevier Science, Amsterdam, The Netherlands, April 2008.

[19] Y. Shoham and M. Tennenholtz. Non-cooperative computation: Boolean functions with correctness and exclusivity. *Theoretical Computer Science*, 343 (1–2): 97–113, 2005.

[20] A. Kobsa. Privacy-enhanced personalization. *Communications of the ACM*, 50: 24–33, August 2007.

[21] M. J. Atallah, H. G. Elmongui, V. Deshpande, and L. B. Schwarz. Secure supply-chain protocols. In *IEEE International Conference on E-Commerce*, pp. 293–302, Newport Beach, CA June 24–27, 2003.

[22] C. Clifton, A. Iyer, R. Cho, W. Jiang, M. Kantarcioğlu, and J. Vaidya. An approach to identifying beneficial collaboration securely in decentralized logistics systems. *Management and Service Operations Management*, 10(1): 108–125, 2008.

[23] V. N. Vapnik. *Estimation of Dependences Based on Empirical Data*. Springer-Verlag, New York, 1982.

[24] M. Atzori, F. Bonchi, F. Giannotti, and D. Pedreschi. k-anonymous patterns. In *PKDD*, pp. 10–21, Porto, Portugal, October 3–7, 2005.

[25] M. Atzori, F. Bonchi, F. Giannotti, and D. Pedreschi. Blocking anonymity threats raised by frequent itemset mining. In *ICDM '05: Proceedings of the 5th IEEE International Conference on Data Mining*, pp. 561–564, Washington DC, 2005. IEEE Computer Society.

[26] C. Clifton. Using sample size to limit exposure to data mining. *Journal of Computer Security*, 8(4): 281–307, November 2000.

[27] Directive 95/46/EC of the European Parliament and of the Council of 24 October 1995 on the protection of individuals with regard to the processing of personal data and on the free movement of such data. *Official Journal of the European Communities*, I (281): 31–50, October 24, 1995.

[28] Standard for privacy of individually identifiable health information. *Federal Register*, 67(157): 53181–53273, August 14, 2002.

[29] L. Sweeney. k-anonymity: A model for protecting privacy. *International Journal on Uncertainty, Fuzziness and Knowledge-based Systems*, 10(5): 557–570, 2002.

[30] P. Samarati. Protecting respondent's privacy in microdata release. 13(6): 1010–1027, *IEEE Transactions on Knowledge and Data Engineering*, November/December 2001.

[31] A. Machanavajjhala, J. Gehrke, D. Kifer, and M. Venkitasubramaniam. *l*-diversity: Privacy beyond *k*-anonymity. In *Proceedings of the 22nd IEEE International Conference on Data Engineering (ICDE 2006)*, pp. 23–34, Atlanta, GA, April 2006.

[32] N. Li and T. Li. t-closeness: Privacy beyond k-anonymity and l-diversity. In *Proceedings of the 23rd International Conference on Data Engineering (ICDE '07)*, Istanbul, Turkey, April 16–20, 2007.

[33] X. Xiao and Y. Tao. Anatomy: Simple and effective privacy preservation. In *Proceedings of 32nd International Conference on Very Large Data Bases (VLDB 2006)*, pp. 139–150, Seoul, Korea, September 12–15, 2006.

[34] M. Nergiz, M. Atzori, and C. Clifton. Hiding the presence of individuals from shared databases. In *Proceedings of the 2007 ACM SIGMOD International Conference on Management of Data*, pp. 665–676, Beijing, China, June 11–14, 2007.

[35] D. J. Martin, D. Kifer, A. Machanavajjhala, J. Gehrke, and J. Y. Halpern. Worst-case background knowledge for privacy-preserving data publishing. In *Proceedings of the 23rd International Conference on Data Engineering (ICDE '07)*, pp. 126–135, Istanbul, Turkey, April 16–20, 2007.

[36] B.-C. Chen, K. LeFevre, and R. Ramakrishnan. Privacy skyline: Privacy with multidimensional adversarial knowledge. In *VLDB '07: Proceedings of the 33rd International Conference on Very Large Data Bases*, pp. 770–781, Vienna, Austria, September 23–28, 2007. VLDB Endowment.

[37] National Institute of Diabetes and Digestive and Kidney Diseases. National diabetes statistics fact sheet: General information and national estimates on diabetes in the United States. Technical Report NIH Publication No. 06–3892, U.S. Department of Health and Human Services, National Institute of Health, Bethesda, MD, November 2005.

[38] American Diabetes Association. Direct and indirect costs of diabetes in the United States. Available at http://www.diabetes.org/diabetes-statistics/cost-of-diabetes-in-us.jsp, 2006.

[39] E. Bertino, D. Lin, and W. Jiang. A survey of quantification of privacy preserving data mining algorithms. In C. C. Aggarwal and P. S. Yu (Eds.), *Privacy-Preserving Data Mining (Models and Algorithms)*. Springer-Verlag, New York, 2008.

[40] AOL search data release reveals a great deal, August 2006.

[41] M. Barbaro and T. Zeller, Jr. A face is exposed for AOL searcher No. 4417749, *New York Times*, August 9, 2006.

[42] R. Kumar, J. Novak, B. Pang, and A. Tomkins. On anonymizing query logs via token-based hashing. In *WWW*, pp. 629–638, Alberta, Canada, 2007.

[43] E. Adar. User 4xxxxx9: Anonymizing query logs. In *Query Log Workshop, WWW*, Alberta, Canada, 2007.

[44] L. Backstrom, C. Dwork, and J. Kleinberg. Wherefore art thou r3579x?: Anonymized social networks, hidden patterns, and structural steganography. In *WWW '07: Proceedings of the 16th International Conference on World Wide Web*, pp. 181–190, New York, 2007. ACM.

[45] M. Hay, G. Miklau, D. Jensen, P. Weis, and S. Srivastava. Anonymizing social networks, University of Massachusets Amherst, Technical report 07–19, 2007.

[46] E. Zheleva and L. Getoor. Preserving the privacy of sensitive relationships in graph data. In *Proceedings of the 1st International Workshop on Privacy, Security, and Trust in KDD (PinKDD'07)*, 4890:153–171, San Jose, CA, August 2007.

[47] M. E. Nergiz, C. Clifton, and A. E. Nergiz. Multirelational k-anonymity. In *Proceedings of the 23rd IEEE International Conference on Data Engineering (ICDE 2007)*, pp. 1417-1421, Istanbul, Turkey, April 16–20, 2007.

[48] C. Bettini, X. S. Wang, and S. Jajodia. Protecting privacy against location-based personal identification. In *Secure Data Management*, pp. 185–199, Trondleim, Norway, 2005.

[49] M. Gruteser and D. Grunwald. Anonymous usage of location-based services through spatial and temporal cloaking. In *Proceedings of the 1st International Conference on Mobile Systems, Applications, and Services*, pp. 31–42, San Francisco, CA, 2003.

[50] F. Bonchi, O. Abul, and M. Nanni. Never walk alone: Uncertainty for anonymity in moving objects databases. In *Proceedings of the 24th International Conference on Data Engineering (ICDE '08)*, pp. 376–385, Cancun, Mexico, April 7, 2008.

[51] M. E. Nergiz, M. Atzori, and Y. Saygin. Perturbation-driven anonymization of trajectories. Technical Report cnr.isti/2007-TR-017, Italian National Research Council (ISTI-CNR), Pisa, Italy, 2007.

[52] F. Bonchi, O. Abul, M. Atzori, and F. Giannotti. Hiding sensitive trajectory patterns. In *6th International Workshop on Privacy Aspects of Data Mining, ICDM'07 Workshops*, pp. 693–698, Omaha, NE, October 2007.

Chapter 19

Analysis of Social Networks and Group Dynamics from Electronic Communication

Nishith Pathak, Sandeep Mane, Jaideep Srivastava, Noshir Contractor,
Scott Poole, and Dmitri Williams

Contents

19.1 Introduction

The field of social network analysis evolved from the need to understand social relationships and interactions among a group of individuals. In the past few years, social network analysis has gained significant prominence due to its use in different applications, from product marketing (e.g., viral marketing) and organizational dynamics (e.g., management) [1,2]. Classical research in social network analysis relied on data collected from individuals via surveys, interviews, and other manual observation methods. In addition to small sample sizes, these data have inherent problems of accuracy and bias. With the widespread use of computer networks (including the Internet), gigabytes of data about electronic communication between individuals are now being collected and are available in large data warehouses, for example, Yahoo, Orkut, MySpace, FaceBook, etc. Collected as operational logs, such data sets provide an unbiased view of social relationships between individuals. This provides an unprecedented opportunity to study large social networks as well as a need to develop new scalable, computational models for analyzing these data. Computer science researchers are now showing an increasing interest in social network analysis and significant effort is being made toward this research. This is demonstrated by the attention to analysis of such data sets, for example, the Enron e-mail data set [3–5].

Statistical models have been the primary tool for the analysis of social network data till now [6]. However, the data sets being collected from online sources have certain characteristics that necessitate developing new analysis techniques. First, the data tend to have high dimensionality. Second, the data are in several forms, including text, hypertext, image, video, and Web clicks. Third, the data have strong temporal characteristics, with the set of variables collected changing often over time. Finally, the data tend to have large volume and be sparse. Based on these characteristics, there is a need to develop scalable techniques for the exploratory analysis of sparse, high-dimensional, and high-volume data sets.

Over the past few years, there has been an increase in interest on research in social network analysis within the data mining community. The basic motivation is the demand to exploit knowledge from copious amounts of data collected pertaining to social behavior of users in online environments. Data mining-based techniques are proving to be useful for analysis of social network data, especially for large data sets that cannot be handled by traditional methods. This chapter discusses two novel problems from social network analysis: (1) cognitive analysis of social networks and (2) analysis of group dynamics, from electronic communication and massively multiplayer game data, respectively.

Cognitive analysis of social networks has evolved from the interest in understanding what an individual's perceptions are about other individuals in terms of who knows who (sociocognitive network) or what knowledge they have (knowledge network). The widespread adoption of computer networks in organizations and the use of electronic communication for business processes have fostered a new age in social network analysis. E-mail communication, for example, is widely used by employees to exchange information. An e-mail server observes all e-mail communication between individuals in the organization. By tapping into such observed communication an analysis of the complete e-mail logs of the organization can be made to determine the perceived social network for each individual, as well as the gold standard (or ground truth) social network.

In the first part of this chapter, the problem of sociocognitive analysis of a social network is presented. This is described using an e-mail communication network, followed by our proposed analysis approach. The results from applying the proposed approach on the Enron e-mail logs are described. The Enron e-mail data set consists of logs of e-mail communication between the employees of Enron before and after the Enron crisis of 2001.

The second part of the chapter describes the problem of modeling and analysis of group dynamics in a social network. Data logs from a multiplayer network-based game, Sony EverQuest2 (EQ2), are being used in our present research on group dynamics. A brief overview of this problem is described and research directions are explained.

19.2 Analysis of Cognitive Networks

19.2.1 What Are Cognitive Networks?

A social network is described as a group of "actors" (or individuals) interacting with each other. Actors' cognitions make up an important component of any social environment and have a profound impact on the social network structure as well as actions of actors in the network. Cognitive networks refer to a representation of actors' social interactions as well as their cognitions that affect and/or are affected by these interactions. Here, the notion of "cognition affecting social interactions" is used in a broad sense and can refer to a variety of things. For example, in studying a group of people in a book reading club, the set of cognitions related to their social links can be preferred genre, preferred authors, or objective of joining the book club (i.e., satisfying a casual hobby, researching a particular author, etc.) for each actor in the social network. The main point is for each actor the factors listed above affect or are affected by the social links. The list is by no means exhaustive and depends on the social network as well as the objective of studying a particular social network. Research involving cognitive networks examines the complex relationship between actors' cognition and the social structure.

19.2.2 Value of Understanding Cognitive Networks

Cognitive networks are usually studied in the fields of sociopsychology, organizational dynamics, and consumer research [7,8]. Cognitive networks are an important component of group behavior analysis, and are particularly useful for the analysis of group consensus development or group decision making [9]. Such research has profound impact in developing techniques for predicting group behavior as well as analyzing the stability of a social group. The focus of this work is in the domain of organizational dynamics, where individual perceptions regarding other actors' social influence play an important part in determining the "health" of a group. For example, it helps identify individuals who command respect among their peers as well as different factions within an organization. In other words, it enables mapping of the perceived "informal hierarchy" in a group, identifying actors perceived to be leaders, handymen, experts, etc. Note that these roles are not formally assigned or might not actually be correct for the actor, since they arise due to the perceptions of fellow actors [2]. Such information will be invaluable for managers as it allows them to build a consensus regarding the roles of individuals within a group. Such consensus enables smooth functioning of the group, as disagreement may lead to formation of factions, dissidents, or general negative sentiments within the group. For example, it may be necessary to build consensus within a group regarding the leadership skills of a certain actor if another less suitable actor is perceived to be a better leader or if possible, have a system where the more qualified person is a mentor for the actor who commands respect among individuals, thus leveraging both their capabilities. Such research can also be used to identify trends regarding upcoming leaderships in a group, people changing factions, etc.

19.2.3 Sociocognitive and Knowledge Networks

There are two special cases of cognitive networks that are of particular interest. The first is, how each actor in a social network perceives the social connections of other actors in the network. For example, knowing all employees in an organization is difficult for any individual due to his/her limited interactions with others, also called the individual's social bandwidth. Thus, in an organization's social network, not everyone directly knows (or interacts) with everyone else [10]. Nor does an individual observe all the communication between individuals known (or unknown) to him directly [11]. The result is that each individual forms perceptions about communication between other individuals, and uses them in their daily tasks. Having correct perceptions for all individuals in the organization would be of invaluable use for the proper functioning of business processes. Such a set of actors each with his perceptions regarding communication between others is called a sociocognitive network (or informally a "who knows, who knows who" network) [12].

The second, referred to as a knowledge network, is about how much and/or what each actor knows about certain topics of interest. By topics of interest we generally mean those concepts that are responsible for the sustenance or existence of the social network. For example, in a book reading club, the topics of interest can be various topics relating to books such as how much each actor knows about the works of author xyz. This is a potential indicator of the level of interest people have in author xyz and it is quite possible that people with higher levels of interest tend to interact among each other or a new person joining such a group will show a rise in his knowledge of author XYZs works. For social networks in organizations, the topics of interest can be about the functioning, goals, or public image. For example, what does each employee in an organization know about the public image of the organization? Actors exposed to positive reviews/articles will develop a perception that the company image is quite good. Such a perception may or may not be actually true, that is, if the company image is actually bad then these actors do not "know" much about the company image. On the other hand, if the company image is positive then these actors are closer to the ground truth. These networks are informally referred to as "who knows what" networks [12,13].

Studies of sociocognitive and knowledge networks look at the perceptions of each actor, how many of them actually know things (i.e., closeness to the ground truth, perceptual realism), and how many of them agree with each other (perceptual congruence).

19.3 Analysis on the Enron E-Mail Corpus

In this section, we briefly introduce our sociocognitive as well as knowledge network modeling and analyses approaches, and use them on the Enron e-mail corpus (see Ref. [14] for further details on both the approaches).

19.3.1 Sociocognitive Network Modeling and Analysis Using the Enron E-Mail Corpus

For sociocognitive networks the modeling phase is a two-stage process. The first stage consists of developing a simplistic model that assumes independence between individual actors' observations. The purpose of this model is twofold. First, it enables us to examine certain basic issues such as data sparseness and dynamic nature of the cognitive states as well as allowing us to define distance measures for the same. Second, it serves as a baseline model, to which we can compare further more enhanced and complex models. In such a model, each observed instance of communication is treated as a Bernoulli trial and every actor estimates a Bernoulli parameter for some actor communicating with another actor. The Bernoulli parameters are themselves dynamic and a time window scheme is used to handle the same. Bayesian update is used to integrate the information gained in one time window with the history of observations. An actor updates his perceptions based only on the e-mails he receives and sends. A fictitious actor that observes every e-mail exchanged in the social network (similar to say an e-mail server) is used as a reference for ground truth. KL-divergence-based measures are used for defining a similarity measure between two actors' perceptions. The analysis phase consists of using the similarity measure to identify groups of actors who agree with each other (i.e., have similar perceptions) as well as actors close to the ground truth (i.e., those that actually know the social network around them).

The sociocognitive network for Enron was modeled using the Enron e-mail corpus and analysis results of the sociocognitive network immediately after the Enron crisis was compared with the same for the previous year (i.e., a time point during normal functioning of the organization).

We construct a graph, called "agreement graph," where nodes represent actors and an edge exists between two nodes if the similarity between their perceptions is lower than a user-defined threshold (see Ref. [14] for complete details on experimental settings). Figure 19.1 shows the agreement graph for October, 2000. It is observed that the graph consists of many small, disjoint components of users. This is because big organizations like Enron usually have many organizational groups with high intragroup and low intergroup communication. Figure 19.2 shows the agreement graph for October 2001, which mainly consists of one large, connected component. This indicates that there is a considerable extent of overlap in social perceptions during the crisis period. The connectivity of the October 2001 agreement graph also indicates that communication (and hence information) is shared among various actors. Such a network is highly conducive toward dissemination of ideas in a social network. In case of Enron, the crisis and related subjects were "hot topics" often discussed in the underlying social network. Note that the number of nodes in the October 2001

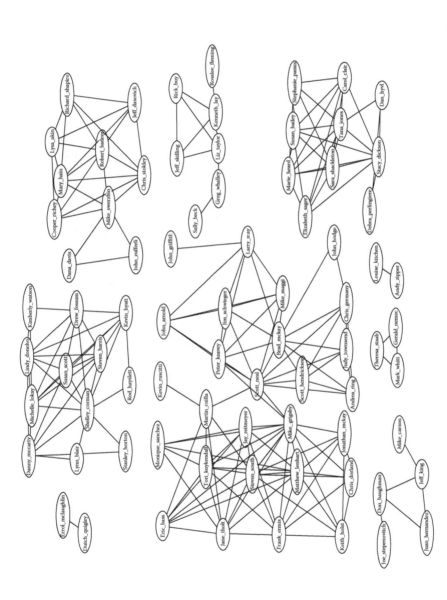

FIGURE 19.1: Agreement graph for October 2000. (From Pathak, N., Mane, S., and Srivastava, J., *Int. J. Seman. Comput.*, 1, 87, 2007.)

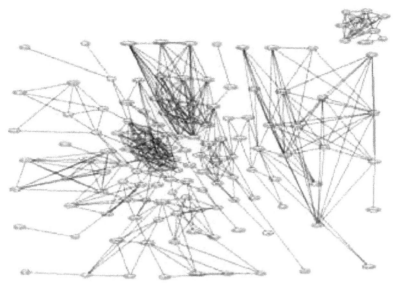

FIGURE 19.2: Agreement graph for October 2001. (From Pathak, N., Mane, S., and Srivastava, J., *Int. J. Seman. Comput.*, 1, 87, 2007.)

graph is much more than that of the October 2000 graph. This is because an actor is included in the agreement graph only if his perceptions have similarity greater than the threshold with at least one other actor.

For analyzing actors' perceptions closeness to reality we simply take the similarity measure between the actors' perceptions and ground truth (a measure which we call r-closeness) and rank the actors in decreasing order of r-closeness. For October 2000, the actors can be roughly divided into three categories. The first category consists of actors who are communicatively active and observe a lot of diverse communications. These actors occupy the top positions in the rankings. These are followed by the second category actors who also observe a lot of communication; however, their observations are skewed which in turn leads to skewed perceptions. The third category consists of actors who are communicatively inactive and hardly observe any of the communication. These actors have low r-closeness values and are at the bottom of the rankings table. Table 19.1 summarizes the percentages of various actors (according to their formal positions) in the different ranges of r-closeness rankings. Using the rankings for October 2000, two sociocognitive network hypotheses of interest to sociologists are studied.

H1. The higher an actor is in the organizational hierarchy, the better his/her perception is of the social network.

From the r-closeness rankings, it is observed that the majority of the top positions are not occupied by higher level executive employees. The top 50 ranks consist of a large chunk of the employee population (around 46.4% of the employees) along with

TABLE 19.1: Users in different rank ranges of r-closeness
(October 2000, $\lambda = 0.5$).

Ranks	N/A (%)	Employee Emp. (%)	Higher Mgmt. (%)	Exec. Mgmt. (%)	Others (%)
1–10	10.3 (4)	4.9 (2)	7.1 (2)	3.4 (1)	7.1 (1)
11–50	17.9 (7)	41.5 (17)	14.3 (4)	31.0 (9)	21.4 (3)
51–151	71.8 (28)	53.6 (22)	78.6 (22)	65.6 (19)	71.5 (10)

Source: From Pathak, N., Mane, S., and Srivastava, J., *Int. J. Seman. Comput.*, 1, 87, 2007.

21.4% of the higher management and 34.4% of the executive management actors (see Table 19.1). A related observation is that most of the higher level executives are communicatively inactive and therefore have fewer perceptions.

H2. The more communication an actor observes, the better will be his/her perception regarding the social network.

It is observed that even though some actors observe a lot of communication, they are still ranked low in terms of r-closeness. The main reason for this is that actors tend to participate only in certain communications and participate less in others. This results in perceptions about the social network that are skewed toward those "favored" communications. Executive management actors who observed a lot of communication showed a tendency for this "skewed perception" behavior.

Table 19.2 summarizes statistics for r-closeness rankings for the month of October 2001. The rankings for the crisis month October 2001 are significantly different from those of October 2000. It was observed that the percentage of management staff among the top 50 ranks increased significantly at the cost of employees being pushed down. Thus, a shift from the normal behavior is observed, indicating that communication perceived by most management level actors is more diverse and evenly distributed as compared to the skewed or no perceptions in October 2000. A possible reason for this may be that during the crisis month, e-mails were exchanged across different levels of formal hierarchy in the organization thus exposing management

TABLE 19.2: Users in different rank ranges of r-closeness
(October 2001, $\lambda = 0.5$).

Ranks	N/A (%)	Employee Emp. (%)	Higher Mgmt. (%)	Exec. Mgmt. (%)	Others (%)
1–10	5.1 (2)	2.5 (1)	3.6 (1)	20.7 (6)	0 (0)
11–50	23.1 (9)	26.8 (11)	28.6 (8)	37.9 (11)	7.1 (1)
51–151	71.8 (28)	70.7 (29)	67.8 (19)	41.4 (12)	92.9 (13)

Source: From Pathak, N., Mane, S., and Srivastava, J., *Int. J. Seman. Comput.*, 1, 87, 2007.

level actors to more diverse communication [4]. Another intuitively appealing reason [4] is that during October 2000, on an average, management people "sent" about 80% and received only 20% of the total communication they were exposed to. In October 2001, there was a reversal and management people sent only 20% and received about 80% of their total communication. Since they observed a lot more communication during the later period, there was a significant increase in the r-closeness ranks of management level actors during October 2001. Finally, management level actors were also lot more communicatively active in October 2001 than in October 2000 (i.e., the volume of communication in October 2001 was greater).

The research presented contributes toward (1) providing a simple, scalable computational for modeling sociocognitive networks for e-mail communication network, (2) proposing a measure to quantify similarities in individual actors' perceptions of social network in such a sociocognitive network and using it to construct agreement graphs between actors, (3) identifying a novel analysis, enabled by social networks on computer networks, for quantifying how well an actor's perceptions reflect reality and proposing a new measure for the same, and (4) illustrating the use of these techniques using a real-world Enron e-mail data.

19.3.2 Knowledge Network Modeling and Analysis Using the Enron E-Mail Corpus

For modeling knowledge networks we first require to solve certain text mining problems. Topic modeling techniques can be used to determine as well as identify occurrences of the topics of interest in the underlying social network [15,16] (or they can be already predefined by the user). Sentiment mining techniques need to be used to quantify the degree to which a given occurrence of a topic is evidence in favor of or against the communicating actors knowing something about that topic [17,18]. The different pieces of evidence can then be combined using Bayes theorem or Dempster–Shafer theory of evidence combination. The knowledge network is represented as a bipartite graph, with actors on one side and topics of interest on the other. The edges can carry labels as a representation of perception. In our modeling approach we chose to represent topics of interest in the form of propositional statements, that is, instead of an abstract topic like company image it is more convenient to use a propositional statement of the form "the company image is good." Such a representation is desirable as how much an actor "knows about a topic" or "what is actually true about a topic" are notions that are not well defined. The use of propositional statements removes this ambiguity as we now have well-defined statements that can only be true or false, and ground truth as well as perceptions can now be represented as probabilities of such statements being true or false. In the bipartite representation we will have actors and the propositional statements on either side of the graph and the edges from an actor to a statement can have the probability with which the actor believes the statement to be true as labels. Once again each actor's perceptions are determined using only the e-mails he/she receives and sends.

Due to lack of data, we modeled the Enron knowledge network for just one proposition statement, "The company image is good," and performed sentiment extraction manually. In modeling the Enron knowledge network we made use of the Dempster–Shafer theory, which is a generalization of the Bayesian probability theory. Apart from the update of actors' perceptions, the key difference is that instead of each edge carrying a label indicating the probability of a statement being true, the label will consist of a two-value tuple indicating the minimum and maximum probabilities (support and plausibility, respectively) of the statement being true. For our experiments we used the labeled data set made available by the Enron Email Analysis Project at the University of California, Berkeley (`http://bailando.sims.berkeley.edu/enron\_email.html`). The knowledge network at the end of years 2000 and 2001 was computed (see Ref. [14] for complete details on experimental settings).

Actors are plotted in the x–y plane with support s along the x-axis and the plausibility p along the y-axis (see Figure 19.3). The line $s = p$ represents points where there is no uncertainty regarding the probability of the verity, of the given knowledge proposition. As we move further above this line, the uncertainty in the belief increases (region of uncertainty). The region m near the origin, that is, points that have uncertainty less than some δ and with s value at most some λ, contains points that believe the proposition more likely to be false with low uncertainty. Similarly, the top-right-hand region n, consists of points that believe the proposition more likely to be true with low uncertainty. Since $s < p$ always, all points always lie above the line $s = p$.

During the year 2000, there were many events such as positive press articles, a highly positive article in *TIME* magazine and talk of the most innovative company of the year award, that sought to improve the company image, as well as certain events such as miscommunication within company resulting in bad press and bad press due to environmental and human rights violation in overseas ventures, that tarnished the company image. The plot for the year 2000 is shown in Figure 19.4. During the year 2001, the company image dropped mainly due to negative press generated during the

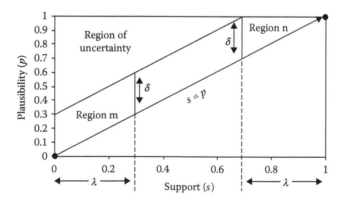

FIGURE 19.3:   Knowledge network as a scatter plot. (From Pathak, N., Mane, S., and Srivastava, J., *Int. J. Seman. Comput.*, 1, 87, 2007.)

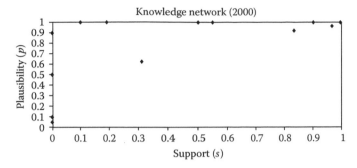

FIGURE 19.4: Knowledge network plot for the year 2000. (From Pathak, N., Mane, S., and Srivastava, J., *Int. J. Seman. Comput.*, 1, 87, 2007.)

California power crisis. However, things started improving when there was talk of a possible merger with a rival company, Dynergy. The plot for the year 2001 is shown in Figure 19.5. The interesting part about the result is the lack of consensus among users regarding the company image. Note the existence of a significant number of points in the regions n and m (see Figures 19.4 through 19.6) for both 2000 and 2001. The number of uncertain people is also quite significant. The fact that the points are pretty much spread out in both the graphs leads us to infer the existence of a lack of harmony among the users' perceptions regarding the company image, throughout both the years.

Thus, we provide a methodology for constructing and maintaining a knowledge network in an electronic communication environment. However, topic discovery and sentiment analysis plays an important role and is the current related research being investigated by us.

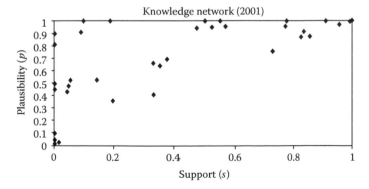

FIGURE 19.5: Knowledge network plot for the year 2001. (From Pathak, N., Mane, S., and Srivastava, J., *Int. J. Seman. Comput.*, 1, 87, 2007.)

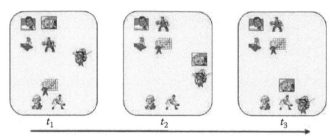

FIGURE 19.6:   Group evolution.

19.4   Group Dynamics: Motivation and Applications

This section describes the motivation to study the group dynamics in a large social network, and explains how analyzing the logs of Sony EQ2 massively multiplayer game will be useful for this purpose. The section closes with a discussion of salient data mining challenges in this research effort.

19.4.1   Group Dynamics

There is considerable evidence of the importance of groups that interact effectively for the global economy. The most important and complex decisions made by governments and organizations occur in group contexts. Consider the coverage of the group deliberations prior to the Bay of Pigs invasion or, more recently, the Challenger and Columbia shuttle tragedies. A central challenge, motivated by emerging developments in IT, is that the nature of groups and how they operate has changed radically. Spurred by globalization, virtual teams have become a staple in governments, businesses, and universities. Even before the recent IT revolution, Hollywood and the construction engineering industry provided early historical examples of the emergence of ad hoc groups that brought together people with different skills from their latent networks for a specific task over a finite time period. Today an increasing preponderance of groups in social, political, and economic contexts are ad hoc, agile, flexible, transient entities that emerge from a larger primordial latent network of relationships for a short duration to accomplish a wide variety of tasks and then dissolve only to be reconstituted with a somewhat different configuration at some later point in time. While there is growing awareness of the socioeconomic consequences of these groups, our understanding of the dynamics of the formation of these groups and their impact on group effectiveness is severely limited.

Example 19.1 Sony EverQuest2 Logs
EQ2 is one of the world's largest massively multiplayer online (MMO) games, developed by Sony Online Entertainment. MMOs comprise tens of thousands of players who are at any one point in time coalescing in thousands of groups to accomplish "quests" and "raids" that involve a wide variety of activities similar to tasks we

undertake in real life such as finding information or materials; making, selling, or buying products and services; and some that are less common such as "killing" other characters or plundering (http://everquest2.station.sony.com). The scale of such a research enterprise poses significant computational challenges in uncovering and analyzing the complexities that govern the dynamics of group behavior in these virtual worlds.

The analysis consists of a network approach to modeling the ecosystem of over-lapping and constantly changing groups that constitute the fabric of contemporary society. Empirically testing such a model using traditional data collection such as manual surveys, poses formidable challenges that have perhaps deterred scholars from embarking on such a theoretical excursion. However, the server logs are a unique resource for mining behavioral traces from the virtual world. Thus, this research aims at applying data mining techniques to analyze the logs of the game, EQ2, to better understand group formation and dynamics. Specific research questions to be addressed include:

- How do networks within the ecosystem of groups enable and constrain the formation of groups?

- How do microgroup processes influence group effectiveness and social identity?

This research promises to usher in a new generation of theorizing and research on the emergence and performance of groups in complex social settings that are unfet-tered by the constraints on the type, quality, and quantity of data that researchers have been heretofore confined to use. It will expand our knowledge of how groups form and operate in larger ecosystems of groups, individuals, and organizations. The analysis of logs generated from virtual worlds poses novel challenges from a com-putational perspective. This requires an interdisciplinary investigation that will result in new (1) information models for modeling the virtual world, (2) data structuring and algorithmic techniques for data access and analysis, and (3) techniques for com-putational efficiency. The knowledge and tools developed in this research will allow researchers to understand more fully, and practitioners to cultivate more effectively, the emergence and performance of ad hoc groups in contemporary society. It will also provide other disciplines with new computational and statistical modeling method-ologies and tools, which should have considerable positive implications for future research in other disciplinary areas.

19.4.2 Traditional versus Proposed Group Analysis

Most previous research on small groups and teams has operated under a restric-tive model that treats groups as well-defined, clearly bounded entities with a sta-ble set of members. The vast majority of experiments on groups and teams take as their unit of analysis a single, small, isolated group whose members are assigned by the researchers. Studies of workgroups and other groups in natural settings, too, overwhelmingly focus on well-bounded, relatively small and stable groups, relying on managers or members to define the groups for study, and assuming that the group remains more or less stable and well-bounded throughout the study. Viewing groups in this way makes conducting research on groups straightforward, because researchers have a well-defined unit of analysis that can be observed relatively easily. It is a simple matter to videotape a five-person group gathered around a table in the experimenters laboratory. It is straightforward to administer a survey to a well-defined work unit (e.g., a nursing unit in a hospital) and the results of the survey clearly apply to this unit. However, groups in their actual settings are much more complex entities than the small, stable sets of people considered in most previous group research [19].

A broader picture of groups that takes their dynamic nature into account views them as part of a complex system of groups and individuals operating as an "ecosystem." Groups in such systems have one or more of the following properties:

- Their membership shifts over time, not only as a function of turnover, but because the shifts are necessary to enable the group to do its work. A group may have core members, but other members who join the group temporarily to advance its work must be considered to have some status in the group.

- Their boundaries are ill-defined, because their work requires them to adapt rapidly to changing demands. Groups can be nested within other groups and in some cases two or more groups must coordinate so closely that they seem to merge into a larger working unit.

- They form for limited-term projects and go out of existence when the project is complete. Members of these project teams are drawn from a pool of available personnel.

- The members may be spread spatially and temporally so that a particular location (such as an office) for the group cannot be specified. Instead the group members come together in different patterns of subgroups as they need to collaborate. These subgroups are often temporary and improvisational, but the members act as a group when they convene and then disband to rejoin the larger group.

- Context, including the demands of task and environment, and the pool of individuals who are potential members of these groups and organizations, exerts a strong influence on the dynamics discussed in the points above. In a real sense, these systems of groups are interdependent with their context.

- The groups often deal with highly complex problems involving a large amount of diverse information. This requires expertise beyond that of its core members and necessitates external linkages to other groups and units.

The small, self-contained, well-bounded groups that are the subject of most group research are special cases within this system, temporarily stabilized versions of the groups just described.

The following illustrates the complex nature of groups and individuals as part of an ecosystem—a large set of N individuals is organized into M organizational units that undertake long-term projects requiring them to carry out various tasks. The membership of these units shifts over time as members enter and exit. Within the units, members take on specialized roles and accumulate experience and skills that can be brought to bear on various tasks that the unit must carry out. Tasks vary from relatively simple and contained ones that can be done by a single person to more complex ones that require a small group to very complex tasks that require larger groups. The members take on tasks as they arise, and at any given time there is a mix of tasks being carried out in the unit, some by individuals, some by small groups, and less often, others by large groups. Some of the groups have relatively stable membership, while others are crews, which have a specific set of roles that can be filled by whatever qualified personnel are available to assign to them (operating room and airline crews are examples). Still other groups are special project teams comprised of members specifically assembled for a particular task. For some tasks, groups are formed that include members from multiple units. Its success in these tasks is an important determinant of the overall effectiveness of the unit in its larger project and of the units standing among other units.

This view of an ecosystem of groups is a considerably different view than that taken by most group research. The basic frame is a set of individuals within a larger context who enter and exit groups. Large groups, the units, have longer term projects that are served by carrying out specific tasks of varying degrees of complexity over a substantial period of time. These tasks are undertaken by smaller groups within and across these units. These smaller groups have limited time frames, shifting memberships, and may grow, shrink, merge with other groups, or go out of existence as the situation requires. The units themselves have longer time frames, but also exhibit the same dynamics as the smaller groups and also relate to one another in the ecosystem. The overall picture is that of a dynamic system of overlapping groups and units.

This conceptualization of groups enables researchers to address all the traditional issues of group research by focusing on internal dynamics of well-bounded groups. It also enables researchers to explore a number of additional issues that are likely to influence the processes and outcomes of individual groups, including the following:

- By taking a longer time frame and considering the pool of members available within units (or within the population) it enables research on the impact of level of member experience garnered within a given group and in previous similar groups on group effectiveness.

- By taking the supply and location of potential members into account it enables research on constraints on recruitment to groups.

- By considering relationships among groups and units, it enables research on competition and cooperation among groups.

- By considering multiple levels of groups, it enables research on the impact of larger units on group processes and outcomes.

- By focusing on groups with shifting memberships it enables research on the effects of member entering and exiting groups and units and its impact on longer term group effectiveness.

- By allowing for multiple units that members can differentially identify with, it enables the study of social identity effects on small group processes and effectiveness.

There is a pressing need to understand groups in their wider contexts and to conduct systematic, meaningful research on them. These types of groups carry out important tasks, including disaster recovery and relief, health care delivery, research and development, complex engineering and design projects, public policy planning and evaluation, and military operations. Groups in context also hold the key to the adaptiveness and agility of modern organizations. They are where the many complicated adjustments that must be made surrounding organizational change and innovation are accomplished. Groups lie in the liminal area between individuals and formal organizations. Ecologies of groups enable small groups to form into larger groups and coordinate their activities to tackle large and pressing problems and projects. They are the points of emergence of organizations.

19.4.3   EQ2/MMO as a Test Bed to Model an Ecosystem of Groups

EQ2 is a fantasy-based MMO in which players compete and collaborate in an ongoing quest for exploration and advancement. Players create a character and advance that character through challenges in a social milieu, typically banding together with other players for help and companionship. The game world prompts players to choose a side in an underlying struggle, and then to specialize their abilities. The conflict between two factions good and evil provides the underlying story line. Each faction has its own home city for players to enter the game, and provides a wide range of races and classes for players to customize their characters. There are altogether 16 races, each with its particular appearance and features. For each character, a class is then chosen to fit some variation of three basic archetypes: damage-dealer, damage-mitigator, and damage-healer. Each archetypal role has different capabilities, weaknesses, and strengths, and the choice of class then determines how players develop their characters and how they will interact with game environment and other players. For example, a priest usually takes the role of healer because of its higher effectiveness in casting healing magic, while a fighter is usually assigned a protective role. In addition, players also select a professional class for their characters to develop "tradeskills." These skills are necessary for characters to craft particular types of in-game items for trade with other desirable in-game items, or for sale in exchange of in-game currency. Performance metrics for groups and individuals in EQ2 involve the success rates for combat, gaining experience, exploring areas, creating items, and gathering resources. Being "killed" is not as final as it is in real life. Instead, it is more akin to a setback that requires players to bide some time and lose opportunities to gain resources before they can rise from the dead. As players rise in ability and power, they are prompted to enter new and unexplored areas. New abilities allow players to deal with and fend off ever more exotic and dangerous creatures and to acquire their accompanying treasures. The goals of players within EQ2 can be broadly characterized as exploring, exploiting, mobilizing, bonding, and swarming. Players often go on quests to *explore* materials or conditions in other parts of the EQ2 world. In order to accomplish this task, they team up with others who might aid them in this exploration. In other instances, players might be on a quest to create items (e.g., a sword, a tunic, or a meat pie) commensurate with their skill level. In this case, they need to "exploit" resources possessed by other players or the environment. Mobilizing directly describes the complex and ever-present functions of group organization and team deployment. As detailed by Ref. [20], group and guild-based dynamics in MMOs follow a regular series of conventions, norms, and patterns.

The basic group unit in EQ2 is an ad hoc cluster called "group" which can contain up to six players. Long-term associations within EQ2 are called "guilds" and come with their own bank, house, chat system, and hierarchy tree. Players mobilize in groups and guilds as they form and dissolve short-term and long-term clusters to accomplish game goals. Some guilds will mobilize more often, and with better outcomes than others. The highest level of mobilization takes place within a "raid," which is the assembly of a large group (up to 70 players at once) to take on a large challenge, usually over several hours. A "raid group" is a complex team requiring specific player roles and skills, and its management is often a daunting task. Reference [21] note that a large number of players who are in MMOs view it as a place to build "bonding" social capital, which is traditional social, emotional, and substantive support. These may, for instance, be geographically distributed family members who are playing together in EQ2 primarily to bond. Reference [22] has referred to bonding in MMOs (specifically World of Warcraft) as the twenty-first century equivalent to playing golf. Bonding may often result in stable networks of players "grouping" for varying quests and tasks. Swarming, or the rapid response to an occurrence or opportunity is also relatively prevalent in EQ2. Ad hoc and guild-based groups may need to respond quickly to game-based events. For example, there might be an invasion by computer-controlled monsters into an area. A game-based message will be sent out to all players in an area, calling them to swarm. Players in EQ2 are given a variety of tools to coordinate their activities. The chief tool is game-based text communication, which occurs in several ways. Players can speak "locally," that is, within a certain radius of the speaker, via person-to-person "tells" akin to instant messaging and in chat channels that span a wide variety of bases. Channels exist for all guilds, ad hoc groups, recruitment functions, general banter, and myriad other game-based reasons. In addition, players also have a list of "friends" that they can reach easily as well as an "ignore" list of players who cannot reach them easily. In summary, the actions, interactions, and transactions in EQ2 share many of the earmarks we associate with the ecosystem of groups as conceptualized in the previous section. The basic frame in EQ2 is a set of individuals within a larger context who enter and exit groups. Players with varying skills, capabilities, and at varying levels coalesce into groups for varying lengths of time to accomplish a variety of activities ranging from exploring, exploiting, mobilizing, bonding, or swarming. The group's performance results in rewards for individuals as well as the group. And, some or all of the members may reconvene as another group at a later time to accomplish a different task. Thus, EQ2 offers an outstanding and unprecedented test bed to investigate the dynamics of group behavior embedded within this ecosystem.

19.4.4   Data Mining Challenges

In EQ2, players participate in a number of activities as members of groups. Players may belong to multiple groups at the same time, based on the type of activity to be performed, and their membership in the set of groups, as well as their attention to each of the groups they belong to, may vary as a function of time. Further, from a group's perspective, its composition as well as cohesiveness may also vary as a function of time. Studying behavior in EQ2 makes it possible to study aspects of their behavior as individuals and as parts of groups, which cannot be studied in other settings, since EQ2 data provides a panoramic view that cannot be collected in the real world. Testing the hypotheses proposed in this project requires the ability to identify the members of a group, as well as all groups a player belongs to at any time. Further, testing the hypotheses also requires computing various metrics over players and groups, their activities, and their evolution over time. Finally, there is a need to perform these computations in a reasonable amount of time, especially since the volume of data captured is extremely high.

19.4.5   Inferring Group Membership and Player Relationships from Game Logs

Consider a set of eight players who participate in different activities over time, with snapshots for times t_1, t_2, and t_3, as shown in Figure 19.6. At t_1 there are two groups with four and three players, respectively, and one player all by himself. At t_2, one member of the bottom group moves to the top group, and one member of the top group joins the isolated player to create a new group. At t_3, the new group created at t_2 joins the bottom group to create a single group of size four. The data logged from Sonys EQ2 is from the perspective of individual players, and not from the perspective of groups. Thus, while it is possible to accurately track the history of individuals, it is much more challenging to do so for groups. The objective is to develop computational techniques for inferring group memberships and interplayer relationships from the game logs and then tracking them.

19.4.6   Metrics for Studying Player and Group Characteristics

Apart from the infrastructure to record and track behaviors of individual players and groups, making comparisons across groups and players would require devising new metrics that can capture the dynamic nature of the network. It has been theorized that people tend to form groups with other people who have similar characteristics that is, homophily [23]. A change in setting in an MMO may bring the different characteristics of the players to the fore which may be important in group formation. Thus, there is a need to determine which characteristics are important, if at all, in determining change in group memberships.

19.4.7 Efficient Computational Techniques for Group Behavior Models

The major interest in this project is to study the dynamics of groups, that is, how they evolve over time and what factors influence these evolutions. After inferring groups and their memberships as well as developing metrics to measure various aspects of the groups and individuals one can then use them to model the group dynamics. The basic problem is that given the groups and their characteristics (such as cohesiveness, goals, size, etc.) at a given time t, can one explain the changes in these groups at time $t + 1$. Changes primarily mean how group memberships vary over time that is, members leaving a group and others joining groups; however, other changes in their characteristics such as group cohesiveness, alignment, goals, etc. can also be studied.

Given the size and fine granularity of the data set (hundreds of thousands of users over a year, measured every millisecond), the tracking of individual memberships across communities as well as the maintenance of various related metrics for player, community, and ecosystem relationships, is a computationally challenging task [24–26]. We outline scalable techniques for computing player relationships, group memberships, and other required statistics as well as present incremental algorithms that can efficiently track changes and maintain them over lengthy time sequences.

19.5 Conclusion

Recording of electronic communication, that is, e-mail logs, Web logs, etc., has captured human processes like never before. Analysis of these logs creates an unprecedented opportunity to understand sociological and psychological processes at a granularity, which were unimaginable just a few years ago. In this chapter, two ongoing projects at the University of Minnesota that explore aspects of this emerging field are described. The first one involves analyzing e-mails to understand sociocognitive and knowledge networks, as well as developing quantitative measures for concepts such as "perceptual congruence" and "perceptual realism." The second one invloves analyzing logs from Sony's EQ2 MMO game to understand the formation and dynamics of group behavior, especially for ad hoc groups.

References

[1] P. Domingos and M. Richardson. Mining the network value of customers. In *Proceedings of 7th ACM SIGKDD*, pp. 57–66, San Francisco, CA, 2001.

[2] D. Krackhardt and J.R. Hanson. Informal networks: The company behind the chart. *Harvard Business Review*, 71(4):104–111, July 1993.

[3] J. Shetty and J. Adibi. The enron email dataset schema and brief statistical report. Technical Report, Information Sciences Institute, USC, 2004.

[4] J. Diesner and K.M. Carley. Exploration of communication networks from the enron email corpus. In *Proceedings of Workshop on Link Analysis, Counterterrorism and Security, SIAM International Conference on Data Mining*, pp. 3–14, Newport Beach, CA, 2005.

[5] M. Berry and M. Browne. Email surveillance using non-negative matrix factorization. *Computational and Mathematical Organizational Theory*, 11: 249–264, 2005.

[6] S. Wasserman and K. Faust. *Social Network Analysis Methods and Applications*. Cambridge University Press, New York, 1994.

[7] M. Kilduff and W. Tsai. *Social Networks and Organizations*. Sage Publications, London, 2003.

[8] J.C. Ward and P.H. Reingen. Sociocognitive analysis of group decision making among consumers. *Journal of Consumer Research*, 17(3):245–263, 1990.

[9] T. Kameda, Y. Ohtsubo, and M. Takezawa. Centrality in sociocognitive networks and social influence: An illustration in a group decision-making context. *Journal of Personality and Social Psychology*, 73(2):296–309, 1997.

[10] R. Cross, N. Nohria, and A. Parker. Six myths about informal networks and how to overcome them. *MIT SLOAN Management Review*, 43(3):67–75, 2002.

[11] M. Heald, N. Contractor, L. Koehly, and S. Wasserman. Formal and emergent predictors of coworkers' perceptual congruence on an organization's social structure. *Human Communication Research*, 24(4):536–563, 1998.

[12] N. Contractor. Multi-theoretical multilevel MTML models to study the emergence of networks. *NetSci'2006*, Bloomington, IN, 2006.

[13] N. Contractor, D. Zink, and M. Chan. Iknow: A tool to assist and study the creation, maintenance, and dissolution of knowledge networks. *Lecture notes in Computer Science*, 1519:201–217, 1998.

[14] N. Pathak, S. Mane, and J. Srivastava. Analysis of cognitive social and knowledge networks from electronic communication. *International Journal on Semantic Computing*, 1(1):87–125, 2007.

[15] M. Steyvers, P. Smyth, M. Rosen-Zvi, and T. Griffiths. Probabilistic author-topic models for information discovery. In *Proceedings of 10th ACM International Conference on Knowledge Discovery and Data Mining*, pp. 306–315, Seattle, WA, 2004.

[16] A. McCallum, A. Corrada-Emmanuel, and X. Wang. Topic and role discovery in social networks. In *Proceedings of International Joint Conference on Artificial Intelligence*, pp. 786–791, Edinburg, UK, 2005.

[17] P. Turney. Thumbs up or thumbs down? Semantic orientation applied to unsupervised classification of reviews. In *Proceedings of 40th Annual Meeting of the Association for Computational Linguistics*, pp. 417–424, Philadelphia, PA, 2002.

[18] X. Bai, R. Padman, and E. Airoldi. Sentiment extraction from unstructured text using tabu search-enhanced markov blanket. Technical Report CMU-ISRI-04-127. Carnegie Mello University, Pittsburg, 2004.

[19] L.L. Putnam and C. Stohl. Bona fide groups: A reconceptualization of groups in context. *Communication Studies*, 41:248–265, 1990.

[20] D. Williams. Why game studies now? Gamers don't bowl alone. *Games and Culture*, 1(1):12–16, 2006.

[21] D. Williams, N. Duchenaut, L. Xiong, Y. Zhang, N. Yee, and E. Nickell. From tree house to barracks: The social life of guilds in world of warcraft. *Games and Culture*, 1:338–361, 2006.

[22] J. Ito. World of warcrack. *Wired*, 14(6), 2006. From http://www.wired.com/wired/archive/14.06/warcraft.html.

[23] M. McPherson, L.L. Smith-Lovin, and J. Cook. Birds of a feather: Homophily in social networks. *Annual Review of Sociology*, 27:415–444, 2001.

[24] P.K. Desikan, N. Pathak, V. Kumar, and J. Srivastava. Incremental pagerank computation on evolving graphs. In *Proceedings of 14th International World Wide Web Conference*, pp. 1094–1095, Chiba, Japan, 2005.

[25] U. Raghavan, R. Albert, and S. Kumara. Near linear time algorithm to detect community structures in large scale networks. *Physical Review E*, 76, 2007.

[26] K.-W. Hsu, A. Banerjee, and J. Srivastava. I/o scalable bregman coclustering. In *Proceedings of 12th Pacific-Asia Conference on Knowledge Discovery and Data Mining*, pp. 896–903, Osaka, Japan, 2008.

Chapter 20

Challenges for Dynamic Heterogeneous Networks in Observational Sciences

Lisa Singh

Contents

20.1   Introduction

In corporate and scientific domains, there exist much data containing interrelated entities that are linked together. While this data can be analyzed by assuming independent instances and ignoring the relationships, the connectivity, relational structure, and associated dependencies can provide valuable insights, leading to potentially interesting data mining results with clearer semantics and higher degrees of accuracy. Different representations exist for domains with large, feature-rich entities and relationships. One natural representation that we consider in this chapter for this interconnected data is a graph. In an age of information overload, graphs give us a tangible, interpretable construct that allows us to more readily incorporate relationships into our analysis. We use graphs as the basis for describing models and abstractions that are useful for state-of-the-art visual mining of public and private graph data.

But graphs are still a very general construct. What should these graphs look like? How much detail is useful in the graph structure for data mining, more specifically visual mining? How much detail should be perturbed or removed in order to maintain

privacy of individuals in a network? Even though simple graphs are easier to analyze
and interpret, more complex graphs are sometimes more beneficial for sophisticated
graph-mining tasks and domain-specific analysis. For example, using multiple node
or relationship types allows for clearer semantic interpretations of clusters and associations, incorporates both node features and graph structural properties when building predictive models, and enables multiple abstractions of the data to help preserve
privacy of individuals and support visual analytics of large graphs.

In this chapter, we consider graph representations and abstractions for dynamic,
heterogeneous networks. A large number of domains contain dynamic, heterogeneous
networks with multiple edge types and relationship types over time, for example,
communication networks, protein interaction networks, social networks, transportation systems, and observational scientific networks. Here, we focus our discussion
on observational scientific networks. These networks have a number of challenges
for future researchers developing data mining algorithms and visual analytic tools,
including high dimensionality, varying degrees of observational certainty, incomplete
data, and highly fluid, dynamic network structures.

We begin by describing the semantics of the data associated with observational
scientific data sets in the next section. We then discuss a generic graph model that
can incorporate constraints useful for visual and graph mining of data generated by
observational scientists. Section 20.3 presents the current state of visual analytics
and mining as it relates to graph structures and describes both algorithmic and visualization challenges. In Section 20.4, we switch gears and consider situations were
the observed graph data need to remain private. This is a difficult problem since there
are many unique features of a graph. We formulate the problem and constraints for
privacy of graphs and identify some of the early work in that arena. Finally, Section
20.5 presents some concluding thoughts.

20.2   Observational Science Motivation

20.2.1   Background Scenario

Observational data is prevalent in many fields including biology, sociology,
medicine, and psychology. We begin by considering a simple observational science
data set where researchers monitor a subject for a specified period of time. Example subjects include wild animals, humans, and planets. Each monitoring period
can be viewed as an event consisting of a number of observations. Events include
tracking a group of animals for a 30 min period, conducting a 30 min psychological evaluation of a person, and taking a snapshot every minute of the interaction
between a planet and its moons. During a single event, researchers watch the subject
or group of subjects, taking notes throughout the process. Sometimes, computers
are used to record observations, but hand notes are common. These observational
data sets tend to contain a large number of events/observations (thousands to millions) and features (hundreds to thousands) for a small number of subjects (tens to
thousands).

It is also not unusual for photos and videos to accompany the more structured data. These data are used for identification of subjects in the wild. For example, if researchers know that certain monkeys are seen regularly together and suddenly the group composition changes, photos can be used to see if bites or injuries on a subject may have caused misclassification or if the community structure actually changed. Using network connectivity in conjunction with image data can help increase the quality of observational results and even help correct errors related to potential duplication. This example also highlights an important feature of observational data—many measurements in the data contain a time element. This time dimension is important for exploring questions regarding community stability and group formation: (1) How stable are these complex graph structures over time? (2) Which modes or relationships change most frequently? (3) What is the topological difference between a multi-featured community at time t_1 and t_2? (4) Why do some communities grow while others get smaller? For more details on long-term animal studies, we refer you to studies on dolphins and whales [1], pronghorn [2], and chimpanzees [3].

20.2.2 Data Representation

The majority of graph-mining algorithms (see Refs. [4,5] for surveys) and visual mining tools (see Ref. [6] for an overview) designed for graphs are developed for unimode, unirelation networks, where each node represents an object of a single type (e.g., an actor/subject, a Web page, or an observation) and each edge represents a relationship of a single type between two nodes in the network (e.g., friendship, kinship, or coauthorship) [7]. More formally, for a graph G containing n nodes or vertices, $G = (V,E)$, where $V = \{v_1, v_2, \ldots, v_n\}$ and $E = \{(v_i, v_j) \mid v_i, v_j \in V, i \neq j, 1 \leq i,j \leq n\}$. Here, V represents a set of nodes of a single type and E represents the set of relationships or edges of a single type, where each edge is defined as a pair of nodes from the set V.

However, in the simple example described in Section 20.2.1, four types of objects exist (observer/scientist, subject, events, and observations within an event), each of which can be viewed as a different vertex or node type. Also, both observations and events may link to more than one subject at a particular time. Therefore, an extended network is necessary to capture multiple node types and multiple edge types. Singh et al. introduced the M^*3 model as the basic data model for Invenio, a visual mining tool for social networks with multiple node types and multiple edge types [8]. In this model, a relation exists for each node type and each edge type. The relations are semantically organized based on actors and events, similar to a traditional affiliation network studied by sociologists. While there are many benefits to the M^*3, there are still some limitations. It does not allow for complex data types (e.g., texts, photos, and videos). Nodes are simple objects and features of nodes and relationships are well structured. It also does not incorporate semantics for time-varying networks. While time can easily be represented as an attribute in the M^*3 model, the model does not support special semantics for aggregation and sophisticated time-varying analysis of dynamic features.

Therefore, we advocate a generic model that captures multiple node and object types (multi-mode), multiple edge types (multirelation), and multiple static and time-varying descriptive features (multi-feature) associated with each. Formally, a more generic graph G' that captures any number of node types and edge types can be represented as $G' = \{V, E\}$, where $V = \{V_1, \ldots, V_{n_{VS}}\}$, $E = \{E_1, \ldots, E_{n_{ES}}\}$, and n_{VS} and n_{ES} are the number of node sets and edge sets in G', respectively. The base case remains a unimode, unirelation graph.

A multi-feature graph has features or attributes associated with each node and each edge in the graph. Some nodes such as the observation event nodes are temporal and will also have a time stamp and a duration time associated with them. This will be crucial for supporting longitudinal graph-mining analysis.

Figure 20.1 shows an example observation network. Each node type is shown as a different shape. Researchers are circles, observation events are squares, observations within an event are diamonds, and subjects are triangles. Other possible node types for these data include photos, geographic locations, and audio clips. For clarity, we show only one link type between different node types and no links between nodes of the same type. In reality, many different link types may exist between any two nodes in the graph. Each node and each edge in Figure 20.1 also has a set of features or attributes associated with it. For example, the animal subject nodes may have the following attributes: birth date, name, gender, mother, father, and pregnancy date for females.

There are a number of advantages to use a graph model with numerous entity and relationship types. First, users can represent a rich feature set for nodes and edges. Next, underlying relational theory supports complex graph structures, allowing users to translate between different graph topologies and abstraction levels. This means

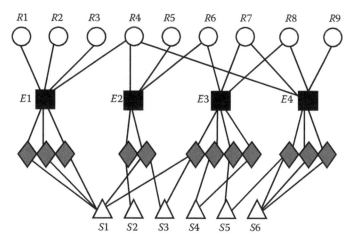

FIGURE 20.1: Observational network with four node types: researchers (circles), events (squares), observations within events (diamonds), and animal subjects (triangles).

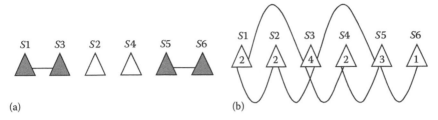

(a)   (b)

FIGURE 20.2: Unimode projections of Figure 20.1: (a) connections between animals observed exhibiting the same behavior when observed together and (b) connections between animals seen together in the same event.

that we can use relational algebra to easily create a subgraph that is projected on a single node type. For our example, we may want to create a unimode network of animal subjects. In this case, each node is a particular animal subject and each link represents animals that are observed together. Figure 20.2 shows two example projections. Figure 20.2a shows connections between animal subjects that have been observed together exhibiting the same behavior. Nodes that have a connection are highlighted in gray. Notice that there are few relationships in this unimode, unirelation representation. Figure 20.2b shows the connections between animal subjects that have been observed together in the same event. Here, all the animals have been seen with at least one other animal. Inside each node is the number of connections an animal has to other animals in the network. This network view highlights the link structure of the animal subject network, without displaying the structure of events or observations.

20.2.3 Challenging Data Features

While one can focus on any single node type, integrating the data can help explore methodological questions, data-quality issues, and graph-mining research questions that are obscured in graphs containing only one node type and one edge type. For example, are certain subjects oversampled by certain researchers? Answering this question requires investigation of three node types: researchers, events, and subjects.

Researchers within disciplines involving observational sciences are interested in individual behaviors as well as group dynamics. Because of the large number of features collected by observational researchers, targeted data exploration is necessary. We have observed that visualization can enhance the process considerably. Researchers can then visually see the results of sophisticated graph-mining algorithms and determine whether or not clusters and predictions coincide with their domain knowledge. They can use visual analytics to enhance their understanding of community structure and alliance creation, information transmission or behavior propagation through the community, and synergies between genetic relationships and community substructure. Further, observational scientists can use advanced statistical analysis on robust graph structures to visually discover patterns that may be difficult to interpret when looking at the statistical results alone.

There are a number of defining features associated with data generated by obser-vational scientists. Here, we identify the most relevant.

1. Because the data are observed, it is incomplete by nature. The behavior of most subjects cannot be monitored 24 h a day. This incomplete ground truth is very similar to terrorist network data sets, where associations, clusters, and classifiers need to be developed using partial information.

2. Many of the observed attributes have an element of uncertainty associated with them. It can occur that a researcher monitoring animals in the field may be uncertain about a behavior that has occurred (e.g., Was animal S1 petting or hitting?) or the individuals involved in the behavior (e.g., Was that S2 or S3 that was jumping?). Are the observations reliable? Using the observational certainty information, is there a relationship between the field condition or the animal subject and the quality of the observation? These uncertainties need to be considered so that confidence in associations, clusters, and predictive models are tempered and new ways to understand and interpret the results are considered.

3. The data are dynamic. Many longitudinal studies of people or animals already have decades of data. Therefore, they are well suited for investigating changing community structures or behaviors over time. Information transmission can also be analyzed in this context. Are behaviors taught based on social rela-tionships or are they self-learned? How are community structures of promi-nent subjects, exhibiting given behaviors, changing over time? How does their community structure compare to the norm of the entire population? Do certain patterns of behavior occur from generation to generation?

4. These data are feature rich and heterogeneous. The dimensionality is large compared to other social network data sets (e.g., blogs and e-mail). Which attributes and relationships are most relevant for pattern discovery, clustering, and classification? Which ones are noisy? How do we integrate knowledge from diverse types of data, for example, minute by minute focal data and snap-shot survey data, for mining applications?

5. Researchers have observational bias. When building predictive models from real data, the sample used is very important. Machine-learning researchers use different techniques to reduce bias in samples that are used to train classifiers. If there are a large number of researchers monitoring subjects, observational bias may be very subtle and difficult to detect. Do some observers have favorites that are oversampled in the population? When there are teams of observers, is the terminology consistent across the team, for example, does "large" mean the same size to all the observers?

6. As more data are collected, graphs will continue to grow. While the number of subjects in the network may be small, the number of observations, rela-tionships, and attributes tend to be larger than blog, e-mail, or communication networks. How do we reduce the graph size prior to exploration while main-taining the properties necessary for accurate analysis?

7. Privacy concerns may not apply to wild animals, but they do to patients. If there are privacy constraints, how must we alter the graph to decrease the likelihood of a privacy breach while still maintaining a reasonable accuracy for meaningful graph-mining analysis? Which abstractions and perturbation strategies balance the goals of preserving privacy with the utility of the data?

Computer science researchers in machine learning, data mining, statistics, and graph theory have begun developing approaches that consider some of these issues. What is missing is an integrated environment that facilitates data exploration as a dynamic, iterative process. An important component of this environment is a sophisticated visual-mining component that incorporates interactive visual exploration of complex data mining results.

20.3 Visual Mining of Complex Graphs

One reason why we like graphs is because they are naturally visual. We can look at them and begin interpretation before any formal analysis begins. While the visualization community has come up with some exceptional visual representations of networks (see Freeman survey [9] and Keim overview [10] for more details), visualization is different from visual analytics and visual mining. Visualization shows a view of the data and provides certain insight resulting from the interface design and layout decisions. The benefits are related to the old cliche, "a picture is worth a thousand words." In contrast, visual mining combines visualization, data mining, and other analytic techniques to support advanced data-exploration tasks [11]. The goal is to help users sift through and manipulate the data more effectively, particularly large or complex data sets, to better understand the data space. Visual analytic and mining tools may serve to help identify and interactively explore clusters or groups, find common structures in the network, compare roles of different classes of people, and visually analyze changes to community structures over time. These capabilities parallel the needs identified in the last section for observational scientists.

20.3.1 Visual Analytic Tools

Over the last few years, numerous toolkits and tools have been developed that use visualization to help represent patterns and results from mining algorithms graphically. Tools fall into two categories, those that have sophisticated statistical analysis using matrix operations [12–14] and those that focus on interactive visualization of unimode networks [15–19] and multi-mode, heterogeneous networks [8,20–22].

The first category of tools is less interactive; their strength is the sophisticated statistical calculations. For example, UCINet calculates social network centrality measures, permutation-based statistics, matrix algebra, and multivariate statistics [13]. StOCNET calculates some similar metrics, but focuses on using stochastic methods to analyze longitudinal data [14]. Finally, Pajek contains sophisticated block-modeling to support analysis of large networks [12].

The more interactive tools lack the sophisticated statistical analysis, but allow users to switch between different visual layouts and levels of data detail with ease. Some tools look at the entire network, while others focus on a piece of the network. Views of graph data range from the more traditional node–edge views similar to Figure 20.1 [8,15,17,18,20,21] to tree-structure representations of subgraphs in the network [19], maps, histograms and nested rectangles [16], and hybrids [22].

Various toolkits have also been developed to help programmers create interactive visualizations and visual-mining tools themselves. The most robust include JUNG [23], Prefuse [24], Piccolo [25], and GUESS [26]. These toolkits support the rapid development of graphic-based applications. JUNG has the largest support for graph mining and path algorithms. Prefuse contains a large number of visual layouts for graphs. Piccolo allows developers to create applications that incorporate different visual and graphic features beyond network-based visualizations with ease. Finally, GUESS contains database support and a simple query language that can be used to focus on analysis and easily change the perspective of a graph.

Even though the tools we have described identify patterns in the graph, zoom in on interesting groups or clusters in the graph, and allow for interactive exploration of the graph, we are missing visual analytic tools that allow us to answer sensitivity or what-if questions: What if we remove this node from the network? What if we add a new member to this clique? What nodes need to be added or removed so the distribution of node degree approximates a power law distribution? These questions are very relevant to group and network stability, information flow, and network characterizations.

While a wealth of tools exist for visualization of graph structures, approaches that integrate measures and algorithms from graph theory with interactive visualizations are still in its infancy. Therefore, the next step is to tightly integrate data mining and visualization so that user-selected subsets and abstractions of the graph can be used as inputs into different data mining algorithms and intermediate results can be visually explored and manipulated, iteratively. Accomplishing this using a flexible framework with a high degree of interactivity that supports a range of analytic tasks is still an open question. One reason is that a platform of this magnitude transcends cutting edge research in many areas of computer science, requiring sophisticated data management and indexing schemes, robust software engineering design, alternative visual paradigms, and scalable statistical and graph-mining procedures.

20.3.2   Developing Metrics for Understanding Complex Structures

Many measures have been developed for characterizing structural or topological features of a graph. Centrality measures are those that are node specific. Some of the more well-known ones include degree (the number of connections an arbitrary node v_i has to other nodes in the network), clustering coefficient (an indicator of the number of neighbors of node v_i that are connected to each other), betweenness (a metric based on the number of shortest paths going through node v_i), and eigenvector (a metric that determines v_i's relative importance in the network based on the importance of its neighbors). More general graph invariants include the number of nodes, the number of edges, the graph density, and the diameter of the graph (the longest shortest path in the graph) [7].

While all these metrics and properties are very important for understanding certain abstraction levels of the graph, not all nodes and edges have the same intrinsic properties in heterogeneous graphs. Understanding the relationship between different node types (modes) and relationship types is necessary to understand the detailed dynamics of the network and the effects of specific graph invariants and properties within and across modes. Therefore, in order to mine heterogeneous networks, we need to extend the unimode, unirelation measures to meaningful multi-mode, multirelation measures. As an example, Singh et al. developed a measure for multi-mode hop expansion [27]. This centrality metric identifies neighborhood size of different modes at different distances from each node v_i. This information can be used to see which nodes have similar positions in the network in terms of distances to other nodes in different modes.

Building on this work, we suggest developing measures that take varying edge types, node types, and feature distributions into consideration. Possible examples include multiedge path length (the number of edges traversed between two nodes in a multi-relational path), strength of connections (frequency and duration of different types of interactions), multi-mode density (a measure of the number of edges connecting nodes in different modes as a fraction of the total number of edges in the graph), transmission rate (path lengths of feature value expansion through different modes), and network turnover (a longitudinal measure that captures affiliation changes over time).

With these topological metrics, we can use the structure to understand the growth distribution of temporal networks. We can analyze the effect of growth rates in one mode on growth rates of others and consider the relationship between attribute features and structural properties of the network. While physicists have been studying the dynamics of network formation and growth [28,29], only the simplest of models are understood. Those findings need to be extended to more complex structures and specialized metrics for measuring individual local community and global network statistics will be vital for exploration of heterogeneous graphs. As we describe in the next section, for large graphs, these metrics can also be useful for eliminating irrelevant or noisy parts of the graph prior to execution of graph-mining algorithms. We now consider possible preprocessing of large graphs.

20.3.3   Preprocessing Prior to Visualization

It is difficult to interpret a graph with a large number of nodes and edges. If the network is well connected, the initial visualization using a traditional layout may appear to be a large black ball containing hundreds if not thousands of nodes. Statistics of node distributions and connectivity structure are useful, but visual analysis of such a large graph is limited. Therefore, initial preprocessing of the graph to identify important components of the graph, hiding irrelevant data, for the specific task of interest makes the problem more tractable [30]. Many techniques have been used to find the important nodes including the following: using structural metrics that capture important attributes of the graph [31,32], using clustering algorithms and blockmodeling to decompose large structures on attribute features or graph-link information [33], applying known compression techniques to graph structures [34], and using graph-matching techniques to identify substructures of interest [35].

Several proposed methods for classification of network objects consider the link structure of the network (see Getoor survey [36]). When considering link-based approaches for prediction in heterogeneous networks, the logical relationship between objects and the probabilistic dependencies between attributes may cause a huge search space for subgraph mining. By removing some of the less relevant components of the data, we can improve predictive accuracy of classifiers and extract smaller, more meaningful clusters and graph substructures from the data, enabling analysts to focus on the most meaningful set of patterns.

In previous work, we showed that predictive accuracy can be maintained on affiliation network (two-mode network) objects if instead of random pruning, the network under consideration is pruned or reduced in size based on attribute values or structural properties like degree and betweenness [32,37]. The goal here was to maximize predictive accuracy on attributes of event nodes in affiliation networks. Standard classifiers were built using pruned networks, where edges were removed based on centrality measures of nodes in the network, feature values, and random sampling. Two affiliation-network data sets were analyzed, an executive corporation network containing board of directors information for a subset of companies traded on the NASDAQ and the NYSE, and an author publication network based on the ACM SIGMOD anthology. For both data sets, pruning on descriptive attributes and graph invariants outperformed random pruning. Further, the underlying networks created using these pruning strategies had significant differences, meaning that each strategy was optimized differently. This finding is also consistent with Airoldi and Carley [38]. They found that pure network topologies are sensitive to random sampling.

Still, further investigation is necessary to determine the role topological structure plays in dynamic, heterogeneous networks in terms of graph-mining accuracy. Is structure less of a predictive indicator for multi-mode networks? Given that no one pruning approach will work across data sets, we suggest selecting a pruning approach prior to subgraph extraction and classification based on local, structural graph invariants (hop expansion, clique structure, clustering coefficient, etc.) and node-specific feature measures (behaviors, gender, lineage, etc.). We can then compare the structural similarities and the predictive accuracies of these pruned networks to the full network to better understand the strengths and weaknesses of the different pruning strategies on networks with specific topological structures.

20.3.4　Graph Mining Applicability to Observational Sciences

Many algorithms have been developed to uncover community substructure, flow of information, and prominent node identification on unimode networks with few, if any, features associated with each node. In the case of unimode networks, various local and global network statistics are used to help interpret network relationships, influence, clusters, or flows. For a recent survey, see Newman [30].

There are a number of problems being explored in the graph-mining community that can benefit from interactive visual analytics and are applicable to research conducted by observational scientists. Here, we describe the most relevant and explain their significance to this domain.

Hidden community identification or group clustering. This problem involves identifying groups of individuals or clusters of individuals that interact frequently together or share some common properties [39–44]. For example, if a scientist is observing a community of monkeys, he may identify a few pockets of 5–10 monkeys that play together regularly. Other significant features may be how often they play or the location where they play. Different unsupervised algorithms have been proposed for identifying hidden communities, including approaches based on subgraph identification, exhaustive search, and greedy heuristics. This problem also has similarity to the graph cut problem [45]. A tangential line of work investigates changes in community structure over time [46–48] and longitudinal network analysis that examines changes to network structural properties over time [7,49]. The networks being used for the analysis contain a single node and a single edge type. We are also interested in extracting unknown or hidden substructures across features and relations. To this end, Cai and colleagues [50] used a linear combination of weighted matrices for each relation to extract unknown community substructures. Because of the volume of data that needs to be analyzed when multiple relations are combined, the preprocessing options discussed in Section 20.3.3 are very relevant here.

Information diffusion and transmission. Here researchers investigate how information spreads through a network [29,51–53]. These papers attempt to find the most influential nodes in the network. How fast will information disseminate if we tell the right people? Who are the right people? Two well-known applications are disease transmission and viral marketing. For animals, behavior transmission is an important application. Approaches included using a global, probabilistic model [51], using a diffusion process that begins with an initial set of active nodes and adds neighbors based on different weighting schemes [52], and using graph invariants [53].

Group formation. The growth of communities in a network and the likelihood that individuals will join a particular community has dependencies to the underlying network structure. Given members in groups, what are the structural features that influence whether an individual will join a particular group? Can we use topological information to determine whether a group will grow or whether the group focus will change? The groups and communities can be viewed as subgraphs of the network, growing and overlapping in complex ways [48,54,55].

Detecting and matching subgraph patterns. In observational sciences that monitor groups of animals, researchers are interested in matching patterns of animal groups based on subgraph structure and feature distributions of nodes and links in a network. For example, does the calf's network emulate that of her mother and is it dependent on the sex of the offspring? The subgraph isomorphism problem looks at matching exact graph structures between two different graphs [56]. Many algorithms have been developed for finding subgraph patterns in massive unimode graphs. Approaches include greedy algorithms [57] and indicative logic programming approaches [58]. For visual exploration, it is important to integrate these approaches with meaningful visualization that can help detect stable subgraphs for more dynamic networks.

Understanding network growth. Many social networks, including the World Wide Web, follow a power law growth distribution [28,59,60]. In order to better understand the growth distribution of temporal heterogeneous networks created from observational scientific data, we need to analyze how growth rates of one relationship or mode affect the growth rates of others and consider how different attribute features relate to the structural properties of the network. How do growth rates of these more complex networks compare to growth rates of known unimode, unirelation networks?

20.4   Complex Social Networks and Privacy

As if the horizon was not complicated enough with the heterogeneity of the data, the dynamic nature of the data, and the graph mining and visual analytic complexities of working with large observational data, a need sometimes exists to keep the identities of the individuals in the data private. While wild animals do not have any well-established privacy rights, human subjects have varying levels of guaranteed privacy. In this scenario, the data need to be released for graph-mining analysis, but some level of privacy must be maintained.

While privacy preservation of data mining approaches has been an important topic for a number of years (see Verykios et al. [61] for an overview), privacy of multirelational medical and social network data is a relatively new area of interest [62–65]. One reason is its complexity. Social networks, human or animal, are not random. This is one reason that anonymization alone is not sufficient for hiding identity information on certain real-world data sets [62,63]. These networks contain topological structures that are identifying marks of the network. If we analyze an unlabeled graph of the Web link structure, finding the Google homepage node may be straightforward because of its dense incoming link structure. This is an example of a unimode network. If we consider complex networks containing more unique features, identification of individuals in the network becomes easier.

How do we combat this? To what degree is network topology a factor compared to node and edge features? Are relationships between nodes more apparent when local neighborhoods have certain topological structures? How can we use the topological structure of complex networks to measure the level of anonymity in the network? To study some of the behaviors associated with social networks, how accurate do the network measures need to be for data mining applications, for example, clustering, community discovery, prominent-node identification, etc. In other words, how much error in the released data is acceptable? While we anticipate many of these topics will be explored soon for unimode networks, a far-reaching goal is to consider privacy preservation in the context of dynamic, heterogeneous networks.

In order to begin to answer these questions, we must first define "What constitutes a privacy breach?" While this may seem straightforward on the surface, many of the authors that have written on this topic have defined different types of adversaries and breaches. In the remainder of this section, we explore different types of attack models, adversaries, and privacy breaches.

Graphs have a great deal of variation. This variation is particularly important in the context of privacy. One may release a single graph or multiple graphs at different time points, depending on the analysis task. Irrespective of the number of graphs, what are the properties of the nodes and edges being released? How many object or node types are there in the network? How many relationship or edge types are in the network? Do the objects or relationships have features?

As the complexity of the data increases, the data become more unique. These unique components can be exploited by adversaries. The goal of any adversary is to determine the identity of one or more individuals or relationships in the social network. In previous work, we investigate ways to determine the level of uniqueness of nodes and edges in a unimode graph by introducing a metric called topological anonymity [66]. This measure combines different structural components, variations of degree, and clustering coefficient to measure the hideability of nodes in the network. If the hideability is low, then perturbation strategies [62,63,65] or abstractions of the original graph [64] need to be investigated.

Since adversaries have varying degrees of information about the original social network, we need to define different adversaries based on their background knowledge. Example adversary-background models include (1) a single adversary that is a member of the network and knows his own degree; (2) a single adversary that is a member of the network, knows own degree, and degree of some neighbors; (3) a single adversary that is a member of the network, knows own degree, and knows if his neighbors are connected; (4) a single adversary that is a member of the network and has insight about a community within the network; (5) a single adversary that is not part of network, but has insight about a community within the network; and (6) two or more adversaries colluding and having varying degrees of information based on Models (1)–(5).

Any of the adversaries listed above may attack the network in different ways. Two possible types of attacks are passive and active [62]. A passive attack occurs when the adversary is trying to learn the identity of nodes after the data are released. In other words, the adversary does not have access to the data before they are released. An active attack occurs when the adversary adds an arbitrary set of nodes to the original data. Edges are placed in a unique structure to targeted users that the adversary wants to identify. Once the data are released, the adversary then looks for a pattern of connections that correspond to a subgraph created by the adversary.

Finally, how can we maintain some level of privacy if a subset of nodes and edges can be labeled correctly by adversaries? As previously mentioned, if the data have breached nodes or edges, then the graph either needs to be altered through perturbation or deletion or generalized, that is, abstracted to hide the individual details of the data. The better approach depends upon the mining task that needs to be executed on the released graph. If the strategy we choose alters the graph significantly, the results of the data mining algorithm will be inaccurate and useless. Further, because real-world graphs have many nodes with more unique centrality measures, random perturbation strategies have a large effect on the accuracy of the released graph [63].

Strategies that incorporate the distribution of the graph invariants into the perturbation strategy may perform better. More research is necessary in this area.

k-Anonymity was introduced for privacy preservation of independent, unlinked data records. Using this approach, each individual should not be distinguishable from $k-1$ other individuals [67]. However, because our nodes are not independent and are linked together, we believe *k*-anonymity as identified in Ref. [67] is difficult to achieve in graphs where clear semantic dependencies exist in the data. We feel that it is even more difficult for the newer metrics of *l*-diversity [68] and *t*-closeness [69]. Two nodes that are indistinguishable across some node structural metrics or whose distribution is similar across different structural attributes do not guarantee that they are across other nodes, particularly path-related measures for nodes in the network. However, if we limit anonymity to local neighborhood structure of a node, *k*-anonymity, *l*-diversity, and *t*-closeness can be an important metrics for improving privacy of a graph.

20.5   Final Thoughts

While we are still investigating ways to analyze simple networks with a single node type and a single edge type, the complexity of today's network data forces us to begin thinking of ways to handle and analyze more heterogeneous data. In order to mine the data, we need to develop robust models that capture the interconnected nature of the data, while allowing for the inclusion of complex features and time-varying attributes. Integrating longitudinal statistical analysis, graph-mining exploratory analysis, and visual analytic approaches to interpret complex, heterogeneous networks with incomplete, uncertain data and potentially, additional privacy constraints is an outstanding challenge. In 2006, a group of data mining researchers created a list of the top 10 data mining challenges [70]. The integration proposed here encompasses portions of six of the challenges mentioned. While researchers are working on these challenges, harnessing and integrating the advances in different areas of computer science in a meaningful, intuitive way are difficult. However, these advances in computer science are necessary to help researchers in other sciences advance their fields at a faster pace than they can today. As the last decade has shown, baby steps in computer science can translate to large strides in other disciplines.

References

[1] J. Mann, R. C. Connor, P. Tyack, and H. Whitehead (Eds.), *Cetacean Societies: Field Studies of Dolphins and Whales.* University of Chicago Press, Chicago, IL, 2000.

[2] J. A. Byers. *American Pronghorn: Social Adaptations and the Ghosts of Predators Past.* University of Chicago Press, Chicago, IL, 1997.

[3] J. Goodall. *The Chimpanzees of Gombe: Patterns of Behavior.* Harvard Univeristy Press, Cambridge, MA, 1986.

[4] D. Cook and L. Holder. Graph-based data mining. *IEEE Intelligent Systems,* 15(2): 32–41, 2000.

[5] T. Washio and H. Motoda. State of the art of graph-based data mining. *SIGKDD Exploration Newsletter,* 5(1): 59–68, 2003.

[6] M. C. Ferreira de Oliveira and H. Levkowitz. From visual data exploration to visual data mining: A survey. *IEEE Transactions on Visualization and Computer Graphics,* 9(3): 378–394, 2003.

[7] S. Wasserman and K. Faust. *Social Network Analysis: Methods and Applications.* Cambridge University Press, Cambridge, United Kingdom, 1994.

[8] L. Singh, M. Beard, L. Getoor, and M. B. Blake. Visual mining of multimodal social networks at different abstraction levels. In *Proceedings of the 11th International Conference Information Visualization,* Zurich, Switzerland, 2007. IEEE Computer Society.

[9] L. C. Freeman. Visualizing social networks. *Journal of Social Structure,* 1(1), 2000.

[10] D. A. Keim. Information visualization and visual data mining. *IEEE Transactions on Visualization and Computer Graphics,* 8(1): 1–8, 2002.

[11] M. Kreuseler and H. Schumann. A flexible approach for visual data mining. *IEEE Transactions on Visualization and Computer Graphics,* 8(1): 39–51, 2002.

[12] V. Batagelj and A. Mrvar. Pajek—program for large network analysis. *Connections,* 21: 47–57, 1998.

[13] L. C. Freeman, S. P. Borgatto, and M. G. Everett. Ucinet for windows: Software for social network analysis, 2002. http://www.analytictech.com.

[14] M. Huisman and M. A. J. van Duijn. Stocnet: Software for the statistical analysis of social networks. *Connections,* 25(1): 7–26, 2003.

[15] M. Baur, M. Benkert, U. Brandes, S. Cornelsen, M. Gaertler, B. Köpf, J. Lerner, and D. Wagner. Visone software for visual social network analysis. In P. Mutzel, M. Jünger, and S. Leipert (Eds.), *Graph Drawing Software,* pp. 463–464. Springer, 2002.

[16] B. Bederson, B. Shneiderman, and M. Wattenberg. Ordered and quantum treemaps: Making effective use of 2D space to display hierarchies. *ACM Transactions on Graphics,* 21(4): 833–854, 2002.

[17] J. Heer and D. Boyd. Vizster: Visualizing online social networks. In *IEEE Symposium on Information Visualization (INFOVIS'05),* p. 5, Washington DC, 2005. IEEE Computer Society.

[18] G. Namata, B. Staats, L. Getoor, and B. Shneiderman. A dual-view approach to interactive network visualization. In *ACM Conference on Information and Knowledge Management*, Lisbon, Portugal, 2007. ACM Press.

[19] C. Plaisant, J. Grosjean, and B. B. Bederson. Spacetree: Supporting exploration in large node link tree, design evolution and empirical evaluation. In *INFO-VIS '02: Proceedings of the IEEE Symposium on Information Visualization (InfoVis'02)*, pp. 57, Washington DC, 2002. IEEE Computer Society.

[20] H. Kang, L. Getoor, and L. Singh. Visual analysis of dynamic group membership in temporal social networks. *SIGKDD Explorations Newsletter*, 9(2): 13–21, 2007.

[21] Netminer ii: Social network mining software. Available at http://www.netminer.com/NetMiner/home_01.jsp.

[22] A. Perer and B. Shneiderman. Balancing systematic and flexible exploration of social networks. *IEEE Transactions on Visualization and Computer Graphics*, 12(5): 693–700, 2006.

[23] P. Smyth, S. White, J. O'Madadhain, D. Fisher, and Y. B. Boey. Analysis and visualization of network data using jung. *Journal of Statistical Software*, W(II) 2005.

[24] J. Heer, S. K. Card, and J. A. Landay. Prefuse: A toolkit for interactive information visualization. In *SIGCHI Conference on Human Factors in Computing Systems*, pp. 421–430, New York, 2005. ACM Press.

[25] B. Bederson, J. Grosjean, and J. Meyer. Toolkit design for interactive structured graphics. *IEEE Transactions on Software Engineering*, 30(8): 535–546, 2004.

[26] E. Adar. Guess: A language and interface for graph exploration. In *SIGCHI Conference on Human Factors in Computing Systems*, pp. 791–800, New York, 2006. ACM Press.

[27] L. Singh, M. Beard, B. Gopalan, and G. Nelson. Structure-based hierarchical transformations for interactive visual exploration of social networks. In *Pacific Asian Conference on Knowledge Discovery and Data Mining*, Osaka, Japan, 2008 Springer.

[28] M. E. J. Newman and J. Park. Why social networks are different from other types of networks. *Physics Review*, 68, May 26, 2003.

[29] M. Boguna and R. Pastor-Satorras. Epidemic spreading in correlated complex networks. *Physical Review*, E 66(4), 2002.

[30] M. Newman. The structure and function of complex networks. *IAM Review*, 45(2): 167–256, 2003.

[31] D. Auber, Y. Chiricota, F. Jourdan, and G. Melancon. Multiscale visualization of small world networks. *IEEE Symposium on Information Visualization*, p. 10, Los Alamitos, CA, 2003. IEEE Computer Society.

[32] L. Singh, L. Getoor, and L. Licamele. Pruning social networks using structural properties and descriptive attributes. In *Proceedings of IEEE International Conference on Data Mining*, Houston, TX, 2005. IEEE Computer Society.

[33] V. Batagelj, P. Doreian, and A. Ferligoj. Generalized blockmodeling of two-mode network data. *Social Networks*, 26(1): 29–53, 2004.

[34] T. Suel and J. Yuan. Compressing the graph structure of the web. In *Data Compression Conference*, Snowbird, Utah, 2001. IEEE Computer Society.

[35] A. Baritchi, D. Cook, and L. Holder. Discovering structural patterns in telecommunications data. In *Proceedings of the 13th International Florida Artificial Intelligence Research Society Conference*, pp. 82–85, Orlando, FL, 2000. AAAI Press.

[36] L. Getoor. Link-based classification. In S. Bandyopadhyay, U. Maulik, L. Holder, and D. Cook (Eds.), *Advanced Methods for Knowledge Discovery from Complex Data*. Springer, 2005.

[37] L. Singh and L. Getoor. Increasing the predictive power of affiliation networks. *IEEE Data Engineering Bulletin*, 30(2): 41–50, 2007.

[38] K. M. Airoldi and K. M. Carley. Sampling algorithms for pure network topologies: A study on the stability and the separability of metric embeddings. *SIGKDD Explorations Newsletter*, 7(2): 13–22, 2005.

[39] G. W. Flake, S. Lawrence, and C. L. Giles. Efficient identification of web communities. In *ACM SIGKDD International Conference on Knowledge Discovery and Data Mining*, pp. 150–160, Boston, MA, 2000. ACM Press.

[40] M. Girvan and M. E. J. Newman. Community structure in social and biological networks. In *Proceedings of the National Academy of Sciences*, pp. 7821–7826, 2002. Academy of Sciences.

[41] M. B. Hastings. Community detection as an inference problem. *Physics Review E*, 74(035102), 2006.

[42] M. E. J. Newman. Finding community structure in networks using the eigenvectors of matrices. *Physics Review E*, 74(036104), 2006.

[43] G. Palla, I. Derenyi, I. Farkas, and T. Vicsek. Uncovering the overlapping community structure of complex networks in nature and society. *Nature*, 435: 814-818, 2005.

[44] S. White and P. Smyth. A spectral clustering approach to finding communities in graph. In *SIAM International Conference on Data Mining*, Newport Beach, CA, 2005. Society for Industrial and Applied Mathematics.

[45] Harary, Frank, *Graph Theory* (1969), Addison-Wesley, Reading, MA.

[46] C. Tantipathananandh, T. Berger-Wolf, and D. Kempe. A framework for community identification in dynamic social networks. In *Proceedings of the 13th ACM SIGKDD International Conference on Knowledge Discovery and Data Mining*, pp. 717–726, New York, 2007. ACM Press.

[47] T. Y. Berger-Wolf and J. Saia. A framework for analysis of dynamic social networks. In *Proceedings of the 12th ACM SIGKDD International Conference on Knowledge Discovery and Data Mining*, pp. 523–528, New York, 2006. ACM Press.

[48] L. Backstrom, D. Huttenlocher, J. Kleinberg, and X. Lan. Group formation in large social networks: Membership, growth, and evolution. In *KDD '06: Proceedings of the 12th ACM SIGKDD International Conference on Knowledge Discovery and Data Mining*, pp. 44–54, New York, 2006. ACM Press.

[49] T. Snijders. The statistical evaluation of social network dynamics. *Sociology Methodology*, 31: 361–395, 2001.

[50] D. Cai, Z. Shao, X. He, X. Yan, and J. Han. Mining hidden community in heterogeneous social networks. In *LinkKDD '05: Proceedings of the 3rd International Workshop on Link Discovery*, pp. 58–65, New York, 2005. ACM Press.

[51] P. Domingos and M. Richadson. Mining the network value of customers. In *ACM International Conference on Knowledge Discovery and Data Mining*, San Francisco, CA, 2001. ACM Press.

[52] D. Kempe, J. Kleinberg, and É. Tardos. Maximizing the spread of influence through a social network. In *ACM International Conference on Knowledge Discovery and Data Mining*, Washington, DC, 2003. ACM Press.

[53] D. Liben-Nowell and J. Kleinberg. The link prediction problem for social networks. In *ACM Conference on Information and Knowledge Management*, New Orleans, LA, 2003. ACM Press.

[54] J. M. Kleinberg, R. Kumar, P. Raghavan, S. Rajagopalan, and A. S. Tomkins. The Web as a graph: Measurements, models and methods. *Lecture Notes in Computer Science*, 1627: 1–17, 1999.

[55] X. Wang and G. Chen. Synchronization in scale-free dynamical networks: Robustness and fragility. *IEEE Transactions on Circuits and Systems I: Fundamental Theory and Applications*, 49(1): 54–62, 2002.

[56] J. R. Ullmann. An algorithm for subgraph isomorphism. *Journal of ACM*, 23(1): 31–42, 1976.

[57] L. Holder, D. Cook, and S. Djoko. Substructure discovery in the subdue system. In *International Conference on Knowledge Discovery in Databases*, New York, 1994. ACM Press.

[58] L. Dehaspe and H. Toivonen. Discovery of frequent datalog patterns. *Data Mining and Knowledge Discovery*, 3(1): 7–36, 1999.

[59] R. Albert, A. Barabsi, and H. Jeong. Scale-free characteristics of random networks: The topology of the World Wide Web. *Physica A*, 281: 69–77, 2000.

[60] M. Faloutsos, P. Faloutsos, and C. Faloutsos. On power-law relationships of the internet topology. In *SIGCOMM '99: Proceedings of the Conference on Applications, Technologies, Architectures, and Protocols for Computer Communication*, pp. 251–262, New York, 1999. ACM Press.

[61] V. S. Verykios, E. Bertino, I. N. Fovino, L. P. Provenza, Y. Saygin, and Y. Theodoridis. State-of-the-art in privacy preserving data mining. *SIGMOD Record*, 33(1): 50–57, 2004.

[62] L. Backstrom, C. Dwork, and J. Kleinberg. Wherefore art thou r3579x?: Anonymized social networks, hidden patterns, and structural steganography. In *WWW '07: Proceedings of the 16th International Conference on World Wide Web*, pp. 181–190, New York, 2007. ACM Press.

[63] M. Hay, G. Miklau, D. Jensen, P. Weis, and S. Srivastava. Anonymizing social networks, University of Massachusetts, Amherst, MA, Technical report no. 07–19, March 2007.

[64] M. E. Nergiz, C. Clifton, and A. E. Nergiz. Multirelational k-anonymity. In *the 23rd IEEE International Conference on Data Engineering (ICDE 2007)*, Istanbul, Turkey, 2007. IEEE Computer Society.

[65] E. Zheleva and L. Getoor. Preserving the privacy of sensitive relationships in graph data. In *1st ACM SIGKDD Workshop on Privacy, Security, and Trust in KDD (PinKDD'07)*, San Jose, CA, 2007. ACM Press.

[66] L. Singh and J. Zhan. Measuring topological anonymity in social networks. In *Proceedings of the International Conference on Granular Computing*, San Jose, CA, 2007. IEEE Computer Society.

[67] L. Sweeney. k-anonymity: A model for protecting privacy. *International Journal of Uncertainty*, 10(5): 557–570, 2002.

[68] A. Machanavajjhala, J. Gehrke, D. Kifer, and M. Venkitasubramaniam. L-diversity: Privacy beyond k-anonymity. In *IEEE International Conference on Data Engineering*, Atlanta, GA, 2006. IEEE Computer Society.

[69] N. Li, T. Li, and S. Venkatasubramanian. t-closeness: Privacy beyond k-anonymity and ℓ-diversity. In *IEEE International Conference on Data Engineering*, Istanbul, Turkey, 2007. IEEE Computer Society.

[70] Q. Yang and X. Wu. 10 challenging problems in data mining research. *International Journal of Information Technology and Decision Making*, 5(4): 597–604, 2006.

... ...
... ...

Chapter 21

Privacy-Preserving Data Analysis on Graphs and Social Networks

Kun Liu, Kamalika Das, Tyrone Grandison, and Hillol Kargupta

Contents

21.1   Introduction

The proliferation of social networks, online communities, peer-to-peer file sharing, and telecommunication systems has created large, complex graphs. These graphs are of significant interest to researchers in various application domains such as marketing, psychology, and epidemiology. Research in these areas has revealed interesting properties of the data and presented efficient ways of maintaining, mining, and querying them. Distributed and ubiquitous computing over these networks, which are essentially graph structures, is also an emerging topic with increasing interest in the data mining community. However, with the exception of some recent work, the privacy concerns associated with data analysis over graphs and networks have been largely ignored. In this chapter, we provide a detailed survey of the very recent work on privacy-preserving data analysis over graphs and networks in an effort to allow the reader to observe common themes and future directions.

In a network, nodes correspond to individuals or other social entities, and edges correspond to relationships between them. The privacy breaches in a network can be grouped to three categories: (1) identity disclosure: the identity of an individual who is associated with a node is revealed; (2) link disclosure: the sensitive relationships between two individuals are disclosed; and (3) content disclosure: the sensitive data associated with each node is compromised, e.g., the e-mail message sent and received by the individuals in an e-mail communication network. A privacy-preservation system over graphs and networks should consider all of these issues. However, compared with existing anonymization and perturbation techniques of tabular data (see, e.g., the survey book [1]), working with graphs and networks is much more challenging due to the following reasons:

- It is difficult to model the background knowledge and the capability of an attacker. Any topological structures of the graph can be exploited by the attacker to derive private information. Two nodes that are indistinguishable with respect to some structural metrics does not guarantee they are on other metrics. Hence, it is not clear what are the most appropriate privacy models for graphs and networks, and how to measure the privacy breach in that setting.

- It is difficult to quantify the information loss. A graph can be worth a thousand words. It contains rich information but there are no standard ways to quantify the information loss incurred by the changes of its nodes and edges. How important are those network measures (e.g., degree, clustering coefficient, average path length, diameter, centrality, betweenness, etc.) to graph-mining applications? (e.g., clustering, community discovery, viral marketing, etc.). How well should we preserve those measures?

- It is even difficult to devise graph-modification algorithms that balance the goals of preserving privacy with the utility of the data. Different from tabular data where each tuple can be viewed as an independent sample from some distribution, the nodes and edges in a graph are all correlated. Therefore, the impact of a single change of an edge or a node can spread across the whole network.

- It is difficult to model the behavior of the participants involved in a network-based collaborative computing environment. Some participants may be quite honest and follow the rules; some may decide to behave dishonestly and exploit the system without contributing much; some may even intentionally try to collude with other parties to expose the private data of a specific individual.

To combat these challenges, several authors have recently developed different types of privacy models, adversaries, and graph-modification algorithms. Unfortunately, none of the work is likely to solve all the problems in one shot. Protecting against different kind of privacy breache may require different techniques or a combination of them. In this chapter, we detail a number of recently developed techniques for each type of the disclosure described above. We hope this survey can offer insight into the challenges and therefore opportunities in this emerging area.

The remainder of this chapter is organized as follows. Section 21.2 describes definitions and notation used throughout. Section 21.3 discusses identity disclosure. Section 21.4 details link disclosure. Section 21.5 presents content disclosure. Section 21.6 discusses privacy issues that arise from multiparty distributed computing, which we believe can serve as a foundation for the research of content disclosure over graphs and network with user interactions. Finally, Section 21.7 outlines future directions and concludes the chapter.

21.2 Definitions and Notation

We model a social network as a graph $G = (V_G, E_G)$, with vertices $V_G = \{v_1, \ldots, v_n\}$ corresponding to individuals and edges $E_G = \{(v_i, v_j) | v_i, v_j \in V_G, i \neq j, 1 \leq i, j \leq n\}$ corresponding to the social relationships among them. We use $\mathbf{d}_G$ to denote the degree sequence of G. That is, $\mathbf{d}_G$ is a vector of size n, with the ith element $\mathbf{d}_G(i)$ being the degree of the ith node of G. A graph isomorphism from G to H is a bijection: $f : V_G \rightarrow V_H$ such that an edge $(u, v) \in E_G$ if and only if $(f(u), f(v)) \in E_H$. A graph automorphism is a graph isomorphism with itself, i.e., a mapping from the vertices of the given graph G back to vertices of G such that the resulting graph is isomorphic with G. An automorphism f is nontrivial if it is not the identity function. Throughout this chapter, we use the terms "network" and "graph" interchangeably.

21.3 Identity Disclosure

The identity disclosure problem often arises from the scenario where the data owner wants to publish or share, with a third party, a network that permits useful analysis without disclosing the actual identity of the individuals involved in the network. Here each individual is represented by a node on the network. A common practice, called naive anonymization, removes the personally identifying information (PII) associated with each node or replaces it with a pseudorandom name. However, as shown later in this section, this simple approach does not always guarantee privacy. Under certain conditions, the attackers can still reidentify the individuals by combining external knowledge with the observed graph structure.

21.3.1 Active Attacks and Passive Attacks

Backstrom et al. [2] considered two different types of attacks on a naively anonymized social network. The first is an active attack, where an attacker creates new user accounts and edges in the original network and uses them to find targets and their relations in the anonymized network. The second is a passive attack, where users of the system find themselves in the anonymized network and discover identities and edge relations of other connected users. These attacks are based on the uniqueness of small random subgraphs embedded in an arbitrary network, using ideas related to those found in arguments from Ramsey theory [3]. Interested readers may observe that identity disclosure often leads to link disclosure. However, in this section we focus on identity disclosure and discuss the latter in Section 21.4.

Next, we give the formal definition of the problem Backstrom et al. studied:

Problem 21.1

Given a social network $G = (V_G, E_G)$ and an arbitrary set of targeted users $U = \{u_1, \ldots, u_b\}$, identify U in the naively anonymized copy of G and hence determine whether edge-relation (u_i, u_j) exists.

The active attack proceeds as follows. Before the anonymized graph is produced and published, the attacker registers k new user accounts $\{x_1, \ldots, x_k\}$ in the system, and it connects them together to create a subgraph H. The attacker then creates links between these new accounts to nodes in the target set $\{u_1, \ldots, u_b\}$, and potentially other nodes in G as well. These links are created depending on the specific application scenario, e.g., by sending messages to the targeted users or adding targeted users to the friends list or the address book of these new accounts. After the anonymized version of G is released, the attacker solves a special instance of the subgraph isomorphism problem to find H that is planted in G. Having identified H, the attacker can locate targeted users $\{u_1, \ldots, u_b\}$, thereby determining all the edge relations among them.

It should be noted that to make the above framework work, the subgraph H has to satisfy the following properties: (1) it is uniquely identifiable in G with high probability, regardless of G's structure and regardless of how it is attached to G; (2) it can be efficiently found from G by the attacker; and (3) H has no nontrivial automorphisms. The proof of the correctness and efficiency of the attacks is rather complicated, and we refer interested readers to Ref. [2] for a better treatment. It has been shown that with $\|V\| = n$ and $k = \Theta(\log n)$ new accounts, a randomly generated subgraph H will be unique with high probability. Moreover, if the maximum node degree in H is $\Theta(\log n)$, then H can be recovered efficiently, as well as the identities of up to $\Theta(\log^2 n)$ targeted nodes to whom the attacker created links from H. In practice, k can be set to values even smaller than the suggested bounds.

The experiments on a 4.4 million node and 77 million edge social network extracted from LiveJournal.com show that, the creation of seven nodes by an attacker can reveal an average of 70 targeted nodes, and hence compromise the privacy of approximately 2400 edge relations among them. The authors further showed that, in the worse case, at least $\Omega(\sqrt{\log n})$ nodes are needed in any active attack to begin compromising the privacy of arbitrary targeted nodes.

The passive attack is based on the observation that most nodes in a real social network already belong to a small uniquely identifiable subgraph. Therefore, if a user u is able to collude with a coalition of $(k-1)$ friends after the release of the network, he or she will be able to identify and compromise the privacy of neighbors connected to this coalition. We refer readers to Ref. [2] for more details.

21.3.2   *k*-Candidate Anonymity and Graph Randomization

Hay et al. [4] considered the problem of reidentifying a known individual in the naively anonymized network. They observed that the structural similarity of the nodes in the graph and the background knowledge an attacker obtains jointly determine the extent to which an individual can be distinguished. For example, if the attacker knows that somebody has exactly five social contacts, then he can locate all the nodes in the graph with degree five. If there are very limited nodes satisfying this property, then the target might be uniquely identified.

Along this direction, the authors proposed a privacy model for social networks, which is based on the notion of k-anonymity [5].

DEFINITION 21.1   k-Candidate Anonymity

A graph satisfies k-candidate anonymity with respect to a structural query if the number of the matching candidate nodes is at least k.

Alternatively, an anonymized graph satisfies k-candidate anonymity if for a given structural query, no individual can be identified with a probability higher than $1/k$.

The query evaluates the existence of the neighbors of a node or the structure of the subgraph in the vicinity of a node. It implicitly models the background knowledge (or the power) of an attacker. In their work, Hey et al. [4] studied two types of queries: (1) Vertex refinement query, which defines a class of queries of increasing power to report the structural information about a node's position in the network. The weakest query $\mathcal{H}_0(x)$ simply returns the identifier (or the pseudorandom name) of node x; $\mathcal{H}_1(x)$ returns the degree of x; $\mathcal{H}_2(x)$ returns the degree of each neighbor of x, and so on. (2) Subgraph knowledge query, which verifies the existence of a specific type of subgraph around the target node. The descriptive power of such a query is measured by counting the number of edges (also known as edge facts) contained in the subgraph.

To protect against these types of attacks, the authors studied a random-perturbation technique that modifies the graph through a sequence of random edge-deletions followed by edge-insertions. While this approach can potentially reduce the risk of reidentification, it does not guarantee that the modified graph satisfies k-candidate anonymity, neither does it guarantee that the utility of the original graph can be well preserved. This technique is further studied by Ying and Wu [6] in the context of sensitive link/relationship protection. They evaluated the impact of edge randomization on some spectrum properties of the graph, and developed a new strategy to better preserve these properties without sacrificing much of the privacy. We detail their technique in Section 21.4.3.

21.3.3   k-Degree Anonymity and Minimal Edge Modifications

Liu and Terzi [7] studied a specific graph-anonymity model called k-degree anonymity, which prevents the reidentification of individuals by adversaries with *a priori* knowledge of the degrees of certain nodes. Note that this is related to the vertex refinement query discussed in Section 21.3.2.

DEFINITION 21.2   k-Degree Anonymity
A graph $G = (V_G, E_G)$ is k-degree anonymous if every node $v \in V_G$ has the same degree with at least $(k-1)$ other nodes.

On the basis of this privacy model, the authors addressed the following problem:

Problem 21.2
Given a graph $G = (V_G, E_G)$ and an integer k, modify G via a set of edge-addition operations in order to construct a new graph $G' = (V_{G'}, E_{G'})$ such that (1) G' is k-degree anonymous; (2) $V_{G'} = V_G$; and (3) $E_{G'} \cap E_G = E_G$.

It is easy to see that one could transform G to the complete graph, in which all nodes share the same degree. Although such an anonymization would preserve privacy, it would make the anonymized graph useless for any study. For that reason, the authors imposed the additional requirement that the minimum number of edge-additions are made. This constraint tries to capture the requirement of structural similarity between the input and output graphs. Note that minimizing the number of additional edges can be translated into minimizing the L_1 distance of the degree sequence of G and G', since it holds that $|E_{G'}| - |E_G| = \frac{1}{2}L_1(\mathbf{d}_{G'} - \mathbf{d}_G)$. With this observation, the authors proposed a two-step framework for the graph-anonymization problem. The algorithms proceed as follows:

1. First, starting from the original degree sequence $\mathbf{d}_G$, construct a new degree sequence $\mathbf{d}'$ that is k-anonymous and the cost $L_1(\mathbf{d}' - \mathbf{d}_G)$ is minimized.

2. Given the new degree sequence $\mathbf{d}'$, construct a graph $G'(V_{G'}, E_{G'})$ such that $\mathbf{d}_{G'} = \mathbf{d}'$, $V_{G'} = V_G$, and $E_{G'} \cap E_G = E_G$ (or $E_{G'} \cap E_G \approx E_G$ in the relaxed version).

The first step is solved by a linear-time dynamic programming algorithm; the second step is solved by a set of graph-construction algorithms which are related to the realizability of degree sequences. The authors also extended their algorithms to allow for edge deletions as well as simultaneous edge additions and deletions. Experiments on a large spectrum of synthetic and real network data sets demonstrate that their algorithms are efficient and can effectively preserve the graph utility while satisfying k-degree anonymity.

21.3.4 *k*-Neighborhood Anonymity and Graph Isomorphism

Zhou and Pei [8] considered the subgraph constructed by the immediate neighbors of a target node. The assumption is that the unique structure of the neighborhood subgraph can be used by the attacker to distinguish the target from other nodes. This observation is closely related to the subgraph knowledge queries discussed in Section 21.3.2. On the basis of this assumption, the authors defined a new notion of the anonymity on graphs, which we call the *k*-neighborhood anonymity.

DEFINITION 21.3   k-Neighborhood Anonymity

A node is k-anonymous in a graph G if there are at least $(k-1)$ other nodes $v_1,\ldots,v_{k-1} \in V_G$ such that the subgraphs constructed by the neighbors of each node $v_1,\ldots,v_{k-1}$ are all isomorphic. A graph satisfies k-neighborhood anonymity if all the nodes are k-anonymous as defined above.

Following this definition, the authors specifically considered the following problem:

Problem 21.3

Given a graph $G = (V_G, E_G)$ and an integer k, construct a new graph $G' = (V_{G'}, E_{G'})$ such that (1) G' is k-neighborhood anonymous, (2) $V_{G'} = V_G$, (3) $E_{G'} \supseteq E_G$, and (4) the information loss incurred by anonymization is not too much.

The algorithm for solving the above problem consists of three steps. First, it marks all the nodes as unanonymized and sorts them in descending order of their neighborhood size. Here the "neighborhood size" is defined as the number of edges and nodes of the subgraph constructed by the immediate neighbors of a node. Then, the algorithm picks up the first unanonymized node *u* from the sorted list, finds the top $(k-1)$ other nodes $\{v_1,\ldots,v_{k-1}\}$ from the list whose neighborhood subgraphs are most similar to that of *u* (we call it subgraph similarity computation). Next, the algorithm iteratively considers every pair of nodes (u, v_i), $i = 1,\ldots,k-1$, and for each pair (u, v_i), the algorithm modifies the neighborhood subgraph of *u* and the neighborhood subgraph of v_i to make them isomorphic to each other. The modification is performed by adding extra edges while keeping the nodes intact (we call it subgraph isomorphism modification). After all the neighborhood subgraphs of these *k* nodes are pairwise isomorphic, the algorithm marks these *k* nodes as anonymized. The process continues until all the nodes in the graph are anonymized.

The information loss is measured by three factors: (1) extra edges added to the neighborhood, (2) nodes that were not in the neighborhood of the anonymized nodes but are now in, and (3) information loss due to the value generalization of the node's label if there is any such operations. Since the subgraph similarity computation and subgraph isomorphism modification are all based on greedy heuristics, there is no guarantee that the information loss is minimal, therefore, the utility of the anonymized graph can only be evaluated empirically.

21.3.5   Personally Identifying Information on Social Networking Sites

So far we have restricted our discussion to the problem of privacy-preserving graph publishing and sharing, and have largely ignored the privacy risks associated with personal information (PI) sharing in the real social networks such as Facebook and MySpace.

While specific goals and patterns vary significantly across these social networking sites, the most common model is based on the presentation of the user's profile and the visualization of his connections to others. As the profile and connection often reveal vast amounts of personal and sometimes sensitive information (e.g., photo, birth date, phone number, current residence, dating preference, current relationship status, political views, and various interests), it is highly likely that a user can be uniquely identified even if he does not openly expose his identity.

In an effort to quantify the privacy risk associated with these networks, Acquisti and Gross [9] combined online social network data and other publicly available data sets in order to estimate whether it is possible to reidentify PII from simple PI. This reidentification may happen, through photos, demographic data, category-based representation of interests that indicate unique or rare overlaps of hobbies. Their research supports the claim that large amounts of private information are available publicly.

21.4   Link Disclosure

The link disclosure problem is centered around the protection of the connection between vertices in a network. Two entities in a social network may have a myriad of connections. Some that are safe for the public to know and others that should remain private. Techniques to solve this problem, while still extracting analytic value from the network, have just started to emerge in the literature. In this section, we describe some recent work in this area.

21.4.1   Link Reidentification

Zheleva and Getoor [10] focused on the problem of link reidentification, which they define as inferring sensitive relationships from anonymized graph data. Graph nodes represent entities that are assumed to have multiple relationships, which are modeled as edges, between them. Edges may be of different types and can be classified as either sensitive or observed. The core problem addressed was how to minimize the probability of predicting sensitive edges based on the observed edges. The goal is to attain privacy preservation of the edge information, while still producing anonymized data that is useful. Utility is measured by the number of observational edges removed. The higher the number of removed observations, the lower the overall utility.

This goal is achieved by employing one of the five anonymization approaches outlined in this chapter. Their first algorithm, called intact edges, removes all sensitive edges and leaves all the observational ones. The second algorithm, called partial edge removal, deletes observational edges that may contribute to the inference of a sensitive relationship. The criteria are left up to the reader to set. They demonstrate this algorithm using a random removal strategy. In the first two approaches, the number of nodes in the graph are unchanged and the edges constructed as links between their anonymized versions. In the cluster-edge anonymization approach, all the anonymized nodes are collapsed into a single node (per cluster) and a decision is made on which edges to include in the collapsed graph. The cluster-edge anonymization with constraints approach uses a more restrictive sanitization technique for the observed edges, by creating edges between equivalence classes if and only if the equivalence class nodes have the same constraints as any two nodes in the original graph. The final approach, called removed edges, removes all relationships/edges from the graph. They recognize that the effectiveness of the approaches depends on the structural and statistical characteristics of the underlying graph. The experiments were carried out on a variety of graphs with varying characteristics and confirmed intuitive expectations, e.g., as the number of observational edges decreased, so did the number of correctly identified sensitive relationships.

In short, Zheleva and Getoor [10] concentrated on an often unexamined aspect of link disclosure—mitigating the risk of link reidentification.

21.4.2 Privacy-Preserving Link Analysis

Duan et al. [11] proposed an algorithm that enables link analysis in situations where there is no stated link structure between the nodes. They constrained their discussion to the domain of expert identification and authoritative document discovery and leverage the observation that a user's level of expertise is reflected by the document they access. Their Secure Online HITS algorithm is an extension of Kleinberg's HIT algorithm [12], where they replaced the 0–1 hyperlink property with a nonnegative value, i.e., a weight, which models the user's behavior.

Given users and their behaviors, whether through access logging systems or other means, they construct a graph such that the users are vertices and log entries represent edges between the two users. Then an eigengap (difference between the largest and the second largest eigenvalues) is computed using their online eigenvector calculation method, which performs in environments where frequent updates are the norm, by estimating the perturbation upper bound and delaying applying updates when possible. Due to the fact that they were logging (possibly) sensitive information from which they build the graph, they augmented their basic algorithm to address the privacy concerns. This was done by leveraging public key encryption to ensure that only aggregate or encrypted data was exposed.

To empirically test the algorithm, they ran it on the Enron email data set [13]. They used the message count between the sender and the recipient as the weight in order to determine if the algorithm could identify the central figures in the social network. The experiments demonstrated that their algorithm provided estimated rankings that closely matched the actual ones.

In short, Duan et al. [11] furthered the state of the art by demonstrating how core principles, like access pattern inference, can be used to construct graph structure, when none appears to exist.

21.4.3   Random Perturbation for Private Relationship Protection

Ying and Wu [6] studied two randomization techniques to protect private relationships. The first one, called Rand Add/Del, modifies the graph by a sequence of random edge-additions followed by edge-deletions. The second, called Rand Switch, randomly switches a pair of edges to produce a new edge set $\tilde{E} \leftarrow E \backslash \{(t,w), (u,v)\} \cup \{(t,v), (w,u)\}$ provided that $(t,v) \notin E$ and $(w,u) \notin E$, and repeats this process many times. The first randomization preserves the total number of edges in the original graph, while the second one maintains the degree of each node.

The authors evaluated, both empirically and theoretically, the impact of randomization on the eigenspectrum of the graph. In particular, they focused on two important eigenvalues: (1) the largest eigenvalue of the adjacency matrix, which is closely related to the maximum degree, chromatic number, clique number, and subgraph centrality of a graph; and (2) the second smallest eigenvalue of the Laplacian matrix (also known as algebraic connectivity [14]), which reflects how well connected the overall graph is, and has implications for properties such as clustering and synchronizability.

Using some theoretical results from Cvetkovic et al. [15], the authors developed the spectrum-preserving versions of Rand Add/Del and Rand Switch. The new algorithms selectively choose the edges that should be added, removed, or switched in order to control the changes of the eigenvalues. The privacy is evaluated by the prior and posterior belief of the existence of an edge. The authors developed closed-form expressions for evaluating Rand Add/Del and Rand Switch, and claimed that their spectrum-preserving counterparts should not differ much in protecting the privacy.

21.4.4   Cryptographic Protocols for Private Relationships Protection

Carminati et al. [16] considered an access control model where only authorized users who satisfy some access conditions are granted right to the resources owned by another user in a social network. Here the resources can be personal profiles, blogs, photos, etc.

The access conditions specify the type of the relationship between the requestor and owner (e.g., colleagues, alumni), the depth of this relationship (e.g., length of the friendship chain), and the trust level (e.g., fully trusted, semitrusted). Since knowing who is trusted by a user and to what extent disclose a lot about that user's personal interests, it is desirable to protect that information during the authentication process.

For this reason, the authors developed a symmetric-key protocol to enforce a selective dissemination of the relationship information during the authentication. This problem is further studied by Domingo-Ferrer [17], who developed a public-key protocol that does the same job as Ref. [16], without requiring a trusted third party.

21.4.5   Deriving Link Structure of the Entire Network

Korolova et al. [18] considered the problem that an attacker wants to derive the link structure of the entire network by collecting neighborhood information of some compromised users, who are either bribed or whose accounts are broken by the attacker.

These users are chosen using different criteria, e.g., uniformly at random (Random), in the descending order of their node degrees (Highest-degree), etc.

Analysis shows that the number of users needed to be compromised in order to cover a constant fraction of the entire network drops exponentially with increase in the lookahead parameter ℓ. Here a network has a lookahead ℓ if a registered user can see all of the links and nodes incident to him within distance ℓ from him. For example, a social network has $\ell = 0$ if a user can only see who are his immediate neighbors; has $\ell = 1$ if a user can see who are his immediate neighbors as well as his neighbors' immediate neighbors. A good example of a social network with $\ell = 1$ is LinkedIn. Experiments on a 572,949-node friendship graph extracted from LiveJournal.com show that (1) Highest-degree yields the best performance while Random performs the worst, and (2) in order to obtain 80% coverage of the graph using lookahead 2, Highest-degree needs to bribe 6308 users; to obtain the same coverage using lookahead 3, Highest-degree only needs to bribe 36 users.

21.4.6   Synthetic Graph Generation

Instead of modifying the graph to have it satisfy some k-anonymity criteria, Leskovec and Faloutsos [19] considered the problem of synthetic-graph generation. That is, given a large graph G, compute the most likely parameters Θ that would generate a synthetic-graph G' having the same properties as G. Hence, the data owner can publish G' without revealing the exact information about the original graph G.

The parameter $\Theta = [\theta_{ij}]$ defined in Ref. [19] is a $n_1 \times n_1$ probability matrix, where $n_1 \ll n$ and the element $\theta_{ij} \in [0, 1]$ indicates the probability that edge (i, j) is present. Given the original graph G, Θ is calculated by maximum likelihood estimation: arg $\max_{\Theta} P(G|\Theta)$. To evaluate this formula, the authors developed a linear-time algorithm (a naive approach would take superexponential time) by exploiting the structure of Kronecker product and by using a sampling technique.

Given the estimated parameter Θ, one can sample an initiator graph G_1 with n_1 nodes, and by recursion produce successively larger graphs $G_2, \ldots, G_k$ such that the kth graph G_k is on $n_k = n_1^k$ nodes. To be more specific, let A_G denote the adjacency matrix of a graph G, we have $A_{G_k} = A_{G_1}^k = A_{G_{k-1}} \otimes A_{G_1}$, where $\otimes$ is the Kronecker product and the graph corresponding to A_{G_k} is called Kronecker graph. Note that this approach assumes that Kronecker graph, which is self-similar and based on a recursive construction, is a good model for the real graph G. We refer interested readers to Ref. [19] and the references wherein for more details.

21.5   Content Disclosure

Content disclosure is normally an issue when the private data associated with a user on the network is disclosed to others. A very interesting example recently arose from Facebook's Beacon service, a social advertisements system where your own expressed brand preferences and Internet browsing habits, and even your very identity are used to market goods and services to you and your friends. For example, adding the latest season of LOST to your queue on Blockbuster.com might have Facebook place an advertisement for Blockbuster straight on your friends' news feeds. This helps Facebook and its partners (Blockbuster in this example) make money because, as Facebook's CEO Mark Zuckerberg extols, "nothing influence a person more than a recommendation from a trusted friend." This may be fine in some situation, but there may be some things that one is not prepared to share with the entire world. From the users perspective, they want to ask how to avoid the disclosure of their personal and private information while still enjoying the benefit of social advertisement, e.g., promise of free iTunes songs and movies. From the company's perspective, they want to know how to assure the users that their privacy is not compromised while doing social advertisement. Privacy concerns regarding content disclosure exist in other application scenarios such as social recommendation, etc.

Protecting against this kind of disclosure is an important research and engineering problem. However, the work in the literature thus far does not take into account the impact of graph structures as other two types of disclosures, but mostly focuses on (1) simple opt-in and opt-out setting and (2) standard data perturbation and anonymization for tabular data. The first approach allows the registered user to determine whether he wants to disable the service, or allow it being used in limited application scenarios. The second approach is more generic and it relies on traditional privacy-preserving data masking techniques [1] to change the data that is to be shared.

21.6   Privacy in Multiparty Distributed Computing

Since users and companies on a social network usually share and exchange some information, or jointly perform some task, we can see a connection between online activities and multiparty distributed computing. Here the graph structure may not play as an important role as in identity and link disclosure problems, but rather the behavior of users on the network and the task they want to achieve determines the extent to which the privacy is breached. Therefore, we believe that the privacy-preservation research in distributed computing can form a foundation for research on content disclosure for graphs and networks. Next, we introduce some work in that area aimed at offering insights into the solutions to content disclosure for graphs and networks.

21.6.1   Secure Multiparty Computation

Privacy-preservation objectives in distributed computing can often be framed as instances of secure multiparty computation (SMC) [20,21], wherein multiple parties, each having a private input, want to compute some function of these inputs without revealing any information other than the function's output. For example, the private input could be each party's income and the computation would return who is the richest. This example is known as the millionaire's problem and was first discussed by Yao [20]. Usually, it is assumed that 1/3 or 1/2 of the parties may be "bad" (or called malicious), while everyone else is assumed to be good (or called semihonest) and they execute the computation protocol as instructed. Although general approaches to SMC were proposed for a variety of settings in the 1980s, the computational and communication complexities hindered the application of SMC to privacy-preserving distributed data mining. In 2000, Lindell and Pinkas [22] designed a two-party SMC version of the ID3 algorithm for constructing a classification tree. They showed that a PPDM task does not have to be cast as a monolithic SMC problem that requires an expensive general SMC solution. Instead, the task may be decomposed into small modules, with each module being implemented with special-purpose efficient SMC protocols. The key to such construction is that we are able to ensure secure chaining of the small SMC components. We prevent information from leaking at the seams between the components by having them produce not public intermediate outputs but rather individual party shares of the outputs. These shares may be fed as inputs to further SMC components. Since Lindell and Pinkas' pioneering work, a variety of SMC solutions for privacy-preserving distributed data mining have been proposed, questioned, and refined. We refer interested readers to Refs. [1,23–25] for a thorough treatment. However, it should be noted that, as of today, a majority of the research in this area is still limited to two-party computation with the assumption of semihonest behavior. Therefore they may not scale well in an application scenario with many malicious participants and large data sets.

A relatively new area of research is the application of game theory to analyze the rational behavior of the participants. Here, we would like to consider what happens if the participants are all trying to maximize their own benefits, rather than being simply bad and good. In Section 21.6.2 we briefly mention some work in this area.

21.6.2   Game-Theoretic Framework for Privacy-Preserving Computation

21.6.2.1   Preliminaries of Game Theory

Before describing the game-theoretic framework for privacy-preserving distributed computing, we first provide a brief background of game theory.

A game is an interaction or a series of interactions between players, which assumes that (1) the players pursue well-defined objectives (they are rational) and (2) they take into account their knowledge or expectations of other players' behavior (they reason strategically). For simplicity, we start by considering the most basic game—the strategic game.

DEFINITION 21.4   Strategic Game
The strategic game consists of

- *A finite set P: the set of players*

- *For each player $i \in P$ a nonempty set A_i: the set of actions available to player i*

- *For each player $i \in P$ a preference relation $\succeq_i$ on $A = x_{j \in P} A_j$: the preference relation of player i*

The preference relation $\succeq_i$ of player i can be specified by a utility function $u_i : A \rightarrow \mathbb{R}$ (also called a payoff function), in the sense that for any $a \in A$, $b \in A$, $u_i(a) \geq u_i(b)$ whenever $a \succeq_i b$. The values of such a function are often referred to as utilities (or payoffs). Here a or b is called the action profile, which consists of a set of actions, one for each player. Therefore, the utility (or payoff) of player i depends not only on the action chosen by himself but also on the actions chosen by all the other players. Mathematically, for any action profile $a \in A$, let a_i be the action chosen by player i and a_{-i} be the list of actions chosen by all the other players except i, the utility of player i is $u_i(a) = u_i(\{a_i, a_{-i}\})$.

One of the fundamental concepts in game theory is the Nash equilibrium.

DEFINITION 21.5   Nash Equilibrium

A Nash equilibrium of a strategic game is an action profile $a^* \in A$ such that for every player $i \in P$ we have

$$u_i(\{a_i^*, a_{-i}^*\}) \geq u_i(\{a_i, a_{-i}^*\}) \quad for\ all\ a_i \in A_i.$$

Therefore, Nash equilibrium defines a set of actions (an action profile) that captures a steady state of the game in which no player can do better by unilaterally changing his or her action while all other players do not change their actions. A game can have zero, one, or more than one Nash equilibriums.

Next, we introduce game-theoretic approaches in three different settings: secret sharing, sovereign information sharing, and multiparty PPDM.

21.6.2.2   Rational Secret Sharing

Secret sharing is one of the main building blocks in modern cryptography. Shamir's secret sharing scheme [26] allows one to share a secret s (a natural number) among n other parties, so that any m of them may reconstruct it. The idea is as follows: party 0, who wants to share the secret, chooses an $(m-1)$ degree polynomial f such that $f(0) = s$, and tells party i the value of $f(i)$, $i = 1, \ldots, n$. Thus $f(i)$ is party i's *share* of the secret. Any m of parties $\{1, \ldots, n\}$ can jointly recover the secret by reconstructing the polynomial using Lagrange interpolation. However, any subset of parties with size less than m do not have any idea what the secret is. The underlying assumption of this protocol is that, at most $n - m$ parties are bad and bad parties cannot prevent the good parties from reconstructing the secret.

While in some situations, it makes sense to consider that some parties are good and some are bad; for other applications, it may be more realistic to view parties as rational individuals who are trying to maximize their benefits. The parties have certain preference over outcomes and can be expected to follow the protocol if and only if doing so increases their expected benefits. In this spirit is the work of Halpern and Teague [27], who considered the secret sharing problem where all parties are rational: (1) they prefer to get the secret to not getting it; (2) they prefer that as few as possible of the other parties get it. The authors showed that, under these assumptions, parties running Shamir's protocol will not cooperate. Using game-theoretic terminology, we say that for any party, not sending his share weakly dominates sending his share. To cope with this situation, the authors developed a randomized secret-sharing mechanism with constant expected running time, where the recommended strategy is a Nash equilibrium that survives iterated deletion of weakly dominated strategies. The results were extended to SMC with rational participants.

Abraham et al. [28] later introduced k-resilient Nash equilibrium, a joint strategy where no member of a coalition of size up to k can do better even if the whole coalition defects. They showed that such k-resilient Nash equilibrium exists for Shamir's secret sharing problem [26], which can be viewed as an extension of Halpern and Teague's work [27] since they did not consider collusion among the parties.

21.6.2.3   On Honesty in Sovereign Information Sharing

Sovereign information sharing [29] allows autonomous entities to compute queries across their databases in such a way that no extra information is revealed other than the result of the computation. Agrawal and Terzi [30] took a game-theoretic approach to address the following problem in a sovereign information-sharing setting: how to ensure that all the rational participants behave honestly by providing truthful information, even though they can benefit from cheating. They modeled the problem as a strategic game and showed that if nobody is punished for cheating, honest behavior cannot be an equilibrium of the game. They therefore added a central auditing device that periodically checks whether any participant has cheated by altering his input. Whenever the device finds out a cheating participant, it penalizes him. The authors derived conditions under which a unique Nash equilibrium is achieved such that every participant provides truthful information. The relationship between the frequency of auditing and the amount of punishment in terms of benefits and losses from cheating was also derived.

A related work is the one by Kleinberg et al. [31], who considered different information-exchange scenarios and quantified the willingness of the participants to share their private information using solution concepts from coalition games. Note that Agrawal and Terzi are interested in quantifying when people are willing to provide truthful information in a game, while Kleinberg et al. are interested in quantifying whether people are willing to participate in the game at all.

21.6.2.4   Game-Theoretic Framework for Secure-Sum Computation

In a multiparty PPDM environment, each participant has certain responsibilities in terms of computation, communication, and privacy protection. However, depending on the characteristics of these participants and their objectives, they can quit the process prematurely, provide bogus inputs, and collude with others to derive private information they should not know. Kargupta et al. [32] also took a game-theoretic approach to analyze this phenomenon and presented Nash equilibrium analysis of a well-known multiparty secure-sum computation [24,33]. The basic idea is again to model the strategies and utilities of the participants as a game and penalize malicious behavior by increasing the cost of computation and communication. For example, if a participant suspects a colluding group of size k', then he may split the number used in a secure sum into $\alpha k'$ pieces, $\alpha > 0$, and demand $\alpha k'$ rounds of secure-sum computation one for each piece. This simple strategy increases the computation and communication cost by $\alpha k'$-fold, which may counteract the possible benefit that one may receive by joining a team of colluders.

21.7   Conclusion and Future Work

This chapter provides a detailed survey of the very recent research on privacy-preserving data analysis over graphs and networks. Due to space constraints, we refer interested readers to Refs. [34–36] for other related work on this topic.

Before concluding this chapter, we present a set of recommendations for future research in this emerging area.

- Develop identity anonymity models for graphs and networks. Much of the existing research for identity disclosure is built upon the notion of k-anonymity. The fundamental research question remains: "What is the ideal base model for privacy-preserving analysis of graphs and networks?"

- Develop efficient and effective graph-modification algorithms for sensitive link protection. A lot of the existing work leverages randomization techniques that change the graph, which is rather heuristic and does not preserve the utility of the graph very well.

- Understand the privacy constraints in the Web 2.0 environment. Develop privacy-preserving techniques to enable core value-added Web 2.0 services, such as social advertisement and recommendation.

- Develop workload-aware metrics that adequately quantify levels of information loss of graph data.

- Create a benchmark graph data repository. This would let researchers compare algorithms to more clearly understand the differences among various approaches.

It is our belief that the future will see a growth in the demand of privacy-protection techniques for not only social network but also other types of networks, such as communication and peer-to-peer networks. As more researchers, engineers, and legal experts delve into this area, standards and theory will begin to take shape. As these are established, the next generation of privacy-preserving data analysis will be a fertile ground for all concerned with the privacy implications in our society.

References

[1] C. C. Aggarwal and P. S. Yu. *Privacy-Preserving Data Mining: Models and Algorithms*, Volume 34 of *Advances in Database Systems*. Springer-Verlag, New York, 2008.

[2] L. Backstrom, C. Dwork, and J. M. Kleinberg. Wherefore art thou R3579X?: Anonymized social networks, hidden patterns, and structural steganography. In *Proceedings of the 16th International Conference on World Wide Web (WWW'07)*, pp. 181–190, Alberta, Canada, May 2007.

[3] P. Erdös. Some remarks on the theory of graphs. *Bulletin of the AMS*, 53:292–294, 1947.

[4] M. Hay, G. Miklau, D. Jensen, P. Weis, and S. Srivastava. Anonymizing social networks. Technical Report, University of Massachusetts, Amherst, MA, 2007.

[5] P. Samarati and L. Sweeney. Generalizing data to provide anonymity when disclosing information. In *Proceedings of the 17th ACM SIGACT-SIGMOD-SIGART Symposium on Principles of Database Systems (PODS'98)*, p. 188, Seattle, WA, 1998.

[6] X. Ying and X. Wu. Randomizing social networks: A spectrum preserving approach. In *Proceedings of 2008 SIAM International Conference on Data Mining (SDM'08)*, pp. 739–750, Atlanta, GA, April 2008.

[7] K. Liu and E. Terzi. Towards identity anonymization on graphs. In *Proceedings of ACM SIGMOD*, pp. 93–106, Vancouver, Canada, June 2008.

[8] B. Zhou and J. Pei. Preserving privacy in social networks against neighborhood attacks. In *Proceedings of the 24th International Conference on Data Engineering (ICDE'08)*, pp. 506–515, Cancun, Mexico, April 2008.

[9] A. Acquisti and R. Gross. Privacy risks for mining online social networks. In *NSF Symposium on Next Generation of Data Mining and Cyber-Enabled Discovery for Innovation (NGDM'07)*, Baltimore, MD, October 2007.

[10] E. Zheleva and L. Getoor. Preserving the privacy of sensitive relationships in graph data. In *Proceedings of the International Workshop on Privacy, Security, and Trust in KDD (PinKDD'07)*, San Jose, CA, August 2007.

[11] Y. Duan, J. Wang, M. Kam, and J. Canny. Privacy preserving link analysis on dynamic weighted graph. *Computational and Mathematical Organization Theory*, 11:141–159, 2005.

[12] J. M. Kleinberg. Authoritative sources in a hyperlinked environment. *Journal of the ACM*, 46:604–632, 1999.

[13] W. W. Cohen. Enron email dataset, http://www-2.cs.cmu.edu/enron/.

[14] M. Fiedler. Algebraic connectivity of graphs. *Czechoslovak Mathematical Journal*, 23(98):298–305, 1973.

[15] D. Cvetkovic, P. Rowlinson, and S. Simic. *Eigenspaces of Graphs, Series: Encyclopedia of Mathematics and its Applications*. Cambridge University Press, Cambridge, UK, 1997.

[16] B. Carminati, E. Ferrari, and A. Perego. Private relationships in social networks. In *Private Data Management Workshop (held in conjunction with ICDE'07)*, Istanbul, Turkey, April 2007.

[17] J. Domingo-Ferrer. A public-key protocol for social networks with private relationships. In *Modeling Decisions for Artificial Intelligence*, Vol. 4617, pp. 373–379. Springer Berlin/Heidelberg, 2007.

[18] A. Korolova, R. Motwani, S. U. Nabar, and Y. Xu. Link privacy in social networks. In *Proceedings of the 24th International Conference on Data Engineering (ICDE'08)*, pp. 1355–1357, Cancun, Mexico, April 2008.

[19] J. Leskovec and C. Faloutsos. Scalable modeling of real graphs using kronecker multiplication. In *Proceedings of 2007 International Conference on Machine Learning (ICML'07)*, pp. 497–504, Corvallis, OR, June 2007.

[20] A. C. Yao. How to generate and exchange secrets. In *Proceedings of 27th IEEE Symposium on Foundations of Computer Science*, pp. 162–167, Toronto, Canada, 1986.

[21] O. Goldreich. *The Foundations of Cryptography*, Vol. 2, Chapter 7. Cambridge University Press, Cambridge, UK, 2004.

[22] Y. Lindell and B. Pinkas. Privacy-preserving data mining. In *Advances in Cryptology (CRYPTO'00)*, Volume 1880 of *Lecture Notes in Computer Science*, pp. 36–54. Springer-Verlag, New York, 2000.

[23] B. Pinkas. Cryptographic techniques for privacy preserving data mining. *SIGKDD Explorations*, 4(2):12–19, 2002.

[24] C. Clifton, M. Kantarcioglu, J. Vaidya, X. Lin, and M. Y. Zhu. Tools for privacy preserving distributed data mining. *ACM SIGKDD Explorations*, 4(2): 28–34, 2003.

[25] J. Vaidya, C. Clifton, and M. Zhu. *Privacy Preserving Data Mining*, volume 19 of *Advances in Information Security verlag*, New York. Springer-Verlag, New York, 2006.

[26] A. Shamir. How to share a secret. *Communications of the ACM*, 22(11): 612–613, November 1979.

[27] J. Halpern and V. Teague. Rational secret sharing and multiparty computation: Extended abstract. In *Proceedings of the 36th Annual ACM Symposium on Theory of Computing (STOC'04)*, pp. 623–632, Chicago, IL, June 2004.

[28] I. Abraham, D. Dolev, R. Gonen, and J. Halpern. Distributed computing meets game theory: Robust mechanisms for rational secret sharing and multiparty computation. In *25th Annual ACM Symposium on Principles of Distributed Computing (PODC'06)*, pp. 53–62, Denver, CO, July 2006.

[29] R. Agrawal, A. Evfimievski, and R. Srikant. Information sharing across private databases. In *Proceedings of the 2003 ACM SIGMOD International Conference on Management of Data (SIGMOD'03)*, pp. 86–97, San Diego, CA, 2003.

[30] R. Agrawal and E. Terzi. On honesty in sovereign information sharing. In *10th International Conference on Extending Database Technology (EDBT'06)*, pp. 240–256, Munich, Germany, March 2006.

[31] J. Kleinberg, C. H. Papadimitriou, and P. Raghavan. On the value of private information. In *Proceedings of the 8th Conference on Theoretical Aspects of Rationality and Knowledge (TARK VIII)*, pp. 249–257, Italy, July 2001.

[32] H. Kargupta, K. Das, and K. Liu. A game theoretic approach toward multi-party privacy preserving distributed data mining. In *Proceedings of the 11th European Conference on Principles and Practice of Knowledge Discovery in Databases (PKDD'07)*, pp. 523–531, Warsaw, Poland, September 2007.

[33] B. Schneier. *Applied Cryptography*. John Wiley & Sons, 2nd edition, 1995.

[34] K. B. Frikken and P. Golle. Private social network analysis: How to assemble pieces of a graph privately. In *Proceedings of the 5th ACM Workshop on Privacy in Electronic Society (WPES'06)*, pp. 89–98, Alexandria, VA, 2006.

[35] D. W. Wang, C. J. Liau, and T. S. Hsu. Privacy protection in social network data disclosure based on granular computing. In *Proceedings of 2006 IEEE International Conference on Fuzzy Systems*, pp. 997–1003, Vancouver, Canada, 2006.

[36] L. Singh and J. Zhan. Measuring topological anonymity in social networks. In *Proceedings of IEEE International Conference on Granular Computing (GRC'07)*, pp. 770, Fremont, CA, November 2007.

Part V

Medicine, Social Science, Finance, and Spatial Data Mining

Chapter 22

Risk Mining as New Trends in Hospital Management

Shusaku Tsumoto and Shoji Hirano

Contents

22.1 Introduction

It has passed about 20 years since clinical information are stored electronically as hospital information system (HIS) since 1980s. Stored data include from accounting information to laboratory data and even patient records are now started to be accumulated: in other words, a hospital cannot function without the information system, where almost all the pieces of medical information are stored as multimedia databases. Especially, if the implementation of electronic patient records is progressed into the improvement on the efficiency of information retrieval, it may not be a dream for each patient to benefit from the personal database with all the health care information, from cradle to tomb. However, although the studies on electronic patient record has been progressed rapidly, reuse of the stored data has not yet been discussed in details, except for laboratory data and accounting information to which on line analytical processing (OLAP) methodologies are applied. Even in these databases, more intelligent techniques for reuse of the data, such as data mining and classical statistical methods, has just started to be applied from 1990s [4,5].

Human data analysis is characterized by a deep and short-range investigation based on their experienced cases, whereas one of the most distinguished features of computer-based data analysis is to enable us to understand from the different viewpoints by using cross-sectional search. It is expected that the intelligent reuse of data in the HIS provides us to grasp all the characteristics of university hospital and to acquire objective knowledge about how the hospital management should be and what kind of medical care should be served in the university hospital.

This chapter focuses on application of data mining to medical risk management. To err is human. However, medical practice should avoid as many errors as possible to achieve safe medicine. Thus, it is a very critical issue in clinical environment how we can avoid the near misses and achieve the medical safety. Errors can be classified into the following three type of errors: (1) systematic error, which occurs due to problems of system and workflow; (2) personal error, which occurs due to lack of expertise of medical staff; and (3) random error. The important point is to detect systematic errors and personal errors, which may be prevented by suitable actions, and data mining is expected as a tool for analysis of those errors.

For this purpose, this chapter proposes risk mining where data including risk information is analyzed by using data-mining methods and mining results are used for risk prevention. We assume that risk mining consists of three major processes: risk detection, risk clarification, and risk utilization, as shown in Section 22.2.

We applied this technique to the following three medical domains: risk aversion of nurse incidents, infection control, and hospital management. The results show that data-mining methods were effective to detection of risk factors.

This chapter is organized as follows. Section 22.2 gives a background of our studies. Section 22.3 proposes three major processes of risk mining. Section 22.4 gives an illustrative application of risk mining. Finally, Section 22.5 concludes this chapter.

22.2   Background

22.2.1   Hospital as Complex Systems

A hospital is a very complicated organization where medical staff, including doctors and nurses, give a very efficient and specialized service for patients. However, such a complicated organization is not robust to rapid changes. Due to rapid advances in medical technology, such as introduction of complicated chemotherapy, medical workflow has to be changed in a rapid and systematic way. Such rapid changes lead to malpractice of medical staff, sometimes a large-scale accident may occur by chain reaction of small-scale accidents.

Medical accidents include not only careless mistakes of doctors or nurses, but also prescription errors, intrahospital infections, or drug side effects. The cause for such accidents may not be well investigated and it is unknown whether such accidents can be classified into systematic errors or random errors. Since the occurrence of severe accidents is very low, case studies are used for their analysis. However, in such investigations, personal errors tend to be the cause of the accidents. Thus, it is very important to discover knowledge about how such accidents occur in a complicated organization and knowledge about the nature of systematic errors or random errors.

22.2.2   Hospital Information System: Cyberspace in Hospital

On the other hand, clinical information have been stored electronically as a HIS. The database stores all the data related with medical actions, including accounting information, laboratory examination, treatment, and patient records described by medical staffs. Incident or accident reports are not exception: they are also stored in HIS as clinical data. For example, Figure 22.1 shows the structure of the HIS in

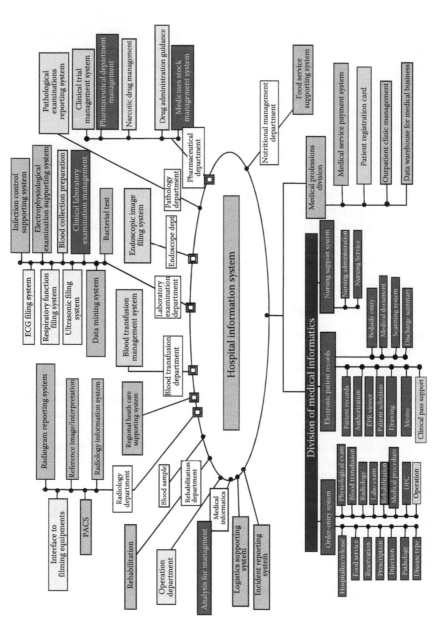

FIGURE 22.1:   HIS in Shimane University Hospital.

Shimane University Hospital. As shown in the figure, all the clinical inputs are shared through the network service, where medical staff can retrieve their information from their terminal.

Thus, this system can be a cyberspace in a hospital where all the results of medical actions are stored with temporal information. This cyberspace can be viewed as distributed large-scale and multimodal spatiotemporal databases.

Thus, dealing with cyberspace in a hospital will be a new challenging problem in hospital administration, and of course spatiotemporal data mining will play a central role in this challenge.

22.2.3 Basic Atom in HIS: Order

The basic atom in HIS is an order, which is a kind of document that conveys an order from medical staff to medical staff. For example, prescription can be viewed as order from a doctor to a pharmacist and an prescription order is executed as follows.

1. Outpatient clinic

2. Prescription given from a doctor to a patient

3. Patient bring it to medical payment department

4. Patient bring it to pharmaceutical department

5. Execution of order in pharmacist office

6. Delivery of prescribed medication

7. Payment

Steps 2–4 can be viewed as information propagation: thus, if we transmit the prescription through the network, all the departments involved in this order can easily share the information and execute the order immediately. This also means that all the results of the prescription process are stored in HIS.

These sharing and storing process can be easily stored as a database by using conventional information technology (IT) and data bases (DB) technologies: thus, HIS can also be viewed as cyberspace of medical orders.

22.2.4 Visualizing Hospital Actions from Data

Let us show the primitive mining results of HIS. Figure 22.2 depicts the chronological overview of the number of orders from November 1, 2006 to February 8, 2008. Vertical axis denotes the number of orders for each day, classified by the type of orders. Horizontal axis gives each date. The plot shows that the temporal behavior of each order is periodical with respect to holidays and very stationary.

Table 22.1 shows the averaged values of the number of orders during the same period. Although these values do not remove the effects of holidays, all the characteristics reflect that shown in Figure 22.2. Records and nursery accounts for 39% of orders and except for them, prescription, reservation of clinics, and injection are top three orders in the hospital.

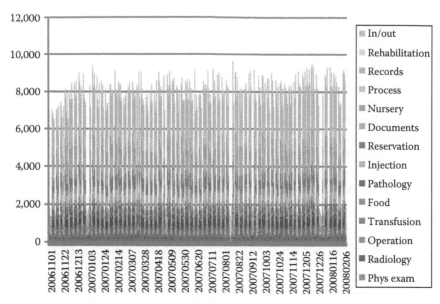

FIGURE 22.2: (See color insert following page 264.) Total number of orders.

Although Figure 22.2 and Table 22.1 overview the total behavior of the hospital, we can also check the temporal trend of each order as shown in Figure 22.3. Figure 22.3 depicts the chronological overview of the average number of each order from February 3–8, 2008. Vertical axis denotes the averaged number of each order,

TABLE 22.1: Averaged number of orders.

Order	Average	Percentage
Prescription	580.6017131	9.91
Labo exam	427.4282655	7.30
Phys exam	94.90149893	1.62
Radiology	227.5053533	3.88
Operation	9.751605996	0.17
Transfusion	10.74732334	0.18
Food	157.2077088	2.68
Pathology	29.37259101	0.50
Injection	507.7002141	8.67
Reservation	555.5010707	9.48
Documents	481.4239829	8.22
Nursery	677.0599572	11.56
Process	432.1541756	7.38
Records	1611.571734	27.51
Rehabilitation	4.35117773	0.07
In/out	51.67237687	0.88
Total	5858.950749	

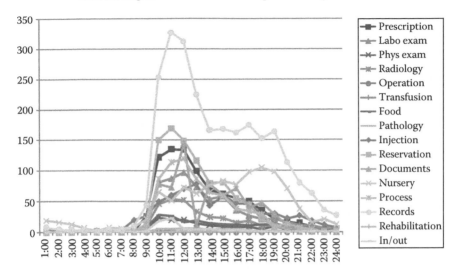

FIGURE 22.3: (See color insert following page 264.) Trends of averaged number of orders.

classfied by the type of orders. Horizonal axis gives each time zone. The plot shows the characteristics of each order. For example, the number of records of doctors have its peak in 11:00 a.m., which corresponds to the peak of outpatient clinic, whose trend is very similar to reservation of outpatient clinic. The difference between these two orders is shown from 1:00 to 5:00 p.m., which corresponds to the activities of wards.

Data in HIS can also capture the trend of the usage of terminals shown in Figure 22.4. Vertical axis denotes the averaged ratio of usage of terminals from February 3–8, 2008. Horizontal axis gives time zone. The plot gives the activity of

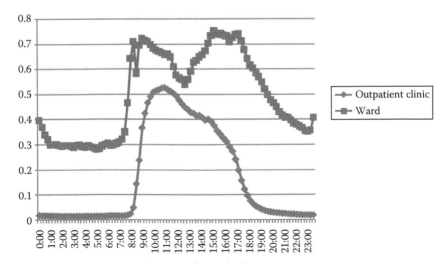

FIGURE 22.4: Averaged usage of terminals.

outpatient clinic and ward. The usage of terminals of ward has two peaks before and after opening of outpatient clinic, which reflects our tuition on the activity in university hospital.

These results show that we can measure and visualize the dynamics of clinical activities in the university hospital by data-analysis techniques. If we can detect some abnormalities different from usual behavior in these measurements, this may give some knowledge about risks in the clinical activities. Thus, it is highly expected that data-mining methods, especially spatiotemporal data-mining techniques, play crucial roles in analyzing data in HIS and understanding dynamics of hospital.

22.3 Risk Mining

In order to utilize information about risk extracted from information systems, we propose risk mining that integrates the following three important process: risk detection, risk clarification, and risk utilization.

22.3.1 Risk Detection

Patterns or information unexpected to domain experts may be important to detect the possibility of large-scale accidents. So, first, mining patterns or other types of information that are unexpected to domain experts is one of the important processes in risk mining. We call this process risk detection, where acquired knowledge is referred to as detected risk information.

22.3.2 Risk Clarification

Focusing on detected risk information, domain experts and data miners can focus on clarification of modeling the hidden mechanism of risk. If domain experts need more information with finer granularity, we should collect more data with detailed information, and apply data mining to newly collected data. We call this process risk clarification, where acquired knowledge is referred to as clarified risk information.

22.3.3 Risk Utilization

We have to evaluate clarified risk information in a real-world environment to prevent risk events. If risk information is not enough to prevention, then more analysis is required. Thus, additional data collection is evoked for a new cycle of risk-mining process. We call this process risk utilization. where acquired knowledge is referred to as clarified risk information. Figure 22.5 shows the overview of risk-mining process.

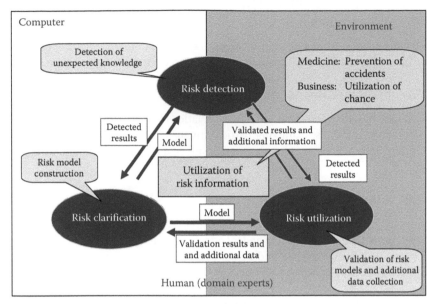

FIGURE 22.5:   Overview of risk-mining process.

22.3.4   Elemental Techiques for Risk Mining

22.3.4.1   Mining Unbalanced Data

A large-scale accident rarely occur: usually such it can be viewed as a large devia-tion of small-scale accidents, called incidents. Since even the occurrence of incidents is very low, the probability of large accidents is nearly equal to zero. On the other hand, most of the data-mining methods depend on frequency and mining such unbal-anced data with small probabilities is one of the difficult problems in data-mining research. Thus, for risk mining, techniques for mining unbalanced data are very important to detect risk information.

22.3.5   Interestingness

In conventional data mining, indices for mining patterns are based on frequency. However, to extract unexpected or interesting knowledge, we can introduce measures for unexpectedness or interestingness to extract patterns from data, and such studies have been reported in data-mining literature.

22.3.6   Uncertainty and Granularity: Granular Computing

Since incident reports include information about human actions, these data are described by subjective information with uncertainty, where we need to deal with coarseness and fineness of information (information granularity). Granular comput-ing, including fuzzy sets and rough sets, are closely related with this point.

22.3.7   Visualization

Visualizing co-occurence events or items may enable domain experts to detect risk information, to clarify the mechanism of risk, or to utilize risk information.

22.3.8   Structure Discovery: Graph Mining

Risk may be detected or clarified only by relations between several items in a large network structure. Thus, extracting partial structure from network hidden in data is a very important technique, focusing on risk information based on relations between items.

22.3.9   Clustering

Similarity may find relations between similar objects that seem not to be similar. Or events that seem to occur independently can be grouped into several similar events, which enable us to find dependencies between events. For this purpose, clustering is a very important techique.

22.3.10   Evaluation of Risk Probability

Since probability is formally defined as a Lebegue measure on a fixed sample space, its performance is very unstable when the definition of sample space is unstable. Especially, when we collect data dynamically, such instablility frequently occurs. Thus, deep reflection on evaluation of risk probability is very important.

22.3.11   Human Computer Interaction

This process is very important for risk-mining process because of the following reasons. First, risk information may be obtained by deep discussions on mining results among domain experts because mining results may show only small part of the total risk information. Since domain experts have knowledge, which is not described in a datasets, they can compensate for insufficient knowledge to obtain a hypothesis or explanation of mining results. Second, mining results may lead to domain experts' deep understanding of workflow, as shown in Section 22.4. Interpretation of mining results in risk detection may lead to new data collection for risk clarification. Finally, human computer interaction gives a new aspect for risk utilization. Domain experts cannot only perform risk clarification results, but also look for other possibilities from the rules that seem to be not so important compared with rules for risk clarification and also evaluate the possibility to design a new data collection.

22.4   Application 1: Prevention of Medication Errors

As an illustrative example, we applied risk-mining process to analysis of nurses' incident data. First, data collected in 6 months were analyzed by rule induction methods, which detects several important factors for incidents (risk detection). Since data do not include precise information about these factors, we recollect incident data for 6 months to collect precise information about incidents. Then, rule induction is applied to new data. Domain experts discussed all the results obtained and found several important systematic errors in workflow (risk clarification). Finally, nurses changed workflow to prevent incidents and data were recollected for 6 months. Surprisingly, the frequency of medication errors has been reduced to one-tenth (risk utilization).

22.4.1 Risk Detection

22.4.1.1 Dataset

Nurses' incident data were collected by using the conventional sheet of incident reports during 6 months from April to September 2001 at the emergency room in Osaka Prefectural General Hospital.

The dataset includes the types of the near misses, the patients' factors, the medical staff's factors, and the shift (early night, late night, and daytime), and the number of items of incidents collected was 245.

We applied C4.5 [3], decision-tree induction, and rule induction to this dataset.

22.4.1.2 Rule Induction

We obtained a decision tree shown in Figure 22.6 and the following interesting rules:

```
(medication error):
If late-night and lack of checking,
then medication errors occur: probability (53.3%, 8/15).

(injection error):
If daytime and lack of checking,
then injection incidents occur: probability (53.6%, 15/28).

(injection error):
If early-night, lack of checking, and error of injection rate,
then injection incidents occur: probability (50%, 2/4).
```

Those rules show that the time shift of nurse and lack of checking were the principal factors for medication and injection errors. Interestingly, lack of expertise (personal errors) was not selected. Thus, time shift and lack of checking could be viewed as risk factor for these errors. Since the conventional format of incident reports did not include future information about workflow, we had decided to ask nurses' to fill out new report form for each incident. This is the next step in risk clarification.

22.4.2 Risk Clarification

22.4.2.1 Dataset

Just after the first 6 months, we had found that the mental concentration of nurses may be important factors for medical errors. During the next 6 months from October

Decision tree: First 6 Months

⌐ Injection error—Injection route trouble (an obstruction due to the bending·reflow,
             the disconnection) = Yes: early-night work (2 −>2)
└ Injection error—Injection route trouble (an obstruction due to the bending· reflow,
             the disconnection) = No
├ Injection error —Pulled out (accident and self) = Yes: early-night (2 −>2)
├ Injection error —Pulled out (accident and self) = No
    ├ Injection error — Interrupts for the work = Yes: late-night (5 −>3)
    ├ Interrupts for the work = No
        ├ Injection error—Lack of knowledge for drugs and injection
        | = Yes: late-night (5−>3)
        ├ Injection error —Lack of knowledge for drugs and injection = No
          ├Injection error —Lack of command on the serious patients
          | = Yes: late-night (3−>2)
          ├ Injection error —Lack of command on the serious patients = No
            ├ Injection error —Lack of attention and confirmation
            | (drug to, dosage by, patient at, time in, route) = No: day-time (6−>4)
            ├Injection error — Lack of attention and confirmation = Yes
              ├Injection error —Wrong IV rate of flow = Yes: early-night work (4−>2)
              ├ Injection error —Wrong IV rate of flow = No: day-time (28 −>15)

FIGURE 22.6:   Decision tree in risk detection.

2001 to March 2002, the detailed interference factors were included in the additional incident report form as the items of environmental factors.

Figure 22.7 shows a sheet for additional information. The additional items included the duration of experience at the present ward, the number of nurse, the degree of

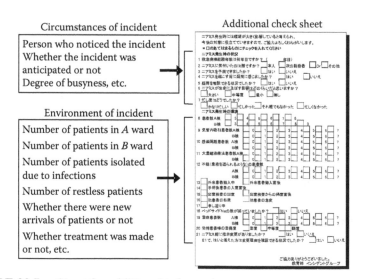

FIGURE 22.7:   Sheet for additional information.

business, the number of serious patients whether the nursing service was interrupted or not, and so on.

We applied C4.5 [3], decision-tree induction, and rule induction to this dataset.

22.4.2.2 Rule Induction

The following rules were obtained:

```
(medication error):
If the number of disturbing patients is one or more,
    then medication errors occur: probability (90%, 18/20).

(medication error):
If nurses' work interrupted,
then medication errors occur: probability (80%, 4/5).
```

By addition of the environmental factors, these high-probability rules of medication errors were extracted.

22.4.2.3 Rule Interpretation

With these results, the nurses discussed their medication check system. At the emergency room, the nurses in charge of the shift prepared the medication (identification, quantity of medicines, etc.). The time of preparation before the beginning of the shift was occasionally less than 30 min., when the liaison conference between shifts took time. In such cases, the sorting of medicines could not be made in advance and must be done during the shift.

If nurses' concentration was disturbed by the restless patients in such situations, double check of the preparation for medicine could not be made, which leads to medication errors.

22.4.3 Risk Utilization

Therefore, it was decided that two nurses who had finished their shifts would prepare medicines for the next shift, and one nurse in charge of the medication would check the dose and identification of medicines alone (triple check by a total of three nurses). (However, heated discussions among domain experts (nurses) are needed for this decision, as shown in Section 22.4.4.) Improvement was applied to the check system as a result of their discussion. During the last 6 months (April to October 2002), incident reports were collected.

After introducing the triple check system, the total number of the medication errors during the last 6 months decreased to 24 cases. It was considered that the nurses' medication work was improved by the triple check system during the last 6 months.

22.4.4   Discussion for Case Study

22.4.4.1   Risk Utilization as Information Sharing

For discussion among domain experts, mining results were presented to medical staffs as objective evidence. Discussion on mining results give a very interactive discussion among the staff of the department of emergency and finally achieve common understanding of the problem on its workflow. Then, it is found that changes in workflow is required for solving the problem: If the staff assigned to the shift cannot prepare medicines, other members who are free should cooperate. However, this idea met a fierce objection in the department at first because of disagreement among nurses about the responsibility of those who prepare medicines. After repeated discussions, it was decided that nurses in charge of medication were responsible for mistakes rather than those who made preparations and nurses in the preceding shift should prepare medicines for the next shift.

During the last 6 months, medication errors were reduced markedly by creating the common perception that liaison (overlapping of shift margins, or paste margins) is important among nurses, and the initial opposition completely subsided. Following this nursing example, we could extend this policy of paste margins, that is, mutual support by free staff members, to the entire department.

This process also shows that information granularity is a very important issue for risk clarification. Items in a conventional report form, such as lack of checking, lack of attention, etc., are too coarse for risk clarification. Rather, detailed description of environmental factors are much more important to evoke domain experts' discussion and their risk utilization.

22.5   Application 2: Infection Control (Risk Detection)

22.5.1   Objective

For the prevention of blood stream infection, we analyzed the effects of lactobacillus therapy and the background risk factors of bacteria detection on blood cultures. For the purpose of our study, we used the clinical data collected from the patients, such as laboratory results, isolated bacterium, antibiotic agents, lactobacillus therapy, various catheters, departments, and underlying diseases.

22.5.1.1   Material

The population for this study consisted of 1291 patients with blood stream infection who were admitted to our center between January and December 2002. The subjects were divided into two groups by the absence or presence of lactobacillus therapy. Lactobacillus group patients were administrated lactobacillus preparation or yoghurt within 5 days from microbial detection in blood cultures, and control group patients never took those preparations. Table 22.2 shows all the components of this dataset.

TABLE 22.2:   Attributes in a dataset on infection control.

Item	Attributes (63)
Patient's profile	ID, gender, age
Department	Department, ward, diagnosis (3)
Order	Background diseases, sampling date, sample No.
Symptom	Fever, catheter (5), tracheotomy, endotracheal intubation, drainage (5)
Examination data	C reactive protein (CRP), white blood cell count (WBC), urine data, liver/kidney function, immunology
Therapy	Antibiotic agents (3), steroid, anticancer drug, radiation therapy, lactobacillus therapy
Culture	Colony count, bacteria, Vitek biocode, β-lactamase
Susceptibility	Cephems, penicillins, aminoglycoside, macrolides, carbapenums, chloramphenicol, Rifanpic, vencomycin (VCM), etc.

22.5.1.2   Analytical Method

As analytical methods, we used decision tree, chi-square test, and logistic regression. If-then rules were extracted from the decision trees. The chi-square test and logistic regression were applied in order to analyze the effect of lactobacillus therapy.

22.5.2   Results

22.5.2.1   Chi-Square Test and Odds Ratio

Chi-square test was applied to evaluate the association between lactobacillus therapy and blood stream infection (bacteria detection on blood cultures). Table 22.3 shows the cross table of the bacteria detection on blood samples and the lactobacillus

TABLE 22.3:   Contingency table of bacteria detection and lactobacillus therapy.

	Lactobacillus Therapy		
	N (Absence)	Y (Presence)	Total
Bacteria Y (detection)	247	55	302
Bacteria N (no detection)	667	322	989
Total	914	377	1291

therapy. In this cross table, its p-value was $0.000000159 < 0.01$. Therefore, the effect
of lactobacillus presence to lactobacillus absence was considered statistically significant. Odds ratio (OR) was calculated as the relative risk of lactobacillus absence to
lactobacillus presence. Probability of bacteria detection on lactobacillus absence is
$p = 247/914$. Probability of bacteria detection on lactobacillus presence is $q = 55/377$.
OR of lactobacillus absence to lactobacillus presence is 2.17 and 95% CI (confidence
interval) was between 1.57 and 2.99.

Since the bacteria detection risk of lactobacillus absence was about 2 (95% CI:
1.57–2.99) to lactobacillus presence, lactobacillus therapy might be significantly
effective to prevent the bacteria detection on blood sample.

Thus, these results showed that lactobacillus therapy might have the effect to the
prevention of blood stream infection.

22.5.2.2 Decision Tree

The following decision tree shown in Figures 22.8 and 22.9 was obtained as the
relationship between the bacteria detection and the various factors, such as diarrhea,
lactobacillus therapy, antibiotics, surgery, tracheotomy, CVP/IVH catheter, urethral
catheter, drainage, and other catheter.

Figure 22.8 shows the sub-tree of the decision tree on lactobacillus therapy = Y
(Y means its presence) and Figure 22.9 shows the sub-tree of the decision tree on
lactobacillus therapy = N (N means its absence).

The target variable of the decision tree is bacteria (Y/N). The first node of the
decision tree is lactobacillus therapy (Y/N). Therefore, lactobacillus therapy might
be the most significant factor for prevention of blood stream infection. In the subtree on lactobacillus therapy (Y/N) = Y (Figure 22.8), the second branch is diarrhea
(Y/N), and the third branch is catheter (Y/N).

On the other hand, in the subtree on lactobacillus therapy (Y/N) = N (Figure 22.9),
the second branch is tracheotomy (Y/N), and the third branch is diarrhea (Y/N) or

```
⊟‑‑ Lactobacillus therapy (Y/N) = Y:
    ⊟‑‑ Diarrhea (Y/N) = N:
        ⊦‑‑‑ Catheter (Y/N) = N: Bacteria : N (74 –>71)
        ⊟‑‑ Catheter (Y/N) = Y:
            ⊦‑‑‑ Surgery (Y/N) = N: Bacteria : N (173 –>149)
            ⊟‑‑ Surgery (Y/N) = Y:
                ⊦‑‑‑CVP/IVH (Y/N) = Y: Bacteria : N (12 –> 12)
                ⊟‑‑CVP/IVH (Y/N) = N:
                    ⊦‑‑‑ Drainage (Y/N) = N: Bacteria : N (17–>13)
                    ⊟‑‑ Drainage (Y/N) = Y:
                        ⊦‑‑‑Urethral catheter (Y/N) = N: Bacteria : N (3–>2)
                        ⊦‑‑‑Urethral catheter (Y/N) = Y: Bacteria : Y (2–>2)
    ⊟‑‑ Diarrhea (Y/N) = Y:
        ⊦‑‑‑ Catheter (Y/N) = Y: Bacteria : N (75–>63)
        ⊟‑‑ Catheter (Y/N) = N
            ⊦‑‑‑ Anti-biotics (Y/N) = N: Bacteria : N (7–>7)
            ⊦‑‑‑ Anti-biotics (Y/N) = Y: Bacteria : Y (14–>9)
```

FIGURE 22.8:   Subtree on lactobacillus therapy (Y/N) = Y.

```
└ Lactobacillus therapy (Y/N) = N:
   └ Tracheotomy (Y/N) = N:
      └ Diarrhea (Y/N) = N:
         └ Anti-biotics (Y/N) = Y: Bacteria : N (428–>356)
         └ Anti-biotics (Y/N) = N:
            └ Catheter (Y/N) = N: Bacteria : N (170–>129)
            └ Catheter (Y/N) = Y:
               └ Surgery (Y/N) = N:
                  └ Drainage (Y/N) = Y: Bacteria : N (9–>7)
                  └ Drainage (Y/N) = N:
                     └ Urethral catheter (Y/N) = N: Bacteria : N (124 –>75)
                     └ Urethral catheter (Y/N) = Y:
                        └ CVP/IVH (Y/N) = N: Bacteria : Y (27–>16)
                        └ CVP/IVH (Y/N) = Y: Bacteria : N (18–>11)
               └ Surgery (Y/N) = Y:
                  └ Drainage (Y/N) = N: Bacteria : N (5–>5)
                  └ Drainage (Y/N) = Y: Bacteria : Y (6–>4)
      └ Diarrhea (Y/N) = Y:
         └ Drainage (Y/N) = Y: Bacteria : N (14–>13)
         └ Drainage (Y/N) = N:
            └ Urethral catheter (Y/N) = N:
               └ CVP/IVH (Y/N) = Y: Bacteria : Y (17–>12)
               └ CVP/IVH (Y/N) = N:
                  └ Anti-biotics (Y/N) = N: Bacteria : Y (15–>8)
                  └ Anti-biotics (Y/N) = Y: Bacteria : N (15–>9)
            └ Urethral catheter (Y/N) = Y:
               └ Anti-biotics (Y/N) = N:
                  └ Surgery (Y/N) = N: Bacteria : N (5–>5)
                  └ Surgery (Y/N) = Y: Bacteria : Y (3–>2)
               └ Anti-biotics (Y/N) = Y:
                  └ CVP/IVH (Y/N) = N: Bacteria : N (2–>2)
                  └ CVP/IVH (Y/N) = Y: Bacteria : Y (12–>7)
   └ Tracheotomy (Y/N) = Y:
      └ Surgery (Y/N) = N: Bacteria : N (19–>16)
      └ Surgery (Y/N) = Y:
         └ Diarrhea (Y/N) = Y: Bacteria : N (2–>2)
         └ Diarrhea (Y/N) = N:
            └ Drainage (Y/N) = Y: Bacteria : Y (13–>12)
            └ Drainage (Y/N) = N:
               └ Anti-biotics (Y/N) = Y: Bacteria : N (3–>3)
               └ Anti-biotics (Y/N) = N:
                  └ CVP/IVH (Y/N) = N: Bacteria : N (2–>2)
                  └ CVP/IVH (Y/N) = Y: Bacteria : Y (5–>5)
```

FIGURE 22.9:   Subtree on lactobacillus therapy (Y/N) = Y.

surgery (Y/N). The decision tree showed that bacteria (Y/N) have the strong relationship with lactobacillus therapy (Y/N), diarrhea (Y/N), catheter (Y/N), tracheotomy (Y/N), etc.

22.5.2.3   If-Then Rules from the Decision Tree

The following significant If-then rules were extracted from the above decision tree between the bacteria detection(Y/N) and the various factors.

```
If-then rule-1:
If Lactobacillus therapy (Y/N) = Y and
      Diarrhea (Y/N) = N and Catheter (Y/N) = Y and
      Surgery (Y/N) = Y and CVP/IVH (Y/N) = Y,
then Bacteria = N. (1.00 = 12/12)
```

If-then rule-1 showed that lactobacillus therapy presence might prevent bacteria detection from blood sample when patient has no diarrhea and has central venous pressure (CVP) catheter and intravenous hyperalimentation (IVH) catheter after the surgery.

```
If-then rule-2:
If Lactobacillus therapy(Y/N) = Y and
Diarrhea (Y/N) = Y and Catheter (Y/N) = Y,
then Bacteria = N. (0.84 = 63/75)
```

It was considered that lactobacillus therapy presence might prevent bacteria detection from blood sample when patient has diarrhea and catheter inserted into the blood vessel. That is, even though patient has diarrhea, lactobacillus therapy might protect patient's normal bacterial flora.

```
If-then rule-3:
If Lactobacillus therapy (Y/N) = Y and
    Diarrhea (Y/N) = Y and Catheter (Y/N) = N and
    Antibiotics (Y/N) = Y,
then Bacteria = Y. (0.64 = 9/14)
```

If-then rule-3 showed that lactobacillus therapy presence might not prevent bacteria detection from blood sample when patient has diarrhea, has no catheter, and has antibiotics. When patient might have diarrhea by antibiotics, lactobacillus therapy could not protect patient's normal bacterial flora.

```
If-then rule-4:
If Lactobacillus therapy (Y/N) = N and
    Tracheotomy (Y/N) = Y and Surgery (Y/N) = Y and
    Diarrhea (Y/N) = N and Drainage (Y/N) = Y,
then Bacteria = Y.
(Confidence: 0.92 = 12/13)
```

If-then rule-4 shows that lactobacillus therapy absence might not prevent bacteria detection from blood sample when patient has tracheotomy, no diarrhea, and has CVP catheter, IVH catheter, and drainage after the surgery.

```
If-then rule-5:
If Lactobacillus therapy (Y/N) = N and
    Tracheotomy (Y/N) = Y and Surgery (Y/N) = Y and
    Diarrhea (Y/N) = N and CVP/IVH (Y/N) = Y and
    Antibiotics (Y/N) = N,
then Bacteria = Y.
 (Confidence: 1.00 = 5/5)
```

It was considered that lactobacillus therapy absence might not prevent bacteria detection from blood sample when patient has tracheotomy, no diarrhea, has CVP catheter and IVH catheter, and no antibiotics

```
If-then rule-6:
If Lactobacillus therapy (Y/N) = N
       and Tracheotomy (Y/N) = N
       and Diarrhea (Y/N) = N and
Antibiotics (Y/N) = Y,
then Bacteria = N.
(Confidence: 0.83 = 428/356)
```

If-then rule-6 shows that bacteria detection from blood sample might be prevented by antibiotics when patient has lactobacillus therapy absence, no tracheotomy, and no diarrhea.

From these rules, there might be the strong relationship between treatment and bacteria detection from blood samples in case of lactobacillus therapy absence.

22.5.3 Discussion

We had an empirical rule that lactobacillus therapy (probiotic product) is effective in patient prognosis. Currently, lactobacillus preparation is used in most departments of our center.

This analysis was conducted to extract background risk factors of blood stream infection in a year data of 2002, by chi-square test, decision tree, If-then rules, and logistic regression.

Antibiotics preparation has antibiotic properties, but it tends to get off balance of the normal bacteria flora and to cause diarrhea. On the other hand, lactobacillus therapy regulates the functions of the intestines and has no side effects. From the results of chi-square test (Table 22.3), its p-value was $0.000000159 < 0.01$. The OR of lactobacillus absence to lactobacillus presence showed that bacteria detection risk of lactobacillus absence was about 2 (95% CI: 1.57–2.99). Therefore, lactobacillus therapy might be significantly effective to prevent the bacteria detection on blood sample.

On the other hand, the first node of the decision tree was lactobacillus therapy (Y/N). Therefore, lactobacillus therapy might be the most significant factor for prevention of blood stream infection. Various significant If-then rules were extracted from the decision tree. From If-then rule-1, lactobacillus therapy presence might prevent bacterial translocation when patient has no diarrhea and has CVP catheter and IVH catheter after the surgery. From If-then rule-2, it was considered that lactobacillus therapy presence might protect patient's normal bacteria flora and might prevent bacterial translocation from the intestinal tract even though patient has diarrhea. Furthermore, If-then rule-4 and If-then rule-5 showed that tracheotomy might cause bacteria detection from blood sample when patient has IVH catheter on lactobacillus therapy absence. As mentioned above, it was reported that bacterial translocation might be caused by antibiotics administration and IVH. Patient who has tracheotomy could not almost swallow down. Furthermore, when the patient has also IVH catheter, bacteria in patient's oral cavity might increase abnormally and the patient's intestinal tract might lose its functions. Therefore, bacterial translocation from oral cavity or intestinal tract might be yielded.

22.6 Application 3: Risk Detection and Clarification in Hospital Administration

22.6.1 Objective

The objectives of this research is to investigate what kind of knowledge can be extracted by statistical methods from the datasets stored in the HIS of Chiba University Hospital, especially useful for future hospital management and decision support. Especially, since the revenue of Japanese hospital is based on NHI (National Health care Insurance) points of Japanese medical care, it is important to investigate the factor that determines the amount of NHI points.

22.6.2 Methods

22.6.2.1 Representation of Discharge Summaries

When the HIS for discharge summaries is introduced in Chiba University Hospital in 1978, a discharge summary is distributed to doctors as a paper sheet for each patient admitted to the hospital. Doctors fill in each sheet just after the patient leaves the hospital, the parts of this sheet that can be coded are stored electronically. A sheet for discharge summary is composed of the items common to all the departments and the items specific to each department. For example, the items specific to neurology consists of the results of neurological examinations and the severity of diseases. The common items consist of those in which codes or numerical values should be filled in and those in which texts should be input. After the doctor in charge fill in those items and submit to the division of medical records, the staff input codes and numerical values into a database system. These processes are continued until a new HIS was introduced in 2000, which means that the nontext items common to all the departments have been stored for about 20 years. There are 16 items for codes or numerical values: patient ID, the department in charge, occupation, height and weight on admission, height and weight just before hospital discharge, a motivation for visit, outcome, autopsy or not, cause of death, the date of first visit, the date of admission, the date of discharge, the name of disease (international classification of diseases [ICD]-9 code [1]), and treatment method. However, height and weight just before hospital discharge are not input in the database. Concerning the items specific to each department, only those of surgery and ophthalmology are stored electronically.

22.6.2.2 Extraction of Datasets from Hospital Information System

The databases in the HIS of Chiba University Hospital are described by MUMPS [2]. MUMPS is a programming language that can construct a database with a hierarchical structure based on a binary tree. By using the characteristics of a binary tree, each item can store several data as a tree, which makes the data management and retrieval more efficient than relational databases. Datasets for analysis are extracted from the database on discharge summaries and the database on patient basic information by using patient ID and the date on admission as keys. The program for extraction is developed by the first author due to the following reasons. Since NHI points, are stored for each patient ID and each month, the total points for each admission for each patient are calculated from NHI points for each month. The total points are combined with the dataset extracted from the discharge summaries by using patient ID and the date on admission as keys. The number of the records of the dataset extracted from the global MRMG, which is a database on discharge summaries, is 157,636 for 21 years from April 1978 to March 2000. The time needed for computation is about 1 h by SUN Workstation (Enterprise 450). Concerning the dataset combined with NHI points, the number of the records is 20,146 for 3 years from April 1997 to March 2000.

22.6.2.3 Methods for Statistical Analysis

Descriptive statistics, exploratory data analysis, and statistical tests were applied to the dataset extracted only from the discharge summaries for the analysis of patient's basic information (gender, age, and occupation), outcome, the number of the days in hospitals, and diseases, including their chronological trends. Concerning the datasets combined with accounting information for 3 years (April 1997 to March 2000), the relations among NHI points and items in the discharge summaries were analyzed by descriptive statistics, exploratory data analysis, statistical tests, regression analysis, and generalized linear model. A statistical tool, R (http://www.r-project.org) was used for these analyses.

22.6.3 Results

Due to the limitation of the spaces, the most interesting results are shown in this section. In the subsequent sections, the results of the whole cases, and two levels of ICD-9 code, called major and minor divisions, are compared. Especially, concerning the results for the major and minor divisions, malignant neoplasm and the following three largest minor divisions of the malignant neoplasm are focused on: neoplasm of trachea, bronchus, and lung; neoplasm of stomach; and neoplasm of liver and intrahepatic bile ducts. In the subsequent sections, neoplasm of lung, stomach, and liver denotes the above three divisions for short.

22.6.3.1 Distribution of Length of Stay

Figure 22.10 shows the distribution of the length of stay of the whole cases, which skewed with the long tail to the right. Thus, the logarithm of the length of stay is taken to tame this skewness. Figure 22.11 gives the result of this transformation, whose distribution is very close to normal distribution: this means that the distribution of the whole cases is lognormal. This observation holds even when the major divisions are taken as sample. It is notable that the nature of this distribution holds even in the minor divisions, three largest diseases.

Table 22.4 summarizes the descriptive statistics of length of stay with respect to the whole cases, major and minor divisions. The natures of these distributions are not

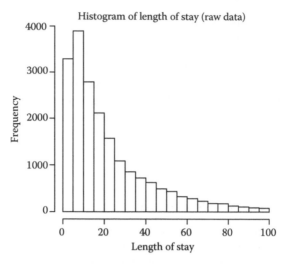

FIGURE 22.10:   Distribution of length of stay (raw data, total cases).

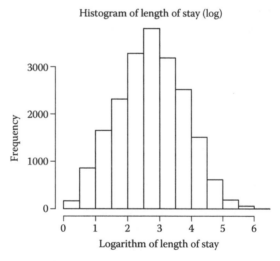

FIGURE 22.11:   Distribution of length of stay (logarithm transformation, total cases).

significantly changed if these cases are stratified by the condition whether a surgical operation is applied to a case or not.

22.6.3.2   Distribution of NHI Points

Since the variance of raw data of NHI points are very large and the distribution is skewed, the raw data are transformed into the median index, which is defined as the ratio of the total points to the median of the whole cases. Figures 22.12 and 22.13

TABLE 22.4: Descriptive statistics of length of stay.

	Average	Median	SD	Skewness	Kuritosis
Whole cases					
Raw data	26.46	16.00	33.67	4.34	34.15
Logarithmic transformation	2.74	2.77	1.06	−0.06	−0.28
Neoplasm					
Raw data	37.54	25.00	38.72	2.90	13.21
Logarithmic transformation	3.19	3.22	0.98	−0.32	0.08
Malignant neoplasm of lung					
Raw data	49.65	39.00	43.42	2.57	10.82
Logarithmic transformation	3.57	3.66	0.88	−0.79	2.00
Malignant neoplasm of stomach					
Raw data	36.44	36.00	19.18	0.46	0.37
Logarithmic transformation	3.40	3.58	0.72	−1.42	2.55
Malignant neoplasm of liver					
Raw data	35.93	33.00	21.40	1.19	2.70
Logarithmic transformation	3.38	3.50	0.71	−1.18	3.03

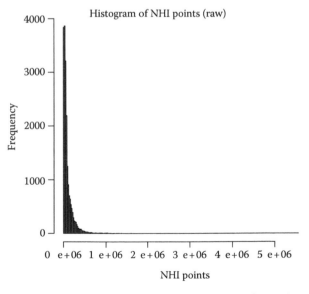

FIGURE 22.12: Distribution of NHI points (raw data, total cases).

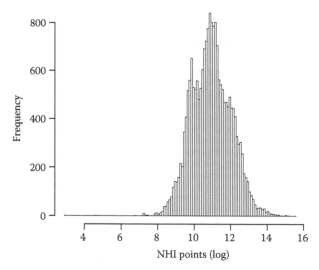

FIGURE 22.13: Distribution of NHI points (logarithm transformation, total cases).

show the distribution of the raw data and that of the logarithm of the raw data of median index. These figures suggests that the NHI points of the whole cases follow lognormal distribution. On the other hand, the distributions for minor divisions are different. The same observations are obtained from the distribution of NHI points of neoplasm.

22.6.3.3   Correlation between Length of Stay and NHI Points

Figures 22.14 and 22.15 depict the scattergram between the length of stay and NHI points of total cases and neoplasm cases that suggest high correlation between two variables. For simplicity, the vertical and horizontal axes show the logarithm of raw values. Actually, the coefficients of correlation are calculated as 0.837 and 0.867, which mean that the correlation is very strong.

Table 22.5 summarized the correlation coeffecients between NHI points and length of stay with respect to the whole cases, neoplasm, and three major types of malignant neoplasm: lung, stomach, and liver. Comparison of the coefficient of correlation between the group with and without a surgical operation shows that the group without an operation has higher correlations than that with an operation, which suggests that NHI points of the treatment methods other than surgical operations should be strongly dependent on the lengths of stay.

22.6.3.4   Generalized Linear Model

Since all the items except for the length of stay are categorical variables, conventional regression models cannot be applied to the study on relations between

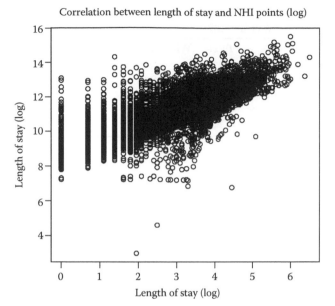

FIGURE 22.14:   Scattergram of length of stay and NHI points (logarithm transformation, total data).

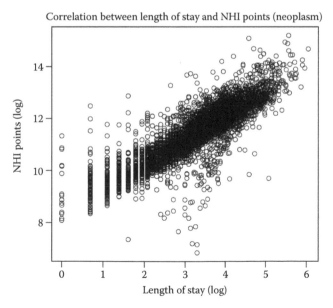

FIGURE 22.15:   Scattergram of length of stay and NHI points (logarithm transformation, neoplasm).

TABLE 22.5: Correlation between length of stay and
NHI points (after logarithm transformation).

	Total	With Operation	Without Operation
Total cases	0.837	0.829	0.779
Neoplasm	0.867	0.844	0.826
Lung cancer	0.838	0.648	0.903
Stomach cancer	0.827	0.738	0.801
Liver cancer	0.711	0.577	0.755

NHI points and other items. For this purpose, generalized linear model [6] was applied to the dataset on combination of accounting data and discharge summaries. NHI point was selected as a target variable and the following four variables were selected as explanatory variables: outcome, treatment method, major division of ICD-9 codes, and the categorized length of stay. The length of stay is categorized so that the distribution of the transformed variable is close to normal distribution, where the width of windows is set to 0.5 for the logarithmic value of the length of stay. Treatment, outcome, and major divisions of ICD codes are transformed into dummy variables to clarify the contributions of these values to a target variable. For example, the outcomes of discharge are split into six dummy variables—D1: recovered, D2: improved, D3: unchanged, D4: worsened, D5: dead, and D6: others. Figure 22.16 shows the results of generalised linear models (GLM) on the total cases, whose target variable is NHI points. All the variables are sorted by the F value. The most contributing factor is the length of stay, whereas the contributions of the other factors are small. Figure 22.17 gives the results of GLM on major division (malignant neoplasm) and three minor divisions, whose target variable is NHI points. Compared with Figure 22.16, the number of factors that gives the significant contributions to NHI points are very small, which suggest that the variabilities of NHI points in major and minor divisions are very low, compared with that of total cases.

22.7   Conclusion

Since all the clinical information have been stored electronically as a HIS, it is now expected that mining such combined data will give a new insight to medical accidents.

In order to utilize information about risk extracted from information systems, we propose risk mining that integrates the following three important process: risk detection, risk clarification, and risk utilization. Risk detection discovers patterns or information unexpected to domain experts, which can be viewed as a sign of large-scale accidents. In risk clarification, domain experts and data miners construct the model

```
Call: glm(formula
    = lognhi0 ~ (loglos0 + sex + age + outcome + adtime)^2,
    data = table)

Deviance Residuals:
    Min         1Q      Median          3Q         Max
-7.17179   -0.34257   -0.05306     0.26980     4.37032

Coefficients:
                    Estimate   Std. Error   t value   Pr(>|t|)
(Intercept)        8.5134576    0.0517890   164.388    < 2e-16 ***
loglos           0 0.8556933    0.0160016    53.476    < 2e-16 ***
sexM               0.1609546    0.0405073     3.973   7.12e-05 ***
age               -0.0038052    0.0008674    -4.387   1.16e-05 ***
outcome           -0.0083361    0.0181751    -0.459   0.646487
adtime            -0.0071641    0.0207570    -0.345   0.729992
loglos0:sexM      -0.0076588    0.0094779    -0.808   0.419061
loglos0:age        0.0006624    0.0001925     3.441   0.000581 ***
loglos0:outcome   -0.0081192    0.0048621    -1.670   0.094960 .
loglos0:adtime    -0.0091114    0.0052452    -1.737   0.082392 .
sexM:age          -0.0003907    0.0004071    -0.960   0.337163
sexM:outcome      -0.0265756    0.0117403    -2.264   0.023611 *
sexM:adtime        0.0049953    0.0110712     0.451   0.651850
age:outcome        0.0011690    0.0002427     4.816   1.48e-06 ***
age:adtime         0.0011459    0.0002167     5.289   1.25e-07 ***
outcome:adtime     0.0136464    0.0056265     2.425   0.015304 *
---
Signif. codes:
        0 '***' 0.001 '**' 0.01 '*' 0.05 '.' 0.1 ' ' 1

(Dispersion parameter for Gaussian family
        taken to be 0.3421949)

    Null deviance: 18087.9  on 15425  degrees of freedom
Residual deviance:  5273.2  on 15410  degrees of freedom AIC:
27253

Number of Fisher scoring iterations: 2
```

FIGURE 22.16: GLM analysis on NHI points (total cases, logarithmic transformed data).

of the hidden mechanism of risk, focusing on detected risk information. If domain experts need more information with finer granularity, we should collect more data with detailed information, and apply data mining to newly collected data. Risk utilization evaluated clarified risk information in a real-world environment to prevent risk events. If risk information is not enough to prevention, then more analysis is required. Thus, additional data collection is evoked for a new cycle of risk-mining process.

```
glm(formula
    = lognhi ~ (loglos + sex + age + outcome + adtime)^2,
    data = data_tumor)

Deviance Residuals:
     Min        1Q     Median        3Q       Max
-4.254140  -0.253159  -0.006586   0.257345  3.272261

Coefficients:
                 Estimate Std. Error t value Pr(>|t|)
(Intercept)     8.3787405  0.1231678  68.027  < 2e-16 ***
loglos          0.9676587  0.0318115  30.419  < 2e-16 ***
sexM            0.0635790  0.0850749   0.747   0.4549
age            -0.0006800  0.0018249  -0.373   0.7095
outcome         0.0149955  0.0366230   0.409   0.6822
adtime          0.0212879  0.0319450   0.666   0.5052
loglos:sexM     0.0270253  0.0161205   1.676   0.0937 .
loglos:age     -0.0005277  0.0003898  -1.354   0.1758
loglos:outcome  0.0109782  0.0071636   1.532   0.1255
loglos:adtime  -0.0412971  0.0086875  -4.754 2.06e-06 ***
sexM:age       -0.0017424  0.0008612  -2.023   0.0431 *
sexM:outcome   -0.0042336  0.0172197  -0.246   0.8058
sexM:adtime     0.0017416  0.0188084   0.093   0.9262
age:outcome    -0.0007851  0.0004409  -1.781   0.0750 .
age:adtime      0.0018626  0.0003839   4.852 1.26e-06 ***
outcome:adtime  0.0053574  0.0072173   0.742   0.4579
---
Signif. codes:
        0 '***' 0.001 '**' 0.01 '*' 0.05 '.' 0.1 ' ' 1

(Dispersion parameter for Gaussian family
   taken to be 0.2561771)

    Null deviance: 4940.4  on 4729  degrees of freedom
Residual deviance: 1207.6  on 4714  degrees of freedom AIC: 6999.4

Number of Fisher scoring iterations: 2
```

FIGURE 22.17: GLM analysis on NHI points (neoplasm, logarithmic transformed data).

As an illustrative example, we applied risk-mining process to analysis of nurses' incident data. First, data collected in 6 months were analyzed by rule-induction methods, which detects several important factors for incidents (risk detection). Since data do not include precise information about these factors, we recollect incident data for 6 months to collect precise information about incidents. Then, rule induction is applied to new data. Domain experts discussed all the results obtained and found several important systematic errors in workflow (risk clarification). Finally, nurses changed workflow to prevent incidents and data were recollected for 6 months. Surprisingly, the frequency of medication errors has been reduced to one-tenth (risk utilization).

References

[1] ICD9.chrisendres.com. Online icd9/icd9cm codes and medical dictionary. http://icd9cm.chrisendres.com/.

[2] P. McCullagh and J.A. Nelder. *Generalized Linear Models*, 2nd edition. CRC Press, Boca Raton, FL, 1990.

[3] J.R. Quinlan. *C4.5—Programs for Machine Learning*. Morgan Kaufmann, Palo Alto, CA, 1993.

[4] S. Tsumoto. Knowledge discovery in clinical databases and evaluation of discovered knowledge in outpatient clinic. *Information Sciences*, 124:125–137, 2000.

[5] S. Tsumoto. G5: Data mining in medicine. In W. Kloesgen and J. Zytkow (Eds.), *Handbook of Data Mining and Knowledge Discovery*. Oxford University Press, Oxford, 2001, pp. 798–807.

[6] R. Walters. *M Programming: A Comprehensive Guide*. Butterworth-Heinemann, Woburn, MA, 1997.

Chapter 23

Challenges for Information Discovery on Electronic Medical Records

**Vagelis Hristidis, Fernando Farfán, Redmond P. Burke,
Anthony F. Rossi, and Jeffrey A. White**

Contents

23.1   Introduction

The National Health Information Network (NHIN) and its data-sharing build-ing blocks, Regional Health Information Organizations (RHIOs), are encouraging the widespread adoption of electronic medical records for all hospitals within the next five years. In addition, the Department of Health and Human Services (HHS) has recently increased funding, and placed pressure on the health care industry to improve the technology involving the exchange of medical information. Many stan-dards and protocols have been introduced that will aid in the process of unifying the electronic medical record into a single architecture. A key component of this effort is the adoption and standardization of electronic medical records (EMRs). To date, there has been little or no effort to define methods or approaches to rapidly search such documents and return meaningful results.

One of the most promising standards for EMR manipulation and exchange is Health Level (HL) 7's Clinical Document Architecture (CDA) [1], which leverages a semistructured format (Extensible Markup Language [XML]), dictionaries, and ontologies to specify the structure and semantics of EMRs for the purpose of elec-tronic data interchange (EDI). This HL7 architecture has been adopted worldwide.

The definition and adoption of this standard presents new challenges to related computer science disciplines like data management, data mining, and information retrieval (IR). In this chapter we study the problem of facilitating information dis-covery on a corpus of CDA documents, i.e., given a question (query) and a set of CDA EMRs, find the entities (typically subtrees) that are good for the query, and rank them according to their goodness with respect to the query. The success of Web search engines has shown that keyword queries are a useful and intuitive information discovery approach. Therefore, we focus in keyword queries in this chapter. Other types of information discovery queries on EMRs not studied here include numeric conditions, aggregation and statistics, classification, and clustering (the last two are closer to the data mining discipline).

As an example, consider the usual scenario where a doctor wants to check possi-ble conflicts or complications between two drugs. Keyword query "drug-A drug-B death" could be submitted to discover cases where a patient who took both drugs died. Note that the word "death" can be specified in many different elements of a CDA document, and also synonyms or related terms like "mortality" can be used instead. The latter can be tackled by leveraging appropriate medical ontologies like Systematized Nomenclature of Human and Veterinary Medicine Clinical Terminol-ogy (SNOMED CT) [2] as discussed below.

To study the challenges and requirements of information discovery on EMRs we have built a diverse research team consisting of computer scientists, medical research doctors, and a partner from the medical informatics industry. The medical doctors provided the domain knowledge regarding the types of queries and answers that are of interest as well as the possible applications of such an information discovery system. Furthermore, they enumerated the different critical dimensions in searching EMRs, like time, location, and type of stakeholder. These dimensions have not been considered in systems for searching general XML documents; however, ignoring these dimensions would significantly limit the use of an EMR information discovery engine.

The key ranking criteria found in current systems as well as in Refs. [3–5] are (a) relevance, (b) quality (authority), and (c) specificity. Relevance to the query has the obvious meaning, while quality represents the query-independent importance of a result. For example, a medication is more important than the name of an insurance company for a clinical researcher. Specificity determines how focused a result is to the query. For example, returning a department of a hospital when the query is only relevant to a particular doctor of this department is worse than returning this doctor object.

It is challenging to define the information discovery semantics for CDA documents such that the three aforementioned key ranking criteria are considered, given the hierarchical structure and specific semantics of CDA, and the common references to outside entities like dictionaries, ontologies, separate text, or multimedia patient data. Medical dictionaries and ontologies typically used in CDA are SNOMED CT [2], Logical Observation Identifiers Links and Codes (LOINC) [6], and RxNorm [7]. We also study how previous work on information discovery on XML data [5,8–17] can be leveraged, and what limitations might exist in this unique domain.

We note that our study does not address the important privacy issues involved in accessing patient information, as required by the United States Health Insurance Portability and Accountability Act (HIPAA) [18]. We envision two possible scenarios. The simplest scenario is that each division of an institution deploys the information discovery engine on its own corpus of EMRs and provides authentication-controlled access to the division's practitioners. The more complex scenario, which is out of the scope of this chapter, is to provide information discovery on a set of interconnected federated databases where elaborate access control mechanisms must be employed [19].

The rest of this chapter is organized as follows: Section 23.2 presents a background exposition of current clinical information standards and a brief survey on information discovery on XML data. Section 23.3 addresses the challenges that we have identified to execute information discovery on a corpus of EMR documents. Section 23.4 presents additional related work. Our concluding remarks are presented in Section 23.5.

23.2 Background

In this section we review key standards used to represent clinical data and EMRs and present previous work on information discovery on general XML documents. In particular, Section 23.2.1 introduces some popular clinical information representation standards as well as clinical ontologies, whereas Section 23.2.2 presents the CDA, which will be the focus of this chapter. Given that CDA is represented in

XML, Section 23.2.3 presents a brief survey on information discovery on general XML documents.

23.2.1   Clinical Information Models, Dictionaries, and Ontologies

The work in Refs. [20,21] described medical informatics as the broad term representing the core theories, concepts, and techniques of information applications in health. We describe the key standards, dictionaries, and ontologies that are currently used in CDA. In particular, we first present the reference information model (RIM) [22], the model from which the CDA documents derive their meaning. Three popular clinical dictionaries/ontologies referred to in CDA documents are presented: SNOMED [2], LOINC [6], and RxNorm [7].

23.2.1.1   Reference Information Model

The HL7 RIM is the grammatical specification of HL7 messages, constituting the building blocks of the language entities and the relationships among them. RIM can be represented as a network of classes, expressed using a notation similar to the Unified Modeling Language (UML) [23]. Its structure can be summarized into six core classes and a set of relations between them, as depicted in Figure 23.1. We include a brief description of each class as follows:

The Act class represents all the actions and happenings—analogous to a verb—to be documented through the health care process, capturing all the events that have happened in the past, that are currently happening, or that are expected to happen in the future. The terms Act, Action, and Activity are all used interchangeably [24].

The Entity class represents any physical thing or being analogous to nouns that takes part or is of interest in the health care and that is capable of participating in an Act. Although it instantiates any physical thing or group of physical things (including living subjects and organisms), it does not include the roles that things can play or the acts that things can perform.

The Role class ties an entity to the acts that it plays or provides, specifying how a particular entity participates in a particular act. Each role is played by one entity, but one entity in a particular role can participate in an act in several ways.

The RoleLink class specifies the connections and dependencies that exist between two different and individual Role objects. The Participation class specifies a relationship between a particular Role instance and a particular Act instance. At the same

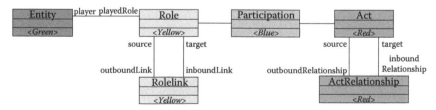

FIGURE 23.1:   RIM core class diagram.

TABLE 23.1:   RIM core classes examples.

Core Class	Example
Act	Clinical observation Assessment of health condition
Entity	Person Chemical substance
Role	Patient Employee
RoleLink	Manager has authority over analyst (using RoleLink for direct authority).
Participation	Surgeon Author
ActRelationship	Theophylline mitigates asthma (using ActRelationship of type mitigates).

time, it connects the Entity playing the Role, to the specified Act, thus expressing the context for the Act in terms of who performed it.

The ActRelationship class associates a pair of Act objects, representing a connection from one Act to another one. Such relationships include "Act to Act" associations, as well as "Source/Target" associations between the objects. Reference [22] states that ActRelationship on the same source Act are called the outbound act relationships of that Act. ActRelationships on the same target Act are called the inbound relationships of that Act. Table 23.1 presents some examples to each core class of the RIM model.

Each Act may be related to any number of Participations, in Roles, played by Entities, at the same time that each Act may be related to other Acts via the ActRelationship class. The Act, Role, and Entity classes may also be specialized into other classes. As an example, the Entity class specializes into the class Living Subject, which itself has a specialization class called Person. Person then inherits the attributes of both Entity and Living Subject. CDA documents (Section 23.2.2) use the semantic definitions from the HL7 RIM, using the HL7 Version 3 Data Types [25] to define the clinical content of the documents.

Since HL7 mainly focuses on information interchange, RIM also provides a set of classes to define a communication infrastructure, including Message Control and Infrastructure (structured documents and components) [24,26].

23.2.1.2   Systematized Nomenclature of Medicine

The SNOMED was created more than 20 years ago as the conjunction of SNOMED RT and the United Kingdom's Clinical Terms Version 3, and has grown up into a comprehensive set of over 150,000 records in 12 different chapters or axes. These concepts are organized into anatomy (topology), morphology (pathologic structure), normal and abnormal functions, symptoms and signs of disease, chemicals, drugs, enzymes and other body proteins, living organisms, physical agents, spatial relationships, occupations, social contexts, diseases/diagnoses, and procedures [2].

Within the disease/diagnosis axis, many disease concepts have cross-references to other concepts in the terminology that are essential characteristics of the disease. These form a useful basis for further formalization and development of a reference terminology [27].

SNOMED has created and is committed to spreading the adoption and implementation of SNOMED clinical terms (SNOMED CT). SNOMED CT is a universal health care terminology and infrastructure, whose objective is making health care knowledge usable wherever and whenever it is needed. It provides a common language that enables a consistent way of capturing, sharing, and aggregating health data across specialties and sites of care. The SNOMED CT structure is concept based; each concept represents a unit of meaning, having one or more human language terms that can be used to describe the concept. Every concept has interrelationships with other concepts that provide logical computer readable definitions, including hierarchical relationships and clinical attributes. Figures 23.2 and 23.3 show subgraphs of the SNOMED CT ontology graph.

At the moment, SNOMED CT contains more than 325,000 concepts, with 800,000 terms in English, 350,000 in Spanish, and 150,000 in German. Also, there are 1,200,000 relationships connecting these terms and concepts.

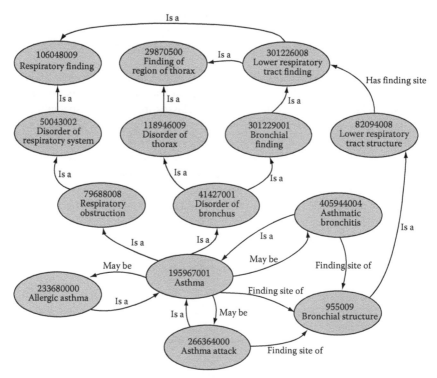

FIGURE 23.2: Partial SNOMED ontology for the term Asthma.

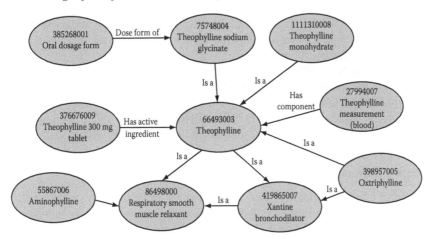

FIGURE 23.3:   Partial SNOMED ontology for the term "Theophylline."

SNOMED CT terms are routinely referenced in CDA documents by their numeric codes, that is, the SNOMED CT vocabulary is referenced as an external domain according to HL7 V3 processes.

23.2.1.3   Logical Observation Identifiers Names and Codes

LOINC is a voluntary effort housed in the Regenstrief Institute, associated with Indiana University. It was initiated in 1994 by the Regenstrief Institute and developed by Regenstrief and the LOINC committee as a response to the demand for electronic movement of clinical data. LOINC facilitates the exchange and pooling of results, such as blood hemoglobin, serum potassium, or vital signs, for clinical care, outcomes management, and research. Currently, most laboratories and other diagnostic services use HL7 to send their results electronically from their reporting systems to their care systems. However, most laboratories and other diagnostic care services identify tests in these messages by means of their internal and idiosyncratic code values. Thus, the care system cannot fully understand and properly file the results they receive unless they either adopt the producer's laboratory codes (which is impossible if they receive results from multiple sources), or invest in the work to map each result producer's code system to their internal code system. LOINC codes are universal identifiers for laboratory and other clinical observations that solve this problem.

The LOINC laboratory terms set provides a standard set of universal names and codes for identifying individual laboratory and clinical results. LOINC codes allow users to merge clinical results from many sources into one database for patient care, clinical research, or management. The LOINC database currently contains about 41,000 terms, which include 31,000 observational terms related to laboratory testing.

Each record in the LOINC database identifies a clinical observation and contains a formal six-part name, a unique name for tests, identifying code with check digits, synonyms, and other useful information.

Currently, LOINC codes are being used in the United States by laboratories and federal agencies and are part of the HIPAA [18] Attachment Proposal [28]. Internationally, LOINC has been adopted in Switzerland, Hong Kong, Australia, Canada, and Germany. Similar to SNOMED CT, LOINC is used by CDA documents as a vocabulary domain, encoding CDA components into a standard database of terms.

23.2.1.4 RxNorm

RxNorm [7] is a standardized nomenclature for clinical drugs produced by the National Library of Medicine. A clinical drug is a pharmaceutical product administered to a patient with a therapeutic or diagnostic intent. The definition of a clinical drug combines its ingredients, strengths, and form. The form refers to the physical form in which the drug is administered in a prescription or order. For example, two possible definitions of clinical drugs are: (a) acetaminophen 500 mg oral tablet, for a generic drug name, and (b) acetaminophen 500 mg oral tablet [Tylenol], for a branded drug name [7].

The purpose of RxNorm is to standardize the information exchange both between systems within the same organization and between different organizations, allowing various systems using different drug nomenclature to share data efficiently. It is intended to cover all prescription medications approved for use in the United States. RxNorm is conformed by concepts, collections of names identical in meaning at a specified level of abstraction. Each concept can be mapped to different string values in different systems, all naming things that are the same. It also provides a linkage to terms from other vocabularies (i.e., the concept Ortho-Novum 7/7/7 21 tablets is a term from the SNOMED vocabulary; it is not within RxNorm at all, except as it is related to RxNorm within the RXNREL table [7]).

23.2.2 Clinical Document Architecture

The CDA is an XML-based document markup standard that specifies the structure and semantics of clinical documents, such as discharge summaries and progress notes, for the purpose of exchange. It is an American National Standards (ANSI) approved HL7 standard, intended to become the de facto electronic medical record.

According to the developers of CDA version 2.0 [1], the following are the main characteristics of the CDA standard:

1. *Persistence*: The clinical documents exist in an unaltered state for a time period defined by local and regulatory requirements.

2. *Stewardship*: A clinical document is maintained by an organization entrusted with its care.

3. *Authentication*: The clinical records are intended to be legally authenticated.

4. *Context*: The clinical document specifies its own default context.

5. *Wholeness*: Authentication of a clinical document applies to the whole instance and the full context. Also, it is a complete and persistent set of information including text, images, sound, and other multimedia content.

6. *Human readability*: A clinical document is human readable.

Some projects already implementing CDA are Continuity of Care Record (the United States) [29], SCIPHOX (Germany) [30], MedEmed (Canada) [31], PICNIC (Denmark) [32], e-Claims Supporting Document Architecture (Canada), Health Information Summaries (New Zealand), Aluetietojaerjestelmae (Finland) [33], and Dalhousie Discharge Summary System (Canada).

Figure 23.4 [34] shows a fragment of the CDA's object model that represents the semantic constructs of the RIM, depicting the connection from a document section to a portion of the CDA clinical statement model with nested CDA entries.

The colors in Figure 23.4 identify these classes with the core classes of RIM as depicted in Ref. [34] (red for Act specializations, blue for Participations, green for Entities, yellow for Roles, and pink for Relationships). As described in Ref. [34], an Act can have zero to many ActRelationships to other Acts, and can have zero to many Participations, each played by an Entity in some Role. A Role relates two Entities; the Entity playing the Role is represented by a solid line and the Entity who recognizes the role is represented with a dashed line. Thus, in Figure 23.4, a "legalAuthenticator" is a Participant of a "ClinicalDocument" Act and is played by a "Person" Entity in an "AssignedEntity" Role that is recognized by an "Organization" Entity [34].

The "Component" class is an ActRelationship that may link the "ClinicalDocument" to the body choice (NonXMLBody or StructuredBody) or the "StructuredBody" to each nested "Section." The "StructuredBody" contains one or more Section

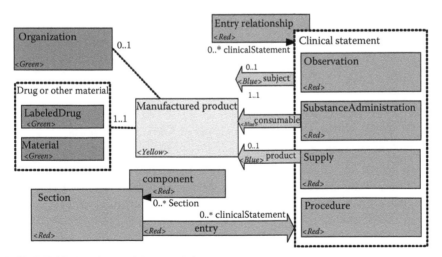

FIGURE 23.4:   CDA object model.

components, each of which contains a human readable title and a "narrative block," the human readable content that has to be populated by the document originator and rendered by the recipient. Each Section can also contain any number of CDA entries and external references. The CDA narrative block is wrapped by the "text" element within the "Section" element, and provides a slot for the human readable content needing to be rendered. Within a document section, the narrative block represents content to be rendered, whereas CDA entries represent structured content provided for a computer. CDA entries encode content present in the narrative block of the same section. The example shows two "Observation" CDA entries, although several other CDA entries are defined.

Figure 23.4 shows, at the right of the Section class, the Entry Relationship, which leads to the clinical statement portion. Each Entry represents structured content intended for computer processing such as decision support applications. Also, the clinicalStatement class contains specializations of the Act class (in this case Observation, SubstanceAdministration, Supply, and Procedure) that will be included in the formal representation [34].

CDA external references always occur within the context of a CDA entry, and are wrapped by the "reference" element. External references refer to things that exist outside the CDA document—such as some other image, some other procedure, or some other observation (which is wrapped by the "ExternalObservation" element). The CDA entry that wraps the external reference can be used to encode the specific portions of the external reference that are addressed in the narrative block.

Figure 23.5 depicts a sample CDA document D_1, which is wrapped by the "ClinicalDocument" element, as it appears in line 2 of this figure. The CDA header (lines 3–29) identifies and classifies the document, and provides information about authentication of the record as well as the participants (patient and involved providers). Figure 23.6 depicts the tree representation of D_1.

The CDA body (lines 31–82), which is wrapped by the StructuredBody element, is the core of the document and contains the clinical report. It can be either an unstructured segment or an XML fragment. We focus this study in the structured XML definition of the clinical report, which is the one providing the most opportunity for high-quality information discovery. Traditional IR approaches [3,4] can be applied to the unstructured scenario.

23.2.3 Information Discovery on General XML Documents

XML has emerged as the de facto standard format to represent and exchange data through the World Wide Web and other heterogeneous environments, spanning a wide variety of domains and applications. The increased popularity of XML repositories and XML documents in general must be accompanied by effective ways to retrieve the information stored in this format. In this section we present an overview of previous work on searching XML documents. This corpus of work will be viewed as the starting point to present the challenges of information discovery on CDA XML documents in Section 23.3.

```
1   <? xml version="1.0" ?>
2   <ClinicalDocument xmlns="urn:hl7-org:v3"
    xmlns:voc="urn:hl7-org:v3/voc"
    xmlns:xsi="http://www.w3.org/2001/XMLSchema-instance"
    xsi:schemaLocation="urn:hl7-org:v3 CDA.ReleaseTwo.Committee.
    2004.xsd" templateId="2.16.840.1.113883.3.27.1776">
3     <id extension="c266" root="2.16.840.1.113883.3.933"/> 4
4     <confidentialityCode code="N" codeSystem="2.16.840.1.11.3883.
      5.25"/>
5     <author>
6      <time value="20040407"/>
7      <assignedAuthor>
8       <id extension="KP00017" root="2.16.840.1.113883.3.933"/>
9       <assignedPerson>
10       <name>
11        <given>Juan</given>
12        <family>Woodblack</family>
13        <suffix>MD</suffix>
14    </name></assignedPerson></assignedAuthor></author>
15    <recordTarget>
16     <patientRole>
17      <id extension="49912" root="2.16.840.1.113883.3.933"/>
18       <patientPatient>
19        <name>
20         <given>FirstName</given>
21          <family>LastName</family>
22          <suffix>Jr.</suffix>
23         </name>
24         <administrativeGenderCode code="M" codeSystem="2.16.
           840.1.5.1"/>
25         <birthTime value="20020924"/>
26        </patientPatient>
27        <providerOrganization>
28         <id extension="M345" root="2.16.840.1.113883.3.933"/>
29    </providerOrganization></patientRole></recordTarget>
30    <component>
31     <StructuredBody>
32      <component>
33       <section>
34        <code code="10160-0" codeSystem="2.16.840.1.113883.6.1"
      codeSystemName="LOINC"/>
35        <title>Medications</title>
36        <entry>
37         <Observation>
38          <code code="84100007" codeSystem="2.16.840.1.113883.
             6.96"
          codeSystemName="SNOMED CT" displayName="Medications"/>
```

FIGURE 23.5:   HL7 CDA sample document.

(*continued*)

```
39        <value xsi:type="CD" code="195967001" codeSystem=
          "2.16.840.1.113883.6.96" codeSystemName="SNOMED CT"
          displayName="Asthma">
40          <originalText><reference value="m1"/></originalText>
41        </value></Observation></entry>
42        <entry>
43         <Observation>
44          <code code="84100007" codeSystem="2.16.840.1.113883.
              6.96"
          codeSystemName="SNOMED CT" displayName="Medications"/>
45          <value xsi:type="CD" code="32398004" codeSystem=
          "2.16.840.1.113883.6.96" codeSystemName="SNOMED CT"
          displayName="Bronchitis">
46          <value xsi:type="CD" code="91143003" codeSystem=
          "2.16.840.1.113883.6.96" codeSystemName="SNOMED CT"
          displayName="Albuterol" />
47        </value></Observation></entry>
48        <entry>
49         <SubstanceAdministration>
50          <text><content ID="m1">Theophylline</content>20 mg
              every
          other day, alternating with 18 mg every other day. Stop
          if temperature is above 103F.</text>
51          <consumable>
52           <manufacturedProduct>
53            <manufacturedLabeledDrug>
54             <code code="66493003" codeSystem="2.16.840.1.113883.
                 6.96"
            codeSystemName="SNOMED CT" displayName="Theophylline"/>
55             </manufacturedLabeledDrug></manufacturedProduct>
               </consumable>
56        </SubstanceAdministration></entry>
57      </section></component>
58      <component>
59       <section>
60        <code code="11384-5" codeSystem="2.16.840.1.113883.6.1"
            codeSystemName="LOINC"/>
61        <title>Physical Examination</title>
62        <component>
63         <section>
64          <code code="8716-3" codeSystem="2.16.840.1.113883.6.1"
              codeSystemName="LOINC"/>
65           <title>Vital Signs</title>
66           <text>
67            <table>
68             <tr>
69              <th>Temperature</th>
70              <td>36.9 C (98.5 F)</td>
```

FIGURE 23.5: (continued)

```
71                    </tr>
72                    <tr>
73                     <th>Pulse</th>
74                     <td>86 / minute </td>
75                    </tr></table></text>
76                    <entry>
77                     <Observation>
78                      <code code="50373000" codeSystem="2.16.840.1.
                           113883.6.96"
                      codeSystemName="SNOMED CT" displayName="Body height"/>
79                       <effectiveTime value="200404071430"/>
80                       <value xsi:type="PQ" value="1.77" unit="m" />
                     </Observation></entry></section></component></section>
                     </component>
81  </StructuredBody></component>
82  </ClinicalDocument>
```

FIGURE 23.5: (continued)

23.2.3.1 Limitations of Traditional Information Retrieval Methods

The traditional and popular text-based search engines cannot deal effectively with XML documents due to a series of limitations. First, text-based search engines do not exploit the XML tags and nested hierarchical structure of the XML documents. Second, the whole XML document is treated as an integral unit and is returned as a whole, which is unacceptable given the possibly large sizes of XML documents, in contrast we would like to be able to return parts of an XML document. A third drawback is the keyword proximity concept in XML, which can be measured in terms of containment edges, in contrast to the traditional keyword proximity search in text and HTML documents. That is, two keywords that may appear physically proximal in the XML file may be distant or unrelated in the tree-structured XML document and vice versa.

23.2.3.2 Previous Work on Searching XML Documents

XRANK [5] computes rankings at the granularity of an element, considering element-to-element links in addition to document-to-document links. XRANK ranks the XML elements by generalizing the PageRank algorithm [35], combining the ranking of elements with keyword proximity.

XSEarch [36] ranks the results taking into consideration both the degrees of the semantic relationship and the relevance of the keyword. XSEarch also adds the power of distinguishing between tag names and textual content. They also disallow results where the same tag name appears more than once in nodes of a vertical result path. Cohen et al. [10] present an extended framework to specify the semantic relationship of XML elements, providing a variety of interconnection semantics based on the XML schema, improving the quality of the rankingof XSEarch. XIRQL [12] utilizes

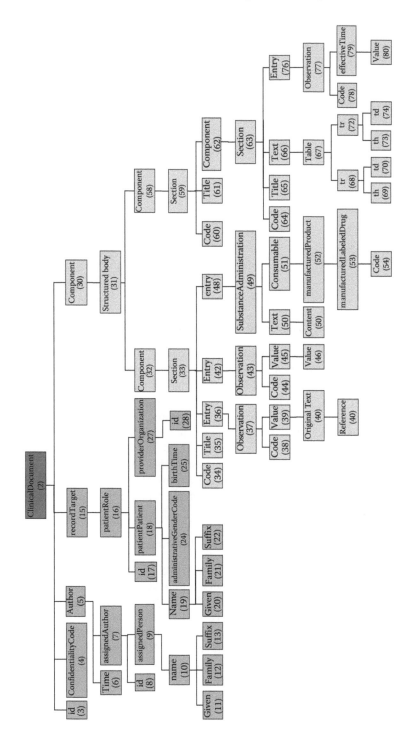

FIGURE 23.6:   Tree representation of document D_1 in Figure 23.5.

a different strategy to compute its ranking, defining index units, specific entity types that can be indexed and used for tf–idf (term frequency–inverse document frequency) computation.

Schema-free XQuery [15] refines the work of XSEarch by utilizing meaningful lowest common ancestors instead of the concept of interconnected nodes, skimming some unrelated, "too inclusive" elements that are not supposed to be returned. Cohen et al. [10] improve this approach even further by including the schema into the framework and discovering interconnection information. Xu and Papakonstantinou [17] define a result as a smallest tree, that is, a subtree that does not contain any subtree that also contains all keywords. Hristidis et al. [14] group structurally similar tree-results to avoid overwhelming the user.

Previous works define a query answer in several different ways. XRANK, XIRQL, and TeXQuery [8] define an answer to be a document fragment (generally a subtree)–the most specific fragment of the XML document is typically the highest ranked answer. In contrast, XSEarch defines the result to a query to be a sequence of XML nodes and null values forming a path that connects the elements that contain the keywords or that satisfy the query predicates. On the other hand, Carmel et al. [11] utilize XML fragments as the syntax to specify the query but their query answers consist of entire documents, not fragments. Pradhan [37] present a flexible algebraic approach for defining results' properties in the query, in addition to a list of keywords.

XKeyword [13] operates on an XML graph (with ID–IDREF edges) and returns a subtree of minimum size that contains all query keywords. The World Wide Web Consortium has proposed syntactic and semantic extensions to XQuery and XPath [8,16] to support full-text search capabilities. Amer-Yahia et al. [9] present an algebra to support such an extension.

23.3   Challenges of Information Discovery on CDA Documents

In this section we present a series of challenges that have to be addressed to effectively perform information discovery on a corpus of CDA documents. For simplicity we focus on plain keyword queries, although the same challenges are valid for semi-structured queries as well—a semistructured query is a query where partial information about the structure of the results is provided. For example, specify that we are only interested in "code" elements under "Observation" elements.

We discuss why the general work on information discovery on XML documents (Section 23.2.3) is not adequate to provide quality information discovery on CDA XML documents. The key reasons are the complex and domain-specific semantics and the frequent references to external information sources like dictionaries and ontologies.

We use document D_1 depicted in Figure 23.5 as our running example, along with the plain keyword queries of Table 23.2.

TABLE 23.2: CDA document queries.

ID	Keyword Query
q_1	Asthma Theophylline
q_2	Substance Theophylline
q_3	Respiratory Theophylline
q_4	Temperature

23.3.1 Structure and Scope of Results

In contrast to traditional Web search where whole HTML documents are returned as query results, in the case of XML documents and particularly CDA documents, we need to define what a meaningful query result is. Previous work has studied different approaches to define the structure of results. A corpus of works [5,8,12] consider a whole subtree as result, that is, a result is unambiguously defined by the lowest common ancestor (LCA) node of the keyword nodes. We refer to this approach as subtree-as-result. For example, XRANK favors deeply nested elements, returning the deepest node containing the keywords as the most specific one, having more context information. In contrast, a path as the result is proposed by the authors in Refs. [36,38–41]; where a minimal path of XML nodes is returned that collectively contain all the query keywords. Note that we use the term "path" loosely to differentiate it from the subtree-as-result approach, because it can be a collection of meeting paths (a tree) for more than two query keywords. We refer to this approach as *path-as-result*.

Example 23.1

To illustrate this challenge we execute query q_1 on document D_1. For the path-as-result approach there are two candidate results depicted in Figures 23.8a and b because of the two appearances of the keyword "Theophylline" in lines 50 and 54. For the subtree-as-result approach, only the subtree rooted at the XML node of line 33 is a possible result.

It is unclear whether the subtree-as-result or the path-as-result is a better fit for searching CDA documents. The discussion on minimal information unit (MIU) below sheds more light to this aspect.

Another issue is the scope of a result, in particular, whether results spanning across EMRs should be produced. For instance, two query keywords may be found on two EMRs authored by the same doctor (the doctor becomes the connection element as discussed in Section 23.3.10. If the query is "drug-A drug-B death" then clearly two-EMR results are not useful since if different patients took the two drugs no correlation between the drugs can be drawn. On the other hand, if the query is "rare-disease-A rare-disease-B" then it may be useful to find a doctor who has treated two patients that have had one disease each. A simple solution to this dilemma is to allow the user to explicitly specify if cross-EMR results are allowed.

Finally, doctors would like to be able to specify the results' schema in some cases, which in turn limits the types of elements searched for the query keywords.

23.3.2   Minimal Information Unit

It is challenging to define the granularity of a piece of information in a way that it is self-contained and meaningful, but at the same time specific. For example, in document D_1 returning the "value" element of line 45 without the preceding "code" element is not meaningful for the user. Hence, the "value" element is not an appropriate MIU, whereas the enclosing "Observation" element could be.

Furthermore, for some queries it is required to include into the result some elements that do not contribute in connecting the query keywords or are part of the MIU of such a connecting node. For instance, the "patientPatient" element should be included in the result of q_1 if a practitioner submits the query, but not if a researcher does. Such personalization issues are further discussed in Section 23.3.14.

Another issue is the static definition of MIU. In XKeyword [41], a "target object" is the equivalent of an MIU and they are defined statically on the schema by a domain expert. Xu et al. [42] also define MIUs in a static manner. Such static MIU definitions are not adequate for CDA information discovery, as the following scenario explains. For the query "Body height" a reasonable result is the "Observation" element in lines 77–81. On the other hand, for the query "1.77" this same element is not meaningful since obviously the user knows that "1.77" is a height value, but the patient who has this height is probably of more interest. Hence, there is a need to dynamically specify MIUs.

Example 23.2

The tight semantic relationship between the nodes in the subtree rooted at the element SubstanceAdministration in line 49 of Figure 23.5 can lead the system expert to consider this subtree as a MIU. In this case, the single result of query q_1 on document D_1 for the path-as-result approach is the one shown in Figure 23.7. If, in contrast, every element in the tree is considered a MIU, then the two paths depicted in Figure 23.8 are the results for this query.

23.3.3   Semantics of Node and Edge Types

It is challenging to incorporate the rich semantic information available for the clinical domain, and particularly for the elements of a CDA document, in the results' ranking process. At the most basic, a domain expert statically assigns a weight to each node and edge type, as in BANKS [39]. In addition to that, we can assign a relevance to whole paths on the schema as explained below. Furthermore, it is desirable that the degrees of semantic association are adjusted dynamically exploiting relevance feedback [43] and learning [44] techniques.

The equivalent of a schema for a CDA document is the CDA Release 2 object model (Figure 23.4), showing the connection from a document section to a portion

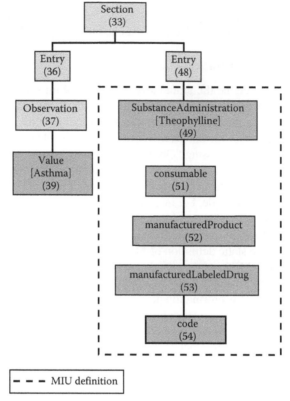

FIGURE 23.7: Result for q_1 using SubstanceAdministration as MIU.

of the CDA clinical statement model [34]. Edge and node weights can be specified on this object model. For example, the relationship between a substance and the patient it was prescribed to may be more relevant than the relationship between the substance and the doctor who prepared the EMR.

As mentioned above, assigning relevance degrees to whole paths instead of single edges can improve the ranking quality. For example, the path Substance Administration $\rightarrow$ consumable $\rightarrow$ manufacturedProduct $\rightarrow$ manufacturedLabeled Drug $\rightarrow$ code could have a higher or equal weight than SubstanceAdministration $\rightarrow$ consumable $\rightarrow$ manufacturedProduct. This is particularly important for cases where a syntactically long path corresponds to a semantically tight association. For instance, the path Substance Administration $\rightarrow$ consumable $\rightarrow$ manufacturedProduct $\rightarrow$ manufacturedLabeledDrug $\rightarrow$ code in lines 49–57 of Figure 23.5 has four edges, but intuitively this sequence of elements will typically appear as an indivisible unit. Hence, this path may be viewed as a single edge for the purpose of ranking. In general, the information discovery algorithm must neutralize the effect of the schema design decisions of CDA by considering a semantic instead of a syntactic distance.

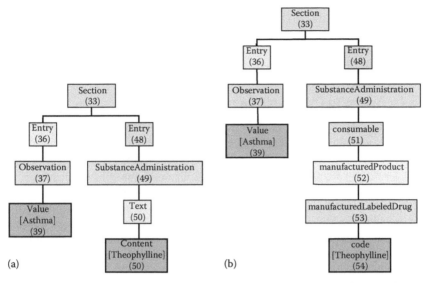

FIGURE 23.8: Atomic path results for query q_1. (a) Path connecting "Asthma" in line 39 and "Theophylline" in line 50; (b) path connecting "Asthma" in line 39 and "Theophylline" in line 54. The highlighted nodes match the terms.

Example 23.3

Consider query q_2 executed over D_1. We can see with this query the need to index and query the XML tags in addition to the values; in this case the keyword "Substance" matches the tag "SubstanceAdministration" in line 49. Figure 23.9 shows

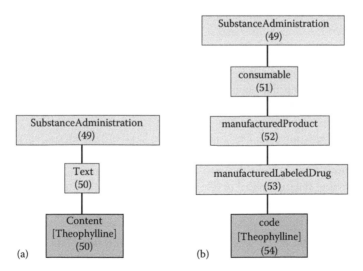

FIGURE 23.9: Path results to q_2. (a) Path connecting Substance in line 49 and Theophylline in line 50; (b) path connecting Substance in line 49 and Theophylline in line 54.

two possible results to q_2. Even though the first result only involves two edges (whereas the second involves four), it could be that the second result is ranked higher if the path SubstanceAdministration $\rightarrow$ consumable $\rightarrow$ manufacturedProduct $\rightarrow$ manufacturedLabeledDrug $\rightarrow$ code is viewed as a single edge.

23.3.4 Access to Dictionaries and Ontologies

CDA documents routinely contain references to external dictionary and ontology sources through numeric codes. As an example, document D_1 includes references to LOINC [6] and SNOMED CT [2] in lines 34 and 38, respectively. Hence, it is no longer enough to answer a query considering the CDA document in isolation, as is done by all previous work on information discovery on XML documents (Section 23.2.3). In this setting, the query keywords may refer to text in the CDA document or an ontology that is connected to the CDA document through a code reference. For example, the query keyword Appendicitis may not be present in the document but its code might be present, so we need to go to the ontology and search for the query keyword there.

On a high level, it would be desirable to view the data graph (the CDA document) along with the ontology graph (e.g., SNOMED) as a single merged graph. An approach to achieve that is the following:

1. View a code node in a CDA document and the corresponding ontology node as a single node, that is, collapse these two nodes. Equivalently, add an edge with infinite weight between them (assuming higher weight denotes higher association).

2. For free text nodes (with no code) v of the CDA document we add an edge between v and each ontology node u with weight equal to the IR similarity between the content of v and u. Only the edges with weight greater than the specified threshold are finally created.

This second technique can be omitted if we assume that the author of the CDA document is including the ontology/dictionary codes where appropriate and there are matching ontology entities for all real entities in the CDA document.

An alternative technique has been described to incorporate ontology information in the query processing [45]. Designed to enable keyword search on data graphs with authority flow semantics, the ObjectRank authority flow algorithm [46] is executed on the ontology graph to rank the ontology nodes with respect to the query, and then uses the terms of the top-ranked ontology nodes to expand the original query.

Example 23.4

Query q_3 executed on D_1 would have an empty result (for AND semantics) if the ontologies/dictionaries were not text searched. However, if the intuition discussed above is applied, the same results as in q_1 are valid, since the query term Respiratory is associated to the term "Asthma" in D_1 through relationships of the SNOMED ontology, as shown in Figure 23.2.

Note that it is challenging to rank results produced by exploiting ontological relationships as discussed in Section 23.3.5.

Performance: The solutions proposed to exploit ontology/dictionary information incur challenging performance issues. Following are two high-level techniques that can be employed to realize the above query semantics:

1. Search all ontologies for the query keywords, find adequately associated codes, and then search the CDA documents for these codes

2. Start searching the documents and for each ontology code encountered, lookup the keywords in the corresponding ontology

Furthermore, it is challenging to develop efficient precomputation and runtime algorithms to facilitate the expensive in terms of execution semantics of the merged data and ontologies graph discussed above.

Another performance challenge arises due to the size of the ontologies. As mentioned in Section 23.2.1, SNOMED CT contains more that 235,000 concepts and 1,200,000 relationships between them. This corresponds to more than 2 GB of compressed data, which will play a role in deciding the execution approach that will be more efficient.

23.3.5   Different Types of Relations in Ontology

We need to assign an appropriate value to each of the relations present in the ontologies. SNOMED CT, for example, has four different types of relationships:

1. Defining characteristics

2. Qualifying characteristics

3. Historical relationships

4. Other relationships

Figures 23.2 and 23.3 include relations such as "May be," "Finding site of," and "Has finding site" in addition to the most common "Is a" relationship. Stricter and stronger relations in the ontology should intuitively have a higher weight.

Furthermore, we need to take into consideration the direction of the edges. For instance, following "Is a" edges specializes and restricts the search on the one direction, but generalize in the other direction, with the risk of returning imprecise terms.

We must also consider the number of incoming and outgoing edges that each node has. For example, some SNOMED CT concepts such as "Duplicate concept" or "Invalid concept" participate in historical relationships and possess a large incoming degree. Navigating these historical relationships to concepts with such large in-degrees may not be beneficial to the information discovery process.

A possible approach to measure the degree of association between nodes of an ontology graph is to execute ObjectRank [46] on the ontology graph, as described by Hwang et al. [45]. In particular, for query q_3 we can place the nodes containing the keyword "Respiratory" in the base set and then execute ObjectRank. If the node containing the term "Asthma" (line 39 of D_1) ends up having a higher score than the node containing the term "Bronchitis" (line 45 of D_1), then the "Asthma" node will be preferred. This process can be further improved by assigning different authority transfer bounds [46] to various edge (relationship) types of the ontology according to their semantic association.

Example 23.5

As an example we execute query q_3 on D_1. We can see in the ontology graph of Figure 23.2 that "Asthmatic Bronchitis" and "Asthma" are both related to "Respiratory," but "Asthmatic Bronchitis" is two "Is a" edges away from "Respiratory," whereas "Asthma" is only one edge away. Hence a result containing "Theophiline" and "Asthma" (line 39) would be better than one containing "Theophyline" and "Bronchitis" (line 45).

23.3.6   Arbitrary Levels of Nesting

We can find an arbitrary number of levels of nesting and recursion in the definition of components and sections, as exemplified in the path component $\rightarrow$ section $\rightarrow$ component $\rightarrow$ section in lines 58–63 of Figure 23.5.

Taking into consideration the semantics of the document, the interconnection relationship rule of XSEarch [36], where the same tag may not appear twice in internal nodes of a result path, cannot be applied since the same tag can appear twice in a vertical path (top-to-bottom). In particular, the rule of XSEarch assumes that a vertical path may not contain the same tag twice, since elements with the same tag name are typically in the same level of the tree. This is clearly not true for CDA documents.

Hence, the XSEarch interconnection relationship should be modified considering semantic information of the surrounding elements. For instance, if we assume that a "component" element represents a hospitalization, then if two keywords with the same tag appear in different components of the same section, the XSEarch rule can be applied, but not if they are in two different sections of same component.

23.3.7   Handling ID–IDREF Edges

CDA entries can include pointers to "content" elements of the CDA narrative block; similarly, "renderMultiMedia" elements of the CDA narrative block can point out to CDA entries. The "content" element can contain an optional ID attribute to identify it, and it can serve as the target for a reference. The "originalText" component of a RIM attribute can then refer to this identifier, indicating the original text. As an example we can find an ID attribute in line 50 of Figure 23.5. A reference to this element is found in the "originalText" element of line 40.

These edge types have been ignored for results computation by previous search strategies like XRANK, which only utilizes the hyperlinks (ID-IDREFs) for score calculation. That is, results are always subtrees ignoring the ID-IDREF edges. We want to exploit these edges in producing the results. A consequence of this issue is the fact that the result can be a graph (with cycles) and not a tree. In this case, we

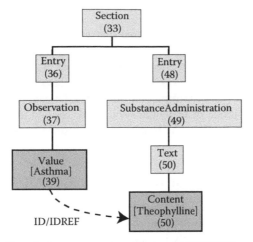

FIGURE 23.10:   Result to query q_1 considering ID/IDREFS.

need to decide whether we break the cycles to return a tree as the answer, since a tree is typically easier to present and reason about. Also, similar to XRANK, ID–IDREF and containment edges could be assigned different weights.

Example 23.6

Example: We execute query q_1 on the sample document D_1. We obtain the two path results depicted in Figure 23.8, but if we include the ID–IDREF hyperlink between elements in lines 40 and 50 of Figure 23.5 we obtain the graph depicted in Figure 23.10, containing a cycle.

In case we decide the best solution is to break the cycles, the next issue is to decide the best edge to remove. The simplest possibility is to eliminate the hyperlink and preserve a path as the one shown in Figure 23.8a. Alternatively, the weights and directions of the edges may be taken into account.

23.3.8   Free Text Embedded in CDA Document

In some cases, plain text descriptions are added to certain sections to enrich the information about the record or to express a real-life property not codified in dictionaries or ontologies. As a first measure, traditional text-based IR techniques [3,4] should be included in the architecture to support such cases.

Another technique to address the coexistence of semi-structured and unstructured data is presented in Ref. [13], where IR and proximity rankings are combined.

In addition to embedded plain text, HTML fragments can also be included to the CDA document, resulting in a mix of semantic mappings. For instance, line 50 in Figure 23.5 describes the full-text description of the dosage for a substance. Due to the complex nature of this description, there is no single entity in the ontology to accurately match it.

Example 23.7

To exemplify this challenge we execute query q_4 on our sample document D_1. Figure 23.11 shows two possible results for this query assuming each element is a MIU. Figure 23.11a presents a free-text entry containing the keyword "Temperature," whereas Figure 23.11b depicts an HTML fragment also containing the keyword. Without additional semantic information, these results cannot be ranked based on their structure; appropriate IR techniques should be applied to solve this challenge. For instance, the second result may be ranked higher since it has a smaller document length (dl).

23.3.9   Special Treatment of Time and Location Attributes

After discussing with medical researchers and practitioners, we found that time and location are critical attributes in most queries. For instance, for the query "drug-A drug-B," the doctor is probably looking for any conflict between these drugs, and hence the time distance between the prescriptions of these drugs for a patient is a critical piece of information. Location is also important since two patients located in nearby beds in the hospital should be viewed as associated because infections tend to transmit to neighboring beds. Clearly, it is challenging to standardize the representation of such location information within an EMR.

Furthermore, time and location can lead to the definition of metrics similar to the idf in IR [3]. For instance, asthma is more common in summer; hence a patient who has asthma in winter should be ranked higher for the query "asthma." Similarly, a patient who has the flu in a town where no one else has it should be ranked higher for the query "flu." These associations are too complex since time can be used to define time, distance, or periodicity. Similarly, location relationships can be specified either within a hospital or across towns.

Finally, there should be a way to specify time intervals in the query, possibly using a calendar interface, and then use the specified time window as an answers filter. Specifying the time–distance between the keywords can also be useful. For instance, the query "newborn heart block" which is often needed at Miami Childrens Hospital, should not return a patient who got a heart block when he was 60 years old but the word "newborn" appeared in his EMR in a description field of her birth day.

```
50   <text>
        <content ID="m1">Theophylline</content>
        20 mg every other day, alternating with 18 mg every other day.
        Stop if temperature is above 103F.
     </text>
(a)
```

```
69   <th>Temperature</th>
(b)
```

FIGURE 23.11:   Free text and HTML fragment results for query q_4. (a) Free text occurrence of keywords on query q_4; (b) embedded HTML fragment is the result of query q_4.

23.3.10 Identity Reconciliation and Value Edges

A single real-life entity (e.g., a medication or a doctor) is duplicated every time it is used in a CDA. Hence, associating two records of the same author, or two patients with the same medication is hard. In contrast, in previous work on searching XML documents, a real-life entity is typically represented by a single XML element, which is linked using ID–IDREF edges where needed. For instance, in XKeyword two articles of the same author have an IDREF to the same author element.

The problem of reference reconciliation has been tackled both in the context of structured databases [47–53] and in the context of free text document collections [50,54–56]. However, focusing on the domain of CDA documents allows manually specifying rules by a domain expert on what types of elements are good candidates for referencing identical real-life objects, in case these elements have identical or similar values.

In particular, we can identify on the schema the elements that have the property that the same value probably means the same real-life entity, so that "value edges" can be added accordingly. Such elements may be the "assignedAuthor," the "patient-Patient," the "manufacturedLabeledDrug" and so on. On the other hand, no "value edge" should be added between two "title" elements. For example, two patients who both have Physical Examination value on the "title" element (line 61 in Figure 23.5) are not related in any way.

As another example, if two medications have the same SNODEM code, they should be associated. However, if a drug and its generic have different SNOMED codes, such associations are hard to establish.

Another challenge involves the use of multiple possibly overlapping ontologies across the corpus of CDA documents. For instance, different codes are used for the term "Asthma" in SNOMED CT and LOINC (195967001 and 45669-9, respectively). Ontology mapping techniques can be leveraged [47–56] (for more details on such techniques see Section 23.4). Furthermore, we can probabilistically extend these initial mappings using metarules like the following [57]: if two concepts C_1 and C_1' match, and there is a relationship q between C_1 and C_2 in ontology O and a matching relationship q' between C_1' and C_2' in ontology O', then we can increase the probability of match between C_2 and C_2'. Hence, code elements in a single or multiple CDA documents that refer to the same or similar real-life entities will be associated through a "value edge."

23.3.11 EMR Document-As-Query

An alternative query type to the plain keyword query is using a whole (or part of) EMR (CDA) document as the query. This approach can be used in order to find similar CDA documents, that is, CDA documents of patients with similar history, demographic information, treatments, and so on. The user should be able to customize and personalize such an information discovery tool to fit her needs. For instance, a researcher may not consider the physicians (author of CDA document) name when matching CDA documents, and could specify that a generic medication should be viewed as identical to the nongeneric equivalent. Previous work on document content similarity [58] and XML document structural similarity [59] can be leveraged to solve this problem. The latter corpus of works is based on the concept of tree edit distance. The best-known algorithm for computing tree edit distance between two ordered trees is by Zhang and Shasha [60] with the time complexity of roughly $O(n^4)$ where n is the number of the nodes in a tree. Chakaravarthy et al. [61] match pieces of unstructured documents to structured entities, whereas we want to match a structured document to other structured or unstructured documents.

Furthermore, such document-as-query queries can be used to locate medical literature relevant to the current patient. In this scenario, the EMR application could have a button named "relevant literature" that invokes an information discovery algorithm on PubMed or other medical sources. Price et al. [62] present a first attempt toward this direction, where they extract all MeSH terms (MeSH refers to the U.S. National Library of Medicine's controlled vocabulary used for indexing articles for MEDLINE/PubMed) from an EMR (not specific to CDA) and then query MEDLINE using these terms. The structured format of CDA documents can potentially allow more elaborate searching algorithms where multiple terms that are structurally correlated can construct a single and more focused query on medical literature sources.

23.3.12 Handle Negative Statements

A substantial fraction of the clinical observations entered into patient records are expressed by means of negation. Elkin et al. [63] found SNOMED-CT to provide coverage for 14,792 concepts in 41 health records from Johns Hopkins University, of which 1,823 (12.3%) were identified as negative by human review. This is because negative findings are as important as positive ones for accurate medical decision making. It is common in a medical document to list all the diagnoses that have been ruled out, for example, state that "the patient does not have hypertension, gout, or diabetes." This creates a major problem when searching medical documents. Today, one has to examine the terms preceding a diagnosis to determine if this diagnosis was excluded or not. Ceusters and Smith [64] propose new ontological relationships to express negative findings. It is challenging to handle such negative statements for an information discovery query in a way that the user can specify whether negated concepts should be excluded or not from the search process.

23.3.13 Handle Extension Elements

Locally defined markup can be used to extend CDA when local semantics have no corresponding representation in the CDA specification. Such user- or institution-defined element types are hard to incorporate to the global semantic information, since it is not possible to define general structural requirements for the results, as in XSEarch [36] and the work of Xu and Papakonstantinou [17].

23.3.14 Personalization

The information discovery engine should provide personalized results depending on the preferences of each individual user. For example, for different doctors, different entities and relationships in the CDA components are more important. For some health care providers, the medication may be more relevant than the observation, or the medication may be more relevant than the doctor name. Also the relationships in ontologies may be viewed differently.

Furthermore, depending on whether a user is a nurse, a pharmacist, a technician, or a physician, the system could automatically assign different weights on edges and nodes of the CDA object model (Figure 23.4) to facilitate the information needs of the users.

23.3.15 Confidentiality of Records

The level of confidentiality of the medical record is indicated by the confidentialityCode element in the header section of the record, taking the values normal, restricted, and very restricted. The value of this element, shown in line 4 of Figure 23.5, may dictate at what level we may return results for an executed query. If confidentialityCode is set to "restricted" but no personal information is contained in the result, then the result could be output. Otherwise, the credentials of the user should also be taken into consideration to validate whether the user has the right privileges to obtain the query results.

As mentioned in Section 23.2.1, LOINC codes are already part of HIPAA [18], complying with the confidentiality standards imposed by the federal government on the insurance and health care industries.

23.4 Related Work

This section reviews some research areas that are related to the problem we are introducing in this chapter, in addition to the XML information discovery techniques reviewed in Section 23.2.3: the testing and evaluation of IR techniques on XML, the problem of automatic ontology mapping, and the limitations of medical ontologies.

23.4.1 INEX

To test and evaluate IR techniques on XML documents, the Initiative for the Evaluation of XML retrieval (INEX) [65,66] was created in 2002 to provide the infrastructure and means to evaluate the retrieval methods and techniques and to compare results, specifically providing a large XML test collection and appropriate scoring methods, for the evaluation of content-oriented XML retrieval systems. For INEX 2007, the test collection consists of more than 650,000 XML-encoded articles from the Wikipedia project, compiling 4.6 GB of textual information. These documents are organized in topics, with relevance assessments defined for each topic. A series of content-only (CO) and content-and-structure (CAS) queries is defined for each topic. The CO queries resemble those used in the Text REtrieval Conference (TREC) [67].

23.4.2 Automatic Ontology Mapping

Even when representing the same domain, information sources may be of heterogeneous semantics, resulting in a necessary mapping between ontologies and schemas in order to compose the information and enable interoperation. This has been a research topic in recent years, providing strategies to compose different and heterogeneous sources, aiming to reduce the impreciseness and errors in such mappings. A large number of articles are listed in Ref. [68]. ONION [69] and Prompt [70] use a combination of interactive specifications of mappings and heuristics to propose potential mappings. GLUE [71] employs machine-learning techniques to discover the mappings. OMEN [57] exploits schema-level information by using a set of metarules.

23.4.3 Limitations of Medical Ontologies

In recent years, one of the hottest research directions in medical informatics has been to address the biomedical terminology problem. Ontologies and description logics have been chosen to tackle this challenge, proving to be an adequate solution. But it has also been shown that description logics alone cannot prevent incorrect representations of the medical terminology, since frequently they are not accompanied of the proper theory to describe them. The inappropriate adoption of the UMLS Metathesaurus [72] has been specifically criticized and questioned in Ref. [73], which cites these three problems: (1) There is a wide range of granularity of terms in different vocabularies. (2) The Metathesaurus itself has no unifying hierarchy, so you cannot take advantage of hierarchical relations. (3) There may be other features of vocabularies that get lost in their homogenization upon being entered into the Metathesaurus. Hahn et al. [74] recognize the value of biomedical terminologies as the starting point for an engineering-oriented definition of medical ontologies, in which the reviewing of concept consistency and hierarchy concludes with the inclusion of missing terms and the correction of misclassified concepts. A new approach has been proposed by Sahay et al. [75], in which they introduce a new level of abstraction to represent a match between a text fragment and an ontology; they facilitate the discovery of medical knowledge by adding semantic annotations (with domain knowledge from the ontology) to the syntactic parse trees from the processed documents.

23.5 Concluding Remarks

We have introduced the problem of information discovery on EMR, enumerating a series of challenges that must be addressed to provide a quality information discovery service on EMRs, specifically on CDA documents. The challenges are related to the semantics of the architecture, the XML definitions of CDA documents, and the convergence of the narrative structure associated with ontologies and dictionaries. More research is needed to address the ability of keyword searches to return meaningful results on CDA documents containing time-dependent relationships.

Guidance is also needed in determining how ontologies can be best used in CDA documents to improve keyword search effectiveness and minimize information discovery times. We hope that this work will spur new research on this topic, which can have a dramatic impact on the quality of health care.

Acknowledgment

This work was supported in part by the National Science Foundation Grant IIS-0534530.

References

[1] HL7 Clinical Document Architecture, Release 2.0 (2004). http://lists.hl7.org/read/attachment/61225/1/CDA-doc%20version.pdf, 2007.

[2] SNOMED Clinical Terms (SNOMED CT). http://www.snomed.org/snomedct/index.html, 2006.

[3] G. Salton. *Automatic Text Processing: The Transformation, Analysis, and Retrieval of Information by Computer*. Addison-Wesley Longman Publishing, Boston, MA, 1989.

[4] R. Baeza-Yates and B. Ribeiro-Neto. *Modern Information Retrieval*. Addison-Wesley Longman Publishing, Boston, MA, May 1999.

[5] L. Guo, F. Shao, C. Botev, and J. Shanmugasundaram. XRANK: Ranked keyword search over XML documents. In *SIGMOD '03: Proceedings of the 2003 ACM SIGMOD International Conference on Management of Data*, pp. 16–27, New York, 2003. ACM.

[6] Logical Observation Identifiers Names and Codes (LOINC). http://www.regenstrief.org/medinformatics/loinc/, 2006.

[7] RxNorm. United States National Library of Medicine. http://www.nlm.nih.gov/research/umls/rxnorm/index.html, 2007.

[8] S. Amer-Yahia, C. Botev, and J. Shanmugasundaram. TeXQuery: A full-text search extension to XQuery. In *WWW '04: Proceedings of the 13th International Conference on World Wide Web*, pp. 583–594, New York, 2004. ACM.

[9] S. Amer-Yahia, E. Curtmola, and A. Deutsch. Flexible and efficient XML search with complex full-text predicates. In *SIGMOD '06: Proceedings of the 2006 ACM SIGMOD International Conference on Management of Data*, pp. 575–586, New York, 2006. ACM.

[10] S. Cohen, Y. Kanza, B. Kimelfeld, and Y. Sagiv. Interconnection semantics for keyword search in XML. In *CIKM '05: Proceedings of the 14th ACM International Conference on Information and Knowledge Management*, pp. 389–396, New York, 2005. ACM.

[11] D. Carmel, Y. S. Maarek, M. Mandelbrod, Y. Mass, and A. Soffer. Searching XML documents via XML fragments. In *SIGIR '03: Proceedings of the 26th Annual International ACM SIGIR Conference on Research and Development in Informaion Retrieval*, pp. 151–158, New York, 2003. ACM.

[12] N. Fuhr and K. Großjohann. XIRQL: A query language for information retrieval in XML documents. In *SIGIR '01: Proceedings of the 24th Annual International ACM SIGIR Conference on Research and Development in Information Retrieval*, pp. 172–180, New York, 2001. ACM.

[13] V. Hristidis, L. Gravano, and Y. Papakonstantinou. Efficient IR-style keyword search over relational databases. In *VLDB'2003: Proceedings of the 29th International Conference on Very Large Data Bases*, pp. 850–861. VLDB Endowment, 2003.

[14] V. Hristidis and Y. Papakonstantinou. Keyword proximity search in XML trees. *IEEE Transactions on Knowledge and Data Engineering*, 18(4):525–539, 2006. Member-Nick Koudas and Member-Divesh Srivastava.

[15] Y. Li, C. Yu, and H. V. Jagadish. Schema-free XQuery. In *VLDB'2004: Proceedings of the 30th International Conference on Very Large Data Bases*, pp. 72–83. VLDB Endowment, 2004.

[16] XQuery 1.0 and XPath 2.0 Full Text. http://www.w3.org/TR/ xquery-full-text/, 2007.

[17] Y. Xu and Y. Papakonstantinou. Efficient keyword search for smallest LCAs in XML databases. In *SIGMOD '05: Proceedings of the 2005 ACM SIGMOD International Conference on Management of Data*, pp. 527–538, New York, 2005. ACM.

[18] Health Insurance Portability and Accountability Act. http://www.hipaa.org/, 2007.

[19] R. Bhatti, A. Ghafoor, E. Bertino, and J. B. D. Joshi. X-GTRBAC: An XML-based policy specification framework and architecture for enterprise-wide access control. *ACM Transactions on Information and system security*, 8(2):187–227, 2005.

[20] W. R. Hersh. Medical informatics: Improving health care through information. *JAMA*, 288(16):1955–1958, 2002.

[21] R. Kukafka, P. W. O'Carroll, J. L. Gerberding, E. H. Shortliffe, C. Aliferis, J. R. Lumpkin, and W. A. Yasnoff. Issues and opportunities in public health informatics: A panel discussion. *Journal of Public Health Management Practice*, 7(6):31–42, November 2001.

[22] HL7 Reference Information Model. http://www.hl7.org/library/datamodel/ RIM/C30204/rim.htm, 2007.

[23] Unified modeling language. http://www.uml.org/, 2007.

[24] HL7 Reference Information Model. http://www.miforum.net/ distillate/rim/, 2007.

[25] HL7 V3.0 Data Types Specification. http://aurora.regenstrief.org/v3dt/ report.html, 2007.

[26] HL7 Reference Information Model Billboard. http://www.miforum.net/ distillate/rim/Graphics/RI, 2007.

[27] K. A. Spackman, K. E. Campbell, and R. A. Cote. SNOMED-RT: A reference terminology for health care. In *Proceedings of the 1997 AMIA Annual Fall Symposium*, pp. 640–644, Nashville, TN, 1997.

[28] C. J. McDonald, S. M. Huff, J. G. Suico, G. Hill, D. Leavelle, R. Aller, A. Forrey, K. Mercer, G. DeMoor, J. Hook, W. Williams, J. Case, and P. Maloney. LOINC, a Universal standard for identifying laboratory observations: A 5-year update. *Clinical Chemistry*, 49(4):624–633, 2003.

[29] ASTM Continuity of Care Record (CCR). http://www.centerforhit.org/ x201.xml, 2007.

[30] SCIPHOX Stenogramm. http://www.sciphox.de/, 2007.

[31] A. Onabajo, I. Bilykh, and J. Jahnke. Wrapping legacy medical systems for integrated health network. In *Workshop on migration and Evoluability of Long-life Software Systems, (MELLS-03) at the Conference NetObjectDays, Erfurt, Germany*, 2003.

[32] PICNIC, Professionals and Citizens Network for Integrated Care. http://www. medcom1-4.dk/picnic/default.htm, 2007.

[33] T. Itl and A. Virtanen. Seamless Care and CDA: Finland (Aluetietojaerjestel-mae). In *HL7 International CDA Conference*, Berlin, Germany, 2002.

[34] R. H. Dolin, L. Alschuler, C. Beebe, P. V. Biron, S. L. Boyer, D. Essin, E. Kimber, T. Lincoln, and J. E. Mattison. The HL7 Clinical Document Architecture. *Journal of American Medical Informatics Association*, 8(6):552–69.

[35] S. Brin and L. Page. The anatomy of a large-scale hypertextual Web search engine. *Computer Networks and ISDN Systems*, 30(1–7):107–117, 1998.

[36] S. Cohen, J. Mamou, Y. Kanza, and Y. Sagiv. XSEarch: A semantic search engine for XML. In *VLDB'2003: Proceedings of the 29th International Conference on Very Large Data Bases*, pp. 45–56. VLDB Endowment, 2003.

[37] S. Pradhan. An algebraic query model for effective and efficient retrieval of XML fragments. In *VLDB '06: Proceedings of the 32nd International Conference on Very Large Data Bases*, pp. 295–306. VLDB Endowment, 2006.

[38] S. Agrawal, S. Chaudhuri, and G. Das. DBXplorer: A system for keyword-based search over relational databases. In *SIGMOD '02: Proceedings of the 2002 ACM SIGMOD International Conference on Management of Data*, pp. 627–627, New York, 2002. ACM.

[39] G. Bhalotia, C. Nakhe, A. Hulgeri, S. Chakrabarti, and S. Sudarshan. Keyword searching and browsing in databases using BANKS. In *ICDE'2002: Proceedings of the 18th International conference on Data Engineering*, pp. 431–440, Washington, D.C., 2002. IEEE Computer Society.

[40] V. Hristidis and Y. Papakonstantinou. DISCOVER: Keyword search in relational databases VLDB '02: In *Proceedings of the 28th International Conference on Very Large Data Bases*, Hong Kong, China, 2002.

[41] V. Hristidis, Y. Papakonstantinou, and A. Balmin. Keyword proximity search on XML graphs. In *ICDE '03: Proceedings of the 19th International Conference on Data Engineering*, Bangalore, India, 2003.

[42] J. Xu, J. Lu, W. Wang, and B. Shi. Effective keyword search in XML documents based on MIU. In *DASFAA, Lecture Notes in Computer Science*, 3882:702–716, 2006. Springer.

[43] G. Salton and C. Buckley. Improving retrieval performance by relevance feedback. In *Readings in Information Retrieval*, pp. 355–364, Morgan Kaufmann Publishers, San Franciso, CA, 1997.

[44] T. M. Mitchell. *Machine Learning*. McGraw-Hill, New York, 1997.

[45] H. Hwang, V. Hristidis, and Y. Papakonstantinou. ObjectRank: A system for authority-based search on databases. In *SIGMOD '06: Proceedings of the 2006 ACM SIGMOD International Conference on Management of Data*, pp. 796–798, New York, 2006. ACM.

[46] A. Balmin, V. Hristidis, and Y. Papakonstantinou. ObjectRank: Authority-based keyword search in databases. In *VLDB, 2004*, pp. 564–575, Toronto, Canada, 2004.

[47] X. Dong, A. Y. Halevy, and J. Madhavan. Reference reconciliation in complex information spaces. In *SIGMOD Conference*, pp. 85–96, 2005.

[48] M. A. Hernandez and S. J. Stolfo. The merge/purge problem for large databases. In *SIGMOD '95: Proceedings of the 1995 ACM SIGMOD International Conference on Management of data*, pp. 127–138, New York, 1995.

[49] A. McCallum, K. Nigam, and L. H. Ungar. Efficient clustering of high-dimensional data sets with application to reference matching. In *KDD '00: Proceedings of the 6th ACM SIGKDD International Conference on Knowledge Discovery and Data Mining*, pp. 169–178, New York, 2000. ACM.

[50] A. McCallum and B. Wellner. Toward conditional models of identity uncertainty with application to proper noun coreference. In *Proceedings of the 6th*

ACM SIGKDD International Conference on Knowledge Discovery and Data Mining, pp. 79–84, Boston, MA, 2003.

[51] S. Sarawagi and A. Bhamidipaty. Interactive deduplication using active learning. In *Proceedings of the 8th ACM SIGKDD International Conference on Knowledge Discovery and Data Mining*, pp. 269–278, Edmonton, Canada, 2002.

[52] S. Tejada, C. A. Knoblock, and S. Minton. Learning domain-independent string transformation weights for high accuracy object identification. In *KDD '02: Proceedings of the 8th ACM SIGKDD International Conference on Knowledge Discovery and Data Mining*, pp. 350–359, New York, 2002. ACM.

[53] W. Winkler. The state of record linkage and current research problems. In *Statistics in Medicine*, (14):491–498, 1999.

[54] J. F. McCarthy and W. G. Lehnert. Using decision trees for coreference resolution. In *Proceedings of the 14th International Joint Conference on Artificial Intelligence IJCAI*, pp. 1050–1055, Montreal, Canada, 1995.

[55] V. Ng and C. Cardie. Improving machine learning approaches to coreference resolution. In *ACL '02: Proceedings of the 40th Annual Meeting on Association for Computational Linguistics*, pp. 104–111, Morristown, NJ, 2001. Association for Computational Linguistics.

[56] D. Zelenko, C. Aone, and A. Richardella. Kernel methods for relation extraction. In *EMNLP '02: Proceedings of the ACL-02 Conference on Empirical Methods in Natural Language Processing*, pp. 71–78, Morristown, NJ, 2002. Association for Computational Linguistics.

[57] P. Mitra, N. F. Noy, and A. R. Jaiswal. Omen: A probabilistic ontology mapping tool. In *Workshop on Meaning Coordination and Negotiation at the 3rd International Conference on the Semantic Web (ISWC-2004)*, Hiroshima, Japan, 2004.

[58] R. K. Ando. Latent semantic space: Iterative scaling improves precision of inter-document similarity measurement. In *Proceedings of the 23rd SIGIR*, pp. 216–223, Athens, Greece, 2000.

[59] A. Nierman and H. V. Jagadish. Evaluating structural similarity in XML documents. In *WebDB 2002: Proceedings of the 5th International Workshop on the Web and Databases*, pp. 61–66, Madison, WI, June 2002.

[60] K. Zhang and D. Shasha. Simple fast algorithms for the editing distance between trees and related problems. *SIAM Journal on Computing*, 18(6): 1245–1262, 1989.

[61] V. T. Chakaravarthy, H. Gupta, P. Roy, and M. Mohania. Efficiently linking text documents with relevant structured information. In *VLDB '06: Proceedings of the 32nd International Conference on Very Large Data Bases*, pp. 667–678. VLDB Endowment, 2006.

[62] S. L. Price, W. R. Hersh, D. D. Olson, and P. J. Embi. SmartQuery: Context-sensitive links to medical knowledge sources from the electronic patient record. In *Proceedings of the AMIA Symposium*, pp. 627–631, San Antonio, TX, 2002.

[63] P. L. Elkin, S. H. Brown, B. A. Bauer, C. S. Husser, W. Carruth, L. R. Bergstrom, and D. L. Wahner-Roedler. A controlled trial of automated classification of negation from clinical notes. *BMC Medical Informatics and Decision Making*, 5(13), May 2005.

[64] W. Ceusters and B. Smith. Tracking referents in electronic health records. In *Proceedings of Medical Informatics Europe MIE*, pp. 71–76, Geneva, Switzerland, 2005.

[65] INitiative for the Evaluation of XML Retrieval. http://inex.is.informatik.uni-duisburg.de/2007/, 2007.

[66] N. Fuhr, N. Gövert, G. Kazai, and M. Lalmas. INEX: INitiative for the Evaluation of XML Retrieval. In *Proceedings of the SIGIR 2002 Workshop on XML and Information Retrieval*, Tampere, Finland, 2002.

[67] Text REtrieval Conference (TREC). http://trec.nist.gov/, 2007.

[68] Ontology matching. http://www.ontologymatching.org/, 2007.

[69] G. Wiederhold, P. Mitra, and S. Decker. A scalable framework for interoperation of information sources. In *the 1st International Semantic Web Working Symposium*, Stanford, CA, 2001.

[70] N. F. Noy and M. A. Musen. The PROMPT suite: Interactive tools for ontology merging and mapping. *International Journal of Human-Computer studies*, 59(6):983–1024, 2003.

[71] A. Doan, J. Madhavan, P. Domingos, and A. Halevy. Learning to map between ontologies on the semantic web. In *Proceedings of the 11th International Conference on World Wide Web WWW*, pp. 662–673, Honolulu, Hawaii, 2002.

[72] UMLS Metathesaurus Fact Sheet. http://www.nlm.nih.gov/pubs/factsheets/umlsmeta.html, 2007.

[73] W. Ceusters, B. Smith, and J. Flanagan. Ontology and medical terminology: Why description logics are not enough. In *Proceedings of TEPR 2003-Towards an Electronic Patient Record*, San Antonio, TX, 2003.

[74] U. Hahn, M. Romacker, and S. Schulz. How knowledge drives understanding–matching medical ontologies with the needs of medical language processing. *Artificial Intelligence in Medicine*, 15(1):25–51, January 1999.

[75] S. Sahay, E. Agichtein, B. Li, E. V. Garcia, and A. Ram. Semantic annotation and inference for medical knowledge discovery. *NSF Next Generation Data Mining (NGDM) Symposium*, Baltimore, MD, 2007.

Chapter 24

Market-Based Profile Infrastructure: Giving Back to the User

Olfa Nasraoui and Maha Soliman

Contents

24.1 Motivations and Introduction

Recommendation systems try to suggest items of interest to a user (e.g., movies or Web pages) based on their user profile [1] which can be explicit (e.g., user ratings) or implicit (e.g., their browsing or purchase history). One of the most successful forms of recommendation is collaborative filtering (CF) [2], which recommends to the current user, items that are of interest to users who are similar to this user, where similarity is based on a correlation-like affinity between the user's ratings or purchasing histories. For this reason, some people think of recommendation technology as a new paradigm of search, since interesting items find the user instead of the user

This chapter is partially supported by National Science Foundation Career Award IIS-0133948.

actually searching for them. As a result, recommender systems are becoming a requisite staple on many e-commerce Web sites, and are bound to connect together the future social Web. Good recommendation systems thrive on the availability of data (e.g., Web sites or products viewed or purchased) to form profiles of the users. These profiles are, in a way, starting to play the role of the user's own digital persona in the Internet marketplace. Yet, despite their success and their broad potential, to this day, unfortunately, a loyal consumer/user of a Web business still cannot own their profile or their persona. Neither can they move it with them freely, as they move from one business or one context to another. However, this profile forms extremely precious information, both to the business and to the users, and it can benefit personalization and combat information overload in a variety of different domains for the following reasons:

1. There are likely correlations between a user's tastes in books, movies, and many other products or content items that are not sold on the same Web site, including food, wine, clothing, sports, arts, content-like news and blogs, as well as music, videos, etc. Hence there is a need for single-profile integration across multiple Web sites.

2. The above correlation can only be enriched if further integrated with many other user profiles in a CF framework, hence predicting a user's interests not only from the same user but also from other similar users' interests by association. Hence, there is a need for multiple-profile integration.

3. Currently, each Web site has a limited view of user profiles (limited to the scope of what is sold/served by this Web site). Extending the scope to other Web sites would give a more global view of a user profile.

4. Currently, each user's scope is limited: only their own profile is available to them, hence there is no sharing with other users. As a result, a user cannot possibly be the one who invokes a CF recommendation. Instead, it is always the server that initiates and benefits from such CF.

All the above reasons make compelling the need for an intermediate solution that fosters both single-profile integration (across multiple Web sites) and multiple-profile integration (across the same Web site), that is, a solution that would stand midway between the server (or the business) and the client (or the user). We propose a market-based profile infrastructure that is based on the creation of a dynamic and distributed market-based system where each user's profile is maintained, updated, and exchanged with other users and especially with online server/merchant agents in a bidding-like system, hence a market-based economy. The principles of this system are as follows:

1. The technical platform consists of an intermediate solution that fosters both single-profile integration (across multiple Web sites) and multiple-profile integration (across the same Web site). The solution would stand midway between the server (or the business) and the client (or the user). This is similar to peer-to-peer (P2P) information sharing: there is no single central control on the user profiles, though there could be a central repository of many user profiles in server communities or clustered repositories.

2. A user, who owns his/her own profile, earns some credit each time that their profile is invoked by a recommendation process (or transaction), hence accumulating credits that can be used toward any purchase within this marketplace, or credit that simply gets accumulated in the user's electronic account (e.g., an e-wallet or paypal account). Although the individual credits may be very small (e.g., a fraction of 1 cent per invocation of the user profile), they may accumulate to a profitable level with a large number of invocations, especially in an increasingly competitive and global e-commerce marketplace. The crediting should work in a similar manner to e-bay auctions, except that interactions would be completely automated.

3. The user, for the first time, not only owns their own profile, but also can sell it like a commodity and benefit from it. The entire solution is enabled by a technical infrastructure that allows such exchange of information to take place. Such a profit has previously been restricted only to the businesses (who frequently sell, buy, and trade user profile data) without any benefit or gain to the user, and without their consent.

Our proposed infrastructure bridges the fields of computer science with economics. This fusion and synergy is enabled by none other than computational thinking, because it is the computational view of the important socioeconomical phenomenon of personalized Internet commerce that allowed us to ask the question of "Whether it is more fair for the minority of businesses with biggest control over the majority of the users' profiles to actually pay them back in the form of a reward?". By shifting ownership to the users, a whole new era of fair start-up opportunity may open up to the majority of (small) businesses, which tend to be located at the long tail, and start with zero knowledge about their users, hence making competition with the few well-established and powerful businesses almost impossible. We propose a framework for not only generating new global knowledge, but also offering it and mining it in a socially responsible way, that is, in a fair manner and with equal opportunity to users (via privacy and rewards embedded in the technical solution unlike all existing frameworks), and equal opportunity to businesses (particularly small and start-up businesses). The resulting profits from this knowledge shift for the first time from the core (servers) to the edges (clients) of the Internet, hence amounting to a paradigm shift in data-mining-based personalization.

Realizing the proposed market-based profile infrastructure requires working on at least four objectives:

1. Technical formulation of a logical and feasible architecture for the above infrastructure based on

   a. Current Internet technologies such as Web service protocols and P2P networks [3]

   b. Additional data collection, routing, exchange, and privacy agents

   c. Market-based agents that serve to implement the credit/payment operations that occur with the invocation of each user profile

2. Analytical study of the dynamics and equilibrium, if any, within this infrastructure under varying scenarios

3. Simulations of the proposed infrastructure under different scenarios and variable parameters to study the effect of each type of data integration and exchange

4. Study of the ethical impacts and interactions with existing regulations from a legal perspective

In this chapter, we focus on the first and most challenging objective (technical formulation), a prerequisite and foundation to the remaining objectives.

From our analysis, it will be obvious how a technical solution will rely in the first place on the power of the people to be willing to become part of a fair, decentralized marketplace that rewards them for each invocation of their profile, thus creating accountability and trust; and in the second place on the power of knowledge discovery/data mining (KDD) techniques that may offer the only way to organize and search this vast, decentralized marketplace in real time, while concealing the user's private data. Thus, KDD would work at the service of both the user and the business, and not only on primarily the latter, as in the current e-commerce status quo.

24.1.1 Challenges

There are several challenging research problems attached to the proposed infrastructure:

1. *Need for distributed computing*: Removing central control calls for a decentralized data infrastructure.

2. *Monetary system to realize the distributed transactions*: Existing finance and market models, current e-commerce infrastructure, e-wallets such as mondex [4]; or paypal accounts.

3. *Physical infrastructure*: Overlaid on existing network structure (e.g., current P2P networks [5]), existing social networking Web sites (e.g., MySpace.com), dedicated distributed repositories affiliated with the user's bank, and earning a commission for their indexing.

4. *Privacy preservation*: Authentication and secure access, privacy-preserving CF, separating the historic profile from the identity and demographics. Existing techniques already exist to handle some privacy issues [6–8].

5. *Ethics/legal considerations*: Who wins, what is fair? Who stores and controls the data? How does this infrastructure interact and play with existing laws even with the users' consent?

24.2   Market-Based Profile Infrastructure

One way to implement the proposed infrastructure is by emulating some ideas both from P2P networks [5] where information is exchanged in a decentralized manner, and from currently operating Web service platforms, where services are advertised/registered via a registration mechanism in a registry, and different actors interact and find each other by checking these registries. Everything else is typically automated by well-controlled ontologies and languages. One main difference between a user profile marketplace and the Web service infrastructure is that the user does not necessarily have a server or a unique URL where they can be reached as in traditional Web servers and Web services. One way to circumvent this limitation is by using the user's own computer or personal device like a cell phone to store such information. Also, an intermediate architecture where user information is logged on their device in real time and then transmitted to one of the several repositories that could be on actual servers/registries, but not necessarily a central server. They could be, for example, superpeers as in P2P networks, which are designated peers that act in a role halfway between a true server and a true peer in the exchange and routing of information.

Recent proliferation of social networking Web sites offers yet another vital carrier and platform for such an infrastructure if a user profile can be stored and invoked securely as part of a market strategy. The social-network-enabled approach would extend the architecture of sites such as MySpace or facebook where each user has their own profile already stored. Hence, it might be possible to actually build a Web service that is an open place where users themselves manage, upload their data/profiles, set options for privacy, and check the amount of credit accumulated. In other words, to each user, there will be a profile (that they will be able to upload using special software that can read from their accounts with proper authorization) and an account (accumulating their rewards). The distributed recommendation system will then be able to search for relevant information from multiple profiles on this Web service, and will deposit credit in their profile. The biggest inconvenience with this approach is the centralized information control exerted by the actual owners of the social networking Web site.

In the future, with the widespread use of radio-frequency identification (RFID) readers and assuming that RFID tags will be required on most merchandize, the collection and exchange of user profiles will be greatly facilitated and automated. For instance, RFID readers can be implanted on the user's personal device, such as a cell phone to integrate even off-line transactions with online transactions. Online transactions can be logged entirely by software on the client computer. However, RFID can bridge the gap between online and off-line worlds, especially if the cell phone equipped with an RFID reader also communicates this information with the user profile's designated repository, be it the user's own computer or one of several remote intermediate repositories. Finally, cell phones (as well as IP addresses of various Internet connected devices) can enrich the user profile by also adding geographical location information. Hence, patterns can be discerned at the local versus global levels for better prediction.

Another possible platform would be based on integrating consumer profiles together with their e-wallets. E-wallets, while still not being widely accepted, have recently been implemented and evaluated based on the existing Mondex card that shares the flexibility and privacy features of cash, while allowing participation in e-commerce even at microeconomical level (very small value transactions) [4].

Privacy must finally be integrated within the above infrastructure. First, there must be a taxonomy of what can be logged or not logged among the user's interactions and purchases. For example, some users do not like to log anything related to their health or to their financial data. These restrictions must be directly implemented on the user's data-collection side, and hence they will be enabled and respected.

24.3   Models of Interaction for Market-Based Profile Infrastructure

Below, we describe a few potential models that can support market-based profiles.

24.3.1   Constrained Markets

We start by specifying the players that participate in a market-based profile system, their roles, and interactions. Like many markets, this market consists at least of sellers and buyers. The item/product sellers are the companies that traditionally sell products, while the item/product buyers are customers who have made prior transactions with these or other sellers. A seller is interested in computing good recommendations for items that they sell based on the profiles of available buyers with matching profiles. A recommendation has a value to the seller if it improves the seller's recommendation model (we will come to this later) or if it results in a sale. The buyers are interested to offer their profile information in return for a reward from the seller. In essence, all the players are sellers: they either sell products (or services or commodities), or they sell their profiles (in this case they are the consumers). Hence, from now on, to avoid any confusion in their roles, we refer to the players as the companies (trying to buy profiles to compute recommendations) and the consumers (who want to earn rewards by selling their profiles). The value of a profile for a company is proportional to its potential for improving the recommendation model, and this can be hard to quantify. A raw recommendation model, whether it is a user–item rating matrix or an item–item association matrix, will generally benefit by increasing its density, or inversely decreasing its sparsity. This is very similar to saying that each additional rating (or item present in a profile for sale) has an incremental value to be added to improve the model. However, not all items are equal, since some valuable items may have very low ratings and are therefore needed more than items that are already densely rated in the recommendation model. For example, items may be valuable as far as they are essential to contribute to forming more accurate distance-based user neighborhoods in user-based CF, or simply because they are of high value (for instance, they have a high profit value for the company). While the latter profit can be easily quantified by a company, the former seems to be related to the densification of the user–item rating matrix as discussed above. Below we formulate the optimization from the points of views of the company and the consumer as primal and dual complementary linear programs.

1. *Company's optimization problem (primal)*: Essentially, companies are in pursuit of buying x_j consumer profiles from each class (j) of profiles that meet certain expectations in terms of which items or attributes (i) they contain, and they want to do so at a minimum combined cost ($c^t x = \Sigma_j c_j x_j$), where c is a cost vector, with c_j, the cost assigned to profile j. The constraints can be formulated as a set of inequalities of the form $A^t x = r$, where matrix A's component a_{ij} is the number of views or rating of item (i) in profile (j), and r_i is the minimum number of desired ratings of item i accumulated from the x profiles.

2. *Consumer's optimization problem (dual)*: Meanwhile, consumers are in pursuit of selling their own profile that contains r_i ratings for each item (i) sought by the company, at the optimal price p_i per item i, while being competitive with the individual requirements (in terms of ratings) and costs for all classes of consumer profiles, given by $\Sigma_i \pi a_{ij} \leq c_j$, $j = 1, \ldots, n$. Moreover, the consumers would like to sell their profile at maximum revenue ($\pi^t r$), since the revenue from selling the items rated in their profile is given by $\Sigma_i \pi r_i = \pi^t r$. The primal and dual problems above are instances of convex linear-programming problems that can be solved efficiently for a unique global solution. For a pair (x, π) to be respective optima for the two above dual problems, it is sufficient that they obey the complementary slackness condition [9], which states that $\pi_i(a_i^t x - r_i) = 0$ for all i, and that $(c_j - \pi^t A_j)x_j = 0$ for all j. Note that A_j is the jth column of A, while a_i^t is the ith row of A. All that this tells us is that there is a potential for equilibrium in the market of companies and consumers; however, it is clear that many assumptions (like the dynamic nature of the bidding process) may not hold.

24.3.2 Computational Issues: Social Networks, Query Incentive Networks, and Game-Theoretic Models

Similar to information retrieval on P2P networks, there could be a finite lifetime and a finite reward on each transaction. According to Ref. [10], using the cosine similarity between users in a user-based CF can be viewed as computing the probability that the two users will ever meet at any location while doing a random walk on the user–item graph (where the nodes are users and items, an edge connect a user and an item if this item belongs to the user's profile, and the user–item links are probabilities of following a certain user–item link). This is easy to verify in the case of binary profiles (user–item vectors consist of 0s and 1s), since $\cos(u_i, u_j) = \Sigma_k u_{ik} u_{jk}/(\Sigma_k u_{ik} \Sigma_k u_{jk})^{1/2} \simeq \Sigma_k P(k|i)P(k|j)$. We may extend this idea to a graph with only users as the nodes, and with the edges or links weighted by the cosine similarity between their user profiles (i.e., their item vectors), or are simply the strength of connection in a social network. The item-based CF version of this problem is when the nodes in the graph correspond to the items only, and we consider two items to meet if they occur in the same transaction at any time. This is particularly the case when the item–item association matrix M is obtained by correlation analysis $M_{ik} =$ correlation (i,k); or by association rule mining of rules of the form $i \rightarrow k$ (a measure of confidence of having an item k given another item i is the conditional probability $P(k|i)$).

Another graph model can be based on the graph that represents a social network (e.g., MySpace). In this case, nodes are linked by social relations, and these relations form the basis for routing a query and searching for an answer. In this case, a search engine can be dedicated to scour and index this social network and be used to query for useful profiles at a later stage. Regardless of which model to use, it is clear that a random walk on a graph model can form the basis for many CF recommendation strategies. In this case, the recommendation process takes place by submitting a query to one or more nodes in the graph, allowing these nodes to pass this query on to their local neighbors, and then waiting for an answer that is returned when a satisfactory answer is found. This is essentially one way to implement information retrieval on a P2P network (such as Gnutella), except that without an incentive for users to participate in such operations, the effective active (responding) network at any time could be very limited.

To answer the search with incentive challenge, Kleinberg and Raghavan [11] formulated a model for query incentive networks. Rather than posing queries to a centralized index of the system, users pose queries to the network itself. Requests for information are propagated along paths through the network, connecting those with information needs to those with relevant answers. In addition, queries are submitted together with incentives for answering them, and these incentives also get propagated along paths in a network, with each participating node earning a portion of the reward, until either an answer is found or the propagating rewards get depleted. In Ref. [11], this type of information-seeking process was formulated as a game among the nodes in the network, and this game was shown to possess a natural Nash equilibrium. Furthermore, the authors tried to understand how much incentive would be needed in order for a node to achieve a reasonable probability of obtaining an answer to a query from the network, by studying the size of query incentives as a function of the rarity of the answer and the structure of the underlying network.

There are several issues that need to be addressed when considering the query incentive network model. In addition to the basic reward setting strategy for each node in the network, the seller must decide the value of the reward to be offered for an answer (i.e., a profile) from the network. This reward can be based on an estimate of the value added by incorporating one more customer's profile into CF. The problem with the above approach is that it may not scale to millions of transactions per second. An index-based retrieval may be the only option on several indexed databases, but the databases need to be refreshed with every user's new transactions. Another game-theoretic approach can be achieved by analyzing the proposed infrastructure when implemented by means of dynamic and real-time automated auctions between companies and consumers. The equilibria of such systems, if they can be derived, can shed light on its promises, as well as whether it provides fair play for all the players, and under what conditions. Auctions offer an efficient mechanism to determine the optimal incentive levels automatically.

Why is a graph-based view of the recommendation process interesting within our framework? There are two reasons for this interest:

1. The graph model supports a distributed profile base, so that no single authority owns all profiles.

2. The graph-based search supports local search where a query is passed from one node to its neighbors, thus limiting threats to privacy.

What are the main challenges facing the graph-based view of the recommendation process? Clearly, the biggest challenge when using the graph-based model would be how to obtain the desired information (the answer): quickly and at a reasonable cost. Different search and incentive strategies, and different properties of the graph in question will largely dictate the cost in terms of time to reach an answer and communication load. However, to answer real-time scalability demands, it would be impractical to perform graph search for each transaction, especially for Web-based commerce.

24.3.3 Proposed Solutions to Answer P2P Structuring and Search Challenges

It is conceivable that these searches could be performed in the ways described below to reduce the computational and communication burdens. Most of these approaches rely on knowledge discovery as a prerequisite for better organization and search in what would otherwise amount to an unfathomable distributed mess. However, their common shortcomings is that none deals with an incentive-based querying, and none considers privacy as even a minor or sideline goal. We start with an overview of existing methods, then proceed to describe our proposed approach, which inherits ideas about self-organization of a decentralized network using not only clustering to break the graph into smaller subgraphs, but also by mining the network value of the nodes in each cluster in order to enable a viral or epidemic local search that could cover the relevant areas of the network in a few hops, and thus in real time.

1. Exploit hybrid P2P network structures/overlays (which are the logical connections between a peer and its visible neighbors) such as distributed hash tables (DHTs) [5], which implement content-addressable distributed data storage, and hierarchical P2P as opposed to pure P2P networks. One example is Chord [12] where nodes are identified with a unique ID, and hold a finger table that points to neighboring (successor) nodes closer in the identifier space. Another example is Pastry [12], which uses routing tables that route a request among root nodes (superpeers) that are connected to leaf nodes that

are numerically closer in the identifier space. Nodes closer together in terms of network locality (either IP hops or geographical location) are listed in a neighborhood set. Both Chord and Pastry have $O(log(N))$ routing complexity (i.e., steps) for N nodes [12]. They also exhibit self-organization of the network connections/overlay. Lately, several more ambitious developments started seeking more intelligent and dynamic self-organization schemes of the network overlay, particularly for information retrieval (where search can target content not only IDs of objects). For instance, Wu et al.'s [13] 6S P2P network for information retrieval tries to dynamically form a social networking type of topology that captures communities of peers with similar searches. This approach uses no DHTs, and in fact starts with a random network topology that is gradually shaped by allowing each peer to learn or refine a model of its neighboring peers that are within its own community. A clustered topology thus emerges according to shared interests and domains. Search finally proceeds using a focused crawler on this topology: that is, crawl to similar (in profile and in query context) neighbors within the self-organizing network instead of blind crawling as in pure P2P search. The main distinction from our problem is that our goal is to keep item lists private. This can be realized by ranking neighbors based on private similarity computations instead of full disclosure of the contents on the peer's list of items. Another conceptual difference is that we deal with baskets of items or interests, while they deal with free text search. Fortunately, in online commerce, transactions or baskets have similar power law properties as text documents.

2. A similar approach to design efficient overlay networks was proposed by Ref. [14] who used hierarchical Dirichlet processes to cluster the user's music files into clusters of styles, and then used these style characterizations to model or profile each peer. Finally, each peer ranks other neighboring peers based on shared styles in their models. These rankings can be used to select which neighbors to forward a query to in a search. Ref. [14] showed that it is preferred to mix this ranking-based selection with random selection, thus resulting in a power-law distributed social network that has more robustness and coverage, while having a smaller diameter. However, privacy will need to be taken into account, since in general any hybridization is expected to pose additional privacy risks.

3. Exploit locality of queries and content to forward searches more efficiently on a P2P network in a way similar to P2P information retrieval (which is content and not merely identifier-based), for example, the ISM (intelligent search mechanism) by Zeinalipour-Yazti [15] that searched text documents on a P2P network using a profiling structure to enhance each peer's knowledge about the potential of other peers to respond to the right query. Queries are routed to a selected set of neighboring peers instead of all neighbors. The selection is based on the profile that captures the kind of queries for which a neighbor has responded well in the past.

4. A distributed CF system for P2P file sharing was proposed in Ref. [16] that computes a dynamic user-content relevance model based on language modeling techniques, and then exploits these models to design self-organizing distributed buddy tables that are later used for distributed item-based and user-based recommendations. This seems to be the most natural approach for our problem, however, it was designed for users to share recommendations without rewards and not for companies to obtain recommendations from users. Thus, a combination of this method with the above explicit P2P search systems should be followed by first forming self-organizing profile networks that can later serve as the dynamic overlays for a P2P exchange network. For instance, a set of superpeers can be formed from clusters or communities of users in a user graph or of items in an item graph. The former would support user-based CF, while the latter would support item-based CF. Each cluster would hold an index of the other clusters, and a global top-level index would hold an index of the superpeers. The most challenging aspect of this approach would be maintaining a high level of decentralization to avoid central control, maintaining and updating the graph (since nodes should be able to move from one cluster to another), allowing clusters to overlap, and ensuring a high level of privacy while forming the self-organizing structure and while providing recommendations.

5. Perform searches in bundles of transactions or users, that is, find the optimal profiles for a batch of transactions. We can use an approach like adaptive query freezing on P2P networks [17], where a query gets frozen with a certain probability that depends on the initiating peer and the system load at the time. Once a small number of hops have been made by this query, it gets frozen, and gets attached to the query response stream of another similar query, as long as it is beneficial to do so. In this way, the frozen query takes a free ride without adding any burden to the system.

6. Perform searches on subgraphs, for example, after an off-line discovery of communities within the original graph [18,19]. A bipartite graph (users × items) consisting of the consumers and their items (purchased or rated) can form the basis for community discovery using a variety of existing techniques. So would the graph (users × companies). Another possibility is a tripartite graph model (users × items × companies) that combines both players via the items bought or sold by users and companies, respectively. However, privacy considerations would need to be taken into account.

24.3.3.1 Proposed Global Solution for Distributed Recommendations in an Adaptive Decentralized Network

Below, we propose a four-step approach to build, adapt the profile network overlay, and search it efficiently. Because the system is dynamic, the steps are repeated periodically, with some of the steps repeated more frequently than others depending on their associated cost. We start by constructing a graph from the user ratings or user profiles that aggregate each user's transactions. This constructed graph forms the initial unstructured overlay, thus a pure P2P profile network. Next, we further structure this overlay by introducing a hierarchical structure similar to DHT-based networks such as Pastry, Chord, or CAN [5]. This means that some of the nodes will be designated as superpeers that point to each other and to a set of successor or leaf nodes in their neighborhood. We determine the neighborhood sets by clustering the graph, hence discovering communities (of similar nodes) within the network. After discovering node communities, we identify the most promising node from each community to act as a superpeer or indexing node. Instead of basing the structure purely on the contents or identifiers of the nodes, we propose to design a structure that optimizes epidemic routing of queries. This is inspired by the idea of viral marketing, a transformative idea that targets marketing promotions toward customers in a similar manner that viruses spread in an epidemic, from one person to the next, or using a social network (modeling nodes as the persons and edges as their connections). The highest potential for vast spreading of a virus tends to occur when hitting highly influential nodes in the social network. The latter nodes are known as influential nodes or nodes with high network value, a concept that is fast replacing the traditional marketing concept or metric known as customer value. According to Domingos and Richardson [20], a customer's network value is the expected increase in sales to others that results from marketing to that customer. We propose to use this method to identify the influential nodes in a P2P network that will cause an initial query to spread epidemically and thus quickly to the neighboring nodes in the network. In other words, we propose a viral routing strategy in P2P networks, with further an adaptive way to structure the network overlay to form links that facilitate this viral communication. However, unlike the approach devised in Ref. [20], our goal is not only to reach as many nodes/users as possible in a few hops, which would optimize the returns to the business, while minimizing the rewards to the customer. Our approach also distributes the incentives/rewards to all the reached nodes that respond when queried in this manner, thus benefiting a significantly larger number of users.

24.3.3.1.1 Step 1 Construct a graph from the user ratings or user profiles that aggregate a user's transactions. Two options arise

1. An item–item graph consists of items as the nodes and the strength of association or similarity (e.g., cos (i_1, i_2)) between the nodes for items i_1 and i_2, as the links between the nodes. The similarity is computed by considering each item as a vector of the user profile indices in which it is present. In order to enable a very simple and efficient accounting (and thus updating the rewards for participating users), each item node stores the IDs of the user profiles that contain this item.

2. A user–user graph consists of users as the nodes and the similarity between their user profiles as the links. In this case, each user profile is a vector of the items present in the profile. Accounting is straightforward here since each user node stores its own user ID.

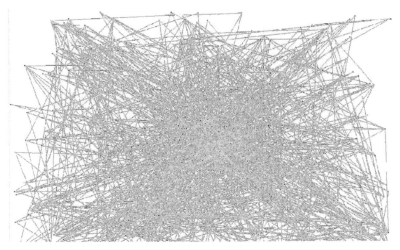

FIGURE 24.1: Social network graph obtained from a subset of the movielens user-ratings data.

We illustrate Step 1 with a subset (to avoid clutter) of the users social network (directed) graph shown in Figure 24.1, obtained from the movielens user-ratings data set [2], after connecting each user to its nearest five neighbors based on cosine similarity, as was done in the study of viral marketing in Ref. [20]. Figure 24.2 shows the ego network or (one-step) neighborhood, consisting of network formed by selecting one particular user's node (in this case for User No. 469), including all nodes that are connected to that node, and all the connections among those other nodes. This illustrates the local overlay structure of a typical neighborhood in a decentralized (P2P) network around one user node. This structure is directly exploited in decentralized search for recommendations. In other words, the decentralized logical structure reflects the social network directly, where the social ties in this case are derived directly from the similarity in the users' profiles. Figure 24.3 shows the one-step neighborhood of a highly connected user node, where the node colors indicate cluster labels. Newman and Girvan's algorithm [19] was used with five clusters.

24.3.3.1.2 Step 2 Cluster the above graphs by discovering communities for instance using spectral clustering on graphs [19]. In order to maintain a stable set of clusters in consecutive clustering results from one time step to another, one can add a stabilizing cluster constraint to the pure cluster optimization constraint as was done for clustering bipartite graphs in Ref. [21]. The approach modifies the criterion to be optimized from the simple snapshot quality, $s_q(C_t, D_t)$ of clustering C_t at time t for data D_t, to the composite of the snapshot qualities in consecutive time steps and history cost functions, $h_c(C_{t-1}, C_t)$, as follows: $\Sigma_t s_q(C_t, D_t) - c_p \Sigma_t h_c(C_{t-1}, C_t)$. $c_p > 0$ is a change parameter that affects the trade-off between the current clustering quality and the continuity of the clustering in between time periods. This approach results not only in a clustering of a static snapshot of the graph, but rather a threaded

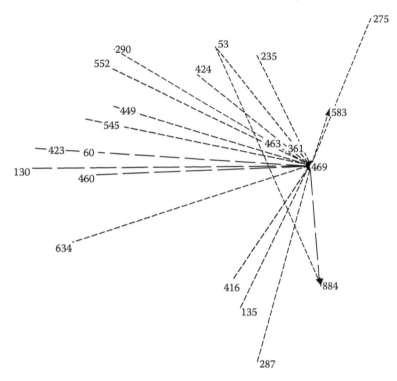

FIGURE 24.2:   Ego network (one-step neighborhood) of one user node illustrating the local overlay structure in the network.

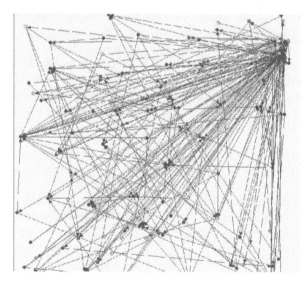

FIGURE 24.3:   Ego network (one-step neighborhood) of a highly connected user node, where the node colors indicate cluster labels. Newman and Girvan's clustering algorithm was used with five clusters.

clustering (from one time step to the next) that evolves with the graph in time. The threaded approach also avoids the need for reclustering a large data set from scratch, and instead does incremental clustering, thus helping to address the scalability challenge.

24.3.3.1.3 Step 3 Consider the nodes that belong to each cluster/community as a set, and identify the top K influential nodes (i.e., with highest network value) to serve as the superpeers in the top level, that route requests toward the rest of the second-level nodes in that community. Domingos and Richardson [20] addressed a related problem in a different context (viral marketing) by modeling markets as social networks, and experimented with the eachmovie CF movie-rating data set, consisting of user-ratings for movies. They set out trying to determine the optimal marketing actions M_i, $i = 1,\ldots,n$ for a set of n potential customers, with buying predicate $X_i = 1$ if customer i bought the product being marketed and $X_i = 0$, otherwise. Assuming that a product is described by a set of m attributes $Y = \{Y_1,\ldots,Y_m\}$. For each customer X_i, there is a set of n_i neighbors $N_i = \{X_{i,1},\ldots,X_{i,n_i}\}$ that directly influence X_i, thus defining a network of customers. Given c, the cost of marketing to a customer (assumed constant), r_0, the revenue from selling the product to a customer if no marketing is performed, and r_1, the revenue from selling the product to a customer if marketing is performed. r_0 and r_1 are assumed to be the same, unless the marketing action includes offering a discount or rebate (which is the case in our context, thus $r_1 < r_0$). Domingos and Richardson [20] try to seek the optimal marketing actions M_i for all customers that maximize the global lift in profit resulting from a particular choice, M of customers to market to, defined as

$$\text{ELP}(X^k,Y,M) = \sum_{i=1}^{n} r_i P(X_i = 1 | X^k, Y, M) - r_0 \sum_{i=1}^{n} P(X_i = 1 | X^k, Y, M_0) - |M|c$$

(24.1)

where
ELP is the expected lift in profit
X^k is the set of customers whose values of X_i is known (i.e., we know whether they bought the product)
$r_i = r_1$ if $M_i = 1$, and $r_i = r_0$ if $M_i = 0$
$|M|$ is the number of 1's in M
M_0 is the vector of all zeroes (thus no marketing at all)

Their most successful search strategy for this optimization (in terms of quality and time) turned out to be a greedy search starting with $M = M_0$, and looping through the M_i's, setting each M_i to 1 if ELP $[X^k, Y, f_i^1(M)] > \text{ELP}(X^k, Y, M)$, until there are no changes in a complete scan of the M_i's. $f_i^1(M)$ is the result of setting $M_i = 1$, and leaving the rest of M unchanged. The probabilities inside the sums in Equation 24.1 are estimated based on training data.

There are several distinctions between our problem and the above viral marketing problem. First, we need to map the above variables to our context. For instance, M_i is not a marketing decision/action of whether to market to customer i, but rather becomes the decision of whether to submit a query containing product Y to node i. Also, $X_i = 1$ would now mean that node i has an answer to a query involving product Y, and the sums in Equation 24.1 become localized in our context, since they are taken over a subnetwork consisting of nodes in the same cluster, instead of the entire graph. In this context, influential customers become influential nodes that would maximize the coverage of a query as it propagates through a subnetwork, during the search. On the other hand, c, the cost of marketing to one customer, is now associated with the incentive or reward to be offered to the initial node to which a query is submitted. r_1 (and r_0) are the estimated profits that a company would reap from actually submitting (or not) a query to a given node. Domingos and Richardson [20] applied this approach successfully to the eachmovie CF data set, modeling the graph of users (based on their ratings' correlations) as a social network. Unfortunately, it turned out that only a small proportion of customers end up receiving the lion's share of the marketing incentives or rewards (a power law distribution). We propose to balance this into a more fair market by sharing the rewards among all the nodes in the network that participate in routing the query from the initial node (that was estimated as having highest network value) to the node that answers this query.

From an optimization perspective, the viral marketing explained above is not directly applicable to our problem, because in our context, the data are decentralized. Thus, optimization would have to be adapted so that the optimization procedure works in stages, propagating from one node to its neighbors. This can be carried out using a message passing broadcast mechanism within each cluster's subnetwork starting from a highly connected node (e.g., a hub). Fortunately, this optimization does not have to be performed in real time with each invocation of CF. Rather, it is applied periodically on the subgraphs corresponding to each cluster separately. The nodes will then be assigned their estimated network values (ELPs) and only the top ranking node IDs will be saved, ready to be used later in real-time CF searches (see Section 24.3.3.1.4).

24.3.3.1.4 Step 4 At search time (i.e., to perform a recommendation from the resulting distributed profile network), the query (which can take the form of a set of items) is initiated at any of the superpeers in the first level, which will route it to the most relevant superpeer, which will in turn forward it to its assigned community nodes. The resulting search is epidemic, and thus fast and efficient even from an incentive point of view, because in a query incentive-based search, the initial reward will be submitted as an incentive to the most influential node that promised to deliver the query to (and share its incentive with) the most relevant nodes via the shortest paths. This strategy should avoid disappointing searches (where the reward is depleted before even reaching relevant nodes), and also optimize the rewards to the contributing nodes, because the shorter the path to the answer, the fewer the nodes that will be on this path, and consequently, the higher the partial rewards that will reach these nodes. Finally, all the nodes that lie on the path (as determined by the identifiers stored in each node) to the final answer receive their partial rewards.

24.3.4 Privacy-Preserving Collaborative Filtering

Privacy-preservation methods can be applied while invoking a user profile to compute similarities for CF. Most CF type recommendations are computed by summing the contributions from multiple users. For example, the method in Ref. [16] is an approach for distributed CF for P2P file sharing. This idea is user-based, meaning that the contributions from each user is pulled at recommendation time. In this case, care must be taken not to reveal the individual user's profiles (i.e., items or *item* weights) while computing the sum. Hence, we turn to privacy-preserving SUM computations (that hide the input) based on a secure-sum protocol as presented in Refs. [8,22].

24.3.5 Economic Issues with Impact on Computational Design of the Proposed Market-Based Profile Infrastructure

Accounting: Since the users should earn rewards or compensations for their profile invocation, one of the issues that need to be solved is accounting. Unlike traditional client/server systems, where accounting is performed by the server that logs all the activities, accounting is much harder in P2P systems. This is because there is no notion of a clear-cut server in P2P networks. All actors (companies and users) are peer nodes. Thus, only peers can gather accounting information in a traditional P2P network. According to Ref. [23], four issues arise: (1) accounting information is distributed throughout the entire system, (2) trustworthy use and storage of this information, (3) behavior rules in incentive-based networks need to be enforceable, and (4) economical use of scarce resources by accounting tasks. Also, three questions must be answered regarding accounting information: (1) How to collect this information (on user's node, company node, or on both)? (2) In which form to collect it (e.g., plain numbers versus receipts, signed receipts, or tokens)? and (3) Where to store it (on company node, user node, or third-party nodes)? All these questions become subject to severe constraints when we take into account the requirements for not only the need for decentralized control of the user profiles, but also the need for sole ownership of a profile by its own user node. According to Ref. [24], one of the main challenges in P2P accounting systems is to bind the accounting information to a real identity, thus making reentries of peers under a new identity costly and hence unattractive. They mention several systems that may solve this problem, including Karma. Another problem is trustworthiness. Trust mechanisms such as Eigentrust [25] may also aggregate peer reputation information in an efficient way. It is unfortunate however that privacy and anonymity may contradict accountability. Hence a trade-off may be considered, for example, a game-theoretic approach to privacy preservation.

Market management: Ref. [24] presents a market-managed P2P system that supports exchange of information beyond file sharing, thus adding the possibility of making peers service providers and service consumers. Service trading was to be managed by market mechanisms, which provide appropriate incentives. According to them, the majority of peer nodes on typical P2P networks are free riders that take and do not give, thus leading to major degradation of performance. They argue that it is hard to use purely accounting mechanisms or payments as an incentive for peers to route/forward all requests to their neighbors. Market mechanisms, however, can lead to efficient and dynamic pricing (hence solving the problem of having to determine the optimal incentive levels). Gerke and Haisheer [24] further present a design and implementation of an open source middleware called MMAPPS (based on JXTA P2P framework), and then presented a specific application, called PeerMart, that uses the overlay network Pastry to enable decentralized auctions for services that is based on mapping typical business processes to core functionalities in service-oriented P2P systems.

24.4   Conclusion

We proposed a market-based profile infrastructure that is based on the creation of a dynamic and distributed market-based system where each user's profile is exchanged with other users and online server/merchant agents in a bidding-like system, hence a market-based economy. One possible solution would stand midway between the server (or the business) and the client (or the user) using a P2P privacy-preserving information sharing, thus ensuring that there is no single central control on the user profiles. A user, who owns his/her own profile, earns some credit each time that their profile is invoked by a recommendation process (or transaction), hence accumulating credits that can be used toward any purchase within this marketplace. The user, for the first time, not only owns their own profile, but also can sell it like a commodity and benefit from it. The entire solution is enabled by a technical infrastructure that allows such exchange of information to take place. Such a profit has previously been restricted only to the businesses (who frequently sell, buy, and trade user profile data) without any benefit or gain to the user, and without their consent.

Our proposed market-based profile infrastructure represents a paradigm shift in personalized e-commerce: from coordination to cooperation (between the online businesses and the multitude of users), from centralization to decentralization (of information, ownership, and control), and from control to incentives, (i.e., incentives for using profiles will create a marketplace with no central control, a marketplace that is enhanced by the power of knowledge that can be extracted, with accountability, from information that is owned by the people, and yet without forcing the people to relinquish this power to businesses).

A sound technical solution will require a suitable orchestration of several powerful KDD techniques that may offer the only way to organize and search the vast decentralized profile marketplace in real time, while concealing the user's private data. Thus, KDD would work at the service of both the user and the business, and not only or primarily the latter, as in the current e-commerce status quo.

The proposed infrastructure presents several challenges for the data-mining and machine-learning communities, particularly in the orchestration of distributed data mining at a massive scale not seen before in other applications, and in tackling the sensitive but crucial privacy and ethical issues that are at stake.

Our future work should consider each objective in detail and implement some of the proposed ideas in a simulated network to study the dynamics of such a decentralized marketplace, in particular from the point of view of the quality of recommendations, and the quantitative benefits to the company nodes and the user nodes. Extensions to a purely user-based marketplace for information exchange between users is also an interesting direction to investigate.

References

[1] M. Pazzani and D. Billsus. Learning and revising user profiles: The identification of interesting Web sites, *Machine Learning*, 27: 313–331, 1997.

[2] J.A. Konstan, B. Miller, J. Maltz, G. Herlocker, and J. Riedl. Grouplens: Collaborative filtering for usenet news, *Communications of the ACM*, March, 77–87, 1997.

[3] T. Suel, C. Mathur, J.W. Wu, J. Zhang, A. Delis, M. Kharrazi, X. Long, and K. Shanmugasundaram, ODISSEA: A peer-to-peer architecture for scalable Web search and information retrieval, in V. Christophides and J. Freire (Eds.), *International Workshop on the Web and Databases*, pp. 67–72, San Diego, California, June 12–13, 2003.

[4] K.Y. Tam and S.Y. Ho, A smart card based Internet micropayment infrastructure: Technical development and user adoption, *Journal of Organizational Computing and Electronic Commerce*, 17(2): 145–173, 2007.

[5] R. Steinmetz and K. Wehrle, What is this "peer-to-peer" about? in R. Steinmetz and K. Wehrle (Eds.), *P2P Systems and Applications*, Springer-Verlag LNCS 3485, pp. 95–117, Berlin, Germany, 2005.

[6] H. Polat and W. Du, Privacy-preserving collaborative filtering using randomized perturbation techniques. In *Proceedings of the 3rd IEEE International Conference on Data Mining (ICDM'03)*, p. 625, Washington, DC, November 2003.

[7] J. Canny, Collaborative filtering with privacy via factor analysis. In *Proceedings of the 25th Annual International ACM SIGIR Conference on Research and Development in Information Retrieval (SIGIR'02)*, pp. 238–245, ACM Press, Tampere, Finland, August 2002.

[8] H. Kargupta, K. Das, and K. Liu, A game theoretic approach toward multi-party privacy-preserving distributed data mining. In *Proceedings of the 11th European Conference on Principles and Practice of Knowledge Discovery in Databases (PKDD)*, pp. 523–531, Warsaw, Polland, September 2007.

[9] C. Papadimitriou and K. Steiglitz, *Combinatorial Optimization, Algorithms and Complexity*, Dover Publications, Mineola, NY, 1982.

[10] E. Cohen and D.D. Lewis, Approximating matrix multiplication for pattern recognition tasks, *Journal of Algorithms*, 30(2): 211–252, February 1999.

[11] J. Kleinberg and P. Raghavan, Query incentive networks. In *FOCS '07: IEEE Symposium on Foundations of Computer Science*, pp. 132–141, 2005.

[12] S. Gotz, S. Rieche, and K. Wehrle, Selected DHT algorithms, in R. Steinmetz and K. Wehrle (Eds.), *P2P Systems and Applications*, Springer-Verlag LNCS 3485, pp. 95–117, 2005.

[13] L.-S. Wu, R. Akavipat, A. Maguitman, and F. Menczer, Adaptive peer to peer social networks for distributed content based Web search, in Social Information Retrieval systems: Emergent technologies and applications for searching the Web Effectively, pp. 155–177, IGI Global, 2007.

[14] A. Fast, D. Jensen, and B.N. Levine, Creating social networks to improve peer-to-peer networking, *KDD'05*, 2005.

[15] D. Zeinalipour-Yazti, V. Kalogeraki, and D. Gunopulos, Exploiting locality for scalable information retrieval in peer-to-peer networks, *Information Systems*, 30: 277–298, 2005.

[16] J. Wang, J. Pouwelse, R.L. Lagendijk, and M.J.T. Reinders, Distributed collaborative filtering for P2P file sharing, *ACM SAC'06*, 2006.

[17] P. Kalni, W.S. Ng, B.C. Ooi, and K.-L. Tan, Answering similarity queries in peer-to-peer networks, *Information Systems*, 31: 57–72, 2006.

[18] G.W. Flake, S. Lawrence, C.L. Giles, and F.M. Coetzee, Self-organization and identification of Web communities, *IEEE Computer*, 35(3): 66–70, 2002.

[19] M.E.J Newman and M. Girvan, Finding and evaluating community structure in networks, *Physical Review E—Statistical, Nonlinear, and Soft Matter*, 69(2):26113–26127, 2004.

[20] P. Domingos and M. Richardson, Mining the network value of customers. In *Proceedings of the 7th ACM SIGKDD International Conference on Knowledge Discovery and Data Mining (KDD'01)*, pp. 57–66, ACM, New York, August 2001.

[21] D. Chakrabarti, R. Kumar, and A. Tomkins, Evolutionary clustering. In *Proceedings of the 12th ACM SIGKDD International Conference on Knowledge Discovery and Data Mining (KDD'06)*, pp. 554–560, ACM, New York, August 2006.

[22] K. Liu, K. Bhaduri, K. Das, P. Nguyen, and H. Kargupta. Client-side Web mining for community formation in peer-to-peer environments. In *Proceedings of the ACM WebKDD Workshop on Knowledge Discovery on the Web*, pp. 130–139, 2006.

[23] N. Liebau, V. Darlagiannis, and O. Heckmann, Accounting in peer-to-peer systems, in R. Steinmetz and K. Wehrle (Eds.), *P2P Systems and Applications*, Springer-Verlag LNCS 3485, pp. 95–117, 2005.

[24] J. Gerke and D. Hausheer, Peer-to-peer market management, in R. Steinmetz and K. Wehrle (Eds.), *P2P Systems and Applications*, Springer-Verlag LNCS 3485, pp. 95–117, 2005.

[25] S.D. Kamvar, M.T. Schlosser, and H. Garcia-Molina, The Eigentrust algorithm for reputation management in P2P networks. In *Proceedings of the 12th International Conference on World Wide Web (WWW'03)*, pp. 640–651, ACM, New York, 2003.

Chapter 25

Challenges in Mining Financial Data

James E. Gentle

Contents

25.1 Introduction

There are many motivating factors for the study of financial data. First and foremost, perhaps, is the profit motive. Investors, speculators, and operators seek an advantage over others in the trading of financial assets. Academics often find a different motive for studying financial data just because of the challenges of developing models for price movements. Finally, government regulators and others are motivated by an interest in maintaining a fair and orderly market. With more and more retirees depending on equity investments for their livelihood, it becomes very important to understand and control the risk in portfolios.

Data mining of stock prices has a long history. Traders have always looked for patterns and other indicators that they think may help to predict stock-price movements. The term "data mining" here refers to exploratory data analysis. In data mining, the analyst is not just fitting the coefficients in a regression model or estimating the autoregressive order in a time series. Although formal methods of statistical inference may be part of the process, in data mining the goals are somewhat less focused. The hope is to discover the unexpected. A common characteristic of an exercise in data mining is the use of data from multiple sources, in different formats, and collected for different purposes.

In the true spirit of data mining, traders have sifted through massive amounts of data from disparate datasets looking for meaningful relationships. A somewhat frivolous example of this was the discovery several years ago of an empirical relationship between professional football wins and losses and an index of stock prices. It was discovered that when the winner of the Super Bowl was a team from the old American Football Conference, the market went up between the date of the game and the end of the year.

Who would have expected such a relationship? It could have been discovered by mining of large and disparate datasets. We must categorize this as knowledge discovery. It actually happened. It is an interesting fact, but it is worthless. Data mining and knowledge discovery must be kept in context.

Another, perhaps more meaningful, discovery that resulted from mining of financial data is called the January effect. Several years ago, it was discovered that there are anomalies in security prices during the first few days of January. There are various details in the differences of January stock prices and the prices in other months (see, e.g., Cataldo and Savage, 2000), but the most relevant general fact is that for a period of over 80 years the average rate of return of the major indexes of stock prices during January was more than double the average rate of return for any other month.

While this discovery comes from just an obvious and straightforward statistical computation, and thus is a rather trivial example in data mining, it serves to illustrate a characteristic of financial data. I call it the uncertainty principle, in analogy to Heisenberg's uncertainty principle that states that making a measurement affects the state of the thing being measured. After the January effect became a common knowledge, the effect seemed to occur earlier (the Santa Claus rally). This, of course, is exactly what one might expect. Carrying such expectations to the second order, the Santa Claus rally may occur in November, and then perhaps in October. (October is subject to the Mark Twain effect, so-called because Twain humorously cited October as one of the 12 months in which it is dangerous to speculate in the stock market. As a side note, the average returns in October have been negative, and two major stock crashes have occurred in October. The average returns during September, however, have been the worst of any month during the past 80 years or so.) As a further parenthetical remark, we should note that any unexpected discovery should be investigated more deeply, and indeed, the January effect has been the subject of many studies of year-end trading.

There are many different types of financial data including balance sheets, earnings statements and their various details, stock prices, and so on. Taking the view that data means any kind of information, we include in financial data the names and backgrounds of directors and other company officers, news items relating to the company, general economic news, and so on. Two major components of financial data are the opinions of financial analysts and the chatter of the large army of people with a computer and a connection to the Internet where they can post touts. This data must be included in the broad class of financial data because they actually have an effect on other financial data such as stock prices. In the following, I use the term "financial data" in this very broad sense.

Three of the general types of financial data are numerical. One type of numerical data relates to trading of financial assets, and for present purposes I restrict this to trading of stock equities and options on those equities. This kind of data is objective and highly reliable. Two other types of numerical data have to do with the general financial state of an individual company and of the national and global economy. These kinds of data, while ostensibly objective, depend on the subjective of the definitions of the terms. (Unemployment rate, e.g., is not a measure of how many employable persons are not employed.) Finally, the fourth type is the text data that is relevant to the trading of stock equities. This includes objective information such as the names of the company officers and products or services of the company. It also includes statements and predictions by anyone with the ability to publicize anything. This kind of data varies from very objective to very subjective.

Data analysts often deal with data that have different levels of accuracy. When it is possible to assign relative variances to different subsets of numerical data, the data can easily be combined using weights inversely proportional to the variance. The differences in the nature of financial data, however, make it difficult to integrate the data in any meaningful way. The totality of relevant financial data is difficult to define. The provenance of financial data is almost impossible to track. Rumors easily become data. Even hard data, that is, numerical data on book values, earnings, and so on, is not always reliable. A price earnings (PE) ratio, for example, may be based on actual earnings in some trailing period or estimated earnings in some period that includes some future time. Unfortunately, earnings, even actual, are a rather subjective quantity, subject to methods of booking. (Even if the fundamental operations of the market were efficient, as is assumed in most academic models, the basic premise of efficiency, that is, that everyone has the same information, is not satisfied. Analysts and traders with the ability to obtain really good data have an advantage.) The integration of data of various types is perhaps the primary challenge in mining financial data.

Finally, a major obstacle to the relevance of any financial data is the fact that the phenomena measured by or described by the data are changing over time.

The primary challenges in the mining of financial data arise from the vast diversity of types and sources of data and from the variation of the data in time. Understanding the temporal variability can be facilitated by mathematical models. The current models are usable most of the time. The models contain parameters, such as mean drift and the standard deviation of the drift in a diffusion process. These model parameters are not directly observable; rather, they must be derived from observable data. Although the models are still very approximate, in some ways the modeling has advanced faster than the statistical methods for estimating the parameters in the models. An example of this is the indirect estimation of the standard deviation using price data for derivatives and the model that relates the price to the standard deviation.

In the next section, I quickly review some general mathematical models of asset prices. And then in Section 25.3, I discuss some of the problems in measuring stochastic volatility, which is one of the most important aspects of financial data, and one of the more challenging features to model. For the issues of mining financial text data, all I do is just point to some references. It is a topic for intensive future research.

25.2   Models of Asset Prices

Anything that is openly traded has a market price that may be more or less than some fair price. In financial studies, a general objective is to measure fair price, value, or worth. For shares of stock, the fair price is likely to be some complicated function of intrinsic (or book) current value of identifiable assets owned by the company, expected rate of growth, future dividends, and other factors.

The price, either the market price or the fair price, varies over time. At the first simple approximation, we assume discrete time, $t_0, t_1, t_2, \ldots$ or $t, t+1, t+2, \ldots$. In more realistic models, we assume continuous time. (And, of course, in really sophisticated models, we would have to revert to some type of discreteness, but at a very fine-grained level.)

The prices of individual securities, even if they follow similar models, behave in a way peculiar to the security. There are more security-specific extraordinary events that affect the price of a given security, than there are extraordinary events that affect the overall market. For that reason, at least as a beginning, we study the prices of some index of stock prices. The S&P 500 is a commonly used index. A graph of the daily closes of the S&P 500 index from January 1, 1986 to December 31, 2007 is shown in Figure 25.1.

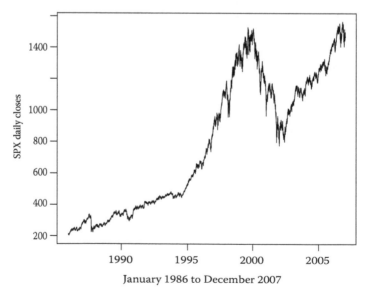

January 1986 to December 2007

FIGURE 25.1:   S&P 500 daily closes (tick marks are at the beginning of the year).

A stochastic model of the price of a stock may view the price as a random variable that depends on previous prices and some characteristic parameters of the particular stock. For example, in discrete time

$$S_{t+1} = f(S_t, \mu, \sigma),$$

where
   t indexes time
   μ and σ are parameters
   f is some function that contains a random component

The randomness in f may be assumed to reflect all variation in the price that is not accounted for in the model.

25.2.1 Modeling Relative Changes of Stock Prices

In the absence of exogenous forces, the movement of stock prices is probably some kind of random walk. A simple random walk could take the prices negative. Also, it seems intuitive that the random walk should have a mean step size that is proportional to the magnitude of the price. The proportional rate of change, $(S_{t+1} - S_t)/S_{t+1}$, therefore, is more interesting than the prices themselves (Figure 25.2), and is more amenable to fitting to a probability model. The event of October 19, 1987 clearly stands out.

A good, general model of a random walk is a Brownian motion, or a Wiener process; hence, we may write the model as a drift and diffusion,

$$\frac{dS(t)}{S(t)} = \mu(S(t), t)dt + \sigma(S(t), t)dB,$$

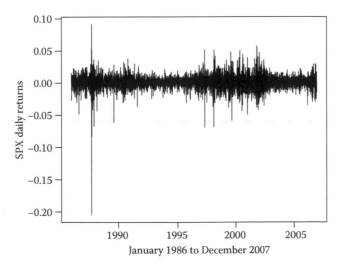

FIGURE 25.2: S&P 500 daily returns.

where dB is a Brownian motion, which has a standard deviation of 1. The standard deviation of the rate of change is therefore $\sigma(S(t),t)$. In this equation, both the mean drift and the standard deviation may depend on both the magnitude of the price $S(t)$ and also on the time t itself.

If we assume that $\mu(\cdot)$ and $\sigma(\cdot)$ do not depend on the value of the state and that they are constant in time, we have the model

$$\frac{dS(t)}{S(t)} = \mu dt + \sigma dB,$$

which is called a geometric Brownian motion. In this form, μ is called the drift and the diffusion component σ is called the volatility. We can estimate μ and σ from the historical rates of return: the mean and the standard deviation, respectively.

Although it is easy to understand the model, it is not so obvious how we would estimate the parameters. First of all, obviously, we cannot work with dt. We must use finite differences based on Δt, but the question is how long is Δt?

We first note an interesting property of Brownian motion. Its variation seems to depend on the frequency at which it is observed; it is infinitely wiggly. The random data shown in Figure 25.3 illustrate the increase in variation at shorter time intervals. (Technically, the first variation of Brownian motion is infinite.) The panels represent the same realized process; the differences are just how frequently the process is observed. From one panel to another in Figure 25.3, straight-line movements are broken into jagged movements. (The paths in Figure 25.3 could be generated by thinning from the higher frequency samples to the lower frequency samples, but they were actually generated in the other direction by a device known as a Brownian bridge.)

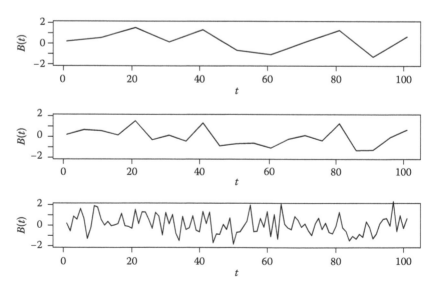

FIGURE 25.3:   Brownian process observed at varying length intervals.

We note that as a model for the rate of return, $dS(t)/S(t)$ geometric Brownian motion, is similar to other common statistical models,

$$\frac{dS(t)}{S(t)} = \mu dt + \sigma dB(t)$$

or

$$\text{Response} = \text{Systematic component} + \text{Random error.}$$

Also, note that without the stochastic component, the differential equation has the simple solution

$$S(t) = ce^{\mu t},$$

from which we get the formula for continuous compounding for a rate μ.

The rate of growth we expect for S just from the systematic component in the geometric Brownian motion model is μ. Because the expected value of the random component is 0, we might think that the overall expected rate of growth is just μ. Closer analysis, however, in which we consider the rate of change σ being equally likely to be positive or negative and the effect on a given quantity if there is an uptick of σ followed by a downtick of equal magnitude yields a net result of $-\sigma^2$ for the two periods. The average over the two periods therefore is $-\sigma^2/2$. The stochastic component reduces the expected rate of μ by $-\sigma^2/2$. This is the price of risk. (We could formalize the preceding discussion using Ito's formula for the stochastic differential equation [SDE].) The geometric Brownian motion model is the simplest model for stock prices that is somewhat realistic.

25.2.1.1 Fitting the Model

Returning now to the problem of estimating a parameter of a continuous-time process, we consider the similar model for continuous compounding. If an amount A is invested for n periods at a per-period rate R that is compounded m times per period, the terminal value is

$$A\left(1 + \frac{R}{m}\right)^{nm}.$$

The limit of the terminal value as $m \to \infty$ is

$$Ae^{Rn}.$$

This suggests that Δt can be chosen arbitrarily, and, since rates are usually quoted on an annualized basis, we chose Δt to be 1 year. Using the formula for compounded interest, we first transform the closing price data $S_0, S_1, S_2 \ldots$ to $r_i = \log(S_i/S_{i-1})$. Now, an obvious estimator of the annualized volatility, $\tilde{\sigma}$, based on N periods each of length Δt (measured in years) is

$$\tilde{\sigma} = \frac{1}{\sqrt{\Delta t}}\sqrt{\frac{1}{N}\sum_{i=1}^{N}(r_i - \bar{r})^2}.$$

We are now in a position to use the geometric Brownian motion drift-diffusion model (with the simplifying assumptions of constant drift and diffusion parameters).

25.2.1.2 Solution of the SDE

The solution of a differential equation is obtained by integrating both sides and allowing for constant terms. Constant terms are evaluated by satisfying known boundary conditions, or initial values. In an SDE, we must be careful in how the integration is performed, although different interpretations may be equally appropriate.

The SDE defines a simple Ito process with constant coefficients,

$$dS(t) = \mu S(t)dt + \sigma S(t)dB(t).$$

We solve this using Ito's formula. Integrating to time $t = T$, we have

$$S(T) = S(t_0)\exp\left[\left(\mu - \frac{1}{2}\sigma^2\right)\Delta t + \sigma\Delta B\right].$$

25.2.2 Modeling Prices of Derivative Assets

For any asset whose price varies over time, there may be a desire to insure against loss, or there may be interest in putting up a small amount of capital now so as to share in future gains. The insurance or the stake that depends on an underlying asset is itself an asset that can be traded. (In the following, we refer to an underlying asset as an underlying.)

There are many ways the insurance or stake can be structured. It most certainly would have an expiration date. It could be a contract or it could be an option. It could be exercisable only at a fixed date or at anytime before expiration. Its price depends on its nature and on the price of the underlying, so it is a derivative asset. (In the following, we refer to a derivative asset as a derivative.) Determination of the fair price of derivatives is one of the major motivations for developing pricing models for stock prices as discussed in the previous section. This section is intended to provide a quick review of the derivative pricing models. More complete discussions are available in many texts, for example, Chriss (1997) or Hull (2005).

Common derivatives are puts and calls on stocks or stock indexes. A put is the right to sell; a call is the right to buy. They are options.

There are various ways that an option agreement can be structured, and so there are different types of options. American style options, for example, carry the right to exercise anytime between the time of acquisition of the right and the expiration date.

How to price a derivative is a difficult question. A model for the value of an option may be expressed as an equation in the form

$$V(t) = g(S(t), \mu(t), \sigma(t)),$$

where

$V(t)$ is the value, that is, the correct price of the option at time t (relative to the expiration date)

$S(t)$ is the market price of the underlying at time t

$\mu(t)$ and $\sigma(t)$ are parametric characteristics of the underlying

g is some function that contains a random component

As usual, we assume frictionless trading; that is, we ignore transaction costs

The randomness in g may be assumed to reflect all variation in the price that is not accounted for in the model.

The price of the underlying will fluctuate, and so the price of the derivative is related to the expected value of the underlying at expiration.

25.2.2.1 Price of a European Call Option

A European call option is a contract that gives the owner the right to buy a specified amount of an underlying for a fixed strike price, K, on the expiration or maturity date, T. The owner of the option does not have any obligations in the contract.

The payoff, h, of the option at time T is either 0 or the excess of the price of the underlying $S(T)$ is over the strike price K. Once the parameters K and T are set, the payoff is a function of $S(T)$:

$$h[S(T)] = \begin{cases} S(T) - K & \text{if } S(T) > K \\ 0 & \text{otherwise.} \end{cases}$$

The price of the option at any time is a function of the time t, and the price of the underlying s. We denote it as $P(t,s)$.

We wish to determine the fair price at time $t = 0$.

It seems natural that the price of the European call option should be the expected value of the payoff of the option at expiration, discounted back to $t = 0$:

$$P(0,s) = e^{-rT} E\{h[S(T)]\}.$$

The basic approach in the Black–Scholes pricing scheme is to seek a portfolio with zero expected value, which consists of short and long positions in the option, the underlying, and a risk-free bond.

There are two key ideas in developing pricing formulas for derivatives:

1. No-arbitrage principle

2. Replicating, or hedging, portfolio

An arbitrage is a trading strategy with a guaranteed rate of return that exceeds the riskless rate of return. In financial analysis, we assume that arbitrages do not exist. This follows from an assumption that the market is efficient; that is, the assumption that all market participants receive and act on all of the relevant information as soon as it becomes available. One does not need any deep knowledge of the market to see that this assumption does not hold, but without the assumption it would not be possible to develop a general model. Every model would have to provide for input from different levels of information for different participants; hence, the model would necessarily apply to a given set of participants. While the hypothesis of an efficient market clearly cannot hold, we can develop useful models under that assumption. (The situation is as described in the quote often attributed to George Box: "All models are wrong, but some are useful.")

There are two essentially equivalent approaches to determining the fair price of a derivative: use of delta hedging and use of a replicating portfolio. In the following, we briefly describe replicating portfolios.

The replication approach is to determine a portfolio and an associated trading strategy that will provide a payout that is identical to that of the underlying. This portfolio and trading strategy replicate the derivative. A replicating strategy involves both long and short positions. If every derivative can be replicated by positions in the underlying (and cash), the economy or market is said to be complete. We will generally assume complete markets.

The Black–Scholes approach leads to the idea of a self-financing replicating hedging strategy. The approach yields the interesting fact that the price of the call does not depend on the expected value of the underlying. It does depend on its volatility, however.

25.2.2.2 Expected Rate of Return on Stock

Assume that XYZ is selling at $S(t_0)$ and pays no dividends. Its expected value at time $T > t_0$ is merely the forward price for what it could be bought now, where the forward price is calculated as $e^{r(T-t_0)}S(t_0)$, where r is the risk-free rate of return, $S(t_0)$ is the spot price, and $T - t_0$ is the time interval. This is an application of the no-arbitrage principle.

The holder of the forward contract (long position) on XYZ must buy stock at time T for $e^{r(T-t_0)}S(t_0)$, and the holder of a call option buys stock only if $S(T) > K$.

Now we must consider the role of the volatility. For a holder of forward contract, volatility is not good, but for a call option holder, volatility is good; that is, it enhances the value of the option.

Under the above assumptions, the volatility of the underlying affects the value of an option, but the expected rate of return of the underlying does not.

A simple model of the market assumes two assets:

1. Riskless asset with price at time t of β_t

2. Risky asset with price at time t of $S(t)$

The price of a derivative can be determined based on trading strategies involving these two assets. The price of the riskless asset follows the deterministic ordinary differential equation

$$d\beta_t = r\beta_t \, dt,$$

where r is the instantaneous risk-free interest rate. The price of the risky asset follows the SDE

$$dS(t) = \mu S(t)dt + \sigma S(t)dB_t.$$

We have then for the price of the call

$$C(t) = \Delta_t S(t) - e^{r(T-t)}R(t),$$

where $R(t)$ is the current value of a riskless bond.

We speak of a portfolio as a vector p whose elements sum to 1. The length of the vector is the number of assets in our universe. By the no-arbitrage principle, there does not exist a p such that for some $t > 0$, either

$$p^T s_0 < 0 \text{ and } p^T S(t)(\omega) \geq 0 \quad \text{for all } \omega,$$

or

$$p^T s_0 \leq 0 \text{ and } p^T S(t)(\omega) \geq 0 \text{ for all } \omega, \text{ and } p^T S(t)(\omega) > 0 \quad \text{for some } \omega.$$

A derivative D is said to be attainable $\bigl($over a universe of assets $S = (S^{(1)}, S^{(2)},\dots,S^{(k)})\bigr)$ if there exists a portfolio p such that for all ω and t,

$$D_t(\omega) = p^T S(t)(\omega).$$

Not all derivatives are attainable. The replicating portfolio approach to pricing derivatives applies only to those that are attainable.

The value of a derivative changes in time and as a function of the value of the underlying; therefore, a replicating portfolio must be changing in time or dynamic. (Note that transaction costs are ignored.) The replicating portfolio is self-financing; that is, once the portfolio is initiated, no further capital is required. Every purchase is financed by a sale.

25.2.2.3 Replicating Strategy

Using our simple market model, with a riskless asset with price at time t of β_t and a risky asset with price at time t of $S(t)$ (with the usual assumptions on the prices of these assets), we can construct a portfolio whose value will have the same expected value as the expected value of the payoff of a European call option on the risky asset at time T.

At time t, the portfolio consists of a_t units of the risky asset and of b_t units of the riskless asset. Therefore, the value of the portfolio is $a_t S(t) + b_t \beta_t$. If we scale β_t so that $\beta_0 = 1$ and adjust b_t accordingly, the expression simplifies, so that $\beta_t = e^{rt}$. The portfolio replicates the value of the option at time T if it has value $K - S(T)$ if this is positive and zero otherwise. If the portfolio is self-financing

$$d[a_t S(t) + b_t e^{rt}] = a_t dS(t) + r b_t e^{rt} dt.$$

25.2.2.4   Black–Scholes Differential Equation

Consider the fair value V of a European call option at time $t < T$. At any time, this is a function of both t and the price of the underlying S_t. We would like to construct a dynamic, self-financing portfolio (a_t, b_t) that will replicate the derivative at maturity. If we can, then the no-arbitrage principle requires that

$$a_t S_t + b_t e^{rt} = V(t, S_t),$$

for $t < T$.

We assume no-arbitrage and we assume that a risk-free return is available. Assuming $V(t, S_t)$ is continuously twice-differentiable, we differentiate both sides of the equation that represents a replicating portfolio with no arbitrage:

$$a_t dS_t + rb_t e^{rt} dt = \left(\frac{\partial V}{\partial S_t} \mu S_t + \frac{\partial V}{\partial t} + \frac{1}{2} \frac{\partial^2 V}{\partial S_t^2} \sigma^2 S_t^2 \right) dt$$
$$+ \frac{\partial V}{\partial S_t} (\sigma S_t) dB_t.$$

By the market model for dS_t, the left-hand side is

$$(a_t \mu S_t + rb_t e^{rt}) dt + a_t \sigma S_t dB_t.$$

Equating the coefficients of dB_t, we have

$$a_t = \frac{\partial V}{\partial S_t}.$$

From our equation for the replicating portfolio, we have

$$b_t = [V(t, S_t) - a_t S_t] e^{-rt}.$$

Now, equating coefficients of dt and substituting for a_t and b_t, we have the Black–Scholes differential equation,

$$r \left(V - S_t \frac{\partial V}{\partial S_t} \right) = \frac{\partial V}{\partial t} + \frac{1}{2} \sigma^2 S_t^2 \frac{\partial^2 V}{\partial S_t^2}.$$

Notice that μ is not in the equation.

Instead of European calls, we can consider European puts, and proceed in the same way using a replicating portfolio, and we arrive at the same Black–Scholes differential equation.

25.2.2.5   Black–Scholes Formula

The solution of the differential equation depends on the boundary conditions. In the case of European options, these are simple. For calls, they are

$$V_c(T, S_t) = (S_t - K)^+,$$

and for puts, they are

$$V_p(T,S_t) = (K - S_t)^+.$$

With these boundary conditions, there are closed-form solutions to the Black–Scholes differential equation. For the call, for example, it is

$$C_{BS}(t,S_t) = S_t\Phi(d_1) - Ke^{-r(T-t)}\Phi(d_2),$$

where

$$d_1 = \frac{\log(S_t/K) + (r + \frac{1}{2}\sigma^2)(T-t)}{\sigma\sqrt{T-t}},$$

$$d_2 = d_1 - \sigma\sqrt{T-t},$$

and

$$\Phi(s) = \frac{1}{\sqrt{2\pi}}\int_{-\infty}^{s} e^{-y^2/2}dy.$$

We recall the assumptions of the Black–Scholes model:

- Differentiability of stock prices with respect to time

- Dynamic replicating portfolio can be maintained without transaction costs

- Returns are

  - Independent
  - Normal
  - Mean stationary
  - Variance stationary

25.2.3 Assessment of the Model for Price Movements

Our focus is on rates of return, because that is the fundamental quantity in our pricing models. Rates of return are not directly observable, and as we indicated before because of the continuous time in the geometric Brownian motion model, there are various ways we may evaluate these derived observations. The lograte returns are shown in Figure 25.4. (The difference rates, shown in Figure 25.2, produce a similar picture.)

The data do not appear to meet the assumptions of the model. Just from the plot in Figure 25.4, without any additional analyses, we can notice three things that violate the assumptions:

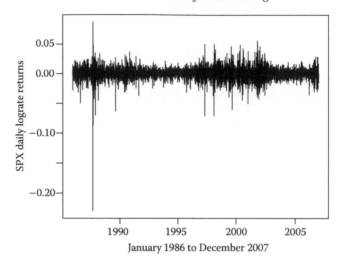

FIGURE 25.4: S&P 500 daily lograte returns (tick marks are at the beginning of the year).

1. Data have several outliers.

2. Data are asymmetric.

3. Data values seem to cluster.

Because of the outliers, the data do not appear to be from a normal distribution. The departure from normality can be seen more easily in a normal Q–Q plot. The plot in Figure 25.5 is a dramatic evidence of the lack of normality.

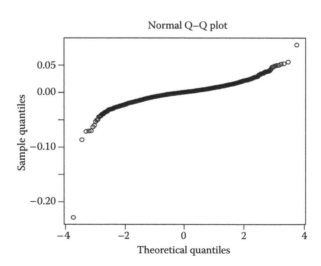

FIGURE 25.5: Q–Q plot of S & P 500 daily lograte returns.

Although the data seem to be centered about 0, and there seem to be roughly as many positive values as negative values, there appear to be larger extreme negative values than extreme positive values. The extreme values are more than what we would expect in a random sample from a normal distribution. The crash of October 19, 1987 is an extreme outlier, but there are others. Finally, the data do not seem to be independent; specifically, the extreme values seem to be clustered. The large drop on October 19, 1987 is followed by a large gain.

All of these empirical facts seem to bring into question the whole idea that the market is efficient. Either basic facts are changing rapidly, or there are irrational motives at play.

The returns in this example are for an index of 500 large stocks. We would expect this index to behave more in line with any model based on assumptions of independent normality than the price of some individual stock. These kinds of violations of the assumptions, however, can be observed in other indexes as well as in individual stock prices. Jondeau et al. (2007) and Rachev et al. (2005) discuss many of the issues of developing models similar to those we discussed above, except without the assumption of normality.

25.3 Volatility

As in all areas of science, our understanding of a phenomenon begins by identifying the quantifiable aspects of the phenomenon and then is limited by our ability to measure those quantifiable aspects.

Most models of prices of financial assets have a parameter for volatility. For a model to be useful, of course, we must have some way of supplying a value for the parameter, either by direct measurement or by estimation. The volatility parameter presents special challenges for the analyst. (Recall volatility is defined as the standard deviation of the rate of return; and, ideally, here we mean the instantaneous rate of return.)

Although often the model assumes that the volatility is constant, volatility, like most parameters in financial models, varies over time. There may be many reasons for this variation in volatility including arrival of news. When the variation is not explained by a specific event, the condition is known as stochastic volatility. Empirical evidence supports the notion that the volatility is stochastic.

Volatility itself is a measure of propensity for change in time. This results in the insurmountable problem of providing a value for a parameter that depends on changes of other values in time, but which itself changes in time.

There are some interesting stylized facts about volatility (see McQueen and Vorkink, 2004):

- Volatility is serially correlated in time.
- Both positive and negative news lead to higher levels of volatility.
- Negative news tend to increase future volatility more than positive news.

- There are two distinct components to the effect of news on volatility, one with a rapid decay and one with a slow decay.

- Volatility has an effect on the risk premium.

The Black–Scholes model and the resulting Black–Scholes formula include a volatility parameter, σ. One use of the Black–Scholes formula obviously is to provide an approximate fair price for an option. This was the motivation for its development. Another formula for the fair price of anything for which there is an active market, however, is the market price. For a given option (underlying, type, strike price, and expiry) and given the price of the underlying and the risk-free rate, the Black–Scholes formula relates the option price to the volatility of the under- lying; that is, the volatility determines the model option price. The actual price at which the option trades can be observed, however. If this price is plugged into the Black–Scholes formula, the volatility can be computed. This is called the implied volatility. The implied volatility may be affected by either the absence of fairness in the market price, or by the market price being correlated to Black–Scholes formulaic prices. In the case of thinly traded assets, the market price may be strongly affected by idiosyncrasies of the traders.

25.3.1 Implied Volatility

Let c be the observed price of the call. Now, set $C_{BS}(t,S_t) = c$, and

$$f(\sigma) = S_t \Phi(d_1) - Ke^{-r(T-t)} \Phi(d_2).$$

We have

$$c = f(\sigma).$$

Given a value for c, that is, the observed price of the option, we can solve for σ. There is no closed-form solution, so we solve iteratively. Beginning with $\sigma^{(0)}$, we can use the Newton updates,

$$\sigma^{(k+1)} = \sigma^{(k)} - \{f[\sigma^{(k)}] - c\}/f'[\sigma^{(k)}].$$

We have

$$f'(\sigma) = S_t \frac{d\Phi(d_1)}{d\sigma} - Ke^{-r(T-t)} \frac{d\Phi(d_2)}{d\sigma}$$

$$= S_t \phi(d_1) \frac{dd_1}{d\sigma} - Ke^{-r(T-t)} \phi(d_2) \frac{dd_2}{d\sigma},$$

where

$$\phi(y) = \frac{1}{\sqrt{2\pi}} e^{-y^2/2},$$

$$\frac{dd_1}{d\sigma} = \frac{\sigma^2(T-t) - \log(S_t/K) - (r + \frac{1}{2}\sigma^2)(T-t)}{\sigma^2 \sqrt{T-t}},$$

and

$$\frac{dd_2}{d\sigma} = \frac{dd_1}{d\sigma} - \sqrt{T-t}.$$

As we have mentioned, one of the problems of the Black–Scholes formula is its assumption that the volatility σ is constant. Because of this, obviously if we substitute the observed market price of a particular option for the Black–Scholes price for that option, and do the same for a different option on the same underlying, we are likely to get different values for the implied volatility. In any event, computing an implied volatility is not straightforward (see Hentschel, 2003).

The implied volatility from the Black–Scholes model should be the same at all points, but it is not. The implied volatility, for given T and S_t, depends on the strike price, K.

In general, the implied volatility is greater than the empirical volatility, but the implied volatility is even greater for far out-of-the-money calls. It also generally increases for deep in-the-money calls.

This variation in implied volatility is called the smile curve, or the volatility smile, as shown in Figure 25.6. The curve is computed for a given security and the traded derivatives on that security with a common expiry. The empirical price for each derivative at that expiry is used in the Black–Scholes formula and, upon inversion of the formula, yields a value for the volatility.

The available strike prices are not continuous, of course. This curve is a smoothed (and idealized) fit of the observed points.

The smile curve is not well understood, although we have a lot of empirical observations on it. Interestingly, prior to the 1987 crash, the minimum of the smile curve

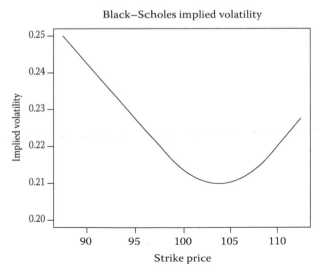

FIGURE 25.6:   Volatility smile.

was at or near the market price S_t. Since then it is generally at a point larger than the market price.

In addition to the variation in implied volatility at a given expiry, there is variation in the implied volatility at a given strike at different expiries. This is a term structure in volatility similar to the term structure of interest rates. The reasons for the term structure of volatility are probably related to the reasons for term structure in interest rates, but this is also not well understood. Gatheral (2006) provides an extensive discussion of the implied volatility function from an empirical perspective.

25.3.1.1 Variation in Volatility over Time

The volatility also varies in time. (This is not the term structure referred to above, which is a variation at a fixed time for events scheduled at different future times.) Volatility varies in time, with periods of high volatility and other periods of low volatility. This is called volatility clustering.

The volatility of an index is somewhat similar to that of an individual stock. The volatility of an index is a reflection of market sentiment. (There are various ways of interpreting this!)

In general, a declining market is viewed as more risky than a rising market, and hence, it is generally true that the volatility in a declining market is higher. Contrarians believe high volatility is bullish because it lags market trends.

A standard measure of the overall volatility of the market is the Chicago board options exchange (CBOE) volatility index (VIX), which CBOE introduced in 1993 as a weighted average of the Black–Scholes-implied volatilities of the S&P 100 index from at-the-money near-term call and put options. (At-the-money is defined as the strike price with the smallest difference between the call price and the put price.)

In 2004, futures on the VIX began trading on the CBOE Futures Exchange, and in 2006, CBOE listed European-style calls and puts on the VIX.

Another measure of the overall market volatility is the CBOE Nasdaq volatility index, which CBOE computes from the Nasdaq-100 index, similar to the VIX. (Note that the more widely watched Nasdaq index is the Composite, IXIC.)

The VIX initially was computed from the Black–Scholes formula. Now the empirical prices are used to fit an implied probability distribution, from which an implied volatility is computed. In 2006, CBOE changed the way the VIX is computed. It is now based on the volatilities of the S&P 500 index implied by several call and put options, not just those at the money, and it uses near-term and next-term options (where near-term is the earliest expiry, more than 8 days away).

The CBOE in computing the VIX uses the prices of calls with strikes above the current price of the underlying, starting with the first out-of-the-money call and sequentially including all with higher strikes until two consecutive such calls have no bids. It uses the prices of puts with strikes below the current price of the underlying in a similar manner.

The price of an option is the mid-quote price, that is, the average of the bid and ask prices. Let $K_1 = K_2 < K_3 < \cdots < K_{n-1} < K_n = K_{n+1}$ be the strike prices of the options that are to be used. The VIX is defined as $100 \times \sigma$, where

$$\sigma^2 = \frac{2e^{rT}}{T} \left\{ \sum_{i=2;\ i\neq j}^{n} \frac{\Delta K_i}{K_i^2} Q(K_i) + \frac{\Delta K_j}{K_j^2} \left[Q(K_j\text{put}) + Q(K_j\text{call}) \right] / 2 \right\}$$

$$- \frac{1}{T} \left(\frac{F}{K_j} - 1 \right)^2,$$

where

T is the time to expiry (in our usual notation, we would use $T - t$, but we can
let $t = 0$)

F, called the forward index level, is the at-the-money strike plus e^{rT} times the
difference in the call and put prices for that strike

K_i is the strike price of the ith out-of-the-money strike price (i.e., of a put if
$K_i < F$ and of a call if $F < K_i$)

$\Delta K_i = (K_{i+1} - K_{i-1})/2$

$Q(K_i)$ is the mid-quote price of the option

r is the risk-free interest rate

K_j is the largest strike price less than F

Hentschel (2003) discusses different methods of computing an implied volatility
estimation, and compares some with the VIX computations prior to 2003 (when the
VIX was based on Black–Scholes).

Figure 25.7 shows the VIX for the period January 1, 1990 to December 31, 2007,
together with the absolute value of the lograte returns of the S&P 500, on a different
scale. The peaks of the two measures correspond, and in general, the VIX and the
lograte returns of the S&P 500 seem to have similar distributions.

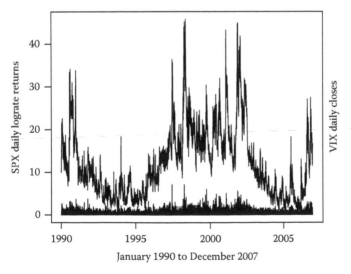

FIGURE 25.7: S&P 500 daily lograte returns and VIX daily closes.

25.3.2   Identifying Volatility Clusters

The identification of change points in a time series has received much attention in the literature. Many of the methods, however, have been based on the assumption that the random component in the data has a normal distribution. Such methods of inference have very low power for distributions with heavy tails, such as the rates of return, as we have seen very clearly in the Q–Q plot in Figure 25.5.

The test of Talwar and Gentle (1981) is less sensitive to the presence of outliers. It clearly identifies changes in volatility in 1987, 1996, 2001, and 2007.

Identification of distributional changes in a random sequence, however, is only part of the picture. The real challenge in mining the data is to determine patterns as they begin, not after the fact. More detailed study of the VIX type of implied volatility and other computed measures of volatility may yield some useful insights.

25.4   Summary: Challenges in Mining Financial Data

Although financial data have been the subject of intense analysis over the years, there are still many remaining challenges. Some of these challenges are in developing better models. Eraker (2004) and Maheu and McCurdy (2004) discuss some of the issues in developing models that accommodate stochastic volatility better.

Perhaps the largest challenge in mining financial data is to make sense of the text data from various sources. The effects of arrival of news on the market in general are discussed by Maheu and McCurdy (2004).

Whether or not Internet chat data are based on an objective analysis, it influences the market in ways that are not understood. Antweiler and Frank (2004) attempt to measure the effects. In order to analyze the effects, and then possibly to predict effects, the first step is to identify sources of relevant data. Many are clear: the recognized stock analysts and the standard financial news services. The weight of individual pieces of data must be estimated and then incorporated into analyses of the effect. A major technical task is to integrate the text data with asset price data and to determine feedback mechanisms.

Financial data of all kinds are streaming data. Mining of streaming data is particularly difficult. Many problems in analysis arise because of the nonstationarity of the data. (See Marchette and Wegman (2004) for discussions of some of the problems in a different setting.)

The main thrust of this chapter has been the need to measure and model volatility of returns. The variability of volatility of stock returns makes planning difficult. This has been one of the most interesting features of recent market activity in which the volatility exhibited extreme swings. Exploratory analyses, both of price data and other types of financial data, including chat data, may identify patterns that presage large volatility. Volatility has implications for portfolio hedging, especially in funds intended for retirement, or actually used for retirement income.

References

[1] Antweiler, W. and M. Z. Frank, 2004, Is all that talk just noise? The information content of internet stock message boards, *The Journal of Finance* **59**, 1259–1294.

[2] Cataldo, A. J. and A. A. Savage, 2000, *The January Effect and Other Seasonal Anomalies: A Common Theoretical Framework*, Jai Press, Stamford, CT.

[3] Chriss, N. A., 1997, *Black-Scholes and Beyond*, Irwin Professional Publishing, Chicago, IL.

[4] Eraker, B., 2004, Do stock prices and volatility jump? Reconciling evidence from spot and option prices, *The Journal of Finance* **59**, 1367–1403.

[5] Gatheral, J., 2006, *The Volatility Surface*, John Wiley & Sons, New York.

[6] Hentschel, L., 2003, Errors in implied volatility estimation, *Journal of Financial and Quantitative Analysis* **38**, 779–810.

[7] Hull, J. C., 2005, *Options, Futures and Other Derivatives*, 6th edn., Prentice-Hall, Englewood Cliffs, NJ.

[8] Jondeau, E., S.-H. Poon, and M. Rockinger, 2007, *Financial Modeling under Non-Gaussian Distributions*, Springer, New York.

[9] Marchette, D. J. and E. J. Wegman, 2004, Statistical analysis of network data for cyber security, *Chance* **17**, 8–18.

[10] Maheu, J. M. and T. H. McCurdy, 2004, News arrival, jump dynamics, and volatility components for individual stock returns, *The Journal of Finance* **59**, 755–793.

[11] McQueen, G. and K. Vorkink, 2004, Whence GARCH? A preference-based explanation for conditional volatility, *The Review of Financial Studies* **17**, 915–949.

[12] Rachev, S. T., C. Menn, and F. J. Fabozzi, 2005, *Fat-Tailed and Skewed Asset Return Distributions*, John Wiley & Sons, New York.

[13] Talwar, P. P. and J. E. Gentle, 1981, Detecting a scale shift in a random sequence at an unknown time point, *Applied Statistics* **30**, 301–304.

References

[1] ...
[2] ...
[3] ...

Chapter 26

Spatial and Spatiotemporal Data Mining: Recent Advances

Shashi Shekhar, Ranga Raju Vatsavai, and Mete Celik

Contents

26.1 Introduction

The explosive growth of spatial data and widespread use of spatial databases have heightened the need for the automated discovery of spatial knowledge. Spatial data mining [1,2] is the process of discovering interesting and previously unknown, but potentially useful patterns from spatial databases. The complexity of spatial data and intrinsic spatial relationships limits the usefulness of conventional data mining techniques for extracting spatial patterns. Efficient tools for extracting information from geospatial data are crucial to organizations which make decisions based on large spatial datasets, including NASA, the National Geospatial-Intelligence Agency (NGA), the National Cancer Institute (NCI), and the U.S. Department of Transportation (USDOT). These organizations are spread across many application domains including ecology and environmental management, public safety, transportation, Earth science, epidemiology, and climatology [3].

General purpose data mining tools like Clementine from SPSS, Enterprise Miner from SAS, data mining extensions from relational database vendors such as Oracle and IBM, public domain data mining packages such as Weka, See5/C5.0 are designed for the purpose of analyzing transactional data. Although these tools were primarily designed to identify customer-buying patterns in market-basket data, they have also been used in analyzing scientific and engineering data, astronomical data, multimedia data, genomic data, and Web data. However, extracting interesting and useful patterns from spatial datasets is more difficult than extracting corresponding patterns from traditional numeric and categorical data due to the complexity of spatial data types, spatial relationships, and spatial autocorrelation.

Specific features of geographical data that preclude the use of general purpose data mining algorithms arc (1) the spatial relationships among the variables, (2) the spatial structure of errors, (3) mixed distributions as opposed to commonly assumed normal distributions, (4) observations that are not independent and identically distributed, (5) spatial autocorrelation among the features, and (6) nonlinear interactions in feature space. Of course, one can apply conventional data mining algorithms, but it is often observed that these algorithms perform more poorly on spatial data. Many supportive examples can be found in the literature; for instance, parametric classifiers like maximum likelihood classifier (MLC) perform more poorly than nonparametric classifiers when the assumptions about the parameters (e.g., normal distribution) are violated, and the per-pixel-based classifiers perform worse than Markov random fields (MRFs) when the features are autocorrelated.

In this chapter we present major accomplishments in the emerging field of spatial data mining, especially in the areas of prediction and classification, outlier detection, spatial colocation rules, and clustering techniques. Spatiotemporal (ST) data mining along with research needs are also briefly discussed.

26.2   Spatial Data

The data inputs of spatial data mining are more complex than the inputs of classical data mining because they include extended objects such as points, lines, and polygons. The data inputs of spatial data mining have two distinct types of attributes: nonspatial attributes and spatial attributes. Nonspatial attributes are used to characterize nonspatial features of objects, such as name, population, and unemployment rate for a city. They are the same as the attributes used in the data inputs of classical data mining. Spatial attributes are used to define the spatial location and extent of spatial objects [4]. The spatial attributes of a spatial object most often include information related to spatial locations, e.g., longitude, latitude, and elevation, as well as shape. Relationships among nonspatial objects are explicit in data inputs,

TABLE 26.1:   Relationships among nonspatial data and spatial data.

Nonspatial Relationship	Spatial Relationship
Arithmetic	Set-oriented: union, intersection, membership, etc.
Ordering	Topological: meet, within, overlap, etc.
Isinstance-of	Directional: North, NE, left, above, behind, etc.
Subclass-of	Metric: e.g., distance, area, perimeter, etc.
Part-of	Dynamic: update, create, destroy, etc.
Membership-of	Shape-based and visibility

e.g., arithmetic relation, ordering, isinstance-of, subclass-of, and membership-of. In contrast, relationships among spatial objects are often implicit, such as overlap, intersect, and behind (Table 26.1). One possible way to deal with implicit spatial relationships is to materialize the relationships into traditional data input columns and then apply classical data mining techniques such as those described in Refs. [5–9]. However, the materialization can result in loss of information. Another way to capture implicit spatial relationships is to develop models or techniques to incorporate spatial information into the spatial data mining process.

Spatial datasets are discrete representations of continuous phenomena. Discretization of continuous space is necessitated by the nature of digital representation. There are two basic models to represent spatial data: raster (grid) and vector. Satellite images are good examples of raster data. On the other hand, vector data consists of points, lines, polygons, and their aggregate (or multi-) counter parts. Spatial networks are another important data type. This distinction is important as many of the techniques that we are going to describe now favor one or more of these data types.

Statistical models [10] are often used to represent observations in terms of random variables. These models can then be used for estimation, description, and prediction based on probability theory. Spatial data can be thought of as resulting from observations on the stochastic process $Z(s) : s \in D$, where s is a spatial location and D is possibly a random set in a spatial framework. Here we present three spatial statistical problems one might encounter: point process, lattice, and geostatistics.

Point process: A point process is a model for the spatial distribution of the points in a point pattern. Several natural processes can be modeled as spatial point patterns, e.g., positions of trees in a forest and locations of bird habitats in a wetland. Spatial point patterns can be broadly grouped into random or nonrandom processes. Real point patterns are often compared with a random pattern (generated by a Poisson process) using the average distance between a point and its nearest neighbor. For a random pattern, this average distance is expected to be $1/(2 \times \sqrt{\text{density}})$, where density is the average number of points per unit area. If for a real process, the computed distance falls within a certain limit, then we conclude that the pattern is generated by a random process; otherwise it is a nonrandom process.

Lattice: A lattice is a model for a gridded space in a spatial framework. Here the lattice refers to a countable collection of regular or irregular spatial sites related to each other via a neighborhood relationship. Several spatial statistical analysis, e.g., the spatial autoregressive model (SAR) and MRFs, can be applied on lattice data.

Geostatistics: Geostatistics deals with the analysis of spatial continuity and weak stationarity [10], which is an inherent characteristics of spatial datasets. Geostatistics provides a set of statistics tools, such as kriging, to the interpolation of attributes at unsampled locations.

One of the fundamental assumptions of statistical analysis is that the data samples are independently generated: like successive tosses of coin, or the rolling of a die. However, in the analysis of spatial data, the assumption about the independence of samples is generally false. In fact, spatial data tends to be highly self-correlated. For example, people with similar characteristics, occupation, and background tend to cluster together in the same neighborhoods. The economies of a region tend to be similar. Changes in natural resources, wildlife, and temperature vary gradually over space. The property of like things to cluster in space is so fundamental that geographers have elevated it to the status of the first law of geography: "Everything is related to everything else but nearby things are more related than distant things" [11]. In spatial statistics, an area within statistics is devoted to the analysis of spatial data, this property is called spatial autocorrelation.

Knowledge discovery techniques that ignore spatial autocorrelation typically perform poorly in the presence of spatial data. Often the spatial dependencies arise due to the inherent characteristics of the phenomena under study, but in particular they arise due to the fact that the spatial resolution of imaging sensors are finer than the size of the object being observed. For example, remote sensing satellites have resolutions ranging from 30 m (e.g., the Enhanced Thematic Mapper of the Landsat 7 satellite of NASA) to 1 m (e.g., the IKONOS satellite from SpaceImaging), while the objects under study (e.g., urban, forest, water) are often much larger than 30 m. As a result, per-pixel-based classifiers, which do not take spatial context into account, often produce classified images with salt and pepper noise. These classifiers also suffer in terms of classification accuracy.

The spatial relationship among locations in a spatial framework is often modeled via a contiguity matrix. A simple contiguity matrix may represent a neighborhood relationship defined using adjacency, Euclidean distance, etc. Example definitions of neighborhood using adjacency include a four-neighborhood and an eight-neighborhood. Given a gridded spatial framework, a four-neighborhood assumes that a pair of locations influence each other if they share an edge. An eight-neighborhood assumes that a pair of locations influence each other if they share either an edge or a vertex.

Figure 26.1a shows a gridded spatial framework with four locations, A, B, C, and D. A binary matrix representation of a four-neighborhood relationship is shown in Figure 26.1b. The row-normalized representation of this matrix is called a contiguity matrix, as shown in Figure 26.1c. Other contiguity matrices can be designed to model neighborhood relationship based on distance. The essential idea is to specify the pairs of locations that influence each other along with the relative intensity of interaction. More general models of spatial relationships using cliques and hypergraphs are available in the literature [12]. In spatial statistics, spatial autocorrelation is quantified using measures such as Ripley's K-function and Moran's I [10].

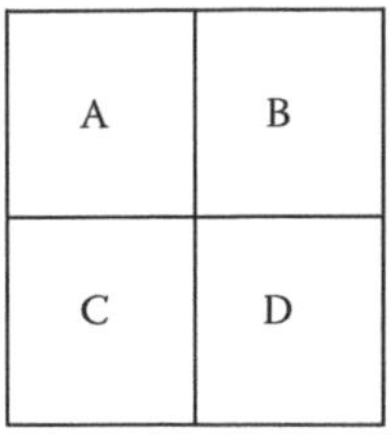

(a) Spatial framework

A	B
C	D

(b) Neighbor relationship

	A	B	C	D
A	0	1	1	0
B	1	0	0	1
C	1	0	0	1
D	0	1	1	0

(c) Contiguity matrix

	A	B	C	D
A	0	0.5	0.5	0
B	0.5	0	0	0.5
C	0.5	0	0	0.5
D	0	0.5	0.5	0

FIGURE 26.1: Spatial framework and its four-neighborhood contiguity matrix.

26.3 Prediction and Classification

Given a sample set of input–output pairs, the objective of supervised learning is to find a function that learns from the given input–output pairs, and predicts an output for any unseen input (but assumed to be generated from the same distribution), such that the predicted output is as close as possible to the desired output. The name "supervised" comes from the fact that the input–output example pairs are given by an expert (teacher). Examples of the supervised learning include thematic map generation (classification) from satellite images, tumor or other organ recognition from medical images, recognition of handwritten characters from the scanned documents, prediction of stock market indexes, and speech recognition. The input–output pairs, also called training samples or training dataset, are denoted by (x_i, y_i), where x_i's are often vectors of measurements over the attribute space. For example, in remote sensing image classification, the input attribute space consists of various spectral bands or channels (e.g., blue, green, red, infrared, thermal, etc.), and the input vectors $(x_i$'s) are reflectance values at the ith location in the image, and the outputs $(y_i$'s) are the-matic classes such as forest, urban, water, and agriculture. Depending on the type of output attribute, two supervised learning tasks can be distinguished:

- *Classification.* In classification, the input vectors x_i are assigned to a few discrete numbers of classes y_i.

- *Regression.* In regression, also known as function approximation, the input–output pairs are generated from an unknown function of the form $y = f(x)$, where y is continuous. Typically, regression is used in prediction and estimation, for example, share value prediction, daily temperature prediction, and market share estimation for a particular product. Regression can also be used in inverse estimation, that is, given that we have an observed value of y, we want to determine the corresponding x value.

Classification can be viewed as a special case of regression. In this section we specifically consider the problem of multispectral remote sensing image classification.

Image classification can be formally defined as finding a function $g(x)$ that maps the input patterns x onto output classes y_i (sometimes y_i's are also denoted as ω_i). The main objective is to assign a label (e.g., water, forest, urban) to each pixel in the classified image, given corresponding feature vector x_j in the input image.

The prediction of events occurring at particular geographic locations is very important in several application domains. Crime analysis, cellular networks, and natural disasters such as fires, floods, droughts, vegetation diseases, and earthquakes are all examples of problems that require location prediction. In this section we present two spatial data mining techniques, namely the SAR and MRF. Before explaining the techniques, we introduce an example application domain to illustrate different concepts in spatial data mining.

26.3.1 An Illustrative Application Domain

We are given data about two wetlands, named Darr and Stubble, on the shores of Lake Erie in Ohio, United States in order to predict the spatial distribution of a marsh-breeding bird, the red-winged blackbird (*Agelaius phoeniceus*). The data was collected from April to June in two successive years, 1995 and 1996 (Figure 26.2a).

A uniform grid was imposed on the two wetlands and different types of measurements were recorded at each cell or pixel. In total, values of seven attributes were recorded at each cell. Domain knowledge is crucial in deciding which attributes are important and which are not. For example, vegetation durability was chosen over vegetation species because specialized knowledge about the bird-nesting habits of the red-winged blackbird suggested that the choice of nest location is more dependent on plant structure, plant resistance to wind, and wave action than on the plant species (Figure 26.2b).

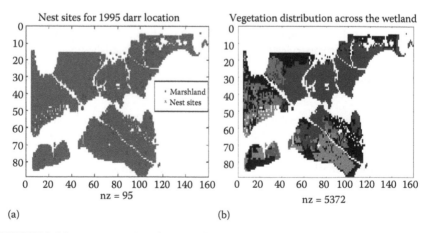

FIGURE 26.2: (a) Learning dataset: The geometry of the wetland and the locations of the nests. (b) The spatial distribution of vegetation durability over the marshland.

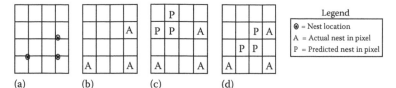

FIGURE 26.3: (a) Actual locations of nests, (b) pixels with actual nests, (c) location predicted by a model, and (d) location predicted by another model. Prediction (d) is spatially more accurate than (c).

Our goal is to build a model for predicting the location of bird nests in the wetlands. Typically the model is built using a portion of the data, called the learning or training data, and then tested on the remainder of the data, called the testing data. In the learning data, all the attributes are used to build the model and in the testing data, one value is hidden, in our case the location of the nests.

The fact that classical data mining techniques ignore spatial autocorrelation and spatial heterogeneity in the model-building process is one reason why these techniques do a poor job. A second, more subtle but equally important reason is related to the choice of the objective function to measure classification accuracy. For a two-class problem, the standard way to measure classification accuracy is to calculate the percentage of correctly classified objects. However, this measure may not be the most suitable in a spatial context. Spatial accuracy—how far the predictions are from the actuals—is as important in this application domain due to the effects of the discretization of a continuous wetland into discrete pixels, as shown in Figure 26.3. Figure 26.3a and b shows the actual locations of nests and the pixels with actual nests, respectively. Note the loss of information during the discretization of continuous space into pixels. Many nest locations barely fall within the pixels labeled "A" and are quite close to other blank pixels, which represent "no-nest." Now consider two predictions shown in Figure 26.3c and d. Domain scientists prefer prediction shown in Figure 26.3d, since the predicted nest locations are closer on average to some actual nest locations. The classification accuracy measure cannot distinguish between the predictions shown in Figure 26.3c and d, and a measure of spatial accuracy is needed to capture this preference.

26.3.2 Modeling Spatial Dependencies Using the SAR and MRF Models

Several previous studies [13,14] have shown that the modeling of spatial dependency (often called context) during the classification process improves overall classification accuracy. Spatial context can be defined by the relationships between spatially adjacent pixels in a small neighborhood. An example spatial framework and its four-neighborhood contiguity matrix is shown in Figure 26.1.

26.3.3 Logistic Spatial Autoregressive Model

Logistic SAR decomposes a classifier $\hat{f}_C$ into two parts, namely spatial autoregression and logistic transformation. We first show how spatial dependencies are modeled using the framework of logistic regression analysis. In the spatial autoregression model, the spatial dependencies of the error term, or, the dependent variable, are directly modeled in the regression equation [15]. If the dependent values y_i are related to each other, then the regression equation can be modified as

$$y = \rho W y + X\beta + \in .$$ (26.1)

where
  W is the neighborhood relationship contiguity matrix
  ρ is a parameter that reflects the strength of the spatial dependencies between the elements of the dependent variable

After the correction term $\rho W y$ is introduced, the components of the residual error vector ε are then assumed to be generated from independent and identical standard normal distributions. As in the case of classical regression, the SAR equation has to be transformed via the logistic function for binary dependent variables.

We refer to Equation 26.1 as the SAR. Notice that when $\rho = 0$, this equation collapses to the classical regression model. The benefits of modeling spatial autocorrelation are many: First, the residual error will have much lower spatial autocorrelation (i.e., systematic variation). With the proper choice of W, the residual error should, at least theoretically, have no systematic variation. In addition, if the spatial autocorrelation coefficient is statistically significant, then SAR will quantify the presence of spatial autocorrelation. It will indicate the extent to which variations in the dependent variable (y) are explained by the average of neighboring observation values. Finally, the model will have a better fit, (i.e., a higher R-squared statistic).

26.3.4 Maximum Likelihood Classifier

Maximum likelihood classification is one of the most widely used parametric and supervised classification technique in remote sensing field [16,17]. Assuming that sufficient ground truth (training) data is available for each thematic class, we can estimate the probability distribution $p(x|y_i)$ for a class (y_i) that describes the chance of finding a pixel from that class at the position $\mathbf{x}$. This estimated $p(y_i|x)$ can be related with the desired $p(x|y_i)$ using Bayes' theorem:

$$p(y_i|x) = \frac{p(x|y_i)p(y_i)}{p(x)}$$ (26.2)

where
  $p(y_i)$ is the probability that class y_i occurs in the image, also know as *a priori* probability
  $p(\mathbf{x})$ is the probability of finding a pixel from any class at location $\mathbf{x}$

Since $p(\mathbf{x})$ is constant, we can omit it from computation and write the discriminant function $g(\mathbf{x})$ by simplifying Equation 26.2 and taking logarithm as follows:

$$g_i(\mathbf{x}) = \ln\, p(\mathbf{x}|y_i) + \ln\, p(y_i), \qquad (26.3)$$

where ln is the natural logarithm. By assuming a multivariate normal model for class probability distributions, the discriminant function $g_i(x)$ for the maximum likelihood classification can be written as the following:

$$g_i(\mathbf{x}) = \ln p(\omega_i) - \frac{1}{2}(\mathbf{x} - \mathbf{m}_i)^t \,\Sigma_i^{-1}(\mathbf{x} - \mathbf{m}_i). \qquad (26.4)$$

MLC is an example of a Bayesian classifier; for more details refer to Refs. [18,19].

26.3.5 Markov-Random-Field-Based Bayesian Classifiers

The MLC presented above is a per-pixel-based classifier and assumes that samples are independent and identically distributed (i.i.d.). Ignoring spatial autocorrelation results in salt and pepper kind of noise in the classified images, we now present MRF-based Bayesian classifiers that model spatial context via the *a priori* term in Bayes' rule. A set of random variables whose interdependency relationship is represented by an undirected graph (i.e., a symmetric neighborhood matrix) is called a MRF [20]. The Markov property specifies that a variable depends only on its neighbors and is independent of all other variables. The location prediction problem can be modeled in this framework by assuming that the class label, $l_i = f_C(s_i)$, of different locations, s_i, constitutes an MRF. In other words, random variable l_i is independent of l_j if $W(s_i, s_j) = 0$.

The Bayesian rule can be used to predict l_i from feature value vector X and neighborhood class label vector L_i as follows:

$$\Pr(l_i|X, L_i) = \frac{\Pr(X|l_i, L_i)\Pr(l_i|L_i)}{\Pr(X)} \qquad (26.5)$$

The solution procedure can estimate $\Pr(l_i|L_i)$ from the training data, where L_i denotes a set of labels in the neighborhood of s_i excluding the label at s_i, by examining the ratios of the frequencies of class labels to the total number of locations in the spatial framework. $\Pr(X|l_i, L_i)$ can be estimated using kernel functions from the observed values in the training dataset. For reliable estimates, even larger training datasets are needed relative to those needed for the Bayesian classifiers without spatial context, since we are estimating a more complex distribution. An assumption on $\Pr(X|l_i, L_i)$ may be useful if the training dataset available is not large enough. A common assumption is the uniformity of influence from all neighbors of a location. For computational efficiency it can be assumed that only local explanatory data $X(s_i)$ and neighborhood label L_i are relevant in predicting class label $l_i = f_C(s_i)$. It is common to assume that all interaction between neighbors is captured via the interaction in the class label variable. Many domains also use specific parametric probability distribution forms, leading to simpler solution procedures. In addition, it is frequently easier to work with a Gibbs distribution specialized by the locally defined MRF through the Hammersley–Clifford theorem [21].

A more detailed theoretical and experimental comparison of these methods can be found in Ref. [22]. Although MRF and SAR classification have different formulations, they share a common goal, estimating the posterior probability distribution: $p(l_i|X)$. However, the posterior for the two models is computed differently with different assumptions. For MRF, the posterior is computed using Bayes' rule. In logistic regression, the posterior distribution is directly fit to the data. One important difference between logistic regression and MRF is that logistic regression assumes no dependence on neighboring classes. Logistic regression and logistic SAR models belong to a more general exponential family. The exponential family is given by $\Pr(u|v) = e^{A(\theta_v)+B(u,\pi)+\theta_v^T u}$, where u and v are location and label, respectively. This exponential family includes many of the common distributions such as Gaussian, Binomial, Bernoulli, and Poisson as special cases.

Experiments were carried out on the Darr and Stubble wetlands to compare the classical regression, SAR, and the MRF-based Bayesian classifiers. The results showed that the MRF models yield better spatial and classification accuracies over SAR in the prediction of the locations of bird nests. We also observed that SAR predications are extremely localized, missing actual nests over a large part of the marsh lands. We also compared performance of MRF against MLC in a multiclass satellite image classification setting. We used a spring Landsat 7 image, taken on May 31, 2000, and clipped to the study region (Carlton County, Minnesota). The final rectified and clipped image size is 1343 lines × 2019 columns × 6 bands. We trained MLC and MRF classifiers using 60 labeled training plots and tested performance using an independent test dataset consisting of 205 labeled plots. The accuracies are summarized in Table 26.2, and Figure 26.4 shows small windows from the classified images.

TABLE 26.2:   MLC versus MRF classification accuracy.

S.No.	CID	C.Name	MLC	MRF
1	1	Hardwood.1	79.82	95.34
2	2	Hardwood.2	82.96	87.18
3	3	Conifer	94.02	96.60
4	4	Agriculture	90.60	93.03
5	5	Urban	53.57	64.29
6	6	Wetlands	93.51	95.15
7	7	Water	100.00	100.00
8	O	Overall	87.05	91.82

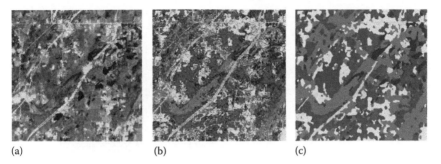

(a)   (b)   (c)

FIGURE 26.4: (See color insert following page 264.) Sample (a) RGB image and corresponding (b) MLC and (c) MRF classified output.

26.4 Spatial Outlier Detection

Outliers have been informally defined as observations in a dataset which appear to be inconsistent with the remainder of that set of data [23], or which deviate so much from other observations as to arouse suspicions that they were generated by a different mechanism [24]. The identification of global outliers can lead to the discovery of unexpected knowledge and has a number of practical applications in areas such as detection of credit card fraud and voting irregularities, athlete performance analysis, and severe weather prediction. This section focuses on spatial outliers, i.e., observations which appear to be inconsistent with their neighborhoods. Detecting spatial outliers is useful in many applications of geographic information systems and spatial databases. These application domains include transportation, ecology, public safety, public health, climatology, and location-based services.

We model a spatial dataset to be a collection of spatially referenced objects, such as houses, roads, and traffic sensors. Spatial objects have two distinct categories of dimensions along which attributes may be measured. Categories of dimensions of interest are spatial and nonspatial. Spatial attributes of a spatially referenced object include location, shape, and other geometric or topological properties. Nonspatial attributes of a spatially referenced object include traffic-sensor identifiers, manufacturer, owner, age, and measurement readings. A spatial neighborhood of a spatially referenced object is a subset of the spatial data based on a spatial dimension, e.g., location. Spatial neighbor hoods may be defined based on spatial attributes, e.g., location, using spatial relationships such as distance or adjacency. Comparisons between spatially referenced objects are based on nonspatial attributes.

A spatial outlier [25] is a spatially referenced object whose nonspatial attribute values differ significantly from those of other spatially referenced objects in its spatial neighborhood. Informally, a spatial outlier is a local instability (in values of nonspatial attributes) or a spatially referenced object whose nonspatial attributes are extreme relative to its neighbors, even though the attributes may not be significantly different from the entire population. For example, a new house in an old neighborhood of

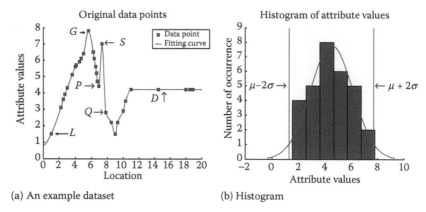

(a) An example dataset   (b) Histogram

FIGURE 26.5:   A dataset for outlier detection.

a growing metropolitan area is a spatial outlier based on the nonspatial attribute house age.

26.4.1   Illustrative Examples and Application Domains

We use an example to illustrate the differences among global and spatial outlier detection methods. In Figure 26.5a, the X-axis is the location of data points in one-dimensional space; the Y-axis is the attribute value for each data point. Global outlier detection methods ignore the spatial location of each data point and fit the distribution model to the values of the nonspatial attribute. The outlier detected using this approach is the data point G, which has an extremely high attribute value 7.9, exceeding the threshold of $\mu + 2\sigma = 4.49 + 2 \times 1.61 = 7.71$, as shown in Figure 26.5b. This test assumes a normal distribution for attribute values. On the other hand, S is a spatial outlier whose observed value is significantly different than its neighbors P and Q.

As another example, we use a spatial database consisting of measurements from the Minneapolis–St. Paul freeway traffic sensor network. The sensor network includes about 900 stations, each of which contains one to four loop detectors, depending on the number of lanes. Sensors embedded in the freeways and interstate monitor the occupancy and volume of traffic on the road. At regular intervals, this information is sent to the traffic management center for operational purposes, e.g., ramp meter control, as well as for experiments and research on traffic modeling. In this application, we are interested in discovering the location of stations whose measurements are inconsistent with those of their spatial neighbors and the time periods when these abnormalities arise.

26.4.2   Tests for Detecting Spatial Outliers

Tests to detect spatial outliers separate spatial attributes from nonspatial attributes. Spatial attributes are used to characterize location, neighborhood, and distance.

Nonspatial attribute dimensions are used to compare a spatially referenced object to its neighbors. Spatial statistics literature provides two kinds of bipartite multidimensional tests: graphical tests and quantitative tests. Graphical tests, which are based on the visualization of spatial data, highlight spatial outliers. Example methods include variogram clouds and Moran scatterplots. Quantitative methods provide a precise test to distinguish spatial outliers from the remainder of data. Scatterplots [26] are a representative technique from the quantitative family.

A variogram cloud displays data points related by neighborhood relationships. For each pair of locations, the square root of the absolute difference between attribute values at the locations versus the Euclidean distance between the locations are plotted. In datasets exhibiting strong spatial dependence, the variance in the attribute differences will increase with increasing distance between locations. Locations that are near to one another, but with large attribute differences, might indicate a spatial outlier, even though the values at both locations may appear to be reasonable when examining the dataset nonspatially. Figure 26.6a shows a variogram cloud for the example dataset shown in Figure 26.5a. This plot shows that two pairs (P, S) and (Q, S) on the left-hand side lie above the main group of pairs and are possibly related to spatial outliers. The point S may be identified as a spatial outlier since it occurs in both pairs (Q, S) and (P, S). However, graphical tests of spatial outlier detection are limited by the lack of precise criteria to distinguish spatial outliers. In addition, a variogram cloud requires nontrivial postprocessing of highlighted pairs to separate spatial outliers from their neighbors, particularly when multiple outliers are present, or density varies greatly.

A Moran scatterplot [27] is a plot of normalized attribute value $(Z[f(i)] = \frac{f(i)-\mu_f}{\sigma_f})$ against the neighborhood average of normalized attribute values $(W \cdot Z)$, where W is the row-normalized (i.e., $\sum_j W_{ij} = 1$) neighborhood matrix, (i.e., $W_{ij} > 0$ iff neighbor (i,j)). The upper-left and lower-right quadrants of Figure 26.6b indicate a spatial association of dissimilar values: low values surrounded by high-value neighbors

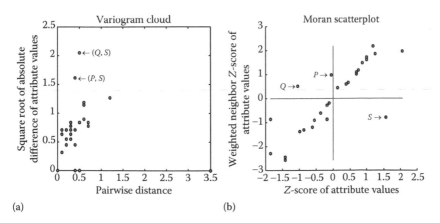

(a) (b)

FIGURE 26.6: (a) Variogram cloud and (b) Moran scatterplot to detect spatial outliers.

(e.g., points P and Q), and high values surrounded by low values (e.g., point S). Thus we can identify points (nodes) that are surrounded by unusually high or low value neighbors. These points can be treated as spatial outliers.

A scatterplot [26] shows attribute values on the X-axis and the average of the attribute values in the neighborhood on the Y-axis. A least square regression line is used to identify spatial outliers. A scatter sloping upward to the right indicates a positive spatial autocorrelation (adjacent values tend to be similar); a scatter sloping upward to the left indicates a negative spatial autocorrelation. The residual is defined as the vertical distance (Y-axis) between a point P with location (X_P, Y_P) to the regression line $Y = mX + b$, that is, residual $\varepsilon = Y_P - (mX_P + b)$. Cases with standardized residuals, $\varepsilon_{standard} = (\varepsilon - \mu_\varepsilon)/\sigma_\varepsilon$, greater than 3.0 or less than -3.0 are flagged as possible spatial outliers, where μ_ε and σ_ε are the mean and standard deviation of the distribution of the error term ε. In Figure 26.7a, a scatterplot shows the attribute values plotted against the average of the attribute values in neighboring areas for the dataset in Figure 26.5a. The point S turns out to be the farthest from the regression line and may be identified as a spatial outlier.

A location (sensor) is compared to its neighborhood using the function $S(x) = \{f(x) - E_{y \in N(x)}[f(y)]\}$, where $f(x)$ is the attribute value for a location x, $N(x)$ is the set of neighbors of x, and $E_{y \in N(x)}[f(y)]$ is the average attribute value for the neighbors of x. The statistic function $S(x)$ denotes the difference of the attribute value of a sensor located at x and the average attribute value of x's neighbors.

Spatial statistic $S(x)$ is normally distributed if the attribute value $f(x)$ is normally distributed. A popular test for detecting spatial outliers for normally distributed $f(x)$ can be described as follows: Spatial statistic $Z_{s(x)} = \left| \frac{S(x) - \mu_s}{\sigma_s} \right| > \theta$. For each location x with an attribute value $f(x)$, the $S(x)$ is the difference between the attribute value at location x and the average attribute value of x's neighbors, μ_s is the mean value of $S(x)$, and σ_s is the value of the standard deviation of $S(x)$ over all stations. The

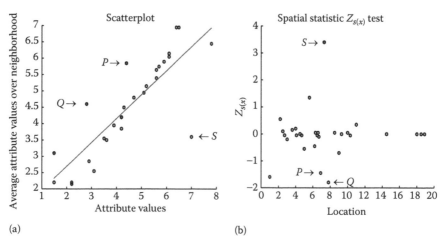

(a)   (b)

FIGURE 26.7:   (a) Scatterplot and (b) spatial statistic $Z_{s(x)}$ to detect spatial outliers.

choice of θ depends on a specified confidence level. For example, a confidence level of 95 percent will lead to $\theta \approx 2$.

Figure 26.7b shows the visualization of the spatial statistic method described above. The X-axis is the location of data points in one-dimensional space; the Y-axis is the value of spatial statistic $Z_{s(x)}$ for each data point. We can easily observe that point S has a $Z_{s(x)}$ value exceeding 3, and will be detected as a spatial outlier. Note that the two neighboring points P and Q of S have $Z_{s(x)}$ values close to -2 due to the presence of spatial outliers in their neighborhoods.

The techniques presented above are based on single attribute. However, multiattribute-based spatial outlier detection is also possible. For example, average and median attribute value based algorithms are presented in Ref. [28].

26.5   Colocation Rules

Colocation patterns represent subsets of boolean spatial features whose instances are often located in close geographic proximity. Examples include symbiotic species, e.g., the Nile Crocodile and Egyptian Plover in ecology and frontage-roads and highways in metropolitan road maps. Boolean spatial features describe the presence or absence of geographic object types at different locations in a two-dimensional or three-dimensional metric space, e.g., the surface of the Earth. Examples of boolean spatial features include plant species, animal species, road types, cancers, crime, and business types.

Colocation rules are models to infer the presence of boolean spatial features in the neighborhood of instances of other boolean spatial features. For example, Nile Crocodiles $\rightarrow$ Egyptian Plover predicts the presence of Egyptian Plover birds in areas with Nile Crocodiles. Figure 26.8a shows a dataset consisting of instances of several boolean spatial features, each represented by a distinct shape. A careful review reveals two colocation patterns, i.e., $(+, \times)$ and $(o, *)$.

Colocation rule discovery is a process to identify colocation patterns from large spatial datasets with a large number of boolean features. The spatial colocation rule discovery problem looks similar, but, in fact, is very different from the association rule mining problem [8] because of the lack of transactions. In market basket datasets, transactions represent sets of item types bought together by customers. The support of an association is defined to be the fraction of transactions containing the association. Association rules are derived from all the associations with support values larger than a user-given threshold. The purpose of mining association rules is to identify frequent item sets for planning store layouts or marketing campaigns. In the spatial colocation rule mining problem, transactions are often not explicit. The transactions in market basket analysis are independent of each other. Transactions are disjoint in the sense of not sharing instances of item types. In contrast, the instances of boolean spatial features are embedded in a continuous space and share a variety of spatial relationships (e.g., neighbor) with each other.

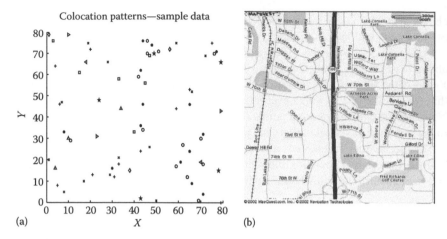

FIGURE 26.8: (a) Illustration of point spatial colocation patterns. Shapes represent different spatial feature types. Spatial features in sets $\{+,\times\}$ and $\{o,^*\}$ tend to be located together. (b) Illustration of line string colocation patterns. Highways, e.g., Hwy100, and frontage roads, e.g., Normandale Road, are colocated.

26.5.1 Colocation Rule Approaches

Approaches to discovering colocation rules can be divided into three categories: those based on spatial statistics, those based on association rules, and those based on the event centric model. Spatial-statistics-based approaches use measures of spatial correlation to characterize the relationship between different types of spatial features using the cross K-function with Monte Carlo simulation and quadrat count analysis [10]. Computing spatial correlation measures for all possible colocation patterns can be computationally expensive due to the exponential number of candidate subsets given a large collection of spatial boolean features.

Spatial colocation rule mining approaches can be grouped into two broad categories: approaches that use spatial statistics and algorithms that use association rule mining kind of primitives. Spatial-statistics-based approaches utilize statistical measures such as cross K-function, mean nearest-neighbor distance, and spatial autocorrelation. However, spatial-statistics-based approaches are computationally expensive. On the other hand, association rule-based approaches focus on the creation of transactions over space so that an *apriori*-like algorithm [8] can be used. Transactions in space can use a reference-feature centric [29] approach or a data-partition [30] approach. The reference feature centric model is based on the choice of a reference spatial feature [29] and is relevant to application domains focusing on a specific boolean spatial feature, e.g., cancer. Domain scientists are interested in finding the colocations of other task relevant features (e.g., asbestos) to the reference feature. A specific example is provided by the spatial association rule [29]. Transactions are created around instances of one user-specified reference spatial feature.

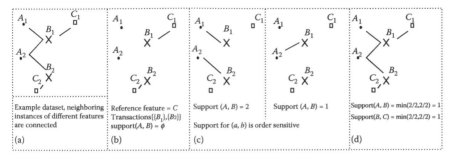

Example dataset, neighboring instances of different features are connected	Reference feature = C Transactions{{B_1},{B_2}} support(A, B) = ϕ	Support (A, B) = 2 Support for (a, b) is order sensitive	Support (A, B) = 1	Support(A, B) = min(2/2,2/2) = 1 Support(B, C) = min(2/2,2/2) = 1
(a)	(b)	(c)		(d)

FIGURE 26.9: Example to illustrate different approaches to discovering colocation patterns. (a) Example dataset and (b) Data partition approach. Support measure is ill-defined and order sensitive. (c) Reference feature centric model and (d) event centric model

The association rules are derived using the *apriori* algorithm. The rules found are all related to the reference feature. For example, consider the spatial dataset in Figure 26.9a with three feature types, A,B, and C. Each feature type has two instances. The neighbor relationships between instances are shown as edges. Colocations (A, B) and (B, C) may be considered to be frequent in this example. Figure 26.9b shows transactions created by choosing C as the reference feature. Colocation (A,B) will not be found since it does not involve the reference feature.

Defining transactions by a data-partition approach [30] defines transactions by dividing spatial datasets into disjoint partitions. There may be many distinct ways of partitioning the data, each yielding a distinct set of transactions, which in turn yields different values of support of a given colocation. Figure 26.9c shows two possible partitions for the dataset of Figure 26.9a, along with the supports for colocation (A, B).

The event centric model finds subsets of spatial features likely to occur in a neighborhood around instances of given subsets of event types. For example, let us determine the probability of finding at least one instance of feature type B in the neighborhood of an instance of feature type A in Figure 26.9a. There are two instances of type A and both have some instances of type B in their neighborhoods. The conditional probability for the colocation rule is: spatial feature A at location 1 $\rightarrow$ spatial feature type B in neighborhood is 100%. This yields a well-defined prevalence measure (i.e., support) without the need for transactions. Figure 26.9d illustrates that our approach will identify both (A,B) and (B,C) as frequent patterns.

Prevalence measures and conditional probability measures, called interest measures, are defined differently in different models, as summarized in Table 26.3. The reference feature centric and data partitioning models "materialize" transactions and thus can use traditional support and confidence measures. The event centric model-based approach defined new transaction-free measures, such as the participation index (refer to Ref. [31] for details).

The colocation algorithm [31] that we discussed above focuses on patterns where the closeness relationships between features form a complete graph [32]. This

TABLE 26.3:   Interest measures for different models.

Model	Items	Transactions Defined by	Interest Measures for $C_1 \rightarrow C_2$ Prevalence	Conditional Probability
Reference feature centric	Predicates on reference and relevant features	Instances of reference feature C_1 and C_2 involved with	Fraction of instance of reference feature with $C_1 \cup C_2$	Pr(C_2 is true for an instance of reference features given C_1 is true for that instance of reference feature)
Data partitioning	Boolean feature types	A partitioning of spatial dataset	Fraction of partitions with $C_1 \cup C_2$	Pr(C_2 in a partition given C_1 in that partition)
Event centric	Boolean feature types	Neighborhoods of instances of feature types	Participation index of $C_1 \cup C_2$	Pr(C_2 in a neighborhood of C_1)

concept was further extended to feature sets where the closeness relationship between arbitrary pairs was allowed, and an efficient colocation mining algorithm was presented in Ref. [33]. The colocation mining was further extended to include geometric objects [34] and ST topological constraints [35].

26.6   Spatial Clustering

Spatial clustering is a process of grouping a set of spatial objects into clusters so that objects within a cluster have high similarity in comparison to one another, but are dissimilar to objects in other clusters. Cluster analysis is used in many spatial and ST application domains. For example, clustering is used in remote sensing data analysis as a first step to determine the number and distribution of spectral classes. Cluster analysis is used in epidemiology for finding unusual groups of health-related events. Cluster analysis is also used in detection of crime hot spots.

26.6.1   Complete Spatial Randomness (CSR) and Clustering

Spatial clustering can be applied to group similar spatial objects together, and its implicit assumption is that patterns tend to be grouped in space rather than in a random pattern. The statistical significance of spatial clustering can be measured by testing the assumption in the data. The test is critical for proceeding to any serious clustering analysis.

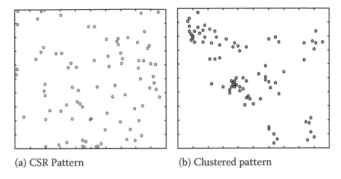

(a) CSR Pattern   (b) Clustered pattern

FIGURE 26.10:   CSR and spatially clustered patterns.

In spatial statistics, the standard against which spatial point patterns are often compared is a completely spatially point process, and departures indicate that the pattern is not completely spatially random. CSR [10] is synonymous with a homogeneous Poisson process. The patterns of the process are independently and uniformly distributed over space, i.e., the patterns are equally likely to occur anywhere and do not interact with each other. In contrast, a clustered pattern is distributed dependently and attractively in space.

An illustration of complete spatial random patterns and clustered patterns is given in Figure 26.10, which shows realizations from a completely spatially random process and from a spatial cluster process respectively (each conditioned to have 85 points in a unit square).

Notice from Figure 26.10a that the CSR pattern seems to exhibit some clustering. This is not an unrepresentive realization, but illustrates a well-known property of homogeneous Poisson processes: event-to-nearest-event distances are proportional to χ_2^2 random variables, whose densities have a substantial amount of probability near zero [10]. In contrast to Figure 26.10a, true clustering is shown in Figure 26.10b.

Several statistical methods [10] can be applied to quantify deviations of patterns from CSR point pattern. One type of descriptive statistics is based on quadrats (i.e., well-defined area, often rectangle in shape). Usually quadrats of random locations and orientations in the quadrats are counted, and statistics derived from the counters are computed. Another type of statistics is based on distances between patterns. One such type is Ripley's K-function.

26.6.2   Categories of Clustering Algorithms

After verification of the statistical significance of spatial clustering, clustering algorithms are used to discover interesting clusters. Because of the multitude of clustering algorithms that have been developed, it is useful to categorize them into groups. Based on the technique adopted to define clusters, the clustering algorithms can be divided into five broad categories:

1. *Hierarchical clustering methods.* These start with all patterns as a single cluster and successively perform splitting or merging until a stopping criterion is met. This results in a tree of clusters, called dendograms. The dendogram can be cut at different levels to yield desired clusters. Hierarchical algorithms can further be divided into agglomerative and divisive methods. The hierarchical clustering algorithms include balanced iterative reducing and clustering using hierarchies (BIRCH), clustering using inter connectivity (CHAMELEON), clustering using representatives (CURE), and robust clustering using links (ROCK).

2. *Partitional clustering algorithms.* These start with each pattern as a single cluster and iteratively reallocate data points to each cluster until a stopping criterion is met. These methods tend to find clusters of spherical shape. K-means and K-medoids are commonly used partitional algorithms. Squared error is the most frequently used criterion function in partitional clustering. The recent algorithms in this category include partitioning around medoids (PAM), clustering large applications (CLARA), clustering large applications based on randomized search (CLARANS), and expectation–maximization (EM).

3. *Density-based clustering algorithms.* These try to find clusters based on the density of data points in a region. These algorithms treat clusters as dense regions of objects in the data space. The density-based clustering algorithms include density-based spatial clustering of applications with noise (DBSCAN), ordering points to identify clustering structure (OPTICS), and density-based clustering (DENCLUE).

4. *Grid-based clustering algorithms.* These first quantize the clustering space into a finite number of cells and then perform the required operations on the quantized space. Cells that contain more than a certain number of points are treated as dense. The dense cells are connected to form the clusters. Grid-based clustering algorithms are primarily developed for analyzing large spatial datasets. The grid-based clustering algorithms include the statistical information grid-based method (STING), WaveCluster, BANG-clustering, and clustering-in-quest (CLIQUE).

5. *Hot spot detection.* One important application of clustering is hot spot detection. Figure 26.11 shows K-means based clustering over crime locations. Several techniques have been applied for crime hot spot detection, including, but not limited to, location indicators of spatial association (LISA) [27], kernel surface estimation algorithms [36], hierarchical clustering, K-means, spatial ellipses. For details, refer to NIJ report [37]. Many of these techniques are available in the popular CrimeStat [38] package.

Sometimes the distinction among these categories diminishes, and some algorithms can even be classified into more than one group. For example, clustering-in-quest (CLIQUE) can be considered as both a density-based and grid-based clustering method. More details on various clustering methods can be found in a recent survey paper [39]. Many of the clustering algorithms discussed here do not take into

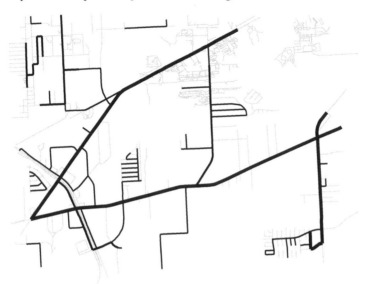

FIGURE 26.11:   Point data and output of *K*-means clustering using CrimeStat.

account the spatial autocorrelation and spatial constraints. Limited studies can be found in the literature to model spatial neighborhood relationships in clustering process. For example, in Refs. [40,41] the conventional expectation maximization approach has been extended by incorporating a spatial penalty term in estimating the likelihood function. Likewise, algorithms for spatial clustering in the presence of obstacles have been proposed in Refs. [42,43]. These approaches show improved clustering results and stress the importance of modeling neighborhood relationships in clustering.

26.6.3   Clustering and Outlier Detection in Spatial Networks

The outlier detection techniques presented so far are most suitable for general spatial databases and time series databases. However, these approaches do not consider the spatial network structure of the dataset, and may not model graph properties such as one-ways, connectivities, etc. Recently, methods are proposed to discover graph-based hot spots, e.g., mean streets which represent those connected subsets of a spatial network whose attribute values are significantly higher than expected. Finding mean streets is very important for many application domains, including crime analysis (high-crime-density street discovery) and police work (planning effective and efficient patrolling strategies). In urban areas, many human activities are centered about ST infrastructure networks, such as transportation, oil/gas pipelines, and utilities (e.g., water, electricity, telephone). Thus, activity reports such as crime reports may often use network-based location references (e.g., street addresses). In addition, spatial interaction among activities at nearby locations may be constrained by network connectivity and network distances (e.g., shortest paths along roads or train networks) rather than the geometric distances used in traditional spatial analysis.

Crime prevention may focus on identifying subsets of ST networks with high activity levels, understanding underlying causes in terms of ST network properties, and designing ST network control policies.

However, identifying and quantifying mean streets is a challenging task for several reasons. One large challenge is choosing the correct statistical model. Many existing ST models assume data normality and either spatial and temporal homogeneity or a well-defined autocorrelation in these domains. A major limitation is the inadequacy of descriptive and explanatory models for activity around ST networks such as train and road networks. Another challenge is that the discovery process of mean streets in large spatial networks is computationally very expensive due to the difficulty of characterizing and enumerating the population of streets to define a normal or expected activity level.

Public safety professionals may be interested in analyzing the ST network factors to explain high activity levels or changes in activity levels at certain highway segments, or to compare prevention options such as check points. Such analysis is not only difficult using existing methods but also may not be statistically meaningful, since common methods such as spatial regression do not adequately model ST network constraints such as connectivity and directions.

Previous studies on discovering high-density regions (i.e. hot spots) can be classified into two main categories based on their statistical interpretability. For example, Ref. [44] defined the hot routes discovery problem in road networks using moving object trajectories. However, discovered patterns in this approach do not have a statistical interpretation such as statistical significance. In addition, this algorithm is designed to process tracks (e.g., GPS tracks) rather than point or aggregate datasets referencing street networks. A distance-based technique to detect outliers in spatial networks is presented in Ref. [45].

Statistics-based methods to identify hot spots can be classified into two categories based on the nature of the dataset: point-based methods [46–53], and aggregate-based methods. Mean streets problem belongs to the latter one. The aim of the point-based approaches is to discover high-density regions from point datasets which show the actual locations of the crimes (Figure 26.11). The point-based approaches focus on the discovery of the geometry (e.g., circle, ellipse, etc.) of the high-density regions [47]. The Spatial and Temporal Analysis of Crime (STAC) tool in the Crime-Stat software, nearest neighbor hierarchical clustering techniques, and K-means clustering techniques are among the methods that use the ellipse method to identify hot spots [49]. Figure 26.11 shows the result of CrimeStat using the K-means clustering method for 15 clusters [49]. Kernel estimation methods have been developed to identify isodensity hot spot surfaces because hot spots may not have crisp ellipsoid boundaries. LISA statistics were proposed to eliminate the limitations of ellipsoid-based and kernel-based estimation techniques [46,48]. The clumping method was proposed by Roach to discover clumped points (e.g., hot spots) from a point dataset [51]. However, these approaches will not be able to discover and quantify high-crime-density regions (e.g., streets) for given aggregate crime data. They also do not consider the spatial network structure of the urban dataset, and may not model graph properties such as one-way streets or connectivity. For example, if all crime events occur along a street of a city, these approaches may tend to divide the street into several ellipsoid clusters or may tend to discover a big ellipse where most of the inside of the area has no activity. Shiode and Okabe extended the clumping method for analyzing point patterns on a spatial network [51–53]. In their approach, if crime point locations on an edge are close enough, they form a clump. A user-defined distance thresh old (or clump radius) is used to check if the points are close enough or not. However, their approach will not be able to discover and quantify patterns for aggregate crime data.

Overall, point-based approaches mainly focus on discovering and quantifying hot spots using point crime data. However, due to the type of crime or concerns for victim security, crime location information may not be released by the authorities and only aggregated crime values may be released for spatial regions, e.g., streets. In that case, point-based approaches, whether they consider the spatial network structure or not, will fail to discover and quantify hot spots since these approaches are dependent on knowing the locations of the crimes. In contrast, statistics-based methods are proposed to discover hot spots (e.g., mean streets) from aggregated datasets referencing urban street networks and taking graph semantics into account.

A novel ST network analysis method is explored to study descriptive and explanatory models for ST network patterns in Ref. [54]. Formally, given a road network $G = (V,E)$ and a set of aggregated crime values on edges E, mean street mining algorithm aims to discover and quantify correct and complete sets of connected subsets of the road network. For example, Figure 26.12 shows mean streets of a part of a metropolitan city in the United States. Each line represents a street and the thickness of it represents the aggregated crime value of the street. In this figure, the thicker the street is, the higher the crime density is. Two algorithms are developed: An

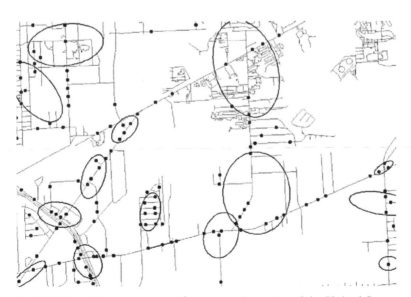

FIGURE 26.12: 12 Mean streets of a metropolitan city of the United States.

apriori-based mean street miner and a graph-based mean street miner. The key idea behind the *a priori*-based method is to discover size $k + 1$ mean streets using size k mean streets. This approach has two pruning strategies: (1) to eliminate unconnected edge combinations, and (2) to eliminate edge combinations that do not satisfy the crime thresholds. This approach will generate size $k + 1$ streets using size k mean streets until there are no more candidate streets. The inputs of the algorithm are a road network $G = (V,E)$, a set of aggregated crime values C_{real}, and a user-defined confidence threshold α. The output is connected sets of streets whose aggregated crime values are no less than their crime thresholds $C_{threshold}$.

On the other hand, in the graph-based approach, the key idea is to generate all possible street sets in a spatial network using path generation algorithms and prune the streets that do not satisfy the criteria. Road networks are often represented as graphs and one method to generate mean streets is to find all possible paths in the graph and then use an appropriate filtering technique to eliminate the connected street sets that are irrelevant. The constraints that need to be satisfied while computing street sets would depend on the users' preferences. For example, in some scenarios, it might be required to generate connected street sets that traverse every edge in the graph at least once. It is also possible that some locations in the road network are designated as start points and endpoints and the connected street set generation needs to incorporate this requirement.

For the *apriori*-based approach, a significant part of the computation time would be spent in generating candidate mean streets without looking at the connectivity of the edges. Experimental results showed that the execution time variation in the graph-based approach is less pronounced. This is more computationally efficient than the apriori-based approach since only the connected paths are generated. The apriori-based algorithm generates candidates without checking the graph connectivity, thus increasing the size of the search space. The execution time of the graph-based approach decreases as the confidence threshold increases. The *apriori*-based approach is computationally more expensive as the confidence threshold decreases because of the increase in the number of mean streets to be discovered. These two methods were evaluated and results were summarized in Ref. [54].

26.7   Computational Issues

The volume of data, complex spatial data types and relationships, and spatial autocorrelation pose several computational challenges to the spatial data mining field. When designing spatial data mining algorithms one has to take into account several considerations, such as space partitioning, predicate approximation, multi-dimensional data structures, etc. These issues are compared against classical data mining algorithms and summarized in the Table 26.4. Computational issues may arise due to dimensionality, spatial join process required in colocation mining and spatial outlier detection, estimation of SAR model parameters in the presence of large neighborhood matrix W, etc.

TABLE 26.4: Algorithmic strategies for SDM.

Classical Algorithms	Algorithmic Strategies for SDM
Divide-and-conquer	Space partitioning
Filter-and-refine	Minimum-bounding rectangle (MBR)
	Predicate approximation
Ordering	Plane sweeping, space filling curve
Hierarchical structures	Spatial index, tree matching
Parameter estimation	Parameter estimation with spatial autocorrelation

We now briefly present a case study with parameter estimation for SAR model. The massive sizes of geospatial datasets in many application domains make it important to develop scalable parameter estimation algorithms of the SAR model solutions for location prediction and classification. These application domains include regional economics [55], ecology [56,57], environmental management [58], public safety [59], transportation [60], public health [61], business, travel, and tourism [62–64]. Many classical data mining algorithms, such as linear regression, assume that the learning samples are independently and identically distributed. This assumption is violated in the case of spatial data due to spatial autocorrelation [65] and in such cases classical linear regression yields a weak model with not only low prediction accuracy [56,57] but also residual error exhibiting spatial dependence. Modeling spatial dependencies improves overall classification and prediction accuracies.

However, estimation of the SAR model parameters is computationally very expensive because of the need to compute the determinant of a large matrix in the likelihood function [66–70]. The maximum likelihood function for SAR parameter estimation contains two terms, namely a determinant term and SSE term (Equation 26.6). The former involves computation of the determinant of a very large matrix, which is a well-known hard problem in numerical analysis. For example, the exact SAR model parameter estimation for a 10,000-point spatial problem can take tens of minutes on common desktop computers. Computation costs make it difficult to use SAR for many important spatial problems that involve millions of points. Because of the high cost of determinant computation, the use of the SAR model has been limited to small problem sizes, despite its promise to improve prediction and classification accuracy.

To estimate the parameters of a ML-based SAR model solution, the log–likelihood function can be constructed, as shown in Equation 26.6. The estimation procedure involves computation of the logarithm of the determinant of (log-det) a large matrix, i.e., $(\mathbf{I} - \rho \mathbf{W})$. Computing the determinant of a matrix is very expensive.

$$\ell(\rho|y) = \frac{-2}{n} \underbrace{\ln|\mathbf{I} - \rho\mathbf{W}|}_{\text{log–det}}$$

$$+ \underbrace{\ln((\mathbf{I} - \rho\mathbf{W})\mathbf{y})^{\mathrm{T}}(\mathbf{I} - \mathbf{x}(\mathbf{x}^{\mathrm{T}}\mathbf{x})^{-1}\,\mathbf{x}^{\mathrm{T}})^{\mathrm{T}}(\mathbf{I} - \mathbf{x}(\mathbf{x}^{\mathrm{T}}\mathbf{x})^{-1}\,\mathbf{x}^{\mathrm{T}})((\mathbf{I} - \rho\mathbf{W}))_{\mathbf{y}}}_{\text{SSE}}$$

$$(26.6)$$

where

y is the *n*-by-1 vector of observations on the dependent variable where *n* is the number of observation points

ρ is the spatial autoregression parameter

W is the *n*-by-*n* neighborhood matrix that accounts for the spatial relationships (dependencies) among the spatial data

x is the *n*-by-*k* matrix of observations on the explanatory variable, where *k* is the number of features

β is a *k*-by-1 vector of regression coefficients

Spatial autocorrelation term ρWy is added to the linear regression model in order to model the strength of the spatial dependencies among the elements of the dependent variable, y.

26.8 Spatiotemporal Data Mining

So far we have discussed techniques that are applicable to spatial data. Like spatial data, which requires consideration of spatial autocorrelation and spatial relationships and constraints in the model building, ST data mining also requires explicit or implicit modeling of ST autocorrelation and constraints. Table 26.5 contrasts ST data mining with spatial data mining. Several ST extensions of classification, clustering, and outlier detection can be found in the literature [71]. In this section, we consider the problem of ST co-occurrence pattern mining and briefly discuss the algorithm recently presented in Ref. [72].

TABLE 26.5: Comparison of SDM and STDM approaches.

		Spatial DM	Spatiotemporal DM
Input data		Complex types	Additional dimension— time
		Often implicit relationships	Implicit relationships change over time
Statistical foundation		Spatial autocorrelation	Spatial autocorrelation and temporal correlation
Output	Association	Colocation	Spatiotemporal association
			Mixed-drove pattern
			Sustained emerging pattern
	Clusters	Hot spots	Flock pattern
			Moving clusters
	Outlier	Spatial outlier	Spatiotemporal outlier
	Prediction	Location prediction	Future location prediction

Mixed-drove ST co-occurrence patterns (MDCOPs) represent subsets of two or more different object types whose instances are often located in spatial and temporal proximity. Discovering MDCOPs is an important problem with many applications such as identifying tactics in battlefields, games, and predator–prey interactions. However, mining MDCOPs is computationally very expensive because the interest measures are computationally complex, datasets are larger due to the archival history, and the set of candidate patterns is exponential in the number of object types. A monotonic composite interest measure for discovering MDCOPs and novel MDCOP mining algorithms are presented in Ref. [72].

As the volume of ST data continues to increase significantly due to both the growth of database archives and the increasing number and resolution of ST sensors, automated and semiautomated pattern analysis becomes more essential. As a result, ST co-occurrence pattern mining has been the subject of recent research. Given a moving object database, the aim in Ref. [72] was to discover MDCOPs representing subsets of different object types whose instances are located close together in geographic space for a significant fraction of time. Unlike the objectives of some other ST co-occurrence pattern identification approaches where the pattern is the primary interest, in MDCOPs both the pattern and the nature of the different object types are of interest.

A simple example of an MDCOP is in ecological predator–prey relationships. Patterns of movements of rabbits and foxes, for example, will tend to be colocated in many time frames which may or may not be consecutive. Rabbits may attempt to move away from foxes, and the foxes may attempt to stay with the rabbits. Other factors such as available food and water may also affect the patterns.

A detailed example: More example MDCOPs may be illustrated in American football where two teams try to outscore each other by moving a football to the opponent's end of the field. Various complex interactions occur within one team and across teams to achieve this goal. These interactions involve intentional and accidental MDCOPs, the identification of which may help teams to study their opponent's tactics. In American football, object types may be defined by the roles of the offensive and defensive players, such as quarterback, running back, wide receiver, kicker, holder, linebacker, and cornerback. An MDCOP is a subset of these different object types (such as {kicker, holder} or {wide_receiver, cornerback}) that occur frequently. One example MDCOP involves offensive wide receivers, defensive linebackers, and defensive cornerbacks, and is called a Hail Mary play. In this play, the objective of the offensive wide receivers is to outrun any linebackers and defensive backs and get behind them, catching an undefended pass while running untouched for a touchdown. This interaction creates an MDCOP between wide receivers and cornerbacks. An example Hail Mary play is given in Figure 26.13. It shows the positions of four offensive wide receivers (W.1, W.2, W.3, and W.4), two defensive cornerbacks (C.1 and C.2), two defensive linebackers (L.1 and L.2), and a quarterback (Q.1) in four time slots. The solid lines between the players show the neighboring players. The wide receivers W.1 and W.4 cross over each other and the wide receivers W.2 and W.3 run directly to the end zone of the

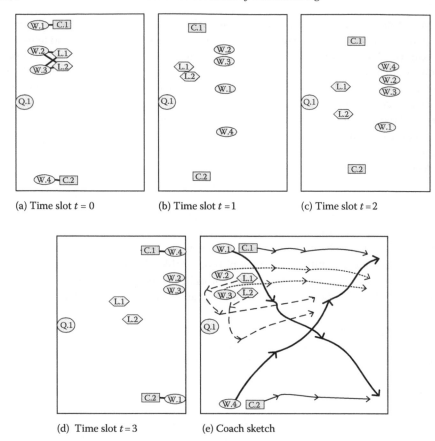

(a) Time slot $t = 0$ (b) Time slot $t = 1$ (c) Time slot $t = 2$

(d) Time slot $t = 3$ (e) Coach sketch

FIGURE 26.13: An example Hail Mary play in American football.

field. Initially, the wide receivers W.1 and W.4 are colocated with cornerbacks C.1 and C.2, respectively, and the wide receivers W.2 and W.3 are colocated with linebackers L.1 and L.2, respectively, at time slot $t = 0$ (Figure 26.13a). In time slot $t = 1$, the four wide receivers begin to run, while the linebackers run toward the quarterback and the cornerbacks remain in their original position, possibly due to a fake handoff from the quarterback to the running back (Figure 26.13b). In time slot $t = 2$, the wide receivers W.1 and W.4 cross over each other and try to drift further away from their respective cornerbacks (Figure 26.13c). When the quarterback shows signs of throwing the football, both cornerbacks and linebackers run to their respective wide receivers (Figure 26.13d). The overall sketch of the game tactics can be seen in Figure 26.13e. In this example, wide receivers and cornerbacks form an MDCOP since they are persistent over time and they occur two out of four time slots. However, wide receivers and linebackers do not form an MDCOP due to the lack of temporal persistence.

There are many applications for which discovering co-occurring patterns of specific combinations of object types is important. Some of these include military (battlefield planning and strategy), ecology (tracking species and pollutant movements), homeland defense (looking for significant events), and transportation (road and network planning) [73,74].

However, discovering MDCOPs poses several nontrivial challenges. First, current interest measures (i.e., the spatial prevalence measure) are not sufficient to quantify such patterns, so new composite interest measures must be created and formalized [75,76]. Second, the set of candidate patterns grows exponentially with the number of object types. Finally, since ST datasets are huge, computationally efficient algorithms must be developed [77].

In contrast to the approaches proposed in the literature, the proposed interest measure and algorithms in Ref. [72] efficiently mine mixed groups of objects (e.g., MDCOPs) which are close in space and persistent (but not necessarily close) in time.

26.9 Summary

In this chapter we have presented the major research achievements and techniques that have emerged from spatial data mining, especially for predicting locations and discovering spatial outliers, colocation rules, and spatial clusters. We conclude by identifying areas of research in spatial and ST data mining that require further investigation. The current research focus is mostly concentrated on developing algorithms that model spatial and spatiotemporal autocorrelations and constraints. ST data mining is still largely an unexplored territory; further research is especially needed for mining trajectory data and streaming data. Further research is also needed to scale these algorithms for large ST datasets. Other important issues that need immediate attention include how to validate the hypotheses generated by spatial data mining algorithms and how to generate actionable knowledge.

Acknowledgments

We are particularly grateful to our collaborators Professor Vipin Kumar, Professor Paul Schrater, Professor Sanjay Chawla, Dr. Chang-Tien Lu, Dr. Weili Wu, and Professor Uygar Ozesmi, Professor Yan Huang, and Dr. Pusheng Zhang for their various contributions. We also thank Xiaobin Ma, Professor Hui Xiong, Professor Jin Soung Yoo, Dr. Qingsong Lu, Dr. Baris Kazar, Betsy George, and anonymous reviewers for their valuable feedback on early versions of this chapter. We would like to thank Kim Koffolt for improving the readability of this chapter.

References

[1] P. Stolorz, H. Nakamura, E. Mesrobian, R.R. Muntz, E.C. Shek, J.R. Santos, J. Yi, K. Ng, S.Y. Chien, R. Mechoso, and J.D. Farrara. Fast spatio-temporal data mining of large geophysical datasets. In *Proceedings of the 1st International Conference on Knowledge Discovery and Data Mining*, AAAI Press, pp. 300–305, Montreal, Canada, 1995.

[2] S. Shekhar and S. Chawla. *Spatial Databases: A Tour*. Prentice-Hall (ISBN 0-7484-0064-6), 2002.

[3] J.-F. Roddick and M. Spiliopoulou. A bibliography of temporal, spatial and spatio-temporal data mining research. *SIGKDD Explorations* 1(1):34–38, 1999.

[4] P. Bolstad. *GIS Fundamentals: A First Text on GIS*. Eider Press, Minnesota, 2002.

[5] J. Quinlan. *C4.5: Programs for Machine Learning*. Morgan Kaufmann Publishers, San Francisco, CA, 1993.

[6] V. Varnett and T. Lewis. *Outliers in Statistical Data*. John Wiley, Chichester, United Kingdom, 1994.

[7] T. Agarwal, R. Imielinski, and A. Swami. Mining association rules between sets of items in large databases. In *Proceedings of the ACM SIGMOD Conference on Management of Data*, Washington, DC, May 1993.

[8] R. Agrawal and R. Srikant. Fast algorithms for mining association rules. In *Proceedings of Very Large Databases*, Santiago de Chile, Chile, May 1994.

[9] A. Jain and R. Dubes. *Algorithms for Clustering Data*. Prentice-Hall, Upper Saddle River, NJ, 1988.

[10] N.A. Cressie. *Statistics for Spatial Data* (revised edition). Wiley, New York, 1993.

[11] W.R. Tobler. Cellular geography. In S. Gale and G. Olsson, editors, *Philosophy in Geography*. Reidel, Dordrecht, 1979.

[12] C.E. Warrender and M.F. Augusteijn. Fusion of image classifications using Bayesian techniques with Markov rand fields. *International Journal of Remote Sensing*, 20(10):1987–2002, 1999.

[13] Y. Jhung and P.H. Swain. Bayesian contextual classification based on modified M-estimates and Markov random fields. *IEEE Transaction on Pattern Analysis and Machine Intelligence*, 34(1):67–75, 1996.

[14] A.H. Solberg, T. Taxt, and A.K. Jain. A Markov random field model for classification of multisource satellite imagery. *IEEE Transaction on Geoscience and Remote Sensing*, 34(1):100–113, 1996.

[15] L. Anselin. *Spatial Econometrics: Methods and Models*. Kluwer, Dordrecht, The Netherlands, 1988.

[16] M. Hixson, D. Scholz, and N. Funs. Evaluation of several schemes for classification of remotely sensed data. *Photogrammetric Engineering and Remote Sensing*, 46:1547–1553, 1980.

[17] A.H. Strahler. The use of prior probabilities in maximum likelihood classification of remote sensing data. *Remote Sensing of Environment*, 10:135–163, 1980.

[18] J.A. Richards and X. Jia. *Remote Sensing Digital Image Analysis*. Springer, New York, 1999.

[19] R.O. Duda, P.E. Hart, and D.G. Stork. *Pattern Classification*. Wiley, New York, 2000.

[20] S. Li. A Markov Random Field Modeling in Image Analysis. Springer-Verlag, New York, 1995.

[21] J.E. Besag. Spatial interaction and statistical analysis of latice systems. *Journal of Royal Statistical Society, Series B*, 36:192–236, 1974.

[22] S. Shekhar, P.R. Schrater, R.R. Vatsavai, W. Wu, and S. Chawla. Spatial contextual classification and prediction models for mining geospatial data. *IEEE Transactions on Multimedia*, 4(2), 2002.

[23] V. Barnett and T. Lewis. *Outliers in Statistical Data*, 3rd edition. John Wiley, 1994.

[24] D. Hawkins. *Identification of Outliers*. Chapman & Hall, London, 1980.

[25] S. Shekhar, C.T. Lu, and P. Zhang. Graph-based outlier detection: Algorithms and applications (A summary of results). In *Proceedings of the 7th of the ACM SIGKDD International Conference on Knowledge Discovery and Data Mining*, San Francisco, CA, 2001.

[26] A. Luc. Exploratory spatial data analysis and geographic information systems. In M. Painho, editor, *New Tools for Spatial Analysis*, pp. 45–54, Eurostat, Luxembourg, 1994.

[27] A. Luc. Local indicators of spatial association: LISA. *Geographical Analysis*, 27(2):93–115, 1995.

[28] C.-T. Lu, D. Chen, and Y. Kou. Detecting spatial outliers with multiple attributes. In *ICTAI '03: Proceedings of the 15th IEEE International Conference on Tools with Artificial Intelligence*, p. 122, Washington, DC, 2003. IEEE Computer Society.

[29] K. Koperski and J. Han. Discovery of spatial association rules in geographic information databases. In *Proceedings of 4th International Symposium on Large Spatial Databases*, pp. 47–66, Maine, 1995.

[30] Y. Morimoto. Mining frequent neighboring class sets in spatial databases. In *Proceedings of ACM SIGKDD International Conference on Knowledge Discovery and Data Mining*, San Francisco, CA, 2001.

[31] S. Shekhar and Y. Huang. Co-location rules mining: A summary of results. *Proceedings of the of Spatio-Temporal Symposium on Databases*, Los Angeles, CA, 2001.

[32] N. Mamoulis. Co-location patterns, algorithms. In S. Shekhar and H. Xiong, editors, *Encyclopedia of GIS 2008*. Springer, New York, 2008.

[33] X. Zhang, N. Mamoulis, D.W. Cheung, and Y. Shou. Fast mining of spatial collocations. In *KDD '04: Proceedings of the 10th ACM SIGKDD International Conference on Knowledge Discovery and Data Mining*, pp. 384–393, New York, 2004. ACM.

[34] H. Yang, S. Parthasarathy, and S. Mehta. Mining spatial object patterns in scientific data. In *International Joint Conference of Artificial Intelligence (IJCAI)*. IJCAI, Edinburgh, United Kingdom, 2005.

[35] J. Wang, W. Hsu, and M.L. Lee. A framework for mining topological patterns in spatio-temporal databases. In *CIKM '05: Proceedings of the 14th ACM International Conference on Information and Knowledge Management*, pp. 429–436, New York, 2005. ACM.

[36] S. McLafferty, D. Williamson, and P.G. McGuire. Identifying crime hot spots using kernel smoothing. In V. Goldsmith, P.G. McGuire, J.H. Mollenkopf, and T.A. Ross, editors, *Analyzing Crime Patterns*. MIT Press, Cambridge, MA, 2004.

[37] NIJ. Mapping crime: Understanding hot spots. http://www.ncjrs.gov/App/Publications/abstract.aspx?ID = 209393.

[38] NIJ. CrimeStat iii. http://www.ojp.usdoj.gov/nij/maps/crimestat.htm.

[39] J. Han, M. Kamber, and A.K.H. Tung. Spatial clustering methods in data mining: A survey. In *Geographic Data Mining and Knowledge Discovery*. Taylor & Francis, Bristol, PA, 2001.

[40] C. Ambroise, V.M. Dang, and G. Govaert. Clustering of spatial data by the em algorithm. In *geoENV I - Geostatistics for Environmental Applications, Quantitative Geology and Geostatistics*, Vol. 9, pp. 493–504, Springer, Geneva, Switzerland, 1997.

[41] T. Hu and Y. Sung. Clustering spatial data with a hybrid em approach. *Pattern Analysis and Applications*, 8(1):139–148, 2005.

[42] A.K.H. Tung, J. Hou, and J. Han. Spatial clustering in the presence of obstacles. *Proceedings of the 17th International Conference on Data Engineering*, pp. 359–367, Heidelberg, Germany, 2001.

[43] X. Zhang, J. Wang, F. Wu, Z. Fan, and X. Li. A novel spatial clustering with obstacles constraints based on genetic algorithms and k-medoids. In *ISDA '06: Proceedings of the 6th International Conference on Intelligent Systems Design and Applications (ISDA '06)*, pp. 605–610, Washington, DC, 2006. IEEE Computer Society.

[44] X. Li, J. Han, J.-G. Lee, and H. Gonzalez. Traffic density-based discovery of hot routes in road networks. In *10th International Symposium on Spatial and Temporal Databases*, pp. 441–459, Boston, MA, 2007.

[45] W. Jin, Y. Jiang, W. Qian, and A.K.H. Tung. Mining outliers in spatial networks. In *11th International Conference on Database Systems for Advanced Applications (DASFAA 2006)*, LNCS, Vol. 3882, Springer, Singapore, 2006.

[46] L. Anselin. Local indicators of spatial association-LISA. *Geographical Analysis*, 27(2):93–155, 1995.

[47] J.E. Eck et al. Mapping crime: Understanding hot spots. US National Institute of Justice http://www.ncjrs.gov/pdffiles1/nij/209393.pdf, 2005.

[48] A. Getis and J.K. Ord. Local spatial statistics: An overview. In *Spatial Analysis: Modelling in a GIS Environment*, pp. 261–277. GeoInformation International, Cambridge, England, 1996.

[49] N. Levine. *CrimeStat 3.0: A Spatial Statistics Program for the Analysis of Crime Incident Locations*. Ned Levine & Associatiates, Houston, TX; National Institute of Justice, Washington, DC, 2004.

[50] J.H. Ratcliffe. The hotspot matrix: A framework for the spatiotemporal targeting of crime reduction. *Police Practice and Research*, 5(1):05–23, 2004.

[51] S.A. Roach. *The Theory of Random Clumping*. Methuen, London, 1968.

[52] S. Shiode and A. Okabe. Network variable clumping method for analyzing point patterns on a network. In Unpublished paper presented at the Annual Meeting of the Associations of American Geographers, Philadelphia, p. 2004.

[53] A. Okabe, K. Okunuki, and S. Shiode. The sanet toolbox: New methods for network spatial analysis. *Transactions in GIS*, 10(4):535–550, 2006.

[54] M. Celik, S. Shekhar, B. George, J.P. Rogers, and J.A. Shine. Discovering and quantifying mean streets: A summary of results. Technical Report 025, University of Minnesota, Minneapolis, July 2007.

[55] P. Krugman. *Development, Geography, and Economic Theory*. MIT Press, Cambridge, MA, 1995.

[56] S. Chawla, S. Shekhar, W. Wu, and U. Ozesmi. Modeling spatial dependencies for mining geospatial data. *1st SIAM International Conference on Data Mining*, Arlington, VA, 2001.

[57] S. Shekhar, P. Schrater, R. Raju, and W. Wu. Spatial contextual classification and prediction models for mining geospatial data. *IEEE Transactions on Multimedia*, 4(2):174–188, 2002.

[58] M. Hohn, L. Gribko, and A.E. Liebhold. A Geostatistical model for forecasting the spatial dynamics of defoliation caused by the Gypsy Moth, *Lymantria dispar* (Lepidoptera:Lymantriidae). *Environmental Entomology*, 22:1066–1075, 1993.

[59] E. Isaaks and M. Srivastava. *Applied Geostatistics*. Oxford University Press, Oxford, 1989.

[60] S. Shekhar, T.A. Yang, and P. Hancock. An intelligent vehicle highway information management system. *International Journal on Microcomputers in Civil Engineering*, 8, 1993.

[61] Y. Yasui and S.R. Lele. A regression method for spatial disease rates: An estimating function approach. *Journal of the American Statistical Association*, 94:21–32, 1997.

[62] P.S. Albert and L.M. McShane. A generalized estimating equations approach for spatially correlated binary data: Applications to the analysis of neuroimaging data. *Biometrics*, 51:627–638, 1995.

[63] S. Shekhar and S. Chawla. *Spatial Databases: A Tour*. Prentice-Hall, Upper Saddle River, NJ, 2003.

[64] R.J. Haining. *Spatial Data Analysis in the Social and Environmental Sciences*. Cambridge University Press, Cambridge, United Kingdom, 1989.

[65] L. Anselin. *Spatial Econometrics: Methods and Models*. Kluwer Academic, Dordrecht, 1988.

[66] B. Li. Implementing spatial statistics on parallel computers. In *Practical Handbook of Spatial Statistics*, pp. 107–148, CRC Press, Boca Raton, FL, 1996.

[67] R.K. Pace and J.P. LeSage. Closed-form maximum likelihood estimates for spatial problems (mess). http://www.spatial-statistics.com, 2000.

[68] R.K. Pace and J.P. LeSage. Semiparametric maximum likelihood estimates of spatial dependence. *Geographical Analysis*, 34(1):76–90, 2002.

[69] R.K. Pace and J.P. LeSage. Simple bounds for difficult spatial likelihood problems. http://www.spatial-statistics.com, 2003.

[70] B.M. Kazar, S. Shekhar, D.J. Lilja, and D. Boley. A parallel formulation of the spatial auto-regression model for mining large geo-spatial datasets. *SIAM*

International Conference on Data Mining Workshop on High Performance and Distributed Mining (HPDM2004), Florida, April 2004.

[71] J.F. Roddick, K. Hornsby, and M. Spiliopoulou. An updated bibliography of temporal, spatial, and spatio-temporal data mining research. In *TSDM*, volume 2007 of *LNCS*, pp. 147–164. Springer, Lyon, France, 2000.

[72] M. Celik, S. Shekhar, J.P. Rogers, J.A. Shine, and J.S. Yoo. Mixed-drove spatio-temporal co-occurence pattern mining: A summary of results. In *ICDM '06: Proceedings of the 6th International Conference on Data Mining*, pp. 119–128, Washington, DC, 2006. IEEE Computer Society.

[73] R. Guting and M. Schneider. *Moving Object Databases*. Morgan Kaufmann, San Francisco, CA, 2005.

[74] M. Koubarakis, T. Sellis, A. Frank, S. Grumbach, R. Guting, C. Jensen, N. Lorentzos, H.J. Schek, and M. Scholl. *Spatio-Temporal Databases: The Chorochronos Approach, LNCS 2520*, volume 9. Springer Verlag, Berlin, Germany, 2003.

[75] Y. Huang, S. Shekhar, and H. Xiong. Discovering co-location patterns from spatial datasets: A general approach. *IEEE Transactions on Knowledge and Data Engineering (TKDE)*, 16(12):1472–1485, 2004.

[76] S. Shekhar, Y. Huang, and H. Xiong. Discovering spatial colocation patterns: A summary of results. In *7th International Symposium on Spatial and Temporal Databases (SSTD)*, Los Angles, CA, 2001.

[77] SSTDM06. First international workshop on spatial and spatio-temporal data mining (sstdm). In *Conjunction with the 6th IEEE International Conference on Data Mining (ICDM 2006)*, Hong Kong, 2006.

Index

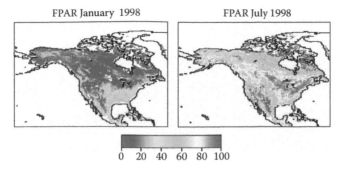

FIGURE 2.2: FPAR data for North America.

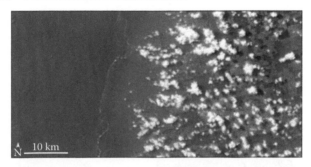

FIGURE 2.5: Deforestation changes local weather. Cloudiness and rainfall can be greater over cleared land (image right) than over intact forest (left). (Courtesy of NASA Earth Observatory.)

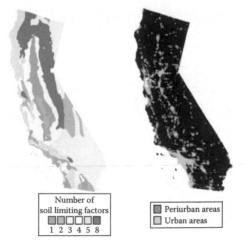

FIGURE 2.6: This pair of images shows the suitability of California soils for farming on the left, and urban areas on the right. The Great Central Valley, where the state's best soils are and most of America's fresh vegetables are grown, is becoming increasingly urbanized. (1: best soil; 8: worst soil). (Courtesy of Marc Inoff, NASA GSFC, and Flashback Imaging Corporation, Ontario, Canada.)

FIGURE 2.7: Urbanization. Between 1982 and 1992, 19,000 sq mi (equivalent to the area of half of Ohio) of rural cropland and wilderness were developed in the United states. This image shows the expansion of Plano (near Dallas) between 1974 and 1989. (Courtesy of NASA Earth Observatory.)

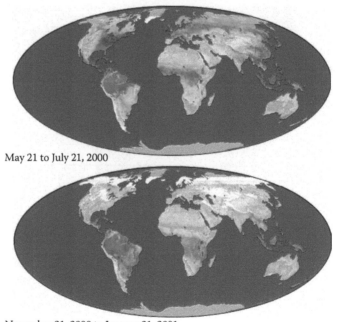

FIGURE 2.8: The MODIS EVI provides a look at vegetation around the globe year round. As the seasons change, the mirror effect of seasonality is seen, and one hemisphere's vegetation is high while the other is low. The images show EVI during two different seasons. Vegetation ranges from 0, indicating no vegetation, to nearly 1, indicating densest vegetation. Gray areas indicate places where observations were not collected. (Courtesy of NASA Earth Observatory, GSFC, and University of Arizona.)

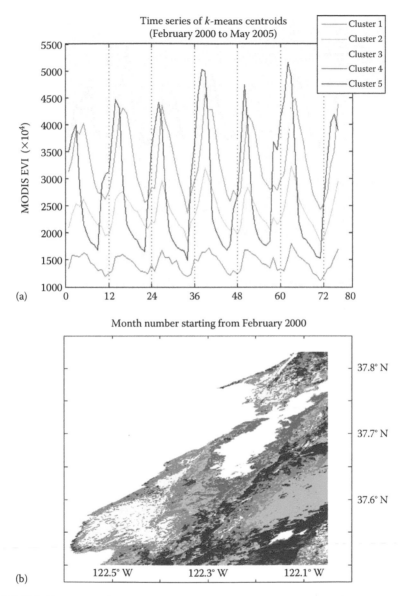

(a)

(b)

FIGURE 2.10: (a) MODIS EVI time series separated as k-means cluster centroids. Attributes of biomass density and interannual variability are defined as follows, with a corresponding land cover type assigned: Cluster 1 is high seasonal biomass density, moderate interannual variability (shrub cover). Cluster 2 is moderate annual biomass density, moderate interannual variability (grass cover). Cluster 3 is high annual biomass density, low interannual variability (evergreen tree cover). Cluster 4 is low annual biomass density, low interannual variability (urbanized cover). Cluster 5 is high seasonal biomass density, high interannual variability (agricultural cover). (b) Map of MODIS EVI time series clusters for the San Francisco Bay Area, defined by the centroid lines and corresponding colors from Figure 2.10a.

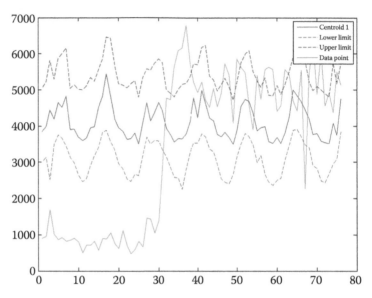

FIGURE 2.11: This figure shows an example of a change point that was discovered by the confidence intervals around cluster centroids methodology.

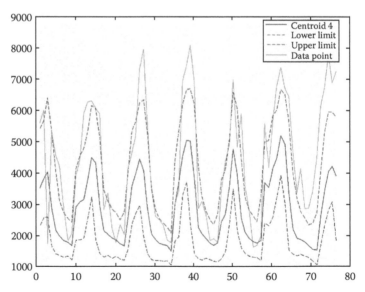

FIGURE 2.12: This figure shows an example of a point that was discovered by the confidence intervals around cluster centroids methodology. It is evident from the time series that this point should not be considered a change point.

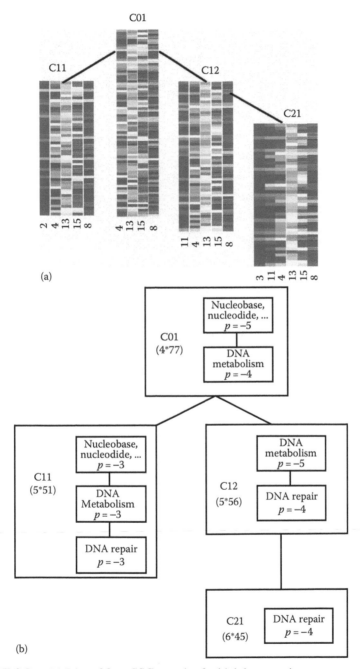

FIGURE 3.2: (a) List of four SSCs, each of which has consistent patterns of their gene expressions and (b) Annotation of each cluster using gene ontology. The significance of each annotation is 10^p.

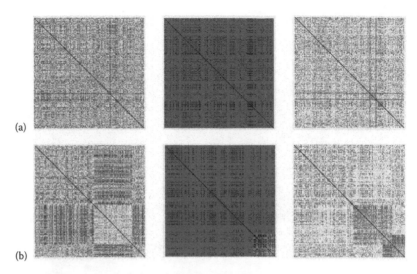

(a)

(b)

FIGURE 3.3: Permutations of weighed dissimilarity matrices. Each row shows two separate dissimilarity matrices on the left and a combined dissimilarity matrix on right. The leftmost column represents the spatial relationships between SNPs according to their sequence position. The center column represents pairwise SNPs correlations weighted by a phenotype level. The top row is shown in the original sequence order, and the bottom row is permuted to expose the clusters resulting from a 50/50 weighting of spatial and phenotype matrices.

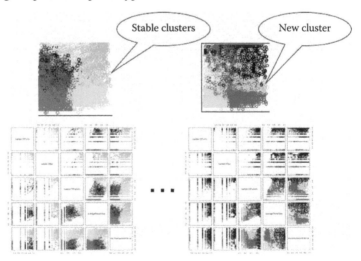

FIGURE 12.2: At the bottom of the figure are two scatter matrix plots (sploms). On the lower left is a splom from a period in which the clusters are stable. On the lower right is a splom as a new cluster emerges after the period of stability illustrated in the left splom. Above the sploms is a blow up in which the new cluster can be seen (the gray cluster).

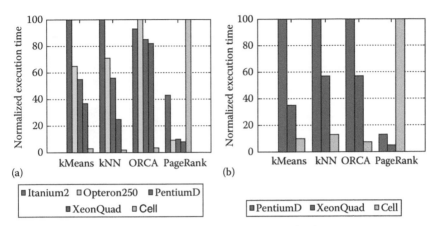

FIGURE 13.6: Performance of Cell against (a) single-core processors and (b) multicore processors.

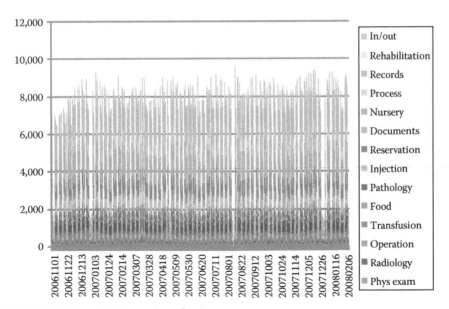

FIGURE 22.2: Total number of orders.

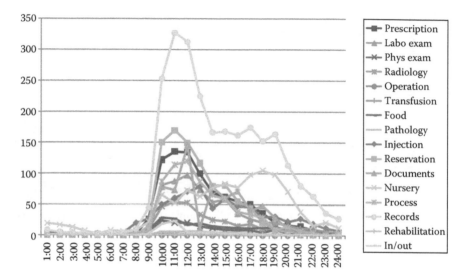

FIGURE 22.3: Trends of averaged number of orders.

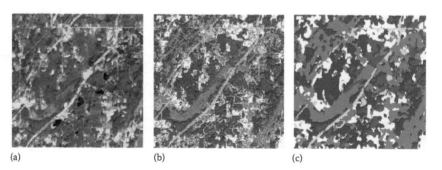

(a)   (b)   (c)

FIGURE 26.4: Sample (a) RGB image and corresponding (b) MLC and (c) MRF classified output.

9 780367 386054